The decade before the First World War witnessed many spectacular archae-
ological discoveries in Egypt. During this period Arthur Weigall, the British
Egyptologist, was involved in the exploration and conservation of the monuments
and antiquities of a region stretching from Luxor to the Sudan border. At a time
when Egypt was being ransacked by private collectors and the agents of western
museums, it was said that without Weigall much more would have been lost
altogether – most notably, the wall paintings in the Tombs of the Nobles. The
enthusiasm and energy of the man and of the books and articles he wrote played
a large part in popularising Egypt and Egyptology, and in promoting the then
radical view that Egypt's antiquities belonged to the Egyptians. When, in 1922,
Tutankhamun's tomb was discovered by his old colleague Howard Carter, Weigall
came into open conflict with Carter's patron, Lord Carnarvon, for his handling
of the question of rights in the tomb, and for his sale of information from it to
the London *Times*. Following Carnarvon's premature death in Egypt it was
Weigall's remarks to the press that led to the notorious story of the 'Curse of the
Pharaohs': a myth that persists to this day. Weigall had many talents: he also
designed theatre scenery, made films and wrote novels. But his real legacy
derives from his passion for Egypt, both ancient and modern – a passion that
informs the whole of his compelling story.

**Julie Hankey** is the granddaughter of Arthur Weigall and has had access to
previously unseen private papers in researching his life.

In memory of my mother, Zippa

**Tauris Parke Paperbacks** is an imprint of I.B.Tauris. It is dedicated to publishing books in accessible paperback editions for the serious general reader within a wide range of categories, including biography, history, travel and the ancient world. The list includes select, critically acclaimed works of top quality writing by distinguished authors that continue to challenge, to inform and to inspire. These are books that possess those subtle but intrinsic elements that mark them out as something exceptional.

**The Colophon** of Tauris Parke Paperbacks is a representation of the ancient Egyptian ibis, sacred to the god Thoth, who was himself often depicted in the form of this most elegant of birds. Thoth was credited in antiquity as the scribe of the ancient Egyptian gods and as the inventor of writing and was associated with many aspects of wisdom and learning.

# A PASSION
# FOR EGYPT

## Arthur Weigall,
## Tutankhamun and the
## 'Curse of the Pharaohs'

JULIE HANKEY

TAURIS PARKE
PAPERBACKS

Published in 2007 by Tauris Parke Paperbacks
an imprint of I.B.Tauris and Co Ltd
6 Salem Road, London W2 4BU
175 Fifth Avenue, New York NY 10010
www.ibtauris.com

In the United States of America and Canada distributed by
Palgrave Macmillan, a division of St. Martin's Press
175 Fifth Avenue, New York NY 10010

First published in 2001 by I.B.Tauris & Co Ltd
Copyright © 2001, Julie Hankey

ISBN: 978 1 84511 435 0

A full CIP record for this book is available from the British Library
A full CIP record is available from the Library of Congress

Library of Congress Catalog Card Number: available

Printed and bound in India by Replika Press Pvt. Ltd

# CONTENTS

**Part One 1880 – 1914**

**Part Two 1914 – 1934**

CONTENTS

# List of illustrations

Endpapers: taken from Arthur Weigall's hand-drawn map of the royal tombs in the Valley of the Kings.

## Text illustrations

## Photographic plates

*The originals of all these illustrations are in the AW archive*

# Egyptian Chronology

I have not attempted to tangle here with the controversies of Egyptian chronology. Where I refer to dates in the ancient history of Egypt, I have derived these from the *Atlas of Ancient Egypt* (1984) by John Baines and Jaromir Málek.

# Acknowledgements

I shall always be grateful to the Weigall family, Alured, Denny, Geraldine, Zippa, and Veronica, for preserving Arthur Weigall's correspondence and for keeping his memory alive. It was however the late archaeologist and scholar Vronwy Hankey whose lively interest in Weigall first led me to understand that he was a figure of significance beyond the family circle and who introduced me to his work.

The help of Dr Nicholas Reeves in setting me on the right path, in suggesting what to read, where to go, and who to write to, and in being unfailingly encouraging along the way, has been invaluable. As an outsider in the field of Egyptology I have relied very much on the interest of insiders. I am grateful to Peter Clayton for his encouragement and in particular for giving me the opportunity to explore in *Minerva* some of the ground developed later; and to David Rohl for communicating his knowledge about and his infectious enthusiasm for Arthur Weigall. I am also grateful to both Dr Aidan Dodson and Dr Nicholas Montserrat for sharing their knowledge of various aspects of the subject with me, and for allowing me to read work in progress. I must also thank Dr Mark Smith for sending me useful literature; and T.G.H. James who went out of his way to try and track down information for me in connection with the bronze statuette.

I am extremely grateful to Margaret Gardiner, the daughter of Alan Gardiner, who generously gave me letters by Arthur Weigall and extracts from letters about him; who told me stories and anecdotes about him and his world; and who brought me closer to him than anyone else outside his family.

Among the archivists who have helped me in my research, I must thank John Larson of the Oriental Institute in Chicago, who as well as expressing interest in Arthur Weigall, and allowing me to quote from James Breasted's correspondence, made an enormous practical contribution by compiling for my use a bibliography of Weigall's work. I am grateful to Dr Diana Magee at the Griffith Institute in Oxford who not only helped me find my way round the correspondence, but pointed me in the direction of relevant published literature. Dr Jaromir Málek, also of the Griffith Institute, was generous with his time, and was always ready to discuss the various political questions so often raised by Weigall's career.

My thanks are due to Marsha Hill of the Metropolitan Museum in New York for locating correspondence by and about Arthur Weigall, often on only the flimsiest guess that there might be something there. I am grateful in the same way to Judy Throm of the Smithsonian Institution in Washington D.C., for combing the Joseph Lindon Smith correspondence. I must also thank Robert Cox of the American Philosophical Society, Philadelphia, for allowing me to quote from Emma Andrews's 'The Journal of the Bedawin'; T.R.S. Allan of Pembroke College Library, Cambridge, for letting me see and quote from the correspondence of Ronald Storrs; and the executors of the late Mervyn Herbert for allowing me to quote from his diary.

My picture of André Charlot was enlarged by James Moore, who knows more about him than anyone, and whose help in tracking down information about his film ventures was greatly appreciated. In this he was assisted by André Charlot's daughter, Joan Midwinter, to whom I am also grateful. And I must thank the staff at the Theatre Museum in London for noticing that James Moore and myself were both interested in the same person, and for introducing us to each other.

For the particulars of the death of Arthur Weigall's father I must thank Colonel M. J. Woodcock, Chapter Clerk to Exeter Cathedral; and for details of his school life I must thank J.C.C. Sworder, Secretary to the Old Wellingtonian Society.

Lastly I owe a great debt to Peri Hankey for helping me in many ways, particularly in the preparation of the script; and to both Graham Greene and my sister Rosalind Ingrams, for reading it so intelligently. My sister has been especially involved, listening, advising and above all enabling me to visit Luxor and the places our grandfather loved.

# Part One
# 1880–1914

# Chapter 1

# 'that violent hullabaloo'
# 1880–1892

'Death of Mr A. Weigall, Tut-ank Amen Curse Recalled', said the *Daily Mail* for 3 January 1934, and the rest of the more sensational newspapers[1] printed much the same kind of thing: Arthur Weigall, famous Egyptologist, has died as a result of the curse of Tutankhamun. Or *possibly* as a result of the curse. Or possibly not as a result of the curse. But one way or another the curse of Tutankhamun was featured in connection with Arthur Weigall's early death at the age of fifty-three.

The curse of Tutankhamun had been a kind of craze ever since Lord Carnarvon, the excavation's financier, had died of an infected mosquito bite in Cairo eleven years before, soon after the tomb's opening. It was said then that, inscribed on the walls of the tomb, was a curse on anyone entering it, and the subsequent demise of anybody at all connected with the excavations was seized on by the newspapers as proof of its potency. Naturally enough, there had been quite a few such deaths, and now here was another, though it was noted, perhaps a little ruefully, that the chief excavator, Howard Carter, remained stubbornly alive.

Arthur Weigall had not in fact been a member of the excavating team. As a young man in his twenties and thirties, during the decade before the First World War, he had been the Chief Inspector of Antiquities for Upper Egypt, where the famous tomb lies in the Valley of the Kings. As such he had been a colleague of Howard Carter and Lord Carnarvon who had been granted concessions to excavate in the area, under Weigall's general supervision, since 1908. Much had happened in the interval – almost the whole story of this book, in fact. By 1922, when Carter first peered through the hole in the outer door of Tutankhamun's tomb, Weigall had undergone many transformations, from archaeologist to theatre set-designer, to song-writer, to film critic. But the most enduring of his metamorphoses had been as an enormously popular writer on modern and ancient Egypt, best known perhaps for his biography of the Pharaoh Akhnaten, the father of Tutankhamun.

When, therefore, news of the discovery of Tutankhamun's tomb broke in November 1922, Weigall was contacted by the *Daily Mail* and asked to go out to Egypt as their special correspondent. He had been away for eight years and when he arrived he found the strange, wild valley almost unrecognizable – tourists swarming, reporters and cameramen everywhere. For the first time, archaeology had become a

3

media sensation. More than that, it had become profitable; for Lord Carnarvon had made an agreement with the *Times* newspaper giving that paper exclusive rights to information relating to the tomb in return for a 75 per cent royalty.

Great difficulties therefore confronted the correspondents of other newspapers sent to cover the story, and Carnarvon found himself at the centre of a huge row, initially about the freedom of the press, but very soon about the whole political question of public versus private ownership. The tomb itself belonged to the Egyptian Government. Was Carnarvon in any position, therefore, to sell information about it? And was such a monument a proper subject for royalty deals struck between newspapers and private individuals? It was a highly charged issue, and the story of it will be told in its place later. It only needs to be said here that Arthur Weigall was a passionate supporter of the public principle. His whole career, as we shall see, had been a battle against the treasure-hunting, 'finders keepers' attitude of much archaeology at that period; a battle to establish the rights of the government of Egypt in Egypt's historical monuments, and the obligations of that government to conserve them for posterity. Weigall's opposition to Carnarvon's deal over Tutankhamun's tomb was therefore only the latest in a long line of such confrontations.

Weigall, in common with every other Egyptologist, denied that there was a curse written on the walls of Tutankhamun's tomb. In an essay he wrote not long after returning from Egypt in 1923, he explained that such curses were very rare, and that they were intended only for the tomb robbers of their day who might damage the tomb and break up the mummy in search of jewellery. Modern excavators, he says, whose 'sole aim' is saving 'the dead from native[2] pillage and their identity from the obliterating hand of time', fall into quite a different category: 'no harm has come to those who have entered these ancient tombs with reverence.'[3] And he leaves it there.

Yet, given the profit motive that Carnarvon had introduced, readers of Weigall's *Daily Mail* dispatches were left with a question hanging in the air. Was the 'sole aim' of the Tutankhamun excavations as he had described it, and had the tomb indeed been entered 'with reverence'? Hanging in the air too was a premonition he had had on the day of the opening, concerning Carnarvon's imminent death. Weigall told the story not in the *Mail*, but in an essay based largely on his newspaper pieces and published with the other mentioned above: how he stood with the other correspondents at the retaining wall of the tomb watching the excavating party descend for the opening of the inner chamber; how there was laughter among the excavators when Carnarvon joked about the chairs down there and about giving a concert in the tomb; and how he, Weigall, suddenly turned to his neighbour and said, 'If he goes down in that spirit, I give him six weeks to live.'

He could not for the life of him think why he said it – 'one of those prophetic utterances which seem to issue, without definite intention, from the sub-conscious brain,'[4] he suggested. Despite his certainty that there was no curse written on the walls of Tutankhamun's tomb, there was a curious ambivalence about Weigall's attitude to these things in general. He writes in one place about hearing 'the most absurd nonsense talked in Egypt by those who believe in the malevolence of the ancient dead'. At the same time, he describes various spooky experiences of his own with a certain relish. All coincidence, of course, – and yet, he concludes teasingly, he likes 'to keep an open mind on the subject'.[5]

In other words, if Weigall did believe that Carnarvon had given offence to the dead, it is possible that in some curiously subterranean manner he half believed, or half hoped, that the dead would take their revenge. Perhaps that is why, according to a friend of his, he didn't really mind that the story of the curse of Tutankhamun got about. Rex Engelbach, the man who succeeded Weigall as Chief Inspector of Antiquities for Upper Egypt, believed that it was in fact Weigall who 'disinterred the old story about bad luck coming from Egyptian tombs': 'when my wife and I protested to Weigall, he said, "But see how the public will lap it up." '[6]

It sounds like a simple piece of opportunism, and it is true that Weigall had always had a nose for what would go down well with the public. But the secret of popular writers is that they share – at least in part – the feelings they address. Engelbach doesn't give chapter and verse for his assertion, but perhaps he is referring to the publication of the story of Weigall's premonition. Weigall himself never said that Carnarvon's death was a consequence of a curse, but maybe he knew his readers would draw their own conclusions.

There is a certain justice therefore in the press notices announcing Weigall's death early in 1934. If Weigall had allowed the idea of a curse to gain a foothold, it is not entirely surprising that he should fall victim to it. His family were upset, of course, feeling that he had been trivialized. He himself would probably have seen the joke. For although, as we shall see, his life was full of passionate causes, he tried at the same time always to keep a light heart.


On the face of it, Arthur Edward Pearse Weigall, born on 30 November 1880, belonged to the kind of family that, commonly at that period, provided the army with its officers, the Church with its vicars, and the Empire with its administrators. The German name, pronounced Wygall, was as English by then as five generations in England could make it. His father's family apparently originated in Nuremberg, some of it migrating to Holland, from where, it is said, the immediate ancestor of the English Weigalls came to England in the suite of William of Orange. Since then they had married English spouses, held army commissions, and taken church livings. Some had become artists, solid society portrait painters and sculptors. One of them, Charles Harvey Weigall, a great uncle, became drawing master to the royal family; another, Henry Weigall, a first cousin once removed, painted the Duke of Wellington. He also painted the Duke's niece, Lady Westmorland, and then her daughter, Lady Rose. Shortly after, Lady Rose and Henry Weigall were married, in Westminster Abbey, to the music of a choir of hidden harps.[7]

Weigall never knew his father, Captain Arthur Archibald Denne Weigall, who died on active service in the Afghan Expedition at Kandahar as Paymaster to the 11th (North Devon) Regiment, in the same year that his son was born.[8] The Captain had been the youngest of five brothers and two sisters born to Cecilia Bythesea Brome and the Rev.

Edward Weigall, Vicar of Hurdsfield and then of Buxton. Two of the five brothers had already died as young men: one had been in the Indian Army and the other in the merchant navy. There remained two more, Mitford Weigall, the eldest, who followed his father into the church, and Albert Weigall, a remarkable man who went to Australia and, as Headmaster of Sydney Grammar School from 1867 to 1912, became known as the Father of Australia. Arthur Weigall, his nephew, met him only once or twice but Albert's biographer notes that he helped his younger brother financially at the start of his army career.[9] The sisters were each married, Geraldine ('a saint if ever there was one') to Thomas Minchin Goodeve ('austere and scholarly'), Barrister-at-law and Professor of Mechanics at the Royal College of Science; and Cecilia ('poor and proud' in her long widowhood) to the Rev. Thomas Wilson, episcopal clergyman at Stirling.[10]

On his mother's side there were aunts, four of them, and a dashing young uncle. These, and Weigall's mother Alice ( always known later as Mimi – with a short 'i', as in Timmy ), were the offspring of an Irish mother, Henrietta Fitzgerald, who it is said, eloped at the age of sixteen with an army medical officer of the name of Cowan, then stationed in Ireland, and later in India and Ceylon (now Sri Lanka).[11] Family legend has it that Henrietta was still so much of a child when she left her parents' house that she took her dolls. Their children were Rose, the eldest, dark and handsome, a catholic convert later in life; Lily, who married a housemaster at Uppingham school; and Mary, a charming red-haired woman, who married a relation of Cardinal Manning. Of Florrie little is known, though Mimi was closest to her as a child. The brother, who was much the youngest, became a soldier, and except for a brief glimpse of him in the following pages, little is known about him.

Here, therefore, were plenty of ordinary upper middle class relations. But although many of the administrators and archaeologists Weigall met later would have shared his kind of background, it was in his case a background merely on paper. None of his uncles or aunts figured in his boyhood. There were no holidays with cousins in country vicarages. Practically speaking there was no close family circle, beyond his mother and his elder sister, Geanie. When Mimi became a widow in 1880, she went briefly to Jersey where her father had retired after years stationed in Ceylon, and there her son was born, named Arthur after his dead young father. But she didn't stay. Very soon she left the island for an extraordinary way of life that isolated her from both sides of the family and indeed from anything that most people of her class would have called respectable.

What happened was that she heard the divine call, and became a revivalist Christian missionary, not only working, but living among the poor, first of south London and then of Salford, near Manchester. She describes the occasion in a tract published in 1889 called *Seeking and Saving, being the Rescue work of the Manchester City Mission*, which she wrote together with a fellow worker, J.W. Macgill. Soon after her husband's death, she writes, a friend involved in work among the poor on Jersey took her one night to what was known as a 'midnight meeting' of prostitutes:

The sights I saw, and the talks I had with the girls of Jersey that night, impressed me deeply and I went home shocked and grieved. Day by day I felt the Lord was calling me to that work, and yet I rebelled. "Any work but that, Lord" was constantly on my lips; but I had learnt to obey, and night after night, after putting my little ones in their cots and hearing their little prayers, part of which was "Oh God, bless mammy, and help her to speak to the poor girls who don't love thee and have no friends", I went out into the wicked streets of that beautiful island of Jersey in search of those sinful ones.[12]

It must have been a wild, unreal time for her, with death and birth coming so hard on each other's heels. Jersey itself was no more home than England – though like all English people abroad at that time, she had been taught to call it 'Home' – and civilian life was as strange to her as it must have been to her parents.

Mimi had been a regimental daughter and wife virtually all her life. Her earliest memories were of the officers quarters in Ceylon where, as little girls, she and her sister Florrie had led a charmed existence. They had been tended by adoring ayahs;[13] stable boys had run beside their ponies as they rode to the Cinnamon Gardens; they had worn rosebud muslin frocks, tied with big sashes, and Leghorn hats draped with sweeping white feathers. Her unpublished childhood memoirs lovingly describe this life, as well as their strange and sometimes dangerous adventures. There were moonlit journeys up to the jungle-covered hills in summer, when exhausted bullocks were roused by fires lighted beneath them. She tells of strange processions of 'natives' painted with the stripes and spots of wild animals. Later, as the wife of Captain Weigall, she had followed his regiment to the Zulu wars.[14] Her son remembered thrilling stories of the Zulu chieftain, Cetewayo, and his impis; she knew the officers who had been killed at the terrible massacre of Isandhwalla, those who fought in defence of Rorke's Drift, and 'nearly everyone in command at Ulundi'.[15] It had been a gay and martial life, full of the sound of bugles, and the music of regimental balls. And underlying everything had been the effortless assumptions and habits of command.

Now she had only a restricted life on a widow's pension to look forward to, marooned with a father and mother retired on half pay. Weigall remembered them as a cantankerous couple, fretting after past glories. In later life Mimi was active, decisive, and dominating. She was much the same as a young woman. For her the only calamity worse than widowhood would have been dependence and inactivity. Here was the answer – a field for action, another Ceylon or Africa, a barbarous pageant flourishing on the underside of Home. And yet it must be said that it became for her a labour of love. She had no political perspective on the problem of poverty, but neither was she a moral martinet. In fact she realized that she could never operate without love, and the fact that she was initially revolted by the prostitutes dismayed her. With a characteristic mixture of downright sense and unashamed emotion, she resolved to ask God what he meant by calling her to work which was so 'irksome' to her:

I went very definitely to Him about it, telling Him all my shrinking from contact with these poor fallen ones, and entreating Him to make me love them; and from that moment I realized a complete change. ... from that hour I have loved these girls with an "unfeigned love" ... Love has a wonderful power. May I recommend all rescue workers to definitely ask and receive this, for it makes such a difference both in one's own experience and in power over these unloved ones.[16]

It was not, of course, unheard of at that time to do what Mimi did. The very poor of late Victorian England lived hideous lives. Drink, disease, crime and destitution were their everyday lot. The gulf between them and the middle classes was so great that they might have belonged to different races and nations. Naturally, there were worried and conscientious people: Christians, Socialists, Christian Socialists, agnostic philanthropists, political scientists and social investigators all agonized over what to do. Young men with university educations now sought livings in darkest London, and with them went volunteer helpers, particularly women.[17] The Homes for orphans, the Reformatories and Penitentiaries for fallen girls, the refuges for girls of virtuous character in moral peril, all proliferated wherever these ladies and gentlemen went. One of the most well-known examples of this phenomenon was the partnership of Henrietta and Samuel Augustus Barnett, who in 1873 took up the living of St. Jude's, Whitechapel, in the East End of London. Together with a large circle of women volunteers, they laboured to improve not only the condition of the poor, but their aesthetic sensibilities, to which end the Whitechapel Art Gallery was established. But many of the volunteers returned to comfortable homes each evening, and led their fashionable lives in parallel. What was unusual about Mimi was that she didn't give herself a way out.

Clapham was no Whitechapel. It had its grand houses and wide green common. But there were parts of it, especially by the railway junction, which were as insalubrious as anywhere in London. The social investigator, Charles Booth, in his great work, *Life and Labour of the People of London* (1902), describes some streets there, 'bad patches' he calls them, which act 'as a moral cess-pool towards which poverty and vice flow in the persons of those who can do no better' and which are 'the despair of the clergy who find it impossible to put any permanent social order into a body of people continually shifting and as continually recruited by the incoming elements of evil and distress.'[18]

Weigall's recollections of this period are grim, particularly of the Clapham house with its pious texts on the walls and brown linoleum on the floor, and 'the terrible street in front and a yard at the back'. Judging by her later work in Salford, Mimi probably joined an extremely Low church, akin to the Salvationists, though Weigall never remembers her wearing the distinctive bonnet. He did however remember her praying that he might become a 'true soldier of Christ', and singing the Salvation Army hymns to him about mansions in the sky 'where the walls were of crystal and the gateways of pearl' and 'where there would be no more sorrow'. Charles Booth describes the efforts of the various churches there, the High, the Broad, the Evangelical, and then finally he mentions a 'small iron mission building which has only recently become a parish church' and which 'seeks to attract the working classes by lively preaching on everyday subjects, with bright music, and the use of the lantern at special services.'[19] Perhaps this was Mimi's hall.

Life among these streets was of course unhealthy, and Weigall's sister Geanie nearly died of diphtheria during this time. When they moved to Manchester, in about 1887, Mimi installed them at some distance from her work, in Chorlton, a rural suburb at that time. Mimi was appointed to the quaintly named post of Lady Superintendent of the City Mission Rescue Work in Salford, and from this period on, Arthur's memories are full and vivid.

Salford in the 1880s and '90s was a desperate place. No one could better describe it than the medical officer for the borough, who wrote in 1886:

> I do not think that the members of the Health Committee can have fully realized the pitiable condition in which the denizens of these wretched areas exist. The greed of successive generations of property jobbers has succeeded in heaping together on an acre of ground, the largest possible number of tenements, without regard either to the health of the occupants, or to the requirements of common decency. The living rooms ... are dark and gloomy in the extreme, and the stagnant air they contain is horribly polluted ... with the foetid emanations from the filth-sodden earth and from the too contiguous cess-pool ...

A helpful footnote explains: 'The earth underneath and around the houses in certain of these older districts is contaminated by soakage from midden cess-pools, and broken or leaky drains.' Consumption, he continues, fever and diarrhoea cause death-rates up to seven times as high as those in healthier parts of the town.[20]

The Manchester City Mission was active in many directions: it ran homes for orphaned or abandoned children, for the care and training of 'fallen' women and prostitutes, and it organized a uniformed Ambulance Corps. This Ambulance Corps was the cutting edge of Mimi's work. It was made up of men largely from the same social class as those it attempted to help, and its job was to make nightly rounds all over the city, intervening in drunken brawls, 'rescuing' prostitutes, and generally administering to the wounded and incapable. Mimi went with them, the only female to do so, although at first she was 'dreadfully frightened', especially of the drunken men. In time, however, the handling of drunkenness became something of a speciality, and she was able to take charge, she says, with no more than a ' "Now then, brother, take hold of my arm, and I'll see if I cannot get you home" '.[21] She would come home after her Saturday nights, Weigall remembered, carrying a harvest of 'pistols, heavy belts, knives, pokers and so forth – which she had taken from the hands of would-be murderers.'

It was the plight of the women in particular that appalled her most, compelled as they were 'to live among knocks, kicks and blows' for the sake of a roof: 'it was high time' she wrote briskly, 'that something was done to put an end to this state of things.'[22] In ten stories of redemption and reclamation – Mary, Kate, Ellen, Hester, Lizzie, and so on, all prostitutes, forced to be so by poverty or by drunk and brutal husbands – Mimi explains how she would persuade these girls to come into the safety of a refuge, where they would be tended by volunteer nurses. From there they would move to a special Home, where they learned various domestic skills, and where they could earn their keep as laundresses, or go on into domestic service. It was a humble goal, perhaps, but better than nothing. At any rate, Mimi seems to have made a deep impression, for twenty and thirty years later, long after she had left the city, she was still writing to 'her girls', and receiving long affectionate letters in reply.

Mimi's voice comes over as firm and shrewd. According to Weigall, she always preserved a dry sense of humour. By contrast, what made the greatest impression on the children was the theatricality of the whole thing: the knives and pokers and blood-stained belts. The set-piece was the Sunday afternoon meeting at the mission hall where their mother preached, to which they were sometimes taken. There they sat, scrubbed clean to the point of itchiness, up on the platform, among the bandsmen and the uniforms – God's elect – watching and watched by rows and rows of the hungry and unwashed:

> I shall never forget the intensity of some of the meetings at the mission-hall: I did not understand it, or take part in it, but I was conscious of it. A man would get up in the crowd and begin to pray passionately, his face upturned, his eyes tight shut, his hands outstretched; and those around him would punctuate his words by fervent cries of "Amen!" or "Alleluia".

But the very intensity of it repelled Weigall: the woman in the front row with one yellow fang, a feather drooping over one eye, who used to smile at him and call out to know whether he was saved; the black-bearded missionary, who stood him on a table and catechized him; the hiss of the gas jets, the smell of dirt and sweat. He was frankly revolted. None of his mother's love for these people rubbed off on him. ' "I hate them, and they smell," ' cries his alter ego, Sebastian, in a semi-autobiographical novel he wrote in his forties,[23] and that just about sums it up.

And who can blame him? In this novel, he describes himself and his sister as wandering 'at the edge of their mother's clamorous dream, hardly yet able to follow her far into it, yet unable to pass out of the reach of its violent hullabaloo'. It was 'an abnormal, hysterical existence'.[24] Furthermore he could see his mother was suffering. He remembers finding her sometimes in tears, her face buried in the pillows and 'to this day I can hear the words she was saying as I crept in: "My burden is more than I can bear, O Lord." ' He remembers her taking him in her arms and saying, ' "O if only your father had lived," ' and then getting out his father's box of sketches and the album of regimental photographs, and describing all the people and places while her tears splashed onto the back of his hand.

Not that the two children weren't conventionally brought up as far Mimi's circumstances allowed. At first she engaged a governess for them, and then, after a move which brought the family closer to Eccles, they each went to day schools there. There were also summer holidays, usually at Red Wharf Bay on Anglesey which was then, before the railway reached it, a tiny village 'wild and primitive in the extreme', he writes. They rented tumble-down cottages – one of which actually did fall down in the wind shortly after they left it. Another had a hole in the bedroom floor through which he and his sister pulled up their morning can of hot water on a string from the kitchen below. Twice, in the winters, they even went to the south of France, to Mentone, where he was overwhelmed by the colours after the grey of Eccles – the blues of sea and sky, the glow of the roof tiles and the oranges on the trees. How exactly Mimi's finances stretched to the Riviera – she drew her widow's pension, says Arthur, 'very little supplemented' – is uncertain. Perhaps there was, in fact, a little help from the family, particularly from Albert in Australia, who had helped his younger brother in the early days.

Manchester was hateful after the Mediterranean, but it was made more bearable by Louie, one of his mother's 'girls'. Louie had made and sold paper windmills in the street and had been brought by Mimi to live in the house and look after the children. Once in charge of them she turned out to be a spellbinder of genius, drawing them both into an extraordinary world of stories and games:

> She was rather self-conscious and shy when other people were present; and at meals she tried to be very genteel. But when she was alone with my sister and me, there would come into her eyes a wild look, and she would begin to smile and move about restlessly, ... and it was then that the magic was wrought. A wonderful atmosphere, which I now picture as quite golden, descended upon us: everything glowed, everything was filled with happiness.

Mimi, Geanie, Louie – it was an exclusively female household. He also made friends among the 'fallen' women at the Home, where Mimi had an apartment for her occasional use, but they would puzzle him sometimes with their odd remarks and knowing looks. Geanie, of course, was never allowed there. In his later years Weigall was always very sure about male and female spheres, and of what should belong to each. Perhaps these early years account for it – the only boy among so many women. And he wasn't just any boy, he was his father's son, his father's substitute almost. The two of them occupied the same sacred ground in his mother's heart, and Mimi would weep over any act of goodness in him as a sign of inherited virtue.

His father's photograph, his sword and medals hung on the wall, as did a Zulu shield and some assegais, or spears:

> Throughout my childhood he was always a legendary figure to me: a man of heroic mould, whose quiet eyes looked down at me from the wall ... a little sternly perhaps, though he was said to have been very sweet in character, and not often aroused to ill-temper. I used to make up wonderful stories about him; and for many years, I remember I had the feeling that he was not dead, but that he would come back one day, telling us how he had only been "reported dead", and how he had remained in captivity amongst the wild tribesmen up in the north.

The boy developed a passion for tin soldiers. With his mother's help, he created an elaborate landscape, with sand and cardboard hills. It was, of course, Zululand, 'to me the chief land of adventure in the world.' Boxes of tin Zulus were on sale everywhere, but not everyone had a father who had fought the terrible feathered warriors themselves, nor a pair of field glasses through which that father had been 'the first officer to see the Zulus coming on that memorable day' at Ulundi:

> I remember I used to stare through them as a child, trying so hard to see what he saw that presently the swarms of black warriors took shape and I seemed to watch them as they came bounding forward over the rolling ground.

Sometimes an old general or a Field Marshall from former days would visit the family, and the boy would wait breathlessly for stories of blood and gore. To watch the soldiers of the XVIIIth Lancers, stationed in Manchester, was a pleasure so exquisite that no greater punishment could be devised by his governess than to hold his head down as they passed. The only member of the family that is ever mentioned in this early part of his life is his mother's younger brother, because he had been in Egypt with his regiment, the XVth Hussars.

Egypt itself appears not to have played a part yet in Weigall's imagination. He would have been too young to take in the battle of Tel el Kebir, which brought the English into Egypt as rulers in all but name; even mad Gordon, so beloved by the British public, and 'martyred' by the Mahdi at Khartoum, would have made little impression on a three year old. But it is interesting that in his fictional autobiography, Weigall alters the place and date of his father's death from Afghanistan in 1880 to Tel el Kebir in Egypt in 1882, and alters his own birth too, to keep the coincidence. Thus British Egypt, springing as it were out of the death of his father, is made to tie in with his own origins.

British ascendancy in the world at large left its mark on him, as it did on most boys of his generation. The Zulu war, the Afghan war, the battle of Tel el Kebir formed a backdrop against which the fluttering Union Jack met an answering flutter in his breast. They were stirring times; Imperialism had entered its most theatrical phase. As James Morris puts it:

> Wars against ... the Afghans, the Boers, the Zulus – the Suez coup – the invasion of Egypt ... – the death of Gordon – ... all these marvellous events, occurring month after month through the decades, had sustained the British people in a condition of flush ... It was like one long, thrilling piece of theatre, with scarcely a flat moment, and a scenario of brilliant daring.[25]

Of course there were those who refused to be flushed, but Weigall grew up with no experience of dissent or doubt. His mother, however unconventional her methods, was no intellectual. She cherished her husband's regimental medals, and the son, his namesake, who would follow in his footsteps. Not until he had experienced the east at first hand did he begin to find another slant on the world.

# Chapter 2

# 'select establishments'
# 1892–1897

Weigall's accounts of himself in his unfinished memoirs and in his semi-autobiographical novel suggest a childhood passed in a city of strangers, while unknown cousins and aunts existed somewhere in a parallel but unvisited world. To some extent this was true, but Mimi never completely lost touch, and when her son reached the critical age of eleven, the larger family came into play. Geanie now had a governess, but a boarding school had to be found for the boy. Mimi turned to one of her sisters, Lily, the one who had married a housemaster at Uppingham. A fellow housemaster, one Walter Perry, had recently moved from Uppingham to become headmaster at a prep school near Malvern. The matter was thus decided. In the summer of 1892, when he was eleven and a half, Weigall entered Hillside School. From the suburbs of Manchester he was translated to the slopes of Malvern Beacon, and for the first time in his life found himself exclusively among boys. Not only that, but among boys of a kind he had not known before.

'Rather a select establishment ... the thirty or forty boys were mainly drawn from the then exclusive grades of English country life.'[1] He was immediately at sea. It baffled him that he should be congratulated by one of the boys on being the only son of a dead father, and commiserated with for having to wait until he was twenty-one before he could have a 'free hand'. The talk was all of horses, hounds, and trout fishing. Under close and pitiless questioning, he revealed a hopeless ignorance of foxes. He tried to make up with the tigers that he imagined his father had shot, but they were no substitute. He wrote to Mimi asking for information about coveys, and the habits of otters. But in time, he became adroit at concealing his background.

Boarding-school life of the period, with its solemn inculcation of 'this great business of ours, of learning how to be, to do, to do without, and to depart', weighed heavily on the under-fourteens. One of the things they had to do without was their mothers. Given that his only parent was a mother, and one that he adored, this bore particularly hard on Weigall. Tears were another disgrace, even tears of rage, as he found on being beaten in an official fight; but extending a gallant hand to a batsman who had just accidentally broken his jaw, and laughing lightly as he slipped in and out of consciousness, made him a hero.

Rewards and punishments were little public rituals. When you were sent to Coventry[2] you were handed a slip of paper with the words of your fate written on it. Everyone, including the masters, knew the form. With the same sense of ceremony, the boy who had hit him 'insisted on my accepting a "token of esteem" from him and some of the others, which took the form of a few quite valuable postage stamps'. Even sex – a darkly fascinating subject that gripped the school and at one point brought it close to scandal – resolved itself eventually in formal set pieces. Apparently Weigall, having been as obsessed as anyone, suffered a sudden revulsion, and resolved to cleanse his mind. To this end, he gathered his friends together and made a formal pact with them to abjure all beastliness. When word of this pact got out, the headmaster delivered a speech to the whole school, in which Weigall – to his 'scarlet shame' – was credited with having restored his faith in boys.

The Anglican service, now encountered for the first time, was another piece of theatre – the gabbled archaic language, the standing up and kneeling down so ceremonious and mechanical, the prayers for the Queen and Albert Edward Prince of Wales. From being an antidote to beer and gin, God suddenly became a courtly figure, enduing 'the Lords of the Council and all the Nobility with wisdom' and delivering the English people from 'sedition, privy conspiracy, and rebellion'. Compared with the rowdy fisticuffs with Satan that he had been brought up on, it was an attractive picture.

In some way related to this was the casual self-confidence of the boys, their offhandedness, which was new and fascinating to him. It dawned on him that being bothered about things wasn't quite gentlemanly. But he couldn't alter himself. He describes sudden fits of frenzy – wild high spirits, riotous rebellion – both here and at his next school, Wellington College. In his last term at Hillside he created a sensation. He had been sent to Coventry, unjustly he maintains, and it had lasted for days, the whole school combining to shut him out of all communication. It had been a shattering experience, and in the end he snapped, smashing a window and dangerously cutting his wrist. He came to be regarded as a maverick, not quite clubbable. And yet, as he explains:

> ... my one desire was to be inconspicuous, that is to say, to be more or less like all the others. Yet I was hopelessly different from them in outlook; and this fact I was at one moment trying to hide, and at the next was defiantly asserting. No wonder I was regarded as a dark horse, for my own mind was a welter of darkness.

According to the headmaster in his autobiographical novel, Weigall's (or Sebastian's) character was at bottom un-English, formed 'during those years you were under the influence of wild people ... who went banging about Whitechapel with tambourines in their hands, like a lot of Italians':

> You do not seem to have grasped the essential fact that English gentlemen stand for something sane and orderly ... Your behaviour has at times been just a little bit – well, Dago. ...

'If English boys, after years of schooling, were still open to brainstorms of reckless youthfulness,' he imagines the man exclaiming, 'then goodbye to their country's prestige and dominion! ... what would become of India and Egypt and Zululand ... which were ruled by the Englishman's sangfroid, dignity and experience?'[3]

Weigall was in fact as much an outsider here as he had been on the platform in the Mission Hall. It was not in his nature to regret or repine, but it is clear that he was not happy. There was one consolation. During his time at Hillside, Mimi and Geanie moved from Eccles to Buxton in Derbyshire, on the edge of the Peak District. Mimi continued her work in Manchester, an hour away by train, but on a reduced scale. Weigall himself saw little more of the slums: 'My mother,' he wrote in his memoir, 'no doubt, felt that the kind of school career she had settled for me was not compatible with my earlier manner of life among the missionaries.' She might have been thinking of Geanie too, who was growing into an attractive and amusing girl. Whatever Mimi's reasons, it was a wonderful change for the children and holidays were magical times, especially at Christmas, when they skated and tobogganed among the snowy hills.

Buxton was where Weigall's paternal grandfather, the Rev. Edward Weigall, had been vicar, although he was no longer alive. Perhaps there were friends of the family that Mimi knew, or perhaps she had already met the curate of Buxton, George Craggs, who was later to become her second husband. Other relations also make an appearance at this juncture of Weigall's life, if only in passing. Now, at fourteen, the question of which school arose again. Wellington College had been established in the 1860s for the sons of army officers, and Weigall would have qualified for a bursary. Besides, his cousins had gone there, the six sons of Henry Weigall and Lady Rose (the daughter of the Earl of Westmorland). Although they were fairly distant, and as a boy Weigall never knew them, Mimi would not have been above feeling that where these particular Weigalls had gone before, her Weigall would do well to follow.

He was withdrawn from Hillside, and a happy Easter term was passed, at home in Buxton, with Craggs coaching him for the Common Entrance: 'I look back to these days with pleasure as some of the happiest I had known,' he wrote. He must have worked too, for the school took him, and in the summer term of 1895 he was put in Kempthorne's House, where the other Weigalls had been. Once again he found himself among a 'select and exclusive' lot of boys, for Kempthorne's had been known as the 'House of Lords':

> We were not allowed to invite any boy from any other House into our sacred precincts ... Certain kinds of rather plebeian sweets, such as bull's-eyes, were not allowed to be bought; and it was considered correct to drink honest English ale with our dinner, however much we might dislike it.

These rules were enforced by the head of House, 'a red-haired Stanley, brother of the present Lord Derby', who was also particularly anxious to uphold the tradition of boxing, and made the boys have three rounds every morning before breakfast.

There were the usual initiation rites and a certain amount of bullying. But Weigall had grown into a very strong boy, not tall, but thick-set, and therefore suffered less than others. Furthermore, the sudden fits already mentioned sometimes took the form of blind rages in which he went berserk with fists and feet, so people were wary of him. But what really made a difference to him was the sense of freedom that Wellington gave him. Each boy had his own small room, and instead being 'one of a squabbling, chattering herd ... the dominant impression I received was of liberty.'

Liberty, it seems, to do nothing in particular. Later in life he worked with almost manic enthusiasm, but at this stage, no one seems to have kindled his interest. Harold Nicolson, who was at Wellington from 1900-1903, wrote that his most lasting memory of the place was of boredom: 'I was bored there as I have never been bored in all my life.'[4] Weigall's experience was much the same, the lack of anything to stir his mind. He had a passion for drawing, which went quite unnoticed by the school. He seems to have been thought of as rather stupid. The Army, which he had always been destined for, faded from his future since there 'seemed little likelihood of my having the brains to pass the exams.' In consequence, he says, he was placed on the classical side of the school, where he languished happily at the bottom of the form with a chum from the same House.

The vacancy was filled by buffoonery. He tells of pocketing a mouse, and then, as it scampered across the master's desk, of diverting all enquiry with a frantic, top-speed improvisation on mice, mouse infestation, the dangers to health, the need for cats, two cats in fact, one for the night and one for the day. Once, he took it into his head with a friend to bellow out the words of the school hymn in chapel so slowly that at the end they were left on their own, trailing out the last phrase into the astonished silence. Weigall had a weakness for farce that lasted all his life. Among his papers there are torn off scraps, envelopes, backs of bills and menus scribbled over with nonsense verses, jokes, cartoons and caricatures. He never lost sight of childhood – at least he hoped not to. Later in his life he railed against the dryness and pomposity of historians and archaeologists, and if he valued anything in himself it was his ability – however intermittent – to keep alive the spirit of Louie, the paper windmill girl. He believed strongly that 'this ability to discover fairy tales in one's modern surroundings is very closely connected with the ability to become excited over one's work.'

Meanwhile, life at home was changing. Geanie, almost grown up, had been sent to a finishing school at Soleur in Switzerland, and Mimi had charmed Weigall's old tutor, the Rev George Craggs, into matrimony. Not liking the name George, Mimi, decisive as ever, renamed her husband Tony. The family moved to Everton, Liverpool, where Craggs became vicar of Emmanuel Church – much to Weigall's sorrow, for he had been happy at Buxton. Thus Mimi entered on new duties as a parson's wife. Weigall imagines her sadness at having to give up Manchester and the considerable position she had made for herself there. Perhaps this was so, for she took up the same kind of work soon enough when Craggs moved a few years later from Liverpool to London. But for the moment she may have been glad of the change.

# Chapter 3

# From pedigrees to hieroglyphs
# 1897–1901

Weigall left Wellington College in 1897, when he was not yet seventeen, and shortly afterwards he paid a visit for the first time in his life to his Uncle Mitford, his father's eldest brother, who was vicar of Frodingham, a country village near Doncaster. Weigall remembered him as

> a stout, grey-bearded man, who laughed a great deal and seemed full of benevolence … a typical squire-parson, connected in my mind with guns and fishing-rods, port and old silver, smooth lawns and stables … he told me little about my father, and contented himself by permitting me to make a copy of the family pedigree, and draw some coats of arms.[1]

One can imagine Weigall searching his uncle's face for a likeness to Mimi's photographs of his father, and feeling closer, in a theoretical way, to the Weigall side of the family than he had ever done before. After all, he might have felt that his father's memory had suffered by Mimi's recent marriage to Craggs, and that he himself was a little out in the cold. Perhaps he pestered his uncle with questions about the family, and the old man, hoping for respite, showed him the family tree and told him to get on with it.

Tracing his way through the various Weigall and Brome branches (Brome was his Weigall grandmother's name), Weigall found himself fascinated, first with the family, and then, it seems, with the whole idea of getting back into history. It may have helped that, according to Uncle Mitford's tree, the Bromes had a romantic-sounding past with aristocratic connections going back to the Plantagenets, the name Brome being a variant of broom, or planta genesta; also that Elizabeth I had given them the manor and lands of Bishop's Stortford, seized from the Church by Henry VIII. Weigall no doubt found these ancestors gratifying after so many years of concealing his origins. The coats of arms must have been a special pleasure.

At any rate when he came home to Liverpool he didn't let the matter rest, but 'at once began to frequent the public library where I read all I could about our history.' If the meticulous work on Mimi's Irish family, now among the family papers, dates from this period, there was something almost lunatic about his new fascination. In little swarms of tiny black letters, the Kings of Leinster and Connaught march across acres of thick white paper, forking and multiplying along beautifully red-inked lines, each with some identifying note: Herema the Calm, succeeded by Iriel the Prophet, born 325 BC, followed by Smiorgioill, whose son, Fiachaiiof, the River of Labruine, was slain at the battle of Bealgadain, 200 BC, and so on and on, until there's no more room at 341 AD.

The bizarre transition from this to Egyptian history is best told in his words:

> Now it happened that I also here read up the family pedigree of my Irish grand-mother; but most Irish families trace their descent from Miletus, their legendary progenitor, and Miletus is said in the old tales to have married a daughter of a Pharaoh of Egypt. Thus I turned to books on Ancient Egypt, and therewith I became so deeply interested in that romantic land that I forgot all about pedigrees and family records, and devoted all my spare time to studying the history of the Pharaohs.

Now that he was interested and was using his hitherto unused brains, he began to feel, almost physically, sensations of intense enthusiasm. Slipping out of the vicarage whenever he could, he pored over the reports in the library on recent Egyptian exca-vations, and felt a thrill that no schoolmaster had ever raised in him.

However, while he was thus absorbed, another kind of future was being plotted for him. Weigall had left Wellington with no prospects: 'To my mother and step-father, I was simply a very backward youth, cursed with an "artistic temperament", fond of drawing and painting, and inclined to develop into a dilettante.' The Army had faded, and neither University nor Art School were thought of. There was probably very little money, otherwise Art School at least might have been considered, for there was a tradition in the family. But if money was a consideration, something less risky had to be found. Of all the solid professions, the one hit upon was accountancy.

Mimi must have been passing the word among her friends and connections. One of the more unlikely of these was an erstwhile violinist in the band at the old Manchester missionary meetings, Ernest Crewdson of Messrs Jones, Crewdson and Yonatt, Char-tered Accountants. This person now came forward with an offer to take Weigall into the London office of his firm, and it was settled that he should be coached for the Preliminary examination. In the January of 1898, when he was just turned seventeen, he managed, to his surprise, 'to pass this rather stiff examination with credit':

> I am sure I don't know how I did it, for my brain was full of other things ... Beside a mass of Egyptological literature, I worked through a great many histories; I taught myself the rudiments of Coptic, Arabic, Persian and Hebrew; I read a lot of Huxley, Herbert Spencer and other great thinkers; and I devoured a mass of books on Biblical criticism. I was obsessed with a passion for knowledge; and my coaching for the examination seemed to be a sort of prison.

But with the passing of the accountancy exam, the prison door shut behind him. Mimi persuaded Craggs to give up his Liverpool living, and to apply for the curacy, then falling vacant, at Christ Church, Lancaster Gate, in London. Thus the whole family moved to a flat in Bayswater – 13, Hereford Mansions – and in August 1898, Weigall joined the army of clerks flowing into the City every day to add up figures from morning to evening.

He did it outwardly without complaint. But 'it was tedious work', he wrote, going through the books of City companies, shops and workshops, hunting for pennies and shillings missing from this or that side of the balance sheet. His description of the lunchtime break is a glimpse into a netherworld:

> You went down a lot of stairs, and presently you walked into a vast room which was thick with smoke. There, at hundreds of marble-topped tables, groups of men were playing dominoes, eating sandwiches, and drinking coffee … I can still see faintly, as through a mist of smoke, the dark-clad figures leaning over the tables, top-hats on the backs of their heads, and slips of paper over their shirt-cuffs, to keep them clean.

Inwardly, however, a mental and emotional revolt was taking place. The last year had been one of extraordinary mental stimulation, and it was impossible to shut down the furnaces now. He used to save his lunch money – two shillings a day – and either go hungry or eat in an A.B.C., a chain of cheap cafeterias, in order to buy books on ancient history or archaeology. He became a member of the London Library, his subscription paid for by Hubert Greenwood of the London County Council, presumably a friend of Mimi's. He read furiously and without method, and he began to suffer agonies of frustration. His days became hateful, and with them the whole straitjacket of social expectation. For the first time in his life, he suffered a revulsion against all the certainties he had been brought up with.

Mimi was of course the nearest representative of these, and it was inevitable that the thing she stood for above everything else – the Christian faith – should be the first casualty in Weigall's revolt: 'My notebooks of those days are full of jeers at the scriptures, and my Bible is scarred all over with notes of interrogation and scoffing exclamation marks.' He managed, heroically, to keep his thoughts to himself, but his crisis of faith, as with so many others of the period, dragged into its vortex the whole of life as he knew it: 'There was nothing to hope for, no way out of the prison in which we were all cooped up; and when we died that was the end of us.' Egypt was his escape, and in the evenings, he says, 'I used to make my nightly flight to the banks of the Nile, and to parade the halls of the Pharaohs with beating heart.' Nothing so practical as a profession in Egyptology crossed his mind. Egypt was simply a secret dream, an enchanted land which released him from the dreary London days and the Bayswater flat.

It is curious how often Weigall's life reads like a novel. Admittedly, the narrative of these early years depends heavily on his own account, and being a born story-teller, he could make even accountancy sound apocalyptic. Just at this crisis, February 1899, there arrived a *deus* – or rather a *dea* – *ex machina*. A woman – an older woman, at that – now entered his life to turn the whole thrust of events in a new direction. Weigall never gives her name, saying only that she was married, that she was in her thirties and that with her husband she was of some importance in intellectual and political circles. He also describes her – slim and freckly, with a lot of teeth and an infectious laugh, dressed in the sage greens and russet browns affected by artistic women at that time. Looking back through the cynical eyes of his middle age he summed her up as 'rather a tom-boy, … [who] liked to regard herself as an airy, fairy, romping, girlish, boyish, child of nature.'

Their first meeting was at a dinner party given by Mimi, which itself throws an interesting light on Mimi's circle at that time. Her work in Manchester had put her in touch with social reformers, and possibly through them with the more intellectual end of fashionable liberalism. At any rate, it was all above Weigall's head, he says, and when the company left the table, he excused himself and went off to his room – not, this time, to his books – but to his other obsession, the meticulous drawing and colouring in of comic mythological beasts. Soon there was a tap on the door and in she slipped, saying that she had come to make friends with him because she had liked him awfully at supper, and did he like her?

And so began a series of shy meetings which speedily grew into a romance. In the midst of his despair and unutterable boredom with life, he found himself dazzled and transported. Until then, he says, he had hardly ever spoken to a woman outside his own household. Suddenly here was one, a woman of the world, who found him attractive. Not only that – and this was the real significance of the affair – she told him he was clever: 'I, clever! … I had always regarded myself as the fool of the family, … but no, she would have it that I was a scholar in embryo, and she told me I ought to abandon the City and go up to Oxford.'

He was obviously an intriguing youth, a strange mixture of ignorance and recondite knowledge, obsessive, enthusiastic, and deeply susceptible. She had been struck by his mythological beasts, and no doubt he showed her the Belloc-like verses that went with them. This was to develop into a long narrative in comic verse, entitled *How Twenty-five Monsters were Found*, which included expertly finished pen and ink cartoons of the two men in the story – a mad professor with a brush of spiky black hair, in search of myths and monsters, and a hapless young man, drawn reluctantly in to this lunatic quest. Some of it may have been inspired by the professors that he began to meet at this time, but some of it clearly comes from a later period when he was in Egypt. But if she saw any of it she couldn't have helped being amused:

Professor Werk is of that class
Of humble men who like to pass
Their lives in deeply thinking.
He loves to sit and write and read
Until he's very ill indeed
And both his eyes are blinking.

Obviously the boy was worth the risk to her reputation, if only for the fun. She, in turn, was a revelation to him. As she went about, taking him to concerts and galleries, reading poetry aloud, she changed the whole aspect of things. His schools had successfully made a Philistine of him, for until he met her he had 'always thought that poetry was effeminate stuff.' To love her was a liberal education, whatever else it was.

But it was a short crammer's course, for all was over by the autumn of that year, 1899. One day he found a note to her from another man, and then his mother found a letter to Weigall from her. There were tears, accusations and admissions, a whiff of possible scandal. In an agony of mind and heart, at least on Weigall's side, they said their last goodbyes. For weeks he was ill, and couldn't work, and soon after he left the City for good. He never saw her again, and at the time of writing his memoir she was dead. But he remained eternally grateful to her for rousing him from his torpor. In an imagined scene on the Day of Judgement, he makes her say to the great Judge: ' "I found him an untutored boy, consigned like a dumb animal to a life's imprisonment in a City office; I left him a grown man, setting out upon a healthy, enthusiastic career. If you please, Judge, I woke him up." '

Whether, in fact, it was all her doing, or whether events were moving in an Egypto-logical direction in any case is arguable, though it spoils the story. She probably gave him the confidence to speak up at home, but Mimi herself must by then have been aware of his consuming interest. At any rate, through a mutual friend, a colleague of her Uppingham brother-in-law, she obtained an introduction to Denison Ross, Professor of Oriental Languages at University College, London. Ross, who had been appointed Professor in 1895 when he was only twenty-five, was a man of huge energy and erudition, a linguist proficient in thirty languages – Professor Werk, by the way, wrote in 'English, French, or Dutch/ With much the same delight, and much/ The same command of spelling.' He too was a lover of nonsense, and a man of enthusi-asms, consumed, wrote Weigall, 'by a very passion of romance which shakes him to his far-distant core; he laughs – or shall I say shouts? – with the merriment of his friends and weeps with their sorrows.' In his autobiography, *Both Ends of the Candle*, Ross says that the young Weigall was sent to him for advice about a career, and that since he had 'a gift for drawing and a taste for things Egyptian', he advised him to take up Egyptology.[2]

Ross was the least discouraging of the three whose advice Weigall sought, and the most cheerful about his prospects. Two other eminent men to whom Ross introduced him were less sanguine. Professor Rhys Davis, the Asiatic and Buddhist scholar, and Percy Newberry, an Egyptologist at that time in charge of a survey of the Theban necropolis, both took the prudent line in favour of accountancy, at any rate for some time longer. However, once he had taken the plunge they were staunch allies, and it was Newberry who gave him his first small piece of professional work: 'He asked me to make some tracings for him at the British Museum, and paid me a couple of pounds for the work, which was the first money I ever earned in archaeology.'

Weigall's future was therefore being actively debated and steps were being taken at the same time as his romance was in progress, by others apart from the lady in ques-tion. So much so, that when the affair ended, and Weigall left the City, he wrote a breathless letter to Newberry confiding the whole thing to him. He wanted to explain that the causes for his decision to abandon accountancy were desperate rather than rational, and that he hadn't done it solely because of Egypt. He says, with perhaps just a touch of pride, that he's been 'terribly in love with a married lady' but that because he sees it's all so wrong he has 'been brave enough to refuse to ever see her again, although I love her with all my heart.' 'Since I took this step (last Friday) I have of course been frantic':

> I shall leave the City, because as you can see it would be impossible for me to exist unless I was doing something which interested me, and helped me to forget myself … for the present I *must* work at Egyptology and drawing – the only things that will take my mind off.[3]

Egypt had taken his mind off the City, and now it would distract him from his love. But he was beginning to want something more practical than dreams. In the same letter he tentatively asks if Newberry could possibly make use of him in Egypt: 'I am awfully keen on Egypt as you know, … I should of course risk the chance of there being no billet going after all, and in the meantime I would work up French, German, drawing, or anything else you might suggest.' The boy was clearly not to be fobbed off with a few tracings. In fact he fairly staggered Newberry at this time by telling him about an article he was writing to protest against the mislabelling of the antiquities in the Egyptian galleries of the British Museum. The man responsible for this was the Keeper, at that time a certain Dr Ernest Alfred Wallis Budge, a prolific scholar and a formidable character to tangle with. Newberry wrote back warning Weigall not to be such a fool:

> Whatever you do be very cautious; it is much easier making enemies than friends … Few know better than I do the absurdities of naming that are to be seen at the British Museum but as a friend, I ask you, is it wise to attack a well-known official? … Nobody knows who you are and whatever you said would have no weight with the *public* against the official keeper of Oriental Antiquities! I am quite sure that Budge would make it very unpleasant for you afterwards and is it worth your making an enemy of him?[4]

Weigall's scoffing comment to this letter foreshadows the battling, crusading spirit of his later career. His mother would have been proud of him: 'It shows the awe in which Dr Budge is held by the English savants. It is said that this round, chubby, spectacled little man can entirely spoil the career of any unfortunate who dares to cross his path … I nevertheless feel it a duty to take up arms against him in so just a cause.'

Perhaps others advised him too, for there is no record of his doing so on this occasion. But Newberry was unwittingly prophetic. Budge's operations in Egypt, exporting antiquities from there for the British Museum collections, came to represent everything that Weigall most passionately and publicly attacked. And although the two men do not appear ever to have clashed directly, by a bizarre twist Budge made a late entry in Weigall's story, and succeeded after his death in making it very unpleasant for Weigall's reputation.

But to return to 1900. For the time being Egypt had to wait. The idea of Oxford had caught on at home, and plans were in train to get him tutored for the entrance exam. It seems extraordinary, in view of Weigall's decided preference for Egyptology, that University College, London was not chosen. Egyptology as an academic discipline was in its infancy, but a start had been made with the first Chair created there, in 1892. Amelia Edwards, author of *A Thousand Miles up the Nile*, and founder of the Egypt Exploration Society (later the Egypt Exploration Fund) had made a provision for it in her will, and the already celebrated William Flinders Petrie had become the first Edwards Professor. But perhaps Egyptology sounded new-fangled then. University still meant Latin and Greek, Oxford and Cambridge. Mimi had always been conservative on educational matters, and no doubt she wished her son to follow in his father's and uncles' footsteps, all Oxford men.

Thus the ludicrous situation arose in which Weigall was being officially crammed for the entrance exams in Latin and Greek, while unofficially he was trying to teach himself oriental languages, Persian and Chinese among them. Quite why he thought he ought to know Chinese is not clear. But although it sounds as though he was thrashing around, in fact, during this year, 1900, he did settle himself to a particular piece of Egyptological investigation, and actually got himself published in the *Journal of the Proceedings of the Society of Biblical Archaeology*.[5] The family had gone to Jersey for some weeks in the summer and Weigall had become interested in the collection of Egyptian antiquities in the museum at St. Helier. Later that summer he 'discovered' another group of interesting objects at the Brighton museum. Finding that neither group had been recorded, he decided to do so himself. With all the confidence of nineteen, and in the hopes of finding more unnoticed material, he followed this up with a paragraph in the *Morning Post*, in which he invited those many visitors to the Nile who might have bought antiquities to communicate with him:

It is … very probable that among this multitude of Egyptian relics … there may be many of value and interest … If the owners of antiquities which they consider to be Egyptian will communicate with me I shall be very much obliged; and should the object in question be inscribed, if a copy or photograph of the inscription is sent to me, I shall be pleased to translate the same … [6]

'Oh! The conceit of youth!!' he comments in the margin of this clipping beside the promise to translate. And indeed the whole thing is a wonderful impersonation of an elderly don writing from his book-lined study. The result was a sad anticlimax: 'An old lady sent me a Chinese teapot, a clergyman sent me a missionaries' copy of St. Luke in the Tamil language, some one else sent me a Zulu bangle.'[7] Much more exciting was a letter from the *Daily Express*[8] asking if they could send a reporter round for an interview. Both mother and son were in a flutter at this brush with fame, but Craggs was unimpressed, and merely reminded his stepson that his exam was drawing near, and that the only thing he ought to be thinking of was Greek.

There were two parts to the entrance examination in those days – the 'Smalls' to the University as a whole, and the 'Matriculation', to the chosen college. New College had been decided on, and very considerately the College decided to wink at his Greek 'unseen', and to give him a special paper on Egyptian hieroglyphs instead. This, as he afterwards told Newberry, was rather an easy paper, and he managed it comfortably.[9] Luckily too, the Greek viva voce turned out to be a passage from St. Luke, which he knew practically by heart in the English anyway. The result was that he passed into New College with honours. Much to his dismay, however, he failed his Smalls, owing to a bad Greek paper. There was a second chance to take the Smalls in the Christmas holidays, and meanwhile the College authorities told him that he could come up as an unattached or non-Collegiate undergraduate. This he did but, as he wrote in his memoir,

> I was depressed, for this failure had been like a blow in the face, and seemed to justify those who said that I ought not to have given up my excellent opening in the City. Moreover, I very soon began to realize that Oxford was not a place at which my knowledge of Oriental subjects would either help me, or be increased. ... On all sides I was told that I ought not to have come up to Oxford, but that I ought to have gone to a German University, ... yet I did not dare to propose the change, for fear of being regarded as incapable of sticking to one thing or of knowing my own mind.

The truth was that he had known his mind perfectly well. Egyptology had been his obsession at least since Liverpool. But he had not known what practical steps to take, and everyone around him had been strangely blinkered. Always one step behind, Mimi had decided on University after launching her son on the City; now she took matters into her own hands again, and after launching him on Oxford, decided on a German University.

So, in January 1901, just after Weigall had taken his Smalls for the second time, Mimi swept him off, together with his sister, and set them down in Leipzig – Geanie to learn German and finish her education, and he to learn German and start his. The idea was that once he had mastered enough of the language, he would enrol under Georg Steindorff, at that time Professor of Egyptology at the University. It didn't quite work out. Germany was intoxicating, just as his love affair had been. The music at the Leipzig Gewanthaus, the art galleries in Dresden and Berlin where he and Geanie travelled in the spring, the Egyptian collection in Berlin, all these things went to his head. He was no more inclined to settle to his German grammar than he had been to his Greek. The trouble was that he was expected to learn things that normally belong in school, at the very moment when he was plum ripe for university:

> I experienced the same excitement I had felt in Liverpool when I first began to read: life seemed a treasure house so crammed with interests that I did not know where to begin ... I remember pacing up and down the galleries of the Berlin Museum, with clenched fists, saying 'Oh, oh, oh!' to myself, like a child at a circus ... I often found it very difficult not to perform a sort of war-dance in the public street.

He did pick up a certain amount of German, and he did work hard at hieroglyphs 'much helped by Steindorff', he says, but he was wildly keen on everything else too. It was becoming clear that he was, by nature, extraordinarily susceptible to art of all kinds, greedy for experience, in love with life. He needed time, preferably the three years of a university education, to explore his enthusiasms. But it never happened. Circumstances combined to tie him down. That spring, both he and Geanie caught smallpox, and when their quarantine was at last over, Mimi took them back to England. It was intended that he should return in the summer and enter the University of Leipzig, but in the meanwhile he obtained an introduction to Flinders Petrie. Within a few weeks he had been offered and had accepted the post of assistant to the great man, and with that ended all idea of a degree, let alone of expanding his soul at leisure.

# Chapter 4

# Egypt 'like a house on fire'
# 1901–1904

Matthew William Flinders Petrie was the first exponent of scientific method in archaeology. In his autobiographical account, *Seventy Years in Archaeology,* he tells a story about himself, aged eight, being horrified by the 'rough shovelling out of contents' at a Roman villa discovered on the Isle of Wight: he 'protested that the earth ought to be pared away inch by inch, to see all that was in it, and how it lay'.[1] This method, taken for granted now, was not prevalent in the nineteenth century, nor at the beginning of the twentieth, and in Egypt, with its tradition of treasure hunting, less than anywhere. The idea that the history of a site lay as much in its sherds and rubbish as in anything more glamorous was not understood. Egyptian scholarship, led by the French, had had huge successes in deciphering the language, but the science of deciphering the ground had been neglected. The ground was important only as a kind of bran tub. Archaeologists simply thrust it aside to get hold of the things. If they were large or beautiful someone would buy them, especially the museums of Europe which were busily collecting ancient empires for their nations as though they were pedigrees. Most of the nineteenth century and the early years of the twentieth century were open season for Egypt's monuments. Indeed as late as 1920, Ernest Wallis Budge, the agent for the British Museum from 1886 to 1913, unashamedly boasted in his autobiography *By Nile and Tigris* of his adventures in smuggling huge quantities of antiquities out of Egypt.[2] One way and another, ancient Egypt was being exported, enriching en route the local thieves and dealers that were necessary to the process, while the Khedives or viceroys of Egypt – a family of Macedonian origin, appointed by the Sultan of Turkey – gave every assistance.

Thus when Petrie first went to Egypt in 1880, he felt that 'it was like a house on fire, so rapid was the destruction going on'. It wasn't so much the export of objects that scandalized him, as the mindless excavation, the destruction, and the indifference to anything that wasn't eye-catching. That and the absence of record keeping:

> ... the observation of the small things, universal at present [he was writing in 1931] had never been attempted ... The science of observation, of registration, of recording, was yet unthought of; nothing had a meaning unless it was an inscription or a sculpture ...[3]

He set himself to salvage what he could, observing so minutely, and recording so copiously that twenty years later, when Weigall was first introduced to him, he was a revered name – the acknowledged father of modern archaeology. The young man arrived for his first interview with some trepidation.

It went like this:

> I went up to the Edwards Library and Museum [at University College, London] where he worked, but at first could not find him. I therefore wandered about, looking at the show-cases; and presently my attention was attracted to one corner of the room, where some inscribed stelae were exhibited in a glass case. ... Desiring to see if there were any inscriptions upon the backs of these stelae, I made a quick movement round the case, and there behind it I found the Professor. He was on his hands and knees, and was just crawling stealthily away towards a dark corner wherein some sacking and other packing materials were heaped. I stood quite still; and to my surprise, I saw him reach out his arm for a piece of the sacking, and attempt to toss it over his hindquarters, just as an elephant throws dust or straw over its back with its trunk.

With a nervous cough, Weigall made his presence known, whereupon the Professor jumped up, bowed low, and having read the proffered letter of introduction, made him welcome. He never mentioned the antics of a moment before. It was only later that Weigall learned that the Professor was well-known for hiding in this way from visitors.[4]

Thus began an association which lasted off and on for many years, marked on Weigall's side by affection and exasperation in equal measure, and furnishing him – as a collector of such things – with much comic material. He began work straightaway, coming into college daily, cataloguing all the hieroglyphic inscriptions in Petrie's collection, and then weighing all his ancient weights, the results of which he published in *The Proceedings of the Society of Biblical Archaeology* in December of that year.[5] This was a work of minute mathematical calculation, and for once, he says, he was grateful for his training in the City – 'the columns of complicated figures had no terrors for me.' He must have proved himself a reliable and enthusiastic student, for the offer of the job as Assistant came quite soon. The work was unpaid, but he jumped at the chance of a real archaeological job and a definite position after the years of dreams and uncertainty. Here was something that Mimi could be proud of, and that Craggs needn't be ashamed of. The cost of travel to Egypt – travel to Egypt! – would be taken care of, as well as board while there, and altogether he was amazed at his good fortune.

At the same time he had a painful sense that this was his last chance. From then on, he says, he literally slaved for Petrie. Every day he accompanied the Professor and sometimes Hilda his wife who worked with her husband, to an A.B.C. for lunch. The Petries were famous for their frugality, and for their horror of time-wasting. Each would open a book beside his or her plate, while the Professor invariably ordered a strawberry ice (' "to cool the stomach prior to eating" '). Next he would bolt two poached eggs, a Bath bun, and two glasses of milk, after which the two of them would wait, reading, while Weigall chewed his way through the remnants of his own food. Petrie always picked up the bill 'with a low bow', and would then stride with great rapidity back to the college, Weigall behind, trying not to trot. Every evening they were the last to leave, locking up together, and as they made their way to their trains, Petrie would stop for another glass of milk.

There were two other Assistants at that time, a little older than Weigall – John Garstang and Arthur Mace – both of whom went on to have distinguished careers, one as Professor at Liverpool University and later as Director of Antiquities in Palestine, and the other at the Metropolitan Museum in New York. They were all friends later on in Weigall's life – though archaeological friendships were fragile things as will be seen – but now they teased the new boy, and called him 'Master Petrie'. Inwardly Weigall chafed and seethed, but he couldn't help himself: his keenness, partly genuine enthusiasm, was also insecurity. Both Garstang and Mace were Oxford graduates. The world was sure to find a place for them, Petrie or no Petrie. Weigall had no degree, and everything depended on how he performed at that instant. Thus, in November 1901, when Weigall embarked for Egypt on the P. & O. *'Somali',* shortly before his twenty-first birthday, his excitement was tempered by the feeling that, 'I was more than ever at school, and directly under the eye of a master whom at all costs I must please.' Luckily the master was to join the ship at Marseilles, so there were a few days of freedom.

Grey England was behind him, golden Egypt ahead of him at last, and the sky was getting bluer by the day:

> One evening there was a dance ... I indulged in a slight but sentimental 'affair' with a girl who was going out to Egypt for the winter; and I remember leaning over the rail with her in the moonlight, and talking about life in a sort of ecstasy of youth. She read me her diary ... I showed her some ... poems, and she said they were 'lovely'. She said she would teach me to dance ... and all one evening we waltzed up and down a secluded corner of the deck, until an angry mother sent her to bed.

All too soon they were in Marseilles, and with Professor Petrie and his wife aboard 'I had to assume again the role of "Master Petrie." ' He was taken in hand. They gave him books: a German essay on anthropology, and a history of Swiss lake-dwellings. Thus ended his days of idleness and romance.

Their destination in Egypt was Abydos, about 250 miles south of Cairo, where there was a royal cemetery in the western desert going back to the period of the First Dynasty, which began about 3000 BC. Petrie had been excavating there for two years, hard on the heels of an earlier excavator, Emile Amelineau, who had given Abydos the bran-tub treatment. Petrie himself tells the story:

> During four years there had been the great scandal of Amelineau's work at the Royal Tombs of Abydos. He had been given a concession to work there for five years; no plans were kept (a few incorrect ones were made later), there was no

record of where things were found, no useful publication. He boasted that he had reduced to chips the pieces of stone vases which he did not care to remove, and burnt up the remains of the woodwork of the 1st dynasty in his kitchen.

The things taken to Paris were scattered as pretty presents by his partners, and finally the greater part were sold by auction.[6]

It was a familiar story, and behind these words against Amelineau lies another implied attack on the body that had granted the concession to him. For since 1858 there had been such a body, the Antiquities Service, a government department set up under the Khedive, Said Pasha, and put into the hands of the French archaeologist Auguste Mariette. The object had been to bring some order into the stampede for antiquities, to keep some for Egypt, and to set up a museum in Cairo, the *Bulaq* as it was known, in which to house them.

The experiment, praiseworthy in itself, had not been entirely successful, at least by later standards. Mariette had become famous for his discovery in 1850 of the avenue of sphinxes, the temple, and the Serapeum at Memphis, a great underground burial chamber for mummified sacred bulls. He was a man of energy and decision, who loved Egypt and its monuments passionately. He was appalled by the neglect and damage they were suffering, and devoted his life to saving them for Egypt. But like the Pharaohs themselves, he operated on a grand scale. Big and beautiful things attracted him, temples, statues, monuments in general. Paring away inch by inch was not his style; nor was recording. Dynamite was a favourite form of excavation. Furthermore the Pasha was a quixotic master liable to cut off funds unless supplied with spectacular objects to give away to visiting grandees. Petrie had seen the results and had continued to watch the operations of the Antiquities Service under subsequent directors. Mariette died in 1881, and had been succeeded by the great Egyptologist Gaston Maspero, then by Grébaut, Loret, and an engineer called de Morgan. Maspero had taken over again in 1899, to continue until 1916. The directorship was the exclusive preserve of France, a fact which inevitably restricted the field. The French engineer de Morgan, for example, had been appointed only because there had not been a French scholar available for the job.

Petrie was not impressed: 'I hear that Mariette most rascally blasted to pieces all the fallen parts of a granite temple,' he writes at one point in his diary; or again, 'It does not say much for Grébaut's regard for antiquities to let so completely ignorant a man [a German looking for silver and gold] to enter a district solely for pillage.'[7] His complaints were frequent and bitter. Abydos was just another example of crass ignorance. The damage caused in the last four years there had been greater than in the last four thousand. Petrie's work in repairing it is worth briefly describing, if only to explain how great the differences were between one kind of excavator and another, and how feelings could come to run so high.

First, he had all the thousands of smashed chips and disregarded fragments gathered up, separated out into the seven different types of stone and spread, group by group, on a long table. Then he had them sorted into rims and bases and middles, and examined for joins. The angle of each fracture was tried against every other of the same angle in the same group, and in this way he was able to find or deduce five hundred different shapes of vessel. These he then drew. The forms thus recorded were seen to evolve one from the next, and by dating them from duplicate references, he traced 'the changes of work and of fashion in each reign'. He did similar work with the clay sealings of jars, sorting and fitting, and then drawing two hundred different designs. These 'formed a picture of the official world and organization of the early dynasties, of which scarcely anything else is known.' The same with fragments of inscriptions. For Petrie's students, it was a strenuous training in the principle of regarding little things, and they must have learnt to curse with him those archaeologists who had contrived to make them even smaller.[8]

Petrie's party arrived on Boxing Day 1901, and Weigall was soon writing to Newberry, at Thebes that winter, to say that he was 'enjoying the work very much. I shall however be glad of a day or two of civilization again. Tinned peas eaten with a knife off a packing case is all very well; but ...! And yet, by Jove, it's worth it – the work is so glorious!'[9] He had been thrown in at the deep end. Petrie had completed his examination of the royal tombs themselves by 1901, but he had noticed another cemetery which proved to be of the Twelfth Dynasty (about 1991-1783 BC) about a mile to the south, and he set the new student to clear it. Thus, suddenly, Weigall found himself in charge of 50 men, with a spade in his hand – Petrie believed strongly that the archaeologist should roll up his sleeves alongside the labourers.

The site lay at the base of limestone cliffs, an expanse of sand marked by four artificial mounds, ruins of some kind. To the west of these, a brick wall was soon noticed, the boundary of a courtyard or *hosh,* running up against the southern cliffs. Immediately the number of men was doubled, an army of village boys was drafted in to carry away the sand and rubbish, and gradually a rectangle of walls, eight or nine feet broad, was revealed, with a shallow stairway leading between the remains of storage chambers, via a causeway and a platform, up to an entrance. Excavations were made in the cliff to see if there was a rock tomb there, but in vain, so the mounds outside the courtyard were tried. These turned out to be fascinating constructions, labyrinthine passages designed to foil the ancient thieves. The shafts down into the rock turned and turned again, were blocked by portcullis-like slabs, dropped into sheer pits, opened into dead ends with false floors. But the old plunderers were wise to these tricks, and very little had been left except for huge granite sarcophagi, their neatly fitting lids hollowed out inside to take the missing wooden coffins.[10]

Again Weigall proved himself a capable student, a fact that Petrie generously acknowledged in his report on Abydos published the following year.[11] To his delight, Petrie promised him the job of contributing a chapter to that report, on the inscriptions from the temple of Osiris at Abydos.[12] This was something normally done by a former student, Francis Llewellyn Griffith, prevented that year by his wife's illness. 'The days fly past,' wrote Weigall to Mimi in February 1902, exuberant with the news about the inscriptions. He had been there three months, and he could hardly recognize himself: 'I have had so many new experiences, I have had to ... get through awful incidents so often, I have had to buckle to so much, that I expect you will find that I've grown up a good deal.' He doesn't say exactly what the 'awful incidents' were, presumably not wishing to alarm her, but he does describe working 'deep down in subterranean passages', adding quickly 'perfectly safe of course'. In fact it turned out to be not quite as safe or jolly as he makes it sound.

These subterranean passages were a series of tunnels leading to the entrance of a royal tomb ninety feet below the desert floor. One evening, after Weigall had left the site for his camp, he was excitedly summoned back. The entrance had been reached. Not only that, but there were others equally interested in the fact. He describes what happened:

> Reaching the mound of sand which surrounded our excavation, we crept to the top and peeped over into the crater. At once we observed a dim light below us, and almost immediately an agitated but polite voice from the opposite mound called out in Arabic, "Go away, mister. We have all got guns." This remark was followed by a shot which whistled past me; and therewith I slid down the hill once more, and wished myself safe in my bed ... after the briefest scrimmage, and the exchanging of a harmless shot or two, we found ourselves in possession of the tomb ... A long night watch followed and the next day we had the satisfaction of arresting some of the criminals.[13]

Tomb-robbing was a traditional and, to the Egyptians, a not dishonourable practice. Any news of a royal tomb spread instantly among the locals and archaeologists had to be constantly on the alert. Petrie was used to this sort of thing. A note sent the next day urges Weigall to get on with the excavation: 'It is absolutely needful to pluck your fowl now you have caught it. We have not spent three months of your time, and £300 to be lost for lack of a fortnight's watching ... The lack of sleep has doubtless crippled you today, coming on top of the excitement ...'[14]

Weigall, it appears was sickening for something. In the end, according to Weigall's official report, the fowl remained unplucked: 'A quick examination of the chambers and passages beyond [the entrance] showed that they were more extensive than those in any tomb known before in Egypt,' and since it was already fairly late in the season, it was decided to postpone the lengthy job of clearing it all out and recording it.[15] Petrie had ended his note to Weigall with this warning: 'Don't trust to brandy,' and then relented – 'though I dare say a little will help you. Feed up well tonight.' The trouble was that it was very difficult to 'feed up well' in Petrie's camps. The food was extremely primitive. Petrie was quite rightly concerned to put every penny to good use, but it seemed to Weigall that he and his wife had turned economy into a fetish, a perpetual game of Red Indians:

> Out in the desert I have known him pretend to be short of water, hoarding a few drops in a little bottle when in fact the supply was plentiful ... I have known him knock a hole in a tin of sardines and drink the oil before opening it, this being done solely to ... demonstrate how a hardy explorer in the waterless desert will make full use of all liquid.[16]

31

Whatever it was that had 'crippled' him at the time of the attempted robbery, by the middle of March he had decided that he couldn't stand another season with Petrie, and that he must look out for another billet. 'I can't go on with Petrie,' he wrote to Newberry, 'I have got so weak and horrid from this beastly food.'[17]

Weigall was 'Master Petrie' no longer. The professor's idiosyncrasies, and worse, his wife, had taken their toll. He describes Hilda in his memoirs as being simply 'impossible', a parody of her husband with none of his charm. A season with the two of them could reduce strong men to incoherent rage. A letter to Mimi written from Cairo in April 1902 describes the reactions to the Petries of Arthur Mace and James Quibell, a former student of Petrie's, and at that time Chief Inspector of Antiquities in the Delta:

> Quibell, a most quiet and silent man, becomes really frightening with regard to them. If one talks very much about them, he turns quite white ... Then there is Mace, also a silent man, who bursts into the most passionate language if one speaks of them, and with wild eyes and clenched fists swears vengeance. They all tell me that I should only have needed one more year with Petrie to hate him as much as I hate his wife, and certainly his behaviour at the end of this season [a reference perhaps to his illness] went a good way towards that.

But it didn't quite, for in the same letter he tells Mimi that he thinks Petrie 'a marvellous man, and one that I am really quite fond of'.

April is a cruel month in Egypt, and it was Weigall's first. He had been left behind in Cairo to receive the boatloads of stuff from the site, so that it could be sorted out by the Antiquities Department – some for Petrie in England, some for the Museum in Cairo, according to a half and half system of division then in force. The boats were delayed, Weigall was hot, depressed and longing for England. It is not surprising that in unburdening himself to Mimi he fell into a fit of irritation. An earlier letter, written to Newberry in February from the camp at Abydos, shows the same new-learnt irreverence in a happier fit of fooling:

My dear Newberry,

Here's a little story for you to tell to the Egyptological world, or to smile over at home.

Professor W.M. Flinders Petrie is a very bad sleeper, and yet for the sake of his health he finds it necessary to take "just a second or so's rest" from the hour of 1.30 until about 3.30. Now during this time the rest of the happy family is making a horrible noise about the courtyard – fitting up pots, copying stelae and so forth, and the Learned Old Gentleman finds it profoundly difficult to sink into sweet oblivion. Also the extraordinary sensations in his inside – due of course to tinned peas and salad oil – keep him painfully alive to the existence of a stomach not yet subordinated to the intellect. And moreover the glaring sun streaming into the hut, the heat, the millions of flies, all combine to annoy him ... Upon retiring to his hut after his ample meal of, let us say, stale peas, sardine oil, aged bread, and eleven oranges, he proceeds to remove all his garments except a coat and a pair of trousers ... Next he takes two lumps of plaster of Paris and thrusts them into his ears (the lumps were made in 1894, I'm told) ... Then, seizing a large green tin from off an upper shelf, he anoints his hair, beard and coat with the famous green powder. And the flies looking dreadfully sick ... crawl off into corners to die quietly. The insubordinated stomach alone remains to be dealt with; and so the Prince of Excavators throws himself upon his bed. ... But, stop a moment, I have omitted to mention the system of dealing with excessive light. The Great Egyptologist has fashioned him a black mask ... and this he ties over his face ... Having now arranged himself upon his bed, his wife steps in to deal with the eccentricities of her husband's world-famed stomach. Simplicity is one of the highest ideals of the Edwards Professor of Egyptology in University College, London; and his wife, following his example, merely lies across the offending portion of his anatomy and the thing is done. The Famous Member of the Imperial German Archaeological Institute sleeps in peace ...

Going in one day to the hut of the Indefatigable Member of the Society of Northern Antiquaries soon after lunchtime, I was horrified to see lying upon the bed a terrible figure curled up, with another equally terrible one lying at right angles above. The face was pitch black, the hair bright green, the beard also green ... one hand was flung out over the hinder portions of the blue lump lying on its face on top; the other clasped a stray hand belonging to the said lump. The atmosphere was thick with powder. Half asphyxiated I coughed and horrors! – the lumps began to move. It was Professor W.M. Flinders Petrie D.C.L. LL.D. Hon. F.S.A. Scot. himself!! I bolted!

Sincerely yours
Arthur E. Weigall.

Newberry probably did pass this squib round the Egyptological world, for it ended up in the papers of Alan Gardiner, the philologist, who in later years became one of Weigall's closest friends.[18] In a way, although it was harmless enough, it was an oddly reckless thing for Weigall to do when his career was still so tenuous, and he needed every friend he could get. But he was never circumspect, not even in his own interests, and a joke or an adventure was always irresistible to him.

By the end of that season he had in fact got himself another friend and another position. Friedrich Wilhelm von Bissing was a German Egyptologist who had been working for Gaston Maspero on the catalogue of the Cairo Museum since 1897. He and Quibell had visited Abydos while Weigall was there, and perhaps they had talked then. At any rate, by the end of the season things were far enough advanced for Bissing to write Weigall a formal letter offering terms – £100 every four months, starting November 1902.[19] Weigall told Newberry that the work would be 'the copying of tombs at Saqqara and elsewhere'.[20] But this poaching was obviously a ticklish business, and Bissing was anxious that Weigall should 'depart from Petrie in as friendly a way as possible'.[21] Later on that summer he writes to say that he is relieved to hear that all is well: 'I am very thankful to Petrie that he is sweet to you: it is certainly not your fault that you are not strong enough to work with him.'[22] This by now was truer than ever, for Weigall contracted typhoid fever some time after leaving Egypt. Petrie's comment on the whole transfer was a gracious regret, 'that I have to congratulate him on passing on at once to a better position.'[23] At any rate Weigall managed to finish his chapter on Petrie's inscriptions, and to help him set up at University College his annual exhibition of things from the season's work.

Then, in the winter of 1902, began one of the happiest periods of his life. Saqqara is a huge necropolis on the edge of the Libyan desert outside the ruins of the old city of Memphis, which was the capital of the Old Kingdom. This is the period from the Third to the Sixth Dynasties, that is from about 2649 BC to about 2150 BC. The first pyramids were built here in the Third and Fourth Dynasties, the most remarkable being the famous Step pyramid of the Pharaoh Djoser. In the Fifth Dynasty (about 2465-2323 BC) tombs called *mastabas* (so named because of their resemblance to the dried mud-brick *mastabas* or benches found outside many Egyptian houses) were made for wealthy nobles and court officials. They were quadrangular structures entered by a single door, consisting of chambers both above and below ground, their walls decorated with reliefs and paintings depicting the agriculture, crafts, and amusements of everyday life at that time. Mariette excavated many of the *mastabas* of Saqqara, and Maspero published a descriptive catalogue of them in 1881. More continued to be discovered, and so there arose the great task of recording and cataloguing. That is what Bissing wanted Weigall for, first in the *mastaba* of Kagemni, or Gemnikai as it was sometimes called, and then two seasons later, in October 1904, in the *mastaba* of Mereruka.

Kagemni was a Sixth Dynasty official, a vizier, and the eight rooms of his *mastaba* tomb are covered in very beautiful coloured reliefs: a row of dancers, for example, bending back almost horizontally, tossing their arms and legs above their heads, as though in the middle of a backwards somersault; fishermen netting fish from reed boats; cattle being herded, their elegant heads and horns overlapping in profile; a suckling pig being weaned by licking milk from the breeder's tongue, and everywhere the birds and beasts and plants of the Nile. It was Weigall's job to photograph, draw and describe in words all these charming scenes, and more.[24] Instead of toiling and burrowing deep underground in the dust and darkness, risking himself and scores of others, responsible for the safety of objects, and constantly guarding against theft, now he was responsible only for himself, and working on material that gave him constant delight. He lived in reasonable comfort, with a servant, in Mariette's old house, a modest structure but with windows east and west for the dawn and the sunset.

Here he was free: he describes himself exploring his domain, walking up to the high vantage points, and sleeping out at night: 'The dark desert drops beneath one; the bed floats in mid-air, with planets above and below. Could one but peer over the side, earth would be seen as small and vivid as the moon.'[25] His jottings from this period, parts of which he used in essays published later, have a jaunty, youthful air as though he were altogether content – happy in his work and exhilarated by the desert. Even getting up in the morning was exciting:

> At 6.30 my man comes with the water, and the mere gong-like noise of the tin bath as it strikes against the floor ... sends a thrill of pleasure through me ... When I come out to my breakfast on the verandah the blue sky and the shining desert greet me, and the fresh north wind puts such a vigour into me – brain and bones alike – that I can hardly allow myself to finish the meal ... but must be up and doing my work before the hands of the clock have got round to eight.

His hermit life suited him for he found the work absorbing, and an inspiration for other kinds of writing. After two seasons there his brain was teeming with literary projects: in one letter he mentions plans for a collection of essays on Egyptian subjects, a diary-like account of life in the desert, even an Egyptian novel, and a book of short stories. None of these are certainly identifiable among the things he published later, but they show how close the scholarly and imaginative sides of him always lay. Perhaps it was here that he added the verses of prophecy to the archaeologist in his *Twenty-five Monsters* story, now that the dust had settled on his subterranean excavations at Abydos:

> You'll go and join some funny band
> Of men who grub about the sand
> Of Egypt, or some other land,
> In search of tombs and temples grand.
> You'll live on peas and salmon canned
> And salad oil, and biscuits, and
> A once-a-monthly buffalo.

A little further on he describes crawling along a tunnel in a 'mummy-pit' and the 'whole beastly show' falling in behind, and sitting in the dark feeling sick. Perhaps this is based on one of the 'awful incidents' he mentioned to Mimi, and certainly there were to be others of that kind later on.

His isolation was not, of course, complete. Saqqara is only about fifteen miles from Cairo: there was a train which brought visitors, and there were always tourists. Besides, in both the winters of 1903 and 1904 there was a party of Petrie's camped at Saqqara, consisting of four women, Miss Hansard, Miss Kingsford (both artists), Miss Eckenstein and Mrs Petrie. In fact after two seasons of virtually building the camp for them, Weigall grumbles rather: 'It's always the same with Petrie: he makes no preparations for his camp ever.'[26] He and Curelly, Petrie's new student – ('a regular adventurer and explorer') – 'simply slaved ... hammering up shelves, bursting boxes open, building walls, and goodness knows what else.' Miss Hansard and Miss Kingsford were fastidious ladies, and he had a pang when he saw them seated in front of their packing cases and tin mugs of weak tea. He turned his own house over to the women one night, sleeping out with Curelly in the November cold, and he was called on regularly for breakfast, lunch and dinner. Petrie at least was generous in his thanks, recognizing that the women 'would have been sadly stranded without you' and offering him a present of archaeological books.[27]

One way and another Weigall made himself useful to Petrie during these Saqqara seasons. A black granite statue of a seated man was stolen from the excavations at Abydos, and Petrie asked him to keep an eye out in the dealers' shops in Cairo. Another time, could he draw some money at Cook's and Son and bring it over when he visits, so as to save one of the students a journey? In early 1904 when Petrie was being unaccountably blocked by Maspero over a concession to dig at Saqqara, Weigall suggested a line of attack which seemed promising: 'I am greatly obliged by your news and impressions,' writes Petrie, '... I must see Maspero, ask his assent to the excellent shape of application which you suggest ...'[28] In the event, Petrie never got his concession that year, but the letter is interesting in that it suggests that Weigall was learning the political ropes of the department.

Cairo, though so close, was a world away, the heart of one of Britain's more exotic imperial possessions – imperial, that is, to all intents and purposes. Though the fiction was maintained that the British were advising the Egyptian government who in turn operated under Turkish dominion, the place was in fact run by the British. Cairo was therefore comfortably arranged for Egypt's administrators with its club – the Turf – and its sports ground, the Ghezirah. There were also the hotels, for Egypt under the British became a fashionable winter resort. Unlike India, it was within relatively easy reach of Europe, a cosmopolitan world, where French was still spoken more generally than English, and with populations of Greeks, Italians and Levantines. Its climate from October to March was perfect, the hotels and Nile houseboats were thoroughly comfortable. One could nose around the bazaars by day and feel oriental, while at night the best Cairo hotels would reproduce the London season. The balls and guest-lists were reported in the *Egyptian Gazette* the next day, and the dresses of the women described – Lady so-and-so in old rose crêpe de chine, and Miss so-and-so, newly arrived, looking exquisite in pale blue satin. With the scarlet and gold of the officers, it must have been a brilliant scene.

On his visits to Cairo, Weigall entered this world, or something like it. Not that he was ever much of a dancer, but he may have looked in on a few of these gatherings. At this stage it is difficult to tell whom he knew and what his connections were. But it was a small world, and one probably only needed to know somebody who knew somebody, and if you were a personable young man with a suit of evening clothes, you would get an invitation. A letter from a friend of the family remarks: 'I hear you are very dissipated in Cairo – going to no end of dances. I am quite glad you are not buried in the desert. I met your mother the other day ...'[29] Weigall must have written a jolly letter to Mimi from Cairo.

But although he was having fun, Weigall was also very conscious of the seriousness of work. The white man's burden was a proud responsibility. The sight, for example, of an official from the Irrigation Department examining a sluice could send a thrill through him, as he told his mother: 'Ruddy-faced, tidily dressed, the natives around him standing back respectfully, not frightenedly – O, he was a goodly sight ... he, and the handful like him, *are* Egypt. At least Egypt would not be much without them.' Writing once from the Turf Club, he described the members he came across as 'hot, red-faced determined men, each with his big work before him and behind him: one gets such a jolly Kiplingy sort of twinge when one sees them all.' It was a twinge that he was soon to feel on his own account.

# Chapter 5

# Private idyll; Howard Carter; public ideal
# 1904–1905

At the end of the Saqqara seasons in 1903 and 1904, Weigall left the heat of Egypt for Europe. He had only two months' leave, so some of the summer months were spent writing up and developing his photographic plates in Munich with Bissing, who was lecturing at the University. By the end of the second season, the tomb of Kagamne was safely captured onto about 60 plates, and Mereruka awaited him on his return in October. But during that summer of 1904, Weigall's life took another sudden turn. He met and fell in love with a young American woman travelling around Europe with her mother.

Hortense Schleiter, the only child of Oscar and Caroline (or Carrie, née Hazlett) of Pittsburgh and then Chicago, was twenty-four when she met Weigall, just six months older than him. She was a beautiful woman, soft and graceful rather than smart and sparkling, with a stately bearing and a gentle manner. As with everything in Weigall's life, it was a headlong plunge for him. In fact feelings on both sides grew to a point so rapidly, that after a mere seven weeks, on July 4th, American Independence Day, they announced their engagement.

The Schleiter women were a curious couple; they had been wandering about from Paris to Vienna, from Munich to Florence, round and round, for at least four years before Weigall met them. They were ostensibly in search of cures for various unspecific ailments – Carrie's kidneys, Hortense's suspected goitre, or sometimes, perhaps, her ovaries – but at the same time they were thoroughly enjoying themselves. Always expected home in the near future, they managed to postpone their return from year to year. In one letter to her unmarried sister, Katharine Hazlett who lived in Chicago, Carrie gives the reason: 'We would dearly love to come home if we were sure we could come back here very soon again.' Carrie was much younger than her husband. The family story says that he had seen her as a child on a rocking chair and had decided then and there that he would propose to her when she grew up. Perhaps after twenty odd years she was bored by him, and a one-way ticket home seemed like death.

Oscar appears to have been a precise and punctilious man; every communication from him records the dates of letters sent and received, and the times of the Atlantic mail steamers; they report his movements, his opinion of the various doctors he visits (a good remedy for the kidneys, he hears, is "Arsenauro" – an arsenic and gold preparation), and the weather, together with its influence on the price of crops and livestock. Useful to the historian, they probably left Carrie cold. As the years pass, these letters become bewildered and finally exasperated. By 1905 he despairs, realizing that his wife would be quite happy to stay in Europe for ever if he would just carry on sending the cheques: 'It is a great disappointment that I must spend my life without a family circle ... My exertions in the past to provide for such an existence in the evening of my days, seem like a failure.'

He himself joined them once or twice, when they were in Germany. His family had originally emigrated to America from Hamburg when he was thirteen, and there was still an Uncle Hermann there. But hotels and travel were expensive, and neither mother nor daughter had much idea of money. Oscar was bound to return home and make as much as he could for them. He was a financier in a modest way, based in Pittsburgh, Pennsylvania, but frequently travelling to Chicago and to cities in Iowa where he had agricultural investments. He was quite successful, but always worried about hard times, and bitterly resentful both of the unions and of the new tycoons that were springing up in the boom years at the turn of the century, and whose fortunes he believed to be dishonestly gained. He may well have been boring, but he seems to have been a kind man, devoted to his wife and daughter, and, in spite of his anxieties, constantly urging them to spare no expense where health was concerned.

Carrie, on the other hand, was enjoying a deferred youth. Their life in Europe was like a play, she says: the constantly changing scene, the people at their various *pensions* – French, German, Italian, American – the little parties and dances arranged by the management, everything set her humming. Her letters to Oscar are dutiful, but to Katharine and cousin Mattie who kept house together in Chicago, she is all high spirits. Berlin, she writes, is 'a moving panorama of officers, civilians and ladies *horsebacking* along', Hortense among them sitting her '*hoss*', she says, 'like a duck'; in Frankfurt 'the swagger German officers are groomed until they look as if they put themselves away in boxes when they get through with strutting around.' As for the Italian lakes and the Swiss mountains, she was enraptured: 'If we only had you-uns along with us to help us chortle in our joy, how glad and gauzy we,' she exclaims.

Carrie's letters ramble miscellaneously around the scenery, foreign customs, how to wash blankets, hats, prescriptions, fashions – all in a gossipy, larky style, with the occasional stroke of brilliance. European oysters, for example – 'A "fake lot",' says she, 'puny, gaunt, shrivelled, lean and cadaverous, with dark, sallow complexions, insignificant puckered up features and squint eyes.' Hortense is less sparky than her mother, more conscientious about galleries and concerts: they've managed only three rooms at the Pinakothek Museum in Munich, she writes in January 1902, and there are '*dozens* of rooms' to go; next Friday they're going to hear Sarasate play the violin, and the other day they went to "Cavalleria Rusticana" which was very fine but rather spoilt by a 'tiresome sort of pantomime of a dozen or so different fairy stories' beforehand. It's from Carrie that we learn how well she looked at the dance in her grey crêpe de chine – a 'sweet gown' – and how many elegant partners she had.

At the end of 1903, a sudden thought struck Oscar, and like a character out of a Henry James novel, he found that he hated the idea of a European husband for his only daughter. He wrote to Carrie advising her to keep well away from American girls who have become 'so-called "Baronesses"', for he strongly disapproves of them. 'The most satisfactory manner of bearing for Americans,' he says, 'is to maintain in a dignified firm manner our American sentiments and remain Americans!' But although Hortense never became a Baroness, she was not to be saved for America.

The next summer Arthur Weigall appeared on the scene with enough time on his hands – Bissing must have let him off – to spend most of his waking hours charming and being charmed by both mother and daughter. Hortense described her feelings to cousin Mattie after their engagement: 'He is a man with whom I can be absolutely and completely *myself* – entirely natural with him, and he with me ... I have never seen anything *overbearing* about him yet, I assure you. I know that he is a wonderful son and brother, and he has a beautiful nature ...' She goes on in this vein, listing his virtues, how well he dresses (he dresses for dinner every evening, but she prefers him in rowing or riding dress), how animals love him (always a good sign), how fond he is of music, how he plays the mandolin, but he didn't have it with him. It's true, she says, that Weigall is 'not a perfectly beautiful surname', but it's very old and good, she says. His ancestors came over with Queen Elizabeth, or was it William of Orange, she can't remember. The best thing about him, though, is that 'he has the keenest sense of humour, fun and nonsense of anyone I ever knew.'

Carrie must have been a sympathetic chaperone. During an enchanted interval at Feldafing, a small town near Munich, Weigall and Hortense became lovers. Both of them have a habit, typical of the period, of etherealizing their feelings, but it cannot disguise their very evident physical pleasure in one another. Weigall entranced Hortense with his descriptions of Egypt, and together they painted an idyllic picture of how their lives would be. She poured it all out to Mattie, the place in the desert called Saqqara, with nothing but the ancient tombs, the nearest village two miles off, 'our house' – not very big, but Arthur is building onto it. Arthur says they can ride from there to the Great Pyramids, and can visit Cairo where there are dances at least once a week. Hortense at this stage wanted to learn drawing and painting, and she imagined working side by side with him. She encloses a photograph of Arthur. The whole thing must have sounded like a fairy story to the two ladies in Chicago, and indeed to Hortense herself.

But she was counting her chickens before they were hatched. Oscar was implacably against the match. Mattie, having studied the photograph under a magnifying glass, and having decided that he looked '*unusually* refined ... determined, energetic, enthusiastic, and good', embraced Hortense's cause. But she was not optimistic. Oscar, she wrote, 'does not want Hortense *ever* to marry *anybody*' and was as little impressed by Egypt as by Europe: 'He says you can get as much out of life in Galva, Iowa as you can out of *any city*. Maybe you can. I think Galva has about two thousand inhabitants, maybe it is a great *art* and *musical* centre ...' Mattie took the view that Oscar was really worried about his own situation. She reports him saying: '"What is to become of *me*? I *know* Carrie will never leave Hortense, and I can't live over there!"' In short, she thought he would do everything he could to break up the engagement.

40

Meanwhile, the other side of the family needed soothing. Poor Mimi was trying to be philosophical, but she was impatient to see her adored son again after his long absence in Egypt and now it looked as though she might have to take second place in his heart. Weigall's attempt to excuse himself for his delayed return on the grounds that it was Carrie that he couldn't abandon, not Hortense, misfired miserably: 'I was eaten up with jealousy *not* at all you say about Hortense, but your saying you felt you *couldn't leave the mother* – I am jealous you should care for her!'

Life had not been easy while he had been away. Mimi and Geanie, left together, had not hit it off. Geanie was an extremely attractive woman, and had many admirers. Mimi was old-fashioned, and Tony Craggs even more so. Earlier that year he had left his curacy in Lancaster Gate to become vicar of St. Saviour's, Shepherd's Bush, and the vicarage there had become their home. Shepherd's Bush was at that time hardly London at all. It took Geanie out of social circulation and threw the three of them more together than any of them could have wished. Geanie had therefore made a rash and hasty marriage in the spring of that year, 1904, to a certain Jack Rutter, a connection that everyone came to regret. He was a vain, dishonest man, a poseur and, on the strength of tea estates in Ceylon, recklessly extravagant.

But the gap that had opened up between mother and daughter went further than Geanie's choice of husband. A whole change in social attitude lay between them, encapsulated just then by a certain well-publicized divorce case of the day. As Weigall explained to Hortense:

… this affair with Lord de la Warr has very much upset Mother. You see the man was divorced from his wife, and married again a very nice girl, who was a friend of ours. Mother cut them all, and my sister has made the quarrel up as far as she is concerned. De la Warr I don't personally know, but I believe he is more fool than knave. Mother thinks Geraldine [Geanie's full name] must be very 'fast' to allow herself to know him – and of course I have to take up the position of peacemaker.

Mimi was always much harder on her own class than she was on the poor. No doubt she thought they ought to set a good example.

Always correct, she now invited the Schleiters to come and stay with them in England. But Carrie was evasive, said she had promised her husband to go to Switzerland for the sake of her health, and that perhaps they would come to England later. The problem was Oscar. It appears that he didn't want Carrie and Hortense to go to England, and he may even have withheld the money for the journey. A brisk correspondence was being conducted to and fro across the Atlantic and the Channel, in which wider financial prospects were also being discussed.

Weigall had only £300 a year, rising possibly, he says, to £400 at the most, but not enough to set up house on anything but a penny-pinching scale. Oscar's general objection to the marriage was given some point by this, which he sharpened further by deploring the remoteness of Egypt and the great expense of yearly travel from Egypt to Europe and occasionally to America and back. Weigall himself couldn't deny that their way of life would have extra costs. Besides, he had a horror of scraping, and Hortense's idea of the simple life probably went no further than love in a cottage – or rather, on the prairie. In fact after four years of hotel life in Europe, she knew nothing about how to manage. Mattie, who did know, had some idea of Hortense's incapacity: 'I cannot imagine Hortense getting along on limited means. It's a *struggle*, and a fearful one if you have to do your own washing, cook, sew, piece and patch, deny yourself.' So Weigall and Hortense both agreed that Oscar must be persuaded somehow to give Hortense £250–£300 a year, according to what Weigall could earn himself. Of course Oscar declined. And so the matter rested. They had wanted to marry that autumn, in October, just before Weigall was due back in Egypt, but as the weeks passed, the prospect faded.

At any rate, Carrie and Hortense did in the end come to England. Carrie was bowled over by London, '*the* City of the World, it is simply stupendous.' They 'went on the underground railway several times – from one end of it to the other.' By the way, she adds, the English don't say '*ce*-ment or *add*-ress, but ce-*ment* and add-*ress*'. And Mimi warmed to Hortense: 'I am quite prepared to be very fond of her. I like her nature and see a great deal to admire and love in her. I am very thankful she is what she is and likely therefore to make you happy.' Mimi sounds rather judicious, but she was taking the long view. She felt that the happiness of a man in his position depended more on his wife than, say, that of a man in the City, who could be much more independent. Perhaps she was remembering the wives of army officers abroad who fretted after England, and was impressed by Hortense's willingness to be enthusiastic about Egypt.

In fact, both Carrie and Hortense were drunk on Egypt. All that winter, which they spent in Paris, Weigall had been writing to them about Saqqara, the house (the extension to Mariette's which he had now blocked off and moved into), his work and his plans. They devoured the books on Egypt he sent them for Christmas, his other present to Hortense being, she informed Mattie, 'some *green beetles* to be mounted in gold,' hastily adding, ' dead – naturally!' 'They smell like nothing on earth,' Weigall had written, 'but I am sure you could have something done to them to stop that, and then you might make them into a necklace, or a pincushion, or a tea-cosy, or an ink pot, or something.'

More than anything else, Weigall brought home to them the strangeness of the place and the unconventionality of his life. He described, for example, a visit from three archaeologists, one of whom was a Scot called Mackenzie, assistant to Arthur Evans in Crete. With 'fierce red moustaches, red face, very tall and rather roughlooking', he was known as 'the Wild Man'. They dined together, and talked late into the night, and as Mackenzie worked his way through a bottle of whisky, he told them stories. After an evening in Candia, he 'always took four glasses of whisky before starting to ride back, and he added, "I have a wee bit pony there, by the name of Hell Fire, and I gallop home on him. Think, man, if I were sober – could I gallop unharmed through the streets of a city and alang a road like a corkscrew, in muckle darkness?" ' After their talk, the four men rode across the desert in the moonlight to the station for the train back to Cairo.

The other day, Weigall says, he came back from visiting Cairo himself, and was amazed to find 'a party of about 70 Americans visiting the tombs, a sight common enough in winter, but till now unseen this year.' 'The big steamers go up the Nile with some 100 people,' he wrote, 'and they vomit out their passengers at all places along the route of interest. It is a luxurious way of seeing Egypt, but what can one see of the real Egypt from the carpeted saloon deck of a steamer?' That was what his letters promised them – the real Egypt. They had themselves spent years looking at 'places of interest' and now he was going to turn the play into real life. As Hortense told Mattie, his letters made her *frantic* not to be there too'.

But there is an ominous note in some of Weigall's letters. He speaks of periods of utter loneliness and depression, of suffering from 'nerves' and 'melancholia'. At those times, his longing for Hortense becomes a kind of madness. At the same time he is passionate about his work. That too was a kind of madness, and the two passions exacerbated each other as he laid his work, as it were, at her feet. He once relayed to Hortense something of Bissing's that delighted him. Bissing had said that he was ' " a hard worker in anything which you take up – often a violent and passionate one"!!' Playing on the words, he asks Hortense what she thinks – is he really 'violent and passionate'? The letter makes no bones about what he means and that she should know. Hortense and his work were the two loves of his life, and at Saqqara he found himself suddenly frightened of the moment when they would meet. Hortense had evidently hinted that his letters were not long enough, and he replied gently explaining that he had so much work to do. 'At Feldafing,' he warned her,

you saw me as I never shall be again except on holidays. You have no idea how I work really. O love, don't you see that my fault is that I throw myself too deeply into everything I do – that I love you too wildly, that I work too intensely, that I expend too much unseen force in writing letters? I have to narrow myself down and hold myself in. You have never seen me become so bursting with enthusiasm about some silly little bit of work that I have to pace about the room.

He seems to have had a sense of foreboding, though neither of them were in a state to take heed.

He was now working hard on the next tomb – Mereruka. He envisaged finishing it by the end of the next season, that is the spring of 1906, but after that nothing was sure. Bissing wanted him to carry on and record the series of *mastabas* at Saqqara known as 'The Street of Tombs', but there was a question over money, and Bissing had recently married so there was less to spare. Besides, Weigall had his own ideas. As it happened, he had taken some photographs of various temple reliefs in Thebes, the ancient city across the river from Luxor in Upper Egypt, for a folio edition to be brought out by the German publisher, Bruckmann. In the course of this work, he found himself so deeply impressed by the beauty and the historical value of the art of the Theban period – that is of the Eighteenth, Nineteenth and Twentieth Dynasties, dating from about 1550 to 1070 BC – that by comparison, the reliefs in the *mastaba* tombs at Saqqara seemed less interesting. He conceived the idea therefore of recording one of these Theban temples in the way that he was doing at Saqqara and he wrote with a proposal to the Egyptologist he admired most on that period, Professor James Henry Breasted.

Breasted was at that time the Director of the Haskell Oriental Museum at the University of Chicago, and he was shortly, in 1905, to become the first Professor of Egyptology and Oriental History in America. In 1903 he had published a book, *The Battle of Kadesh,* about the great military campaign of Rameses II against the Hittites in Syria in 1285 BC. Rameses' victory at the battle of Kadesh is commemorated no less than four times in reliefs on the walls of temples in Egypt: the Temple of Rameses II at Abydos, the Temple of Luxor, the Ramasseum, and the temple at Abu Simbel. Weigall must have been thinking of these reliefs in particular, for he talks of the great battle scenes of the period, and of the Ramasseum as a possible choice of temple. His enthusiasm is palpable – 'I felt I would give anything to be able to work on these' – and it drives him on, in a way that was very characteristic of him, to envisage in such detail how he would do it all, that by the end of the letter he seems to have persuaded himself that nothing could possibly stand in the way:

> All the scenes in the temple would be photographed with a camera similar to the one I am now using, i.e. carrying plate 24 × 30 cent. in size. Then a classification of the objects would be made in drawing as I have done at Kagemni, and a complete list of hieroglyphs, showing the different forms; and also drawings would be made of all those scenes which, owing to their position could not be photographed. Then full plans and sections would be made, with a complete list of the wall blocks, to show how they are laid. And finally a detailed description would be made without reference to the photographs; and thus every detail would not only be reproduced as the camera has seen it, but it would be described as the eye has observed it under varying lights. Thus no possible mistake could be made, and the publication could be regarded as absolutely final.

A little later, as he enlarges on how easy it would all prove, on how convenient Chicago would be for him now that he was about to marry someone from that city, and on how he could work with Breasted in the summers, he suddenly pulls himself up short: 'I hope the scheme does not sound very impracticable to you. I am so enthusiastic over the subject, and so keen to have the chance of recording some of these scenes that perhaps I overstep the bounds of reason.' [1] In the end nothing came of it. The letter, written in October 1904, wasn't answered until February 1905. Breasted was interested – 'exactly the kind of thing we should like to see done' – but excavations in Babylon would absorb all their current funds for several seasons to come.[2] This was the first of many schemes in Weigall's life, conceived in a blaze of enthusiasm, and planned in such detail as to rout all possible opposition. But he was to be disappointed again and again. In any case it didn't really matter, for between the two letters came a far greater change in Weigall's fortunes.

In order to explain this revolution in Weigall's life, it is necessary to describe something of the administration of archaeology in Egypt at that period. Since the British occupation of Egypt in 1882, and increasingly over the next twenty years the number of European visitors to Egypt had grown enormously. By 1898 Thomas Cook and Son were said to be bringing in 50,000 tourists a year, and every year more.[3] These were not hardy travellers. The Nile was an effortless conveyance, and Cook pampered its clients. The French traveller Pierre Loti has left a bitter and witty account of the British tourist in Egypt at this period: loud, unlovely 'Cooks and Cookesses' in cork helmets and green spectacles, drinking whisky and soda in the temples and eating sandwiches out of greasy paper. He describes the river at Luxor lined with Cook's three storeyed barracks, as he calls their ships, whistles blasting and dynamos throbbing; and Aswan, like Kensington Gardens, all 'so British in its orderliness and method', green painted railings and neat flowerbeds, and the great cataract silenced by the new barrage.[4]

These tourists wanted their places of interest to be in good nick. The work of clearing out, cleaning up, and stabilizing temples, shrines and pylons (temple gateways) was thus carried out as much for their sakes as for the monuments themselves. Arab huts that huddled round and on top of temples, mountains of desert sand packed inside, everything was now being cleared away. Retaining walls were being built, railings and steps constructed, the whole place done over. The yearly reports of the Director General, Maspero, are full of accounts of such works:

> The development of Aswan as a winter resort has busied me in making sure that the few ancient monuments that are there are fit to be seen and easily accessible – the only one in the town itself that I know of at present, the Ptolemaic temple of Isis discovered forty years ago by Mariette, was almost disappearing beneath rubbish. On my orders, Mr Carter has had it cleared ... and a retaining wall built ... Actually, the temple is in good condition and it could become a point of interest to the residents and travellers passing through.[5]

The tourists also meant brisk trade for the dealers, and gave a fresh incentive to their suppliers for whom robbing the sites of excavations, and carrying out illicit digs, were a way of life. Archaeologists were not, of course, the only people disturbing the ground and uncovering antiquities. The British were attempting to make Egypt more productive which meant digging more irrigation canals and bringing more land into cultivation. The population was growing, more houses were being built, more drains laid, and more stone quarried. Everywhere there were rich pickings in 'antikas', as they were called. Furthermore, as irrigation turned the desert into real estate, land prices were rising enormously and government property, potentially rich in antiquities, was constantly under threat of seizure by private individuals. All this put the work of the Antiquities department under strain and in 1904 the Government of Egypt increased the budget of the Department of Antiquities so as to fund the appointment of two more Chief Inspectors.

The Inspectorates were regional posts, originally created in 1899, only two of them at first, dividing between them the whole of Egypt from the Delta to the border with Sudan. The first appointees had been James Quibell based at the Museum in Cairo, whom Weigall had already met, and for the southern region, Howard Carter, based in Luxor – Maspero's 'Mr Carter', who was to become famous years later for his discovery of the tomb of Tutankhamun. Now, in 1904, the boundaries were to be shifted to make room for a third region in Middle Egypt, and a French scholar, Gustave Lefebvre, was appointed Chief Inspector there. In addition to that, Saqqara was to have its own Inspector. The arrangement had always been that after three or four years Quibell and Carter would change places, which they did in November 1904; but after only a few months in Luxor, Quibell was moved again, this time to Saqqara. Thus the southern inspectorate fell vacant, and at the end of January 1905, the person appointed to fill Quibell's post was Arthur Weigall.

It was an extraordinary compliment to such a young man with such a short experience of Egypt. Far more eligible for the post was Arthur Mace, Weigall's old fellow-student under Petrie and now his main rival. As Weigall explained to Hortense before he was chosen: '[Mace] has been in the country 8 years (to my 4), is 32 years old, and has done some work for the Govt. ... at present [he] is assistant to Reisner the American excavator, but himself he is English. He is *very nearly certain* to get the post, and I am rather glad ... I should far rather stay in my present job if it wasn't for the question of money.' Perhaps the reason for Weigall's appointment was simply that he was thought to be the best man for the job. And yet there are suggestions that the situation may have been more complicated than that. Following them up takes one through the politics of archaeology in Egypt at the time, a minefield of personal and national ambitions and animosities that Weigall would himself have to traverse in time. It also throws light on the early stages of Weigall's relationship with Howard Carter, a fluctuating business that affected Weigall, on and off, for much of his life.

Archaeology in Egypt at that period was conducted against a background of fierce national rivalries, mainly between Britain, France and Germany, as though it were a microcosm of the international political situation. Germany had long been well represented with Emile Brugsch in charge of the Museum, and with Ludwig Borchardt responsible for the task of compiling the General Catalogue. Over them had been the French, as we have seen, the post of Director General always going to a Frenchman. It was a tradition that owed itself to the special cultural relation between France and Egypt going back to Napoleon and his academy of Egyptological *savants*. So strong was French feeling on the subject that the British and French Entente Cordiale of 1904 which defined two spheres of influence – French Morocco for British Egypt – contained a proviso that the Director General of the Egyptian Antiquities Department should always be a Frenchman. Though the odds had always been against it, it had always been possible until then for other nations to hope that they might one day put one of their own men in.

Meanwhile, Britain had gained the political ascendancy in Egypt, and although there were British excavators at work in the country, there was a feeling in some quarters that she was not adequately represented in the Department of Antiquities itself. A letter, written in 1899, by a certain Somers Clarke (who will be more fully introduced in chapter seven) to the Egyptologist Francis Ll. Griffith, expresses just this complaint:

There is no doubt that … Lord Cromer [the Governor of Egypt or British Agent] – is much more alive to matters connected with the antiquities than of yore and there is a wish to get more Englishmen of influence into the Museum and Antiquities Department.

… It is really a deplorable thing that we are not better represented in Egypt which is now overrun by German and French students and professors … The Germans push their people and are doing it more than before just because they see we are getting strong in the saddle …

Letter-sketch of James Quibell

Letter-sketch of the young Carter

The letter speculates about the recent opportunities created by the proposal to establish a regional Inspectorate – in which case, he says, 'Quibell would most probably have one of the places … [and] there would then be a vacancy at the Museum.'[6] In other words, the Inspectorate was seen from the very beginning as an opening for the British, with Quibell and Carter the first Antiquities officials to carry the Union Jack into the provinces.

Quibell was in fact not especially suited to that role. Weigall describes him to Hortense as 'a middle-aged sleepy old fellow, nice and kind, a good archaeologist and a bad administrative official.' Carter, on the other hand is 'young, ill-tempered, knows nothing of archaeology, but is a magnificent organizer and policeman.' He then illustrates his point by telling a story about Carter once pursuing an Egyptian who had disobeyed one of his rules, thundering after him on horseback as far as the man's house, jumping the wall that surrounded it, and landing bang among the chickens. He rushed in, apparently, seized the man's dagger from him, grabbed him by the ear and handed him over to the police. The offence had been begging. Weigall's tone is half admiration, and half incredulity at Carter's recklessness over something so small.

And now, here he was, in early January 1905, staying with Weigall at Saqqara, on a tour of inspection in his new – that is, Quibell's old – district. Weigall was instantly fascinated by the whole style of the man, which he described for Hortense:

The other day he came up here to lunch and dinner – rode up in rather grand style, with a train of secretaries and people behind him. He held an inspection of guards and gave millions of orders and made new rules and generally set the place on a new footing, thank goodness! I was *delighted* with the marvellous way he administered. One could feel the firmness and strength of the man.

It is a side of Carter that has not, I think, been particularly noticed by his biographers. Carter was a man of little formal education, so that a rather plummy manner he affected later in his life is often put down to his long association with Lord Carnarvon. But in fact, years before he met Carnarvon, he showed that a taste for authority was as natural to him as to any public school boy sent to administer the 'natives'.

Weigall's letter describing all this also describes Carter's present plans and ambitions. He doesn't say where his information comes from, but it is likely that it came from Carter himself. Their meals together were probably spent talking shop. After all, there was much to discuss. As we have seen, the Entente Cordiale had just confirmed the French as the ultimate block on British careers in the Antiquities Department. Whatever the source, Weigall tells Hortense that when Carter's exchange with Quibell had fallen due, Carter had at first asked to stay on at Luxor; but that when the Anglo-French agreement was signed he at once wished to resign. Weigall's interpretation of that drastic decision was that Carter must have been hoping 'to step direct from Luxor into the Directorship at Cairo – a mere exchange of Inspectorship being quite beneath him.'

However (the letter goes on), another idea then occurred to Carter. He withdrew his resignation, carried out the exchange and went to Cairo where he proceeded to establish himself at the Museum in quasi-Directorial style. He

*actually rebuilt* [Quibell's] office, made it twice as big as the Director's, engaged two secretaries and three messengers (whereas the Director had two messengers and no secretary) issued an order that every letter and document for the Dept. was to come to him, not to the Director, and that every rule etc. made by the Dept. was to be sanctioned by him ... But he realized that in three years or four, Quibell would exchange back to Cairo; so he had to get him out of the way. And this he seems to have done by turning him into a Museum's curator at Cairo (the appointment is not made yet) and by putting somebody else as inspector at Luxor, who will be second to him (Carter) and will not have the right to exchange. The next thing is that Carter will receive a bigger salary and more power and thus the Anglo-French agreement will be annulled in value.

I think it is all splendid, for as you know, I admire Carter immensely as an official though I rather dislike him as a man.

All this is surprising in view of the friendly relationship that undoubtedly existed between Carter and Maspero. On the other hand, Maspero was a skilful operator as well as being a scholar of eminence, and he probably felt himself to be less threatened than this account suggests. The archaeological world was full of people who wanted his job, and over the years he would survive many attempts to sideline him – including some from Weigall himself. Besides, Maspero's active benevolence towards

Carter belongs to a time when, as we shall see, Carter had seriously upset his own chances of ever being a danger to him. All the same, it is odd that Maspero should have allowed Carter to get away with any of it. Perhaps the point here is not so much whether Weigall's account was correct (though he certainly believed it to be) but that it is possibly a reflection of Carter's own picture of himself.

As for his feelings for Carter as a man, Weigall was not alone. Carter's latest biographer, T.G.H. James,[7] has well documented his mixture of charm and cussedness, and like many others who knew him, Weigall over the years would shift frequently between like and dislike, admiration and exasperation. 'He always seems on the lookout for slights,' Weigall told Hortense, 'and woe be to the man who does anything which could possibly suggest that Carter wasn't quite so important an official as he believes himself. I have known him turn white in the face with rage because he was introduced to another person second, and not first. ... You know, sweetheart, he once was very rude to me at Luxor, and I threatened then to break every bone in his body if he was rude again.' But here at Saqqara, Carter was not at all rude, and somehow, Weigall writes, 'I forgot to do anything but like him very much!'

The following week, Carter made another arrival 'in his usual ceremonious way', and Weigall was again dazzled by him:

> Carter had to see a case at a neighbouring village and so I went with him. The case was one of land encroachment, that is to say a native had extended his garden wall onto an open space which should have been left vacant owing to its having antiquities on it ... We rode into the village, Carter on his horse, then I on a donkey, then his secretary, then some head man, and then four guards. When we got to the place some chairs were brought out and Carter and I sat and held a regular *durbar*. You must imagine us sitting in the shadow of a palm, then in front of us in the hot sun the crowd of Arabs, and behind them the fallen pillars partly submerged in a greeny pond in which ducks were splashing about; and finally in the background the mud huts and palm trees rising up to the blue sky ... It was a delicious scene ... the mere fact of sitting in judgement – just one white man administering justice to all that crowd of natives ...

So much power, so picturesquely wielded! It was in the midst of Weigall's thrill over these performances that Carter chose to give him the latest inside information: 'Carter told me in confidence what I had anticipated in my last letter. Quibell is to give up the Luxor Inspectorship and is to come and live at Saqqara, being engaged in excavating for the Govt. here. Carter is to remain as head-Inspector, as now; and there is to be a new Inspector at Luxor. The candidates for the Inspectorship are Mace and myself; and the former has the best chance.' Three days later, on 13 January 1905, he tells Hortense that he has sent in a letter indicating his willingness to take up a government post. Though he was in two minds about it himself, 'Carter advised me to do this as he thought it might tip the balance in my favour.'

Why was Carter so anxious to get Weigall appointed to this post? It must be remembered that, at the time, he believed that it would be subordinate to his own. He may well have thought that the young man was good material; but he may also have preferred a frankly admiring junior – one incidentally, without a degree – to Mace, a more experienced scholar-archaeologist of his own age, who was much more obviously part of the archaeological establishment than Weigall. Carter had first come to Egypt at the age of seventeen, as a 'tracer' or draughtsman working for Newberry, and although over the years he taught himself a great deal, he was never regarded as a scholar. Neither was he, in that strictly hierarchical world, regarded as a 'gentleman'. Weigall was a 'gentleman', true, but he might still have seemed a more likely subordinate than Mace.

Weigall himself never makes any comment about Carter's social standing. In fact, in Saqqara he was impressed not only with his administrative abilities, but with his social aplomb as well. In the evening of the day of the 'durbar', the omdeh or headman of the village invited both men and two Englishwomen, artists from the camp Petrie had established that year, Miss Hansard and Miss Kingsford, to a great feast at his house. It was an elaborate occasion, and it gave Carter a chance, as an old hand in Egypt, to show his green English colleagues just how such things were done. Weigall's description of the whole scene brings him vividly before us:

> The omdeh is a fine-looking man and a thorough gentleman. He wears the usual long flowing robes and silk turban, and is unspeakably dignified and grand. Carter is used, though, to native dinners, but I was pretty nervous about it, as Carter told me awful stories of your host handing you the eye of the roasted sheep as a dainty morsel!
> The omdeh sent donkeys up for us, and we started off in a delightfully romantic procession, headed with lanterns and tailed with the crowd of guards ... The moon was young, and the stars gleamed between the palm trees as we passed through the groves. Then we clattered through the village, all the dogs barking and the people lined up to see our procession pass. Finally we turned into a side alley and then through a great stone doorway into a courtyard, at the far end of which ... our host stood to greet us.

He goes on to describe the Frenchified reception room, the stilted conversation in Arabic, and finally the arrival of a huge tray of food carried on the head of a servant. Then came the rituals of washing and eating, the host choosing succulent portions with his fingers and passing them to his guests, the endless succession of dishes, all of which had to be sampled, until at last, after the fourteenth course, they all subsided into a stupor of satiation. 'Carter behaved splendidly – grunted and groaned, and expressed his excitement about the next dish – called to the servants to hasten as he could not contain his excitement longer; and finally at the end he threw himself back and groaned "Ah! – my stomach is as full of food as your head of wisdom, O Omdeh!"'

> At the end of the meal more soap and water was brought round, but this time Carter also washed out his mouth and spat into the basin, and then muttered under his breath to us, 'You *must* do the same.' So we all had to! Then came cigarettes and

*tea* and more talk, though we all felt too *absolutely stuffed* to do more than grunt a few remarks. About eleven, we all rode home; and that night I dreamed dreams of battle, murder and sudden death!

The dreams of battle, murder and sudden death, so lightly mentioned there, were the effects of indigestion working on a drama that had occurred earlier in the afternoon. The now famous 'Saqqara incident' – famous at least to historians of Egyptology – which was to cause so much diplomatic trouble at the Agency, and which in the end cost Carter his job, had managed to fit itself into the afternoon between the durbar and the omdeh's banquet.

Carter's official account of it is reproduced by T.G.H. James in his biography, so I will use Weigall's words from his letter to Hortense written two days after it all happened. The scene returns, then, to the durbar, after which Carter and Weigall joined Miss Hansard and Miss Kingsford for tea, taking it out 'onto the rocks near the cultivation':

While we were at tea a guard came flying up to fetch Carter as he said they were having trouble with some rowdy tourists. So he went off, and when we joined him an hour later we found everybody in wild excitement ...15 French tourists had tried to get into one of the tombs with only 11 tickets, and had finally beaten the guards and burst the door open. Afterwards they came to the verandah of Mariette's House, which is open to the public and had barracked themselves in there. At this stage, Carter arrived on the scene, and after some words ordered the guards – now reinforced – to eject them. Result: a serious fight in which sticks and chairs were used and two guards and two tourists rendered unconscious. When I saw the place afterwards it was a pool of blood. Carter behaved very well and was very moderate in his treatment of the brutes on the whole, and he only ordered the guards to use force after one of them had been knocked down by a tourist. As soon as they had been turned out of the house he called them off, for of course he could not touch them while they were on the open ground outside, but only as long as they were on Govt. ground inside the house. At last they all went off carrying their wounded with them, and throwing a few stones back as a parting salute. Carter promptly sent off telegrams to the police etc., and a messenger came up later to say they had been arrested at Bedracheyn ... Next day (yesterday) the commander of the police arrived, and Carter and I spent nearly eleven hours sitting, hearing and giving evidence ... Carter was of course rather nervous about it all, for he felt that he might be considered to have been too violent in ordering the guards to turn them out; but I haven't the slightest doubt how the case will go. I can see the French being fined £1,000, or doing a few months' hard labour. I only wish I had been in the fight – I am prehistoric enough to love a scrap of that kind. But I never arrived on the scene till all was over except the shouting.

Weigall's prophecy did not come true. The tourists complained to the French consulate, the newspapers took up the story, France's honour was felt to have been injured by the raising of 'native' sticks against her subjects, and the whole thing threatened to become an embarrassing diplomatic incident. In the end, in order to avoid a row with the French, Lord Cromer asked Carter to apologize. To everyone's astonishment, and in the face of repeated pleas, Carter refused. As a mark of displeasure, he was sent to Tanta, a dull town in the Delta, and finally in October of that year he resigned from the Service altogether.

In the context of the national rivalries outlined here, there is something painfully ironical about Carter's fate. He had done his duty, and here he was being expected to apologize to the French Consul at the request of the British Agent. Weigall saw it straightaway. 'The latest thing is that Carter has been asked by the Govt. to apologize to those French scoundrels whom he so very properly kicked out of Sakkara ... The matter has just lately been up for trial, and the committee found that it was Carter's duty to say he was sorry. Sorry, that is to say, for doing his duty.' However, as the days passed and Carter's refusal to apologize became a serious embarrassment, Weigall began to wonder:

... the machine of govt. has been put out of gear for a couple of days by his refusal. Knowing what a good man he is they have all tried to make him do this apology business, and four ministers have talked to him in turn but still he says "No", and Maspero tells me that his face is like that of a martyr, for he thinks he is dying for the sake of honour and morality. Well, so he is in a way but if you come to think of it, it is really *pride* that keeps him from sacrificing himself for his country. It is so small a thing that they ask – merely that he shall say that he regretted the incident but that he thought he was in the right. The Consul will then say, "It is nothing – don't mention it," ... Poor Carter, perhaps he may yet climb down – though I don't say I shall admire him less if he doesn't. In fact naturally all our sympathy is with him, but we all feel that he is childishly proud, and lacks broadness of mind.

Meanwhile, Weigall had his own decision to make. When they came to offer him the job, he was in a ferment. It turned out that Weigall's post was not to be subordinate to Carter's, and not to have a lower salary, as he had feared. He desperately needed the money, for Oscar's sake, and he wrote anxiously to Hortense for her views. But feelings were mixed on her side too. In spite of being desperately proud of him – 'How can I tell you how unspeakably proud and glad you have made me?' – she couldn't see their Saqqaran idyll slip away without a pang. She had hoped so much that they would have a little time 'when we should be quite alone together ... and for a while should not have any pressing duties to our fellow men ... And that we should live there so freely and simply and joyously.'

Their courtship had flourished on these dreams. Transferring her thoughts from Saqqara to the immensely more public and official life of Luxor seemed to her like pulling flowers up by the roots. But she worried for his sake too. He had told her, she reminds him, that the Inspectorship 'would entirely end your archaeological work – that you were tempted however, to take it *on account of the steady income* – that you really preferred on the whole to do excavating work.' She thought 'that you had this year become, more than ever before, absorbed and interested in your archaeological work and had such a lot of big plans for it and for writing etc. that you felt you *could* not and ought not to give it up.'

Hortense is referring here to a basic distinction in Weigall's mind between the life of a scholar and the life of a government official. From the very beginning Weigall had formed a clear picture of what the Inspectorate should be. It was not in his view an extension of the field he already occupied, not an opportunity for freer scope as an archaeologist. It was allied but distinct, at once more limited and more general. It required the archaeologist in him to refrain, and instead to provide the framework in which archaeology could thrive. Administration, supervision, conservation, and policing were the main features of it, and in a region that stretched from Nag Hamadi, about 400 miles south of Cairo, to Wady Halfa on the Sudanese border, there would be little time left over for private interests.

Nothing so strict and absolute had been the rule before this. Carter had carried out excavations of his own while on the job, and there would in the future be at least one occasion when Maspero would urge Weigall to do the same. Weigall refused then, on the grounds that he had 'always felt that the work of an inspector was to inspect and safeguard and not to excavate.'[8] And yet it was not all a matter of self-denial. Weigall's imagination was fired by the ideal of public duty. Carter's example had triggered his own inherent sense of romantic imperialism. Now he himself had the chance to bring about order and justice and to serve his country. 'The Kipling feeling has taken me by the shoulders,' he writes, 'and I am being pushed forward into the vastness where somehow the individual seems to fall away, and all I realize is that I am an Englishman, and my country has chosen me to do a piece of work.'

From our position a century or so later it is hard not to smile and to realize the genuine ardour of this. Hortense caught the spirit of it herself and in her next letter exclaimed that although one part of her felt sorry to lose Saqqara, another part understood 'more and more keenly … that the reality is far *more* beautiful and vastly richer, fuller and wider than the other … It must be a wonderful thing to feel that one is working, not so much on one's own account, as on behalf of one's country.' They were both in a highly wrought state, exalted by their love for each other and inclined to see everything in a heroic glow. Weigall had a genius for enthusing himself, for throwing himself forward into an imagined situation, and seeing the whole thing complete in its ideal form. But his different roles clashed sometimes. Hortense speaks at one point of his various aspects – the scientist and student, the artist, and the public spirited administrator. Among all these, she says, 'there must be civil war sometimes!' It was a perceptive remark, and his life was to prove her right.

# Chapter 6

# Yuya and Tuya, and Weigall 'Bashmufetish'
# 1905

So for the moment, with his mind at last made up, the public servant was in the ascendant, and Weigall poured the energy of all his other enthusiasms into that one channel. And after all, Hortense too, together with Carrie, was determined to be proud and ambitious for him. Carrie, in fact, had been bursting with delight from the start, and she wrote off to Chicago exclaiming: 'Girls, Girls, *Girls*! ... a telegram from Arthur came, and the whole face of the world has changed! ... It meant a wonderful beautiful story. Once upon a time a young man, very gifted and wise sat in his house in the Desert ...,' and she goes on to tell the whole thing. Hortense was bowled over by the fact that he had been 'passed over the heads of men with so much more experience in point of *time* – and so much older. ... Arthur, I don't know *how* to tell you how happy such an honour to you makes me.' She may have put her finger on something when she added, 'It must be rough for the unsuccessful one.' Mace in fact wrote a sporting letter of congratulation: 'I must make a brief interval in my clothes-rending and ashes and sackcloth execrations, and send you my hearty congratulations.'[1] Nevertheless it can't have been pleasant to be pipped to the post by Master Petrie.

Weigall was in no mood to worry about that; Oscar was his concern now. At last he had triumphant information about income, increments, pensions and perks: a free house, a horse and its upkeep, and travelling expenses. Furthermore he was no longer offering Hortense a hut in the desert, but a position in 'one of the large tourist resorts [which] from November to April is a pleasant and gay place to live in.' In fact, as he points out to Hortense, Luxor was scarcely more than an Arab village, with three large hotels dumped down in it. But Oscar wasn't to know, and he proceeds gravely: 'There are several large hotels and all modern conveniences. There is an English Church and hospital with resident chaplain and doctors. The climate is said to be the best in the world. ... Aswan [is] an equally fashionable place during the winter months. ... There will be no lack of society for your daughter during the winter.'

At the same time Hortense and Carrie were trying to get Oscar to let them visit Egypt. Weigall himself could not leave the country at all during the first year of his appointment. The government's conditions of employment were much harsher than Bissing's. It was extravagant of course for the Schleiters to come, because they could not stay much beyond April – the months between April and October were considered too hot for women. But if they couldn't come soon, when the weather was clement, they would have to wait until October, when it was hoped the wedding would take place, in Cairo. A whole year would then have passed since Hortense and Weigall had last seen each other; but there would be no point in marrying in the spring only to part for the summer. There was consternation both in Berne and Shepherd's Bush.

Meanwhile, Weigall's work was providing them with wonderful proof that Egypt might have the edge on Iowa. A few days after his arrival in Luxor on 5 February 1905, a discovery of a flight of steps cut into the rock was made in the Valley of the Kings, the great royal necropolis on the west bank of the Nile in which the pharaohs of the Eighteenth, Nineteenth and Twentieth Dynasties were buried, with all their gold about them. The Valley was government property, together with all the tombs and their contents, but the permit, or concession, for excavating in the Valley together with certain privileges and obligations, had been granted in 1903 by the Antiquities Department to a wealthy, elderly American amateur, Theodore Davis from Newport, Rhode Island.

The work of clearing the steps down to the entrance took some days, for they had been buried deep beneath a mound of stone chippings from two later tombs close on each side, those of Rameses III and Rameses XI. When the door was finally struck, it so happened that Weigall had to take charge, for Quibell was at Edfu, further south. He had been called away from Luxor to attend on the King's brother, H.R.H. the Duke of Connaught who, as commander-in-chief of the British Army in Egypt, was making his annual visit. Weigall was thus suddenly in at the deep end again, contemplating the dangers of attack and robbery, particularly through the night. As he knew from his experience at Abydos, any news of a discovery in the Valley of the Kings, usually accompanied by rumours of gold, flew instantly round the villages from which the diggers came. A force of local police and guards or *ghaffirs* was always placed at the entrance to newly discovered tombs, day and night, but a European official was also required to be on the spot, sleeping there on the sand with the guards.

Theodore Davis published an account of this excavation two years later, and later still Weigall wrote a piece about it for *Putnam's Magazine*.[2] The following extracts are from Weigall's letter home,[3] and though it differs in some details from Davis's account, it has the merit of having been written contemporaneously. Weigall was intensely conscious of witnessing a rare occurrence, and terribly excited, as were his family, who made two copies of his letter to send to one another. He starts in the evening of the first day when the steps were finally cleared as far as the door. He was with Davis:

and we crawled in together, into the slanting passage which appeared to lead down right into the mountain. As soon as we got in we found lying on the floor a lovely staff with an enamel top, and some other antiquities. We followed the passage down some distance, down another flight of steps, and then we came to a doorway, bricked up and sealed with a seal which we at once recognized as that of the Priests of Amen of the XVIIIth dynasty. There was a small hole in the corner of this brick wall; and it was evident that a man had been into the tomb and robbed it, and had thrown aside the staff etc. in his hurry to escape. The fact that the mouth of the tomb was covered with XIXth dynasty rubbish undisturbed showed plainly that the man had been in about 1300 BC and that after that date nobody had entered the place.

Davis went back to his *dahabiyeh* and made contact with Maspero, who happened to be visiting Luxor. Meanwhile Weigall settled down for the night. The valley is a desolate place and even more so at night, especially with the risk of attack. He had been on Davis's *dahabiyeh* earlier that day, and had said that he rather dreaded sleeping there. At that, an American painter, Joseph Lindon Smith, and his wife Corinna, offered to keep him company. According to the diary of Davis's companion, Emma Andrews, who accompanied him for more than a decade on his trips to Egypt, Corinna was 'wildly enthusiastic' the next day, and 'said that the night had been one of the most beautiful she had ever spent.'[4] Poor Hortense; it was just the Saqqara-like adventure that she would have loved.

Maspero was always quick to exploit the tombs as good theatre, especially where the audience was distinguished and influential. On this occasion he was in luck, for here was the Duke of Connaught – too good an opportunity to let slip. He sent word that he wanted the formal opening to take place when the royal presence could be secured. Archaeology at that time relied heavily on private money, and if the discoveries of one rich man could be made to attract others, so much the better. It was a precarious method of funding, and Weigall always deplored Maspero's failure to push for proper government support.

Maspero himself arrived in good time with Davis, Emma Andrews and their guests. As they all waited for the Duke, he, Davis and Weigall reconnoitred:

We slipped and slid [continues Weigall's account] down the long, steep passage to the blocked door, and with some difficulty we crawled into the inner chamber. For some moments we couldn't see anything much, but as our eyes got used to the candle light we saw a sight which I can safely say no living man has ever seen. The chamber was pretty large – a rough hewn cavern of a place. In the middle of the room were two enormous sarcophagi of wood inlaid with gold. The lids had been wrenched off by the plunderers and the coffins inside had been tumbled about so that the two mummies were exposed. The plunderers had evidently very hurriedly searched the bodies for the jewels but had not touched anything else. All round the sarcophagi – piled almost to the roof – were chairs, tables, beds, vases, and so on – all in perfect condition ... a tomb has never been found before with the things in such perfect preservation or in anything like such large numbers. In one corner a large chariot – quite perfect – as clean as a London hansom – lay; and by it a huge bedstead of inlaid wood, something like Chippendale. Here there was a group of lovely painted vases – here a pile of gold and silver figures. In one corner were some jars of wine, the lids tied on with string; and among them was one huge alabaster *jug full of honey still liquid* [this turned out to be natron, an embalming substance, not honey]. When I saw this I *really* nearly fainted. The extraordinary sensation of finding oneself looking at a pot of honey as liquid and sticky as the honey one eats at breakfast and yet *three thousand five hundred years old*, was so dumbfounding that one felt as though one were mad or dreaming. The room looked just as a drawing room would look in a London house shut up while the people were away for the summer ... There were lovely gold and wood arm chairs with cane bottoms. There were cushions stuffed with feathers and down – as soft as though they were only made yesterday.

Maspero, Davis and I all stood there gaping and almost trembling for a time – and I think we all felt that we were face to face with something which seemed to upset all human ideas of time and distance. Then we dashed for the inscribed objects and read out the names of Prince Auai and his wife Thuaie [variant spellings] – the famous mother and father of Queen Tiy. They had been known so well and discussed so often that they seemed old friends ... But nobody had ever expected to see them; and as we looked at the mummies – Princess Thuai with her hair still plaited and elaborately dressed, and Prince Auai with his eyes peacefully closed and his mouth a little open – an awful feeling came over me. All three of us very soon crawled out of the tomb and into the sunlight – one step from the seventeenth century[5] before Christ to the twentieth century after Him.

Outside, others in Davis's party were waiting their turn to enter. Emma Andrews noticed that Weigall 'came up pale and breathless' – the bad air, perhaps, but also excitement.[6] Then Joe Lindon Smith and his wife Corinna went down:

To show you how impressive the sight was [wrote Weigall] I must tell you that Mrs Smith burst into a torrent of tears ... Then after a while ... Davis came in again. But he had hardly looked for more than a minute when he cried "O my God!" and pitched forward in a bad faint. Smith and I fanned him and were pretty badly scared as he is an old man. And when he fainted a second time we shouted for help and all carried him to the surface ...

I am afraid you will think us all very hysterical, but you have not experienced the blank, utter amazement of finding oneself carried back and dumped into the 17th century BC!

But Hortense was equally moved by what she read: 'I felt like someone in a dream and I grew first cold and then hot as I read, and when the letter was finished my cheeks were so crimson that Mamma thought I had fever! I can't get over the marvellousness of it – I don't wonder that people fainted and cried! ... It is too dumbfounding to think that the honey was still liquid – how *could* it be!'

Davis then went home, and Weigall started on the inventory of the contents:

I was hard at work and filthy dirty and hot when Maspero came to the door of the tomb and called to see me. I hurried up and brushed myself clean on the way, and when I got to the surface Maspero said "the Duke of Connaught" and I found myself being led up to a large party of people, and presently I was shaking hands with the Duke. ... I took the whole party down one by one, but didn't let them go further than the entrance of the burial chamber as the place was so littered with objects.

He then had to give them a guided tour of the other tombs ('the Duke was awfully nice and quite informal – begged me to keep my hat on') after which came tea with his daughters. On returning to the tomb, he found yet more people had arrived:

A gruff, rude old man began to talk very fast to me and I soon discovered that he was the Duke of Devonshire ... Then came some Egyptologists and a mixed crowd of foolish English and French Dukes, Marquises, etc. for Luxor at present teems with them. A little dark man asked me to take him down but I got out of it. He proved to be the Crown Prince of Norway, afterwards.

In his autobiography, *Tombs, Temples and Ancient Art*, Joseph Lindon Smith has a story of the Duke of Devonshire arriving at the tomb, preceded by an equerry who got off his donkey simply by straightening his legs and letting the donkey walk away; and of the Duchess being tipped off her litter because she had prodded the front bearers with her umbrella, while omitting to make a sign to the back bearers.[7] Smith clearly took a dim view of Dukes, so he might have embroidered the tale, but the point is that Maspero's weakness for them meant that work in the tomb was constantly inter-rupted. The social tact of archaeologists, soothing and satisfying august and over-heated personages, counted for much in those days.

Quibell returned in the evening of the day of the opening, and the next day more archaeologists and artists were drafted in to help with the task of clearing and recording:

By this time, with two such exciting days and two bed-less nights in the open, and the Turkish-bath like temperature of the tomb, I was pretty tired. People kept coming to see the place (with special invitations from the Director or somebody) and just after lunch the Empress Eugenie [widow of Napoleon III] arrived. Quibell and I hurriedly tidied ourselves and we showed her round – a very hot, cross, old lady she was too.

The next day, Wednesday, they worked as steadily as they could, coming across

... some exquisite bits of furniture. One piece was a little chest made entirely of inlaid wood, the inlay being jasper, blue porcelain and gold, in beautiful patterns. It had a charming lid, and inside were some jewels. It looked as though it had been made yesterday. The lady Thuai has a fine face ... Poor soul how she must have hated having an electric lamp blazing in her eyes after 34 centuries of darkness.

On Thursday the treasures continued: 'The things are more and more wonderful. Today we have carried out into the daylight a large trunk made of wicker work, with trays inside for clothes – all as a perfect as a modern thing. We have also got a nice gold and ivory bedstead, and another jewel case.'

But the VIPs continued to buzz round like wasps at a jam pot:

I awoke this morning about 7 o'c ... [and] was cleaning myself up about 8 o'c when the Duke of Connaught arrived and said he wanted to see the tomb again. So I took him down with his a.d.c. and a Sir Somebody Mackenzie. The Duke was most delightful and was enormously interested in the tomb ... When at last we got to the surface we found the Duke of Devonshire had come again, with a Mr and Mrs Maguire – South African millionaires I think. His Grace looked very old and groggy. ... I got pretty angry with him, as he would tread so carelessly and nearly broke some of our antiquities ... We had hardly got to work again when the Crown Prince of Sweden or Norway arrived ...

After we had got rid of him we worked pretty hard until sunset ... As I write now I am pretty dead tired as you can imagine. The Arabs believe that we have found £20,000 worth of gold and an attack is possible; but we now have masses of police and guards. As a matter of fact the market value of the stuff in the tomb is at least £50,000!

Ten hectic days or so later, on 25 February, the work was completed, and the Valley of the Kings was quiet again. Weigall's last letter describes the scene:

All around me the cliffs rise in a stately circle, dark against the latest colours of the sunset. The stars are just showing; and things down here are almost as quiet as they – except for the scrappy conversation of the policemen and guards who are sitting over their fire near the tomb; with just one unfortunate man standing sentry – a rather lonely looking figure, half leaning on his rifle with its fixed bayonet – fixed goodness knows why, for I hope all danger of a raid is over.

Though the discovery of the tomb of Yuya and Tuya was followed by other important discoveries, this was always the one he looked back on as having had the greatest dramatic interest.

How much of all this was related to Oscar is not known, but no doubt Carrie and Hortense made the most of it. They must have worked on him relentlessly, for Hortense got her way in the end. By February 1905, Oscar had consented to their marriage, and by the middle of April the ladies were in Luxor. As for Weigall, in spite of his desire to have Hortense with him, he had begun to feel a little nervous at the thought. The last time he had seen Hortense had been among sympathetic members of his family, and before that, anonymously in Feldafing. Luxor was a different matter. Its European component was a tight little circle, alarmingly interested in appearances and gossip. Hortense and Carrie, free spirits that they were, had little experience of social busybodies, and the thought that they might, in their innocence, treat Luxor as another stop on their European merry-go-round, had given him a fright. He had written from Saqqara warning her against doing anything that might be questioned or discussed. Of course we will let everyone know we are engaged; but we mustn't be seen about in any particularly idle sort of way!! The winter society of this place consists of the Doctor, the Chaplain, Mr Davis and party (from Newport), Mr Tytus and party (New York) and Mr Bird and party. All of these are American millionaires who each have *dahabiyahs* (house boats). Then there is a Mr Mond and his family – a millionaire English Jew … Then the excavators of the English Exploration Fund; and several more or less permanent people such as the different officials who are in that district, and the more regular of the English visitors. Besides these, there are about 20,000 European (chiefly American and English) tourists who only stay a week or so. Except for the last named, all these people will be only too glad to discuss us, and you may be sure that anything against us will go into my dossier. Every official out here has his dossier at the ministry, and the secret service agents report the most minute details which are all noted and filed. Had I been an official at Feldafing, my dossier would be pretty startling!

Hortense's regret over Saqqara must have given her another stab. Worse, he goes on to describe the atmosphere of his new work, which already seemed to be casting a shadow over him.

I wonder how you will like me in a tarboush (or fez) … I have to wear it on all occasions when I am doing official work, and one has to keep it on in the house when doing things officially; and also one has to resist one's natural inclination to take one's hat off to a lady, but has to salute instead!

I have been having rather a nervous time since Wednesday when I was appointed, and I rather hate the guards with their "Bashmufetish" this and "Bashmufetish" that. 'Bash' of course means 'Pasha' or 'Chief', and 'Mufetish' is 'Inspector'. Everybody is so d-d polite! … At Luxor during the winter I shall have to wear gloves – g*loves,* think of it! – … and never again shall I be able to whistle the piercing notes of "O-o- Tommy-Tommy Atkins" … as I do here when I go tramping over the open sand …

In fact, when Carrie and Hortense did arrive he gave them a wonderful time, and no doubt whistled as freely as ever as he went up the Valley of the Kings with them. Hortense must have had fun, for though she reports as dutifully as ever about the beauties of the monuments, she lets herself go about her dresses, with illustrations showing just how the shoulders went, and the ribbons. Carrie, by contrast, is the po-faced one, at least to Oscar – Oscar never heard his wife's true voice in her letters. She assures him that Arthur has proved himself to be all that she had thought him, both in mind and disposition, and that she believes him to be not only a fine young man, but a remarkable one.

The visit was over in six weeks, the women returned to Germany, and for the third time in a year the lovers were separated. But if it was agonizing for them, for Mimi it was almost worse. She longed for her son. She begged Weigall to persuade Maspero to let him come to England in August for the wedding. But as he explained, he couldn't afford to annoy his boss. In fact it is possible that just then, Weigall was trying especially hard not to be annoying. At the end of May there had come a surprising enquiry from Maspero: Howard Carter was unhappy at Tanta where he had been sent in the aftermath of the Saqqara affair, and wished 'he had not left Luxor to come to a place where he was often at a loss what to do'. Would Weigall consider swapping Luxor for Tanta? Maspero continues:

> The manners and customs of the people in Lower Egypt differ in several aspects from the ways of the Saide [Upper Egypt], and his affray at Sakkara has disgusted him with Cairo and the neighbourhood ... Each residence has its advantages and drawbacks. Luxor is immensely superior during the winter, but horribly hot in the summer and completely dull. Tanteh is dull at all times, but it is one hour from Cairo, and that is a good thing to think of, since you are to be married and events happen to newly married people which may require prompt medical investigation, etc.
>
> I leave the matter to your consideration ... If all considered you prefer staying at Luxor, well and good, I will find some means to tell Carter in an incidental way that he is to remain at Tanteh. Pray consider yourself and your future only in the matter, and do what you think will be best for your interests.[8]

Carter's biographer, T.G.H.James, describes how solicitous Maspero was for Carter's future after the Saqqara affair, and how Carter battled on, refusing to admit fault or defeat, always hoping for reinstatement. This letter to Weigall is an extraordinary illustration of both these things. Weigall remarked to Hortense that he thought it 'rather a kind letter', referring no doubt to Maspero's tact in leaving the decision entirely to Weigall. It is also extremely 'kind' to Carter. Were it not for its great courtesy, Weigall would have been justified in feeling outraged; and if Carter had in any way manoeuvred for it, it was a lot to ask of Maspero. Of course Weigall replied immediately that he wanted to stay where he was. Maspero – who must have expected such an answer – replied assuring him that he would explain the situation to Carter in such a way that neither party need feel embarrassed when they next met.[9] All the same, the situation worried Weigall, for he feared that Carter would continue to agitate. Instead, he resigned from the service altogether a few months later.

Mimi, meanwhile, bravely swallowed her disappointment about the wedding. She quoted St. Paul on self-sacrifice, and threw herself into her work among the poor of Shepherd's Bush. It was single mothers, just as it had been in Salford, though without the midnight patrols and the revivalist meetings. In one letter, she had just been with 90 of 'her mothers' for their annual outing to Epping Forest, a long journey in horse-drawn wagons – 'they like it long and noisy!' In another she describes her hunt for the young man responsible for 'ruining' one of her girls:

> I had to go to an office in the City and ask to see a young gentleman, one of the clerks. A smart looking boy came out and said he was Mr Osborne. I said, can I

speak to you privately at which he looked as if he would die ... I told him to get his hat on and come out with me, which he refused to do. So I said, you don't want the office boys to hear my business, do you. Get on your hat and come with me, which he meekly did, and we walked over London Bridge together. I said "Your son was born last Thursday" ... I could not help feeling sorry for the boy, just 20. Still, he was a brute to ruin this poor little girl of 18. All I want him to do is to help provide for the child. The girl won't marry him, as she hates him ... of course I blame her too – unless a girl is drugged which does not often happen and seldom when the man is only a boy. These old men, well up in that sort of thing, can manage a drug – but seldom between a boy and a girl ... These rescue cases do require time and money to deal with them properly, and I get very tired sometimes over it.

Weigall was now working furiously in the heat, very conscious of the sheer size of his district, the vast unvisited areas to the south and east of Luxor. His experiences at Abydos and at the tomb of Yuya and Tuya had taught him that before anything else, his first task must be security. The most consummate tomb robbers had always lived at Thebes; there were whole families who lived by thieving, their intimate knowledge of the area handed down from father to son. The most famous example of this was the el Rassoul family. Long before, in 1871, the el Rassouls had found a tomb in the cliffs behind Deir el Bahri, Hatshepsut's funerary temple, in which lay the now famous 'royal cache': 16 royal mummies hidden in ancient times to protect them from tomb robbers. Slowly over the years they had released its goods onto the market. But the appearance of several well-preserved papyri aroused suspicion, and after intelligence gathering, interrogations and even torture, one of the el Rassoul brothers gave the secret away. In 1881, Maspero being away, the Curator of the Museum, Emile Brugsch, became the first European to step inside the hiding place and lay eyes on the astonishing stack of all the most famous Eighteenth- and Nineteenth- Dynasty Pharaohs.

But short of interrogation and torture, Europeans were at an impossible disadvantage. Furthermore, when Weigall arrived he found the existing body of guards slack, slovenly and possibly corrupt. He sacked the lot, drafted in new ones, drilled them, and put them in uniform. Hortense was alarmed: couldn't he keep at least the good ones, and she did hope that the new uniform would be picturesque. Judging by Carter's military methods at Saqqara, it is odd that his guards should have been slack. But it was notorious how lightly the ghaffirs carried their foreign discipline, and perhaps they had slipped during Quibell's kindly interregnum.

But, as Weigall travelled about, and saw what had to be done, he couldn't help reflecting on Carter in general. As he wrote to Hortense in September 1905:

Carter ... has gone down in my estimation a lot since I have seen his work here. He did splendid work at Luxor; but when you come to think that he only visited about 20 of the 250 sites in his district, and only knew of the existence of 100 although he was here for 12 years[10] one can hardly admire him as an *Inspector*, and as I always said, I don't like him as a *man*. I now only admire him as the cleaner of the Theban monuments, and even in that respect I don't think he did anything extraordinary considering that he lived 100 yards from his work for several years and the things that had to be done hit him in the eye, so to speak, whenever he went out.

Carter himself might have conceded that he was more interested in excavation than inspection, and in later years, when Weigall saw his work as an excavator, he ranked him with the best. In his disappointment, he seems to have forgotten that he could indeed like him as a man.

With all those neglected sites, the ones at Luxor must have seemed the least in need of attention. And yet there was Davis, an amateur, excavating in the Valley of the Kings, whose daily operations were allowed by Maspero to be directed by a local 'reis', or foreman. No professional archaeologist was in charge. This was really the classy end of treasure hunting. Davis bore the cost of his excavations, and in turn was granted certain plums from the tombs – not strictly by right, but Maspero never really insisted on the distinction between right and favour. Since the Antiquities Department was always strapped for cash for excavations, Maspero was happy to accommodate wealthy individuals so long as they let the Museum have some good things. When Davis made no claims on the contents of a tomb, he was treated as a great benefactor. It was a cosy bargain. During the winter months Davis lived on the *Bedouin*, his comfortable houseboat or *dahabiyeh*, with his companion, Mrs Emma Andrews, a cousin of his wife. Periodically he rode his donkey up the valley to visit the excavations, and in general passed the time in a state of pleasing impatience, in the hopes that his men would strike lucky.

The Chief Inspector was, of course, ultimately responsible, but by the nature of his job, he could only keep a general eye on things. As we shall see, Maspero's casualness on the question of supervision was to become one of Weigall's bugbears. He felt that between them, Maspero and people like Davis perpetuated amateurism, and ignored the obligation both of the Antiquities Department and of the excavator towards Egypt's antiquities. He was not alone, of course. Only the year before, Petrie had published a handbook for archaeologists, *Methods and Aims in Archaeology,* in which he had stated as a cardinal principle of scientific archaeology, that excavations should be supervised by a knowledgeable person, trained in the techniques of recording and preserving:

To undertake excavating, and so take the responsibility of preserving a multitude of delicate and valuable things, unless one is prepared to deal with them efficiently ... is like undertaking a surgical operation in ignorance of anatomy ... To remove and preserve only the pretty and interesting pieces, and leave the rest behind unnoticed, and separated from what gave them a value and a meaning, proves the spirit of a dealer and not that of a scholar.[11]

This comes perilously close to Davis's spirit, and Weigall was deeply suspicious of him. Some years later he wrote an article called the 'Morality of Excavation' (one of

Petrie's chapters was entitled 'The Ethics of Archaeology') in which he enlarged on many of Petrie's points. In speaking of the importance and real difficulty of accurate and comprehensive record-keeping, he tells a story against himself:

Some years ago I excavated a few tombs in Lower Nubia ... I photographed the contents *in situ*, recorded the positions of the skeletons and all the objects placed around them, measured and photographed the skulls ... Some months later, I showed the skulls to a certain savant ...

"I notice in these pictures," said he, " that some of the front teeth are missing from the jaws. Had they dropped out in the grave, or had they been knocked out during life? You could, of course, tell from the condition of the jawbone." And it was with considerable shame that I was obliged to admit that I had not made the required observations. The point was an important one. Certain African tribes break out the front teeth for ornamental reasons, and the origin and geographical distribution of this strange custom, which can now be traced back to Pharaonic times, is a matter of far-reaching value to ethnology.[12]

If a relatively conscientious and informed archaeologist could make such a mistake, Davis without supervision could do infinite damage.

But, in fact, until Quibell and Weigall took over, it had not been a great problem. Howard Carter's interest in excavation had saved Davis from himself. Carter had actually taken charge of Davis's men on a daily basis, making some spectacular discoveries – most notably the tombs of Tuthmosis IV and of Queen Hatshepsut. But this had had its cost from the point of view of the Inspectorate as a whole. It was impossible to be both excavator and Inspector. Weigall raised the whole issue with Maspero: 'I pointed out to our Director General that only recognized archaeologists should be allowed to work, and at my request he readily invited Mr Davis to employ an archaeologist to work for him, which was at once done.'[13]

This makes it sound smooth enough. But Davis's letter to Weigall, confirming the new arrangement in June 1905, suggests that there had been some discord:

I have now arranged with M. Maspero to the end that "Ayrton" shall be employed by me to conduct explorations in the Valley. I know that you will be glad to escape the bother of looking after my work or at least until I find a tomb when doubtless the contents will be turned over to your care. It seems to be the best manner of conducting the explorations, and certainly will make life more harmonious![14]

"Ayrton" was Edward Russell Ayrton, an English archaeologist, just 22, who had been trained by Petrie at Abydos the year after Weigall left, and who had recently been working with the Swiss archaeologist, Naville, at Deir-el-Bahri. Weigall had met him while he was at Saqqara, and again when he had come over to help with the tomb of Yuya and Tuya. His appointment under Davis established a major point of principle, enshrined in the terms of Davis's new contract for the concession of the Valley of the Kings drawn up that November.[15] But the universal application of that principle was to be fragile in practice, and Weigall had a constant fight with Maspero to get him to observe it. If the excavators had money, Maspero was inclined to indulge them and to let them go it alone. On two occasions Weigall refused western amateurs for Upper Egypt – a Mr Dow Covington and a Mr Whittaker – to whom Maspero then gave concessions in Middle Egypt.[16]

As for the 250 sites, Weigall made a start that summer. He wrote in July to Hortense about one particular expedition, camping out over several days and nights in the desert on both sides of the Nile between Esneh and Edfu, south of Luxor. It had been quite a procession, with camels and donkeys and guards and the sub-inspector, the object being 'to see the little cemeteries that occur every few miles along the desert, and to map them, and make notes about them, and see they are not being plundered'. They had been plundered, of course, and Weigall had confiscated 'antikas' hidden in Bedouin tents, and had dealt sharply with local omdehs. The story was repeated throughout his territory to the south of Luxor to Aswan, and on through Nubia to Wady Halfa. In his annual report for that year, Maspero makes mention of Weigall's journeys, in which he reconnoitred 'the great number of archaic and prehistoric cemeteries' and, with the co-operation of the police, put them under 'a stricter surveillance than has been possible until now'. These cemeteries, Maspero goes on,

> have in effect, been ransacked and ruined during the last fifteen years by diggers in the pay of the Luxor and Keneh dealers: the objects which they have obtained and sold to the tourists separately without provenance, are almost all lost to science. The measures taken with the help of the Ministry of the Interior may not save everything that remains, but they will at least slow down the destruction until scholars can come and explore these sites methodically.[17]

It was an example of the value of inspection to archaeology, though it can't have made Weigall any friends among the Bedouin in the desert, or the dealers who paid them.

Similarly, Weigall may have fallen foul of the irrigation officials – the very men he so admired – who wanted to dig a canal straight through the middle of the plain of Thebes, bisecting the necropolis at Gurneh, where the Tombs of the Nobles are. The work was begun, and Weigall describes the dealers gathering and sitting round at a little distance, patiently waiting for their moment – a vivid glimpse of how closely the work of engineers affected the antiquities market. Failing to halt the engineer in charge, Weigall sent a telegram warning Maspero. After hurried meetings in Cairo, the thing was stopped, and the course of the canal altered.[18] The two episodes gave him his first taste of the powers and responsibilities of authority, and the other parties in both cases may have bristled a little at this commanding young man of twenty-four.

In fact, it wasn't easy for him. During those first months of his new job, he writes of the difficulties of asserting his authority, of being cheated and taken advantage of by guards and sub-inspectors, and of being forced against his nature into treating them 'like dogs', as Carter had done. He writes of eight-hour journeys in the blazing sun, of his mouth filling with 'a white sort of leathery foam', and of feeling 'deathly sick'. Hortense mourned the loss of his youth and freedom, and implored him not to forget that it will still be in their power, when they are together, to shut out the world like two carefree children. Her imagination still ran on Saqqara lines, still conjured up the picture of nights beneath the stars in desert camps, of journeys into the remote south where they could be alone in caverns beside the Nile, the first man and woman in a Garden of Eden. Whether he smiled at that lost world, or thought that perhaps he could find it again with her, is impossible to tell.

It had been an extraordinary year: they had left each other wrapped in romantic dreams, and now they were to meet in the stark light of public office. Apart from their six weeks together in April and May, all their adjustments to each other had been made by letter. But the wedding was drawing near, and he had arranged a honeymoon trip by boat from Cairo to Abu Simbel. It may not have been Paradise, but it was a pretty good substitute. In early October, Carrie and Hortense arrived in Egypt and on the 11th Hortense and Weigall were married at last. Carrie told the Chicago ladies all the details, the clothes, the hats, the shoes – and Arthur's face: 'very lofty and extremely solemn.' She also assured them that they all went to church on ostriches. As the married couple sailed away up the river, Carrie went back alone to Shepheard's Hotel, her long holiday away from Oscar over. She was to join them later in Luxor, and stay for Christmas, but America could not now be avoided for long. Before she went however, she was determined, she told her sister, to buy her return ticket for Europe.

# Chapter 7

# The flooding of Nubia; the Tombs of the Nobles
# 1906–1907

For Weigall the journey into Nubia, the country south beyond Aswan, was both work and play. He mentions it in various reports as though it were a tour of inspection, a continuation of the work he had started that summer on the ancient remains between Luxor and Aswan. All the same he didn't disappoint Hortense, for even if he was keeping an eye out for cemeteries and potsherds, she was a well-trained sightseer by now, and what better guide than a lover. Becalmed just a few miles short of Abu Simbel, she wrote back to Carrie to say that they were having 'a most tremendously, extraordinarily, unheard-of-ly good time'. The country they passed through is now at the bottom of Lake Nasser, but in 1905 it was still desert with the merest strip of cultivation along the river. In one of his essays Weigall described this now lost land: 'rugged and often magnificent ...'

> ... the rocky hills on either side group themselves into bold compositions, rising darkly above the palms and acacias reflected in the water. The villages, clustered on the hillsides as though grown like mushrooms in the night, are not different in colour to the ground ... Now we come upon a tract of desert sand which rolls down to the river in a golden slope; now the hills recede, leaving an open bay wherein there are patches of cultivated ground ... now a dense but narrow palm-grove follows the line of the bank for a mile or more, backed by the villages at the foot of the hills.[1]

The Nubians were different from the Egyptians, darker, their features more aquiline. The women wore their robes draped over one shoulder, and their hair in hundreds of tiny plaits, the ones across the forehead stopped with lumps of beeswax. The men carried spears, and sometimes even battleaxes, but they were not fierce – on the contrary, a cheerful race, Weigall says, and peaceable. Not many letters survive from the couple, but one can catch a whisper of them sometimes in Mimi's and Carrie's answers: there had been a freak storm, Hortense had lost her shoes, they had sailed paper boats on the Nile – going in for the 'simple life' rather, remarked Mimi dryly.

But apart from the paper boats, Weigall's visits to this region, now in October and again in May and September of the following year, had a serious object, for they were

A reach of the Nile on the way to Abu Simbel

part of the preliminaries for the grand project of the decade: the first raising of the Aswan dam, which itself had only recently been completed, in 1902. Under the British, the agriculture and hydraulics of Upper Egypt were in the process of being transformed. Instead of the annual inundation which for thousands of years had spread rich Nile mud over the fields, leaving the rest of the year dry, now the flow of water was being regulated, held back over the winter, and released during the summer. Unfortunately this meant that some of the temples, forts and cemeteries of Nubia were being flooded during the winter to a greater height than before, and now, with the proposed raising of the dam, more would be. It was an urgent matter, therefore, to estimate the likely damage and to make recommendations for minimizing it.

Much damage had already been done. In 1901, a year before the completion of the first dam, the Department of Public Works had taken in hand the consolidation of the foundations of the temples on the island of Philae, but nothing else had been done either by them or by the Antiquities Department to strengthen the other Nubian temple foundations or to protect the cemeteries, or at least to excavate and record them before they were flooded. At the same time there continued the steady destruction of all these monuments at the hands of villagers who plundered cemeteries, removed masonry blocks and dug at mud brick foundations for fertilizer. The digging out of mud-bricks, or 'sebakh', for fertilizer was a custom that worried archaeologists throughout Egypt, for it is certain that the 'sebakhin', as the diggers were called, found valuable matter other than nitrates. In Weigall's time there was an attempt to control the practice by a system of licences, but it was impossible to check illicit digging entirely, and certainly not in regions such as Nubia where the Department had made so little impression.

The general destruction was assisted by European visitors who carved their names on the monuments and scrambled over cracked and unsteady statues to pose for photographs. The situation had been worsening over several years, both before and after Maspero's second term as Director General in 1899, and those who knew what was happening pointed an accusing finger at the Antiquities Department. One such was Somers Clarke, an architectural archaeologist, known for his work on English cathedrals (he was made Surveyor of the Fabric of St Paul's cathedral in 1897), but who also took a special interest in Egyptian archaeology. He had visited Nubia in 1894-5 and again in 1898-9, and had deplored both threats – the plundering and now the flooding. As he recalled in a paper presented to the Society of Antiquaries in 1908:

> It was known that whilst some of the temples stood upon rock, others rested merely upon the alluvium, a perfectly adequate substratum if unattacked by water. The attention of the Department of Antiquities was called to these facts; indeed based upon my second visit to Nubia in 1898-9, I made a long report to the Director stating the deplorable condition in which I found most of the temples, and the active destruction going on at the hands of the villagers. Nothing was done.[2]

In 1899 Maspero would have been the Director, just installed, to whom Somers Clarke's report was addressed. But as Maspero says in his own account of the situation in *Les Temples Immergés de la Nubie* (1911), he felt that the first claims on his attention were the Cairo Museum and the Egyptian provinces. He had an impossible job. Somers Clarke himself conceded that Maspero's museum, unlike the Louvre or the British Museum, extended for a thousand miles beyond the walls of the one in Cairo. Certainly there is nothing in Maspero's annual *Rapports* for 1899 and 1900 to show that Clarke's Nubian warnings were in the forefront of his mind. In 1901 he did send his Chief Inspector, Howard Carter, to Nubia, but by then it was late in the day, the dam was nearing completion, and Carter's brief – to judge by the outcome – was to make only a cursory report on six of the temples together with rough estimates of the cost of restoration. Furthermore, Maspero admits that he did not follow up these estimates with the Department of Public Works. It was not until 1904-5, after the dam had been completed and when talk of raising it had begun, that Maspero himself made a visit, and even then his report was confined to sixteen temples.[3]

What Weigall did, during 1905-6, in the short time that was left before the decision to raise the dam was made in 1907, was to mount the investigation that should have been carried out six years before. It was, as he explains in the Preface to his resulting publication, *A Report on the Antiquities of Lower Nubia* (1907), a very rushed job, and in the circumstances, addressed as much to the Public Works Department as to the archaeologists:

> the material was rapidly collected ... and has been put together without reference to more than the half-dozen books that happened to be accessible. Few of the questions have thus been 'worked up'; and no doubt errors will be found by the

Egyptological reader. The copying of the inscriptions, the writing up of the text, and the preparation of the plates has occupied little more than two months, in which the greater part of the days was spent walking over the country.[4]

Nevertheless it was more comprehensive than anything previously attempted. It gives an account of the history of Nubia, and of the people who lived there in ancient times – the 'Pangrave' people as they were known, from the shape of their graves. There follows a description of the temples, the reliefs and inscriptions on their walls, and their history, together with a rough idea of what works were needed to preserve them; the same for the cemeteries, ancient quarries, fortresses and other ruins; and finally it provides facsimile drawings of sherds and rock inscriptions, together with about two hundred photographs of the sites and monuments. Somers Clarke, referring to it in his Society of Antiquaries paper, said that 'no such compendious collection illustrating Nubia has before been issued. Mr Weigall is to be congratulated on the great industry and care he has displayed.'[5]

But there was a sting in his congratulations, for he points out that, though the author no doubt had no such intention, his very descriptions of the remains amounted to a severe criticism of the Department of Antiquities. In fact, Weigall could scarcely have avoided realizing it. Of the temple of Dabod, for example, he wrote:

One matter which, like so much in Lower Nubia, was never reported to the Director-General, should here be recorded. Almost the whole of the south side of the temple, and a great part of the fallen doorway on the east of the temple, has been systematically quarried away: and as the photograph here published shows that the doorway had not fallen a few years ago, this quarrying must have occurred within quite recent years. About 250 large blocks have been entirely removed.[6]

And of the temple at Derr:

The temple is excavated in the cliffs at the back of the town, and thus forms a convenient place for the depositing of rubbish and filth. The officials of the town had hardly heard of the Antiquities Department ... The temple lies open to the world and has no watchman appointed by the Antiquities Department ... The preservation of the temple is not good. The open hall has been much damaged and all the pillars have disappeared apart from their bases.[7]

Of the temple at Amada:

Much requires to be done to protect the temple against native thieves or European vandals. It now stands quite open and unprotected, and a great deal of damage has been done to it in recent years. Over the reliefs on the doorpost, an employee at the Derr Police Station painted a large numeral in red paint a short time ago; and this the writer had removed, though a bad stain remains. When censured the employee stated that he had no idea that the place was anything but a convenient landmark. Across one of the finest reliefs 'W.W. 1905' has been heavily cut in large size and there are many other tourists besides W.W. in Egypt against whose vulgarity the temple must be protected.[8]

He does not openly blame Maspero – indeed he excuses him on the grounds that these matters were not reported to him. But he must have pondered again, just as he had done in Thebes, on Howard Carter's role, and ultimately – for there was no escaping it – on Maspero's failure to use his Chief Inspector properly in Nubia.

Weigall learned early on in his relations with Maspero to cultivate what he called 'the gentle art of disobedience'.[9] By treading delicately, he says, he was sometimes able to push through reforms and projects in his district in spite of his Director, and even against his wishes; furthermore, he could sometimes persuade him that they emanated from himself:

In 1906, when it was decided to raise the height of the dam at Aswan, no adequate steps were taken to protect the ancient remains in Lower Nubia, and I received *no orders whatsoever* on the subject. I therefore wrote a report on the condition of these remains, and, having informed Sir William Garstin [Adviser for the Department of Public Works] about it, was told to attend at Aswan in 1907 when the official meeting was held on the subject. The Director General [Maspero] submitted a report to that meeting asking for £17,000 for the necessary archaeological works. I submitted a note privately, asking for £65,000. I then obtained leave to publish my report and added a preface to it ... stating that our Director General had ordered me to go to Lower Nubia to make it, which was absolutely untrue, since he never even knew that I had made it. I then told him that I had asked for £65,000 in accordance with *his* wishes which was again untrue, and I did not tell him that I had seen his report asking for only £17,000. The larger sum was voted for the work, and the Director General was, and still is, firmly of the opinion that it was voted at *his* request.

It has been mentioned that the administration of archaeology in Egypt was closely entangled in politics – both intergovernmental and interdepartmental. Weigall quickly grasped the importance of this. As a member of the Antiquities Service and as an employee of the British government he in fact straddled two lines of power, and to achieve anything he had to know how to manipulate them. For although, as we have seen, the Antiquities Department was the special preserve of the French, it was part of the British Agency as a whole, being subsumed within the Ministry of Public Works. It was thus answerable ultimately to a British Adviser.

In his *Reminiscences*, A.H. Sayce, the Oxford Professor of Assyriology from 1891 to 1919, sheds much light on the relations of the two powers, and on the position of the Department of Antiquities between them. Owing to poor health Sayce had since the 1880s spent his winters on the Nile in a *dahabiyeh* fitted up with a large working library. He knew all the archaeologists and the chief Agency officials in the Egypt of his day, and was often consulted by them. According to him, the British Agency regarded the Antiquities department as important only in so far as it could be used as a lever on the French – 'the continuance or extension of French influence in it being used in exchange for some political equivalent.' The British were interested only in those departments 'which contributed to swell the revenue', Thus:

> Finance held the first place, irrigation upon which the prosperity of the country depended came second, while law was third. On the other hand, matters like education and archaeology ... were neglected; the Department of antiquities was tolerated only in so far as it could be made useful in bargaining with France ... Lord Cromer was once provoked into saying to me: "My dear Mr Sayce, I wish there were no antiquities in this country; they are more trouble than anything else."[10]

The Antiquities Department was a political pawn, therefore, and it was further embarrassed by its position within the very department in which the actual political ascendancy of the British was most triumphant. For it was from the Public Works Department that the great engineering and irrigation projects were initiated and controlled. The water engineers were the aristocracy of British officialdom. As G.W. Steevens wrote in *Egypt in 1898*: 'Egypt is, of all others, the land of the engineer: he makes or unmakes it, enlarges or diminishes it, according as he fails or succeeds in managing the Nile. The British engineers are making – quite literally and visibly and palpably making – Egypt.'[11]

Weigall had seen for himself how little they bothered to take the Antiquities Department into account when they had tried to cut a canal through ancient Thebes. Here, in Nubia there needed a huge injection of energy and determination to get them to listen to the archaeological claims of so remote and unstudied a region. And yet Maspero was strangely reluctant to push his claims with the British – a hesitation which comes out, for example, in his not asking for the money Carter had estimated in 1901 for the six Nubian temples in his report. Maspero explained himself years later by saying that Sir William Garstin had already agreed to give him L.E.22,000 (L.E. stands for Egyptian pounds) to strengthen the Philae temples, and he could not therefore ask for more.[12] Actually, the figure L.E.22,000 appears in the Report on the consolidation of the Philae temples published at the time (1901) by the Public Works Department as its own figure, out of which Maspero was allowed L.E.3,000 for work on the superstructure. It is symptomatic both of Maspero's habit of misremembering and of the rivalry between the two departments that he should have represented the larger figure as the budget given specifically to him. He admits that, out of this amount, he 'abandoned' ('j'abondonnai') L.E.18,000 to the engineers in the Public Works Department (incidentally, L.E.1,000 seems unaccounted for), but adds that he only did it because he wasn't at that time fully aware of the technical skills of the men under him.[13]

In the light of these departmental rivalries, coloured as they always were by national rivalries, Maspero's hesitation in asking for money is less strange. After all, asking only emphasized the subordinate position of the Antiquities Department within the Department of Public Works. Weigall explains:

It has been the policy of the Department to stand aloof from the Government as much as possible. The Director General endeavours to make it a sort of separate French society, and there are few people who even know it is a government department. The isolation in which it is kept causes it to be regarded as a sort of Institute for cranks dependent upon the support of old ladies. Letters are almost invariably addressed to me by tourists as director of the "Society of Antiquaries" or something of that kind. Thus the work that the *Government* is doing is being ignored, and this has the effect of lowering our prestige very considerably. In certain large reports of mine, I have headed the title page: – Ministry of Public Works, Department of Antiquities, but our Director General has always cut out the words relating to the PWD.[14]

Weigall's 'Institute of cranks' slyly introduces a quite separate criticism, for it doesn't necessarily follow from Maspero's isolation that he should attract cranks. And yet his aloofness from the Government did nothing to promote the image of the archaeologist as a professional. It was galling to find colleagues such as Somers Clarke able to make brutal comparisons, as in the following passage where he compares the two departments at the time of the raising of the dam:

As soon as Captain Lyons [who organized the Geological Surveys of Egypt from 1897–1909] had received his instructions to set in hand the researches, he very wisely sought out specialists in their several spheres, so that each department of the work should be carried forward in a thoroughly efficient manner.

It is but too well known that a great deal of investigation in Egypt is carried on by men who are more of amateurs than of scientific workers. With wonderful energy and devotion they often throw themselves into the undertaking, but the mental atmosphere is more suited to that of a prolonged picnic than of a serious occupation. Some, again, are permitted to undertake work who have absolutely no qualifications whatever beyond that of powerful influence or a fine name, whilst others are but traders who hope, by selling half … of what they find, to pay the cost of their labours; the Antiquity Department coming off with what it can get of the remaining half.[15]

The relations between the Antiquities department and the Ministry, and the national and personal sensitivities that they embodied, affected Weigall at every turn. Maspero was essentially a scholar, who occupied a post that cried out for administrative vision. Weigall was not really a scholar – as he was the first to admit – but he had learnt from Petrie about the principles of archaeology and he thought boldly and comprehensively about their administrative implications. Theodore Davis and the question of concessions to amateur archaeologists was only the beginning; conservation was next, and Nubia was a glaring example of how necessary it was to think big.

But for the moment, there were no campaigns; all was tact and discretion. Weigall was in the early months of his job, still getting used to the detail, the sheer miscellaneous diffuseness of it – a drunken ghaffir here, a non-ticket-paying tourist there, a lady friend of a minister to attend to tomorrow, ant-eaten wooden steps to be replaced, and so on. Regulating the conduct of his guards along English public school lines was a particularly thankless task, and the tourists didn't help. He tried, for example, to abolish the custom of bakhshish or tipping. On one occasion, he tells Hortense, he found a tourist about to give a tip and the guard 'just about to take it when he saw me, and instantly pushed the money ostentatiously from him and said "No" in a voice of thunder. The poor little tourist was terrified and fled.' He could laugh, but in his report to the Egypt Exploration Fund for the year 1905-06 he wearily conveys the daily grind which pushed all the interesting projects into corners: 'The main part of my time has been taken up by the administrative side of the work; for the endeavour to keep things up to the mark, in a country where the tendency to slide back is so pronounced, occupies most of one's days.'[16]

By way of compensation there was 'the most delightful game of being married'. As he wrote to Carrie, 'It gets more interesting by the minute.' The house was newly built, just finished in the summer of 1905, for until then the Inspector had lived in a small building at a spot called Medinet Habu, on the west side of the Nile in among the ruins. Now he was to be installed in quite a large residence, with servants' quarters and stables, all on one floor for the moment, but a second storey was planned. It was on the east side of the Nile, about a mile outside Luxor towards Karnak, and overlooking the river. Hortense was rapturous about it and about everything Weigall had done. It was 'so cosey and homey and pretty,' she wrote to Carrie, 'it is so delightful to be in *my own* house!' After five years of wandering, domesticity was an adventure in itself.

Not that there was much of a challenge, at least not immediately. Carrie, who joined them on their return, and the servants who came with the house, shielded her still. She was to discover that servants are not necessarily a blessing, but for the moment all went smoothly, meals arrived from the kitchen, and the only task was to arrange everything prettily, and fill the rooms with flowers. Both Weigall and Hortense had an eye for a charming room – absolutely no dados, or stencilling, they had told each other – and now they brought it all together to their taste. Mattie was enchanted: '… floor cushions are lovely, I think, and tiled floors must be a *joy* … Oh is your house *Oriental* and *velvety*?' And to have a servant standing at the door 'with a feather duster in hand', she says, must be 'very oriental'. The servants were not only colourful in themselves – Abdu, the chief factotum, wore a long white robe tied with a red sash, and a red tarboush – but they sprang their own ideas on the household. During the night before Christmas they were busy, and Carrie describes the 'gorgeous sight [that] burst on our view' on Christmas morning, the drawing room blazing with red banners and sugar cane stalks decorating the doors and windows.'

Now with all the glass and china unpacked and a wife across the table, Weigall could entertain in some style – though Hortense felt a little nervous at the prospect. She describes a small party they gave after Christmas for Theodore Davis and his guests. Everything had been exquisite: the tablecloth embroidered with white roses, the glass bowl filled with 'purplish brownish chrysanthemums', the dinner service with Arthur's crest in black. She was particularly delighted with 'the sweetest little glass pitchers' for water – the latest thing, she understood, in London. And with her 'Vienna' dress, which Arthur always begged her to wear. As for the food, she lists all seven courses but quite how it had all been done, she had no idea. As she told Mattie, she must find out how the cook made the pine nut and raisin turkey stuffing.

The crest is a revealing touch. Mattie was mightily impressed – 'Do tell me about Arthur's *crest,* what it is like ... he must have had an earl or some titled being in his family to have a crest.' One remembers the strange upbringing Mimi had given him in Manchester, his feeling of social inferiority among the boys at his prep school, and to some extent at Wellington. Egypt likewise had thrown him among a wealthier and at times more aristocratic set of people than he would have met in England. Society at that time was rigidly snobbish, and Egypt got a concentrated dose of it. His letter to Oscar immediately after his appointment shows what kind of world he thought he was up against:

In my new work it will be necessary for me to be introduced to many of the royal-ties who pass through Luxor each year; and on the occasion of such a visit I shall be obliged to entertain the personage at lunch or dinner ... Could you therefore see your way to allowing Hortense to be presented to the King in London?[17] My mother would present her, I am sure, and would arrange all the formalities ... A lady who has been presented has a social position quite undisputed, and this would make matters much more simple for her in Egypt. It is of course not really neces-sary; but undoubtedly it would be a great advantage to her.

Oscar wouldn't countenance it. It represented the old world at its most ridiculous and decadent, and he wrote to Hortense to 'please dispense with that London farce. I feel as if anyone is rather disgraced than otherwise to be presented to that notorious former Prince of Wales.' Whether Weigall's crest or Hortense's unpresented status made the slightest difference to them in Egypt, it is impossible to tell. Certainly he collected many admirers, some of them titled. But what impressed people about him was his knowledge and love for the ancient monuments, and his charm.

On Weigall's return from Nubia in November, Maspero had asked him to occupy himself in Thebes for the time being because the Department couldn't pay any more travel expenses. Davis was now safe in Ayrton's hands, but there was still plenty to do in Thebes. There was the Luxor temple to tidy up, tourist roads to be made, and always, everywhere, the constant battle against thieves. He tells Hortense about 'burgling' a tomb one night to test the guard, and found that the man didn't even wake up; at Karnak he 'put in a "control-watch" installation, which obliges the ghaf-firs to make ten automatically-registered patrols of the whole of the temple each night.'[18] But apart from these routine chores, there was a particular part of the Theban necropolis that was in more urgent need of attention than anywhere else: the Tombs of the Nobles – or, more properly speaking, their mortuary chapels.

Honeycombing the low hills between Hatshepsut's temple at Deir-el-Bahri and the Ramasseum, these rock chambers were excavated for the great nobles of the Eight-eenth Dynasty. They were not tombs as such, for the mummified bodies were buried separately. Their function was to contain painted scenes depicting aspects of life which would then accompany the deceased into death. Thus, just as in the mastabas of Saqqara, the ancient world was recreated: musicians and dancers, workmen treading grapes, servants fetching water, potters, labourers receiving their wages, as well as priests making sacrifices and subject nations paying tribute. Sacred and secular, historic and quotidian, it was all there, a storehouse for the scholar.

These chapels were to become Weigall's love, and over the next six years he spent as much time as he could among them, safeguarding, repairing, numbering, describing, cataloguing, and writing about them. In time, he drew the Egyptologist and philologist Alan Gardiner into his enthusiasm and the two of them worked together to produce a catalogue, which was published in 1913. But for the moment he was on his own, and in the early months of 1906 he began his first systematic study of them. It was sad work. During the nineteenth century western travellers and copyists had, in their enthusiasm, wrecked many of the frescoes. Some had taken wet squeezes – that is, they had pressed wetted paper onto the paintings so as to take coloured prints – draining the colour from the originals and leaving streaks and smears behind. Some had outlined the paintings in heavy lead pencil in order to make tracing easier. Others had squared them up, again in heavy pencil, so as to make reduced copies. Sometimes the walls were blackened with soot from the candles and magnesium flares lit by visitors wanting to see them more clearly. Or with smoke from the cooking pots of people actually living in the chapels, the Gurnawis as they were called, after Sheikh abd'el Gurneh, the hill in which most of the chapels are to be found. As the trade in antiquities developed, the Gurnawis had for years been hacking pieces out of the wall-paintings to sell to the dealers who supplied the collectors and the museums. Tombs that had been filled with sand and debris over the centuries, and had therefore been safely lost, were now being dug out and left open and vulnerable.

Percy Newberry, Weigall's old friend and mentor, had carried out a survey of the Theban necropolis during the years before Weigall's appointment, and had made a particular study of these chapels, one of which he published in his *Life of Rekhmira, Vezir of Upper Egypt under Thothmes III and Amenhotep II circa 1471–1448 BC* (1900). In the course of that time he had involved a millionaire Englishman, Robert Mond (Weigall mentions him to Hortense in his letter describing the residents of Luxor), a chemical scientist with a keen interest in Egyptology. Mond had begun to finance the work of clearing and recording the tombs, and with his help, Carter, then Chief Inspector, had begun to get lockable iron grills fixed onto some of the tomb entrances. But the problem was urgent. When Weigall first came to his post, only eight out of about two hundred chapels had been furnished with grills.

The destruction and neglect of the Tombs of the Nobles was a revelation from which Weigall never quite recovered. He developed a reputation for arrogance among his colleagues, and it is true that a sense of deep indignation against many in the Egyptological world did come over him when he looked about him in Gurneh. It shocked him that scholars, interested amateurs, funding institutions, and the Antiquities Department itself, should have known what was going on and yet not have taken adequate steps to prevent it. Nubia was one thing, relatively little visited or studied.

But this was in the heart of one of Egypt's best-known attractions. Robert Hay, the antiquarian and copyist, had drawn here in the 1820s and '30s; Karl Lepsius, the German archaeologist and his team of draughtsmen had worked there in the middle of the century; John Gardner Wilkinson had taken notes there and made beautiful watercolour copies for his great work *The Manners and Customs of the Ancient Egyptians* (1837). Wilkinson's book was the Victorian encyclopaedia of ancient Egypt. Amelia Edwards, the founder of the Egypt Exploration Society, had Wilkinson's illustrations almost by heart since childhood, and when she visited Egypt in the 1870s, she wrote movingly of her old friends on the walls of these chapels. And yet, while so much had been done to *record* these monuments, nothing had been done during the nineteenth century, and very little since, to *preserve* them for the future.

And so, at that late hour, Weigall set himself to salvage what was left. Nothing special was required, no skill or knowledge, nor even very much money. That was the galling thing about it:

> As soon as the doorway has been exposed an iron gate has been built onto it, fastened with a heavy padlock, a number has been nailed up outside the door, and the monument has been placed in the charge of the ghaffir. ... Anybody could have done the work: most people a great deal better than I. Yet no one set about it ... practically all the mortuary chapels could have been protected by the expenditure of a sum less than that employed, for example, in the single work of clearing out of the temple of Deir el Bahri by the Egypt Exploration Fund in the nineties.[19]

Of course these iron grills were not entirely proof against thieves, but the point was that they forced the notoriously lenient local magistrates to treat robberies not as 'contraventions' carrying very light penalties – a small fine, a day or two in prison – but as burglaries with the possibility of several months' or even years' imprisonment. A further 'contravention' which Weigall tackled was illegal midnight excavation by the Gurnawis in the vicinity of the chapels. With fifty pounds given him by Robert Mond he had a wall built, nearly 1200 metres long, entirely surrounding the eastern face of the hill Sheikh abd'el Gurneh, and thus enclosing the majority of the important tombs: 'Since a wall had to be surmounted, any native who even entered the enclosure might be charged with burglary; and thus these tombs at all events will never again be without the strong support of the law in their protection, so far as that goes.'[20]

However, the real challenge was the hearts and minds of those directly or indirectly responsible for the destruction in the first place. Outright severity against the fellahin (peasants) was often counterproductive, as Weigall learned soon after his arrival in Upper Egypt, when he was warned by one of them that he would take his revenge not on the Inspector, but by vandalizing the wall-paintings themselves.[21] Weigall therefore tried to influence opinion among the more educated Egyptians, in the hopes that they, in turn, might bring about a change in the general ethos that condoned robbery:

With the willing assistance of the Mamur of Luxor I called a meeting at the Police Station of the various Luxor notables, and asked them whether they would contribute money and their influence towards the protection of the tombs. ...

Could they sit still, I asked, while these monuments of their civilization were destroyed? And could they actually encourage such destruction by purchasing these ill-gotten antiquities to sell them to tourists? These tombs were admired, visited, written about, by Europeans; and yet the descendants of the men who made them stirred not a finger to save them ... at the end of the meeting, some £50 was subscribed, with which a number of tombs were repaired and safeguarded.[22]

Weigall also had separate conversations with one or two of the dealers, and 'extracted from them the promise that they would not buy fragments which they knew to be stolen from standing monuments.'[23]

The problem was by no means solved, but something at least, was being achieved. And money was now coming in. Weigall regarded it as 'an extraordinary circumstance that the safeguarding of these most important monuments in Egypt should have been carried out by an official of the Department of Antiquities with money that was not official', but nevertheless it was welcome. Apart from Robert Mond and the people of Luxor themselves, the donors were Albert Lythgoe, on behalf of the Metropolitan Museum of New York, von Bissing, Griffith, Newberry, Alan Gardiner, the King of Saxony, and several others. By the end of the 1907 season some 50 chapels had been fixed with doors. By 1908, there were 70. Year by year more and more were added, until in January 1912 Weigall wrote triumphantly that some 200 chapels were now safeguarded.[24]

All the same, there was another dimension to the whole problem which could on occasion defeat all these measures: namely, the western Museum. In an essay entitled 'Archaeology in the Open', published a few years later in 1911, Weigall enlarges on the whole question of museums, their function, the kind of archaeology and scholarship they fostered, and their effect on the countries contributing to their collections. In particular he deplored the fact that they created a market in stolen antiquities. He describes, for example, the theft of a beautiful relief of Queen Tiy sculpted on the wall of a tomb that had been discovered some years before in 1900. After photographs had been taken of it, the tomb had been buried again for its protection. However, in 1908 Weigall decided to re-open the tomb, only to discover that robbers had entered it in the interim and hacked the relief out. It had been taken to a dealer who had sold it to the Royal Museum in Brussels. Weigall reproduces two photographs of this relief, before and after, showing not only the damage done to it in cutting it out, but further damage in the form of inscriptions chiselled out so as to remove clues as to its place of origin. He goes on to give several further instances of reliefs, wall paintings and inscriptions being chopped out of walls, sold to dealers and on to museums in London, Leyden, Bologna, Brussels and elsewhere; and he confesses to feeling nothing short of 'black murder in his heart' at the sight of the gaping holes created in order to adorn the walls of these European museums.[25]

It must have been a cruel shock, then, to return to Egypt from his summer leave in England in 1906 and see the tomb Maspero describes in his *Rapport* for that year, after thieves had broken in. This disastrous attempt, says Maspero, was caused

> by the reckless enthusiasm of savants, or their agents who, in order to supply the European museums, ask the local dealers for pieces of a certain period, and point out to them certain known tombs as examples of what they want to buy. The purveyors never hesitate to attack these self-same examples, and it is thus that, in order, so it is said, to facilitate the study of antiquity by European and American archaeologists, the annihilation of the most precious monuments is unwittingly caused.[26]

But there were years of work ahead in the Valley in which to build up a head of steam against such practices. The job was proving to be an odd combination of long-term vision and crisis management. Now suddenly it was dams again, and everything that went with them. Flooding had been the chief threat, but quarrying for the rock to build the dam was potentially just as bad. With the ancient inscriptions in the rocks at Aswan about to be blasted to pieces, Weigall personally took a pot of paint and a brush and numbered all the places that were to be preserved.[27] Pierre Loti, when he saw these white painted numbers, was horrified – another example of British municipal utilitarianism, he thought – and he excoriated the 'English Egyptologist' who had dreamt up the idea. No one told him that it had been done to prevent the inscriptions from being blasted out of existence.[28]

Now there was something more worrying still, a request from the Department of Public Works to use the ancient quarries on the east side of the Nile at Gebel Silsileh for another barrage further north, at Esneh. These huge quarries between Aswan and Esneh (now destroyed by modern workings) had been opened by the Pharaoh Akhnaten for his great building programme at Thebes, and they were famous for the record they preserved of the skill of the ancient Egyptian labourers: 'Both for their vast extent and on account of the care and perfection of workmanship displayed in the cutting of the stone,' wrote Weigall, 'they are amongst the greatest monuments of human labour known.'[29] Amelia Edwards had visited them a generation before and she describes them vividly in her book *A Thousand Miles up the Nile* (1877), huge amphitheatres of amber-coloured sandstone, on which

> the chisel-marks and wedge-holes were as fresh as if the last blocks had been taken hence but yesterday ... But the most wonderful thing about Silsilis is the way in which the quarrying has been done ... the sandstone has been sliced out smooth and straight, like hay from a hayrick. Everywhere the blocks have been taken out square; and everywhere the best of the stone has been extracted and the worst left. Where it was fine in grain and even in colour, it has been cut with the nicest economy. Where it was whitish, or brownish, or traversed by veins of violet, it has been left standing. Here and there, we saw places where the lower part had been removed and the upper part left projecting ... Compared with this puissant and perfect quarrying, our rough-and-ready blasting looks like the work of savages.[30]

This was precisely the kind of blasting that now threatened these quarries. White paint was not going to do the trick here, and another confrontation loomed.

This time, though, the irrigation people asked first: no less a person than the Under Secretary of State for Irrigation, A.L. Webb, applied for a permit to quarry there. Weigall refused. To Webb's protest, Weigall replied:

> You mention in your letter that by refusing a permit my Department interferes with the commercial development of the mineral wealth of the country. My Department contends, of course, that by the destruction of the ancient quarries you would damage the archaeological wealth of the country. All persons will see the matter from one or other of these standpoints, and therefore I think it necessary for you and myself to satisfy the demands of the divergent interests which we represent by actually meeting on the spot and making the compromise there.[31]

This proposed visit duly took place:

> I visited the site with Mr Blue, Mr Webb and others and when asked for them [the quarries], I said that I could *not* offer them either of the two great quarries to be reopened. They quite agreed that it would be wrong to work them, and some other concessions were given instead. A short time afterwards Mr Webb, while passing the place, allowed the men to begin work in one of these two old sites. I heard of this, and offered my resignation if the work was continued. It was stopped, and neither of the two great quarries was touched.[32]

In Weigall's report to the Egypt Exploration Fund for the 1906-7 season, there is no hint of the extremes to which he had gone. He simply says that new quarries have been opened, that they are under supervision so that nothing of value will be damaged, and that he has closed the two ancient quarries with iron doors, visitors now having to show admission tickets before entering.

The other thing he doesn't mention is the row he had with Maspero. Maspero appears to have taken a much softer line than Weigall with the Public Works Department. In his *Rapport* for 1906 he clearly envisages a programme of quarrying at the ancient site, though he suggests that only the least interesting parts of the site will be conceded – or at least that those are the places that will be taken first. It is difficult to decide from his account whether he would have yielded up the ancient workings themselves if the engineers had asked, but he certainly doesn't say that any part of the site was out of bounds, nor does he mention iron doors and tickets. Those seem to have been entirely Weigall's measures. But however one interprets Maspero's *Rapport*, there was in practice a gap between Weigall's and Maspero's view of the matter. Webb's infringement seems to have left no doubt in Weigall's mind that his boss was not on his side, and he wrote to Maspero, throwing down the gauntlet:

> If you find it impossible to prevent these quarries being sacrificed I hope you will not think it incorrect if I ask you to let the transaction be made without passing

through my office, as I have taken a somewhat firm attitude about giving the concession, and I find that I am unable to hand over for destruction the monuments which your writings, and those of other archaeologists, have taught me to regard of value.[33]

The result appears to have been a victory for the ancient quarries.

But this kind of incident leaves a residue of resentment behind. Weigall had written to Hortense about the small world of the resident community in Luxor. It was an equally small world among the officials. Like people who lie down in front of bulldozers, Weigall was beginning to be a thorn in the side of the authorities.

# Chapter 8

# Another royal tomb: Queen Tiy? Akhnaten? 1907

Nubia and the Aswan dam project brought together a particularly quarrelsome combination of people – French, English, archaeologists, engineers and surveyors. It is impossible now to fathom precisely what was going on, but letters from Weigall to Hortense written in the October of the following year, 1907, give an idea of the jockeying and mutual suspicion among some of these men. Weigall was on his way back from his second holiday in England since his appointment, leaving Hortense behind with Mimi at the vicarage. It had been a particularly hard wrench for he was leaving not only Hortense, but their first baby, a son born on 4 August 1907, whom they named Alured, the Anglo-Saxon spelling for Alfred. Weigall's letters from the train across France and Italy to Brindisi cry out against the separations that his way of life forced on them, but by the time he was settled on the P & O steamboat he was sufficiently resigned to look about him.

It was an interesting boatload, a microcosm of Empire: a dapper sub-governor of the White Nile province who lived in a grass hut and who longed to write of his experiences, were it not that the army regarded writers as 'bally idiots' and it might ruin his career. There was the over-civilized Ronald Storrs, the future Governor of Jerusalem, at that time not long down from Oxford, eking out his salary in the Audit Department of the British Agency in Cairo with articles on opera for the *Egyptian Gazette*. Weigall, who later became a close friend, was already acquainted with him, but as if to confirm the governor of the White Nile's fears, an army man on the boat exploded at the mention of him: that bounder, he said, 'with his vulgar smattering of artist's talk and his penny-a-line articles on music and art … thought he would insult his regiment by patronizing them at their own mess.' There was a learned governor of a Sudan province; an old Indian civil service hand; a couple of friendly artillery subalterns and – the most important passenger on board – Sir Eldon Gorst, going out to take up his post as

Lord Cromer's successor. Weigall spent some time observing and sketching him for Hortense's amusement.

Besides these, two other passengers were of particular interest, one of them Mrs Lyons on her way to join Captain Lyons of the Survey Department, and the other a man who worked for him. This man, wrote Weigall,

> told me, by the way, never to trust Lyons too far, as he is not awfully straight, which gives me food for some thought. He says Lyons is trying to be made Minister – I mean Advisor – of Science, and wants to create that Ministry, which will include the Survey and Antiquities, thus making Lyons Maspero's chief. It might be good in some ways. ... I have talked a little to Mrs Lyons ... she says neither Lyons nor Reisner [an American archaeologist, and Director of the Nubian Archaeological Survey from 1907–1909] went to Nubia after all. I wonder whether they are going at all, or whether Lyons was advised not to go owing to Maspero's possibly taking offence, and there being trouble between the English and French consulates.

Another letter to Hortense, written later in the month after a flying visit to Cairo, takes up the story again, when it appears to have crept closer to himself personally:

> Maspero had asked me to make a report on Philae, and had referred to Capt. Lyons' baseness. In the Club I saw Lyons and got into conversation. So I said, "O, by the way, I've to go up to Philae to make a report, and in case anything I say may be misrepresented I should like to tell you what I *am* going to say exactly." He said he was going up with a whole lot of Survey men to make a scientific report on Philae also, so I said the best thing for me to do would be to say almost nothing. Lyons said "Well of course, we all know that Maspero will stick you up on a wall for us both to shy things at, but I'll see that you fall soft." Words of terrible omen! He then said that Maspero is almost certain to distort everything I say about Nubia so that it may be used against Lyons and his work; but he said he'd know how much to believe. But anyway, my role is to keep off Nubia while this fighting is going on, I think. Fortunately, in my Nubian report [not yet published] I have said much in favour of Lyons' work. Lyons says it is a disgrace the way our Dept. is tackling its side of the job. Well, I've done with Nubia more or less, except as concerns the territory above water level, and now I'm for the Eastern Desert ... Hurrah!

Weigall was planning a trip across the eastern desert to the Red Sea that autumn. Nubia was no longer on his conscience; he had done what he could. But why should Maspero have wanted to make an Aunt Sally of him over Philae – or was Lyons being 'not awfully straight', for reasons of his own?

Weigall had been no rebel over Philae. There had been an outcry about the proposed flooding of the temples, and many lovers of Egypt, Pierre Loti among them, had charged Britain with vandalism and economic self interest. Whatever Weigall might have thought about Britain's economic motives, he had for once agreed with the official line taken by the Department of Antiquities over the monuments. He had faith in the work of underpinning that had been carried out. If the temples were structurally safe, he was prepared to accept the modern claims of agriculture. The objectors had got things out of proportion, he said, and were mistaken in their belief that the temples were in danger. Egyptian monuments with their feet in the water were a common sight anyway, because of the yearly inundation. Admittedly, Philae would be up to its neck, and remain so for longer, but for seven months of the year it would stand high and dry and open to tourists. True, there had been some slight disintegration of the sandstone since the first dam had been built, and the hieroglyphs inscribed on the blocks had become somewhat blurred; but once the salts in the stone had disappeared, this would cease. He could point to the sharpness of the inscriptions on the sandstone blocks of many Pharaonic quay walls that had been submerged since ancient times.[1]

This surely would have been music to Maspero's ears. The only battle between them was over the capitals on the columns in the Hall of Isis. These were painted, and the colour was therefore bound to wash off. In his essay, 'The Flooding of Lower Nubia', Weigall expressed the hope that they might still be saved, 'removed and replaced by dummies, or else most carefully copied in facsimile.'[2] But Maspero never acted, and when the essay was reprinted in 1924, Weigall still felt bitterly enough about the loss to add the words: 'I urged very strongly that these capitals should be removed ... but Sir Gaston Maspero did not think the loss justified the expense.' No doubt he had made his feelings very clear to Maspero at the time, but whether that explains Captain Lyons's words it is impossible to say.

As for Lyons's own fight with Maspero, the details are probably irrecoverable now. There was an ancient rivalry between the two of them going back to the days when Maspero was being wooed from his retirement to take the job of Director General for the second time. One way and another the Directors since his first retirement had failed to win the respect of Egyptologists, and the custom of a permanently French Director General had been questioned more than once. In 1898 the outgoing Director, Loret, had been so generally disliked that Cromer had actually been prepared to flout the tradition. According to A.H. Sayce, Lord Cromer asked him to sound out Maspero as the only respected French Egyptologist suitable for the job: '"We must get rid of Loret," he said, "but if another Frenchman is appointed, it must be Maspero. I want you therefore, to write to him privately and persuade him to come, pointing out that if he will not accept the post we shall appoint Lyons."'[3] With the honour of France at stake, Maspero had returned – while Lyons presumably had retired hurt. It is unlikely that Weigall knew anything about Maspero v. Lyons, otherwise he would have seen the irony and significance of Lyons now manoeuvring for a post above Maspero for himself. In any case it doesn't really matter. The point is the atmosphere of backbiting, conspiracy, and bad faith. No wonder Weigall was glad to be shot of it all, and away into the eastern desert.

As it happened, he was by that stage embroiled in another disagreement, but at least it was over a matter of archaeological opinion rather than departmental politics. In the January of that same year, 1907, Theodore Davis's archaeological minder,

Edward Ayrton, discovered a tomb in the Valley of the Kings which would set the archaeological world alight. Ayrton's men were working through the debris that lay at the foot of the rocks to the south of the tomb of Rameses IX. The first indication of anything to come was a group of pots buried in the debris, and then, beneath them, the square corner of what turned out to be a flight of steps, sloping down to a doorway, blocked by a drystone wall. On January 7th Ayrton was sure enough of a possible royal discovery to spend the night, as Weigall had done, outside the entrance with the American painter, Joe Lindon Smith for company. The next day Emma Andrews, who was again in Egypt keeping house for Davis on his *dahabiyeh*, wrote in her diary:

> All of us went over to the Valley this morning – found Mr Ayrton had cleared enough to show a small chamber which he thought was the whole tomb. But after lunch it was found that a doorway which had been sealed up as that in the tomb of Touyou and Iuia led to a corridor. In removing some of the blocks of stone which hindered progress, a fine broken alabaster vase and some bits of gold foil were found, so the work for the day was stopped, as it was too late to open it, the guards and police were sent for … Mr Weigall and his wife were already camping in the valley … Joe Smith and his wife also stayed.

This description is a little confusing in the light of Ayrton's account, which does not mention any 'small chamber' just inside, and suggests that the inner door was right up against the inside of the rough outer door. Confusions like this between all the accounts are unfortunately typical. That night was quite like old times, like the nights in February 1905 that Weigall and the Smiths had spent together before the tomb of Yuya and Tuya, though this time Hortense was with them, having arrived in Egypt towards the end of November, with Alured, then nearly four months old.

Wednesday, January 9th, was the great day of entry. Davis's party joined the campers, and the three men, Davis, Ayrton, and Weigall went down the steps alone, leaving their wives and guests above in the sunshine. It must have been then that they looked properly at the sealings of the inner doorway, for Emma Andrews, waiting with the other women, noted the cry of 'Tutankhamun' among the other exclamations that drifted up to them from below. In an article written that same year for the October issue of *Blackwood's Magazine*, Weigall mentions the fact that 'the entrance was blocked with stones, and sealed with the seal of Tutankhamun, a fragment of which was found; and it was in this condition that it was found last January.'[4] Then, from the shadows below came more exclamations, '"Ateu! the rays of the sun" … and at last Mr Davis's voice rang out, "By Jove, Queen Tiy and no mistake."'[5] Davis wrote of this particular moment: 'It is quite impossible to describe the surprise and joy of finding the tomb of the great queen and her household gods, which for these 3,000 years had never been discovered.'[6]

Tiy was the daughter of Yuya and Tuya, and the mother of Akhnaten, the Pharaoh who overthrew the ancient polytheistic religion of Amon, and established Aten-worship in its place. Davis's euphoria at the apparent discovery of this Queen clearly

swept them all up. The puzzle of an ancient and official re-entry into the tomb signi-
fied on the inner door by the seal of Tutankhamun, the son of Akhnaten, was for the
moment thrust into the background. As they peered over the inner doorway, the
archaeologists saw, lying on the rubble that filled the corridor beyond, a gold-covered
and inscribed wooden panel and a door, in a very fragile condition. These were
jammed sloping across the whole width of the corridor, and in order to get past, says
Weigall, we 'made a bridge of planks within a few inches of the low roof, and on this
we wriggled ourselves across into the unencumbered passage beyond.'[7] They carried
electric lamps with them, and it was then that they saw, incised on the panels, scenes
of Aten worship – the royal family embraced by the hands on the rays of the sundisk
– and the names of Queen Tiy and her husband Amenophis III, in their cartouches,
or oval frames. The figure and cartouche of their son Akhnaten, however, had been
carefully erased. When they reached the chamber beyond, they found other similar
gold-covered panels and doors leaning against the walls and lying on the ramp of
rubble that sloped into the room from the corridor. These had the same scenes and
names and erasures, and where the foil still adhered they could read enough to show
that they were the dismantled sides of a great wooden shrine, made by Akhnaten for
his mother, and intended to contain her coffin.

There was, however, no other funeral furniture in the tomb, apart from some small
objects and a coffin. This lay, not in the middle of the room, where the shrine would
have stood, but to one side, on a wooden bier that had collapsed beneath it, jerking
the lid off a little, and exposing the head and feet of a mummy. The body was in a
very decayed state. The flesh had almost completely rotted away, leaving just the skull
and bones 'protruding from the remains of the linen bandages and from the sheets of
flexible gold-foil in which, as we afterwards found, the whole body was wrapped.' In
fact the whole tomb was in a mess. The shrine was in bits, plaster and masonry had
fallen in, and water had seeped in through cracks in the roof. Woodwork had decayed;
when Davis rashly fingered a tooth of the mummy,[8] it crumbled instantly. Now, as the
outside air came down the passage, the fragile gold leaf that covered so much of the
wood, began to flake off. When Emma Andrews went down into the tomb a few days
later, she saw drifts of it lying on the ground. But the coffin lid still glowed with gold
and with an inlaid feather pattern of lapis-blue glass and carnelian, very like the one
found later on one of Tutankhamun's coffins. Down the lid ran an inscription giving
the titles of Akhnaten marked out in semi-precious stones, though his cartouche was
always cut out.

In spite of that, however, no one thought to wonder about the identity of the
mummy, or why the name of Queen Tiy herself was not on the coffin. If it had been
erased, why was it allowed to stand on the shrine? There were other oddities too: for
example, the exact circumstances of the ancient entry, clearly not a robbery since so
much gold had been left; the lack of funeral furniture for the Queen; the titles of
Akhnaten (though the name itself had been erased) on the coffin and on the gold foil
bands encircling the mummy which were found later.[9] No one at this stage doubted
that the body in the coffin was Queen Tiy's, and the idea that two burials might have
taken place in the same tomb did not occur to anyone. When at last the coffin lid was

lifted away, the body was seen to be lying in the pose associated with women, one arm straight down by the side and the other across the breast. A certain Dr Pollock and a visiting obstetrician examined it on the spot, and confirmed Davis's joy by pronouncing the anatomy female.

Nothing could be moved without injury. A photographer was brought from Cairo to photograph the tomb, and Joe Lindon Smith started painting some of the things *in situ*. 'But even before the first quick record had been finished,' wrote Weigall, 'some of the scenes on the gold, showed signs of dropping to pieces.'[10] They did what they could: 'It was all under Ayrton's charge,' wrote Emma Andrews comfortably, and Davis was having the panels treated with paraffin to keep the gold on.[11] On the 25th January they managed at last to lift 'the coffin off the mummy without much damage', and finally on the 27th, she records that all the treasures from the tomb have been packed up in boxes and carried to their *dahabiyeh* to be transported down the river to the Museum in Cairo: 'Weigall and Ayrton on horses led the way, and a long procession of Arabs carrying the boxes – and the sun striking the rifles of the accompanying sailors. It was really a most impressive sight.'

One wonders what these Arabs must have thought. Walter Tyndale, a visiting English painter working in the Valley at the time of the discovery, recorded the intense speculation of the locals: 'The very air seemed thick with news! News that Ayrton was knee-deep in gold and precious stones, feverishly filling petroleum tins, pickle pots and cans from Chicago with the spoil ... That every one connected with these excavations is doing it simply for the plunder is a rooted idea in the native mind which neither proof nor argument can disturb ...'[12] It was suspicion of just this kind that was to fuel the row over Tutankhamun many years later. Meanwhile, as they watched their ancient treasure being packed off to Cairo, some of the local people would have taken comfort in the fact that they had already sold back to Davis some small objects from the tomb which had taken a detour on their way out.[13]

During the next few weeks a stream of visitors came to the *dahabiyeh* to see the things, rich Americans and English chiefly, among them Lord and Lady Carnarvon, brought to tea one day by Weigall, and Lord and Lady Cromer. Davis had given Mrs Andrews what he thought was the Queen's crown, a gold vulture with curving outspread wings that had been found round the head of the mummy, to keep 'in the closet at the head of my bed!' There had been a magnificent necklace round its neck and bracelets round its wrists; there was an exquisite little statuette of a girl carrying a pot on her shoulder; four 'canopic' jars, intended for the mummified viscera of the deceased, which had been found in a niche near the coffin, furnished with stoppers in the form of beautifully sculpted heads. There was, in other words, plenty to hand round the tea table. Maspero must have been pleased with the interest shown by so many distinguished visitors, and when he came to tea himself, Mrs Andrews records charming gestures of generosity between him and Davis: 'Maspero delighted Theo by saying they wanted him to have one of the canopic heads and he hoped he would choose the best one. Theo replied he would not do that, but would choose the one having a stain across the head, caused by dripping water.'[14] At last the season drew to an end, the Davis *dahabiyeh* sailed off, the various archaeologists took their leave, and Weigall was left, he tells us, 'to send the bones, soaked in wax to prevent their breakage, to Dr. Elliot Smith, to be examined by that eminent authority.'[15]

Grafton Elliot Smith, an anthropologist and anatomist, had been Professor of Anatomy at the Cairo School of Medicine since 1900, and he specialized in the study of royal mummies. A bombshell awaited them all:

It may be imagined [wrote Weigall] that my surprise was considerable when I received a letter from him reading – "Are you sure that the bones you sent me are those which were found in the tomb? Instead of the bones of an old woman, you have sent me those of a young man. Surely there must be some mistake."

When the news reached him, Davis was devastated. The Alma Tadema tendency was still strong in Edwardian times. They dwelt on the beauty of queens, the romance of gold, on palaces and pleasure-gardens and other fairytale trimmings. Nefertiti, whose famous bust had not yet been discovered at that time, has eclipsed Queen Tiy in our day, but that potent myth, the mystery of the East, clung to Tiy in the same way. Queen Hatshepsut had been another. Her great terraced temple at the foot of the cliffs at Deir el Bahri had recently been cleared. Howard Carter discovered her tomb in 1903, lying behind the temple in the Valley of the Kings, and Davis had paid tribute to her by financing the excavations. Now with Queen Tiy, he seemed to have another prize. She lived at the height of the Egyptian Empire, and together with her husband, Amenophis III, seemed actually to share in the divinity of the gods they represented. They built a palace at Medinet Habu, and under them Thebes had become a fabled city, adorned with the spoils of an Empire which stretched from Syria in the north to Somaliland in the south, a city where gold was said to be as plentiful as dust.

Davis never brought himself to accept fully that he hadn't found her, though he was bound to include the views of Elliot Smith in his publication about the tomb in 1910. Walter Tyndale who visited the tomb was similarly affected: delighted at the thought of a queen – 'arrayed as she might have been when Amenhotep the Magnificent led her to the marriage feast ... [with] that immovable expression on her face which the contemplation of the vanity of all things might have produced' – then dashed at the news from the laboratory – 'a sad disillusionment was in store.'[16] Ayrton's contribution to Davis's book, perhaps in deference to his employer's feelings, avoids any mention of the fact that the mummy was not Queen Tiy's.[17] Under the same illusion, Weigall himself wrote an article for the September issue of the *Century*, in which he described Queen Tiy as 'the beautiful heroine of an almost fairy-like story'.[18]

But when Elliot Smith pronounced his verdict, he corrected himself in time for the next *Blackwood's Magazine*. More than that, he threw the cat among the pigeons by arguing that the mummy was the heretic king himself, Tiy's son, Akhnaten. This is the Pharaoh whose elongated head and swelling stomach strike even the most casual tourist, and whose religious revolution from polytheism to monotheism has made him seem to some Egyptologists like a forerunner of Moses. He ascended the throne in about 1353 BC, and was later branded with heresy by the polytheistic priests of Amon, a god who, together with all the company of animal gods in Egypt, Akhnaten had cast out in favour of Aten, the sun-god.

Setting aside the popular allure of queens, this Pharaoh was arguably the greatest prize of all to the Egyptologist, particularly at that period. Historians since have revised, and in some cases exploded, the views of the early 1900s,[19] but Akhnaten was interpreted at that time as a benevolent philosopher-king, a follower of the Simple Life, a freethinking religious sophisticate, a poet and artist, and, most captivating of all, a family man devoted to his charming wife Nefertiti, and their daughters. After a long line of indistinguishably stiff and inexpressive Pharaohs, it seemed that here at last was a knowable individual. In his *History of Egypt* published the year before, James Breasted had in fact called him 'the first *individual* in history'.[20] Petrie too had written of Akhnaten in the same spirit in 1896, after his excavations at Amarna,[21] the site where Akhnaten created a new city to replace Thebes, until then the centre of the powerful orthodox priesthood.

Besides, there was no denying the originality of the art of Akhnaten's reign. The old formalities, the conventional rituals and martial exploits of earlier Pharaohs give way to scenes of intimacy, of the royal family at play, kissing, caressing, disporting themselves while their subjects look on in adoration. The paintings in the private chapels at Amarna, like the ones at Gurneh, had attracted European visitors and copyists for much of the nineteenth century, most recently the English painter Norman de Garis Davies, whose six volumes of tracings and commentaries, *The Rock Tombs of El Amarna*, were being published yearly by the Egypt Exploration Fund from 1903 onwards. Akhnaten was thus emerging from ancient obscurity as a uniquely modern figure, or so it seemed, and Weigall's excitement at the possible discovery of his body took hold of him as powerfully as Theodore Davis's excitement at the supposed discovery of Queen Tiy.

Weigall's conviction was more than wishful thinking. It seemed to him that the state in which the tomb had been found, and the nature of its contents, now began to make some sense. It was known that after the death of Akhnaten, his city at Amarna was abandoned, and that some time later the old Amon priesthood at Thebes pronounced anathema on him and all his works. Just as he had in his time erased the name of Amon from every public monument, now his own name and figure were cut away wherever they appeared. In order to explain the ancient entry of Tiy's tomb, the erased names of Akhnaten, the dismantled shrine, the position of the coffin, and the lack of funeral furniture, Weigall had had to suppose, for his article in the *Century Magazine*, that some of the anti-Aten officials

> went up to the Valley of the Tombs and excavated the sepulchre of Queen Tiy. They threw down the walls of stone, wrenched the golden doors off their hinges, and entering the shrine, lifted out the inner coffin and mummy, and placed it on one side. They then hacked out the name of Akhnaten in the inscriptions, and destroyed his figure in the scenes. Queen Tiy's figure and name, however, they left untouched, for her influence in the [religious] revolution had never been publicly

recognized; but nevertheless they had such a lack of love for her memory that they did not scruple to strip the tomb of some of its furniture. One panel of the gold-covered door and one side of the outer coffin they dragged out of the tomb and up the passage; but near the entrance they abandoned their work, and left these two pieces lying across the ruins of the wall which had blocked the mouth. They then carefully walled up the doorway again, out of some tardy feelings of respect for the dead, and hid the steps and mouth of the tomb with stones.

It is clear from this passage that Weigall was having some difficulty: were these priests out for Tiy as well as Akhnaten? If they respected her why did they try to deprive her of her furniture, the things that were essential to her well-being in the after life? But if they were prepared to go so far as that, why did they leave her name untouched, and not erase her memory along with her son's? And then they had 'tardy feelings' of respect as they walled up the doorway again. The theory creaked, however smoothly he expressed it.

But now Elliot Smith's evidence seemed to make everything clear. Weigall's revised theory was that Akhnaten was originally buried in the tomb he had cut for himself at Amarna, but that some time after his death, when his city was abandoned, his body was brought from there to Thebes. His mother's tomb was then opened to receive his coffin which was placed beside her shrine. At that time Akhnaten's religion was not yet overthrown, but during the reign of Tutankhamun, when Amon was restored, the priestly iconoclasts entered the tomb in order to erase Akhnaten's name and remove the queen's body in its coffin, together with its furniture, from the polluting proximity of her son. That is why her shrine was dismantled, for an attempt had been made to remove it with her coffin. That is why there was very little of her funeral furniture in the tomb. The erasures of Akhnaten's name and figure from the shrine and every-where else were explained as they had been before; but now the other facts, unex-plained until now or not mentioned, could also be understood – Akhnaten's title, 'the beautiful child of the sun' on the coffin lid, and, as it transpired, on the inside of the lid and shell, though his actual cartouche was cut out from both. There were also the 'magic bricks',[22] so-called, with Akhnaten's name still legible, and the gold foil bands that encircled the body lengthways and across, which were inscribed with Akhnaten's titles, though there too the cartouche had been cut out. [23]

Weigall set out his position in *Blackwood's* with a lot more besides about the reign of Akhnaten and the chronological implications of Elliot Smith's anatomical findings. For these findings showed not only that the body was male, but that – as far as it was possible to tell at that time – it was of a man of only 25 years old. Here was more fuel to the fire, and from now on the arguments flew in three directions. While Davis was fighting for his lost queen, some archaeologists were sceptical about how all the events of Akhnaten's life, political, religious and reproductive (there were *six* daugh-ters), could be packed into so short a time. During the following decades a succession of scholars re-examined the coffin, the inscriptions, the erasures and the bones, and another candidate emerged, namely Smenkhare who reigned as Akhnaten's co-regent for a time. Indeed it appears that a sort of musical chairs of coffins and mummies may have taken place, the coffin found in the tomb (known as KV55, KV standing for King's Valley) having been made for one person (one of Akhnaten's wives, Kiya), and then occupied by another, either Akhnaten or Smenkhare, or possibly by each in succession. Present opinion remains split between these two Pharaohs, the nearest approach to a compromise being the suggestion that even if the bones aren't Akhnaten's, the ancients who reburied them thought they were.[24]

At the time, however, Weigall's argument implied a precociousness in Akhnaten, and in particular a sexual maturity in him and Nefertiti that some found difficult to imagine. The Rev. A.H. Sayce, for example, wrote to Weigall complimenting him on his article ('its clear and attractive style made the dry bones live') but disagreeing with its conclusion. He accepts Dr Elliot Smith's verdict 'that it represents the body of a man of 25 or thereabouts, but what I don't believe is that it is the mummy of Khu-n-Aten [a variant spelling]. Apart from the difficulty about the daughters (which requires further hypotheses in order to be got over) I do not see where was the time for the successive architectural works at Thebes, Sheikh Sayyid and Tel-el-Amarna which were constructed during Khu-n-Aten's reign.'[25]

Weigall, now in a state of high excitement, was vehement: 'No difficulty', 'Rot!', 'Rotter!' he scribbled in the margins of this letter. There was no problem with the daughters, he had dealt with them already, pointing out that they started young in those days. It was known for example that Amenophis III was old enough to hunt lions at the time of his father Tuthmosis IV's death at the age of twenty-six; not only that, but that he was married a year later to Queen Tiy. Tuthmosis had probably been a father at the age of thirteen or so, and Amenophis a husband at about the same age. Where was the difficulty in Akhnaten's being a father of two at the age of fifteen? And if you can father children at fifteen, why not build cities and overturn religions? Besides, there was a romantic strain in Weigall which cherished the notion of the boy king, the visionary youth.

Meanwhile, Elliot Smith had jumped in with both feet too, insisting not only that the body was male and young, but that the skull was anthropologically consistent with Akhnaten's portraits. Davis, for his part, was not taking any of this quietly. A letter from Weigall to Hortense written shortly after his arrival from England buzzes with the subject. He had been at his hotel for only an hour and a half, he says, but he was already bursting with news:

> I hear that Davis is furious about Queen Thiy, and is trying to get Elliot Smith to alter his opinion. Elliot Smith is deluged with articles and cuttings sent by Davis from every conceivable paper and magazine to him to read – all trying to show it is Queen Thiy. Elliot Smith is very angry, and is *absolutely certain* that the body is of a man of 25, and not only that but the jaw and head can now be reconstructed and are identical with the portraits of Akhnaten. He says it is a young man answering to Akhnaten in every anthropological way, and only awaits historical information as to whether the identification is possible from our point of view. ... my article really is a cinch (is that how you spell it?) coming as it does in the middle of the controversy, and being the first to show that the body can be Akhnaten's historically. Only of course, Davis will be *mad*, as it seems he is viciously fighting the idea of it being anybody but Thiy ... Aren't

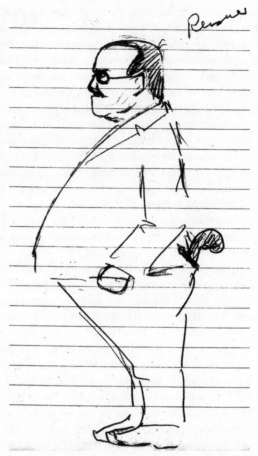

George Reisner of the Nubian Archaeological Survey

people *idiots* to dare to contradict Elliot Smith, when they know nothing of his science! I am awfully bucked by it all! and am mightily pleased at having had the audacity to change my views and correct the Century article at once, though I see now what an ass I should have looked if Elliot Smith had changed his opinion.

Print cannot convey the dash of Weigall's handwriting, the underlinings, the swirl of it. There is a sort of absurd innocence about his self-congratulation, and his eagerness – dancing about, fists up – for an archaeological showdown.

A week later he wrote again, this time from Luxor, from where he had made a visit to a cemetery where Reisner was working, the American archaeologist mentioned earlier, who was in charge of the Nubian Archaeological Survey. Elliot Smith was there too, examining bones again, and others of the Survey, busy mapping. The lavishness of Reisner's camp made him green: 'He has an enormous camp of tents – at least 40! He has a steam launch and every other luxury which we ought to have if only Maspero would get a wiggle on.' But he was delighted with the impression his article seemed to have made on them all. Quibell had written to say that he was 'mightily pleased' with it, and now he found that at Reisner's camp it was 'much liked all round': 'I have convinced them all about Akhnaten.' Then, in an odd touch, he adds – 'which is strange, as it is so popular in style.' It was a doubt that nagged him from time to time, for he knew that he had a talent that way, and yet he was well aware that the scholars looked askance at it.

One of the things he was especially pleased about was a conversation with Dr Pollock, the doctor who had originally pronounced the bones to be female: 'I saw Dr Pollock in Luxor the other day, who denies that he ever thought it was a woman, and says he and the other doctor could not be sure. Elliot Smith has written to the *Times* saying that it is very bad luck on these doctors having opinions of theirs quoted which could only have been formed in the most adverse circumstances.' When at the end of the month Elliot Smith was prepared to stretch the upper age limit of the body to a possible 28, Weigall felt that all controversy was now over: 'so now this concession clears off the slight difficulties that Sayce and others feel about the history and settles the matter finally. If we split the difference and call him 27 there is ample time for everything.'

Altogether he was in a state of high exuberance, and to add to it he had a stroke of chronological luck. Hortense, as always, is his audience – perhaps a little bemused by her excited husband in the baby-dominated vicarage in Shepherd's Bush :

In my article I make out that Amenhotep III could only have been 49 at his death, and this is an essential point to the argument in favour of Akhnaten only being 25. But when I wrote this I quite forgot that Elliot Smith was examining that king's mummy also, and could prove or disprove my statement in one fell swoop. What was my delight then when he said that 49 was the exact age he had attributed to the bones!

O for a chance of writing yet another article on the subject with all these new points which so encourage and confirm what I said.

Instead of another article the idea grew into a book, and in 1910, the year when Davis's record of Queen Tiy's tomb came out, Weigall's biography of Akhnaten was published. He dedicated it to Davis whom he slyly called 'the discoverer of the bones of Akhnaten'.

But in the cold light of the morning after, or rather of the decades after, it must be said that it is a pity that Queen Tiy's tomb got caught up in such violent feelings. Modern scholars all agree that the proper recording of it suffered at the hands of its discoverers, and naturally the blame falls on the professionals involved – Ayrton, Weigall, and ultimately Maspero. Perhaps the row over the unknown body distracted the archaeologists from the job in hand. It took Davis a long time to publish his official account, with contributions from himself, Maspero, Ayrton, Elliot Smith and Daressy (assistant keeper at the Cairo Museum, who compiled a catalogue of the contents). Weigall was conspicuously not invited. And the whole thing when at last it did emerge was disappointing: 'Perfunctory in the extreme,' writes Cyril Aldred, a modern biographer of Akhnaten, 'no plans or dimensions are given, the descriptions are slipshod and incomplete.'[26]

The contemporaneous descriptions from Weigall and Ayrton were also slipshod and incomplete. There is in fact an explanation for this which, as far as I know, no one has yet pointed out. Theodore Davis's contract with the Department of Antiquities imposed a legal restraint on anyone else writing about any tomb discovered under Davis's auspices. It stated that while Davis had no right to any of the objects in the tombs he might discover, he reserved to himself exclusively the publication of the discovery ('M. Davis se réserve seulement de publier la trouvaille').[27] Davis took this very seriously, and there survives correspondence between him and Weigall over a magazine article Weigall wrote about a tomb discovered the following year, the tomb of Horemheb, which shows how much of a stickler the old man could be:

March 19, 1908

Dear Weigall,

I have your letter and MS. I am very much pleased with your treatment of the tomb, but I must ask you to correct the erased matter on the first page as it will suggest to many readers that I am paid for the work, or that I am exploring on sites named by the Museum etc.

If you desire to say more than the simple paragraph as it now stands, you can say that I donate all objects found in the tomb to the Museum. ...

If you accept my suggestions, or rather exclusions, I shall be glad to have you publish as you propose and will allow you to publish the photos of such objects as we may agree upon.

Weigall would have choked at Davis's lordly offer to the Museum of objects that were already its own property. Two days later, he received this:

March 21, 1908

Dear Weigall,

On reflection I have concluded to say to you that I think it would be entirely proper for you to end your article with a statement to the effect that you are able to publish the article owing to my courtesy. Of course you will express it as you please but on the lines I have stated.

I do not want it to be understood that you have an *ex officio* right to publish etc. before my book appears. Trusting you will think well of my suggestion,

Very truly yours,
Theo M Davis[28]

The situation would have been the same in 1907 over the tomb of Queen Tiy. The only person within Davis's control, without an '*ex officio*' right to publish, and yet qualified to do so was, of course, Ayrton, and two articles by him did appear that year, though they hardly do more than Weigall's pieces.[29] He too must have been held back by Davis's overriding solicitude for his book. In his copy of Davis's contract, just after the clause allowing Davis the exclusive right to publish his finds, Weigall has pencilled in the words '*in book form*'. One imagines him infuriated by the fact that no one had thought to put that phrase in when the contract was drawn up, so as to leave people like Ayrton and himself free to write articles about Davis's excavations.

In the light of all this, Weigall's archaeologically thin and atmospheric articles about Queen Tiy's tomb are hardly surprising. It was presumably only *because* they were sketchy that Davis passed them at all. And he kept a close eye. Two years after Queen Tiy's tomb was discovered, Weigall was given a clutch of Egyptological books to review for the *Quarterly Review*. Characteristically, Weigall seized the opportunity to rehearse the arguments about the identity of the mummy in KV55. Davis, who had still not published his own book, suspected as much and, as Weigall reported to Hortense, 'Old Davis called this morning, and asked for, and I had to give him, the Quarterly Review article!' Just checking. Luckily Weigall had been perfectly correct in the article and had stopped himself from saying anything precise about the tomb with the words: 'Mr Davis's publication must not be anticipated here by a description of the 'find'.'[30]

It is some time later, therefore, in the biography of Akhnaten, published in 1910 after Davis's volume, that we first hear about the gold foil ribbons encircling the mummy and inscribed with Akhnaten's name. They are a footnote only in the *Black-woods* article, and the *Quarterly Review* piece doesn't mention them at all. But by far the most detailed of Weigall's accounts comes much later, after Davis's death, in the preface and the concluding chapters of the 1922 edition of the biography, and in an article he wrote that same year for the *Journal of Egyptian Archaeology*. It is here that, among other things, Weigall mentions the 'magic bricks' for the first time; where the particulars about the foil ribbons or bands are described; where he gives, again for the first time, a translation of the prayer, composed he thinks by Akhnaten, that appears inscribed in gold at the foot of the coffin; and where he offers his interpretation of the vulture 'crown', as it was catalogued by Daressy – not a crown, he says, but a collar, or pectoral, accidentally shoved over the body's skull by the collapse of the coffin. It was a view borne out by a later find, that of Tutankhamun himself, who was provided with a similar pectoral.

Piecemeal and delayed as all this information was, it only goes to show the damaging effect on scholarship of Davis's intellectual rights. In fact the whole subject of rights became one of Weigall's most anxious preoccupations, and he explored its general implications later when he described the attitude of scholars towards the tombs at Gurneh. Later still, when Lord Carnarvon actually sold to *The Times* his supposed rights to information from the tomb of Tutankhamun, Weigall must have had a sense of déjà vu.

But apart from Davis's contract, the relation in which the three men found themselves – Weigall, Davis and Ayrton – was bound to have a malign effect on their work. Their functions were hopelessly ill-defined and overlapping. Davis, as we have seen, had had the concession for the Valley of the Kings long before Weigall was appointed, had financed the work himself, and had enjoyed great independence from the Department. A series of remarkable discoveries and Maspero's gratitude and generosity had only encouraged Davis's sense of autonomy. Then, with Weigall's appointment, a new regime had been imposed, and Davis was obliged to employ a trained archaeologist. This archaeologist was paid by Davis, but answerable ultimately to the Department, which practically speaking meant the Inspector. It would have needed remarkable forbearance for each of these three men not to have felt that the others were encroaching on his territory. No doubt Davis held so jealously to his right of publication precisely because his autonomy as an excavator was no longer complete. For his part, Weigall would burst with irritation at Davis from time to time, and Ayrton was similarly irritable with both the others.

None of this was a surprise to Weigall. As he says in his preface to the 1922 edition of his biography of Akhnaten:

> ... for diplomatic reasons I kept in the background, and to a great extent left the clearing of the tomb [Tiy's] in his [Ayrton's] efficient hands ... When Mr Davis published the results, he ... preserved a strict silence in regard to my own part in the work; and I should like to explain that this was ... due to his very understandable objection to the restrictions which my Department rightly obliged me to impose upon him.

It was the same the following year, over the tomb of Horemheb. Weigall's contribution that year to the Egypt Exploration Fund's Archaeological Reports said very little about the new tomb, and when the editor, Griffith, asked why, he explained:

> With regard to Horemheb I purposely did not say much about it, because my position is such a very delicate one in regard to Davis. I insist on the formality of supervising his work on behalf of the Govt ... Davis naturally dislikes this, and, though we are good friends, I find it very difficult to prevent him running the Tombs of the Kings as a social affair. Ayrton behaved as badly as he could while there [Ayrton had since resigned from Davis's employ], being entirely under Davis's thumb; and also on his own account resenting my appearance on what he considered his own field. ... It is always very difficult for us all in these excavations, and I must not complicate matters by reporting on the discovery of the Horemheb tomb which Ayrton would regard, no doubt, as a personal affront. Would he not himself supply details?[31]

But for now, Weigall's frustration with Davis could not take away from his present euphoria. As we have seen, Nubia was honourably behind him, his imagination had been kindled by the 'discovery' of Akhnaten, and his reputation stood high amongst some at least of his colleagues. Almost more important than that, he had found out that he could write for the general public. Encouraged by the complimentary remarks made to him by friends outside the archaeological world (Ronald Storrs was one), he told Hortense that 'I'm beginning to think that whether it's Science or not it is both profitable and pleasing to cultivate the Art of letters.' He was in the mood to write more, and his desert trip would give him something to write about.

After that, Hortense and the baby were expected back in Egypt, and he was *'mad'* to see her. All his letters throughout this period, full as they were with the anxious excitements described in this chapter, were equally full of his longing to see her again. He was as eager about her as about Akhnaten, planning for her arrival, rearranging the bedrooms for the baby and its nurse, and always liable to fall into black rage and despair should Hortense leave so much as half a week without writing to him.

arrival home.

# Chapter 9

# The Eastern Desert; 'odium archaeologicum'
# 1907–1908

Weigall's journey across the eastern desert was more than an escape from quarrels about tombs and dams. One of the constant themes in his writing about the desert is the escape from civilization, by which he meant not just modern civilization but a particular kind of Egyptian civilization. Here in the desert, he seems to say, where the ancient trade routes with the east ran, and where the Romans quarried their white granite and purple porphyry, you leave not only modern life behind, but you also encounter another kind of history: an Egypt of merchants rather than Pharaohs, of prospectors instead of priests, of miners, stone masons, road builders, Roman legionaries and medieval caravan masters.

> Travelling in Egypt one sees so many remains of the solemn religious ceremonies of the ancient Egyptians, and reading at home one meets with so many representations of the sacred rites, that it is a real relief to come across some relic ... of human energy and toil ... One has heard in the imagination the rhythmic chants, has smelt the heavy incense ... Glum Pharaohs have stalked across the picture, raising their stiff hands to the dull gods; ... Here there are no mysteries ... One does not pace through holy places whispering "How weird!" but stick in hand, and whistling a tune down the wind, one follows in the footsteps of the bold caravan-masters ...

He hints at an analogy between the luxury and ceremony of ancient Egypt and the rich pleasures of modern Europe. As he summons up the picture of the whistling traveller, stick in hand, he urges the tourist to shed both civilizations and join him in the company of men doing a man's work, men uncannily like the energetic irrigation officials of the British Empire that he so admired: 'when the amusements of the luxurious hotels have given out, and the solemnity of the ancient ruins have begun to pall, the spirits ... of the captains and caravan-conductors, are always to be found waiting on the breezy hill-tops behind the island of Elephantine, at the head of the Nubian highway.'

These extracts come from a piece[1] inspired by a Nubian excursion into the western desert, in which he tells the story of a certain prince Herkhuf of Elephantine (the island opposite the town of Aswan) who, in about 2250 BC, explored and opened up a road to the south:

> Let the visitor to Aswan step out some afternoon from the hall of his hotel, where the string band throbs in his ears and the latest Parisian gowns shimmer before his eyes, and let him take boat to the little western bay behind the ruins of Elephantine. ... At the top of the hills to his left he will presently see ... a large isolated boulder ... and making his way up the hillside towards this boulder, he will suddenly come upon a paved causeway ...

This, says Weigall, must be Herkhuf's high road south, though he says he has never come across any reference to it. But the point here is not so much the discovery, as the appeal to the hotel guest with the sound of the string band in his ears. Weigall wants to take him beyond the enclosed garden of the Nile valley, as he calls it, and out into the bare hills. He wants to lead his readers 'straight into the boisterous breezes of Egypt'. Then, he says, 'the walls of their rooms would fall flat as those of Jericho; and outside they would see the advancing host of the invaders – the sunshine, the north wind, the scudding clouds, the circling eagles, the glistening sand, the blue shadows and the rampant rocks.' [2]

These articles about the desert, collected and published in 1909 by Blackwood's as *Travels in the Upper Egyptian Deserts*, are some of the most vivid things he wrote, and they introduced him to a large, educated, general public. It must have helped enormously that there was no-one like Davis breathing down his neck. There were no contracts here, none of the jealousy over rights to objects or publications that so bedevilled the Valley of the Kings. Here instead was a vast unvisited wilderness in which he could write about places 'which no other European eyes have seen.' A couple of nineteenth-century Egyptologists, Lepsius and Golenischeff; the German botanist and explorer, Schweinfurth; these and modern mining prospectors and surveyors were all the Europeans who had ever penetrated the region. This, in spite of the fact that the eastern desert is no Sahara, and that with a guide who knows the wells, and with camels to carry tents and provisions, it is not a dangerous under-taking.

The desert was where Weigall always felt closest to the ancient world. With scarcely a modern mark on it, Time, he said, seemed to be at a standstill there. The ancients, on the other hand, had left plenty of marks: 'No matter in what direction one travels, hardly a day passes on which one does not meet with some ancient activity. Here it will be a deserted gold-mine, there a quarry; here a ruined fortress or town, and there an inscription upon the rocks.' [3] And all of them -- at least the inscriptions – as fresh and clean as yesterday. Even the ruins might have only just collapsed. Walter Tyndale, the painter mentioned in the previous chapter, was thoroughly disappointed by just that. Together with two other artists, Charles Whymper[4] and Erskine Nicol, he accompanied Weigall on his expedition to the Red Sea in November 1907, and in his book of travels, *An Artist in Egypt* (1912), he wrote that a desert ruin is 'a depressing sight': 'No growth to hide the shapeless bits of fallen masonry are there, neither moss nor lichen to give it the beautiful colouring associated with the remains of bygone structures. A shrine which may have crumbled in centuries ago might have fallen in the day before yesterday.'[5]

But it was just this sense of the day before yesterday that Weigall loved. Egypt was the perfect place precisely because there was no moss. He had no interest in mists. Far away and long ago gave him a thrill only if he could actually finger it. Sitting on a rock beside a grafitto scratched there by a Roman soldier, he knew he was resting on the exact spot, in the same shade, looking at the same hills as the soldier had done. One of the things that moved him most was the sight of some great quarried blocks of a blue and olive-green stone called tuff, lying on the sand ready to be collected and marked with the Caesar's address but, for some reason, never dispatched.[6] By the same token, he was not given to meditations on the human condition. Faced with the shattered visage of Shelley's Ozymandias, he would probably, in imagination at least, have put it back together again. The nearest he came to a philosophical idea was to say, as he had done in his piece about Yuya and Tuya, that our notion of Time was all wrong: 'A door seems to open in the brain, a screen slides back, and clearly one sees Time in its true relation. A thousand years, two thousand years, have the value of the merest drop of water in the ocean.'[7]

There were four expeditions into the eastern desert. The first was in March 1907, to the Roman porphyry mines at Gebel Dukhan some 27 miles from the Red Sea, opposite the southern end of the Sinai Peninsula. He went at the invitation of the Director of the Department of Mines who was preparing a report on the possibility of re-opening the old workings, and understood the need (this would have pleased Weigall) to liaise with the Department of Antiquities. His second was really the return journey, but by a route which he took on his own account without the Mining Director. It went through the Roman granite quarries of Mons Claudianus, as it is known, and past the old Egyptian and Roman gold mines of Fatireh. Then came his journey with Tyndale, Whymper and Nicol in November 1907, to the sleepy Red Sea town of Khossair, via the quarries of Wady Hammamat where tuff was found. And finally, in March 1908 he journeyed, this time with Hortense, by way of El Kab just south of Edfu to the rock temple of Wady Abad built by King Sety I (c. 1306 BC) near the numerous gold workings in the desert to the east.

Weigall was at heart a proselytiser. The fact that people didn't come to the desert was almost an affront – an affront to Egypt and its history. 'There will come a time,' he prophesied hopefully, 'when one will travel to the quarries by automobile.'[8] Meanwhile, all he could do was to write, emulating the explorer whose description of a journey across the Sahara caused a young reader to exclaim afterwards that 'his nose was covered with freckles'.[9] The review of his book in the *Westminster Gazette* (6 October 1909) obviously gave him special pleasure, for in his cuttings album Weigall has underlined these words: 'None, I think, has realized the fascination of the desert more fully than Arthur E.P. Weigall. ... The sights, the sounds, the very air of the desert, visit the senses of the reader with a keenness that is almost painful.'

To the modern reader, Weigall's deliberate cadences, his poeticizing style, his archaisms such as 'the elder days', and history 'writ' upon the rocks, can be irritating. On the whole his contemporaries found these things felicitous, though there were some who did not. What saves him is his own fascination for everything he saw. His zest and his keen eye survive his 'fine writing'. He describes the afternoon shadows, each camel footprint 'a basin filled with blue shade'; as the sun 'bombards' his helmet, and the wind 'charges' him from the flank, suddenly a blazing white butterfly zigzags across the sky, darkening the blue by contrast. He notices the ground strewn with 'yellow fragments of sandstone, orange-coloured ochre, transparent pieces of gypsum, carnelian and alabaster chips, and glittering quartz'. A fellow travel writer, Norma Lorimer, wrote to congratulate him, especially on these 'delightful sounding things'.[10] But his alabaster and carnelian were exact, not mere Wildean flourishes. In among the stones, he picks out the wiggly lines of lizards, the footprints of wagtails, vultures, eagles, desert partridges, the short jumps of jerboas, the 'dainty padmarks' of jackals and foxes, 'the heavier prints' of hyaenas, and the occasional gazelle.[11] 'I think page 7 is ripping,' wrote Lorimer, and page 7 is indeed the footprint page.

But more often the scale is larger, the wild contortions and colours of the mountains he passed through:

On the right the line of the valley drew the eyes over the dim, brown waves of gravel to the darkness of the rugged horizon. Behind, and sweeping upward, the sky was golden red; and this presently turned to green, and the green to deep blue. On the left some reflected light tinged the eastern sky with a suggestion of purple, and against this the nearer mountains stood out darkly. In front the low hills met together, and knit themselves into shapes so strange that one might have thought them the distortions of a dream. ... Then in the warm perfect stillness ... there came – at first almost unnoticed – a small black moving mass, creeping over an indefinite hill-top ... Presently, very quietly, the mass resolved itself into a compact flock of goats ... there arose a plaintive bleating and the wail of the goatherd's pipe ... Behind the flock two figures moved, their white garments fluttering in the wind, changing grotesquely the form and shape of the wearers. ...[12]

It is, of course, a set-piece (and more laboured without my excisions), but distinct and particular, as well as grand and strange. In the days before wide angle lenses and Technicolor cinema, that kind of writing had a place.

Weigall ravished his readers in the manner of his time, with sunsets and solitudes, thrilled them with the suggestion of ghostly voices whispering from behind rocks and recesses. Yet at the same time he insisted that the mystery was no such thing, that just out of earshot were not whisperings, but the shouts of the people who used to live and work there. That is the real strangeness. And so having caught his readers by his wordscapes, he makes them listen to his translation of 'a very interesting tariff of taxes imposed on persons using the road during the Roman occupation';[13] or of the inscription about the personnel records of an expedition sent by Rameses IV to quarry tuff from Wady Hammamat, together with the supplies that were sent with it;[14] they must understand the methods used by the Romans to extract gold from the rocks,[15] and hear the story, carved in the rocks near Sety's temple, of how he came to build it.[16] He was especially excited to find three carved cartouches on the road to Hammamat, one of Queen Tiy, one of Amenophis IV and one of that king under his adopted name, Akhnaten, all placed together above the symbols of sovereignty and below the rays of the sun's disk. This showed, he believed, that Akhnaten came to the throne while his mother was still queen, and confirmed that he was still 'but a boy of tender years' on his accession. He only just refrains from buttonholing his reader about the whole argument, letting him off with a reference to the October number of *Blackwood's* instead.[17]

These articles are in fact full of information, the result of extremely hard work. He may have gazed dreamily in the evenings, and been charmed by birds and butterflies, but he spent his days notebook in hand. Walter Tyndale describes long days spent making very slow progress, zigzagging across burning, barren valleys while Weigall went from one rock inscription to the next,[18] patiently copying the decipherable and the indecipherable alike: and one can see the results, strange runic marks and signs, among the illustrations to the collected volume. In fact, to a modern reader, a walk round a ruin with Weigall is as good as any sunset. Here he is at the porphyry town at Gebel Dukhan:

> A fine terrace runs along the east side, and up to this a ramp ascends. Passing through the gateway, one enters the main street, and the attention is first attracted by a fine imposing building on the right hand. Here there are several chambers leading into an eight-pillared hall, at the end of which a well-made and well-preserved plunge-bath eloquently tells of the small pleasures of expatriated Roman officers. A turning from the main street brings one into an open courtyard, where there are two ovens and some stone dishes to be seen ... it does not require much imagination to people it again with that noisy crowd of Greek, Roman, and Egyptian quarrymen. One sees them prising out the blocks of purple porphyry from the hill side high above the valley, returning in the evening down the broad causeway to the town, ... In the middle of the valley there is a well ... A gallery, the roof of which was supported by five pillars passes in a half circle round one side ... Here the workmen could sit in the shade ...

And so he goes on, building up the picture touch by touch, the wagon trains loaded with provisions, the soldiers patrolling the road back to the Nile, the river barges to take the porphyry down to the sea for transhipment to the Roman galleys, and finally, after all the toil and sweat, the 'thoughtless implacable men, dipping their jewelled fingers into the basins of purple porphyry as they reclined in the Halls of imperial Rome'.[19] One then turns to his photographs and has to hand it to him: for there, at least to the untrained eye, instead of imposing buildings and columned halls, is only a jumble of broken down masonry, with here and there a pillar still unfallen.

When the collection came out in book form in September 1909, it was an instant success. There were one or two complaints against his purple, but everyone was agreed on his powers of observation and his historic imagination. One of the best things about it, they said, was the author's 'own intense enjoyment of the desert': 'Mr

Weigall is a desert enthusiast. He has felt its spell. He has rejoiced in its burning days and starry nights … He loves it for itself, not less than for its human monuments.'[20] Whether Weigall loved the desert most, or the monuments in it, the reviewers couldn't decide. *The Manchester Guardian* (8 December 1909) wrote that wherever he went, 'Mr Weigall carries the reader with him; in his company the dead past lives again. Yet we suspect that the desert itself is more to the author than all its departed glories.' But in fact the two things were inseparable, the landscape led inexorably to its history, and it was impossible for him to look at one without feeling the other: 'To those interested in the olden days the rocks hold out an invitation which one is surprised to find so little responded to; but let any one feel for an hour the fine freedom of the desert, and see for an hour the fantasy of the hills, and that invitation will not again be so lightly set aside.'[21]

The last expedition, in March 1908, was made with Hortense, and one can detect a special rapture about Weigall's descriptions this time. It was the first time they had been alone together on a trip since their honeymoon. After their long autumn separation, from the end of August to the end of November, she had returned to Egypt, as we have seen, with the baby Alured and a nurse. The house would never be quite the same. Married life was no longer, if it had ever been, a private game played by two romantic children. In early January, Mimi had joined them for two months. Now she was gone, and the baby too had been sent home with the nurse ahead of Hortense. She wept bitterly, but would be returning to England herself in May. This journey was like another honeymoon, and just the kind of adventure Hortense had always dreamed of. When they reached Sety's temple, they spent two days there at the ruins of a large fortified Graeco-Roman station built on the plain nearby. Here time slipped past, Weigall wrote, 'in a half-dream of pleasure':

At dawn, at noon, at sunset – all day long – this fortress in the Wady Abad is beautiful; and for those who love the desert, there is here and in its surroundings always some new thing to charm. The walls of the enclosure, and beyond them the pillared portico of the temple sheltering under the rugged brown cliffs, form as delightful a picture as may be found in Egypt. … the hours race by at an absurd speed … There was a flight of cranes, which sailed overhead … Why should my memory recall so charmedly the passage of a hundred birds?

He notes a hyaena in the red dusk; a vulture as bright against the sky as the painted vultures inside the temple; black and white stonechats fluttering among the rocks; the sparkle of the sand on the plain outside the fortifications, and the blue of the shadows within.

But again, there was more here than fauna and flora. The place was remote, and not immediately on the way to anywhere but the mines. Weigall wondered why Sety had decided to build a temple at this particular spot, and the answer seemed to him to lie in the quantity of archaic pictures scratched in the cliff face near the temple. Here were strangely shaped, high-prowed boats, with stick-like men and animals and shrines on board. The boats were like the arks used in ancient religious rites, and it seemed therefore that the place had long been sacred. He leaves it at that,[22] but the mere fact that he had been interested enough to copy what he saw is an example of the importance of record-keeping. In the middle of the twentieth century, and again more recently, Weigall's copies have played a significant part in a debate about the possible foreign origins of Egyptian civilization.[23]

Mimi's visit to them just after Christmas gives us a glimpse of the life they returned to in Luxor, for she described the whole scene with characteristic verve to her daughter Geanie. Weigall had met her off the boat at Port Said, and had whirled her round the sights – the Pyramids, Cairo, the races, the bazaar, a dinner and a dance: 'Such women and such dresses,' she had exclaimed. Then they had gone up by train to Luxor, where Hortense met them, looking much thinner, says Mimi, now that she had stopped nursing the baby, and 'has some good stays on'. One can imagine Mimi's searching eye. After describing the house and garden, she comes to Abdu, their manservant:

> ... all the household turn to Abdu as their stay and comfort, their guide and coun-
> sellor. He is a charming sight to behold too, in flowing white robe, and red sash and
> shoes, and 'tarboush', and then in the afternoons he appears in a dark red flowing
> robe and looks even more lovely. ... This morning Hortense and I walked out with
> him to see the native market and he walked in front and hit the camels on the head
> if they came too near, and pushed the donkeys away, and kept calling out some-
> thing in Arabic which I suppose meant that the Queen of Sheba and her daughter
> in law were coming through their midst. One poor woman he smacked over her
> ears because she and her baby came too near. He bargained for beads, and bought
> us sugar cane, and seemed wonderfully relieved when he got us safely home. That
> market was an interesting sight. Crowds of Arabs have been crossing the Nile all
> the morning in boatloads, and others streaming along the dusty path past the
> house, with their goats and donkeys and camels. ... We drove over to see the
> wonderful Temple of Karnak yesterday at sunset. It is past describing ... I was
> much impressed at the guards' behaviour when Arthur came along. They presented
> arms and looked absolutely terrified and the head man dropped his gun, and
> followed us with an awe-struck face, and if Arthur spoke to him he nearly died, and
> evidently was thankful not to have had his head cut off at any rate for that one day.

Obviously Weigall's ideas of discipline had taken root, at least when he was looking. Mimi also mentions a curious fact about Hortense. Having described the baby Alured, she adds that 'Hortense grabs him up and carries him upside down in her usual way, and no matter how he cries only says – oh my son, son, but otherwise is quite unmoved.' It is the first sign of a cloud that was to hang between Hortense and Weigall later on, when it became clear that Hortense had no idea at all of domestic management. Servants and nurses masked the fact for some time yet, but it was something that Mimi and Geanie seemed already to have noticed between themselves.

But for Weigall, the return from the desert to Luxor and domestic life meant a return to professional vexations too. Among the letters waiting for him were those already quoted, from Theodore Davis, telling him what he could and could not put in his article about the tomb of Horemheb. These letters, though no doubt irritating, were at least relatively friendly. But it had been a particularly acrimonious season between the three men – Davis, Ayrton, and Weigall. As we have seen, the Akhnaten affair rankled with Davis, and Weigall's *Blackwoods* article explaining his theory must indeed have made him 'mad'. On the other hand, Davis was having an uncommonly long run of luck: first Yuya and Tuya, then Queen Tiy, and now in early 1908, Ayrton had come upon a deposit of beautiful gold and silver jewellery embedded in the silt of a previously flooded tomb, each piece inscribed with the names of Sety II and Queen Tawosert. There were alabaster and pottery vases too, a sandal, and two curious silver 'gloves', more like mittens without the thumbs. Davis shook them upside down, and out poured eight little rings.[24] The jewellery is now thought to have been made by Queen Tawosert for a child originally buried there, but because no body or coffin was found (water having rotted everything perishable) it was assumed that the pieces were some sort of salvaged cache belonging to the queen herself.

Perhaps the discovery, so soon after the Akhnaten affair, put new steam into Davis's defiance of Weigall. Whatever it was, he appears to have been more than ever resentful of Weigall's 'interference' in the Valley. His letter informing him of Ayrton's find is extraordinarily cold and formal:

5 January 1908

Dear Sir,

I beg to advise you that I have this day discovered what I suppose to be a large tomb. Owing to the request of Sir Eldon Gorst [Lord Cromer's successor] I shall not open or enter the tomb until the 17th inst.

Will you kindly exercise your rights and duties under your Inspectorship in the matter of guarding the site of the tomb and oblige

yours truly
Theo M Davis.[25]

Davis was probably trying to keep Weigall at arm's length from Ayrton's work, and to confine him to security matters. Whatever it was, Weigall was obviously incensed, for he wrote to Maspero asking him to intervene in some way. While he was at it, he must have added that Davis was an amateur and a treasure hunter, that every Egyptologist of worth knew it, and that such a state of affairs reflected badly on the Antiquities Department. That much, at any rate, can be guessed from Maspero's reply, dated 17 January 1908, the very day of Gorst's visit. Maspero, of course, was just as interested as Davis in putting on a good show for the British Agent, and he opens his letter to Weigall with the hope that 'the tomb of Queen Tawosert proved worthy of the queen and that the diplomatic party enjoyed the sightseeing.' As for Weigall's complaints, his answer is a masterpiece of charming evasion:

> I will speak with Davis myself, and I think that we may arrange everything peacefully. Only do not call him an amateur: he has Ayrton with him, who is able to do as well as most of the people who think they are Egyptologists. Of course, all the people who do not find a royal tomb are a little angry with Davis for finding them, but I have not seen that any of those who are hard on him have ever given us the whole of their finds, and published the account of it in such a splendid and complete way. If, given the profit which comes for the Museum and for Egyptology, they think that our Service has amateurish ways of doing its duty, let them think so and say so: I do not care for myself, and you may refer them to me. I shall give them my reasons for acting as I am, and my candid opinion of their sayings. It will be done with all the courtesy of which I am capable in such a case.[26]

Maspero's courtesy was notorious, and Weigall must have torn his hair out. *Of course* other Egyptologists did not give the whole of their finds; the law that applied to sites other than the Valley of the Kings allowed them to keep half. Davis's concession was of a different kind; it embodied a different principle. It is significant that Weigall's copy of Davis's contract dates from exactly this period. A note across the top of it is dated 19 January 1908 and initialled by Maspero. Presumably the combined effect of Maspero and Davis drove Weigall to ask for a copy for himself, to study. What he read there couldn't have been clearer: not only did it say, as we have seen, that 'Mr Davis shall not have any right to any of the objects enclosed in the tomb or monument that is discovered; such objects, together with the monument or tomb itself remaining the property of the Department of Antiquities', but also that 'The work is to be carried out under the control of the Department of Antiquities, which shall have the right not only to oversee the works but also to correct their progress if it judges that this would be useful for the success of the enterprise.' In other words, the Inspector could not be legitimately cold shouldered.[27]

Maspero and Davis both belonged to the old world, and there was no budging them. It was a world in which the Antiquities Service felt itself beholden to rich individuals who were kind enough to excavate and give whatever they felt they could to the nation. In return, the Antiquities department buttered them up with gifts and gratitude. No doubt Maspero smoothed Davis down in this way, and persuaded him to accept Weigall as his representative, for Emma Andrews' diary mentions Weigall as a member of their party on the *dahabiyeh* and in the Valley fairly frequently over the next weeks. Weigall would simply have had to swallow his rage.

Meanwhile Ayrton was also suffering from Davis's style of operations. Gorst's visit to the opening of Queen Tawosert's tomb (or so it was thought to be) brought him up against precisely what Weigall meant about Davis's amateurism. Gorst himself set the tone of frivolity. According to the American archaeologist, Herbert Winlock[28] who was working for the Metropolitan Museum at Deir el Bahri, and who visited Ayrton at the time, Gorst had written to Davis to say that 'he had heard that the latter's men found a royal tomb every winter and [requested], as he intended to be in the Valley of the Kings in a few days, that all discoveries be postponed until his arrival.' Unfortunately, in the course of the days leading up to the official opening, Davis realized that he did not have a 'large tomb' to show him, and he did not think that the jewellery on its own was 'sufficiently spectacular' to show Gorst.

Davis therefore fell back on some jars that Ayrton had uncovered in a pit a few weeks before, in one of which he had found 'a charming little yellow mask'. According to Winlock, 'Everybody thought they were going to find many more objects in the other jars,' and so the vessels were lined up neatly in front of Ayrton's house in the Valley, ready for Gorst's entertainment at a lunch party to be held there. The day arrived, and Emma Andrews recorded in her diary, 'a very pleasant lunch' with the Gorsts, and their secretary and Mrs Weigall – Weigall himself is not mentioned, but then nor is Ayrton who must have been there. What she does not say either is that the opening of the jars was a fiasco.

Winlock, who came over to see Ayrton after everyone had gone, picks up the story:

What in the morning had been fairly neat rows of pots were tumbled in every direction, with little bundles of natron [a substance used in the embalming process] and broken pottery all over the ground. The little mask which had been taken as a harbinger of something better to come had brought forth nothing, and poor Ayrton was a very sick and tired person after the undeserved tongue-lashing he had had all that afternoon. Sir Eldon complimented Mr Davis on his cook, and that is the last of him as far as this story is concerned.

In fact, as Winlock's painstaking work subsequently revealed, the jars contained extremely interesting material connected with the final burial ceremonies of Tutankhamun, whose tomb was concealed nearby. All Davis knew was that the stuff was not eye-catching, and that Ayrton had let him down in front of the highest official in the land. It must have struck Ayrton then, if it hadn't already, that this was no way to carry on serious archaeological work.

The Tawosert jewellery was stowed on board Davis's boat, like the things from Tiy's tomb the previous year, and again it attracted a stream of visitors who came and went with their daughters and friends and hangers-on, and usually with Weigall in attendance. It was a large and time-consuming part of his duties, to 'be so good' (as all the little notes to him say) as to put so and so – a friend of a minister, a friend of a friend – in the way of seeing the sights. After the Gorsts came the Devonshires once more, and Emma Andrews' diary for 18 January gives a vivid picture of the kind of scene he witnessed:

We had the whole Devonshire party to tea this afternoon to see the find. The Duke and Duchess, her daughter Lady Gosford, and Lord Gosford and their daughter Lady Theodora Guest – with Mr Weigall ... The Duke, now a very old and broken man, is of course a great personage ... The Duchess, so celebrated in her way, was a wonderful old woman – painted and enamelled, with reddish wig, an old black hat, with painted lips – very keen to see everything. ... I heard the Duchess talking to Mr Davis about how much the Gorsts enjoyed their lunch yesterday in the Valley House, and I knew from what she said that she intended Theo should invite them also to lunch there, and I don't think he will be able to escape it.

At the end of the month, a note from Sir Arthur Webb (with whom Weigall crossed swords over the quarries at Gebel Silsileh) informs him of the arrival of Sir Ernest Cassel, the financier behind the Aswan dam, and friend of the King: 'Could you kindly see him, and put him in the way of visiting the temples?'[29] The next day there he is, in Emma Andrews' diary, on the *dahabiyeh*, with his daughter and an Italian Princess and Weigall. A month later came the Connaughts: 'Quite an imposing array,' writes Mrs Andrews on March 2. 'Several mounted guards arrived before them – and the Duchess and Princess Patricia arrived first,' then a lady in waiting, followed by various military figures, and finally, the inevitable 'Mr Weigall': 'They looked at the gold find, and then went on deck for tea.' And so it went on. Poor Emma Andrews often sounds weary of the constant crowds. When at the end of the season Davis left for Cairo, and on March 17 handed the gold over to the Museum, one sympathizes with her final words in that day's entry – ' A good riddance.'

In the midst of all this, on 22 February 1908, came a note from Ayrton saying that 'we have just found another tomb', and asking for a night guard.[30] This turned out to be the tomb of Horemheb, the last thing the three tense and irritable men needed just then. But a discovery will not wait, especially in the high season, when the hotels are full and the *dahabiyehs* are moored and the aristocracy of Europe are on hand. The entrance was made a week later, and once again it is a story of scrambling over rubble, backs scraping against the roof of the passage, of hot foul air, and of stunned silence at the bottom. At the end of the corridor, the three men, together with two others found themselves 'at the brink of a large rectangular well, or shaft'. Weigall's account describes them peering around by the light of their electric lamps at

> wonderfully preserved paintings executed on slightly raised plaster. Here Horemheb was seen standing before Isis, Osiris, Horus and other gods; and his cartouches stood out boldly from amidst the elaborate inscriptions. The colours were extremely rich ... we were able to climb down [the shaft] by means of a ladder, and up the other side to an entrance which formed a kind of window in the sheer wall ... there was nothing so impressive as this view across the well ... and through the window-like aperture before one, a dim suggestion could be obtained of a white-pillared hall.[31]

Horemheb was a general who seized power after the brief reign of Ay, the little known Pharaoh who succeeded Tutankhamun. His tomb had been plundered, and the pillared hall was a chaotic scene of smashed fragments. Parts of the roof had fallen in too, and Weigall remarks casually that 'other parts appeared to be likely to do so at any moment.' It must have been a fearful thing going down into these tombs, and this was worse than some, for it had a further passage leading down through the floor of the first room. The large burial chamber at the end of this corridor was also littered with fallen rock slabs, and the pillars that supported its roof were crumbling.

But here in this second chamber was a prize, a great pink and white granite sarcophagus, covered with finely cut inscriptions and, at the four corners, the figures of Isis and Nephthys carved in relief, their wings spread out protectively across the right-angle, like the ones later discovered on Tutankhamun's sarcophagus. Paintings leapt out at them in the glare of their lamps, and in front of one of them was a little wooden statue of a god, hands upraised as if 'in horror at the sight of us ... gasping with surprise and indignation.'

It was, as always, a strange and thrilling experience: 'One cannot describe the silence, the echoing steps, the dark shadows, the hot, breathless air; nor tell of the sense of vast Time and the penetrating of it which stirs one so deeply.'[32] It was also extremely uncomfortable – hot and suffocating. Weigall doesn't say whether he ever felt more than discomfort on these occasions, but it is perhaps significant that a few years later he began to suffer horrible attacks of claustrophobia. To make matters worse, this particular tomb proved over the next few weeks to be cursed too, though not by any ancient taboo. The Egyptologist Somers Clarke, once exclaimed to Weigall 'Why do the archaeologists so furiously rage together?', adding that Lord Cromer had once warned him that the 'odium archaeologicum' was even worse than the 'odium theologicum.'[33]

On this occasion it was Ayrton who snapped, letting fly at Weigall who had brought some visitors to the tomb. They were not aristocrats for once, but professional colleagues, none other than Dr Elliot Smith himself and a fellow anatomist. Though the letter Weigall wrote later to Griffith is philosophical enough about the behaviour of Ayrton and Davis at the time of Horemheb, he was put out at the time. He wrote to Mimi, now back in England: 'Ayrton, who apparently didn't like having them there, had quite a row with me, and was awfully babyish and rude ... He is a funny chap, and I am rather glad he is leaving. He is always so frightfully on his dignity.' The outburst had obviously made quite an impression, for Joe Lindon Smith who was staying with Weigall, also wrote to his mother: 'Ayrton has suddenly gone mad. I can hardly explain his babyish action otherwise – he has gone out of his way to insult Arthur by word of mouth as well as by letters ... We think he has gone off his head really.'[34]

Ayrton was no doubt strung up because of Davis; perhaps the sight of Elliot Smith, the destroyer of Davis's dream of Queen Tiy, and therefore of a peaceful working atmosphere, was too much for him; perhaps it seemed, in his sensitive state, that Weigall was gloating over him and Davis by bringing Elliot Smith at all. The weather was also suffocating, 'with those nasty hot south winds and stuffy clouds,' as Weigall told his mother. At any rate, Ayrton resigned soon after, and went back to his former employer, Naville, who was excavating now for the Egypt Exploration Fund at Abydos. His successor was a Welsh artist and excavator, Harold Jones, who had worked with John Garstang and who seems to have possessed the qualities of gentleness and good nature so rare in that irascible world.

# Chapter 10

# Gaiety; Akhnaten; and Howard Carter again
# 1908–1909

In the circumstances, one can understand the impetus behind Weigall's search for another Egypt, away from the overcharged expectations and bitter disappointments of tombs. Besides, Davis's discoveries were feeding into the old popular myth of a funereal Egypt. Now, just when they and the 'odium archaeologicum' were casting a blacker shadow than usual, Weigall was seized with the desire to do for the whole subject of archaeology (by which he meant Egyptian archaeology) what he had done for ancient Egyptian history: that is, to blow away the dust and ashes from the popular view of it, and drag it out of the academic corner which at that time it still occupied.

Nowadays, since Tutmania, so-called, and television and mass tourism, it is difficult to realize that Ancient Egypt was not yet a popular interest. Weigall was to write many years later, that the man in the street discovered antiquity only with the discovery of the tomb of Tutankhamun.[1] Before that, it was an atmosphere merely, something picturesque and Biblical: there were traveller's books, David Roberts's lithographs, Wilkinson's watercolours, and for spectacle, Alma Tadema, or perhaps a gorgeously mounted production of *Antony and Cleopatra*. But otherwise it was regarded as a subject for Doctor Dry-as-dust. As one reviewer of Weigall's books put it: 'Mr Weigall is a fascinating writer on a fascinating subject. Ancient Egypt fascinating, you say; why it is all sand and mummies. It may be, but let anyone read Mr Weigall's [books] …'[2]

Weigall sums up the common view of archaeology itself in a mock speech given by the secretary of some local archaeological society to introduce Professor Blank:

"Archaeology," he says in a voice of brass, "is a science which bars its doors to all but the most erudite; for to the layman … the dead will not reveal their secrets … To-night, we are privileged; for Professor Blank will open the doors for us that we may gaze for a moment upon that solemn charnel-house of the Past in which he has sat for so many long hours in inductive meditation."

This comes in a piece provocatively entitled 'The Necessity of Archaeology to the Gaiety of the World'[3] in which he argues that archaeology is not – or rather that it

110

should not be – the peculiar pursuit of Casaubon-like antiquarians holding up the rags and bones of distant cultures like trophies. On the contrary it is, properly speaking, an intensely imagined, dramatic encounter with the past, and the archaeologist should no more think of pointing to the raw material of his trade than the artist would exhibit the blobs of paint on his palette. The archaeologist is really a historian, a story-teller. A catalogue of scarabs, and an analysis of their glaze is all very well, he writes in another related article, but it is only so much data until it can be made to tell 'the history of a period, of a dynasty, of a craft'.[4] The archaeologist's business is life, not death; he is in love with it, whether past or present hardly matters. In fact Weigall defied his reader to believe that the archaeologist has any particular attachment to the past at all. Warming to his theme to the point of recklessness, he maintained that the archaeologist

> has turned to the Past because he is in love with the Present. He, more than anyone, worships at the altar of the goddess of Today; and he is so desirous of extending her dominion that he has ventured, like a crusader, into the lands of the Past in order to subject them to her. ... His whole business is to hide the gap between Yesterday and Today ... The Present is too small for him; and it is therefore that he calls so insistently to the Past to come forth from the darkness to augment it.[5]

Weigall was a born polemicist. He ran with his subject, dropping into purple prose and out again into slapstick, caricaturing, dramatizing, and arguing hard all the way. The Mission Hall exhortations he heard so often as a boy are sometimes distinctly audible.

But his picture of the common idea of the archaeologist probably looks more like caricature now than it did then. Long before this time, Weigall had had a conversation with the Egyptologist, Alan Gardiner, who later became a close friend, about the relative claims of archaeology and philology. They had disagreed and Gardiner had become heated, for he wrote a letter apologizing. This letter is an interesting exposition of the then current attitude towards archaeologists, and it shows just how paradoxical Weigall's later claims must have seemed. It was written at about the time of Weigall's first season at Saqqara, in the winter of 1902.

> In speaking of the rival claims of Archaeology and Philology [Gardiner wrote], I certainly did take rather a narrow view of the former at the moment. I had in my mind the usual conception of archaeology, – that which a brilliant Greek scholar had in view when he spoke of "Aegean crockery". He surely had no thought of the Parthenon, nor did I think of Karnak and all the tomb-paintings of Benihasan and Thebes. But these are inextricably associated with work in the study: they are not included in the ordinary conception of archaeology. Archaeology to nine tenths of Archaeologists means the study of materials, pots and pans – the merest skeleton-shape of a people's existence. Philology may, it is true, be construed just as narrowly: but in fact I believe it is not. ... Why do we say that we know more of the

111

XVIIIth dynasty than of the 1st? The answer is obviously that we have the writings of the [XVIIIth dynasty] … But do not imagine that I do not value archaeology. Bones are certainly as essential as flesh and blood. But flesh and blood are the *more* important. I cannot give up my opinion.[6]

Weigall also thought them more important, but he claimed them for the archaeologist too, and being a man of extremes, he went further and reversed Gardiner's assumption that the study was a place for the imagination at all. Certainly he would never have conceded that the tomb-paintings of Benihasan and Thebes were properly associated with the study.

The only place in which Egyptology could be studied properly, Weigall argued, was Egypt. It was his constant refrain. The land and its ancient culture were one, an obvious enough point where monuments and rock inscriptions are concerned, but he meant more than simply the remains themselves. He meant the landscape too, the people, their crafts, even their character. Or take the sun: 'Who that has not wandered in such a valley as this to watch an Egyptian sunset', he asks at one point, 'can realize what death meant to the old Egyptians?':

They joined the barque of the sun and passed like him through the regions of the night: their death was like his setting. … In western cities the sunset is usually unobserved. The light of day fades in a slow process, and the moment when the sun sinks behind the horizon passes unnoticed. But Egypt is dominated by the sun, and the moment of his setting is the affair of every man … To us was made known at that hour much about ancient Egypt that can never be made known to the professor in his western study; and the merest tourist in the land is a better scholar than he.[7]

Weigall believed the modern Egyptians to have descended in an unbroken line from the ancient Egyptians – or at least in a less broken line than, say, the modern Greeks from the ancient Greeks or the Italians from the ancient Romans. It was true of the Nubians too, he said, and he had noted it in his Report. In fact, the only thing he had really regretted about the flooding of Nubia was that it had been done before carrying out any proper research on the modern Nubians. What little he knew seemed to point to connections between modern Nubia and ancient Egypt which would now be lost to the historian for ever:

In Lower Nubia it is the custom for the husband to go to the wife's house after marriage, instead of the wife going to the husband's house as in Egypt. This is perhaps an ancient custom descended from the Pharaonic days when women were the legal owners of property … The pottery used in Lower Nubia is extremely ancient in form, and the baskets carried on the women's heads constantly call to mind the ancient Egyptian scenes … These customs are so fast dying out, and when the water is raised they will so quickly disappear … that there is very urgent need for their recording. Perhaps the most serious objection that can be made to the presence of the reservoir in Lower Nubia is that the raising of the water has led to the routing out of the inhabitants from the ancient mode of life before that life had been studied.

Notice that his reasons for regret are strictly anthropological and archaeological, not in the least humanitarian: 'It is to be hoped that just as the constructing of the dam here was urgently necessary for Egyptian agriculture, so the study of this historic people will be considered now as urgently necessary for Egyptian archaeology.'[8]

It was a favourite argument, and when he came to write about Egypt, he used it to reinforce his contention that the archaeologist on the spot had a special insight denied to the Egyptologist in his western library. For there, all around him, was the live continuation of what was depicted on the walls of the monuments:

> When the sailors cross the Nile they may often be heard singing *Ya Amuni, Ya Amuni*, "O Amon, O Amon", as though calling upon that forgotten god for assistance. At Aswan those who are about to travel far still go up to pray at the site of the traveller's shrine, which was dedicated to the gods of the cataracts ... The hair of the jackal is burnt in the presence of dying people, even of the upper classes, unknowingly to avert the jackal-god Anubis, the Lord of Death. A scarab representing the god of creation is sometimes placed in the bath of a young married woman to give virtue to the water ... The huts or shelters of dried corn stalks, so often erected in the fields, are precisely the same as those used in prehistoric days, and the archaic bunches of corn stalks, smeared with mud, which gave their form to later stone columns, are set up to this day, though their stone posterity is now in ruins ...[9]

His examples multiply: modern modifications of ancient words, widespread belief in magic, agricultural methods, wedding-rites and so on, all recognizable as survivals of ancient practices. In a charming passage he describes modern Egypt alive with its own ancient hieroglyphs:

> The letter *m*, the owl, goes hooting past. The letter *a*, the eagle, circles overhead; the sign *ur*, the wagtail, flits at the roadside, chirping at the sign *rekh*, the peewit. Along the road comes the sign *ab*, the frolicking calf; and near it is *ka*, the bull; while behind them walks the sign *fa*, a man carrying a basket on his head ... and thus that wonderful old writing ceases to be mysterious, a thing of long ago, and one realizes how natural a product of the country it was.[10]

The homebound European Egyptologist is deprived of these points of reference:

> The Egyptologist who has not resided for some time in Egypt is inclined to allow his ideas regarding the ancient customs of the land to be influenced by his unconsciously-acquired knowledge of the habits of the west ... It is of no value to science to record the life of Thutmosis III with Napoleon as our model for it, nor to

describe the daily life of the Pharaoh with the person of an English king before our mind's eye ... Avoid Egypt, and though your brains be of vast capacity ... you will yet remain an ignoramus in many ways ...[11]

Weigall's insistence on the relevance to the archaeologist of modern Egypt was exceptional then, as was its corollary, the argument against the whole idea of museums. In his view, not only did they encourage armchair scholarship and kill the imagination – 'the bird-trap, once the centre of such feathered commotion, is propped up in a glass case as 'D, 18, 432' '[12] – but they destroyed the very culture they purported to preserve:

The resident in Egypt, interested in archaeology, comes to look with a kind of horror upon museums and to feel extraordinary hostility to what may be called the museum spirit. He sees with his own eyes the half-destroyed tombs, which to the museum curator are things far off and not visualized. While the curator is blandly saying to his visitor: "See, I will now show you a beautiful fragment of sculpture from a distant and little-known Theban tomb," the white resident, with black murder in his heart, is saying: "See, I will now show you a beautiful tomb of which the best part of one wall is utterly destroyed that a fragment might be hacked out for a distant and little-known European museum."[13]

What enraged Weigall was that the legitimate functions of the museum – firstly as places for public exhibition and instruction, and secondly as 'homes for stray cats and dogs', i.e. for objects already loose on the market and without provenance – were being forgotten in the stampede to build up complete and original collections. The fact that there were strays was a misfortune, not a reason to collect, and thus encourage more strays. And for educational purposes, good facsimiles and reproductions were perfectly adequate. If authenticity is required then, of course, 'Egypt itself is the true museum for Egyptian antiquities.'

But the curator has generally the insatiable appetite of the collector. The authorities of one museum bid vigorously against those of another at the auction which constantly goes on in the shops of the dealers in antiquities. They pay huge prices for original statues, vases, or sarcophagi: prices which would procure for them the finest series of casts or facsimiles ... And what is it all for? It is not for the benefit of the general public, who could not tell the difference between a genuine antiquity and a ... reproduction ... It is almost solely for the benefit of the student or scholar who cannot, or will not, go to Egypt. Soon it comes to be the curator's pride to observe that savants are hastening to his museum to make their studies ... The archaeologist may complain that it is too expensive a matter to come to Egypt. But why, then, are not the expenses of such a journey met by the various museums? Quite a small sum will pay for a student's winter in Egypt and his journey to and from that country. Such a sum is given readily enough for the purchase of an antiquity; but surely right-minded students are a better investment than wrongly-acquired antiquities. [14]

These articles (later republished and added to for his 1911 collection *The Treasury of Ancient Egypt*) appeared in the monthly periodicals, widely read both in Britain and America. He was always meeting people in trains and boats, friends and strangers, who had seen one or other of them. They established him as something more than a picturesque travel writer: a critic as well as a romantic, opinionated and controversial as well as poetical. Museum curators in particular would have taken note – no one more so than Wallis Budge at the British Museum, whom Weigall of course never names, but whose connections with illicit dealers were notorious at the time. Lythgoe and Mace too, at the Metropolitan Museum in New York, might have raised an eyebrow.

Weigall's pieces are uneven, overlapping, and in some areas very dated now – for example, in their curious obsession with archaeology as a hygienic and muscular pursuit, chosen by healthy young men (it was always men) clothed 'in the ordinary costume of a gentleman'.[15] But even that was part of an attitude that hasn't dated, shared in one way or another by all his essays – namely that Egyptology should not be allowed to become an eccentric pursuit, a coterie subject, a backwater unrelated to matters of general human interest. The young man in gentleman's dress was really a bid for the mainstream.

Weigall wanted to cultivate a new constituency of public interest, and just as he tried to rescue the ancient Egyptians from their reputation for weirdness and mysticism, so he tried to rescue the subject from cranks and antiquarians. In fact so urgent was Weigall's sense of the relevance and essential modernity of his subject that two of the essays in *The Treasury of Ancient Egypt* argued for the importance of archaeology to modern politics. Tendentious and naive, these pages scarcely bear re-reading now, though Cromer, in a long letter of thanks for his copy, obviously thought them the most interesting things in it.[16] No doubt Weigall wanted to move the subject up the political agenda, but whatever his motive it demonstrates his instinct against introversion.

Hortense left Egypt for England in May 1908 with no very clear idea when Weigall would be able to join her. In fact they were not to see each other again until September when Weigall took his leave, and then only for seven weeks, for he had to return alone, leaving her behind in a London nursing home. From that autumn on, for about two years, there began an extraordinary period of ill health for Hortense: first an operation to remove a goitre, then, early in February 1909, a complicated and nearly fatal miscarriage, and then in the autumn and winter of the same year, an operation to investigate suspected appendicitis, followed by a rupture of the intestine. Two of these operations kept her in England during the cool season, just when she would have been in Egypt, and the miscarriage, though it began in Luxor, took her almost as inaccessibly to Cairo for two months.

Weigall pined for Hortense. He speaks of burying his head in the clothes she has left behind, of wandering about the empty rooms with a lump in his throat, and finally arranging to do as much as he can out in his district where her presence will haunt him less. But even then there were the nights, and his dreams, so that at times the loneliness was almost unbearable. Not only the loneliness, but his enforced celibacy, about which he is quite frank with her. Sitting in the shadow of a temple wall, or under the desert rocks whose inscriptions he was copying, or in a hot train trying to keep his pencil steady, he wrote letter after letter to her, straining after ways to say how desperately he missed her: 'If only I loved you calmly! – but you make me *boil* so.'

During the summer of 1908 he spent long weeks in the south of his district – at Edfu, Gebel Silsileh, Aswan and Kom Ombo – accompanied by the painter Walter Tyndale again, and by another artist, F.F. Ogilvie. While Weigall was inwardly boiling for Hortense, externally they all boiled together – at one point the temperature reached 124 degrees in the shade. Mosquitoes and sandflies made it almost impossible to sleep, and when they did, the moon – 'the beastly moon burning into one's eyes' – would wake them again. The letters are full of memories of times together, of plans for getting away, of hopes and doubts about when Maspero will let him go, and when the other Inspectors will come back from their leaves so as to release him – they covered for one another in the summers. But the strain of living on memories and fantasies of the future sometimes reached breaking point.

Weigall, a faithful correspondent himself, was exacting. He wanted her to write every day. Occasionally she lapsed. Her letters were long, but she sometimes left longish gaps between them, once as much as ten days. Passionate and lonely as he was, an interval of more than three days would plunge him into violent misery. A kind of reckless despair would overwhelm him, and there was nothing for it but to thrust her brutally from his mind: 'Your words of love which would be so dear to me in frequent letters are so much dust and ashes to me in a letter which has lain on your table unposted for all those days ... I can't tell you how I feel when I read your trivial excuses about being occupied with baby's food, or having had to go out ... reason tells me to forget and not to worry, to live my own life ... I sometimes wish to God I didn't love you so madly, Hortense.' Hortense's failing was vagueness, and it would have been perfectly possible for her to forget to post a letter she had written days before. Small comfort to Weigall, of course, but then Shepherd's Bush had its trials too, and perhaps there was some excuse for her distractedness.

It was a household of babies, mothers, grandmothers, and nurses. Weigall's sister, Geanie, gave birth to a daughter, Betty, in the July of 1908, just short of Alured's first birthday. It had been a difficult birth, and then a breast abscess had developed. She lay upstairs, fainting with pain if she was so much as carried to the window, which she was once, in order to watch the infants of the parish poor having the annual Treat that Mimi had organized for them in the garden. Meanwhile Hortense and the rest of the house were also worried about Alured, who was sickly and not eating well. Altogether, it was a large, noisy, and anxious household: two babies, two mothers, two nurses for the babies, an extra nurse from the hospital (to look after Geanie), three household servants, Geanie's husband and of course, Mimi herself and her husband, Tony.

The next year, Carrie, Hortense's mother, joined them, and the two grandmothers found themselves at variance on how to bring up children. Hortense was miserable. Her letters have not survived, but in everyone else's she figures as patient and suffering, going out to drawing lessons, not sticking to them, drifting down to breakfast at a quarter to ten instead of eight, and feeling ill. She had, early in 1909, suffered her near-fatal miscarriage, and now in the summer and autumn there were new pains, so severe that, according to the doctors, an operation was unavoidable. 'She really ought not to be worried by anything,' wrote Geanie. 'Baba [their pet name for Alured] exhausts her, and after one of his fits of crying Hortense looks like a white distracted image of despair.'

Weigall followed all this with anxious sympathy, but he could never have understood the sort of haze in which Hortense seemed to be living. He was himself an immensely vigorous and disciplined man: up early, completing his quota of pages whatever the temperature, doing his official business, going out on inspections, writing personal letters to Mimi, Geanie, Carrie and Hortense, and always seizing the stray moments, on station platforms, in trains and boats, to get on with whatever was in hand. During the summer of 1908, when Tyndale was collapsing from the heat (in the end he had to be taken to hospital), Weigall was using the early mornings to write the biography of Akhnaten he had started, and the late afternoons to ride out to the cemeteries in the desert on his tours of inspection. During the middle and hottest part of the day, while Ogilvie took a siesta, he found the energy to paint: 'I'm madly interested in it and look forward to the afternoons. I work naked of course, and simply drip in spite of its only being 95. The subject is in sandstone, and I am trying to make what Tyndale calls "a play of colour" ... and so I am treating it in browns and blues and the effect is good.'

Somewhere in the day, he also managed to fit in a gruelling regime of gymnastics to get rid of his 'bulging tum' – something he never quite conquered – ten of these (stick figures illustrating what he means) 25 of those, 40 of these, 'ending up with a 300 paced run with arms above head.' In fact, Weigall seems to have thrived in conditions that laid other men flat. Hortense, in her graciously vague, procrastinating and disorganized way, lived in an entirely different atmosphere. All the same, she always managed to win him back, for as soon as a letter from her did arrive, he was as loving as ever – if not quite by the next post, then by the one after that.

And yet, over these years, a more insidious threat to their marriage was at work. Living so much apart from her, Weigall began to create her in his imagination. Little by little he worked her up into a ministering angel. He was in many ways an iconoclast, shrewd and witty, but he was also sentimental and deeply coloured by the ideals of his time: the Empire was a force for good, for example, Motherhood was sacred. Notions such as these always lurked, particularly round Hortense. As their separations continued, the two of them were never able to get used to each other. They had no time to be ordinary. The moment always loomed when they would have to part. And such partings! she languishing in a hospital in London or Cairo, about to be operated on by grave-faced doctors, he facing the perils of southern Egypt, where a snake bite or sunstroke, or the endemic cholera could so easily strike. Gradually their love began to exist on a level with Life and Death. No wonder they sometimes misunderstood and bewildered each other. Every now and then, after they have parted, he writes apologizing for having been 'beastly'.

But no woman could live up to the image he had of Hortense. On his way back from England in 1909 he wrote:

> All during the journey to Cairo and all today I thought steadily about you darling heart ... I love you utterly, unspeakably, with all the deeps of my whole being, and I shall love you for the whole of eternity – right through death and everything else ... I feel more than I have ever felt what a truly *good* and *great* woman you are, and I feel the honour of being your husband so keenly that I could cry with it. ... If only I could be worthy of you: it makes me want worldly things, I am so filled with ambition, for your sake and at the same time I am filled with higher thoughts – you are a sort of religion to me, darling.

The nineteenth century was over, but Weigall was still carrying its baggage, and Hortense seems to have been content to have it laid at her feet. The whole thing was unreal.

What was real, though, was that just at this period, from about 1908 onwards Weigall's energies for work, for writing, for people, for travel, for sheer physical slog, reached new heights. While he craved and yearned after Hortense, he was also striking out new paths. And he was enjoying life, in spite of himself. In the same letter that he declares her to be his religion, he says 'personally I am as fit as a fiddle, and frightfully enthusiastic, and keen, and healthy and energetic. I don't know what to do to work it off.' In fact he had been working almost without stopping since the summer before. The article already mentioned on the tomb of Horemheb, another on 'The Temperament of the Ancient Egyptians' (in which he argued that the ancient Egyptians were really like the modern French, fond of dancing and wine), the piece on 'The Eastern Desert and its Interests', the *Quarterly Review* article, and a few others that were published the following year – these were only a fraction of his output. They were written partly for the pleasure of it but also, with growing urgency, for the money. He and Hortense were living beyond their means. Being ill and having babies was expensive. In two months, between the middle of June and the middle of August 1908, he started and finished his biography of Akhnaten, 50 to 60 thousand words. It was a labour of love, but he also needed the £100 down.

He wrote it, he says (only half apologetically) 'partly in the shade of rocks beside the Nile, partly at railway stations or in the train, partly amidst the ruins of ancient temples', without the benefit of 'an English study where books of reference are always at hand'.[17] Besides these, there were his official publications: a catalogue of the weights and measures in the Cairo Museum, a report on the condition of the tombs at Gurneh for the *Annales du Service des Antiquites* and, for the same publication, a report on the Temple of Redesiyeh (as Sety I's temple in the Wady Abad used to be known), and notes on the inscriptions and artefacts found throughout his district. In the intervals, he was at work on another project – his *Guide to the Antiquities of Upper Egypt*, a densely detailed and informative volume, 600 pages of small print, intended for the use of visitors to the monuments. As we shall see, it was to occupy him on and off over two years, and was finally published in 1910.

In all this formidable programme, the biography of Akhnaten was the most important and exciting to him. Though there were times during that summer of 1908 when he was heartily sick of it – along with everything else, the heat, the scorpions, the bats in the temple-roof at Edfu whose droppings fell onto their supper – he wrote it, he tells Hortense, in a happy state of 'No-conscience', during a clear lull in his other work: 'It *is* such a relief to feel like this. ... I think it is due to the fact that I have exactly reckoned out how long it will take me to finish Akhnaten, and have given myself a daily task of exactly so many pages. Except for the Guide, I have nothing else on hand, and all I had intended to do is done, or is up to date as far as I can carry it for the present.'

At last he could indulge the mood of the previous autumn, when he had written his *Blackwood's* article about Akhnaten: 'Oh for the chance of writing yet another article.' He was borne along by the thrill of having found the man (so he thought), and of having been his champion against the doubting scholars. That, and by his genuine admiration, for he held the view that Akhnaten was the prototype of Christ no less, a prophet who, alone and without example, anticipated later religions by substituting a pure and abstracted idea of the Deity for the anthropomorphic barbarities of polytheism. At the same time he was a poet whose prayers celebrated the hand of God in every flower and lamb and hatching egg-shell, and a patron of artists whose sculptures, reliefs and paintings rival those of ancient Greece. Bloodshed was not in his nature, it seemed, for his generals pleaded in vain for more troops. In short, not only was he a Christ, but a nineteenth-century Romantic, with a touch of Hamlet thrown in.

The story, as Weigall tells it, is highly sentimental: Akhnaten, the religious Teacher, the gentle, simple, loving pacifist who lost an empire and gained his soul, and who was reviled in death and finally excommunicated – his 'poor twittering shadow ... hunted and chased by the relentless magic of the men whom he had tried to reform'.[18] But as he tells it, the story doesn't end there. It hangs suspended across the centuries, until the great moment of the discovery of the tomb, so that the reader is made to feel that only now, with this last episode and its coda in Elliot Smith's laboratory (and by extension, its post-coda in Weigall's book itself) can Akhnaten's soul be laid to rest. Weigall's own involvement is thus made integral to the life, in a sense the climax of it. So much so that he even wrote the book backwards. As he explained to Hortense: 'I am working hard at the Akhnaten book ... Of course I have written the last chapters first, and have made them d'd thrilling. I can never *work up* to a climax: I like to start with it!'

He was pleased with the book, though he realized that his great theme – the identical nature of Akhnaten's religion with the Christian understanding of God – had been compromised to suit the sensitivities of his public. He admitted to Hortense that his own religious notions had wandered so far, that he could scarcely trust himself. Perhaps she would be able to tell whether he had struck the right note?

> I am anxious to know what you will think of the chapter on religion – I haven't any idea whether I am orthodox or not in my views. I take it that as Aton is in every way described like our God, and as there is no attribute of our God which is not applied to Aton, therefore Aton *is* God as we understand Him; and I speak of the Aton-worship as a sort of pre-Christian revelation ... I have been careful to speak of Christianity as having the only true conception of God, and of Aton being God *because of* its likeness to the Christian idea. But of course, in my heart I feel this attitude is simply playing to my audience, for I laugh at the very idea of Christianity being in sole possession. I had no idea how far I had strayed from the orthodox point of view: ...

Just how little it took to offend the British public at this period is illustrated by an incident that happened that summer in the temple of Kom Ombo:

> The other day, Abdu came to ask whether a girl from the village might be allowed to walk round the temple, as it was mid-summer and she thought if she walked round it then she might produce a child. So she came muffled up and was led round by her young husband, and touched the walls with her fingers at various places ... It never occurred to me to refuse the request, but Ogilvie was loud in my praises for it, and said it was so *un-English* of me!!

Apart from his treatment of religion in the book, Weigall's main worry concerned its style:

> I wish it didn't read so slightly and so easily, for no one would believe that the sentences have received such careful thought as regards their matter. The whole thing is an entirely new reading of the life, and nobody will ever realize that. It reads like a very simple story of Caesar for the young, or Martha Peddigrew's stories from History for Children; and yet I've been so d-d serious about it, and have put a lot of work into it, so that in fact I can't sleep o'nights – just as I was in Nubia after doing the report.

He was most proud of the fact that 'I've got ten times more historical facts out of the monuments than were known' – his reward for scrambling among the rocks copying inscriptions, and for researching every monument for his *Guide*.

But he didn't think people would notice that either, a fate he both lamented and courted. He deliberately wrote for the general public, keeping the whole thing 'very light', as he explained to Hortense, 'and in the style of the Blackwoods article. So I shall have it distinctly as a sketch to introduce the gent. to people.' He refused to make a parade of his learning, but at the same time he couldn't help a twinge at the thought that he wouldn't be given his due. In the event he was right, for when the book was published in 1910, he was heaped with praise of the sort he could have expected, but only occasionally did someone notice the scholarship he tried so hard to hide.

Weigall returned to Luxor from time to time during this summer – once to deal with troubles at Karnak that Maspero had asked him to sort out. It was just the kind of awkward situation that typified an Inspector's life. The French Egyptologist, Georges Legrain, was established there, much in the same way that Quibell was at Saqqara. Since 1895 he had been engaged in the enormous work of clearing, restoring and excavating the complex of temples, a task that would occupy him until his death in 1917. It was delicate work, clearing temples at that time, for it usually meant clearing people – that is to say, buying them out of and then destroying their houses, built, as they were, on top of and within the ruins. Relations between Legrain and the locals were not good. There had been a row between him and one of the Egyptian sub-Inspectors the previous autumn, when Legrain had accused him of stealing a statue. Weigall had had to intervene then, and now the local villagers were bringing an action against Legrain 'for destroying their land'. Legrain, Weigall continues in a letter to Hortense, 'of course says "it is the vengeance of the village against my honour", to translate his French phrase! – and he accuses my wakil-shek of ghaffirs of instigating it. So I am in the difficult position again of having to offend Legrain if I find the man innocent.'

In the event, the villagers dropped their charges. Weigall found that Legrain was right in supposing that the *wakil-shek* had been vengefully behind them, but wrong in the first place to insist that the man should pull down a certain wall of his house. Weigall fined the man for trying to avenge himself, but he knew it would look unfair: 'I say A was wrong to force B to do a certain thing, and B was wrong to revenge himself on A for A's wrong action!! However I had it elaborately explained to him that I had fined him for trying to revenge himself in a round about manner, instead of coming to me direct like an honest man with his complaint. But that is small comfort when your pay is docked!' Legrain and Weigall remained on good terms, but it was just the kind of thing that might have turned nasty, especially if honour was at stake.

There was someone else at Luxor at that time, who might well have been feeling frayed. Ever since his failed attempt to get reinstated at Luxor in Weigall's place and his subsequent resignation from the Antiquities Service in late 1905, Howard Carter had been picking up a living as best he could, mainly as a painter and copyist, but also possibly as a dealer in antiquities on behalf of friends who respected his knowledge and experience. Luxor was his old territory, and he was there now, in the summer of 1908, living, as Weigall wrote to Hortense, mainly with the manager of the local bank at Luxor, a man called Losco. During his bachelor months, Weigall tended to shun the house at Luxor and often took his meals at one of the hotels, usually the Winter Palace, sometimes staying on into the night, talking and occasionally making music, himself on the mandolin, with whoever could sing a song or play an instrument. Over the years he had come across Carter from time to time in these hotels, and he

Ogilvie, Dr Clark and Weigall with their instruments

mentions the fact to Hortense, rarely to say anything more than that they had talked, or that Carter had been 'cordial'. On the whole, and in spite of what both of them must always have had in mind, the picture for these years – 1906 and 1907 – is genial.

I mention this because Carter's biographer, T.G.H.James, has developed a theory that Weigall did whatever he could to thwart Carter. Working back from the disagreement that arose between them at the time of the discovery of the tomb of Tutankhamun, T.G.H.James supposes that Weigall had always been hostile to Carter, and even finds (mistakenly) the seeds of this hostility in the events of 1905 at Saqqara. Without being aware of Carter's desire to swap with Weigall in Luxor, James could not have known that Carter was more likely to be hostile to Weigall than the other way round. However, according to T.G.H.James, Weigall as Inspector deliberately withheld help from Carter when he needed work, and slighted his achievements when at last, in early 1909, he was reinstated as a professional archaeologist attached – as Ayrton had been to Davis – to Lord Carnarvon. In this way, James makes it appear that the Tutankhamun affair (which will be dealt with in its place) merely continued a personal vendetta, and had little to do with matters of principle.

It is true that when Weigall first took up his post in southern Egypt, he saw that Carter had not been an especially energetic Inspector – as distinct from archaeologist. It is also true that at a time when he was trying to persuade the dealers not to trade in stolen goods, Weigall would have looked warily at any antique collector's agent. But although his professional opinion of Carter held – as one Inspector of another – his personal feelings for him were, as we have seen, more open, variable, and at times sympathetic, than James makes out. There were times when tempers flared, but that was common among archaeologists. Early in 1908, at the time of Ayrton's outburst against Weigall at the tomb of Horemheb, Joe Lindon Smith wrote to his wife to say that 'Carter and Ayrton both seem to hate Arthur, and have absurd grievances against him.'[19] But these 'hates' came and went. A row could be followed shortly by a jolly evening at the hotel only to be followed by ructions a week later, and so on. Ayrton in fact made it up very nicely with Weigall. In 1909 he was appointed to the Archaeological Survey of Ceylon, and when Weigall wrote a letter of congratulation, Ayrton thanked him, assured him that he had forgotten all about 'our little fracas' and that they must shake hands across the water.[20] Weigall and Carter went up and down in the same way, though the following contretemps does suggest that Carter was less willing than either Ayrton or Weigall to forgive and forget.

Until now it has been unclear what exactly occurred, for only a couple of letters about the episode from Carter to Newberry have been available. They were written in the late summer of 1909, a few months after Carter had been appointed as assistant to Lord Carnarvon, who had recently taken up archaeology. T.G.H. James quotes these letters, creating the impression that somehow Carter was a victim of Weigall's spite. In one of them, Carter complains that Weigall has just written him an 'unpleasant letter', accusing him of 'negligence and acting against the interests of the Dept.', and that he has 'put a man into the M[edinet] H[abu] house. Isn't it beastly.' (The Medinet Habu house was the government house that Carter had occupied when he was Inspector, and which Maspero was now lending back to him.) Whether Carter minded more about having to share the house, or about Weigall's accusation, is not clear, but he adds that he shall have to involve Maspero, which he doesn't like to do after all his kindness to him.[21]

Weigall's correspondence now explains what it was all about. The man that he put into the Medinet Habu house was Gordon Jelf, a young assistant, just down from Oxford, who was paid for by Robert Mond to help Weigall in his work at Gurneh. The accusation against Carter was that he had re-employed for his excavations some men, in particular a certain Reis Muhammed, whom Weigall had dismissed for robbery. In a letter to Hortense, Weigall takes up the story as it unfolded one evening at the house of a friend called Cooper, where he encountered Carter as a fellow-guest:

Carter was very cordial and seemed quite content and delighted about having Jelf with him. I was therefore most surprised to hear from Jelf afterwards that Carter had said to him that he was surprised at my 'nerve' at putting another man into *his* house, etc etc, but that since it was so, and since it wasn't Jelf's fault they might be good friends, but that he would have it out with me at Cooper's that night! Having it out consisted in being extremely polite and saying he was perfectly content, which pleases me in that it shows that he is (like all of us) a barker with very little bite. You know I had written to him asking him not to employ men I had dismissed (apropos of the robbery in that tomb). He says he would like to talk this over with me when I go to Gurneh tomorrow as he thinks I have 'made a mistake'. So tomorrow I expect some heated words.

That was written on Saturday, 25 September 1909, and on the next day, Sunday, Weigall and Carter had their conference. Weigall's next letter continues:

He was very nice, and spoke of himself as being bad tempered and liverish and getting old and so on, and quite worked on my feelings. He said Carnarvon had appointed the people I had dismissed, not he, which I think is an excuse. He (Carter) saw Maspero on his way across France, and mentioned the matter, and Maspero said he would like them to employ Reis Muhammed. So now I shall have to see Maspero when he comes out, and insist on them not doing so. Carter says he is perfectly willing not to employ him if Maspero is willing too. It is very petty and it annoys me. Carter was quite nice too about the Medinet Habu house. He said that Maspero had definitely lent him the whole house, and I said Maspero had definitely told me he had lent only one half of it. So we agreed that Maspero was a wicked old man, and left it as it was, and said we'd be friends in the future. I think he really means well, and he certainly was just as nice as he could be to me.

A happy ending, one would have thought.

But a few days later, Carter wrote to Newberry, giving an account of his meeting with Weigall and of his interview with Maspero which is scarcely recognizable:

Weigall has behaved stupidly. My existence I fear will always be an irritation to him. Why I do not know for my intentions towards him have, I may say, always been to his welfare than otherwise. I shew [sic] his letter to Maspero when in Paris. He was disgusted and ever so kind. Maspero had nothing whatsoever to do with the placing of the man Jelf or rather boy (not a bad little chap) in the house here. However I have made the matter right and have now taken him in as a guest.

... I gave Weigall a good quiet talking to in regard to his insinuations and accusations and I think his private feelings were somewhat uncomfortable. I have acted and shall act friendly to him and I told him any time that he had a grievance against me to come direct and tell me before he came to any conclusions and I hope he will though I fear not.[22]

Weigall's grievance was plain enough. It had nothing to do with Carter's existence, only with his re-employment of a dismissed man. It had been expressed as directly as Carter could have wished, in fact, judging by his first complaint to Newberry, too directly for his liking. As for Maspero, a letter from him to Weigall written later, in the middle of October, does indeed advise turning a blind eye to Muhammed Reis, though it scarcely expresses 'disgust'. He says he is pleased that Weigall has 'arranged matters with Carter' and regrets that Carter 'did not use diplomacy enough in the affair, which [with a glance at the Saqqara business] was the original cause of his resignation'. On the question of the dismissed Reis, he asks whether it wouldn't be better to leave the man where he is, with Lord Carnarvon?

To begin with being occupied with Lord Carnarvon he does not roam about and try to excavate secretly on his own account. ... If you have him sent away, he will try to revenge himself on the monuments, breaking them and encouraging other people to break them. It seems to be safer to leave him at his present work: it is only for one or two years more, and when Lord Carnarvon drops him, having finished the excavations, he will of course begin to steal antiquities, but having no special motive to revenge himself, he will not think of defacing the reliefs or destroying the tombs ...

Weigall knew well that revenge was a real danger, but since the man had already committed a robbery he could not be relied on even if he were re-employed, though robbery was not as bad as defacement. On the other hand, to reinstate him would be a green light to any future transgressor, besides leaving Weigall's authority (and Maspero's) in tatters. Maspero seems not to have been completely convinced by what he was saying, for he leaves the final decision to Weigall with the assurance that 'if you think it is better to dismiss the Reis, I shall write immediately to Lord Carnarvon.'[23]

This curiously convoluted story may have been 'petty' as Weigall says, but it offers a vivid snapshot of the complications involved in excavating, and also of the peculiar personal relations among some of the archaeologists in Thebes at that time. It does seem that in this instance Carter's liver had got the better of him. Also, that Carter was not content to treat it as a professional matter between himself, Weigall and Maspero. His eagerness that Newberry should think ill of Weigall, and believe that Maspero did too, is striking.

Weigall probably never guessed that this was how the story was being represented, for he went on believing himself to be on good terms with Carter at least for that season. Certainly Carter didn't let on that he was still disgruntled. As it happened, a friend of Weigall's, Norman MacNaghten the chief of police for Upper Egypt, bought one of Carter's drawings for £30 at about this time, and, as Weigall told Hortense, 'immediately afterwards other people who had seen it came over and bought everything he [Carter] had – cleared him out. So he says he won't paint again this year! He thanked me most profusely! He and I are great friends now.' Presumably Carter's thanks were for the introduction, and there is a letter from him giving Weigall the news of the sale to MacNaghten and signing off with 'I must thank you again.'[24]

In fact it was the dislike of others for Carter rather than Weigall's own that could cause real embarrassment. For example, two months after the affair of the dismissed Reis, at Christmas in 1909, a group of friends – Howard Carter, Percy Newberry and his wife, Losco, Weigall, a Dr Clark who played the violin, and several others – all dined together at the Winter Palace Hotel. At midnight they sang songs and carols, and then 'Clark stood up in the middle and fiddled to us':

After Clark had played, Carter handed him a penny with a sour sort of face. Clark completely lost his temper and simply sliced him up, and refused to play again until he had left the room. So presently Carter went off to bed! It was quite a scene and I had to explain to Carter afterwards that I was not to be associated with the views of my guests and wished to stand apart from any quarrel. "*What* an unfortunate manner poor old Carter has," said Newberry. And that is about all there is to say. I rather like Carter myself, just now.

Howard Carter in
the wilderness

T.G.H. James's more serious accusation, that Weigall did nothing to help Carter when it was possibly within his power to do so, turns out on closer inspection to be equally frail. In fact, there are grounds for believing the reverse – that Carter's appointment in early 1909 as Lord Carnarvon's assistant, actually owed itself, directly or indirectly, to Weigall. To understand how it might have come about, one must go back a little.

It has been seen that one of Weigall's principal tenets was that a concession to excavate should never be given to an amateur without a trained archaeologist to supervise the work. The appointment of Ayrton as archaeologist for Davis was an example of the new regime that Weigall instituted in his district, and it was his constant object to ban all amateur excavations of the kind that had been normal before his arrival in Luxor. During this time, Lord Carnarvon had been visiting Egypt in the winter months, and as we have seen, Weigall had escorted him to Davis's *dahabiyeh* to see the old man's finds from the Valley of the Kings. Carnarvon soon developed an interest in Egyptian antiquities himself, and so applied for his own concession at Thebes for the 1906-07 season.

As Weigall explained later to Griffith, the editor of the Egypt Exploration Fund's archaeological reports: 'Two years ago Lord Carnarvon asked Sir William Garstin to obtain him a digging concession. Maspero having approved the application, Sir William wrote to me telling me to find him a site.' Now this was precisely the kind of concession that Weigall disapproved of, but it was an order, and to refuse Sir William Garstin, Adviser at the Public Works Department, would have meant giving offence to the last court of appeal in Weigall's often difficult dealings with Maspero. There was nothing for it but to comply, and he did it in the safest and most useful way he could, as he told Griffith:

Fearing that he might do damage to a good site ['good' meaning full of movables], I placed him on the rubbish-mounds of Shekh abd'el Gurneh, where of course he worked for a season without finding anything, though I had hoped that he might find a good painted tomb, which would have been a useful find, without much to damage in it.[25]

Carnarvon found nothing more than a mummified cat, though according to Lindon Smith who was staying with Weigall at the time, he was very excited about his cat.[26] T.G.H. James, on the other hand, suggests that Carnarvon was put out by Weigall's unfair and ungenerous choice of site for him.[27] In fact there is no sign of coolness between them. On his way back to England, Carnarvon wrote to Weigall filling him in on his negotiations with Maspero over a possible site for the following season and described their fruitless search in the Cairo Museum for a map of the Dra abul Naggah area (near Gurneh). He promises, on his return, 'to bring out a learned man as I have not time to learn up all the requisite data'.[28] In the event, Carnarvon never did bring out his 'learned man', and the conclusion of his 1907-8 season brought just the kind of disaster that Weigall had feared.

Among the things that Carnarvon uncovered during that season was a tablet – known now as the 'Carnarvon tablet' – on part of which is a text relating to the rebellion of a Theban king, Kemose, against the Hyksos, a foreign power that ruled Egypt from the north between about 1640 and 1532 BC. It was a little documented period, and the tablet was therefore important. Weigall brought photographs of it back to England in the autumn of 1908, and sent them to Griffith in Oxford. When Griffith came to work on them, he found that parts of the text had flaked off, and he wrote to Weigall to ask about the condition of the original. Weigall's answer was to tell the story of Carnarvon's concessions, ending up with the inevitable disaster:

> Towards the end of the work I had to go away, and when I returned to Luxor Lord Carnarvon had gone, leaving his antiquities in my office. There was a basket full of odds and ends amongst these, and stuffed anyhow into the mouth of the basket was this tablet, in two pieces, and I am sure this rough handling is responsible for some of the flaking. A sadder instance of the sin of allowing amateurs to dig could not be found. Lord Carnarvon does his best, and sits over his work conscientiously; but that is not enough.[29]

Griffith's reply agrees that 'the mischiefs are unavoidable. Excavations, repairs and all the rest are on the wrong principle':

> It is grievous to think the plaque may have been perfect when found. I have worked at it again since I wrote to you ... The three lines from the middle are a great loss. [There follows a rough translation of the text] ... It is the most important document we have next to the El Kab Ahmosi inscriptions ...
>
> Mace is in Oxford and Gardiner will be here for a few hours on Monday and I look forward to meeting you later.[30]

It is likely that the whole subject was discussed among all four at one time and another that autumn.

In the light of all this, it is not surprising to find Carnarvon provided with an experienced archaeologist the very next season, nor is it surprising that the man should be Howard Carter. Carter, experienced and available, was the obvious choice. T.G.H. James's theory that Weigall would have regarded the appointment as a personal slight and that Maspero would probably not have consulted him in making it, does not bear examination.

In fact Weigall had at least two meetings with Maspero in Cairo in May 1908, that is at the end of the season in which the Carnarvon tablet was found. He had just seen Hortense off on the boat train to Port Said, and he tells her in his next letter that he called on Maspero, who 'says that the inscribed tablet from Carnarvon's work is a copy of the instructions of Ptahhotep, and also a new story [the Hyksos text] which is interesting.' A few days later he tells her that he has 'had a long talk with Maspero about all sorts of things', including Maspero's plans for retiring and his wish to be succeeded by Lacau, a French philologist based in the Cairo Museum. In the context, with the damaged tablet fresh in their minds, it is difficult to believe that Weigall would not have brought up the subject of Carnarvon's future as an excavator, the desirability of an Ayrton-like assistant, and that Maspero, in confidential and wide-ranging mood, would not have canvassed with him the possible candidates.

There is in fact a piece of evidence that might possibly refer to Weigall's active recommendation of Carter. The story of the quarrel between Weigall and Carter at the time of Tutankhamun will be treated later, but there is a moment in it that is relevant here. During a lecture tour in America that Weigall gave after the discovery of the tomb, Carter attempted to place a denigratory story about Weigall in the American press. In one of Weigall's notebooks there is the draft of a letter that he wrote to Carter, in which, among other things, he reminded him that he was 'under some old obligations' to himself. There would have been no point in saying this privately and confidentially, unless he could be sure that Carter knew what he meant. Of course one cannot know for certain, but there is at least a possibility that Weigall was here referring to his influence in getting Carter his post with Carnarvon. Nothing else, at any rate, suggests itself.

But however Carter's appointment came about, the point is that the arrangement was exactly what Weigall could have wished, and one that he would have engineered if necessary. Weigall admired Carter's abilities as an excavator, and when in 1911 he wrote a confidential report on the Department of Antiquities to Dupuis, the new Adviser to the Public Works Department, he lists Carter among those whose excavations he thought were models of good practice: 'As examples of good excavation I may mention the work done by Dr Reisner for Boston, Dr Lythgoe and his party for New York, Carter for Lord Carnarvon, Quibell for our Department, Borchardt and other Germans.'[31]

There is one last point. T.G.H. James claims that Weigall, 'inspired perhaps by hostility towards Carnarvon and later Carter', was 'exceptionally ungenerous' about their work in his annual reports to the Egypt Exploration Fund.[32] This entirely misunderstands the nature of those reports. All the Inspectors sent in general summaries of their work in their areas, and referred only briefly to the excavations undertaken by archaeologists outside the department. It was up to these archaeologists to send in their own reports. Sometimes they did and sometimes they didn't, the Inspector could never be sure, but in any case it was important not to pre-empt them. We have already seen, from Weigall's experience over Horemheb, how careful Inspectors needed to be about the work of others.

In fact, Weigall's reports mention Carter and Carnarvon no more briefly than they mention anyone else, nor are his references any more 'ungenerous' than those of other Inspectors, including Carter himself when he was Inspector. A typical summary might be:

> In my inspectorate the excavations of Monsieur Clermont-Gannau and of Herr Dr Zucker at Elephantine were continued, and the latter did some work in the Kom Ombo cemeteries; M. de Morgan opened a few tombs at various places between Esneh and Sisileh; and Dr Randall-MacIver worked in Lower Nubia. You will doubtless have had special reports on these and on Dr Reisner's excavations.[33]

As for the success or otherwise of excavations, to mention the fact was not a question of compliment or denigration. Lefebvre, for example, the Inspector for Middle Egypt, signs off a report on a generally unspectacular season with the wry comment: 'That's all. I hope to give you better news next year and announce some precious discoveries.'[34] It was all par for the course.

Weigall had many faults, but vindictiveness was not one of them. Of course there were rows, but as we have seen it was almost a joke at the time how much the archaeologists 'furiously raged together', and Weigall's feelings for Carter always included a portion of professional respect.

# Chapter 11

# Maspero; the Autocrat of Thebes;
# Akhnaten's curse
# 1909

Weigall's relationship with Maspero was also more complicated than the simple one of boss and subordinate that is implied by T.G.H.James. In 1913 Weigall prepared some notes for a book of Egyptian reminiscences which he never wrote, among them some pages devoted to Maspero, with the comment on the cover, 'These are about Maspero ... but I discontinued them because I felt they were rather unkind.' By 1913

Gaston Maspero, Director-General of the Antiquities Service

the Director General, despite his high reputation as a scholar, was an embattled man, under attack from all sides as an administrator. Weigall was as fierce in his criticism as the rest, but he had no wish to hurt him personally.

For just as Carter made it difficult for people to like him, so Maspero made it difficult for people to dislike him. Joe Lindon Smith remembered him as 'full of fun … very gallant with ladies … [he] displayed the enthusiasm of a boy at each new "find" … the charm of his personality was unforgettable.'[1] Even at his most irritated, Weigall could not disagree. He wrote to Hortense on one such occasion in early 1911: 'Maspero was very sweet and very inconsequent … He certainly has the power of smoothing one down when one is ruffled, and the exerting of that power is the only obvious sign that one has made any impression on him!'

Weigall knew well enough that he was himself an irritant, the *enfant terrible* of the department. From the very beginning he had laid down principles, thrown down gauntlets, and refused to settle for a quiet life. Maspero, on the other hand was slowing down. This was his second term of office, he was nearing retirement, and his mind, as we have seen, was already on the choice of his successor. Weigall's notes on Maspero are in the form of an open letter to Macdonald, then Adviser to the Public Works Department, and he starts by describing how he himself must have seemed to the old gentleman:

Dear M,

You say in your last letter that you have heard me spoken of as the spoilt child of the Department, and that my chief is said to have treated me with greater tolerance than he showed to the other Englishmen in his service. This, however, was due to the almost pathetically eager desire on the part of Monsieur Maspero to hold me in a condition of enforced quietude. … it must have been most aggravating to him in his days of well-deserved half-speed, to be aroused by my barbarous outbursts of Anglo-Saxon energy. I know that on countless occasions I have sorely tried his inherent good-nature; and though his perfect manners have never permitted him to 'wash my head' – a term which he was constantly using to me in recounting his stern behaviour to those officials whose offences I had to bring to his notice – I know that he has hotly denounced me to others as a 'new broom', a knight-errant, and an enthusiast. I was never quite sure whether he liked me or detested me.

When Weigall wrote this Maspero probably detested him, for the knight-errant was then tilting at the entire administration of the Department, with plans for nothing less than a complete overhaul. It was a bitter fight, as we shall see, but there was still even then, a residuum of exasperated affection.

Maspero's charming letter to Weigall soon after the birth of his first son conveys something of the footing they were on:

I am afraid I am becoming too lazy: it is now some weeks I want to write to you and I postpone it from day to day for no reason except that the weather is so good and the sky so fresh that I feel not ready to do anything … First of all, how are Mrs Weigall and her baby? … I remember that when Henry (now twenty-three years of age) was born, my wife kept wondering for months how it was that he was there: from time to time she doubted whether it was not a doll of a special kind, only it cried so lustily that there was no mistaking its being a real boy. I wish we were still at that time: he has passed his last examination, and in two months' time he is going away to China. I envy you, when I think that you still have long years to keep your child with you, while we are parting from ours, for how many years I do not know.[2]

Even Maspero's business letters are rarely without some personal, even fatherly touch. Take good care, he might say, of such and such a lady when she comes to Luxor – she comes of a good family, knows everyone in Paris, and 'has a great deal to say on everything';[3] try not to close any of the tombs to tourists, even if they are being worked on – think how annoyed you'd be if you had only three days in Luxor; I myself, he says, have managed to keep all the rooms open at the Museum, even when they were being rearranged.[4] On one occasion, in December 1908, Maspero confesses himself at a loss over the competing demands of Lord Carnarvon and Petrie for the same piece of land at Thebes. He comes up with a compromise which he asks Weigall to put to them.[5] (It seems to have worked, for both Petrie and Carnarvon were excavating at Thebes that winter.) Sometimes Maspero ends with a word to say that he will discuss things later when they meet, and in fact he seems to have preferred word of mouth, possibly because archaeological matters were often too delicate for letters. Once, though, he forgets himself so far as to confide his opinion of a colleague: 'I will write to Legrain strongly … otherwise I can reprove him … in words, but autant en emporte le vent. What a fool he is!'[6]

We have seen Maspero and Weigall discussing 'all sorts of things' in Cairo. On his annual journey up the Nile, Maspero would visit his Inspectors, and there are glimpses of him playing with the Weigall children, or sitting in the Luxor garden talking expansively. Joe Lindon Smith recalls him coming to stay one winter when he and his wife were also guests of the Weigalls. The two Egyptologists, wrote Smith, 'discussed the problems of the Antiquities Service. Maspero was frank in what he said to those whose discretion he trusted, and our talks covered a wide range of subjects in the quiet evenings at the Inspector's house.'[7] In the light of all this, James's suggestion that Weigall was in some way ignored by Maspero and 'out-manoeuvred in his own parish'[8] by the Carnarvon and Carter team, seems wide of the mark.

As has been pointed out, Maspero's new arrangement for Carnarvon might have been designed to meet Weigall's wishes. With Carter's appointment, his ban on amateurs was complete. Carnarvon was now safe; Davis was being looked after by Ayrton's successor, Harold Jones, a young Welshman who had worked in Nubia with Weigall's old fellow student under Petrie, John Garstang; every other excavation was in the hands of professionals funded by government or academic institutions. Private money was necessary, but in Upper Egypt none of it went into private unsupervised excavations. In fact, Weigall in 1908-09 was so much in command of his 'parish', so determined that it should be a model of good practice, that a friend half humorously referred to him as 'the autocrat of Thebes'. Autocrat or not, his early contentious initiatives were at last bearing fruit.

Nubia too, where he had been as active as at Thebes, was no longer the neglected area that it had been on his arrival. Weigall's Nubian Report, published at the end of 1907, had been well received, as has been seen from Somers Clarke's comments. In the spring of 1908, Professor Sayce wrote to congratulate him, in particular on his elucidation of a little-known ancient Nubian people called, from the shape of their graves, the Pan-grave people: 'Your Report ... is the best thing of the kind that has ever been done. We have now got Nubian archaeology on a secure footing, and the mystery of the Pan-grave people is thereby cleared up.'[9]

Weigall's Report had not, in fact, set out to clear anything up. Apart from being a sort of emergency survey for the attention of the Aswan dam committee, it had been intended merely as a preliminary step, to suggest areas for excavation and study by other archaeologists. It had started the ball rolling, and there were now well-run excavations both north and south. Randall MacIver, director of an expedition sent by the University of Philadelphia, and Leonard Woolley (known later for his work at Ur in Mesopotamia) were excavating a large cemetery in Upper Nubia; in Lower Nubia, French, English and German archaeologists were copying temples in danger of being inundated by the raising of the Aswan dam; at the same time, the Conservateur-Restorateur of the Antiquities Service, Signor Barsanti, was repairing them and strengthening their foundations. By the end of the 1909-10 season, Weigall could report with confidence that Lower Nubia, at any rate, 'is now as well looked after as any other part of my district, instead of being the most neglected part, as it was when I was sent to report upon its general condition in 1906.'[10] As for all the inscriptions threatened by the quarrying at Aswan and Gebel Silsileh – Weigall had marked and numbered over a thousand at Aswan alone – none had been lost, and the Director General of Reservoirs had allowed him extra ghaffirs as watchmen.

Above all, Weigall's own special project, the safeguarding and recording of the mortuary chapels of the nobles in the hills of Shekh abd'el Gurneh and, a little to the north, El Assasif, was at last gathering pace. Now, with the rest of his district in good working order, he and his sub-inspector, Mahmoud Effendi Rushdy, could afford to spend more time there. A word is due to Rushdy. He was clearly an extremely capable man. Weigall always wrote admiringly of him, and in one of his later schemes for reorganization Rushdy was to become a key figure. A few of his official memos have survived, usually about repairs and estimated costs, but sometimes drawing Weigall's attention to something new or at risk. In one of a series of notes made after an inspection in the valley of the kings, he intriguingly mentions the protection of the piece of rope (now gone) by which the ancient robbers had pulled themselves out of the shaft and into the tomb of Tuthmosis IV. Another informs Weigall of a chapel at El Assassif, with 'fine inscriptions' that he has 'tried to reserve for the Department'. It can only be entered, however, from inside the house of a native, so 'I intend to pay the man one or two pound bakshish and in this way we shall have it. I think when you go to the place you will be pleased.'[11]

The situation of these mortuary chapels is extraordinary. Many of them lie among the houses of the villagers, their entrances sometimes, as here, accessible only from within the houses themselves. Weigall relates a gruesome incident that happened not long after he was appointed, in which an entire family was suffocated – each attempting to rescue the one before – by the noxious gases issuing from a tunnel they were trying to excavate from inside the house.[12] Weigall's old employer, von Bissing, once told him how in 1896 'he was led from inside a native house through underground tunnels to one chapel after another, all apparently deeply buried from the outside.'[13] It was a difficult question to decide whether chapels were safer buried or exposed, and Weigall decided that although he should not go in search of unknown buried ones, he had to expose and safeguard those known to villagers, or else they would be raided secretly.

Maspero could spare him little money, but Robert Mond, the British industrial chemist and Egyptophile, continued to be a generous contributor, among other things paying for Gordon Jelf to help Weigall at Gurneh during the 1909-10 season. By wangling 50 pounds here and 50 pounds there from other individuals and institutions, Weigall got by. The immediate need was for lockable doors. By the end of 1908 70 chapels were thus secured, compared with eight when he first arrived, and in his report to the *Annales du Service* ('A Report on the Tombs of Shek Abd'el Gurneh and el Assasif') for that year he could announce that 'there is not a single valuable tomb at Shekh abd'el Gurneh or in El Assasif which now remains open or in such a condition that the full penalties of burglary could not be applied to a native entering or damaging it.'

The love that he felt for these chapels, and his outrage at the neglect and damage they had suffered, have been described in an earlier chapter. In a draft version of a report he wrote later and never published – perhaps because it was too angry – he summed it up: 'In these mortuary chapels are preserved examples of the finest painting, the most superb sculpture, of ancient days … On the walls … are shown the habits, manners, customs, industries, arts, crafts and so forth, of the ancient inhabitants of Egypt, represented in such detail that a student who studies here for a few months learns more of old Egypt than ever his books could teach him.' And yet:

> There on the Theban hillsides, during the second half of the Nineteenth Century (a period which in Egypt itself is the disgrace of Egyptology), the chapels have been permitted to rot and decay, to be hacked to pieces by antiquity robbers, stained and spoilt by the elements, and disfigured by … the work of copyists, until less than half of what kindly Time had preserved to us is now in our possession.

It seemed to him incomprehensible that these tombs, disappearing as they were, had still not been properly studied: 'I can count on the fingers of one hand the living Egyptologists who have come to Thebes to make a real study of these amazing chapels and tombs.'[14]

There was one Egyptologist in particular that Weigall wanted to come to Thebes – his old acquaintance, Alan Gardiner, with whom he had argued over the relative merits of philology and archaeology. Weigall had been tempting him with inscriptions for some time: 'At Wady Hammamat, [he writes in January 1908] I've got several new inscriptions of secondary importance and one or two of first rate value on which I shall be awfully glad to have your opinion.'[15] He was no doubt thinking of the cartouche with the name of Queen Tiy and the two names of Akhnaten. But Gardiner was working with Randall MacIver in Upper Nubia that winter, and though Weigall suggested he come out again in the summer he was disappointed. Early the following year, 1909, Weigall proposed the summer again, this time trailing the ostraka (inscribed sherds of clay or stone) from Davis's and Petrie's previous season's excavations at Thebes, adding in a postscript, 'We might also publish together the tomb (with inscriptions) of Rames [i.e. Ramose] which I have recently cleared.'[16]

This now famous Gurneh tomb was made for Ramose, the Vizier of Egypt during the early reign of Amenophis IV (later Akhnaten) and possibly during the reign of Amenophis III. Its walls are of white limestone, sculpted and painted with unusual liveliness and grace. It was a period when the conventions had loosened, but not to the point of caricature typical of Akhnaten's later reign. The chapel was still half buried in Weigall's time, though it had been known about since 1860, and in a rare moment in his *Guide to the Antiquities of Upper Egypt*, he drops his strictly impersonal tone and reveals his own part in uncovering it: 'The present writer discovered the beautiful reliefs upon the east wall, and enclosed them in 1908, partly at the expense of the Department of Antiquities and partly at that of the Metropolitan Museum of New York, U.S.A.'[17]

But Gardiner seems to have been unwilling to risk the southern Egyptian summer for in his next letter Weigall tries to reassure him:

> Couldn't you find it in your heart to come out with me at the end of July? The worst of the summer is then over. I am not going to be strenuous at all, for my doctor tells me I have overdone ... My camp is quite comfortable and nice ... while at Aswan and Luxor the house is cool and I have the same servants as in the winter ... at Gebel Silsileh you will find much to do, and at Gurneh you must work on all the new tombs. The Ramose inscriptions are most interesting. And then there are the ostraca. You won't mind the heat: in August the water rises and it is quite bearable ... [18]

In his autobiography, *My Working Years* (1962), Gardiner says that what finally persuaded him was Weigall's blunt statement that it was no use 'smugging away over books in Berlin when the material indispensable for your studies is perishing in Egypt in double quick time.'[19] That struck home, says Gardiner, and on 9 September 1909, he joined Weigall at Luxor. Thus began one of Weigall's happiest periods in Egypt, both professionally and personally, and one that on his side too, Alan Gardiner remembered with pleasure: 'I look back on the months spent on exploring and numbering the tombs of the nobles of the Eighteenth Dynasty onwards as one of the happiest and most useful periods of my life. Weigall was a witty and charming companion ...'[20] But before coming to it, this chapter must take a diversion – almost impossible to avoid when archaeology was so mixed up with society and entertainment.

During the season of 1908–09, while the tomb of Ramose lay open waiting for Gardiner, Weigall had staying with him Joe and Corinna Lindon Smith. Joe Lindon Smith's letters home are full of news and gossip about the archaeological world at Luxor: Davis, Ayrton, von Bissing, Petrie and his 'eccentric Madame', the Carnarvons expected soon, Robert Mond also, and later various American millionaires.[21] Weigall rigged up some scaffolding in the tomb, and allowed Smith to paint one of his uncannily accurate *trompe-l'oeuil* copies of the reliefs. One of the millionaires to visit Egypt that season was J.P. Morgan, who whirled into town and then, to Smith's disgust, 'incontinently left, having seen almost none of the monuments and tombs – and none of the renowned paintings by one Smith who had a sneaking hope that the banker might see his picture of Ramose and covet it.'[22] It had to be said that the rich had their drawbacks: Robert Mond, for example, was a wonderful patron, but according to Smith, would talk everyone into a stupor.[23] He also had a tendency to splutter. Someone asked Weigall once how he would survive on one occasion, to which he replied cheerfully, 'I'll give him spit for spat.'[24]

Hortense was now back in Egypt, restored after a goitre operation in London; Weigall was working on the Gurneh tombs on his own, and so she and the Smiths decided to cross the river and camp with him. Weigall's camps, as he told Gardiner, were comfortable affairs, and were frequently swelled by friends, tourists, officials, archaeologists, passing through for a night or two. Smith remembered Ayrton and Carter among them – the latter inclined to be moody, but full of good stories. Everyone, he says, slept under the stars in 'army cots placed in a row', and used the nearby late Rameses tombs as dressing-rooms. One of these, he says, was a studio for himself, and also a study for Weigall, in which he revised his book on Akhnaten.[25]

It was at this time that the four friends hatched an idea for an entertainment. As they rambled along the paths connecting valley to valley, they came across a mysterious place gouged out of the cliffs at the far end of the Valley of the Queens. They used to visit it at night and once as they sat there, Weigall struck a match to light his pipe: 'As the flame flickered, the dark shadows fluttered like black hair in the wind, and the promontories jutted forward like great snouts and chins. An owl startled by the light half tumbled from its roost ... and went floundering into the darkness, hooting like a lost soul.'[26] At once Smith, who had had experience of mounting plays and pageants in America, exclaimed '"What a stage for a play!"' Everyone leapt at the idea. The story of Akhnaten and his excommunication by the ancient priests was in the air. What about a play, there in the open among the rocks, at night, to cancel the anathema pronounced on Akhnaten's soul?

Joe Lindon Smith many years later, and Weigall just three years later,[27] each told the story a little differently, but essentially the plan was to use the natural amphitheatre[28] in the cliffs to enact with fire and music, costumes, wigs and masks, the lifting of that curse. Hortense was to be Akhnaten himself, standing high on a crag above the stage. Smith was to be Horus, the hawk-headed god of the underworld, and Corinna, Akhnaten's mother Queen Tiy, his intercessor with the gods. Ogilvie, the painter, was to compose and play weird music on his guitar, and when he wasn't doing that he was to manage the fire effects. While Smith made the wigs and masks and the women sewed the costumes, Weigall wrote the script, which was in blank verse, and composed the invitation.

This last was a learned spoof, drawing on the papers of a late Professor Gustav Schnuppendorf, among which a copy of a demotic inscription had supposedly been found recording ancient sightings of a Pharaoh's ghost, 'accompanied by the very fearsome image of a man with the head of a bird'. Fragmentary inscriptions and translations of inscriptions found at later periods are then quoted so as to reveal when exactly and at what time of year these ghostly appearances happened, and after much astronomical figuring the invitation finally asks the recipient to be present on January 26, at 6 pm, 'to observe whatever phenomena may take place':

> Food will be provided at the usual dining hour, and since our inscriptions state that the hour of the appearance is that immediately after sunset, it is hoped that those who will be present will be able to return to their respective dwelling places about nine o'clock. As only a few persons (all experienced in Egyptological and Psychological matters) are being invited, there will be no difficulty in providing an escort for the return journey to Luxor.[29]

It was just the sort of thing to delight Maspero, a *jeu d'esprit* for the amusement of Egyptologists and potential patrons – scholars, aristocrats, and plutocrats. Furthermore, there was to be a special and unexpected guest to give the occasion a touch of glamour. The actor-manager Beerbohm Tree was visiting Thebes that year. According to Smith, Weigall met him, told him about the play, and he asked to see the script: 'When we asked him to come to the performance, he told us he would change his plans accordingly, and could he bring his manager?'[30] In short, everything promised well: the invitations were sent out, decorations arranged for the river bank and at the 'theatre', cushions especially made up in gay cloth for the audience to sit on, and the turkeys ordered for supper after the show.

But it was not to be. At the last rehearsal almost everyone was mysteriously struck down, Akhnaten and Tiy ending up as emergency cases at Cairo hospital, and the rest afflicted in some way – anything from 'flu to Ogilvie's mother's broken leg. The story quickly became legend, for everyone leapt at the notion that the players had been cursed by the ancient priests of Amon. Soon Weigall found that complete strangers seemed to know all about it: on his way back to Egypt from his summer leave that year, for example, he told Hortense that he heard someone say to his wife, '"That man Weigall is on board I see," and then he began to describe our play and how you and Corinna had got ill etc etc. Presently he turned to me and asked if I knew which was Weigall!' Incidentally, the man turned out to be Dr Derry, Elliot Smith's assistant, and his successor as Professor of Anatomy – a fascinating man, Weigall says, who knew a great deal about the reproductive organs of humans, whales, and hermaphrodites.

At Christmas 1910, a story came out in *The London Magazine* by one Lilian Theodosia Bagnall, partly based on the cursed play. She wrote to Weigall ostensibly to tell him that she was a fan of his biography of Akhnaten, but really to advertise her story, 'founded,' she said, 'on what I was assured was a true set of incidents ... told while I was in Egypt, a few weeks after the events took place ... I have embroidered on this.'[31] Weigall himself had, by then, worked the whole thing up into a set piece: my 'great stunt is to take people to the cave and tell them the story of the play – it never fails to go down,' he told Hortense.

At the time, however, it was not at all amusing. Corinna had developed an extreme case of opthalmia, and Hortense's crisis turned out to be an ectopic pregnancy from which she only narrowly escaped death. The play itself was the last thing on anyone's mind. Incidentally, it is clear from Smith's letter home to Corinna's parents, that her eye had been giving her trouble several days before the play.[32] He makes no mention of the melodramatic details that emerge in his book published so many years later – a terrific thunderstorm during the last rehearsal, and the dreams of both women about a statue of Rameses II smiting each of them with his flail. Weigall says nothing about storms or dreams. In general he was scornful of spiritualists and mysticism, though after the Curse of Tutankhamun craze in 1923 he published a couple of strange stories.

The Tutankhamun phenomenon was only the most notorious, for there had long been a fashion for Egyptian curses and mysteries. At one time Weigall had actually to take steps in his official capacity to stop tourists from worshipping the black lion-headed statue, Sekhmet, the goddess both of fertility and pestilence, at Karnak:

> It actually became the custom for English and American ladies to leave their hotels after dinner and to hasten into the presence of the goddess ... [Once], a well-known lady threw herself upon her knees before the statue, and ... cried out, "I believe, I believe!," while a friend of hers passionately kissed the stone hand and patted the somewhat ungainly feet ... a kind of ritual was mumbled by an enthusiastic gentleman; while a famous French lady of letters ... made mewing noises.[33]

The 'enthusiastic gentleman' was none other than the Inspector of Karnak himself, Georges Legrain, the 'fool' of Maspero's outburst. Two letters survive – carbon copies for Weigall's attention – sent from Maspero to Legrain listing various complaints against him and ordering him to desist from such exhibitions of showmanship.[34]

It might be said that the whole business of Egyptian archaeology in those days verged on showmanship anyway. But one had to do it in style. Carnarvon, for example, gave a huge banquet in the Hypostyle Hall at Karnak in the spring of 1909, lit both by electricity and the moon, in which the waiters were dressed as extras out of Aida. Joe Lindon Smith describes it in his book, and he mentions a particularly magical effect. He and Maspero were standing together: 'We both looked at the great court and the standing figures of Ramesses where we had recently feasted. The table had vanished, so had the chairs. There was no sign of anyone's having been there. Maspero rubbed his eyes: "An unexpected and a perfect climax!" he said.'[35]

Like a latter-day Prospero, Carnarvon knew how to carry such things off. Likewise in the case of Weigall's play, everything had been thought of to make it a charming evening. By contrast, Legrain's seances were merely ridiculous, and Maspero was not amused.

# Chapter 12

# Alan Gardiner at Gurneh;
# high life in Luxor
# 1909–1911

Gardiner's arrival at Gurneh marked more than the beginning of a scholarly collaboration. At the end of it they produced a catalogue of the tombs of the nobles, but a
catalogue is a pale expression of a friendship. Whatever Weigall was expecting in
September 1909, he found something quite unlooked for.

Sir Alan Gardiner is now known to scholars as the great Egyptological eminence of
the twentieth century, the author of hundreds of articles and dozens of books, his
*Egyptian Grammar* being perhaps the most famous. But this was not the Gardiner
Weigall knew. In 1909 he was barely 30, only a year older than Weigall, and, as Weigall
reported to Hortense 'a delightful companion ... full of beans always and quite
refreshing.' In fact they instantly recognized each other as fellow spirits: 'He is
absurdly like me in many ways, and we keep saying to each other "I wish you wouldn't
take the words out of my mouth."' The only difference between them that Weigall
felt at all keenly was that Gardiner was wealthy. Bumping along on £600 a year,
desperately dependent on writing for *Blackwoods* and the other periodicals, Weigall was
agog when he discovered just how wealthy. 'It was so funny just now,' he wrote to
Hortense, 'hearing him complaining that his shares weren't paying well this year and
that he was hard up. After pumping him I found that the trouble was that he only had
£3000 this year instead of the usual £4500. I had no idea he was so rich.'

Before starting work at Gurneh, Weigall took Gardiner to Philae to see the
German archaeologists, Junker and Koch, and on the return journey they stopped at
the ancient quarries at Gebel Silsileh. Weigall had been there before with Hortense,
and they had clambered among the rocks to see the shrines – 'their' shrines as they
had become. This time, the inundation was at its height, and the only way the two
men could get about was to swim: 'So we undressed and stepped in at the place where
we step down always to get to our shrine. Then we swam across the big crack in the
rock where we used to climb up and down, and then climbed into our two shrines,
dived out of the window of the second one ... and swam along southwards ... It was
quite delicious, and we had a rattling good lunch afterwards.'

If there was any shyness between the two it must have melted away then. They
continued on their way, and stopped a few days at El Kab, where they camped in the
tombs, Gardiner copying inscriptions and Weigall drawing scenes for the manners

and customs book he always hoped he would write one day. It was very hot, and they went about in pyjamas. In this relaxed fashion, they seem in a few days to have reached ground that the manners and customs of Edwardian society might have reserved for a while yet : 'Gardiner is really *very* nice. He is quite original in his point of view, very frank and outspoken, rather immoral I fear, and inclined to think it man's legitimate right to have "affairs".' Weigall was curiously innocent, easily startled by such things, and a little later he is relieved to be able to report that when Gardiner says 'seduction' he only means 'flirtation'. So that was all right.

Gardiner educated Weigall in other ways too, though Weigall was pleased to discover that he could be useful in his turn:

I am amazed at his knowledge of the language and of all the references to inscriptions, and he is amazed at my knowledge of the scenes on the monuments, so we want to do manners and customs together; then I find he knows so much about the lists of ancient towns, and he finds I know so much about the actual known remains of towns, so we want to do old geography together; and so on. He has lots of material but can't write; I have some ability to write, but no material. It is all great fun, and I have a new impetus for work.

A month later he finds that his knowledge of the tombs has 'increased enormously'. He was fizzing with excitement. Here was a scholar, who was also turning out to be a friend, and not only a friend but an ally. Gardiner contributed £50 that season towards lockable grills: 'We have opened all the remaining Mond tombs, and Gardiner has expropriated one family from a tomb, dug out another and discovered a third. The tombs actually numbered and safeguarded now run from 1 to 117 without a break.' Added to that, he tells Hortense, 'Gardiner ... has told me that so many of my theories about things are worth publishing.' No one from inside the Egyptological world had ever actually encouraged his enthusiasms.

But his friend had news for him. One day in camp Weigall announced that he was about to make 'a good list of tombs with the full titles of the owners in hieroglyphs, so that they would be at once identified.' Gardiner replied, '"O but that is beyond you." I simply gasped, but he went on to explain that there were only about three people in the world who *could* copy an inscription correctly, and of those, only two knew what the titles really meant, and of those two only one could fill in the lacunae, and that one was not absolutely infallible.' Scholarship, it seemed, was a mountain he could never scale, and those who could reckoned their journey in decades: 'I implore him to give me material to make readable – for he seems to like my article writing very much – he says he can't hope to publish his literary fragments for ten years or so, which means I can't hope to write on Egyptian character.'

He was dismayed, and yet he took comfort in the fact that he seemed to have a nose for history: 'I seem to have learnt from him only to unlearn everything; but curiously enough I find my judgement comes out triumphant, and what I think is so, is generally near the mark.' The fusion of imagination with scholarship, the intuitive leap from a set of given premises – it was this kind of mental audacity that had served him, he felt, in his (supposed) identification of the body of Akhnaten. It might have been at about this time, when he was regularly wandering over the hills between the Valley of the Kings and Gurneh, that he made another 'discovery' of the same kind – namely of the tomb of Amenophis I.

There is no absolutely unambiguous candidate among the royal tombs for this early Eighteenth Dynasty Pharaoh, and a few years later Carter, who had been searching for it on and off since 1904, put forward a different solution. Both men used the evidence provided by a papyrus (known as the Abbot papyrus) dating from the reign of Ramesses Xth, which gives an account of an inspection of royal tombs known to have been plundered. In the course this account the tomb of Amenophis I is said to be 120 cubits down from a high point north of the palace of 'Amenhotep of the Garden'. It all depends of course on which palace and which high point, but Carter's choice requires a good deal of gymnastic and tendentious measuring.[1] Whereas Weigall's candidate has the merit of falling in with the papyrus very plausibly.[2] It was KV 39, a well-known but never identified tomb on the slope above the southernmost end of the Valley of the Kings, and 120 cubits exactly below the high point of the village used by the workmen of the necropolis (whose special patron Amenophis was).

The tomb was never properly excavated in Weigall's day, and indeed had to wait until 1989 when John Rose started his five-year excavation of it. It appears that it was used as a staging post for royal mummies on their way to the 'royal cache' at Deir el Bahri, but nothing has been found either to link Amenophis I to the tomb, or to rule him out. Rose keeps an open mind on the matter, believing that the Abbot papyrus and the tomb's position at the head of the valley makes Amenophis 'as good a candidate as any other royal personage'.[3] In contrast, Aidan Dodson takes the view that since all the material from the tomb is of mid-Eighteenth Dynasty date, it is most probably the burial-place of members of the family of Amenophis II, whose name appears on some of its foundation deposits.[4] KV39 thus remains an enigma, though there is still a chance that, after all, Weigall was right.

Whatever Gardiner thought of him as a scholar, Weigall was reassured by the general opinion of him he felt his friend was forming. As he told Hortense: 'He leaves me with the feeling that I am a decent inspector, a decent common-sensed person, fairly sound on Egyptological things in general, uncommonly well-acquainted (as is natural) with the monuments, likely to be of use as a writer, but quite hopeless as a scientific Egyptologist as far as details of syntax etc go. ... it is something of a blow to me to find I can never be a scholar.' Given what he felt about the limitations of pure scholarship, his mortification sounds a bit trumped up. The point was, that although they saw eye to eye on matters of principle, their talents were diverse, and there was plenty left over after scholarship for each to admire in the other. For example, Weigall always had on hand drafts and plans for novels and plays. As it happens, he had just finished a play when Gardiner joined him: 'Gardiner likes it very much,' he told Hortense, 'he is a severe critic, and so I am very bucked that he classes it as "First rate".' Weigall often talks of Egyptology as 'a phase' of his mind and character. There were other 'phases' – administrative for example, or aesthetic or imaginative, and one remembers Hortense's remark about the civil war in Weigall's nature between the scientist, the administrator, and the artist.

She was right, but it was not always war. On the contrary, having other sources of inspiration was sometimes just what he needed. One morning, feeling 'sick of tombs' he decided to go on a huge walk from temple to temple – Medinet Habu, the palace of Amenophis III, and Deir el Bahri – then all over the hills between the Valley of the Queens and the Valley of the Kings and back, running much of the way, he says, so great was his feeling of elation. At last he scrambled 'up the back of Shekh abd'el Gurneh and dropped down the other side into the camp': 'It wiped away the stodge of days of tracing, and filled me with a mad desire to travel and write about travel.'

Great surges of energy and excitement like this would often come to the rescue, and during his weeks with Gardiner he would sweep his friend up in them too:

It was a lovely windy evening and we were both walking off our want to see our wives. So we scrambled about and shouted and sang in the wind and let off steam ... I wish you could see us two *fooling* about together. He is the first man I have ever been able to play the ass with. Yesterday we climbed up to the Shekh's tomb, and danced in circles in the moon round it, chanting "ticky-tick, ticky-tick, chickabee-chickabor." We generally climb hills together and then actually *chase* each other down them, as though we were aged ten. And we make the most hopeless jokes ... hysterical with laughter about it ...

Being able to fool and work and talk with Gardiner during these seasons was a lifeline for Weigall. The years from 1909 to 1911 were a turmoil of literary, archaeological, and administrative aspiration for him, of public success, private depression, and the strain of celebrity. Not only was it a relief to have a sympathetic comrade, but it steadied him to know where his real strengths and weaknesses lay.

Suddenly the past five years of work were bearing fruit – four books published in two years: *Travels in the Upper Egyptian Deserts*, *The Life and Times of Akhnaton*, *A Guide to the Antiquities of Upper Egypt* and lastly a collection of essays entitled *The Treasury of Ancient Egypt*. To his surprise, he was reviewed everywhere and at length, in the dailies and in the monthly periodicals, in the provincial press, in America, India and Australia, and in the English language Egyptian press. When the first reviews came out, he was 'utterly appalled': 'It's like suddenly finding yourself the only person talking at a dinner party. I simply *dread* the appearance of Akhnaten now ...' But he needn't have worried. On the whole the critics were favourable, sometimes even rapturous, though there were reservations too, and the response to the *Treasury* volume was altogether more mixed.

As we have seen from the coverage of his book of desert travels, when they praised him it was for his historic imagination, for his picturesque pen, and for his ability to make scholarly information interesting and alive. When they demurred it was for the excesses of those qualities: his flights of historical speculation and his high-falutin' style. As the critic of the *Times* (12 May 1910) remarked in his review of the biography of Akhnaten:

Mr Weigall would perhaps be wise to curb his exuberant fancy; there is a page of fanfaronade about Pan and the nymphs and the cedars of Lebanon, the hymns of Adonis and the rose gardens of Persia, as embodied in the dreams of the idealizing Pharaoh, that may well make the judicious grieve.

All the same, the critic was prepared – as they all were – to accept Weigall's idealizing picture of Akhnaten as a religious thinker almost indistinguishable from Christ, a pacifist even at the cost of his empire, a prophet no sooner dead than reviled in his own country. In fact the reviewers took off into flights of their own:

> The pity of it is that the sublime conception died with its founder ... Yet who can tell? ... At least the author of this singularly beautiful book – at once a reconstruction from the original sources of a scholar deeply versed in Egyptian archaeology and history and himself a partner in many discoveries, and also an eloquent and illuminating exposition of a learned subject by one who is himself an idealist gifted with insight and sympathy – has done much to set 'the world's first idealist' in his true place as the voice of God in a barren land.

This was the *Times*, but many other papers struck the same organ notes. Clearly the subject itself – a lofty soul straining after Truth – touched a contemporary nerve still vibrating to the theme of faith versus materialism. *The Irish Times* (9 April 1910), for example, underlined the book's modern relevance by opening its review with a dialogue in which someone asks a clergyman 'what would happen if anyone tried to run an Empire on Christian lines'. It is Empire Sunday, and the vicar irritably replies that he has just preached a sermon about it. But, says the other, the 'white man's burden' does not quite take account of Christ's dictum that his kingdom was not of this world. The vicar retorts that that is all Tolstoyan nonsense, and begins to dilate on the need for a strong navy. From there the reviewer moves smoothly into what he takes to be the real subject of Weigall's book: the failed experiment in Christian imperialism, and concludes on a note of high moral melancholy:

> Mr A.E.P. Weigall has ... given us a very great book on which a few people will meditate with wondering sorrow, at which a few more will raise their eyebrows in contemptuous incredulity, and of which a great number, being very eagerly occupied about the things that, according to Akhnaten, do not really matter, will never hear at all.

As for Weigall's scholarship, the *Athenaeum* (7 May 1910) makes a point of the new information contained in the book, and goes into some detail:

> [Weigall] gives a clear idea of the development of the Aten-worship as exemplified in the inscriptions in the tomb of Ra-mes [Ramose] on the one hand, and Khuenaten's [Akhnaten's] own statements on the other ... So, too, he tells us many things which can only have been discovered by a close and critical inspection of the

monuments, such as the first and last appearance of the Aten, or sun-disk upon them; the abandonment of the convention by which the queens of Egypt are repre-sented as about a third of the height of the king; the careful avoidance in Khuen-aton's spelling of the names of the gods, of any ideograms capable of bearing a doctrinal interpretation; and the changes in the doctrine itself evidenced by the introduction in its later days of the name of Ra.

But whether or not they noticed these things, the surprise was that a biography of someone so remote was possible at all. No one had attempted it before, and the very idea suddenly brought the ancient Egyptians within range. Furthermore, wrote the *Manchester Courier* (15 April 1910), in a field where, apart from the writings of Maspero and Breasted, 'the dry and unilluminating methods of archaeology have reigned supreme', Weigall's book provided 'the best of good reading.' Everyone agreed it would reach people most scholars failed to reach.

In fact the book was to have an impact far beyond anything Weigall could have imagined, for it attracted followings in circles of people of which he knew little or nothing. Spiritualists, mystics and even theosophists he had experienced in plenty; but Freud and his disciples looking for iconic historical figures on whom to demonstrate the universality of the Oedipus complex would have surprised him. As for the nudists and neo-pagans of Germany in the 1920s and 1930s, for whom the sun-worshipping, nature-loving, non-Judaeo-Christian Pharaoh was a potent totem, he would have found them both ridiculous and appalling. In *Akhenaten: History, Fantasy and ancient Egypt*, Dominic Montserrat analyses these and other culturally constructed versions of Akhenaten, and argues that the partly Syrian genealogy given by Weigall to Akhnaten (through his mother, Queen Tiy, and his paternal grandmother, Mutemua or Mutemwiya) served racist attempts to Aryanize him.[5] If so it was unwitting. Weigall's conjectures were not racial in intent – he certainly never uses the word Aryan. They were part of his search for the religious lineage of the Aten or Aton, as he spells it, which he thought might have been related to Adon or Adonis, the god of vegetation especially venerated in Syria.

In the same month as the *Life and Times of Akhnaton*, there appeared Weigall's *Guide to the Antiquities of Upper Egypt*. Here was the reason for his minute knowledge of the monuments. As he says in his preface, 'Each chapter has been written actu-ally in, or in a few cases, a stone's throw away from, the temples or tombs therein described … .there is no antiquity or ancient site, however small, here recorded which has not been personally seen or examined.' The book is crammed with infor-mation: Weigall walks and talks the tourist through every courtyard and pylon, in and out of the chambers and corridors of every tomb, describing and interpreting every inscription, relief, painting and architectural feature of note, left and right, top and bottom. It was fuller than the contemporary Baedeker and Murray, though Weigall does draw upon them, and because of his own involvement, it was more up to date with the most recent archaeological work. And of course, nowhere else were Nubia or the tombs of the nobles – not at that time on the tourist trail – so comprehensively treated.

It is still regarded as the most intensive compendium of information about the antiquities in that region, and when it came out there was virtually unanimous applause for its fullness and the plainness of the writing. As the *Egyptian Gazette* (13 May 1910) put it, Weigall 'must have been sorely tempted at times to indulge in 'tropes', as is evident from his last two books ... but he has not given way once and has written in a restrained and practical style exactly what the tourist wants to know.' This is not quite true, for the book has its moments. For example, at Kom Ombo,

> Some Egyptian temples are top-heavy, some crowded, some squat; but here the lines wonderfully combine the sense of stability with that of grace. ... one's eye is carried through doorway after doorway, to the grey altar of the sanctuary at the end; and once again one is conscious of the simple beauty of the Egyptian rectangular gateways set off against the curves of cornice and capital.[6]

The *Athenaeum* (10 September 1910) noted that it was an innovation for any of the Inspectors to produce a guide book, and the *Egyptian Gazette* (13 May 1910) wished 'the Government would transfer Mr Weigall to the Delta, which sadly needs similar treatment.' Likewise, the *Nation* (1 September 1910, New York edition) wanted the same thing done for Middle Egypt, 'particularly Assiut, Beni Hassan, Tell el-Amarna, Saqqarah, and Gizeh'. But the compliment that might privately have pleased him most, came from James Breasted, to whom the book was dedicated, and who wrote to say that apart from its being a vade mecum for the tourist, it would also prove 'a useful book of reference on the table of every Egyptologist ... a catalogue placing important documents in tombs and temples ...'[7] At last the monuments themselves had achieved the status of documents; the archaeologist was on a level with the philologist. It had been a huge labour, and one which had sometimes threatened to overwhelm him. Writing once to Hortense about arrangements for meeting, he suggests that after all they should put it off 'as I could then finish the Guide first, if I *ever* finish the beastly thing. I am so sick of it, and it is so *endless*.' Now he could bask.

But in fact his very success had a sting in its tail. The higher his reputation as a writer, the more he was forced to realize that as an employee of the Department he had reached an impasse. There was no promotion for the Chief Inspectors. As long as the Director General's post was reserved for a Frenchman, the ladder was blocked. And yet he was now in his prime, conscious of his abilities, and in need of a wider field of operations.

He began casting about. He looked at his Inspectorate, and he looked at the others. In fact, during the three summers from 1909 to 1911 he was obliged to cover Middle Egypt while Lefebvre was away, and for the last summer, when Campbell Cowan Edgar was absent from the Delta, he did the same there. Temporarily he became, in effect, the Inspector for the whole of Egypt. He found much to depress him. Weigall was by nature incapable of merely standing in. He could not help carrying the battle for administrative reform beyond his own border. The Inspector for Middle Egypt, Lefebvre, for example, was a respected scholar, a classicist and an expert on hieroglyphs. His published output was prodigious. But, as Weigall knew, such things had administrative consequences. In a letter to Hortense he describes what he found:

> I went to the Assiut tombs [in Middle Egypt] and scrambled about mountains until sunset and much enjoyed it. The tombs were filthy and full of bats, and the ghaffirs filthier and altogether "d—n Lefebvre!" say I. At Meydum the other day I found the ghaffir living in a tent made of rags and straw like a Bishari, unspeakably filthy, and I wrote at once asking for a hut to be built for him. In not a single place am I saluted. Each ghaffir bows and *kisses the hand* of the [sub-] inspector and utterly ignores me and I suppose that is what Lefebvre lets them do.

It didn't matter personally; it was a question of the status of the post itself. If the Inspectors were there to give effect to certain principles, they needed to be men of authority. By the end of these tours of duty in Middle and Lower Egypt, Weigall became convinced that the scholarly temperament was not suited to the post. What was needed was someone to make people jump and look lively.

It therefore occurred to him, in a flash of hopelessly naive logic, that everyone should be allowed to do what they did best: that Lefebvre and Edgar should be transferred to the Museum which was understaffed and where they could pursue their scholarly labours, and that he, as Chief Inspector for the whole of Egypt, should be given the opportunity to replicate the model of Upper Egypt in the Delta and Middle Egypt. It was, perhaps, a breathtaking piece of Empire-building, but he did genuinely want the chance to reform the other districts. He knew that concessions to excavate were being granted there to European amateurs and collectors and to Egyptians interested only in selling their share to the dealers. It was no use killing dragons in the south if they could take refuge further north.

Weigall floated the proposal in his confidential report to Dupuis already mentioned. He asked for no rise in salary, simply the appointment of a trained English university graduate as an assistant. And he explained his thinking:

> ..the Inspector must be known to be active and likely to appear at any moment at any place. He must work with the police, and make the fact that he is an officer of the judicial police very apparent. He must ride out to the scene of a crime well mounted and accompanied by police officers and men; he must be on friendly terms with all the Mudirs, Mamurs, Judges and so forth. The Inspectors of the Interiors [i.e. the chiefs of police] must be his friends and companions; he must be known at the ministries and acquainted with the means of getting things pushed through quickly. He must in short be an ordinary English official, just like other officials, and not an obvious scholar and recluse ... It is not the reading of hieroglyphs that is wanted in an Inspector, so much as the ability to protect those hieroglyphs; it is not a scholar that is needed, but a policeman.

The point about being seen as 'an ordinary English official' had been driven home to him by his friendship with the Inspector for the Interior in his district, Norman MacNaghten.

He soon noticed the effect. In a letter to Hortense, he describes one morning coming down blearily to breakfast after a very late night, and finding to his horror all the Luxor notables packed into the drawing room: 'The fact that the Mudir is a friend of mine ... has brought all these others, I suppose. Or it may be that I have more influence than I used to have ... partly perhaps because MacNaghten is such a friend of mine.'

Some time in 1910, MacNaghten was transferred to Assiut in Middle Egypt, and while Weigall was there covering for Lefebvre, the two men carried out just the sort of joint enterprise that Weigall had had in mind when he wrote to Dupuis. MacNaghten, the son of a clergymen, was, like Weigall, a man of reckless energy – in fact people thought him mad, as Weigall sometimes notes in his letters. They had spent the previous day together, he tells Hortense, inscription hunting in the old alabaster quarries near Assiut ('I found a nice one of Queen Aahmes Nefertari'), and the next day they went to Amarna 'where I am dragging Norman to help to find out who smashed the locks of some of our tombs, and I trust the people (and later Lefebvre) will be impressed at this pounce of an armed force on the offending village.' It was an old trick of the ghaffirs, Maspero had told him: 'Those outrages are frequent,' he wrote, '... they are perpetrated in order that we may dismiss the ghaffirs and have new ghaffirs appointed – probably the breakers of the locks.'[8]

The idea was not necessarily to catch the culprits, but at least

to make a demonstration in force ... the horses were waiting and we rode down to the river, Norman and myself, a police officer, three mounted police, three omdehs, and endless town – and antiquity – ghaffirs ... we were seven hours in the saddle altogether, so must have done at least 40 miles – right through the heat of the day. It was great fun and we did a lot of good and caused a stir that will not soon be forgotten. I find Lefebvre's men all so very slack and quite unaccustomed to working with the police at all.

Weigall was obviously itching to lick them all into shape, as he had done at Thebes.

Weigall's energy has been remarked on. There was something exorbitant about it at this period. It was more than a robust constitution – as far as that goes, he writes from time to time of a 'wobbly' heart. It was an expression of character, of enthusiasm, of a greed for life and experience. He was approaching thirty, intensely conscious of the shortness of life and of its being 'so hatefully full of interest'. He describes for example, in a letter to Hortense, an expedition he made in August 1909, again during a tour of duty in Middle Egypt, with some Egyptian sub-inspectors. One day he noticed some rocks overlooking the river in the distance and longed to go there. It was a very remote spot, and to everyone's dismay he insisted on visiting it. They were up at five the next day and after a journey of some hours by train, horse and boat they arrived : 'I had to lie to cover my shame at making them all come here; and I said I had heard of certain inscriptions on the rocks. As luck would have it I came across a huge pair of cartouches of Sety II, each twelve feet high ... Rather interesting as Sety II is not a common cartouche at all. Then I walked miles but found nothing else, but enjoyed myself thoroughly.'

After the return boat journey, they walked back as hard as they could in the noonday sun to catch the train. The horses met them half a mile from the station, so they galloped the last bit, Weigall 'simply shouting inside for the pleasure of it all'. After all, they missed the train. As his custom was, he had already written some of this letter by then, using every pause in the day's activity to put it all down, and he continued it on the platform:

> Of course, the trouble with me is that I can't look ahead, and I start out on these sort of excursions without realizing what it will mean. Today's outing – very early start; ride; hours in open boat; climb up mountain; 2 mile walk along rocks; hours in boat back; 3 mile walk at hottest time of the day; ride; 1 and a half hours wait in station – is really a serious undertaking in summer, and one would never do it if one thought; and it is only because I'm a fool that I do do it. Again, when I saw the cartouches, I went straight up the side of a house, so to speak, till I reached them; and it was only then that I realized I was on a giddy height, and then of course I was green with fright. It's the same thing that makes me lose Halma games with you: I don't see ahead. Now the trouble is I don't see back either. The past is done and the future hasn't come, and it's all *present* ... Perhaps in a way I can attribute my love of ancient times to this love of the present. I want to turn past into present for the enlargement of the present. ...

This, clearly, is the germ of that piece mentioned earlier entitled 'The Necessity of Archaeology to the Gaiety of the World', in which Weigall replaces the death-loving antiquarian of popular tradition with the life-loving archaeologist who raises the dead and cancels the passage of Time. But it is interesting to see the paradox emerging not as an elegant intellectual conceit, but as a sudden thought struck out of violent physical energy, the sweat still on it.

The irony is that he hardly needed to enlarge his present. His life had begun to fill up with people who, rather to his surprise, were suddenly finding him clubbable. Until then, he had never imagined himself fitting naturally into the male world. Now, his bachelor existence laid him open to it, and he found himself playing host to all sorts of officials passing through on their way up and down the river. 'You would laugh to see the place full of policemen – orderlies in uniform getting baths ready for the muffetisheen ... the hall table with all the tarboushes upon it! And the piano goes all day, and every room has its noise of singing and whistling.' He was drawn in spite of himself into their cheery way of life: 'My entry into the bar causes a scene of soul-stirring enthusiasm – I am shouted at by one group to come and have a drink, and by another group to come and play billiards ... I am called Old Man, and Dear Old Chap ... and altogether I seem to have reached the height of my ambition – to be a popular bar-loafer.'

Weigall could never resist working these scenes up, but sometimes they can be strangely evocative. For example, he describes taking a group of Cairo men to the Tombs of the Kings in the dark, all of them terrified that the locals would ambush them, 'none of them knowing anything about the wild and woolly Gurneh':

... so I rode ahead, and they came in a silent group a few yards behind, ready to bolt if I met "the ambush". However, when we reached the lights of [Harold] Jones's house, they cheered up and we had a merry dinner in front of the house. ... Then they sang quartettes ... singing indiscriminately "Swany river", "O dem golden slippers", "Abide with me", "Can a woman's tender care", "She sells sea shells", "Peace perfect peace", etc – all quite charming softly sung in parts.

Clubbability was one thing, but celebrity was more dangerous. Weigall's books and their wide coverage in the press were now putting him in the spotlight. He began to get fan mail, people wanted to meet him, to be shown the sites by him. He told Hortense: 'It's a good thing that Gardiner so thoroughly squashed me as regards my scholarship, for ... I am *adored* by all the old fogies, and called Doctor and Mr Inspector and Director and all sorts of things.' To Gardiner he wrote: 'I am doing dragoman [i.e. guiding] till I could weep.'[9] 'Doing dragoman' for the kinds of people confided to his official care involved him in much more than guiding, of course. He was sucked into their world, the world of the hotels, of tea and tennis and the races and dinners. Tennis, incidentally, was a revelation:

O! It's such absolute fun [he tells Hortense]. ... What I love best is to hit a ball so that it sings through the air, and my opponent has to leap into the air with hands flying to save himself! – a very uncultured and brutal sort of pleasure, I fear. I serve one ball and then simply have to sit down and *cry* with laughing ...

His letters to Hortense are full of these sudden rushes of enthusiasm and nonsense: a lecture down the tombs to a large party of Americans who insisted on addressing him as Doctor Weigall, and telling one another each other to be quiet so that they could hear – 'Now, doctor, let me recapitulate the points. Do I rightly understand that so and so ...' Sometimes the letters groan with the endless introductions to uncongenial people: 'He is said to be a snob, and she is like a camel, and his sister is cross-eyed,' he writes of one party. Occasionally there would be a curiosity: 'An *impossible* little man with painted face and eyebrows – he is very old and tries to look younger.' But more often they buzz with excitement. Paint, incidentally, was a ticklish matter for either sex: 'I went on to the Winter Palace in order to fix up a proposed trip to Edfu with Countess Contardone ... She is such a delightful woman in spite of powder and a little paint I fear. She is lady in waiting to the Queen of Italy and tells the most amusing stories of Italian court life.'

On Thursday I took the Duchess of Sutherland and Miss Gordon-Lennox ... over to Der el Medineh. They both rode their ponies astride, and looked so awfully nice. The Duchess has been a beautiful woman ... she swears rather, and is rather like Lady Carnarvon in her talk; but she is better read and is keenly interested in arts and crafts and such things. ... We lunched with the Carnarvons, and afterwards ... the Carnarvons gave a big dinner, to the Sutherlands and others, and I was flattered and made vain for the evening by being given the place of honour at the table. I *am* a ridiculous baby about that sort of thing, for although I never mind being given a back seat, I do *beam* when I'm given a front one.

As it turned out, this Duchess of Sutherland had a sister-in-law who was (he explained to Hortense) Lady Rose Weigall's niece, 'so I was admitted to her rather frigidly kept circle, and we all became on the jolliest terms at once.'

It was a tight world, but it wasn't all frigid, even among the nobs: the Countess Contardone, for example, Lord Esme Gordon Lennox and his wife, and Robin and Lady Helena Acland-Hood ('he a tall, red-haired, gentle, consumptive man ... both awfully keen'), and many others. They started out as people with letters of introduction, but they quickly became friends. Perhaps Hortense had predisposed him, but Weigall also found Americans especially fascinating, a relief after the stiff reserve of the English: 'They thrill me as English people never do. There is such a vast world of resource behind them, and you feel it's all leading somewhere, and not up against a blank wall as it is in England.'

One particularly interesting American was Theodore Roosevelt, who visited Egypt in March 1910. Weigall spent three days with him and his party, showing him the sights, and on one occasion racing horses with him in the desert. Some journalist picked up the story of the race, and Hortense sent him a cutting. Weigall was amused that Roosevelt was reported as having won, 'when *I* won easily.' But Weigall did more than show him the sights and race horses with him.

Shortly before Roosevelt's arrival in Egypt, the Egyptian Prime Minister, Boutros Pasha, a Coptic Christian appointed by Sir Eldon Gorst (Cromer's successor), had been assassinated by Moslem Nationalists. When Roosevelt arrived in Cairo after his visit to Luxor, he gave a speech to the largely Nationalist students at Cairo University in which he reproved the Nationalists for assassinating Boutros Pasha, told them that a mere constitution wouldn't necessarily give them democracy, and that they wouldn't be ready for self-rule for several generations yet. There had been high hopes among the Nationalists of this great Democrat, and Roosevelt's speech was deeply disappointing to them. In fact it is still remembered by Egyptians as a betrayal of the principles for which America was meant to stand.[10] But there is one intriguing sidelight on this story. In the letter to Hortense in which Weigall describes his race with Roosevelt, he adds this: 'Roosevelt's speech at the University, to which I was god-father, has made the greatest impression, and has caused consternation among the nationalists. I feel as proud of it as I read it as if it had been my own. And it's simply *thrilling* to read my own suggestions in it.'

Weigall, as we have seen, espoused the imperialist ideal, and although after the First World War he came to accept the right of the Egyptians to govern themselves, in 1910 he still believed in the benevolent influence of the British in Egypt. Weigall and Roosevelt clearly discussed these matters; but did Weigall really have a hand in arranging Roosevelt's appearance at the University? Did he contribute in some way to the speech? Or did Roosevelt's views simply happen to coincide with his? We shall probably never know the answers. At any rate, the two men do seem to have hit it off uncommonly well together – well enough for Weigall to venture jokes with him at J.P.

Morgan's expense. One of Roosevelt's thankyou letters (for 'the delightful days we spent in Egypt') continues a piece of nonsense Weigall had written to him, and addresses him as 'my dear "Chief" Weigall':

It is with real regret that I think of your lost opportunities, and that I might have seen you hung with beads and carrying a spear! If you see your fellow savage, Theodorum Daviz, give him my love. I think particularly good is the fact that the unfortunate Mr [Harold] Jones is believed to be preparing a tomb for Mr J.P. Morgan, with my approval ...

With hearty thanks, not only for the book [presumably the life of Akhnaten] but for your most amusing letter, and even more for the kindness you showed me when in Egypt.[11]

In the following year *The Treasury of Ancient Egypt* came out, and Roosevelt reviewed it in his periodical *The Outlook*: an 'exceedingly interesting' book, he wrote, 'truthful with the truth that comes only from insight and broadminded grasp of essential facts ... it teaches certain lessons which it is of capital importance to learn and apply.'[12] And he went on, in 1912, to deliver a lecture, 'History as Literature', to the American Historical Society, in which he mentions Weigall, alongside Breasted and Maspero, as one of the few who were able to bring history to life.[13]

But in spite of everything, by early 1911, Weigall was beginning to suffer. Hortense had been in Cairo all over the Christmas of 1910, having their second son, whom they called Denny. His letters to her become frantic scribbles, consisting mainly of his social diary, and full of apologies for not writing more often. The adulation was gratifying, but there always nagged at the back of his mind the fear that, after all, he wasn't getting anywhere:

... everybody slobbers over Akhnaton and is "honoured" to know me ... and I get surrounded by crowds of admiring females ... But though I like it in some ways, I am *never* happy, and long for the quiet of October and November and for the time to do some writing. I *never* wake up happy, but always deadly depressed and weighed down with a sort of anxiety that never leaves me ... And of course my mania all the time nowadays is the feeling that there isn't any *future* in this present job.

His sister Geanie, now separated from her husband, had come to stay early in December, while Hortense was away, bringing her two-year old daughter, Betty. She played hostess for him, dazzlingly, and seems to have raised the temperature a degree or two all round him. He told Hortense that she was 'a *profound* success and everybody is crazy about her. Geraldine certainly is extraordinarily beautiful just now, and it really is surprising how brilliant she is in keeping a crowd amused and how she becomes the *centre* of things wherever she goes.' It was a year when European monarchs and their entourages were particularly thick on the ground, and his days were spent putting them together with parties of appropriate and amusing aristocrats and plutocrats, and taking them round the sites. Day after day, night after night, never a meal at home: 'It is all really quite bewildering. *And* the flattery! – and the fuss! ... The people *clamour* to know me!!!' They also clamoured to know Geanie. His house was besieged with men-friends, 'all hanging round ... pretending they had come to see me and bringing the most rotten excuses for the visit!' It was Geanie who had leisure to write and to observe, and the diary[14] she kept of her Egyptian holiday gives us the fine detail of Weigall's whirling days.

What one realizes is that, for all the glitter, much of it was deadly dull. Like her brother, she felt exhilarated by the place, the sharp air and light and colours, and was amazed by the strange wildness of the Valley of the Kings – much wilder then, without tarmac and coaches. She was enchanted too, by spectacles such as Karnak by bonfire light: 'perfectly lovely as the fire was arranged to show only the glow and light without seeing the actual fire itself.' But while some of the people she met were cultivated and amusing, many were heavy going, and her diary often finishes off the record of some great dinner with the remark, 'The whole affair bored me terribly.' There were awful duties, like entertaining the Bishop of Tokyo and his wife and two daughters to tea – 'a most ageing affair' – and then showing them the tombs in the Valley of the Kings next day.

And there was Theodore Davis. He invited them both to dine on his *dahabiyeh*, and it was

a glorious sensation to be pulled swiftly over the dark waters on a perfect starlit night, without a sound from the crew ... one felt one were being conveyed to Cleopatra's *dahabiyeh* and that out of the night a scene of glorious splendour awaited our coming instead of which a fussy old butler dragged us on board, and his still more fussy old master bored us with lengthy discourses on the obvious ...

The diary is full of ridiculous characters – a certain Mrs Livingstone, for example, scolding her daughter: 'Now then, Aleda Livingstone, turn right round and look at the sunset, we haven't paid 5000 dollars to come all this way and have you standing with your back to the view.' Or Mr Back, the parson from Ramsgate who stood in the tomb open-mouthed, listening to Weigall and saying 'Yes yes yes I see I see I see until one felt dizzy'; or the woman – a Mrs Gordon – who was convinced that she had been cursed by a mummy in the British Museum. Apparently, she had suffered a string of calamities, among which was a shipwreck when she was said to have 'hung with her teeth in her nightie to some rocks all night': 'Last night Mr and Mrs Gordon introduced themselves ...She is tall and thin, with ... shaggy eyebrows which she darkens with soot, and rows and rows of teeth absolutely made for hanging on to rocks with.'

The European monarchs were also a hazard. Prince Rupert, the Crown Prince of Bavaria, had a slight speech impediment, and on one occasion Weigall, Geanie and the Prince were joined by Lord Carnarvon:

The Prince lisped and Lord Carnarvon spoke with no roof to his mouth or something equally curious, and neither could understand the other and they stood close together and literally wrestled with the words! While Arthur and I stood by and threw in a suggestion every now and then to help things out! The Prince ran back after saying goodbye to ask me to come to Aswan with Arthur and have lunch with him at Phylae … He gave me one of his radiant smiles and ran (he never walks) up the passage.

The King of the Belgians didn't have an impediment but he 'speaks English very badly and there were long pauses in the conversation that were very trying. The Minister with him I decided was deaf and dumb … [his] only speech was "Do you fond of hinting?"', by which they discovered he meant "hunting". The women of the Belgian party proved more congenial: the queen, the queen's sister (the Crown Princess of Bavaria, married to Prince Rupert) and her aunt, Princess Marie. Geanie thought them 'the most charmingly unaffected and simple people imaginable' and gave the queen high praise – 'dainty and small and very fascinating'. It is as well that she was small, for according to the diary Weigall took her to the Valley of the Kings and 'carried [her] up and down everywhere piggyback!' He also arranged a visit to the temple at Karnak by moonlight for them, and 'of course Arthur has absolutely won their hearts and they all love him.'

Sometimes these kinds of people could tell a good story. There was another prince, a Spanish boy who looked scarcely more than 16, who 'amused us at lunch by his open discussion of affairs in Spain':

He described going motoring with [King] Alfonso and as they were starting they heard that there was to be a demonstration of socialists and a general uprising. So the king ordered the car to be driven to the scene … "Of course we knew there might be bomb throwing, but it's really far more exciting than racing or any other form of sport, and we Spanish know no fear." So they drove right through the mob, and got out at the Church and walked through the people and went in to pray, and when they came out the whole aspect of the scene was changed and they were received with cheers without one hostile glance.

The boy fell madly in love with Geanie – as did many others. In fact, she seems to have spent much of her time 'managing' (as she put it) importunate men. Sometimes it was innocent enough, young men at dances holding her too tight and trying to bite her ear. Once, she went to a fancy dress ball at one of the hotels dressed as a Bacchante, and in the middle of dinner received a telegram from an anonymous 'Bacchus': "Even tho' your skirts are scanty / Welcome loveliest Bacchante."[15] At other times it was more frightening. Losco, for example, the local bank manager with whom Carter lodged in his wilderness years, gave her some difficulty. She and Weigall had been invited to dine:

Losco sat at the head of the table … his face rather flushed with the excitement and his eyes giving the … curious impression of being too hot … Whenever I surprised a direct look, I felt it burning through me ... After dinner he followed me out onto the little balcony and began in rather a harsh tone of voice ... "You are the sort of woman who would enjoy driving a man mad, and sit and laugh in your horrid disdainful manner, when the poor brute was breaking his heart." ... I discovered he was smarting under what he chose to call my indifference to him ... and attributed it to his "inferior position"! ... Burning desire is written all over him, and a horrible cruelty behind it all – and in spite of the fact that the man is out of the reckoning ... there is that about him which makes one sit up with a start and cry "danger" with every bone in one's body!

Losco was right. Geanie was disdainful. As a small town bank manager and a Jew (casual anti-Semitism was very common then) he was indeed 'out of the reckoning'. Carter, whom Geanie also met, suffered from the same kind of chip as Losco, and it is tempting to imagine the two of them comparing notes about the snooty Weigalls. Geanie found Carter almost as sinister, though not in the same way: 'I do so dislike Carter, his manners are so aggressive and every word he utters is veiled with thin sarcasm.'

There was another of Weigall's circle who was less easy to dismiss: Ronald Storrs. Storrs was an elaborately cultivated man, well-read, knowledgeable about music, and a collector of fine things. He had met Geanie in Cairo when she first arrived and now they were fellow-guests at another fancy dress dance: 'Storrs was like a raging lion seeking whom he might devour and quite determined to have me as his prey ... but in spite of hating the man, his force and dominating personality was a thing to fear':

He is an amazing creature – everything he does is done with the quickest and fiercest precision – To see him peel oranges is almost an indication of his character. He eats 12 oranges for breakfast and peels them with his fingers, ripping the skin off with practised skill, and dividing the fruit and spitting out the stones so swiftly that 6 oranges have disappeared before one has had time to eat *one*. Then his curious dislike to seeing a plate or knife or fork beside him is so odd and the *moment* he has finished he flings the empty dish aside. When he plays the piano he beats the heart out of his music relentlessly ... When alone in his rooms, he plays Bach in the morning *naked* ... The fancy dress dance was a fearful failure ... the hot pursuit of Ronald Storrs and his impassioned speeches, all made me *sick* ...

Perhaps because her effect on them was so extreme, Geanie seems to have found most men either ridiculous or hateful. Women on the other hand fascinated her, at least women with any sort of flair and style. The Countess Contardone, for example. They met in her hotel room 'where we sat and talked and smoked':

She wore a cherry coloured chiffon tunic over a cherry satin skirt and I think I should have cried with disappointment if she had worn any other colour. She fascinated and delighted me. She had converted a very commonplace hotel bedroom into a charming comfortable apartment with about three touches, and it gave the greatest satisfaction. She herself was complete and the atmosphere was restful, and one felt that the woman had achieved so much in life that one's interest in her never flagged. I should think there is nothing that woman hasn't done, and she knows her world backwards and words of wisdom flow from her mouth. I envy her with all my heart, because she has the enthusiasm and keen sense of enjoyment of the *right* things, and yet she has all the vanity and fastidiousness of a smart woman.

The Countess might almost have stepped out of a novel by Edith Wharton – an older Madame Olenska, perhaps, from *The Age of Innocence*.

One feels, reading the diary, that Geanie was in many ways infinitely more sophisticated than her brother. She thoroughly understood the sexual game that was being played all round her. She herself was an adept. Nothing surprised her and she knew to the last inch how to keep matters in hand. She had an affair of her own, but that was for herself and her diary. By contrast, when Weigall found himself surrounded by 'admiring females', he is thrown into a fluster of surprise, gratification and self-questioning. As with the matey men, he wants to tell someone. Unfortunately, that 'someone' was usually his wife.

Unhappily married middle-aged mothers, young girls visiting Egypt to forget their unrequited loves, even young wives, were all quite ready to flirt with him, he found, and he wrote it all down for Hortense: their little gestures of sentimentality, the half-closed eyes, hand to brow, the sighs in the darkness under the moon. He wondered whether she thought him hot-blooded, or cold-blooded, to be so flirted with and yet, he assures her, so resistant. Sometimes a known 'bad woman' would make an appearance, always beautifully dressed and well-mannered. He was surprised to find himself occasionally the object of their attentions. Again he wondered what it meant to be a 'bad woman'. Once in Cairo, someone had pointed out a well-known courtesan to him, a certain Elise, about whom it was said: ' "When a new English official comes to Cairo he has to do three things. First to meet Elise, second to join the club, and third *if he has time* to leave a card on Lord Cromer." '

Weigall, as we have seen, was curiously simple-minded about such things. He had been entirely wrapped up in Hortense – body and soul, as he would have said – and he assumed he could examine such questions in a spirit of scientific enquiry. It was easy to place Elise, just as it was to place Mimi's 'ruined' girls – about whom, incidentally, she continued to write him letters. But he was now living in a world thick with sexual innuendo about people of his own class. Weigall heard tales of Agency life in Cairo, of adultery in high places, and in conversations here and there he picked things up, often about people he knew: 'It's all rather beastly', he tells Hortense. At the same time there were others even simpler than himself – Gordon Jelf, for example, the young assistant that Robert Mond had sent him. One evening in camp, the talk turning to such things, the boy burst out saying that he couldn't imagine how civilized men could bring themselves to perform the sexual act even with their wives. Weigall was shocked at his priggishness. The whole subject, which he had thought sublime, was turning out to be altogether more tricky.

Egypt was a particularly hot spot for such an education. Like France, it was where scandalous women went to escape the unforgiving hostesses of London. The very people whose names had been paraded before the public in the divorce courts were likely to be found in the hotels of Cairo, Luxor and Aswan the following season. In January and February 1910, a certain Mrs Atherton was staying at the Winter Palace Hotel. Mrs Atherton had been divorced by her husband on the grounds of adultery, and she had recently been named as the co-respondent in another notorious divorce case. The entire *Times* reading public for 1906 and again for 1908 and 1909 had been transfixed by the case of Stirling v Stirling, and would have been minutely acquainted with Mrs Atherton's private affairs: the interconnecting bedrooms in her house, the exact position of her bathroom, the monogrammed handkerchief found under her pillow, and so on. Her treacherous French maid, Therese Dagonne, was a mine of information for the prosecution. To the delight of the spectators, she revealed that her own lover was the valet of her mistress's lover. Stirling himself was a lieutenant in the Scots Guards who had married an American actress after seeing her in an Adelphi show called *The Earl and the Girl*. Four years later, he had met the now divorced Mrs Atherton, and his wife had consoled herself with a Lord Northland of the Coldstream Guards. The two Stirlings made a dash for the divorce courts, and thus provided months of entertainment to the British public.[16]

It so happened that Mrs Atherton was acquainted with parts of Weigall's family, for she had been a friend of Lord de la Warr and his wife, who was a friend of Weigall's sister Geanie, and she also knew one of Mimi's sisters. When Weigall was introduced to her early in January 1910, she made much of this connection and fell into a tone of familiarity which completely disarmed him. She was not the 'flashy, fleshy' type, he told Hortense, but 'a charming looking woman ... tall graceful and *very* refined', and now that he was talking to her, she didn't appear to be bad at all. Could it be that she was 'a good woman with bad morals?', he suggests hopefully. She had broken the rules, yes, but she had suffered for it. Did she deserve still to be cut by everyone, by old friends, including her greatest friend, his Aunt Minnie? 'One's chivalry simply revolts ... I don't see why she should suffer unless the man can suffer too.' Wishing to make up for his aunt's pharisaical narrowness, he offered Hortense by way of compensation: 'I took the first opportunity,' he wrote, 'of saying "I do wish my wife was out [in Egypt]: she would have so enjoyed meeting you."'

When Geanie heard this, she was outraged, for while she had no patience with the social conventions, she knew a good deal about Mrs Atherton, and told Hortense that she was not fit to sit in her dustbin, let alone her drawing room. Nevertheless, Weigall argued it out with Hortense, faithfully describing his expeditions to the monuments with the beautiful Mrs Atherton, the little dinner parties to which he made a point of inviting her, and his indignation at the people who refused – Newberry, for example, who wouldn't come one evening because, he said, his wife's people would be shocked.

All this looked very different to Hortense, ill and weak after her operation that winter. Mimi saw the signs, and wrote Weigall a fierce letter:

I *never* have seen Hortense so downhearted and utterly miserable as she was all Sunday ... your letter came and she seemed very worried over it and her hand shook and she suddenly said she was so cold and so we went upstairs and I encouraged her to talk about you. You see she will never discuss you ... but she did talk to me a little and said she was 'uneasy in her mind'.

Of course old boy you know you have rather tried her by these descriptions of women and *your interest in them!!* ... I know she does not want you to think she is *jealous* but after all I don't know how she can help being so ... you out there having such a jolly time, and made so much of, and she suffering and dull – dull – ... you like to feel that you tell each other everything ... Well let it be *told* and not written, for while you are watching expressions on the face of the listener, you can quickly fill in bits, or leave them out.

... If it were me I would give you a good dressing down in one line and tell you you were not to look at another woman or girl. ...

Hortense was temperamentally incapable of giving Weigall a dressing down, and wrote him long moral disquisitions instead. Geanie on the other hand bluntly compared Mrs Atherton to Belladonna, the wicked heroine of a sensational book of that name by Robert Hitchens. Weigall compared her to Pinero's second Mrs Tanqueray. And that, in the last analysis, was the nub of it. Morality was by the by. Mrs Atherton's predicament was an interesting situation, and it pricked his curiosity about life:

I suppose it is the dramatic instinct in me. I like to *live* certain scenes; and I find myself inclined to play with fire for the purpose of learning what it is like. I want to know this person or that, because I think that person is interesting, and ... whether I *ought* to know the person is quite overlooked. ... I should revolt at anything nasty, you know, but I do enjoy rubbing shoulders with the world.

Weigall must have seemed to Hortense an infuriating mixture of artist and undergraduate: heedless of others, obstinately confident of his own immunity and full of reckless curiosity. Her letters seem to have made no difference, nor Mimi's, for he remained fatally attracted to interesting situations, and always assumed that Hortense should listen in the same spirit.

But if she couldn't quite join in, she might have taken comfort in the fact that Weigall's habit of total immersion in the present was bound to move him on to another present. It was the nature of Egypt that people passed through and it was the nature of his job that the focus was always changing. In the midst of his absorption in Mrs Atherton's case, his friend Gardiner, who had left Gurneh for the Cairo Museum in early November, came back, and Weigall joined him on the other side: 'It is extraordinary [he wrote] ... We only came over here yesterday, and I feel as though the Winter Palace Hotel did not exist, and all the crowd of people I've been with these last few days has faded quite out of mind.' It was a temperament perfectly in tune with the Egyptian landscape.

# Chapter 13

# 'Egyptologists are themselves ... the worst vandals'
## 1910–1911

Not that Weigall's life revolved solely round the twin poles of Gurneh and the Winter Palace Hotel. He might have got his district into good working order, but the price of that was eternal vigilance. The prohibition against inexpert archaeologists, for example, was never safe. Among Weigall's collection of memoranda for his (never written) book of official reminiscences, there is a note belonging to this period: 'Excavations started at Aswan by permission from M. without informing me.' One imagines the level of blood pressure behind that faint scribble. Again, during this 1910–11 season, Weigall seems to have played some part in thwarting a certain Whitaker who had applied for a concession to dig at the Palace of Amenophis III at Thebes. Weigall told Gardiner that he had explained his action to Newberry who had been expecting to work there too, and 'he agreed that Whitaker was not really very desirable as an excavator.'[1] The concession was given to Winlock of the Metropolitan Museum instead, and a little later, in a letter to Hortense, Weigall was able to report with a certain wry satisfaction that 'Whitaker and Newberry have got a concession to dig near Akhmin (Sohag) [in Middle Egypt], so will go off soon, and good riddance.' So much for Maspero and Middle Egypt.

Archaeologists on the one hand, thieves and vandals on the other, and Maspero's handling of both, were a perpetual worry. At the end of 1910 an attack was made on an important tomb at Anaybeh in Nubia, about 130 miles south of Aswan. It had belonged to a certain Pennut, Superintendent of the Temple of Horus in the reign of Ramesses VI. The walls of his tomb were painted with scenes representing exchanges of gifts between Rameses VI and Pennut, and others showing Pennut before the gods with his wife, who was a singer at the temple at Anaybeh. Weigall had described these at some length in his *Report on the Antiquities of Lower Nubia ... 1906–7*, and had warned then that 'the tomb at present stands open and an iron door must certainly be placed on it in order to protect it.'[2] Four years later, in his *Guide*, he simply repeats: 'The tomb at present stands open.'[3] Just too late to change the text, the place was vandalized.

The aftermath is instructive. Soon after, a Greek dealer in possession of all the fragments was arrested. Maspero, however, was terrified (as Weigall explained to Gardiner) that the arrest was illegal and that 'the Greek could sue us'.[4] In his notes on

Maspero, entitled 'The Gentle Art of Disobedience', Weigall continues the story, explaining that the Director then ordered Weigall to hand back the stolen fragments to the Greek. Weigall refused. Meanwhile, the Egyptians who had actually done the deed were thrown into prison. At which point, Weigall resorted to trickery. He asked the Egyptian Governor of Aswan to write to his Ministry to complain that a Greek was being rewarded for a crime for which two Egyptians were suffering. Fearing a Nationalist outcry, Maspero climbed down and 'consented to my retaining the stolen fragments and dismissing the Greek with a warning.' But Maspero had the last word: 'The fragments were never replaced in the walls. They were sent to the Cairo Museum during my absence on leave; and there I found them, a couple of years later, mixed up with all manner of other fragments from different ruins. They are now set up in the portico of the Museum as nameless objects from an unknown site.' In the circumstances, an Egyptian museum was no better than a European one; the paintings belonged in the tomb either way, he felt.

The laxity of the law, further enfeebled by Maspero's fear of using it, was one of Weigall's bitterest complaints. Again among his memoranda is a copy of a letter he wrote to one of the ministries, presumably the Ministry of Public Works, urging them to lean on the judges. It is, he wrote, 'a very serious duty of the present Govt. to hand these monuments on intact to the next generation ... I think the Ministry might do good by giving instructions that such cases should receive the closest attention of the judges ... The loss of works of art of this kind is a matter which is sufficiently ethical to demand the intervention of the law in its most subtle form.'[5] Weigall was working his way round Maspero, in despair at getting anywhere by direct approach. In fact it is during this year, 1910–1911, that he found himself seriously at a loss over the Director General.

As far back as May 1908, Maspero had been contemplating his retirement and had spoken to Weigall of Lacau as his choice of successor. Two years later, Weigall tells Hortense that the subject was being raised by 'the committee' – a body made up of Agency officials and archaeologists to which the Department of Antiquities reported – and that they had actually discussed whether an Englishman could be appointed 'by treaty with France'. Weigall's name had been mentioned, but he had been considered too young, and among the French candidates, Lefebvre was favoured. But it was all in vain. Maspero, no doubt determined to ensure Lacau's succession, hung on.

The consequences for the department of this waiting game were disastrous. Maspero, according to Weigall, was simply filling his space. In January 1911, when he was in Luxor on his annual progress through the Inspectorates, Weigall found it impossible to interest him in the work at Gurneh. 'I have seen rather little of him,' he wrote to Hortense, 'for he is *so* lazy and has only been over to the tombs of the kings with Davis, to the Palace with Winlock, and to the Temple of Sety with Barsanti [who was restoring it] – that is his three weeks' work. He says he hasn't time to see the Gurneh tombs!' A little later, in a letter to Lord Cromer thanking him for a book he had just sent him – his *Ancient and Modern Imperialism* – Weigall said that 'I can never get him to do anything while he is with me but play with my children or tell me, or them, long stories of old days. The Department is thus in a sort of coma ... such really disgraceful things happen that I was on the point of resigning on one occasion last winter, and it was only the assurance of Dupuis that something would be done that kept me from doing so.'[6]

Perhaps the occasion was when Maspero – juggling with houses as he had done with Carter and Jelf – had proposed turning Rushdy out of the government house at Gurneh, to make way for Barsanti, whose work on the Temple of Sety was nearby. 'I wrote most wildly to Maspero,' Weigall told Hortense, 'in a blind rage!', and an extract from that letter survives: 'I repeat that I cannot and will not hold myself responsible for the safety of Gurneh unless the native inspector is properly housed at Gurneh so that he may spend a great part of his time there.'[7] It wasn't Rushdy that Weigall was thinking of so much as Gurneh. Three weeks later Maspero 'gave some money to build on new rooms … for Mahmoud Eff. So *that* is all right,' he told Hortense. No doubt Dupuis lay behind the extra funds.

Apart from crucial matters of this kind, the miscellaneous pressures of the job continued. It was at this time that Somers Clarke made his remark about the archaeologists furiously raging together, though he was probably not thinking of Maspero and Weigall. Complicated quarrels were proceeding on other fronts too, and although Weigall was not a party to them, he was obliged to act as referee. They are hardly worth recalling, other than as they illustrate a society bristling with moral censoriousness. People seem to have been extraordinarily ready to call one another other brutes and bounders. There was one quarrel between the painter Walter Tyndale and a certain Semenowski, who had an agreement to take casts of the reliefs at Der el Bahri for the Chicago Museum. The Antiquities department had lent them a house for the purpose, and this together with the exact terms of their agreement caused a row that spilled over into piles of correspondence between Weigall and both parties and the painter Nicol, who seems also to have been involved. Both he and his friend Howard Carter held strong views as to who was in the right. Bearing in mind the free way in which, unknown to Weigall, his behaviour had been discussed on another occasion, there is a certain irony in his trying to see fair play on this one: 'Nicol and Carter [he told Hortense] still stick to it that Tyndale is a liar and a scoundrel, and I told them with some sharpness that it was at any rate not *perfect* justice to down a man when you hadn't heard what he'd got to say for two years.'

Then there were interdepartmental rows: the temple at Esna was at that time being dug out from under a mass of houses which had been bought up and demolished. Now the Local Land Commission was allowing the mamur of Esna to sell licences to traders to set up booths where the houses had been, thus defeating the whole object. The Ministry said that it would stop the licences only if the Antiquities department compensated the Local Land Commission for the loss of rents. Weigall objected.[8] And so it went on – encroachments, irritations, exhausting confrontations.

But against that, there was progress too: for example plans for the establishment of a museum at Aswan to house the antiquities discovered during the dam works. In the summer of 1910, Weigall explained to Hortense how he was trying to get the Finance department to build it:

with dam workmen and dam funds, as a permanent memorial of the Gov't's interest in the history of the land they've flooded. I do hope they'll see it ... It would be splendid to have a series of rooms chronologically illustrating the whole history of Lower Nubia, and masses of photos on the walls of everything found there, and all the temples there etc. And good examples of complete burials of each period in the middle of each room. ...

And he added, characteristically, that 'we should have a modern section also'. At that time Malcolm Macdonald, who later succeeded Dupuis as Advisor to the Public Works Department, was in charge of the dam works, and he wrote to Weigall assuring him that he would 'be delighted to help you all I can in founding a Museum for the Nubian Antiquities somewhere in Aswan. I will have whatever plans are required for estimating purposes drawn out and ... will ask permissions to assist you in every way with carrying out the building with the aid of men and materials from the permanent staff of the dam.'[9] It was an example of what Weigall meant when he emphasised the importance of being on good working terms with officials from other departments. The museum did get built, and Maspero for one was pleased, for the archaeologist, Cecil Firth wrote a few years later to say as much. Firth was completing his archaeological survey of Lower Nubia at the time and was staying at Aswan, working at the Museum so as 'to finish the plates for my Reports'. Maspero visited and 'liked the Museum,' wrote Firth, 'although it was not on orthodox lines. No red case linings and so on.'[10]

Nubia was always of special interest to Weigall, and he kept a careful eye on developments there. He needed to. Towards the end of 1909 the Nubian villagers displaced by the dam wanted to quarry stone to build new houses. But the rocks, as Weigall knew better than anyone, were full of inscriptions. Maspero seems to have gone ahead regardless, as a terse note implies: 'Dept. gave a map for new villages in Nubia without telling me.'[11] Another battle, and another small victory, as he tells Hortense: 'I have to go up probably [to Nubia], to give the villagers concessions for quarrying stone to build the new villages. I insisted that I and nobody else must give these concessions, as I knew the inscribed rocks etc.'

This was in October 1909, and he finally made the journey at the end of February the following year. A small steamer had been provided specially for him, and he was able to get beyond Abu Simbel and back in less than a week: 'So different from the old *dahabiyeh* journeys when it took a month to get to Abu Simbel!' Earlier days came back too when he stopped to look at Cecil Firth's excavations some 70 miles south of Aswan, at the cemeteries in the desert where the '"pan-graves" ... roused my old enthusiasm greatly.' There was nothing nostalgic about Abu Simbel, however. Barsanti, the Department's chief restorer, had been at work there, and had cleared away the drift of sand in front of the main temple 'to make a wide, level drill-ground', which you reached up a flight of steps 'with a sort of Brighton embankment on either side'. The whole place was covered in cement:

*Six tons* ... distributed over *one* of the colossi. What could sound more awful?, [he asks] and yet somehow it was just what was wanted. It is so vast that its *grandeur* was

161

the thing that appealed, not its *picturesqueness*, and now of course it looks ever so much *grander*, and it doesn't seem to matter that it looks less picturesque ... The place is unquestionably ten times more impressive, and it is impressive *because* it is clean and clear and exposed.

On his way back he stopped at Toshkeh, where a great battle had been fought 20 years before, between the Anglo-Egyptian army and Nejumi, a Mahdist Sudanese general. The place was 'covered with bones and old clothes etc': 'Behind each big rock you see a lot of cartridges and generally a skeleton, as though some Dervish had used it as a shelter while he was sniping at our men, and had finally been killed there.' Further north, at Korosko, he saw the tracks, still visible in the sand, of the carts and gun-carriages used by the army of General William Hicks, annihilated by the Mahdis in 1883.[12] Egypt's modern history lay as beguilingly preserved as its ancient remains.

In April of the following year, he repeated the journey to grant quarrying concessions, this time accompanied by Ronald Storrs, Geanie's tormentor. Weigall found him excellent company: 'very clever and interesting and unscrupulous,' he told Hortense. Their journey to Abu Simbel and back was marked by one of those baptismal bathes, like the one with Gardiner, but this time at sunset in the ruins of Philae. 'We had a most *marvellous* bathe,' he told Hortense, 'swimming all round the temples, in and out of the shrines, floating through the doorways into pillared courts, and drifting through the halls and colonnades. It *was* a sensation.' So much so that they both published accounts of it – Weigall a year later in *The Cornhill Magazine*, and Storrs 25 years later, in *Orientations*, his autobiography:

We reached the sunken colonnade just before sunset [wrote Storrs] and could not resist throwing off our clothes, diving into the Nile and coming up underneath the lintels into the dim painted shrines. The sun refracted from the green water struck up against the gods and goddesses moving along the frieze and "quivering in the waves' intenser day". The animals turned this way and that, and the merry little god Bez danced once more for joy in the birth he personified.[13]

This was the beginning of a friendship that became closer over the next few years, though time and distance separated them later.

But Weigall's love of Nubia was never as complicated and passionate as his love of Gurneh. He hankered after Gurneh. Once in the summer of 1911, when he was covering for Edgar and Lefebvre in the Delta and Middle Egypt, he made a flying visit back to Luxor. It was July, 'like a furnace,' he told Hortense, 'and I arrived feeling like nothing on earth. However I dashed straight over to Gurneh nevertheless, with Mahmoud Effendi, and rode about the tombs till 12:30 or so. ... I love that necropolis passionately, and felt awfully happy pottering around it again, and seeing the new tombs that have been expropriated.' Not even a suggestion from Maspero that he should personally excavate a promising site near the Valley of the Kings could tempt him away from Gurneh. In his E.E.F. report for 1909-10, Weigall tells of finding in 'another valley' (presumably the western valley off the main Valley of the Kings) 'a great deal of evidence ... to show that the Pharaohs of Dynasty XXI were buried there':

> I therefore offered the site to Mr Davis, who will work there this coming season. I should have liked to have conducted the work there myself, especially as Sir Gaston Maspero offered me the money to do so; but I have always felt that the work of an inspector is to inspect and to safeguard, and not to excavate.[14]

The following season, 1910–11, Gardiner was not in Egypt, so Weigall carried on at Gurneh as best he could on his own, in spite of the mad social life that was threatening to engulf him. But it was lonely work and he charged Gardiner not to forget 'to get used to the idea that you are coming here next Sept. 1st'.[15] It was not just that he was solitary – after all there were others at work in Thebes. His isolation was more fundamental. His blind rage with Maspero over Rushdy's house was a symptom of it. Whatever his reputation with the public at large, his work at Gurneh was not getting professional recognition. Admittedly, he was as exacting over Gurneh as he was as a lover, and nothing less than his own boundless enthusiasm would have pleased him. But the whole point of his work there was that it was not complete until it was put to use. Its object was inherently open-ended, an exercise in conservation, not scholarship.

His Nubian report had been the same, its purpose to point the way for others, and very soon after its publication, teams of scholars were at work, surveying, excavating, and conserving. But at Gurneh, where he was so much more closely and personally involved, this was not so. A note of desperation sounds in his news for the E.E.F. in 1909–10. After explaining what has been done to make the tombs available to scholars, he addresses them directly: 'I would remind Egyptologists that they now have at Thebes a vast collection of tomb paintings and reliefs such as has never been accessible before, and there awaits publication and classification a mass of material without a study of which no one can attempt to discuss the manners and customs of Ancient Egypt.'[16] But apart from Gardiner and Newberry (who had helped locate and identify tombs in the 1909–10 season) and Norman and Nina de Garis Davies who were copying there, there was no rush for the newly opened tombs.

Maspero had always been disappointing. He had consistently failed to produce enough money over the years for their conservation; he had been prepared to risk further vandalism by removing Rushdy from permanent residence among them; and we have seen that he omitted even to visit the tombs when he was in Luxor in January 1911. Griffith, who in the winter of 1909 coincided with Gardiner in Cairo, was also inclined to give Gurneh a miss. He was working on the ancient Nubian script, known as Meroitic, and he wrote to Weigall to arrange a meeting with him about a couple of inscriptions that Weigall had found in Lower Nubia. Towards the end of the letter, he does say that 'your work among the tombs is much praised, and I shall be glad to see it with my eyes',[17] but Gardiner told his friend that Griffith 'had half thought of skipping Luxor'. It was only Gardiner's intervention – 'I insisted on his seeing your work' – that made him change his mind.[18]

Some time later, Gardiner, in a letter written from the camp at Gurneh to his wife, Hedi, commented on Weigall's standing among his colleagues. In the course of describing their work together, he says:

> If it had not been for Weigall there would now be hardly a decent picture to look at on the tomb-walls; and even [de Garis] Davies, on the spot and with the clear evidence of all this before his eyes, does not possess the big mindedness to recognize what Weigall has done and how culpable many of our Egyptologists have been and still are. ... If only I were one of those men who can impart a little of their enthusiasm to others, who can thrill, and awake a response in lethargic imaginations. Weigall can do this, but the pedants simply shut their ears and say he is no scholar ... .[19]

The cruel irony is that it was probably precisely because Weigall had put his efforts into awakening the imagination, rather than into writing books of pure scholarship, that his colleagues felt free to ignore him. Once identified as a popular writer he could be comfortably overlooked, even, for example, on so gritty a subject as weights and measures. As Weigall explained to Gardiner:

> [Borchardt] told me he was working a good deal on weights, so I asked him how he liked my paper on them in the Catalogue. He replied saying he had not read it but that he supposed Griffith's notes in the P.S.B.A. still remained the only important literature on the subject. I restrained myself manfully, though my hand was on my hip pocket, and answered that I quite agreed. So much for *one* bit of hard work![20]

He could put a brave face on it, and perhaps, after all, he did not mind all that much about weights. But it left him feeling all the more sensitive and embattled on matters that were closer to his heart.

It is perhaps this that explains his brittleness under criticism from Gardiner – not criticism of his scholarship, for he had become quite humble about that – but of the application of his principles. During the summer of 1911, while Weigall was working all over Egypt in all three districts, Gardiner wrote to him about a conversation he had had with Norman de Garis Davies. Gardiner clearly knew Weigall's passionate nature well enough by then, for he opens cautiously:

> Now don't be angry if I report to you frankly what Davies said to me; you know how apt he is to depreciate, a habit of his which it would be petty of you to treat too seriously. He seems to deprecate your digging out so many Theban tombs without proper European supervision that the fragments are carefully preserved. Of course heaps of fragments always do fall from the walls, and I do think it possible that in your zeal for conservation you may be overreaching yourself a little. Remember that the conclusion we came to was that it was very desirable to dig up and protect tombs that have been known to Egyptologists and are known to the natives; it is quite a different matter with tombs that have not been known

hitherto ... I am sure you will not take offence at my betraying a fear which I think may have some slight foundation.[21]

But Weigall did take offence. He was quite ready to admit that, without a Gordon Jelf to help him (Mond funded Jelf for one season only) he had to rely heavily on Rushdy – but Rushdy, he wrote, was 'an honest and capable man'. He also agreed that fragments did fall loose, and that they were liable therefore to be stolen: 'Though I can honestly say that I don't think they are, and I have certainly never heard the faintest rumour of a single piece being lost.' What he really took exception to was the suggestion that he dug out new, that is to say previously unknown, tombs:

I have *never* opened a tomb for the sake of opening one. I have cleared out and safeguarded *only* those which in my opinion were in danger. ... Remember this always: tombs that are *buried* are in far greater danger than tombs that are not ... For example, the tomb of the gardener which you saw in 1901, under Newberry's old house, was buried under two metres of rubbish. When I dug it out it was much damaged by robbers, who had got in God knows how.

Having disposed of that question he returns to the other, of whether or not to act at all in the absence of a European assistant: 'It makes me smile to hear this criticism of Davies's offered as though it were something I had overlooked. Why, man, I have given it – the whole question – the most serious and eager thought, and I have decided that there is only one thing to do, namely to safeguard every tomb of which the natives have any inkling, and to do the work as rapidly as possible and with whatever staff I have at my disposal, however bad.'

He had lived with 'the whole question', with the ethics of archaeology for so long, he had fought for it against his own and other departments, he had written about it, made enemies over it, laid his job on the line for it – suddenly, one realizes that Gardiner's mild reproach has dropped into a boiling pot of bitterness and frustration: 'I have fits of extreme depression about our work; and there are times when the *daily* struggle with Maspero and others on matters of principle get[s] on my nerves to such an extent that I don't know what to do. It sometimes seems to me that my work becomes nothing more than a sort of unlistened-to *teaching* all the time.'

The other day, he says, the German philologist Spiegelberg actually 'patted me on the back, and said he was *surprised* and glad to find such views held by me (on some small matter we had talked about)'; and now he, Gardiner, was reminding him of 'an *elementary* rule (i.e. not to dig out tombs while others remain to be protected with the money).' It was too much: '*When* will you all understand that, though an ass and though no scholar, my views, my principles, my doctrines, are *sound*':

All this may sound very conceited and all that; but you must remember that since you were here I have for two years fought and fought and struggled and struggled to uphold the morals of our work, *daily* giving my judgement and opinion on some matter of principle, and never backed up or helped. And thus principles have come to be the one thing I stand for and represent. I have no other *raison d'être*. Well I must stop this bosh and go and bathe. All the best and good wishes to you old chap ...[22]

Of course there was something absurd about this outburst, as Gardiner gently pointed out in his reply. All he meant, said Gardiner, was that it would help to have another Jelf, in fact he knows of a schoolmaster who wants to go to Egypt for his rheumatism, couldn't Mond be persuaded? 'Anyhow don't fret your soul over any remarks I may make. ... It's very irritating but doesn't matter much.'[23] But Gardiner was speaking from the calm heights of philological endeavour – from Hampshire what's more – not from the long hot conflict on the ground. He couldn't have guessed just how much it did matter, nor how great a load of frustration he had triggered. He was sympathetic, but the iron had not really entered his soul. Over the last year, Gardiner says, he has had news that 'has been more than depressing': 'O how I wish one could effect something to prevent the utter destruction that is going on everywhere. I am growing more and more convinced that Egyptologists are themselves for the most part the worst vandals ... the trouble is that small fry like myself can do so little to prevent damage done by our many-initialled Professors!'[24] But Weigall couldn't throw up his hands like that. He had defined himself professionally as part of the fray. His whole function was to do battle against vandals, many-initialled or not, and there was no refuge from it in the quiet of academia for him.

In his E.E.F. news for 1910–11, Weigall promised a report on the tombs at Gurneh, adding a plea: 'I beg your readers to look at [it] ... in order to realize the immense value of these Theban mortuary chapels ...'[25] But although he wrote a draft, he never published this report. The Introduction to the catalogue which came out in 1913 was written by Gardiner, and is quite different in conception. In fact Weigall's draft shows that he was embarked on something more ambitious than a report. Though he wrote, as so often, in the heat of passion, he was nevertheless trying to do two serious things: firstly, to examine the pathology of scholars, and secondly to offer an apologia for the principles of conservation and stewardship. The substance of this second theme, with glancing hints at the first, did, in fact, appear as part of a periodical article entitled 'The Morality of Excavation', in the summer of 1912, reprinted and enlarged in 1923 for a collection of his essays, *The Glory of the Pharaohs*. But the whole subject was too charged and dangerous for a formal report. Either he lost heart, or else he forced himself to hold his tongue (rather as he did over his notes on Maspero).

We have seen how furiously he deplored the neglect and destruction of these tombs over the years. It depressed him profoundly. When he came to writing his draft, he was unable to describe the calamity without laying the blame, and unable to exclude from that blame a large portion of contemporary Egyptologists. He doesn't actually name them, but those who had actually worked on the tombs, taking notes, making copies, publishing, even cleaning and conserving a few here and there, would have recognized themselves – Carter, for example, Newberry, and as the man in overall charge, Maspero himself. It was the absence of any systematic programme, anything matching the scale of the problem, that so scandalized Weigall. The fact that he, with help from Gardiner, Rushdy and Jelf, had squeaked in on private money, in the nick of time, before total destruction, could not redeem the others from not having done it long before.

At the heart of his argument lies a critique of the whole ethos of scholarly appropriation. The real explanation for the calamity, he says, is selfishness, an assumption that a tomb 'belongs' to its discoverer in some sense. This assumption is particularly dangerous because it is apt to slip into the further notion that the records made in a tomb by its discoverer take priority not only over the records of others, but over the thing itself. In this way the monument is rendered virtually superfluous – its value transferred from the original to the derived version.

> When an Egyptologist has made considerable notes and copies in some one ruin, he comes to feel that the monument is to some extent his own property. He, perhaps has discovered it; he knows every inch of it; he has theories about it. And should another savant now walk into the place and also evolve theories ... the former scholar feels that it is something of an intrusion ... Now this instinct is to a large extent the cause of the mischief. The first instinct of the Egyptologist should lead him ... to realize that he shares it with all the world, present and future. It should be his primary desire ... to throw it open to all scholars, safeguarded and protected.

He almost apologizes for saying anything so elementary, and yet the record is there:

> Most of the scholars ... who have worked at Thebes in the past considered it necessary only to make their notes, drawings, tracings, copies, and so forth, for their own use, retaining the while a firm hand on their personal right to certain monuments. ... I do not hesitate to say that before a single note was made, steps should have been taken to protect the ruin for the benefit of those who should come after. ...
>
> Did they not understand that their duty lay not so much in filling their perishable notebooks with fascinating notes, as in handing on intact to a better equipped generation the monuments which it is evident that they so much appreciated? ... The selfishness of their work is past belief. ...

A few of the chapels have been beautifully cleared and cleaned, restored and safeguarded, he says, but the very completeness and exquisiteness in those cases (and he mentions Newberry's tomb of Rekhmara, though without naming Newberry) have been at the expense of all the others. Until all of them are at least safe, he argues, it is frivolous to use the limited money available on cleaning every nook and corner of one or two.

Another related reason for the catastrophe, he says, is the desire to possess more, and to be the first on virgin ground:

> Some people are disturbed by a very passion to make new "finds" ... This is a very useful tendency in its rightful place, but ... in general it is wrong to unearth new

monuments or antiquities until those already uncovered are studied and safe-guarded. ... I cannot help feeling that this tendency ... is due to a kind of selfish-ness, a sort of grabbing at the plums.

Having thus analysed the scholar's psychology, he allows his own experience to enter the argument:

> I do not set forth a doctrine that is ideal. I myself (with many a pang, it is true) have thrown open to scholars every monument which I have discovered, retaining abso-lutely no personal rights whatsoever. ... many new and important discoveries have been made; new reliefs and paintings have been exposed; new material of a fasci-nating nature has been brought to light almost every day. ... I have forced myself to invite archaeologists to consider every monument ... as the property of the scien-tific world, unencumbered by reservations or private rights of any kind whatsoever.

Much later, in 1922, when the tomb of Tutankhamun was discovered, and Carnarvon sold 'his' rights to information about the tomb to the *Times* newspaper, Weigall was forcibly reminded of his old arguments. He published then, and was damned. Perhaps in 1911 he instinctively expected no less, and recoiled.

Weigall was composing this draft at roughly the same time as he was writing his confidential report on the Antiquities Department for Dupuis. The two documents were intimately connected in his mind, for they both concerned the collective failure of scholars and administrators, past and present, to establish the practice of archae-ology in general (rather than in particular instances) on any formal basis of principle. Of course there were exceptions, and he names them to Dupuis, but no one had yet succeeded in turning the best practice into the officially required norm. As we have seen, he saw conservation as paramount – no monuments, no archaeology. But other principles – record-keeping, law enforcement, the retention of antiquities within the host country – followed close behind. He was not, of course, the first to formulate these principles. Petrie had outlined many of them long before in his *Aims and Methods of Archaeology*. Many people had deplored the destruction of the monuments, and their export to other countries. The origin of the Antiquities Department itself, and the founding of the museum in Cairo, owed themselves to Mariette's resolution to put an end to such depredations. But after Mariette, Weigall was the first to dedicate himself professionally to campaigning for what others simply articulated.

Now, in the summer of 1911, he was in a position to see the story of Gurneh repeated on every side. The excavations of European adventurers and native dealers amounted to 'nothing more nor less than legalized plundering':[26]

> The worst case of this occurred lately at Assiut [in Middle Egypt]. A native named Said Bey obtained a permit to excavate from our Department ... Ahmed Bey Kamal, an old Egyptian employee at the Museum, half blind and not having a rudimentary knowledge of scientific methods, was told to go and look after him. Magnificent antiquities were found, and Ahmed Bey was allowed to make the

division himself with Said Bey who was to sell his half [the other half going to the Museum], which at least put a grave temptation in the way of both men to make a deal with the balance on the side of the originator of the scheme. Said Bey's share of the spoil was sold for hundreds of pounds. One statue alone fetched £300. No record was made of the work, but as a sop to the archaeologists a brief catalogue of the antiquities was drawn up – of no use to anybody. This really scandalous piece of work was authorized by our Director General. ...

Weigall continues the tale of incompetence with chapter and verse, winding up with the final outrage that antiquities of prime importance were being allowed to leave the country: 'The worst case of this was allowing the Boston Museum to take the magnificent statue of Menkaura out of the country without it even being looked at. This case I believe was brought to the attention of Sir Eldon Gorst.'[27]

The remedy he proposed to Dupuis has been described in the previous chapter. Nothing came of it. Maspero would certainly have squashed the idea of an Egypt-wide Inspectorate, realizing that such a post could become a stepping-stone to his own. But Weigall's work in the Delta, in place of Edgar that summer, had brought him into much closer contact with the Advisors and with the workings of government in Cairo. A whole new perspective had opened up for him; he was able to gauge how matters stood between the Antiquities Department and the other Ministries, to get a better feel for the lines of power and influence, and to try out how far it was possible to push for reforms in spite of Maspero. As he explains to Gardiner:

Maspero becomes more and more impossible scientifically, and I have now taken to dealing direct with the ministers more or less behind his back; but it is a dangerous game, and though I get things done a good deal, I fear I incur his displeasure. The Govt. is well aware that things are not going right, and have told me so very plainly, and (this is very private) my views were asked and given on the question of who should be allowed to excavate and who not.[28]

Although the ministries were more receptive to him than his own department, he knew that they all, in the end, had to come to terms with Maspero and the claims of the French. And behind Maspero there lay another dimension still: the political masters of the ministers. We have seen Weigall writing to Cromer about the 'coma' into which the department had fallen under Maspero. Cromer, though retired, continued to take a close interest in Egyptian affairs, and was often consulted by his successors. He was now president of the E.E.F. and there survives a letter to him about Weigall's complaints from Lord Kitchener, the Agent who succeeded Gorst in 1911. Broadly in sympathy with Weigall, the letter nevertheless throws a cold light on the likely outcome of all his endeavours. 'So far as I can gather at present,' writes Kitchener:

Something more ought to be done for the better preservation of monuments and sites which the Department has not been able to take in hand, in order to prevent the dispersal of objects of value. I am informed, however, that more stringent regulations would be opposed by the Powers, whose agents are easily able to secure antiquities in the present state of things, and that without their consent they cannot be introduced.[29]

Simple really. Museums were symbols of national prestige. The *status quo* suited the Powers: the British, the Germans, the Italians, the Americans, the Russians, just as much as the French. It was something that Wallis Budge had known all along, as he explains in his autobiography. The impetus behind his missions to Egypt had been the example of the museums of Russia, France and Germany. As a result they were supported by Government money.[30] Lord Cromer had objected then to Budge's activities – not for Egypt's sake, but for fear of offending France – but even he had been impotent. Kitchener felt himself in much the same position.

But at least Weigall was being listened to. And yet that too added to the strain. It meant more ears to bend and more doors to knock on. Weigall's life was now whirling him in and out of depression and euphoria. Despairing about his department and his job, he was nevertheless high on the thought that he could save both at the same time; angry and bitter about Gurneh, he could still take enormous pride in his work there; ignored by the scholarly world, he was exhilarated by his social and literary celebrity. Through it all, he was also going about his job, now temporarily expanded three-fold, while at the same time discovering new fields for pressure and persuasion in Cairo. The days were full of excitement. But there was something ominous in those words to Hortense: 'I never wake up happy, but always ... weighed down with a sort of anxiety that never leaves me.' With no close friend in Egypt that summer, with neither Hortense nor Gardiner to listen or advise, alone in the raging heat, talking endlessly to himself in letters, he began to go under. On 15 September 1911, back at last in Gurneh and about to start work with Gardiner again, he suddenly came to a shuddering stop. It was, he wrote to Hortense two days later, what 'once or twice I have feared, a complete breakdown.'

# Chapter 14

# Breakdown; the bronze; the war for Egypt's heritage
# 1911–1912

Weigall's letter to Hortense about his sudden collapse shows how difficult it was at that period to admit to nervous breakdown, or even to find the language for it:

> I hate to talk about it and am so utterly ashamed of it ... I went through the most awful experience of my whole life the night before last at Gurneh ... I was alone and quite happy, sitting on the plateau looking at the stars. Then suddenly it came: an absolute *horror*. It was not exactly fear, but just *horror*. ... I paced up and down with the perspiration absolutely running off me, telling myself not to be a fool ... It all sounds so *absurd*, doesn't it?

The next day he went back to Luxor in time to meet Gardiner and recovered a little. 'But I can't tell you how I dread the thought of going back to dear old Gurneh, in case the associations should bring back the mood.'

In the event Gardiner needed to work at the Luxor temple before going over to the other side, so Weigall could postpone his return. He began to feel much better, and to dismiss the whole thing as a passing spell: 'It was pure nerves, nothing else – due to being alone for some days ... and the absolute isolation of the place I was in.' Hortense was at that time spending the summer at Ramleh, a coastal resort near Alexandria, with the children and Mimi who had come out to Egypt again. Weigall had arranged to go and see them briefly, and on the return journey to Luxor was seized with a second attack of the horrors. There was nothing for it, but to return to Cairo immediately and apply for sick leave.

He wrote in misery to Gardiner:

> My dear old chap, I don't know how to find words to tell you of my decision ... I feel too utterly sick at having to give up Gurneh ... Believe me I would not have done this if I saw any way out of it, for I'd rather be working with you than anything else ... I had ... a pretty bad time in the train, and then all yesterday ... utter, utter depression, and heart all wrong – couldn't eat a thing, couldn't sleep. And when at last I found I could hardly stand ... and was getting all sorts of nightmarish thoughts into my head, I decided that the only thing was to take Phillip's

[the doctor's] most emphatic advice and quit. ... I suppose it is what is called a nervous breakdown ...[1]

During the rest of the year, Weigall remained in Cairo working at the Museum and then, at the beginning of January 1912, returned to England on sick-leave for eight months. Gardiner was thus left to continue alone at Gurneh and eventually to bring together all their joint work on the catalogue of the tombs for the publication itself in 1913.

After this first extreme episode, Weigall rarely referred to his panic attacks. The general assumption at that period was that 'nerves' were a failure of moral fibre. When Mimi first heard the news, she told him his nerves '*must be got over*, ... you will have to ride this horse with a bit and snaffle and let him understand you are *master*.' It just needed an exertion of the will. Gradually Weigall learned to disguise his condition, but for the rest of his life, he never felt entirely safe. In the autumn of 1912, when he returned to Egypt after his sick-leave, it was all still fresh, and he lived in dread. 'Nobody,' he told Hortense, 'not even myself would know that I was like this, so long as I do routine work in Cairo.' But, 'when I tell you that I can hardly make up my mind to face a solitary walk round the Pyramids, you will realize what I am like.' For the first time, he finds a name for his sufferings: 'It is this awful agoramania! – a sort of horror of open spaces and unfamiliar ground.'

The only real therapy, or analgesic, that he knew of was work. During the following two and a half years, until he retired in April 1914, he kept the demons at bay by flinging himself into a fury of accelerating activity. What exactly the demons looked like, why they were plaguing him, how they related to the rest of his life, these were things he couldn't bear to examine. Sometimes in moments of reflection, he seems to have recognized this blind desperation in himself. During a severe bout of dengue fever in early 1913, he reverts to his old theme of living only for the present, seeing neither before nor after. But he does it with a difference this time:

> For so long now, hardly consciously, I have clung to the present to escape the darkness of the future and *nothing* in the way of entertainments or places in prospect has interested me. ... it is only during the last week or two that I have been able to *look forward* at all without a sort of horror – not of any one thing, but of life itself. I've lived all this last year just for each moment. My work, my schemes, my everything, has all been done in and for the enthusiasm of the moment and I have never dared to see where the road was leading.

This momentary lifting of the curtain owed itself partly to a great friendship with a certain Doctor Edward Madge, 'a nerve specialist' Weigall calls him, who appears to have been 'court doctor to half a dozen royalties', and in particular to the Rumanian royal family.[2] Weigall found him extraordinarily inspiring and sympathetic: 'He rather reminds me of the travelling rat in The Wind in the Willows, for he talks along and you never quite know if he has said a thing or only suggested the thought ... he knows how to deal with me and has given me back the *joie de vivre* ... which I had lost. ... [he] just quietly makes you feel that all gates are unbarred and all things possible to all men.'

Weigall had reached a crossroads in his life. He spent the rest of that year, 'sizzling over', as he put it, with schemes for administrative reform, for archaeological rescue work, for rationalizing the Museum, for educational programmes (including one for training specifically Egyptian archaeologists), all of which he pursued with extraordinary energy and tenacity down every possible corridor of power. But at the same time there was an undertow pulling in quite another direction, which in the end allowed him to see the road ahead more clearly. And it also allowed him eventually to leave the service without a pang, in spite of all his unfinished work there.

It was simply his aesthetic sense, his gift for being moved by anything beautiful – in nature, in art, in people. As with everything in his life, it acted upon him with an almost physical immediacy. One remembers him stamping and dancing with joy outside the Berlin Museum. He changed very little over the years. During his period in Cairo, he began to put together a book about Egyptian art – simply as art – an aspect of the study of ancient remains which he felt had been neglected. As he told Hortense the work sometimes made him 'feel all trembly and gone at the knees. It is the great excitement of new and intense *pleasure* in things.'

It wasn't really new. It was more that his way of life had given him no time to cultivate it. Moments of physical delight were as common as air with him. The letters are full of the beauty of Egypt, and by the same token they are also full of disgust – at tasteless rooms, or at people, ugly, squint-eyed, fat, or smelly. Bad taste was an outrage. Even charm could scarcely compensate for that: 'his wife is charming,' he says of someone, 'but both have vile taste and have terrible pictures etc, and an *awful* Japanese screen as the chief feature of their little drawing-room.' Going to stay in Lefebvre's house the summer he was covering for him, Weigall describes the general pokiness of the place, 'its oilcloth covers and its fans and cheap plates nailed to the walls', all sending 'shivers through me', and the garden, where the 'little beds and stupid paths' were little better. Then suddenly 'the moon came out and shone on the flowers and then great white moths came and fluttered about, sipping the flowers, and their *eyes* could be seen sparkling as they hovered.' In an instant he was happy, and a poem formed in his mind which, however, went no further than 'O Hortense!'

It was a quality Gardiner sorely missed when he was alone at Gurneh. Early in 1913, he wrote to his wife Hedi: 'Do you know, I often miss Weigall here. He had a gift of making me feel, or making me articulate my feelings about the beauty of the world; and this was one reason I loved his companionship. He may be material; in some ways he is. But I fancy all *real* people are; and nearly all the poets. It is the sense of life that makes them so, the need of living.'[3] Whatever Gardiner meant by 'material', Weigall was probably demonstrating it with a vengeance at that moment.

When he moved from Luxor to Cairo, he came, in effect, from a small town, little more than a village in the desert, to a city of treasures – the bazaars and shops full of exquisite carpets, textiles, pots and sculptures from all over the Middle East, the drawing-rooms of his friends glowing with their choicest wares. Cairo came to mean not just the centre of political life, but of aesthetic pleasure too. 'O my dear,' he wrote to Hortense, shortly after arriving,

> you don't know what Cairo means to me nowadays! ... the facilities for shoving things through the ministries, the opportunities for discussing things with the authorities, and above all the feeling of being right on the spot. Then also I am simply *crazy* now about getting some nice rooms and filling them with beautiful things. I am mad to buy ikons and tiles and embroideries and Greek statuary and Persian paintings and all the things that please one so much in Rattigan's house, or Home's, or Storrs', or Hornblower's – the things one couldn't get in Luxor.

Ronald Storrs and Frank Rattigan (the father, incidentally, of the playwright, Terence) were both at the Agency: Rattigan, Diplomatic Secretary, and Storrs still Oriental Secretary, though his chief was now Lord Kitchener, Sir Eldon Gorst having retired, gravely ill, the year before.

Gorst had been a brilliant but rather joyless intellectual whose political brief had been to begin the transfer of administrative functions from the British to the Egyptians. This had won him few friends among the British and, unfortunately, his aloof manner and general lack of style had won him few friends among the Egyptians either. By the time he came to retire, political unrest among the Nationalists had killed off all thoughts of further liberalization, and Field Marshall Lord Kitchener, the very antithesis of Gorst, was appointed to replace him. Dubbed 'the butcher of Khartoum', he was remembered bitterly by Nationalist Arabs for his expedition to the Sudan to relieve General Gordon. But hero or butcher, he had a force of personality that added a zest to the life of Cairo in the years immediately before the First World War. He filled the Agency with his collections of porcelain, Byzantine icons and Chippendale, built a new ballroom, and with the flourish of a man who had once aspired to be Viceroy of India, he changed the servants out of Gorst's livery of chocolate and yellow and put them into scarlet and gold.

Both Rattigan and Storrs in their autobiographies say that Kitchener's one great interest outside his work was collecting antiques. 'In his love and pursuit of the fine arts, more especially the decorative and antique,' wrote Storrs, 'he surpassed all who had gone before or have come after him.' Twice a week Kitchener would visit the bazaars, and on his return to the Agency, almost run up the steps in his eagerness 'to undo his parcel and to ring for one or more of the staff to approve his purchases.'[4] They were all, as Rattigan wrote 'bitten with the craze for Egyptology, and seized every opportunity to add to our collections.'[5] They discussed their enthusiasms endlessly, vying with one another, and jealously guarding their acquisitions against one another's envy: 'Lord K came to tea with me on Tues.,' wrote Storrs to his mother, 'and had a look at my things, which he praised with a studied moderation that made me apprehensive of subsequent overtures for purchase.'[6]

Here then was a congenial society in many ways, and it seems that Weigall was made welcome among them. Luxor may have been the outback, but his years among ancient paintings and reliefs had educated and refined his eye. His letters begin to talk of all sorts of objects, from all over the region: Graeco-Roman terracotta heads, sixteenth-century gilded Persian book-covers painted with flowers, two figures said to be from Syria which he saw at once were Cretan, a beautiful head of Akhnaten lying unregarded in a dealer's shop. He began to pride himself on being able to identify the special and unique, and then to be both thrilled and appalled at how easily he could become, if he chose – of all things – a successful dealer.

When Weigall arrived back in Egypt in 1912, he was seriously short of money. His sick-leave had been on half pay and, to his surprise, some of the articles he had written so as to break even had been rejected. He put it down to nervous exhaustion. Blackwoods did offer him a good price for a book-length collection of them, but that lay in the future, and although he was deep in another biography – of Cleopatra – the work was going slowly. There were other projects, for example a commission from Fisher Unwin to write a book on modern Egypt, and the book on Egyptian art already mentioned. But none of these was earning yet. His position was officially Inspector of Antiquities for Lower Egypt, and Edgar, his predecessor, was to take his place in Luxor. But the headquarters for the Delta was Mansourah, and Weigall had no intention of burying himself away in a provincial town like Mansourah. Cairo was the only place he could operate from, but in Cairo there were no free house and servants.

Hortense had stayed behind in England, for she was expecting her third child the following March. The family had always stayed with Mimi, but now, with another baby on the way, they needed their own house. Hopelessly impractical, she took the lease on a house far too expensive for them, on Boar's Hill outside Oxford. The two of them were in a desperate hole, staving off creditors in both countries, while Weigall lived in daily fear of his friend Home, the bank manager. He was at his wit's end; every letter at this period begins with a panic about money, how to last a little longer, how to pay off one debt and postpone another, and always how to persuade Home to let him carry on with his overdraft.

There was, therefore, a strong temptation on him to make use of his knowledge and his eye for fine works of art. At the same time he felt uneasy at the thought. Those two Cretan figures for example:

The thing is, shall I make a profit of a few hundred on these or not? Certainly they are foreign goods. Certainly no price is too high for them since they are unique? Why not? Why not? Can *you* see any reason why not? *I* can't, though I *feel* there is *something* against it. Perhaps it is simply one's natural dislike of being a tradesman – but if that's all it is, one must get over it. And yet all the time there is the feeling of *joy* at beating others at their own game, by one's knowledge. I had no idea the use of knowledge could be so thrilling! It is all so *easy*, so *frightfully* simple. Do you know, I believe I should absolutely *adore* being a dealer!!

It is as though he realized he was at the start of a slippery slope. A little later in the same letter he says that he saw a head of Akhnaten in a shop just as a demand arrived from the painter, Ogilvie, for repayment of a loan of £100. He also owed Robert

Mond another £50. He bought it, intending at first 'to get somebody to buy it for a museum at the price I gave', but decided instead to offer it 'for £150 more than the price' to an American millionaire he knew, Edward Tuck – with the condition, he adds, 'that it should be bequeathed to a museum.' Tuck agreed by telegram, and so 'Next week I pay Ogilvie and Mond (and remain myself in my broke state, by the way!')[7]

Although Weigall frets over this – 'I can't help feeling that I have fallen from a pedestal' – he doesn't seem to realize how far he has indeed fallen. 'And yet what have I done?' he asks. 'I have used my brains, and spotted a work of art that others have overlooked (it has been in dealers' hands for years, I am told) ... I have broken no rule or law. And yet?' But he had broken a rule. Egyptian antikas, even 'stray' ones from dealers' shops, had to be shown to Maspero first, in case they should be wanted for the Museum.[8] His insouciance is extraordinary. One is tempted to think that he was not quite himself at this period. These confessions to Hortense about the Akhnaten head and the Cretan figures come in the same letter in which he describes his fever and depression, and the wonderful Dr Madge.

But, even setting aside the Egyptian origin or otherwise of these objects, it should have been obvious to him at once 'why not'. The Akhnaten head is the only case in which he seems to have been guilty of actual wrongdoing; but in both cases it was as he feared – there was *something* against it.' That 'something' was 'bad form', a prohibition no less absolute for being vague. His airy dismissal of it as something that one must 'get over' was never going to save him from the gossip of the clubs and the dinner tables. But more than that, his professional position and his crusade against the dealers should have made it impossible for him, of all people, to be seen to deal at all. It was a step calculated to delight his enemies. As it happened, apart from the instances related here, Weigall did resist the temptation to deal. But he might as well have been hung for a sheep as a lamb, for one of them – not the Akhnaten head, curiously, but a bronze statuette from the Roman period – was enough to destroy his career.

As with many things in Weigall's life, the story of it was an adventure in itself. Midnight ambushes and skirmishes had always been part of the job but on this occasion the chase was peculiarly complicated and protracted. The account of it that he published many years later[9] leaves out the names of some of the actors, and I shall therefore quote not from this, but from the less discreet draft for it found among his papers. In the beginning it was merely a case of recovering a stolen antika:

One of my inspectors came to me in Cairo one day [in November 1912], and reported that strange events were taking place by night at a certain point upon the Suez canal. Some Bedouin ... were said to be in possession of some fine antique bronzes which were believed to have come from Turkey or Syria; and a certain Bulgarian dealer, named Nikola Yamani, was endeavouring to purchase these and to bring them secretly into Egypt for sale. I therefore gave the inspector the necessary instructions, with the result that as soon as Nikola had made his purchase he was asked to bring his objects to the nearest office of the Department of Antiquities, which happened to be at the town of Zagazig, and there to give me the opportunity of buying them from him for the Cairo Museum. Now it so happened that Mr Frank Rattigan, at that time Second Secretary at the British Agency, was anxious to finance some excavations amongst the ruins of the ancient Bubastis, near Zagazig; and when I went ... to look at these bronzes, he came with me to look at the site of the proposed excavations.

The coming of the Diplomatic Secretary, shining in the reflected glory of his chief, Lord Kitchener, was telegraphed to the Egyptian provincial governor, who lived at Zagazig; the Governor met us, and took us in semi-state to lunch with him. Nikola Yamani saw the procession, thought the whole might of the British Empire had come to seize his antiquities, dashed off to the Inspector's office, bribed the native clerk in charge to hide the one and only really fine piece in the collection, and then sat down to await our arrival. ...

Weigall then saw the remaining bronzes, decided that they were not worth purchasing for the nation, and after Maspero had been consulted, they were officially rejected. Yamani returned to the clerk to reclaim his treasure, only to find that his stratagem had backfired. The clerk had in the mean time quietly sold the thing, and swore blind that he had never set eyes on it. In despair Yamani decided to come clean with Weigall: 'I listened to that wicked clerk,' he said, 'who told me that Lord Kitchener's Secretary would certainly seize the one good bronze for England.' It seems that the clerk had positively inveigled Yamani, so Weigall promised to do what he could to recover the bronze:

The clerk was arrested, but denied all knowledge of the stolen antiquity; Nikola, meanwhile, more or less burgled the house of the clerk, and was chased out by the inmates at the point of a revolver ... I then invited Mr Rattigan and my friend Mr Ronald Storrs, Oriental Secretary at the British Agency, to help me, my idea being that the fear of the redoubtable Lord Kitchener, which had been the cause of the trouble, might now be employed to some purpose.

What followed was a tale of desperate daring and devilry, which Weigall merely indicates in broad terms:

... our trapping of the Arab dealer and holding him prisoner while a certain hiding place of his was searched; false scents which he caused us to follow up; our final exasperation with him, and the giving of a time limit in which he was to confess if he wished to save himself from the deepest and darkest dungeon in Cairo. Suffice it to say that, one minute before the time limit expired, the man confessed that he had bought the missing bronze from the Zagazig clerk, and had sold it to a well-known Italian dealer.

Eventually they got it back and Rattigan saw it for the first time. He described it to Weigall, who 'discussed with Maspero the desirability of purchasing it for the nation'.

Maspero 'objected, however, to spend public money on an antiquity found outside Egypt, and he therefore gave Nikola permission to dispose of it as he pleased.' The bronze was of 'a boy dressed in the ancient costume of Armenia or Media, and wearing the royal crown of Armenia ... and it evidently dated from Roman times.' It was apparently very beautiful, at least the letters written at the time say so, though the published account emphasizes its interest and originality rather than its beauty.

It is at this point that the story becomes murky. Yamani promptly offered the bronze not to any of the dealers from whom it had been recovered – and who presumably would have objected to paying twice for it – but to the three who had rescued it for him. Neither the draft nor the published account confess the whole truth here, merely saying that Rattigan bought the bronze himself and that he offered to share any profit he might make on re-selling it with Weigall and Storrs. The published account comes to a discreet close soon after, but the draft goes on to say that the three of them 'made no secret' of their intention 'to sell it and sell it well', that the dealers through whose hands it had originally passed 'now gnashed their teeth', and that finally 'on Lord Kitchener's advice, we offered it to Mr Pierpont Morgan' – the American steel king, multi-millionaire, prodigious collector and President of the New York Metropolitan Museum. Unfortunately Morgan died in early 1913, and the bronze was finally sold, years later, for 'a rather disappointing sum'. Who bought it, when, and what for, Weigall doesn't say.

But neither of these versions is as candid as it might be. The letters to Hortense, written as the adventure was unfolding, fill in and correct the picture. Rattigan's purchase and offer of a share of the profits did occur, but not in relation to the stolen bronze. Weigall explained to Hortense that he showed Rattigan the other bronzes, the ones that Yamani had shown him:

> I arranged the bargain, feeling that there was no harm in doing so, since Maspero had refused them for the Govt. New York [i.e. the Metropolitan Museum] has offered Rattigan £600 for them, and he insists that Ronald and I and he shall share the profits! since we were all in it together. So I ought to get £50 or so, which one side of my brain says is disreputable, and the other side says is perfectly all right. What do you think? There is nothing against it that I can see, and yet I don't like to be mixed up in even innocent sales of this kind. Yet we want the money badly enough ...

Soon after this was written, the existence of Yamani's hidden bronze became known. Weigall's next letter, written after its recovery, shows that his whole frame of mind had shifted, and in a tone of rather forced jubilation, he describes a different arrangement altogether. He had been reluctant to dip a toe in before, but he was now in up to his neck:

> Those bronzes I told you about in my last letter have produced a story like a fairy tale. One of them was stolen, and I never saw it; but I worked until I got it back, and found to my delight that it was not an Egyptian antiquity at all, but a Persian

Arthur Weigall's mother, Mimi, as a young woman

Arthur Weigall, aged about 20, c. 1900

Weigall's first excavation, at Abydos, under Petrie, 1901–2

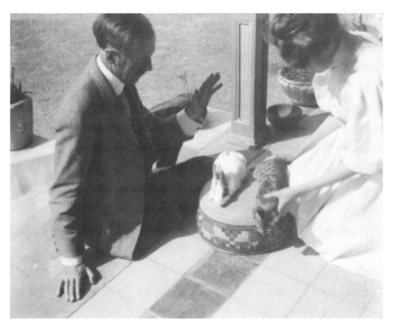

Theodore Davis, a wealthy American amateur archaeologist, on the verandah of
Weigall's house at Luxor, with Hortense and pets

Edward Ayrton in the Valley of Kings. In 1905, at Weigall's insistence, he was
appointed by Maspero to supervise Davis's excavations

Weigall emerging from the newly discovered tomb of Horemheb, 1908

Arthur Weigall beside a statue of the hawk-god
Horus in front of the Temple of Edfu

From left to right: nurse, Hortense with her first-born son, Alured, on her lap, Oscar and Carrie
Schleiter, her parents, in the vicarage garden, Shepherd's Bush, August 1907

Hortense in Luxor, c. 1905

Hortense with her second son, Denny, early 1911

Interior of the house at Luxor, with Hortense

Arthur Weigall, Chief Inspector of Antiquities, at Thebes: c. 1910

At the Tombs of the Nobles. From left to right, Hortense, Mimi, Weigall, Charles Whymper (a bird painter) and a friend. February 1908

Weigall's sister, Geanie, with her daughter, Betty, in Luxor. March 1911

Geanie in the garden at Luxor. December 1910

Ronald Storrs, Oriental Secretary at the British Agency, on board the steamer from which he and Arthur Weigall swam among the drowned temples at Philae. April 1911

The Queen of the Belgians (centre) and Princesses, in the Valley of the Kings. March 1911

The King of the Belgians (left) and Arthur Weigall at the Ramesseum. March 1911

The Valley of the Kings, with Arthur Weigall walking up the path

Arthur Weigall standing with the Governor of the province in front of the tomb of Tutankhamun. This was the frontispiece to his *Tutankhamun and other Essays*, and by including the Governor in it, Weigall was underlining the fact that, despite Lord Carnarvon's monopoly agreement with *The Times*, the tomb belonged to the Egyptian Government

Arthur Weigall sitting on the retaining wall of the tomb of Tutankhamun taking notes for his *Daily Mail* articles

thing, and in no way concerned the Govt., but came from somewhere in Turkey. Rattigan, Storrs and I bought it together for £800, and we are offering it to [Pierpont] Morgan ... The delightful thing is that it is nothing to do with my business, and my conscience is clear – as easy in fact as it would be if I'd bought and sold some old English furniture. ... It is a *glorious* figure of a Persian god, Greek period [he obviously changed his mind about exactly what it was] – lovely flowing robes – absolutely unique. The full story of how I got it is too long to tell you, but it was *the most* thrilling thing. ... Keep this *dead dead* secret ... I am sending you my report of the affair for Maspero. Please type it and return quickly ... I don't want it done here, owing to the need for secrecy. The report of course does not tell the final fact of our purchase of the stolen thing from Nikola for £800. Maspero need never know that.

The letter is thick with the atmosphere of impending scandal, and whatever he says about his clear conscience and the rights and wrongs of it technically speaking, he is gripped by the dread of exposure.

Unfortunately, the task of selling it seems to have fallen more heavily on Weigall than the others, not only because he had contacts in the museum world, but also because it was he who recognized just how remarkable it was. As he explained to Hortense:

There is a great London dealer here called Hirsch who has seen our bronze and has told us that if we can let him have it for £12,000 he thinks he can sell it at once to the Berlin Museum. This shows that our original price of £18,000 or £20,000 was not too high, but it also shows that we (who have no knowledge of *how* to sell it) can't expect to get that top price ... You know it was I who fixed the price at £20,000, simply by instinct. Ronald and Frank thought from £2,000 to £3,000 originally and I am rather proud of having seen at a glance the artistic merit of the piece, for after all I knew very little about Perso-Graeco-Roman art; but now this great connoisseur has confirmed my opinion ...

Weigall's estimate sent the whole affair into another dimension. Suddenly the thing was potentially and nerve-rackingly newsworthy. Over these months, photographs of the statuette were put into the hands of Hirsch, and two other international dealers of the period, Kalekian and Duveen, who took them to Paris and New York. Kalekian, wrote Weigall, 'says we ought to get more than £20,000 and he is the richest dealer in the world and ought to know.' Such enormous sums could not be hushed up for ever and the active involvement of Weigall was bound to raise suspicions.

£20,000 was their will-o'-the-wisp. As the weeks and months went by without a sale, Weigall's letters return again and again to the argument for dropping to 17, 15, 12, even to eight thousand pounds, simply to get the sale and the anxiety over quickly. And yet just as often, he reminds himself of the market value of the thing, the price that the dealers would certainly ask, and all his wisdom evaporates: 'Duveen would certainly ask for £20,000 if he were selling it ... It is so sickening when one *knows* that £20,000 is a fair price, if only we could find the buyer, and could *wait.*' At first, their one hope of bypassing the dealers lay with Pierpont Morgan, towards whom they could make their own overtures – at least Weigall could, for Morgan was advised by old colleagues of his, Lythgoe and Mace. Unfortunately, this brought him very much out into the open, exactly where he didn't want to be, and the impossibility of his position becomes painfully clear in the correspondence he then entered into.

Arthur Mace was in Cairo in November 1912, very soon after the bronze was recovered, and Weigall wrote to tell him of it, 'in case Morgan would like to buy it.' He mentions that Kalekian is seeing 'the owner' tomorrow, and that he believes the price to be between £15,000 and £20,000.[10] He doesn't, of course, say that he is part-owner himself. Having seen it, Mace then wrote to Lythgoe in New York, describing the situation as he understood it. Clearly the odour of 'bad form' hung over Rattigan as well:

Rattigan is rather shy of the business, as he's never sold anything before, and doesn't want it to get out in Cairo lest he should get the reputation of being a dealer. He's one of Lord K's secretaries, and I fancy does not want him to know. He says he would far rather sell it privately than through a dealer for that reason. I promised I would not mention it to anyone but you. ... He says he's badly dipped [i.e. short of money] at present owing to the Balkan War.

If Weigall was right, Kitchener knew well enough, and it was Cairo at large that worried him more. Mace then goes on to describe the object and we learn that it is '27 inches high, in very good condition, and good work ... I've never seen anything in the least like it. Have you?' (Weigall was sending photographs by the same mail) It is, he says, quite outside their province (both of them worked in the Egyptian department of the museum) so he suggests showing the photograph to Edward Robinson, the Director. He thinks that the price is very high, but that since Rattigan intends to sell as soon as he can, Morgan ought to be given the chance to bid for it, 'as it might be one of those chances that one would hate to have missed.'[11]

In January 1913, the great plutocrat arrived in Egypt, where he regularly visited during the winter months, viewing the American excavations that he financed, and setting the dealers alight with his huge purchases. Lythgoe and his wife were of the party, and Weigall wrote reminding him of the statuette. Two and half months had passed since the first flush of excitement, and in that time gossip must have begun to circulate, for he is clearly embarrassed: 'I am a little shy of calling your notice to it, for I rather feel that I might appear 'interested' in the sale, at least so a kind friend hinted to me! I must say here, therefore, that my only interest is in the object itself and in my friendship for Rattigan, for whose sake I do want to get a purchaser.'[12]

Weigall was his own worst enemy. Storrs, the highest ranking of the three, and the closest to Kitchener, was the only one to keep himself out of the story and he did so, it seems, by being virtually silent and invisible. They must all have decided that he was too high a flyer to risk exposure. But given that Weigall's function in the trio made him highly audible and visible, it would have been better to have admitted his 'interest' straightaway, and have faced the music. After all, he had a case. It was not an Egyptian object.[13] He had, even so, informed Maspero of it. Maspero had turned it down. Weigall's only 'crime' was against convention and 'good form'. Later that year, in the autumn of 1913, when distorted versions of the story had become public property, Weigall's ultimate boss, Malcolm Macdonald, the Adviser to the Department of the Public Works, asked him to contradict it. This he did, in writing, though still concealing the fact ('at Rattigan's request,' he tells Hortense) that anyone other than Rattigan had bought it. Macdonald's reaction is instructive, for it shows that Weigall could indeed have come clean without irreparable damage to his reputation. Weigall told Hortense that 'Macdonald said of course he couldn't see under the circumstances what would have been wrong even if *I* had bought it; but anyway he was glad I hadn't, as it might have been considered bad form.'

As it was, Weigall got the worst of both worlds. He neither concealed his interest, nor had the satisfaction of telling the truth. He could not, therefore, pre-empt scandal (by the time Macdonald called for a contradiction, the word was that Weigall and Rattigan had *stolen* an Egyptian statue), and he laid himself open to anyone who might want to destroy him. As it happened, one of Weigall's schemes, the most important in fact during these Cairo years, was calculated to make him enemies. It became the subject of fierce dispute between Maspero, Weigall and the Agency during 1912-13, and drew protests from many prominent Egyptologists.


This is how it came about. Weigall was now entirely disillusioned, and had no faith in Maspero's ability or willingness to implement the ideals on which he had made such a stand in Upper Egypt. All round him he saw concessions going to unqualified people – Rattigan, incidentally, was one of them – and Weigall disapproved. He also saw the portions allowed them by Maspero's lenient divisions disappearing into private hands abroad via the dealers of Cairo. It was a self-nourishing circle that bypassed the Department of Antiquities to a large extent, and while everyone else had a share of the profits, the Department had to hold out its begging bowl to rich benefactors and hope for generosity from the Finance Department.

Weigall thought he could see a way out. It was, briefly, that the Museum itself should enter the field by becoming the greatest dealer of them all. It was a revolutionary idea, 'the biggest thing I've done yet,' Weigall told Hortense: 'It's been in the back of my mind for years, but it only really dawned on me properly one day in the museum when I saw how many things we had that we didn't want, and how cramped we were for room, and at the same time what vast prices Morgan etc were paying dealers for the very things we could supply.'

Incidentally, J.P. Morgan's visit to Luxor three years before, in 1909, may have helped form his thinking – the same occasion, when to Lindon Smith's disgust Morgan failed to see his picture of Ramose. The great man had, in fact, been much more interested in the Luxor dealer Mohammed Mohassib, the man who, according to Morgan's biographer, Herbert Saterlee, 'controlled the antiquity market of upper Egypt'. Lythgoe of the Metropolitan Museum introduced the two men, and was instrumental in bringing off an important deal between them: the sale of an unusually fine series of objects, found by locals at Tell el-Amarna.[14] Weigall would surely have heard about the transaction, and have drawn his conclusions about the interdependence of dealers, collectors and Museum curators.

But to return. The opening paragraphs of his formal proposal to the Agency put the commercial facts as bluntly as possible, as though he wanted to shock the Agency into thinking in unaccustomed ways:

> The dealers in Egypt at present make enormous profits each year by the sale of antiquities. From the Sale-Room of the Cairo Museum, however, very small profits are made, owing to the fact that only worthless objects are there to be obtained. The dealers are thus without competition, and all persons who are engaged in buying antiquities for foreign museums or collections go always to them, and never come to us, ...
>
> I propose that the sale of the antiquities by the Cairo Museum should be vastly extended, and that the work should be put on business lines.

It was a complicated proposal, not least because it was designed to kill several birds with one stone:

1) To help all the museums of the world to obtain the class of Egyptian antiquities which they require, and to form collections suitable for the needs of their public.

2) To put a check on robbery by preventing foreign curators' indiscriminate purchases from dealers.

3) To relieve the Cairo Museum of its surplus stock which takes up much room and is badly looked after owing to the vast size of the collection.

4) To make our surplus stock of important antiquities accessible to the public all over the world by selling historic or artistic objects exclusively to public museums or large collections, and selling only unimportant objects to private collectors or tourists.

5) To add to our funds by the proceeds of these sales, which would amount to several thousand pounds a year.

6) To spend a part of the money thus obtained by purchasing from dealers any objects which obviously ought not to be allowed to leave the country ...[15]

At first sight, Weigall had come a long way from deploring the export of Egypt's heritage to foreign museums. But he was a pragmatist as well as an idealist; museums and their buyers weren't going to go away. Besides, as we shall see, his scheme envisaged the Cairo Museum's having much tighter control on everything of importance. Above all, a closer acquaintance with that Museum had shown him that, at the rate the land was being excavated, it was physically impossible for the existing collections to be properly housed, exhibited and cared for, let alone the additional things that were coming in season after season.

As he wrote to Gardiner: 'At present we are weighed down with duplicates and our space is so limited that I see no way of properly exhibiting the important things, except by obtaining more room. Yet it is impossible to expect the Govt. to spend money on building a larger museum. The present building is too new for that.'[16] But it wasn't just a matter of space. The proposal talks about objects being 'badly looked after' and indeed many years later, at the time of the discovery of Tutankhamun's tomb, he was shocked to find just how badly they had suffered. He described the Museum then – 'built beside the Nile in a climate having a humidity which rises to 80 per cent, with an annual mean of 70 per cent' – as being 'entirely unfit to receive' the Tutankhamun treasure at all.[17]

Lying at the root of the problem, Weigall felt, was the *ad hoc* manner in which the Museum collections had been, and were being, built up year by year. This he put down to the way the divisions were carried out, a system full of casual, gentlemanly courtesies, connivances, and chance. Having had personal experience of it, he was able in his proposal to describe the amateurish methods he had himself been obliged to use:

[In Upper Egypt], I generally made the selection of what the Museum wanted, visiting the excavations for this purpose and going through the finds in the rough before they were cleaned or shown to advantage. I had no idea what the Cairo Museum required ... in any one class of objects, for my work gave me very little opportunities for visiting the Museum; and I therefore made a quite casual selection ... of what happened to strike me as being needed by us. Other excavators, considering that I was severe in my selection, preferred to take their finds to Cairo, where often only a few boxes were unpacked for inspection. Other excavators did not show their finds at all, but the selection was made at Cairo by means of photographs.

The result was that there was no logic to the Cairo collections. They were 'absurdly overstocked in one class of objects and miserably deficient in another class': 'For example its collection of ancient weights and measures is not half so complete as is Prof. Petrie's collection of these objects in London; yet all the fine specimens which he has got have passed out of Egypt with our nominal sanction, simply owing to the Museum's representative not knowing what weights we had got and what we wanted.' It was impossible, he maintained, to make a sensible selection without a detailed and comprehensive knowledge of what the Museum possessed. There needed to be someone, specifically employed for the purpose, who was based at the Museum, had studied its collections, and who could make the selection there, at the Museum, with everything on hand for reference and comparison. Of course this was a job he saw himself doing, for he chafed still at the dead-end post of Inspector.

If the Museum collections needed rationalizing, the first step was a thorough weeding, a commission of Egyptologists being appointed to decide on the selection. The surplus could then be sold, duplicates of the best things to museums and public institutions and the 'worthless ... little blue things', as he phrased it to Gardiner,[18] to tourists and private collectors. This would be a one-off clear-out. But thereafter, as new things came in, why not build upon the arrangement? Why not continue to create a superfluity for the Museum that could then be sold on the same basis? At present, although the law said that the Government would take half of everything found, and give half to the excavator, in practice Maspero usually allowed the excavator to keep much more than half. This was good for the serious, 'scientific' excavators who thus had plenty to take back to their subscribers – often museums – but it was also good for the unserious profiteering excavators who had plenty to take to the dealers.

What Weigall saw was that if the Government applied the law to the letter, and insisted on a strict half and half division, the serious excavator would be inconvenienced, true, but more important, the loot-hunter might actually be deterred. At last he had found a way round Maspero's inveterate leniency in granting concessions. As he wrote to Gardiner:

Do you think that our taking a full half from them [i.e. the institutional excavators] will ruin them? Will their institutions refuse them funds if they don't get more than their half share? If so, all I can say is that their institutions are not worthy. But actually I know it will make no difference to them – they will be annoyed and that is all ... I know it is hard on the scientific excavators, [but] I feel that they ought to be public-spirited enough to submit to this more strict interpretation of the law, in view of the fact that it is the *only* way of sitting on unscientific workers. Can you suggest any other means ... you might struggle for a generation before you could get any law passed to restrict the kind of excavator who now works ...[19]

By the same token, of course, Weigall's system would channel a greater part of the traffic in antiquities through the Museum, and thus give it the kind of control over the flow and destination of antiquities that now rested so largely with the dealers. What he envisaged was that the Museum would take half the value of the whole, even if this meant that it took valuable duplicates and unimportant objects as well as important ones. Then the most needed and wanted things, chosen in the context of the existing collections, would be added to the Museum's permanent stock (space having been created by the initial weeding), and the remainder, after being photographed, catalogued and priced (a little below the dealer's prices) would be divided into two classes, just as in the initial clear-out: insignificant things for sale to private individuals; and duplicates of the more important classes of object for sale only to foreign museums.

These ideas, but chiefly the divisions at Cairo and the half-and half rule, caused consternation among archaeologists: the first because it was inconvenient and time-consuming, to pack, unpack and repack sometimes very frail objects; and the second because financial ruin was predicted if subscribers were disappointed. As to the larger questions Weigall was addressing, the coherence of the Museum collections, the role of Government in controlling the antiquities market, these seem not to have interested the archaeologists. Protests were sent to the Agency, one in particular from Thomas Eric Peet, soon to be Lecturer in Egyptology at Manchester University, and at that time working for the Egypt Exploration Fund at Abydos. He wrote complaining to the Financial Adviser, Lord Edward Cecil (who passed the letter on to Weigall for comment), in precisely the way Weigall had predicted: namely, that a strict half and half division 'will certainly damage our subscription list and possibly in the end ruin us.' More seriously, perhaps, Peet feared that objects that derive their interest from being kept together – tomb-groups as they are called – would be split up. Weigall's answer to this last point is not extant, though given his understanding of the problem, it would be surprising if he hadn't thought about it.

Much of the rest of Peet's letter, however, is written under some misunderstanding, and in that respect he stands, perhaps, for many other archaeologists. The scheme obviously went so far against what people were accustomed to that it appeared wilder than it really was. Peet doesn't appear to realize that the sales of important objects were to be restricted to public institutions and museums, that their whereabouts would therefore be public knowledge, and that a complete record of each object and the circumstances of its discovery would be made before it was sold:

> To an archaeologist nothing is so precious as the proper keeping of scientific records [writes Peet] ... We fear that the system of open sale ... will render this no longer possible and make it impracticable to keep trace of what we find. ... This system would present a sad contrast to our present method of dealing with our finds, in which every tomb-group is sent unbroken to a properly authorized public museum with a complete record of the circumstances of its finding ... [20]

At that point in the letter there are red underlinings and marginal marks, either Weigall's or Cecil's, which indicate that some reply was meditated.

Gardiner also seems to have thought that important objects were to be made available to private collectors, and that the excavators themselves would be unfairly cut out. Weigall replies:

> You don't seem to understand that the whole scheme is based on the selling of this stuff [i.e. anything important] to *other museums,* and I have put in the strictest clauses to prevent sales to private collectors or private persons ... I quite agree that the excavator from whom we have taken our full half shall have the first right to buy any object which we have taken from him but which we do not intend to exhibit. I had not put that clause in, simply because I imagined that the thing would happen naturally; for the excavator would naturally say during the division, "I say, let me have first chance of buying that thing," and we should naturally say, "Certainly." However, I *will* put it in.

Weigall was particularly anxious to persuade Gardiner. He knew he was going out on a limb, and that there would be a howl from the archaeologists, and more than ever he needed Gardiner's fundamental faith in him:

I can't have you in opposition to me, old chap – Believe me, I may seem impulsive and all that sort of thing, but I really have got something behind it, something fairly solid; and in any scheme which I propose I want to feel that you at least see its good points, and don't oppose it simply because it seems revolutionary. You always laugh at my schemes ... but I do give them enormous thought and take enormous trouble about them, and I *do* believe in them![21]

Whether Gardiner came round to Weigall's way of thinking it is difficult to tell, but he did write to his wife Hedi at just this time, January 1913, in a way that suggests that his faith still held. He was in Luxor, alone, and 'distinctly in the blues': 'There is not any Egyptologist who combines real enthusiasm, humour and common sense as Arthur does and one feels now that the place is abandoned to its fate.'[22]

But, in any case, by the time Peet and Gardiner were making their objections, the scheme was being considered, as we have seen, at the highest levels in the British Agency. The frantic letters that Weigall wrote to Hortense about debts and the bronze statuette usually contained updates on the Sale-of-Antiquities Scheme. He was never under any illusion that Maspero would be against it, and he was therefore pushing it as hard as he could, and with some success, at the Agency. But for every Advisor converted, Weigall paid the price of Maspero's goodwill: 'Maspero was much against my great scheme when I saw him; so I saw Cecil again who sent for him and talked it over, and he says he thinks it just possible that Maspero may do it. He has sent him on to Kitchener, and it still all hangs in the balance. But I expect K. won't push it, although *extremely* keen on it, I know, and recently wrote telling Cecil *he* must push it through. They all so funk a row with M.'

The following week, after Maspero's meeting with Kitchener, Weigall wrote again: 'K. has seen Maspero and has told him that the scheme *must* go through at once. Maspero was all against it and I am now awfully afraid that M. will propose some modified form of it to K., and spite me by leaving me out of it ... I expect now that K. has been rather short with him, he (M) will be rather sick with me.' Over these months one has the feeling that Maspero was becoming seriously rattled by Weigall. It was hardly what he was used to, having these British lords telling him what he *must* do. Clearly, Weigall had been able to exploit Kitchener's natural interest in antiquities, and the Agent was taking a view on matters that previous Agents had left well alone. By bringing the two parties into direct confrontation, Weigall was upsetting the delicate balance of power between them.

But beyond that, Maspero could be forgiven for feeling that Weigall's scheme was itself a veiled attack on him. Although in one sense Weigall was attempting to give proper controls to the Museum, and thus to the Director General of Antiquities, in another he was undermining Maspero's power of discretion, his room for manoeuvre. All Weigall's stringency and method, his insistence on the half and half division, his ban on the profiteering excavator, his commercial logic – so alien to the traditions of cultural institutions – threatened precisely those personal gestures of generosity, those unpredictable caprices, severities and leniencies by which Maspero expressed his charm, his patronage and his power.

Isolated in Upper Egypt, Weigall had been just tolerable. But now he was bringing his war to Cairo, waging it under Maspero's nose, and dragging in the British Advisors. Points of principle on which he had been obliged at Luxor to make a relatively solitary stand were now table talk among the politicians. Weigall told Gardiner, for example, that a certain Lord Dudley wanted to have a digging concession near Thebes 'as he would like to have a little "flutter" (that is his word).' He, Weigall, had written to Maspero to say that unless he insisted on Dudley's employing 'the best possible archaeologist to do the work – Firth, I suggested – I would have to offer my resignation':

Last night I was dining with Cecil, and Lindsay, the new Under Secretary, and they brought up the subject, and I told them of my ultimatum to Maspero; and they both said that they were glad I'd put it as strongly as that and would back me. I've got Cecil *entirely* round to our point of view nowadays and he feels *most strongly* about it all. I think I can safely say that Kitchener, Cecil, Lindsay, Goschen and Macdonald (i.e. the Advisors) are all now completely with us as regards the wrong sort of excavation.[23]

'Endless talk at dinners and lunches', as Weigall put it in the same letter to Gardiner, was beginning make a difference.

But winning against Maspero was dangerous. In a hundred ways, he could turn all Weigall's victories to dust and ashes. Almost every letter of triumph is balanced by another of despair, and thoughts of leaving the Service altogether were not far from his mind. For example, Hortense received the same sort of letter as Gardiner about the British Advisors all being ready to listen to him, and yet:

You have no idea of the discouragements ... Maspero checkmates me every time. If I had at all a free hand I would stick to the Service gladly; but I don't see there is any chance ... I feel so impotent and I beat so at the bars all the time. And Maspero *must* be getting annoyed with me. He told Gardiner that I tried to teach him "where the sun stood at noon", which shows he thinks me too pushing; and yet he is always sweet to me. I think he is a little afraid of me, because he knows how well I stand with the English authorities ...

Whether or not Maspero was a little afraid, he was certainly extremely annoyed, so much so that within a few months it became evident that, like Henry II and Thomas à Becket, he had let it be known that he would be grateful to anyone who would rid him of this turbulent Inspector. The story of this will be told in the next Chapter.

# Chapter 15

# Scandal, schemes, and Egyptology for Egyptians 1913–1914

Howard Carter was at this time excavating for Lord Carnarvon in the Delta at the ancient Hyksos city of Xois, or Sakha as it is called in Arabic. Although it was an uncomfortable site, humid, snake-infested, unprovided with smart hotels and unvisited by society, Carnarvon had nevertheless been persuaded that it was promising. 'It is well thought of by the Cairo dealers,' he wrote to Newberry from England – a nice instance, incidentally, of the close eye kept by the dealers on the sites, of Carnarvon's interest in their opinion, and of his assumption of like-mindedness in Newberry. Furthermore, he says he has heard about the place from Wallis Budge. He 'showed me some things that came from Sakha … He seemed to know a good deal about the matter,' and Carnarvon signs off with his racing flourish: 'I am just off to Newmarket' – a characteristic farewell that Weigall noted later in an essay on Carnarvon.[1]

Carter's and Weigall's professional paths therefore crossed once more, excavator and Inspector working in the same region. There is no sign that they had much to do with each other personally, but Weigall would have been pleased to have a 'scientific' excavator at work in the Delta. When he took up his post as Inspector there, he realized that the antiquities in Egypt's great area of cultivation were disappearing faster than anywhere else in the country. More and more land was being ploughed and irrigated, and yet at the same time the Department of Antiquities seemed curiously phlegmatic. As Weigall explained to Hortense:

> … whenever a fellah wanted a bit of our ground which adjoined his fields to be cultivated he applied to buy it, and Maspero used to say "Yes; give us £5 to make soundings, and if we find no antiquities we will sell it to you." Hundreds of acres have gone this way, and the excavations were being done by our own native inspectors who made a hole or two, pocketed the £5, stole whatever antiquities they found, and handed the ground over to the purchaser. I've stopped that dead, and thereby saved Heaven knows how many papyri etc which would have been ruined by the irrigation of the ground.

The correspondence for this period frequently mentions a 'Delta scheme', but without giving the details. In the letter to Gardiner about the sale-of-antiquities plan, the two ideas appear to have tied in, at least at the point of the strict half and half division: 'I am very anxious to get people to work in the Delta on the easy terms I proposed. So if we are severe in regard to the Upper Egyptian sites we shall make them all the more ready to take up the Delta business, which at the moment is the most urgent in Egypt, considering the rate at which the tells are being lost.'[2]

The 'tells' were mud-brick mounds, acres wide, the remains of ancient cities to archaeologists, but to the local *sebakhin*, quarries for fertilizer. Weigall seems to have urged a systematic rescue programme, as he had done at Gurneh, with incentives in the form of easier terms. In November 1912 he was writing to Hortense to say that 'the Delta scheme is keenly approved by K, but Maspero is somewhat in the way ... I expect it will go through; and work on Tell Basta will begin soon if it does.' He showed the proposal to the American archaeologist Reisner, whom he had known from the period of the Nubian Survey, and who was now Curator of the Egyptian Department of the Boston Museum. Reisner wrote back to put in a bid for Sa el-hagar – the ancient Delta city of Tanis – if all went through satisfactorily.[3] Another archaeologist, Gerald Wainwright, one of Petrie's assistants, also wrote to say he'd 'heard rumours of a Govt. scheme to dig the Delta sites' and could Weigall 'submit my name as a candidate for any work there may be going.'[4]

In other words, the idea was gaining some currency by the time Carnarvon ceased work at Sakha, so that Carter's proposal to carry on in the Delta for the 1912–13 season, at Tell el-Balamun, may have owed something to it. Weigall may himself have put in a word for the Delta to Carnarvon. In a letter to Hortense he describes calling on the Carnarvons as they passed through Cairo early in 1913: 'Lady Carnarvon gave me her photo and kissed her hand to me when I left – so startling, as she and I have always been rather stiff and formal with one another. Lord Carnarvon has bad headaches, and seems ill. I like him *very* much always.' What Weigall didn't know was that, at about this period, Howard Carter had hostile plans for him.

It will be remembered that Lythgoe's arrival in Cairo in January 1913 prompted a letter from Weigall about the bronze. The American party was on its way through to Thebes, where Winlock of the Metropolitan Museum was working. Edgar, the Delta Inspector who would have been responsible for Carter's work at Sakha, was in Luxor too, having taken over from Weigall. Cecil Firth was also in the district. Firth was at that time in correspondence with Weigall, anxious to know of possible openings in the Department and therefore of any career moves that Weigall might be contemplating. Perhaps neither Lythgoe nor Mace was entirely discreet – as indeed they had no special reason to be. At any rate, all these people were to figure as disseminators of damaging tales about Weigall. At the end of the season at Tell el-Balamun, in May 1913, Carter paid a visit to Luxor. No doubt he had already heard about Weigall and the bronze from Edgar, and now the sociableness of Luxor provided the yeast to ferment the story. On May 9th, he wrote the following letter to Lythgoe:

Dear Lythgoe,

Do you still feel disposed to show the documents you have regarding Weigall and the proposed sale of the bronze? If so will you either give them to Maspero or to me to send to Maspero? They will be used against Weigall.

Weigall seems to be causing a lot of trouble and Maspero says he ought to be dismissed. I am telling you this so that you may know the full consequences in the event of your giving them up. Personally I think that such disgraceful proceedings on the part of an English Inspector of Antiquities should be stopped but one hates to have to do such a thing. Maspero I know will be grateful and will use every discretion.

Yours sincerely,
Howard Carter

In any case please treat this as confidential.[5]

Carter speaks of Weigall causing 'a lot of trouble', which is an odd phrase to use about his efforts to sell the bronze. Perhaps he meant that in causing talk, he was causing trouble, for it reflected upon the Department. But the story did not really break publicly until later that year. Or could Carter have been referring to Weigall's activities in other areas, in particular his sale-of-antiquities scheme? Certainly this was troublesome to Maspero, and to anyone such as Lythgoe (or indeed to himself, as an occasional dealer in antiquities) who would have been alarmed at any proposal to restrict the export of antiquities, and block the traditional sources of supply. And yet, 'disgraceful proceedings' seems to point to the bronze again. In that connection, did Carter know that the statuette was not Egyptian and not stolen? One is reminded of his tendency to call names, as in the Semenowski versus Tyndale case. Whatever the answers, what comes through strongly from the letter is that he and Maspero were acting together, that Maspero was using Carter as his agent, and that Carter was happy to oblige.

It is unlikely that Weigall ever knew about Carter's part in his fate. Years later, at the time of the discovery of Tutankhamun's tomb, when Weigall figured prominently in the press campaign to break Carnarvon's exclusive deal with the *Times*, there were attempts to re-run the scandal in order to discredit him. Weigall wrote to Carter at that time (the letter mentioned in an earlier chapter) referring to these efforts, but he doesn't appear to realize that he was addressing one of the chief players in the original drama. In fact he was out of the way, on leave in England, when Carter wrote to Lythgoe, and only when he returned, in October 1913, did he realize how busy people had been in his absence.

Hortense, having left the children with Mimi, had accompanied him this time in order to pack up the house in Luxor and establish some sort of household in Cairo. Weigall wrote to her in Upper Egypt, to say that he had had a visit from Cecil Firth, 'who had a long talk with me yesterday. He says Ronald Storrs sent for him and dressed him down for spreading tales about me. He seemed quite honestly good-natured and not intentionally libellous!' This is Storrs's sole public appearance in relation to the statuette affair, the irony of it only matched by the wonder of being stabbed so affectionately in the back by Firth. In another letter to Hortense, he reports that someone has told him that 'there were many stories in Mansourah emanating from Edgar about me.' Meanwhile, Winlock was winging the gossip to Newberry.

Winlock's letter, which also discusses the situation at the department in general, explains why Weigall's fate was so interesting to everybody. The Curator of the Cairo Museum, Emile Brugsch, who had been at his post for about thirty-two years, was about to retire. After years of departmental immobility, career opportunities were in the wind. There was excitement among the archaeologists, to which Weigall's story gave a relish: not only the pleasures of *schadenfreude* but the possibility of another vacancy. 'The talk of Egypt has been the Service des Antiquites,' wrote Winlock:

> Brugsch has resigned to take effect on January 1st and the Weigall affair has created such a scandal that it has got into the papers. Ratigan [sic] has been promoted to Berlin and everybody said it was to clear the Agency's reputation a bit. There were the wildest of speculations as to Weigall's fate. That gentleman has shown a great deal of ingenuity to say the least having kept the Gazette posted with little personal items about himself and how Maspero had promised him Brugsch's place if his health held good.
>
> Meantime the government tried to make Maspero do something definite and as he would not K. and Macdonald took things in their own hands and settled it all without him. Daressy becomes administrative head and Quibell scientific head of the Museum. Firth takes Quibell's place. Weigall – so Maspero told me – was asked to resign from April 1st and until then is to be inspector of Galoubia where there are no antiquities but an insane asylum and the Cairo Purification Plant. Weigall says to people – not to me for he doesn't speak to me any more – that he has been forced to resign because of his health but that the government is so disgusted that gossips should have spread stories about him and a bronze statue that they have insisted on his staying on until it all blows over!! The result is that there is only one vacancy ...[6]

Clearly Winlock doesn't believe a word of Weigall's gloss. But in fact, Maspero had indeed offered him Brugsch's place, as far back as November 1912, when it was originally thought Brugsch would be retiring. And when, later on, Maspero appeared to change his mind, the Agency did try to cook up something else for him.

To go back a little. When Weigall returned to Egypt in the autumn of 1912, it was generally understood that he was not going to be satisfied with the Inspectorate of the Delta for long. He was firmly entrenched in Cairo, either proposing schemes that had implications for the department as a whole, or, if they concerned the Delta in particular, that needed the consideration of the authorities in the capital. In fact it is remarkable how much he threw himself into the new Inspectorate, even though he saw it as a dead-end. What he called 'the Delta scheme' has been mentioned: only a few years before, such a project would have filled pages of excited description. Now one has to look in the asides, the postscripts, or the notes scribbled across letters received, to discover what they were. For example, on a letter from one James Dixon, an archaeologist who had worked with Peet at Abydos for the Egypt Exploration Fund, Weigall pencilled the explanation: 'I offered him a job on a 'model' excavation we are starting, run by Egyptians under the eye of an Englishman – my idea – much taken up by K. It's to show that if Egyptians work scientifically they will get concessions as much as Europeans do.' For the period it was an extraordinarily far-sighted and imaginative idea, however patronizing that 'eye of an Englishman' might seem now. But this note, and a passing mention in a letter to Gardiner, is all one ever hears of it; though, as we shall see, he did write much more about the whole Egyptianizing idea in another project he was working on at this time.[7]

But, as Weigall knew from experience, if initiatives of this kind were to succeed, they needed to be promoted from a position of greater power than an Inspectorate. Maspero – for the time being at least – seems to have been prepared to accommodate him by moving him into the Museum and onto a higher career ladder, perhaps in the hope that it might keep him quiet. At any rate, just when Maspero was being harassed by the ministers over the sale-of-antiquities scheme, summoned hither and thither by Cecil and Kitchener, Weigall wrote to Hortense to say that 'Maspero was so keen to shut my mouth before he saw K. that he voluntarily offered me Brugsch's job in the Museum, which would make me second man in the Dept ... he could hardly have known what he was talking about, for the Germans insist on putting a man in in Brugsch's place.'

Maspero probably understood perfectly well what he was doing – blocking the Germans being part of it. A few weeks later Maspero was still keen, in spite of the fact that Kitchener was too, and that he, Kitchener, linked the move specifically with the sale-of-antiquities scheme:

Maspero has told me verbally of his keen wish for me to come into the Museum, and he has made me go and see Macdonald and Cecil etc, and everybody has agreed to it, and K. has said that I am to go into the Museum with the avowed object of carrying out my great selling scheme, combining both jobs, and he has told Cecil to write me a letter which I have just received, saying that as regards salary, perhaps I shall be given an extra allowance for carrying out the scheme ...

In fact the whole idea had become so definite in Maspero's mind that he let it be known more widely. Cecil Firth wrote to Weigall in early 1913 to say that 'Maspero when here seemed to think you would be likely to come into the Museum when B[rugsch] fell out of his niche (or finally lay down between the shafts).'[8]

Nothing came of all this. In the end, Brugsch decided to hang on for another year, perhaps like Maspero hoping for a suitable German successor to emerge. By the time the whole question became live again, the scandal had broken, and the antagonism between Maspero and Weigall had become as open as the good manners of both parties allowed. Actually, whether the statuette affair had any material effect on their relations, or whether it simply enabled Maspero to wage old wars by other means, is hard to tell. But certainly, by the autumn of 1913, we hear no more of Maspero wanting Weigall in the Museum.

But the Advisors remained loyal to Weigall – loyal or, as with Rattigan, anxious to clear the reputation of the Agency. Weigall was an employee after all, and an Englishman; if Rattigan could be actually promoted, Winlock needn't have boggled at the idea of the Agency closing ranks in Weigall's defence. Whatever the reason, as soon as Weigall had sent Macdonald his account of the statuette affair, and had contradicted the various versions of what had happened – that the bronze was Egyptian, that it was government property, that he had failed to inform the authorities, that he had smuggled it out of the country – then the Agency did what it could to find him something: 'He [Macdonald] took my letter to Lord K. and Cecil, and last night I saw him again, when he told me all was well, and that Lord K. had decided that whether Brugsch resigned *or not* I *must* be given a job at once, so as to correct the bad impression of the stories ...'

There is an irony at the back of all this in the figure of Brugsch himself. It was generally understood that Brugsch belonged to the bad old school of archaeology, more interested in acquiring spectacular objects for the Museum than in scholarship, and as liable as Theodore Davis to destroy anything that wasn't alluring to the eye. There was also a strong suspicion that he had for years been helping himself to items from the Museum collections. The archaeologist Leonard Woolley tells how Carnarvon once bought a couple of antikas, only to remember afterwards that he had seen them in the Museum. When he revisited the display case, he found that it was indeed empty, and went to Maspero. Maspero confessed that he knew they had gone, but that he had not taken any steps: 'Carnarvon knew what that meant; it meant that the things had been stolen by the Sub-Director, who was a German [i.e. Brugsch], and to have accused him would have caused an International incident that they couldn't possibly afford.' [9] Brugsch represented the German interest as unassailably as Maspero represented the French, and no amount of shady rumours could topple him.

One archaeologist who did try to deal fairly by Weigall was, surprisingly, Norman de Garis Davies, who, as we have seen, had worked at Gurneh with him and Gardiner. He clearly didn't consider himself a close friend but nevertheless, as he wrote to Gardiner, he suspected that the gossip about Weigall was 'a fine example of uncharity believing all things and hoping all things': [10]

I wrote to him frankly lately and told him he expected too much of his friends if he expected them to believe in him *in toto* when an explicit narrative about him was widespread in Cairo and uncontradicted by him or by his superiors and of which moreover a small part at any rate was supported by documentary evidence. He took it pretty well and finally wrote me his whole account of the matter. I am inclined to think that if roseate and a little reserved it is true and that the tale Firth and Winlock and no doubt others are telling with most attractive detail and Defoe-like picturesqueness is a myth engendered on the intense dislike he has aroused.

W. says he has made all right with his superiors and they have promised to scotch the scandal. But among his superiors he does not seem to reckon Maspero! And I don't think *he* yearns to set Humpty Dumpty back on the wall ... (I dislike F[irth] *intensely* and distrust him).[11]

Davies's mention of 'documentary evidence' is arresting: it reminds one of Carter's letter to Lythgoe. Was this the evidence that Lythgoe was asked to provide? Did Lythgoe therefore accede to Carter's request for documents, and did Maspero use them, as Carter promised, against Weigall? Nothing suggests that Weigall ever faced any open challenge from Maspero. Did Maspero, therefore, 'use' the documents in a different kind of way altogether, i.e. leak them? And if so, was it in order to create, or at least to fuel, scandalous speculation? Like Storrs, Maspero was a consummate diplomat, and it would be surprising if he left any tracks. As for the 'intense dislike', it was probably all Weigall could expect after a career spent making waves. Like all evangelists – like Mimi herself, though Mimi's girls were no doubt more tractable than archaeologists – Weigall couldn't see something wrong without leaping in to put it right, with all the ardour, and even arrogance, of absolute conviction. Very often he was right, but no one ever made friends by being right.

But there may also at this particular period have been a certain hardness and edge to him. It was a bitter time. His sick-leave in England had given him the longest period with Hortense that he had ever had, and it had not been a success. Over the years, she had allowed herself to slip into a chaotic way of life – herself, the children and the house uncared for and unkempt. The pedestal he had put her on had become a little cracked and chipped. They were out of step with each other. He had knocked about a bit since the days when he had called her his religion, while she had remained somewhat self-consciously the keeper of the moral flame. He consoled himself in England with an affair, and now, after his frank revelations about various flirtations in Luxor and Cairo, she was jealous and aggrieved. He justified himself on the grounds that he was only a mortal man – with the emphasis rather complacently on *man* – and she reproached him with betraying her trust. When he returned to Cairo in 1912 and again the next year, he argued it out with her in letter after letter, trying, it seems, to shatter her innocence, to drag her into the modern world where affairs and flirtations and prostitutes (a deliberately brutal touch, that – though he promises that unlike most Englishmen in Cairo, he has never visited one) are all part of a man's life, quite separate from home and family.

Had she been quicker on her feet, she could have demolished him, and the irony is that he probably would have admired her for it. The novels he was to write later often feature plucky women who make devastating attacks on male assumptions. But Hortense was slow to provoke. He was fond of her, but he no longer wanted a Pre-Raphaelite goddess, still less a dishevelled one. He wanted someone, as he put it, 'smart and alert and clean and orderly'. Her replies belonged to another world: 'Your letters are profoundly cold and serious, and come as solemn church bells ringing through my wild sleigh bells, on a cold and frosty morning! Very fine and deep and good and comforting and clear, but not wild.'

His own wildness fascinated him, but it was in reality more desperate, less simply jolly than he implies there. He loved the idea of family life and despite the long separations, had come to adore the children, especially his eldest son, Alured, who had first enchanted him during the months in 1910-11 when Hortense was in Cairo having their second son, Denny. Alured had stayed in Luxor then, and when his aunt Geanie had come to visit with her daughter Betty, the two noisy children had virtually taken over the house – much to Weigall's delight. His spell in England in 1912 brought home to him how much he had missed, but it did so at the very moment when it seemed to be slipping away. Everything – career, wife, and home – was turning to dust and ashes.

And now something happened that was at least as bad as the failure of marriage and career. One of the reasons for de Garis Davies's letter about Weigall to Gardiner was that he had understood the friendship between the two men to be in peril, and he wanted to urge Gardiner to stand by Weigall over the business of the statuette: Weigall, he wrote, 'is capable of making a real fool of himself, and feeling it acutely when it is done.'[12] The two friends had indeed had a blazing row. It had arisen at the time of Gardiner's final preparations for the publication of the catalogue of the Tombs of the Nobles.

The quarrel was particularly painful because it was all about the very thing that they had both agreed was irrelevant to the great object of disinterested science: intellectual property. It was the possessiveness of other scholars that had led to all the evil at Gurneh, so that to find themselves quarrelling over who did what in initiating and carrying out the cataloguing of the tombs was peculiarly humiliating. Gardiner had been left alone for the winter seasons at Gurneh ever since Weigall's collapse in September 1911. By the time the catalogue and Introduction were finished in September 1913, he had come to regard them as basically his own work, accomplished with help from Weigall. Actually, he had seen it in that light for some time. In a letter to Professor J.H. Breasted at Chicago, written in January 1913, he describes his recent work in Egypt and his whole attitude towards the conservation and recording of the monuments as though they were the result of his own independent assessment of priorities: 'During recent visits to Egypt I had gradually come to the conclusion that the essential task of Egyptology now is the publication of the monuments of Egypt – after, at least, their very preservation has been ensured. In particular I have interested myself in the private tombs at Thebes, and with Weigall's help, I believe that I have started a rather important piece of work.'[13]

Fortunately Weigall would never have seen this letter, but he was bound to discover the attitude that informed it sooner or later. The more so since Gardiner himself seems genuinely to have been unaware of how hurtful it was. In September of that year, Gardiner wrote to Weigall to say that '*my* Topographical Catalogue of the Theban Tombs is just going to press' [my italics], and although Weigall held his fire, one can imagine the twinge it must have given him. Finally, in October, Weigall saw the proof sheets, and in the midst of a high fever, at 2 a.m. one night, he annotated them with what Gardiner called 'insolent remarks and contemptible insinuations' and sent them back.[14] It is a pity Weigall didn't change his mind, as he sometimes did on such occasions. There is for example a long and furious letter to Petrie written in 1909, detailing various acts of inconsiderateness, at the top of which Weigall has written – 'not to be sent, just to let off steam'.[15] It is a pity too that they could not have met, Weigall being in Egypt at the time, and Gardiner in London.

The 'insolent remarks', for which Weigall apologized, seem to have been prompted by his feeling that Gardiner had 'by an oversight, rather done me down':

> Perhaps it is because the slaving away at those tombs for years during the heat of summer that you have never known, and during periods of great loneliness and lack of help, has impressed the whole subject on my mind. I know and fully admit your great work, but I do think the cataloguing work and the careful ferreting out which you have done cannot obliterate all my preliminary labours; and I feel that you were not very thoughtful when you took seriously my tactful and flattering remarks to you suggesting that I had done so little that I hardly felt that my name could dare stand beside yours on the title page!

That was a rash mistake of Weigall's, and it took them some time to sort out the matter of the title page, Gardiner insisting that he needed Weigall's specific permission to put his name there, and Weigall coyly evading a direct answer. What Weigall really minded was not so much the title page but the wording of the Introduction:

> It will *absolutely* satisfy me if only you will say "we" and "Weigall and I", etc; but what drives me *mad* with rage is when you state as *your* views the principles which I was working out in the sweat of my brow and which I gradually and slowly evolved, and then insinuated into your at first hostile mind in those long discussions we had at my camp at Gurneh.[16]

Rather wearily, as though dealing with an unreasonable child, Gardiner said he would see what he could do, though it was too late to recast the whole thing, and he refused to admit that he had been in any way ungenerous. It was simply 'a disinterested piece of scientific work, which was merely impressed with my name because someone must take the responsibility ...'[17] Gardiner was cool and lofty, Weigall was heated and emotional. In the end, after a detour when Weigall played with the idea of publishing two separate volumes and pretended to try to remember which bits of which tomb lists had been made by whom, and whose notes had been used as the basis for what, they arrived at some sort of harmony. Gardiner made the necessary adjustments to the Introduction, Weigall finally said he did want to have his name on the title page, and the book came out as their joint work. But there remained in Weigall, even after they had shaken hands and made up, a sense of loss and disappointment. It comes in a postscript to one of the letters, squeezed in across the top and along the margins, a passionate afterthought:

As regards the Introduction here returned, you have defended yourself perfectly and have shown yourself perfectly correct: you manage to give my full due to me, however, in such a way that it looks as though you didn't feel a word of what you say. At first I thought it was deliberate. Now I see it is a sort of literary self-restraint. O Alan, I fear I'm a journalist, and you are one of those nasty careful, cautious scholars! But why on earth *should you give me my due?* Weren't we going to stand up together to the world and say "This is our work. Let the *world* give US our due"? I seem to remember those words spoken by you one night in the old tent. ... I object to the whole idea of your *thanking* me, so to speak. I wanted Egyptologists to thank us both, side by side, we two who were friends and who, of the whole world, alone saw eye to eye about the ethics of archaeology.[18]

The quarrel was not, in the end, fatal. They continued to meet and talk in England during the war, and at one time even established a weekly habit of it. And after all, the catalogue was not the only fruit of their collaboration. Before Weigall left Luxor, and together with Robert Mond, they had begun to push for the creation of a new post – an Inspectorate specifically for the Tombs of the Nobles at Gurneh, like Quibell's at Saqqara. They were successful, and the post, funded by Mond, was filled by the Petrie-trained archaeologist, Ernest Mackay. The two of them could pat each other's backs over that at least, without worrying about intellectual property.[19] But there was no denying that Gardiner's career, as it advanced, took him inexorably among scholars and many-initialled professors. Talk of 'we two' standing up against them soon became a piece of impossible romanticism, if it wasn't already. They grew apart, but they never quite lost sight of each other, and the memory of a real friendship remained.

It is extraordinary to think that during this hectic period, Weigall was also writing his biography of Cleopatra. He rarely mentions it in the letters, beyond the fact that it is going slowly – and no wonder. Nevertheless, it was ready by the end of 1913, and he was correcting the proofs by February 1914. On the face of it, Weigall could hardly have failed with a glamorous subject like Cleopatra. But on historical matters as in everything else, he had a talent for controversy, and he chose to challenge the popular view of her. With Akhnaten he had been pretty safe. There had been no orthodox opinion to overthrow. Cleopatra on the other hand was one of the most mythologized women in history.

In ancient times the record had been written by her political enemies, and the view that she was a dusky siren who seduced the upright Caesar and ruined the great Antony had persisted until modern times. The stature of Caesar and Rome depended, at least in part, on the depiction of Cleopatra and Egypt as a side-show, whose only importance was to serve as a warning against passion in the affairs of men. In 1902, the historian Charles Oman summed up the attitude: 'The whole [Egyptian] episode is unworthy of Caesar; the conqueror of Gaul should not have placed himself in the position to be besieged for months by a Levantine rabble [in the palace at Alexandria]. Still less should he have lapsed into his silly and undignified entanglement with Cleopatra.'[20] Weigall set himself to overthrow all this.

Far from being irrelevant to Caesar's purposes, Egypt was absolutely central, he maintained: 'Egypt ... was the granary of the world, the most important commercial market of the Mediterranean, ... the gateway of the unconquered kingdoms of the Orient.'[21] The journey up the Nile that Caesar took with Cleopatra in her sumptuous barge, with four hundred attendant vessels, had always been regarded as yet another example of his foolish enslavement, but Weigall maintained that it was an expedition to determine the resources of the country. Weigall's own knowledge of the land, of the wheat fields of the Delta, the ancient quarries and mines of the eastern desert and Nubia, and the trade routes across to the Red Sea, led him to believe that Caesar's focus was bound to shift from the lands to the north and west towards those to the south and east:

> Egypt has always been a land of speculation, attracting alike the interest of the financier and the enthusiasm of the conqueror; and Caesar's imagination must have been stimulated by those ambitious schemes which have fired the brains of so many of her conquerors, just as that of the great Alexander had been inspired three centuries before. ... he may perhaps have considered the expediency of carrying Roman arms into the uttermost parts of Ethiopia; of crossing the Red Sea into Arabia; or of penetrating, like Alexander, to India and the marvellous kingdoms of the East. Even so, eighteen hundred years later, Napoleon Bonaparte dreamed of marching his army through Egypt to the lands of Hindustan; and so also England, striving to hold her beloved India ... fixed her gaze upon the Nile valley ...[22]

To some, this kind of history writing was intolerable. The reviewer for the *Nation* wrote witheringly: 'It would be hard to find a book of serious intent in which "must have been", "might have been", "possibly", "probably", and other such symbols of lack of evidence are so persistently made the cornerstones of imposing structures of alleged certainty.'[23]

Weigall saw *realpolitik* as well as romance, in Caesar's – and after him, Antony's – interest in Cleopatra. Of course, he was hardly the writer to discount romance, but he was unwilling to take the nearest way and present his heroine as a scheming voluptuary. In the first place, he points out, Cleopatra was not a dusky Oriental at all; she was a Ptolemy, a Macedonian Greek, supposedly descended from one of Alexander's generals, and therefore as likely as not to have been fair-haired and blue-eyed. As for her reputation as the very type of sensual decadence, there is no evidence that she was worse than anyone else at that time:

> At an age when the legal rights of marriage were violated on every side, ... Cleopatra, so far as I can see, confined her attentions to the two men who, in sequence each acted towards her in the manner of a legitimate husband, each being recognized in Egypt as her divinely-sanctioned consort.[24]

As far as sexual licence goes Caesar himself, says Weigall, could have taught her a thing or two. When he met Cleopatra, he was a seasoned womanizer of fifty-four, and she at twenty-one, a woman 'so far as we know ... of blameless character'.[25]

This was a blow to his readers. One of Weigall's fans wrote to him to say she felt a little disappointed that he hadn't managed to find any *affaires de coeur* in Cleopatra's life beyond Caesar and Antony. The *TLS* critic used the same point for a piece of sarcasm calculated to hit Weigall where it hurt: 'There are many Cleopatras in History – a round dozen in fact – but there is only one in Romance; and we should have thought it impossible to make that one dull, if Mr Weigall had not shown us how.'[26] In short, Weigall was a spoilsport. But he needed to be, in order to clear the way for his real argument, a case for her importance as a formative influence in the creation of the Roman Empire.

Weigall's discussion of Cleopatra's role, as distinct from her personality, is the most interesting part of the book. Not that he himself makes the distinction in so many words. In fact, he is pulled in both directions at once, weakening his discussion of her political importance by trying, against odds of his own making, to be vivid about her character. He relies heavily on Plutarch for her appearance, her voice, her charm, her wit, and so on, but, in order to sustain his idea that she was not an accomplished man-eater, he falls heavily into the trap of turning her into a child-woman, a harum-scarum dare-devil, and later into a plucky little mother in the nursery among her babes. In her book *Cleopatra: Histories, Dreams and Distortions* about the Cleopatra legend, Lucy Hughes-Hallett identifies this line in Weigall with a general trend at that period,[27] the most famous example of which is the infantilized heroine of G.B. Shaw's play *Caesar and Cleopatra*.

But Weigall's Cleopatra is really a shrewd politician, aware of the dynamics of power and economics in the region, and motivated by the desire to protect the Ptolemaic dynasty. Her claim that Caesar was the father of her son Caesarion, and then, after Caesar's assassination, her marriage to Antony, were both intended to promote the Ptolemys by turning them into Caesars. Rome had the military power but it needed Egypt's wealth. Cleopatra's apparently mad extravagance – melting priceless pearls in vinegar and so on – was in fact a calculated stratagem for advertising Egypt's bottomless purse. Weigall surmises that Caesar could not have lived at close quarters with Cleopatra without having distinctly unrepublican thoughts: 'She represented monarchy in its most absolute form, and in Egypt her word was law. The very tone of her royal mode of life must have constituted new matter for his mind to ruminate upon.'[28]

The idea was not entirely new. A few years before, the historian Giuglielmo Ferrero had written in passing that 'the Queen of Egypt plays a strange and significant part in the tragedy of the Roman Republic ... She desired to become Caesar's wife and she hoped to awaken in him the passion for kingship.'[29] But Ferrero had left it at that. Weigall's development of the notion was largely speculation, and as such abhorrent in some quarters. But it was not implausible speculation. Though there are no actual documents to prove it, Weigall makes the whole thing hang together with some conviction.

The critic of the *Saturday Review* (20 June 1914), was prepared to 'receive his political fancies as inspired history'. The philosopher and historian John Beattie Crozier wrote to say that although he had flattered himself 'that there was hardly anything worth knowing [about Rome] that I did not know already', Weigall's book 'has been a real surprise to me. I could check nearly every statement you make *separately* but the *unification* which you have given me is a new and *real* acquisition. I am recommending it to all my historical friends. In many ways it is most admirable, and in itself would dispense any ordinary reader from resorting to any other books.'[30]

The press as a whole was congratulatory, though not always so knowledgeably. They found it a wonderful story, dramatically told, with living characters, a form of praise which of course Weigall would have welcomed. But the *Saturday Review* (20 June 1914) was perhaps the most perceptive when it said that Weigall's imagination was best when it was 'politically active'. It was the imagination of the 'natural historian' – and by implication, not of the novelist. The critic could 'unreservedly praise' his portraits of Caesar and Antony and Octavian, about whom so much more is known, but Cleopatra herself was unconvincing: 'Frankly, we do not see the woman he describes.'

One can only imagine that *Cleopatra* was written very early in the mornings, for during this time Weigall was leading the same sort of social and dragoman life that had so overwhelmed him in Luxor. From the drifts of invitations and menu cards among Weigall's papers, one has the impression of a society constantly dining and lunching at the hotels, arranging little expeditions, playing tennis, meeting one another at musical evenings (one of Storrs's special attractions was the composer Ethel Smyth), introducing friends, daughters, brothers-in-law, thanking profusely, flattering, gushing, apologizing. Outside the circle of archaeologists, Weigall appears to have aroused the very reverse of intense dislike. The same energy that made him such an uncomfortable colleague made him a fascinating companion. He had a gusto, an irrepressible flair that irritated the scholars and alarmed the administrators, but charmed his friends. 'If I were to try to tell you how badly we all miss you here,' wrote one from Luxor, 'and how often I hear it said around me – I should become tired! You have no idea what a mainspring of *all* our enjoyment you were!' People 'go about with your book [the *Guide* ] everywhere. I simply can't tell you how much we all pine for you – everyone moans that you are ungetatable for the present – and in reality I think you can't realize what a tremendous loss you are to us!'[31]

In fact Weigall kept an archaeological eye on Luxor, even from Cairo. A letter from Thomas Cook and Son thanks him for his advice, assures him that they will furnish their dragomans with information on the Tombs of the Nobles, and promises not to send parties to the Valley of the Queens. Weigall scribbled a note on the bottom of this letter saying that 'I advised them not to, so as not to damage Nefertari', the highly decorated tomb of Ramesses II's Queen.[32] But the demands of the tourists at hand were pressing. The voices, with their elaborate self-deprecations barely disguising their insistent demands, can almost be heard through the trailing handwriting – 'Do you remember two wandering females? we are going to the Fayoum, and wondered if you knew of some antiquarian who just might be persuaded …?', 'Could you tell me if some lesser clerk could show us the Museum, on *no* account are you to do it yourself', 'Lady so-and-so is dying to meet you, would it be a bore …?'

There were people with no other introduction than the fact that they had read his books, they had heard him spoken of. Others approached his friends for an introduction: 'Dear Mr Storrs, … When will you bring Mr Weigall to see me? We long to know him. …'. A certain Sir Claude MacDonald wanting to be shown round the Museum wrote to Storrs: 'I understand that the greatest living expert or one of the greatest is a Mr Weigall. I wonder could he be persuaded to show us over? I understand he is a great friend of yours and that if anybody can persuade him you can.'[33] Storrs sent him the letter – 'O beautiful words!!' Weigall scribbled in the margin.

Weigall was by this time acquainting himself closely with the collections, perhaps in preparation for his sale-of-antiquities scheme, and had embarked on another Guide for the use of visitors. He worked at it steadily through the winter of 1913–14, and by March 1914 had finished the manuscript on all the lower galleries. But, as he told Hortense, he then heard that 'all the Old Kingdom galleries, i.e. the best ones, are to be closed for two years, so it is no use publishing it till then.' It was the story of all these last months. When he left Egypt in April 1914, it was in mid-sentence, so to speak. Half-a-dozen irons were in the fire, and he still thought he would be coming back the following season, if not in Government service, then as a private person, excavating, researching, even perhaps as the head of an Institute that he had long been meditating. He never stopped spinning off ideas; as one fell away, another would emerge, and sometimes he would juggle two or three at the same time. The Inspectorate of all-Egypt died soon; the Delta scheme and the sale-of-antiquities scheme sprang up. These were joined by a proposal (prompted by complaints from tourists to the Pyramids) to overhaul the chaotic ticket system run by the Bedouin, licensees of the Department by long tradition. Each of these initiatives began to fade for one reason or another, but he pressed on without a backward glance. Apart from a spurt of anger at the failure of the Pyramid plan – much money was involved and he sniffed corruption – it is almost as if the only way to avoid defeat was to rush on. Now, in early 1914, he was engaged on one last project.

In fact, he had thought about it as far back as 1907, and had drawn up an outline in December 1911, just before he went on sick-leave. It was a proposal for an Institute of Archaeology, rather along the lines of the British Schools in Rome and Athens, with offices in London and Cairo, to be funded by private donation. It was to be equipped with a library, with complete collections of photographs, maps and plans of the ancient sites, with the services of philologists, ancient historians, and experts in modern archaeological method – in short with everything necessary to provide a scientific training to students of archaeology, both European and, significantly, Egyptian. That was the backbone of it, but there were also to be specific pieces of work undertaken by the Institute, particularly in the areas of conservation, copying and recording.

It could be said – and he did say it, privately – that this Institute was a final attempt to promote those principles of scientific archaeology and conservation to which he had failed to convert the Department of Antiquities. Thwarted in his attempt to repeat the Upper Egyptian model, baffled by Maspero's intransigence, barred from the post of Director General, he was now trying his last throw: to side-step the Department altogether and create a parallel institution. As he wrote to Cromer, to whom he sent his outline with an invitation to become the Institute's patron: 'The main objects which the proposed Institute would have in view would be just those which I see no chance of our Department adopting; and the Institute relieves the Govt. of the delicate task of interfering in the administration by itself doing the work left undone.'[34]

Cromer's answer was cautious, pointing out that there were already existing organizations, such as the Egypt Exploration Fund, and that it would be best to work through them.[35] But the E.E.F., later the Egypt Exploration Society, was essentially a fundraising body for excavations and their associated publications. Furthermore it had shown itself to be not entirely in the vanguard of the new school of archaeology. It was in protest against just this that Petrie had broken with the E.E.F in 1905, and had founded the British School of Archaeology in Egypt (with offices in London, not Egypt).[36] But his society was also essentially a fundraising body for his excavations.

Weigall's proposed Institute was to be only marginally concerned with actual excavation. 'Excavations are conducted far too freely,' he noted in the prospectus, 'and with far too little preparedness ... they are undertaken on a scale wholly disproportionate to the number of trained archaeologists available.'[37] The Institute's real object was to create good excavators. Petrie had long been doing this on the hoof. Now Weigall was proposing, in his characteristically methodical way, to formalize it:

When Egyptologists such as those conducting excavations for the Egypt Exploration Fund or British School in Egypt wished to take new students to Egypt, as almost every year they do, the Institute would undertake, free of charge, to give them some preliminary training ... the want of proper scientific training in those who now take up Egyptology professionally is almost invariable; and until a sound basis is supplied, the science ... will remain in its present chaotic and erratic state.

It is difficult to remember now, when every profession is barricaded behind formidable qualifications, that such a point ever needed to be made.

But Weigall went further and argued also for a specifically Egyptian body of expertise:

No steps of any value whatsoever are being taken to educate the Egyptians to understand and appreciate their ancient ruins and the history which they reveal, nor is any attempt being made to educate them to fill the posts of inspectors in the Department of Antiquities or any other Egyptological posts ...

He proposed that an Egyptian, his old sub-inspector Mahmoud Effendi Rushdy, should deliver courses of lectures on Egyptology at the Egyptian University in Cairo, and he wanted to have, attached to every excavation, a trained Egyptian student.

Weigall was thinking not so much of politics here as of Egyptology. He had always seen a connection between modern and ancient customs and manners, and felt that Egyptian archaeologists would be an asset, because better than Europeans at interpreting what they saw.

So, apart from the provisions covering training and education, it is not surprising that Weigall's prospectuses (there were two different drafts) discussed the study of the manners and customs of ancient Egypt. This, he felt, was 'the most important branch of Egyptology, and that which has most bearing upon the modern Egyptians.' A second project therefore, was to be a study of the manners and customs of modern Egyptians, and this was to be carried out by Egyptians: 'Native clerks in government employment, and others, will be invited to write up accounts of various customs which come under their notice, and these reports or articles will be put into English and published in annual volumes, thereby forming in time a corpus which will be of extreme value to ethnology.' The plan sounds bizarre now, but given the conditions of the time it was a practical way of making use of the means to hand.

No one in the administration of antiquities at that time was thinking remotely along these lines[38] and this in spite of the fact that the whole question of the position of Egyptians in their own country was being urgently debated by British politicians and officials both at home and elsewhere in the Agency. The theory had always been that the British were in Egypt temporarily, called in as a result of the country's financial crisis, continuing there merely as advisors, and retreating gradually into the background until such time as the Egyptians themselves were ready to take control of their own affairs. However during Cromer's reign, far from preparing the Egyptians for power, the British had arrogated more of it to themselves, and had increased their presence throughout the whole of the administration both at the centre and in the provinces. Their stated reasons were admirably altruistic and benevolent, but the fact was that as time went on the Egyptians began to feel aggrieved, and the cause of the Nationalists was strengthened. As we have seen, when Cromer retired after 25 years, the Liberal Government appointed Sir Eldon Gorst with the brief of reversing British encroachment.

Storrs, who was at the Agency under all three Agents – Cromer, Gorst and Kitchener – thought the transition 'essential if Great Britain was ever to redeem her promise of ultimate Evacuation and (in the opinion of some of us) no less essential even if we were to remain in Egypt for ever.'[39] All the same, as he explains in his autobiography, it was an extremely difficult and delicate process for both the British and the Egyptians, and, in practice, resentment and obstruction bedevilled it at every level of officialdom on both sides. The whole subject therefore, was live – not to say electric – at the Ministries when Weigall moved to Cairo. As we have seen, it was not new to Weigall, and on practical grounds he would have agreed with Storrs. He had always felt, from the first years of his appointment, that the only solution lay in drawing the Egyptians in, so that the issues became theirs too. Training Egyptian students was the logical next step.

Weigall knew his project for an Institute would get nowhere without the endorsement of the Agency, and that they in turn could not act in downright opposition of

Maspero. There are several diplomatic sentences in the prospectuses about working side by side with the Antiquities department, acting as a link between it and the various bodies representing the different nationalities, and so on. He knew only too well what would be said. But the objection had already been made. When Cromer replied to Weigall's invitation he sent a copy to William Garstin, one time Advisor to the Public Works Department, to which Garstin replied: 'I entirely agree with what you say in your letter. I cannot see how an Institution like that proposed by Weigall could help clashing with the Antiquities service. ... It looks rather as if Weigall were trying to find a post for himself, and suspect that is what it really means ... I do not expect anything will come of this proposal.'[40]

Garstin was right in a way: it was an attempt at finding a post for himself. But it wasn't cynical and self-serving, which is rather Garstin's implication. Nor did the proposal die straightaway. Weigall tweaked it about, and got many people interested – Professor Sayce, Gardiner, and above all Petrie, who was prepared to lend it his name, as a sister body to his own, sharing certain facilities, but with each retaining its independence. There was interest too among the laity, especially from the wife of the General in command of the British forces in Egypt, Lady Byng, a new and cordial friend. It was real in Weigall's mind up to the last minute. It was his habit to draw up his schemes in meticulous detail: patrons pencilled in, committee members appointed, times of meetings, rents, salaries, expenses, cleaning ladies, closing times, half day holidays. There is a curious melancholy in reading that the Institute would be open from 10am to 4pm, and close on Wednesday and Saturday afternoons.

In the end, as with so much else, the idea did die. Petrie wrote in May 1914 with the news that it had been scotched: 'I am sorry to say that the scheme we talked about when we last met does not seem likely to come to pass. First I had objections from the side of your Committee; and then I found that the views and feelings of various officials in Egypt would not be favourable for the scheme. I am very sorry that we shall not have the benefit of your accumulated knowledge.'[41] And he adds a postscript inviting him to write for his new journal. The unmistakable shadow of Maspero falls across these lines.

But the remarkable fact is that Weigall himself never repined. He had suffered disappointments in his work, character assassination from friends and colleagues, money worries, domestic breakdown, and perhaps worse than anything, the row with Gardiner. Whatever triumphs he might have looked back on were already melting away. In a rare moment of explicit regret, he told Gardiner that he was 'rather disgusted ... everything has slid back in Luxor ... robberies, slack ghaffirs, etc.'[42] And to Hortense he wrote that he thought his life had been 'all on the wrong tack, and that I ought to have given much more time to writing and the arts, and much less to administrative work which literally goes to pieces the second one's back is turned, and has no quality of duration.'

But the letter in which he says this is bursting with excitement and hope, with news about a new play he's been writing, or rather a mime, for he calls it a 'wordless play'. He's done all the sketches for it and now he wants to build the models and sets at once. He has also written quite a lot of songs and wants to get them properly set. The play he showed Gardiner at Gurneh, which he calls 'the Miriam play', altered a hundred times since then, is with an agent in London, and the book about Egyptian art is progressing. Meanwhile the proofs of his biography of Cleopatra have been corrected, and he expects to finish his history of modern Egypt by the end of May. Far from lamenting his fate, he was buoyant: 'Of course Egyptian air does make one live at a high pitch. I have been perfectly raving mad this whole winter, and fuller of ideas than ever before. It is partly due, I think to the fact that I now don't waste time enthusiastically inventing schemes for the Dept. which never come off; but with equal enthusiasm I now make schemes along more artistic lines ... which my mind was too exhausted to do before.'

He speaks of waking up happy in the mornings, of looking forward to England. He hadn't given up on Hortense at all, though admittedly it was always easier for him to think fondly of her from a distance. She was expecting again, the baby due shortly in May, and he was longing to see Alured and Denny, now that they were a little older, and the baby girl, Geraldine, born in March 1913. Suddenly he noticed a different atmosphere round him. Everyone at the Agency was being nice to him. No doubt they were relieved to be seeing the last of him: 'It is as though I were no longer to be feared diplomatically,' he writes – but perhaps there was something infectious in his new-found ease and cheerfulness. Kitchener 'has been speaking nicely about me, so I'm told,' and Weigall was taking parties of Kitchener's friends and family round the Museum several times a week: 'Three of them made me take them round *twice* and a man called Sir George Arthur came on all *three* mornings.'

And so, on the 5th of April 1914, Weigall embarked for England, with the words of his old friend the Advisor for Public Works, Malcolm Macdonald, ringing in his ears:

Macdonald was so good to me that I feel I would do anything in the world for him ... He said the Dept. was good enough for Firth and Quibell and Edgar, but not for men of *my* energy ... "... I've watched you kicking and kicking and kicking at the pricks; and I'm glad you've at last kicked yourself free. You'll never regret it. ... I've asked His Highness to give you a good decoration – you ought to have had it before, but that darned old fool Maspero objected. Now that you're leaving, I can give it to you myself, direct." I really felt quite chokey when I left!

In a few months the Service duly informed Weigall that 'Son Altesse le Khedive' had deigned to confer on him 'la decoration de 3me classe de Medjidieh.'[43] He also received an Austrian decoration, the Cross of the Order of Franz Joseph, though when war broke out it was cancelled by the British as having come from an enemy government.

But in spite of a degree of genuine goodwill from official quarters, the story that stuck to Weigall – and sticks, when his name crops up[44] – was that he left Egypt under a cloud, as a result of the statuette scandal. He himself seemed remarkably equani-mous about it, and it is possible that the cloud was not so much governmental as the creation of the archaeological world. The scandal had clearly been extremely wounding, as wounding in fact as some of his colleagues could possibly make it. It was never spoken of in the family, or only whispered as something dreadful. But others continued to talk, for the tale stayed alive and can be found as late as 1939, virtually unrecognizable. It comes in the autobiography of an acquaintance of Weigall's, Douglas Sladen, a travel writer, political commentator, and one time editor of *Who's Who*: 'Weigall ... was an extremely interesting man,' he writes, 'who was said to have lost his post in Egypt by assisting Kitchener to smuggle his wonderful collection of curios out of Egypt.'[45]

Weigall would have enjoyed that, had he lived to read it. But for the moment his mind was casting forward to the next stage, and all the clouds lay behind him. He stopped at Nice for a week, dreading the cold of England, he said, in spite of his longing to see the family. He was still thinking about and working on the scenario for his wordless play, and wanted time. Sharing Weigall's cabin on the boat had been a writer, Algernon Blackwood (no connection with *Blackwood's Magazine*), whom he had known in Cairo where he had been part of a semi-mystical circle that Weigall had slightly despised – the 'whole set are rather dotty', he had written to Mimi 'with their "New Thought" (Health, Wealth and Flatulence, you know) and spiritualism etc.' Algernon Blackwood had offered to send Weigall's scenario to a friend of his in London, a popular dramatist of the day called Louis Parker. Parker is forgotten now but he was well-known then for devising civic and patriotic pageants, a genre much in fashion in Edwardian England. While still in Nice, Weigall received a reply from Parker in which he offered to meet him and to help in any way he could. He found the play extremely interesting, 'a weird and powerful subject'.[46]

Thus, before even touching foot in England, Weigall, indefatigable as ever, was already taking the first steps in a new career, though at the time he wouldn't have cared to call it that.

# Part Two
## 1914 – 1934

# Chapter 16

# From Egypt to the West End
# 1914–1916

Egyptology wasn't over for him, though archaeology and its administration were. At the time he was happy to say goodbye, but the country and its people always remained in his heart. It is difficult to assess his achievement precisely. His survey of Nubia and his rescue work at Gurneh were of crucial importance – indeed, it is arguable that it is largely because of him that the wall-paintings at Gurneh were not all hacked out and sold to foreign museums in the early years of the twentieth century. These are definite and tangible successes, and it was no doubt in recognition of them that he received medals and honours from foreign governments – there was a German order as well, the Red Eagle, fourth class – though conspicuously not from his own. Beyond these pieces of work, it is also true that many of his aspirations came to be realized, though whether he had a direct hand in hastening them one cannot be sure. The professionalization of archaeology, the importance of conservation, above all the involvement of the Egyptians themselves in preserving their past, these are the things that Weigall strove for. But they were bound to come about in time. History was on his side. Perhaps it could be said with greater certainty that Weigall changed the climate of opinion – both at Government level and among the general public.

Climates of opinion are necessarily vague things, but occasionally a detail turns up that gives it definite shape. One such is a description of J.P. Morgan having lunch with Kitchener at the British Residency in January 1913. It was during his last visit to Egypt before he died, and according to his biographer, his host took the occasion:

> to speak rather sharply about the antiquities that were taken out of the country by Americans ... They [Morgan and his party] all got the impression that he wanted to convey to Mr Morgan and Peter Jay [the American diplomatic agent in Egypt] in an unofficial way, the fact that if he could prevent it, he was not going to permit any more of the best things to go to the Metropolitan Museum.[1]

Weigall wasn't present, but one can almost hear his voice.

But more broadly, he had a real gift, as a writer, for inspiring a wide general public – mostly European and American – with an interest in the country, both in its past and in its present, and for educating it in the issues raised by archaeology. This is not an

209

incidental or trivial accomplishment, and after the war he would continue what he had begun. The very survival of archaeology in Egypt depended in part on work of this kind. Egyptologists, as Gardiner wrote to his wife, tended to dismiss Weigall as a 'mere' popularizer, but they could not ignore the importance of private money. In 1920, for example, when the Egypt Exploration Society won the concession to excavate at El Amarna, Akhnaten's city, the person they turned to for help was Weigall. 'We shall need all the resources we can possibly lay hands on,' Alan Gardiner wrote to him, 'in order to make the expedition as good as anything the Americans can do. Will you help us with some propaganda? No one could possibly help us more than the author of the *Life and Times of Akhnaten*. Newberry is going to write to you on the subject ... Do help us, please!'[2]

Two years later, when the second edition of the *Life and Times of Akhnaton* was about to be published, H.R. Hall, at that time Assistant Keeper at the Department of Egyptian and Assyrian Antiquities in the British Museum, also wrote to ask Weigall to 'boost the E.E.S. and the Amarna digs in your book, on the re-edition of which I congratulate you.' His letter exactly expresses the mixture of need and contempt that the scholarly world felt for Weigall's talents. He himself, says Hall, wouldn't be any use at making an appeal – far too hard-boiled for the 'Great British Public'. 'Ah me!' he writes. 'I fear I am unregenerate: no uplift about *me*. No enthewziasm, no mystery, no ghosteses, no One God, no primeval Egyptian wisdom, no unlucky mummies, no signs of the zodiac, no reincarnation, no abracadabra, no soulfulness about *me*!' In his view, Akhnaten – whom he dubs old Crackpot, Crackernaten, and Crackitaten – was a 'prig', 'a Montessori prig', at that; whereas Weigall's Akhnaten was a 'thriller' for the 'movie public'. 'But,' he adds, 'each to his taste, and as brother augurs, we can carefully place our tongues in our cheeks and wink our dexter eye at one another.'[3]

For all its wit, the letter has a snide undertow: the best that can be said for Weigall's book, it implies, is that it is not written in good faith. Weigall's colleagues often took this line. They recognized that he understood the Great British Public, whose interest and money they needed. They themselves frankly despised that public, and if they didn't despise Weigall, it was only because they fancied he had his tongue in his cheek. In fact Weigall's attitude was less easy to define, as we shall see in connection with his writings after the war.

But to return to 1914. Weigall would have been in no mood for retrospective summings up. His face was set in a new direction, and all his ambition now pointed to the theatre. The course of someone's life usually emerges with hindsight, but Weigall had a habit of taking his corners very deliberately and self-consciously. From accountancy to archaeology, from archaeology to administration, and now from administration to the theatre, each step was taken as though it were the first on a fresh journey. Of course the archaeologist was in the administrator, the artist in the Egyptologist, and perhaps surprisingly, the accountant in all of them. Costings and breakdowns accompanied all his schemes and although in his private life he could never keep money for very long, he always knew where it had gone.

Now in April 1914, although his biography of Cleopatra was about to be published and his history of modern Egypt was still being written, he knew himself to be on the brink of something different. It was still Egypt, but an Egypt for the eye and ear and imagination. He had already, as we have seen with the Akhnaten play, become fascinated by the idea of staging Egypt. It is as though writing about it was not enough; he wanted to show it to people physically. At the same time, he needed to make money. The theatre seemed the place where both purposes could be fulfilled.

The East at that period was very much in fashion. A series of plays and spectacles with eastern settings had been making a stir on the London stage since at least 1911 when the German director, Max Reinhardt, had brought to the Coliseum a wordless play called *Sumurun*, adapted from the Arabian Nights. Weigall missed it, but he would have heard of it, and his notion of a wordless play might have arisen from it. In fact *Sumurun* was the flavour of 1911. 'Saki' (H.H. Munro) brought it into a short story called 'The Peace Offering', about country house theatricals.[4] In the story, the play was to be conceived 'in the Sumurun manner', full of 'weird music, and exotic skippings and flying leaps and lots of drapery and undraperey. Particularly undrapery.' In Saki these things become irresistible opportunities for comic disaster; but at the Coliseum all went smoothly. The critic of the *Times* (20 February 1911) was enchanted:

The like of this marvel has surely never been seen in London before! It presents harmonies of colours that are now suave and tender, now ablaze and dazzling – the quiet hues of an old Persian rug and the glitter of gems; it has purity of outline and grace of movement. Then it tells a dramatic story of love and jealousy, revenge and death with most eloquent silence ... Sumurun['s] ... eyes twinkled like stars through the faint mist of her veil. When they fell on Nur-al Din they grew soft and she paused straight and slender like a palm tree against the moon. Then of a sudden she fled like an antelope ...

This was exactly up Weigall's street. Moonlight, dazzle, palm-trees, he knew them all.

Showing at about the same time was another Arabian Nights play, *Kismet,* by Edward Knoblauch, starring Oscar Asche, who later wrote his own Oriental entertainment, *Chu Chin Chow,* a musical fantasy with camels and donkeys, which became a huge success in 1916, running non-stop until 1922. In between, he toured Australia with a spectacular *Antony and Cleopatra,* whose dancing girls and negro slaves, lion-skins and cushions, outdid even Beerbohm Tree, who had produced a famously lavish production of that play at His Majesty's in 1906–07. But perhaps most fascinating of all was Diaghilev's Russian Ballet, which visited London first in 1911 and again in 1914.

They created a sensation. Two months before Weigall's arrival in 1914, Hortense writes to say that she is being taken to see them. Everyone was fascinated by Bakst's sets and daring costumes, and their macaw-like combinations of colour. A souvenir programme from the 1916 American tour of the Ballet Russe survives among

Weigall's papers (sent, possibly, by one of Hortense's family) complete with a series of Bakst colour reproductions. *Scheherezade*, starring Nijinsky and Karsavina, left the *Times* critic lost for words:

> There is a gorgeous savagery about the whole thing quite incommunicable in words ... The music, the movement, the stage pictures all combine to carry one into a strange atmosphere in which life and death are nothing more than the expression of intense emotion, followed by its sudden cessation.[5]

He went again and thought that *Scheherezade*, with its 'riot of colour and its extraordinary combination of sensuous languor and intense physical energy [was] the most enthralling work which the Ballet has produced here up to the present.'[6] Clearly the public was ripe for anything exotic Weigall might concoct.

But it wasn't easy. He had few contacts, and had served no apprenticeship in the theatre. There wasn't even a Petrie, as it were, to show him the ropes. It was obvious that he needed something more persuasive than the scenario of a wordless play. He needed to make the models of the sets, and to get theatre managers to come and look at them. Melfort, the house on Boar's Hill which Hortense had so rashly leased in 1913, was no use to him. London was the only possible place, and he urged Hortense to move with him, adding that the children would benefit from being closer to Mimi and Geanie and Betty.

It was probably just this that turned her against the idea. By now both Mimi and Geanie were aware that all was not well between the two of them, and their letters to Hortense are full of well-intended hints and suggestions. Geanie writes to ask for her measurements, head, neck, waist and so on, and promises to send her a selection of smart hats and coats and skirts from which to choose. Mimi writes that it might be a good idea to flatter Arthur by involving him more in the management of the children. Hortense's side of these conversations is missing, as usual, but one suspects that she may have been wary of their closer scrutiny in London. Besides, as it will emerge, she took a high and serious view of Weigall's talents, and always felt that the theatre was beneath him. Perhaps by keeping the family close to Oxford, she was making a point.

But without a degree the universities were closed to Weigall, even supposing he wanted an academic post. He took a studio in London, first in Redcliffe Road off the Fulham Road, and then at 117 Fulham Road itself. All that May and June he worked on his models, visiting the family as often as he could. Alured, his eldest son, aged seven in 1914, remembered him coming to Melfort and painting ideas for scenes on huge sheets of cardboard on the dining-room table, and then in the afternoons digging a sunken garden and making brick paths between formal beds. But 'regularly we would hear him say "Got to go up to town today"' and so he would be off. Or it would be arranged that Alured would go up to the studio, a wonderful place, he recalled:

> one very long room, a bath and geyser at one end. At the other, workmen were employed to make a fairly small room separated from the rest by a light partition

painted black, an Eastern shaped doorway cut in it and hung with a black curtain. The necessary furniture and a blue damask-covered divan bed completed his bedroom. In the long centre space, his working table. The whole of one side against the wall, his models. Their wooden frames were made to his specification, complete with electric lighting, and stage plans and all measurements for any theatre he knew they would be used for.[7]

This sounds as though Weigall had the models built for him, but at the beginning he relied solely on his own ingenuity. 'Darling,' he writes to Hortense, 'I've been working without a pause all day through, and now feel muzzy and awful ... I've completely set up one of the stages and have taught myself by many mistakes how to do it and how best to fix the pieces together. I am surprised by how well it looks, even without the lighting.' The lighting, however, was all-important, and when Hortense herself came to visit the studio in June (a month after her second daughter, Philippa, was born – soon to be known as Zippa) he was careful to time things so that she came in the evening: 'You *mustn't* see the models by day first!'

It was a slow and frustrating business. People came, were interested, even impressed, sometimes wildly complimentary, and promised him introductions to yet more people. Louis Parker introduced him to Stanley Bell, Beerbohm Tree's manager; and his old Cairo friend, Dr Edward Madge who had helped him so much at the time of his breakdown, introduced him to Oscar Asche, fresh from his tour of Australia with *Antony and Cleopatra*. Weigall's biography of Cleopatra came out in June, receiving much publicity. Perhaps he had hopes that his famous eye for local colour would serve in this new world, and that Asche would use him for a London production of his *Cleopatra*. But they were dashed. As he wrote to Hortense, 'Oscar Asche has asked me to come down to his theatre and discuss scenery with him, which is hopeful. He was enthusiastic but they have postponed *Cleopatra* till next year.'

In the same letter, he writes in great excitement to say that 'the chairman of Earl's Court and producer of the *Miracle* came to see the models, and seemed quite settled about taking it for the Empress Hall.' This was F.H. Payne, who had put up the money for another of Max Reinhardt's wordless spectacles, The *Miracle*, about a medieval German nun and a statue of a Madonna that comes to life, which had been staged in December 1911 at the Olympia.[8] The Olympia, then under the management of the showman, C.B. Cochran, was an arena where equestrian displays were often put on, with seating for eight thousand spectators, but which for Reinhardt's purposes had been transformed into the interior of Cologne cathedral. The Empress Hall at Earl's Court was also huge, the stage 80 feet wide, and a British Empire Exhibition was being planned there for later in the year. It seems that Weigall's piece was to form part of the Exhibition, and Payne, he says, was offering him '200 performers, mostly real natives; orchestra of 120 instruments; unlimited funds. Performance twice a day, and 5 months' run whether a success or a failure. My profits probably many thousands of pounds. So naturally I am very anxious.'

A glimpse of his social life at this period comes with this letter, sent from Hill Hall, at Epping, the country house of Mary Hunter. Mary Hunter was the sister of Ethel

Smyth, whom he had met with Ronald Storrs in Cairo, and her husband had been Director of the Egyptian coastguard service when Weigall was in Egypt. Osbert Sitwell knew her, and described her in his autobiography as 'the Edwardian hostess, *in excelsis*': 'in the highest degree she was lavish: and if her house was a little over-exuberant, the curves and gilding of chair and table a little over-emphasized, the velvets a little too complicated in pattern, these were faults of taste indicative of her epoch.'[9] To this setting came the fashionable and artistic society of the day, and Weigall met there among others, the composer Percy Grainger, the novelist George Moore, and the art historian Bernhard Berenson. It is curious to think of these men pausing momentarily from their talk to pronounce upon his situation: 'Mary Hunter and everybody here advise me strongly to accept if the offer is definitely made,' he told Hortense.

A few days later, at the end of July, there came a follow-up letter from a certain Gaston Mayer, assuring Weigall that 'after certain indispensable formalities have been accomplished, I feel sure the directors will be pleased to carry out your project of producing your spectacle in the Empress Hall. The matter rests forcibly in abeyance until the Exposition proper has been formally decided upon and that can only be a matter of a few weeks now. I will keep you *au courant*.[10] Less than a week later, on 4 August 1914, Britain declared war on Germany.

It seems extraordinary to us who know about the carnage of the next four years, that life went on so blithely. But for most people it did, and even a ringside seat onto the deliberations of the great, gave Weigall more of a frisson of excitement than a premonition of doom. 'I lunched today with Harry Cust,'[11] he told Hortense:

and many English and foreign diplomats and generals were present. They gave no hope, but all expressed confidence that we should win. Germany apparently did not think we should fight, but it seems certain we shall. This knowledge *may* make for peace, but all seem to think it is a prearranged plan on Germany's part. We land 200,000 men in Germany the day war is declared ... It is the biggest crisis since Napoleon's time; and all the foreigners say they look to us to repeat Wellington's exploits. It was very thrilling ...

For some weeks both the war and Weigall's prospects continued to seem, if not thrilling, at least fairly optimistic. In September the Earl's Court management was still in communication, signing off with the remark that 'the war situation certainly looks more hopeful.'[12] By November, after the first battle of Ypres, all that had changed. The Exhibition was cancelled.

Mimi's letters now tell of interminable journeys in troop trains, and of news from a nursing friend about the 'indescribable wounds' – though her friend adds that 'it is too wonderful how cheerful the men are.' Weigall's theatrical affairs thus drifted on without anything definite materializing. The war, perhaps unsurprisingly, is largely absent from the letters of this period. After all, Weigall was seeing his family fairly frequently, and when he wrote it was about immediate matters, plans, work in hand. The letters are not discursive, like the ones from Egypt. There is one moment, however, in a letter to Hortense's mother, Carrie in Chicago. The occasion was the birth in July 1915 at Melfort of her latest granddaughter, Veronica, the last of Weigall's three daughters, and he takes the opportunity to reassure her:

> Here at Oxford you would hardly know a war was going on, except for the number of wounded in the streets of the town. But of course there is a general atmosphere everywhere of seriousness, and a kind of exaltation of the thoughts, if I can so call it, which makes us all very sober and determined to rid the earth of this pest. ... It is very curious to notice how patriotism has become quite lost in the general desire for the welfare of all mankind. We believe we are fighting for nothing less than the whole human race, and it is hard for us to understand why America does not join in.

This rather grand tone was very common during the First World War, and Weigall became even grander in print. An article for the *Fortnightly Review,* which came out that October (he was no doubt meditating it when he wrote to Carrie) talked about the war as an elemental clash of civilizations: Teutonic materialism versus English idealism, the cold head versus the warm heart, mechanical logic versus feeling and sentiment. No doubt he felt all this genuinely enough, but if the hero of his semi-autobiographical novel, *The Not Impossible She* – published much later in 1926 – is any reflection of himself at the time, Weigall was also partly repelled by this kind of mood music. Sebastian, his alter-ego:

> was not in the least interested in military matters, nor did the arbitrament of war appeal to him as anything but organized vulgarity and doltishness ... He detested the death-or-glory sentiments of some of his associates ... War was a silly waste, unworthy of man's intelligence, and the only satisfactory feature of his participation in the trumpery business was that, in doing so, he was helping to end it.[13]

Sebastian does join up, but Sebastian's creator didn't. There was no pressure, of course, on married men until 1916, and there were also health reasons, but all the same it is possible that Weigall felt a little defensive at the time, when so many were rushing to enlist. A long letter from Ronald Storrs in Cairo, whose views he had sought on the subject of Anglo-Egyptian relations, winds up with the reassurance: 'I think you are perfectly right to remain where you are: there are "Other Fronts" than the fighting line, and who shall say that one is more necessary than the other.'[14]

One of the other fronts Storrs meant was probably Weigall's series of articles begun in November of 1914, also for the *Fortnightly Review,* a political and historical analysis of the situation in the Near East. The general reader in England had probably very little idea of the brew of conflicting loyalties – religious, cultural, political, and pragmatic – that characterized Egypt at the time, and the monthly press digests of the periodical output often mention Weigall's articles as particularly valuable. With great clarity, he explains the extremely complicated situation between Turkey, now in on the German side of the war, and Egypt, nominally part of the Turkish Empire but actually under British control. At the end of the year, the British did declare Egypt a Protectorate, but until that happened, the anomaly of British control in Egypt was more glaring than ever. He unravels the history of British involvement in Egypt, the feelings of the Egyptians for the British on the one hand and for the Turks on the other, the cultural sympathies of the Egyptian upper classes for the French (now allies against the Germans) and, behind and above everything, the overriding importance of Islam.

During 1914, Weigall had been writing and correcting the proofs of his *History of Events in Egypt from 1798 to 1914*, and these periodical articles are clearly spun off from that book, though angled now specifically on the political and military implications for Britain. In May 1915, the book itself was published, giving the general reader the nineteenth-century background and filling out the personalities and achievements of the three British Agents. In fact it is really a series of character sketches of the various rulers of Egypt, and as such is relatively lightweight. It has an almost cartoon-like quality, full of anecdotes, and as easygoing as the flow of an after-dinner raconteur.

Reading it now, its British bias is striking – especially over the infamous Deneshwai incident.[15] But there are things in it that were daring for the time. The chapter on Eldon Gorst, for example, is a generous defence of a man who was generally abused by British officials for attempting to transfer power to the Egyptians. And of Cromer, Weigall wrote:

> In no disparaging sense it may be said at once that he did not trouble himself to understand the Egyptian mind, nor to study the prejudices and temper of the people over whom he ruled. He never learnt to speak Arabic ... and he made no effort to adapt his manners to the habit of the land. When he retired in 1907 he knew as little of Egyptian thought outside the range of his official experience as he did of Arabic grammar.[16]

There is a good deal of glozing praise for Cromer on either side of this passage, and one reviewer took him to task for appearing to approve of these shortcomings.[17] But the passage needs to be read between the lines. Weigall's expression, 'in no disparaging sense', is just the kind of phrase he would have used before saying something damaging about Maspero. On the whole the war-time press were not critical of Weigall's chauvinism, and one is not surprised to learn that, according to Ronald Storrs, the book found an enthusiastic readership among the British officials in Cairo: 'You will be interested to hear that the younger generation, including the High Commissioner, of the Residency are brought up upon your history of the country they are attempting to govern.'[18]

That was another world. Weigall had written both *Cleopatra* and his *History of Events in Egypt* in a former incarnation; now, here he was, among a new cast of people, London stage managers, actor managers, and theatrical financiers. He was pursuing his next project, this time a full length play to be called *Omar Khayyam*, a proper scripted drama in three acts, and with lots of opportunities for picturesque eastern scenery, for which he was also making the models. The plot was based on the eleventh-century Persian story of Hassan-as-Sebbah, also known as the Old Man of the Mountains, who formed a religious order called the Sect of the Seven with the object of dethroning the Sultan of Persia and incorporating the Persian Empire into the dominions of the Caliphs of Egypt. For this purpose he laid out, in a valley below the mountain fastness which was his headquarters, a garden according to the description of Paradise in the Koran. Having drugged with hashish his devotees, or 'assassins', he then persuaded them that it would be theirs for ever if they murdered those who stood in his path.

Apart from two juvenile parts, male and female – Hassan kidnaps a beautiful young girl who has to be rescued by a beautiful young man – there were two not quite equal older male leads: Hassan and Omar Khayyam. Omar was the Astronomer Royal whose function is chiefly to make philosophical remarks in ornate Persianese, and to quote prophetically from Edward Fitzgerald's famous 1859 'translation' of his poem. Weigall tried to interest a number of prominent actors in one or other of these characters, and during the spring of 1915 both Beerbohm Tree and Oscar Asche seriously considered producing the play. Tree wanted to play Omar and Asche wanted to play Hassan, but as actor managers of their own companies they couldn't both be in it together. Depending on which took the play, Weigall would have to rewrite it so as to foreground one or other of these roles.

The negotiations were complicated by money. Asche had just taken over the lease on His Majesty's Theatre from Tree and was nervous: 'People do not jump at investing money in plays,' he told Madge, who appears to have acted as go-between, and 'Actor managers who have theatres on their hands ... are obliged to keep them going.' Of the two, Tree seems to have come closest to doing it, for he was still writing in June 1915 to say he 'would like to talk to you about Omar Khayyam after our new play is out.'[19] But in the end neither actor took the play. There is about the whole thing an awful sense of déjà vu: the excitement of a great scheme, the flurry of correspondence, the real hope, all in the end melting away.

But in the process of drumming up interest, Weigall's models had been seen by a great many people, and he was already getting a name for himself, not as a writer or deviser of plays, but as a set designer. And that, in the end, is how he got his first break. How exactly it came about is unclear, but in the autumn of 1915, the balloon went up. Suddenly he had contracts for three shows in West End theatres: the Palace in September, the Alhambra in October, and the Playhouse in November. It was not what he had had in mind, but as Oscar Asche had feared, money wasn't being invested in plays. These were not plays, either wordless or scripted. They were 'revues', a term covering a hybrid form that the newspaper critics of the day struggled to define. It had originally been a French genre, consisting of topical turns, sometimes satirical and political, and held together by a compère or a commère. But in London so many indigenous shoots sprang up within it, so many of the old music hall and pantomime artists brought to it their own distinctive styles, that the *Stage* (23 September 1915) could declare of one of them that it was also 'musical comedy, burlesque, comic opera ... ballet, extravaganza, pantomime and vaudeville by turns – a little of each and nothing long.'

217

Weigall's souvenir programme for *Now's the Time*, signed by the cast

By 1915 the theatres and hippodromes of Leicester Square, Cambridge Circus and Shaftesbury Avenue were all showing revues, and many of the foremost talents of the day were writing for or appearing in them. Irving Berlin wrote songs for them, as did Ivor Novello and Nat Ayer, whose song 'If you were the only girl in the world ...'

came into a 1916 revue called *The Bing Boys are Here*, and is still remembered along with 'Tipperary'. It was sung by the popular comedian George Robey, drawn in to revue from the music halls, and Violet Lorraine, another favourite of the day. Many of the names are remembered now only by theatre historians, but others have survived: Gertrude Lawrence, Noel Coward's leading lady, Beatrice Lillie, Fay Compton, Cicely Courtneidge, and Jack Buchanan. The character of these revues varied enormously, some being nearer to pure spectacle, while others, especially the small-scale 'intimate' revues pioneered by the Frenchman André Charlot, were witty and sophisticated. It was, after all, the form that nurtured Noel Coward. Whatever the quality, *The Times* (1 September 1915) concluded that it was 'evidently to be the form of entertainment associated in theatrical history with the great war.'

It is curious how seriously the press treated such ephemeral theatre. J.T. Grein of the *Sunday Times*, for example, more at home with Shaw and Ibsen, devoted many column inches to these snappily titled pieces (*Bric-a-Brac, Now's the Time, Look Who's Here*, and so on). In the case of Weigall's first show, for example, he fondly discusses its nostalgic atmosphere, 'the pit-a-pat of those nursery days, long behind us, to which the mind turns back so willingly.'[20] This was a reference to a song called 'Toy Town' sung in front of Weigall's set by Gertie Millar dressed as a black and white striped jumping jack, surrounded by a chorus of the same, all wearing shock-headed wigs. The effect must have been strange – indeed Grein calls the song 'eerie' – for Weigall's scene was not of a nursery but of a twilit Italian garden, 'amethyst merging into chalcedony, behind black cypresses that grew beside the balustrade of a marble walk.'[21] The *Tatler* (29 September 1915) called it 'the most beautiful scene of all ... so exquisite as to make a success of the revue without anything else. When the curtain rises you hear a sigh of rapture go all round the house.' Weigall's effects were achieved chiefly by light and colour. They were his hallmark, and every review for show after show makes the point. His mind's eye seems to have been full of the light of Egypt still, even when the sets themselves had nothing to do with that country.

Apart from these reviews, from the memories of his eldest son and a few useless black and white photographs in the illustrated magazines, there is frustratingly little to go on. But there is a fragment of something Weigall calls *Castles in Spain*, a musical comedy he was writing in the winter of 1915-16, in which he describes his stage effects. One scene set in 'a fantastic ballroom' gives us a rare glimpse of his scenic imagination:

> The columns are black, the walls white, the floor black with a yellow border. Eight large black candle stands, four on each side, are ranged along the sides. At the back, the hall is open and the starlit sky can be seen.
>
> The hall at first is lit with a strong rose-amber light, which intensifies the deep blue of the sky outside. On each of the candle-stands are four large yellow candles, such as are used in churches, and these are lit (electric lights). Later in the scene the sky at the back becomes golden with the dawn, and at the end it becomes the full blue of morning. These three changes of lighting form the feature of this scene, and the costumes are arranged to go with the three different colours of the background.

Another scene, 'the Spanish Bazaar in London', got up by the Spanish Embassy, becomes an excuse for more displays of colour and light:

> The scene represents a hall in blue tiles, in the Moorish style. There are three huge arched doorways at the back, with blue doors which are at present closed. Above the middle door is a large opening through which the starlit sky can be seen. The men and girls in the opening chorus are all dressed in blues and emerald greens ...

After several songs and choruses and intervals of dialogue,

> ... the three great doors at the back of the stage are thrown open revealing a mass of yellow orange trees in the full light of the rising sun. Thus we get the effect of this blue hall with the yellow light beyond. Many of the ladies of the chorus, who have had blue opera cloaks on, now reveal the lining of these cloaks which is of orange colour.
>
> Presently a number of little orange trees are brought on, and placed in a regular pattern on the stage, and the girls dance between them. The troupe of jugglers whom we have used three times in the previous scenes [notably in a tennis scene] throw coloured balls like oranges to one another, so that one gets the effect of a moving mass of yellow against the blue setting.

One can well imagine the effect on an audience, especially in wartime.

Apart from the influence of Egypt, there is also a feeling of Edwardian chic about his sets, their plain bright colours and simple shapes in deliberate reaction to the elaborate effects of the Victorians. In his novel, *The Not Impossible She*, Weigall has a set-designer called Moira, whose ideas on the subject are of course his own. He makes her abhor the general custom of painting 'with mud':

> Moira, however insisted on the employment of clean brushes and pure pigments, and as a result she placed before the audience a brilliance of colour which startled the eye.
>
> Her second device was the use of simple architectural effects, wide expanses of a single colour, and compositions in clear-cut right angles, in place of the 'mess', as she termed it, which was the result of the more florid and ornate designs then prevailing.[22]

If Weigall was modern, it was in a distinctly middlebrow sense. He would never have understood the violent discords of a contemporary like Mikhail Larionov, one of Diaghilev's designers, or the cubist experiments of Picasso, whose designs for the ballet *Parade* were first seen in Paris in 1917. The revolution against 'mess' had, in any case, already begun, with the simple, soaring architectural shapes of Edward Gordon Craig, and the clean, uncluttered, Japanese-inspired Shakespeare of Harley Granville-Barker. Indeed one critic of Weigall's set for the December revue, *Samples*, actually compared it with Granville-Barker's productions at the Savoy.[23] It consisted of an arrangement of 'plain white square columns, set around Stonehengewise, with top pieces and poplars and a sunset at the back', and according to the *Referee* (5 December 1915), it 'won a round of applause on its own account.'

He now found himself an overnight success. All the big popular entertainment companies were making offers. C.B. Cochran, who had managed and promoted Reinhardt's *Miracle*, and was now the general manager of The Empire, Leicester Square, wrote to compliment him on his scene at the Palace, and to 'talk about scenery' for the next Empire show.[24] The stage manager at the London Coliseum also wrote saying that 'Mr Stoll has requested me to let you know that he will be at your studio at 3.30 on Friday afternoon next.'[25] This was Oswald Stoll, of Moss and Stoll, whose Empires were going up all over the country, and who had built the Coliseum in 1904 as a music hall, showing four times daily.

These vast people's palaces were being built in all the big cities, replacing the old music halls that had grown up in the back rooms of pubs. Four years before Stoll's Coliseum, Edward Moss had built the London Hippodrome, originally as a circus, though it was also equipped with a water tank for aquatic shows. Now it was a ballet and variety house, and its manager, Albert de Courville, famous as a producer of spectacular revues, wrote to Weigall wanting an 'arrangement ... for seven scenic or other effects', adding that 'it is necessary that I should have the offer of these things exclusively.'[26]

During the next two years, Weigall worked with all these managements, but the person with whom he had most sympathy, artistic and personal, was André Charlot. Charlot never wrote about himself as C.B. Cochran did, which is probably why he has been largely forgotten. But in his day he was the king of revue, and according to Bea Lillie, his shows 'brightened up London as nothing else quite did.'[27] His distinction was an eye for real talent and after his death Cochran recorded the 'big debt of gratitude' owed to him by the playgoer 'for the introduction of those fine artists, Jack Buchanan, Gertrude Lawrence, our most glamorous actress, and Beatrice Lillie, one of the few living players to whom I dare apply the word 'genius' in its proper sense without apology.'[28]

As it happened, Weigall's first Charlot revue, *Now's the Time*, included the young Beatrice Lillie, dressed, as she often was during the war, as a young man – on this occasion, in tails and top hat as Lord Lionel Lyonesse. However, this was not yet 'intimate revue', but a huge spectacle at the Alhambra, another Leicester Square theatre, part of Stoll's syndicate, of which Charlot was then the managing director. To give an idea of the sort of thing these revues were, here is the *Observer*, describing *Now's the Time*. The connecting thread was a sort of H.G. Wells time machine, by means of which two modern cockneys are taken:

> to the Garden of Eden ... where they find Adam and Eve quite ready to come down the ages and see what modern life is like ... Eve appears again at a smart dress-maker's (where a madman is having a *succès fou* as a designer of gowns) ... meanwhile Bill [one of the cockneys] has got to Elizabeth's days, where he "takes on" the Virgin Queen and sees Shakespeare and others writhing under an infliction

of ragtime, while Drake sings a patriotic song. They get too to a century hence, a fearful age in which everyone is known by a number instead of a name and old ladies and all take terrific excursions in air ... Later we go back to Egypt and see a golden-haired Cleopatra fascinate Antony under the sardonic eyes of the Sphinx. The ballet is by Arthur E.P. Weigall, and very effective it is ...[29]

Cleopatra's golden hair is a nice touch. It wasn't only the ballet that Weigall devised, but the set and the Sphinx and the lighting too. Weigall's son, Alured, remembered being taken to the first night, and being enchanted by the 'luminous blue night sky' of the Egyptian scene. The next morning, both Weigall and the dancer, Phyllis Monkman, were singled out in the notices, the *Sunday Herald* (17 October 1915), for example, expressing a general view that 'the scenes that interested most were ... Good Queen Bess's Old London and Good King Weigall's bit of old Egypt (with Sphinx).' The *Sunday Times* for the same day went so far as to say that 'there was no measure of praise too high for Mr Arthur Weigall and others responsible for the wonderful ballet *The Spirit of Egypt*. It approached perfection.'

Weigall stayed with Charlot for his next show, *Samples*, at the much smaller Playhouse, for which he designed his Granville-Barker-like 'Column Hall'. But he had to take whatever work came his way, and in early 1916 he was back in Leicester Square, this time at the Empire, not as it happens a Stoll theatre but under the management of one Alfred Butt. By this time, Weigall had signed up with an agent, Carl Leyel, and it is clear from their correspondence that, despite Weigall's success, managers were trying to get him on the cheap. Butt was asking for a big crowd scene for his show, *Follow the Crowd*, for which Weigall was to design not only the set, but the costumes for some 70 people. Leyel was asking for £50, plus a couple of guineas per costume (presumably there weren't 70 separate designs), but Alfred Butt would hear of nothing over 35 guineas altogether. Weigall caved in, much to Leyel's disgust, who warned him that Butt was adept at playing off principals against agents, and that he was not to be trusted.[30]

The truth was that Weigall was in desperate financial straits. In the middle of January he was writing to Hortense to tell her he hadn't got the train fare to Oxford. He had '2/6 in the world and the week's wages to pay the charwoman tomorrow! I shall have to pretend I'm away and tell her not to come tomorrow ... I do wish to heaven we hadn't these terrible money troubles, darling; for as far as enthusiasm for work goes I am in an awfully elated state, and should be so happy. But the actual fact is that I shall have to pawn something tomorrow!' The whole letter swings wildly between elation and despair. Alfred Butt, while trying to screw him down, was also 'tumbling over me as far as politeness goes – lent me his car the other day, and generally makes a fuss over me, which is of course only his diplomacy, but still is very nice':

Tom Reynolds, the producer at the Empire, told me Butt wanted to secure me for 5 years and 'won't rest till he has done so', and the assistant producer said 'everybody here's gone mad – stark mad – about your work'. ... Meanwhile the Alhambra and

Stoll are naturally anxious to have a look in, to spite Butt, and Charlot has asked me to see him tomorrow, which I hope means something.

What seems to have happened is that Weigall had attained a celebrity which far outstripped the level of fees usually paid to set designers. The magic of the marketplace was a step behind, and certainly not helped by Weigall's own gentlemanly inhibitions. In explaining to Hortense how tough he had been with Butt, he gives himself away: 'I have been having a battle royal with Butt, for I told him that his prices were too small for me, and although I didn't work for money, still I must have fair payment.' It seems that he wanted his set-designing to be understood as a sideline, not as his profession – and, in a way, this is really how he saw it himself. He was incapable of doing anything less than wholeheartedly, but as he explained to Hortense later that year, 'I never intended to be a scenic artist, and the fact that I made a hit with my scenes was really only a side issue, and I used it to get my feet established in theatrical circles.'

He wanted really to be a playwright: revues first, to be followed in time, if the public mood changed, by serious dramas. Money came into it, for he had realized by then that it was the writers, not the designers, who were profiting from the shows. But he also felt that there was something inherently futile about set-designing: 'It all seems rather a waste of time to make one scene after another – all the time without a moment for anything else and I can only justify it on the grounds that it is only earning a living till better things come on in the authorship line and therefore has to be done with as good a grace as possible!'

Outwardly he cultivated an air of gentlemanly dilettantism, as one newspaperman discovered when arriving at his studio for an interview:

Mr Weigall is one of those curiously active men who, by a paradoxical freak of nature, invariably seems to have a dislike for work of any kind. If you go to see him at his studio he apparently has nothing more strenuous to do than light a cigarette and offer you a cup of tea. After a course of careful and cautious questioning it will be discovered that he is writing political articles for the *Fortnightly*, composing music, doing a bit of scientific research, writing the fourth act of a play, arranging for the production of a new ballet, and doing a few odd jobs at the British Museum to fill in any "spare time" he may have.[31]

This being so, he may well have pulled his punches with sharks like Butt. Not only that, but in other small ways, Weigall's studied nonchalance was probably bad policy. Charlot, for example, still owed him money in January for *Samples* – did he chase it hard enough? A manager called Raymond Roze asked him for a little scene which, he told Hortense, 'I consented to do ... for £25 "for friendly motives", and he wants it in a hurry.' This was while he was still in the middle of doing Butt's big crowd scene.

This scene, called 'At the Farm', was a fascinating challenge. Weigall described it to Hortense as being 'very startling and white and bright'. It 'gives me a feeling of confidence rather,' he continued, 'for it is the first ordinary full-light scene I've done, and the first that has no lighting effects and dodges. And again it's my first attempt at dressing a whole crowd and making a big stage picture of varied colours.' The costumes had been an exciting departure for him, and as with set design, he had had to teach himself on the spot: 'I find inventing and drawing costumes is quite fascinating. This morning the costumiers came to the studio with all the stuffs for my Empire set of dresses, and I pretended to know all about it.'

His general confidence was not misplaced. After the first night, he wrote elatedly to Hortense, 'the show went with a gallop, and was an instant success. My scene was much applauded ... Charlot was there, and congratulated me very warmly, and asked me to see him this week. Butt and everybody was very nice. Mother and Geraldine [Geanie] liked it very much I think, though Mother was shocked at the jokes!' Perhaps one of the things that shocked Mimi was Fay Compton's 'disrobing' song called 'Take a little bit off' – though it must have been only a very little bit, for the hallmark of these shows was that they were 'funny without being vulgar'.[32] Or perhaps it was 'God Save the King' sung by chorus girls and men in a 'regular rhapsody of mingled ragtime and patriotic effect'.[33] The music and lyrics throughout were by Irving Berlin, and the characters in Weigall's own scene sang and danced entirely in ragtime, the hottest thing from America. Altogether it was a wacky evening, one song, for example, being accompanied by six men on a 30 foot keyboard. But for all that, the critic for the *Stage* (24 February 1916) thought that 'perhaps the best feature of all is the At the Farm scene, a delightful stage picture in glowingly bold colours, that might have been painted by a child in a nursery after having been designed by the skilled hand of an adult, Arthur Weigall, to wit.'

The pace was relentless. Now it was Charlot and Stoll at the Alhambra again with a garden party scene (set and costumes) for *The Bing Boys are Here*, for which he was at last being offered a reasonable fee – £100. The Bing boys were two bumpkins, played by the comedians Alfred Lester and George Robey, up from Binghampton on a visit to London. Together with the rest of a starry cast – Violet Lorraine and Phyllis Monkman among them – they and their ludicrous adventures entertained the audience so thoroughly that very little newspaper space was devoted next day to the scenery. Weigall's scene is occasionally noticed – the *Tatler* (3 May 1916) said that 'as usual Arthur Weigall's scene is the one the loveliness of which lingers longest in the memory' – but actually the scene that attracted most attention was by the designer Laverdet, a copy of the recently built Mappin terraces at London Zoo, 'painted with the kind assistance ... of the Zoological Society'.[34] Nevertheless, there were warm letters and telegrams of congratulation from Stoll and Charlot, and offers of yet more work from each: for Stoll at the London Opera House in July and for Charlot at the Comedy Theatre in December.

Weigall's name was now synonymous with set design, so much so that a new verb temporarily entered the language. The critic for the *Sunday Herald* (23 July 1916), writing about a show at the Palace in which Weigall was not involved, informed his readers that M. Flers, the designer, would on this occasion 'Weigall' it. Annoying for M. Flers. And yet, would Weigall himself have been entirely happy with the remark? That summer, Alan Gardiner invited Howard Carter, who was in England, to dinner and suggested an evening at the *Bing Boys*.[35] They must both have known of Weigall's new incarnation, and one wonders how they viewed his success. It probably seemed like the end of Egyptology for him, and if they went to the show, Carter might have looked at Weigall's name in the programme with a private smile of triumph.

# Chapter 17

# Experiments in theatre and film
# 1916–1918

The worst of it was that, in spite of his press notices and the contracts for work, Weigall was still barely managing to survive. The letters at this period show him literally going without food, cadging from his sister and mother and, more ominously, suffering from 'nerves'. Just after Butt's show *Follow the Crowd*, for example, he writes to Hortense to say that he has been sitting alone in his studio 'nearly in a state of collapse' and feeling 'terribly nervy'. He felt defeated. 'It is awful,' he continues, 'that the best years of our lives should be ruined by these worries, but I feel sure that some day soon I shall score. The real successes I've had *can't* go on producing nothing but a few pounds.' It was like Egypt all over again – heady success combined with despair, and a constant racking around for a way out. He had realized then that, if he wanted to climb, he must make his own ladder. The same was true now, though it was food and rent rather than promotion that he was after this time.

Set designing didn't pay, nor did straight plays. True, he didn't give up on *Omar Khayyam* until after the war, and showed it to all the managers he worked with and a number of actors besides. Eventually, in 1923, he published it as a novel, *The Garden of Paradise*, in which form it proved to be a popular success. But in the meantime, the only theatrical way forward was in revue. The writers, librettists and managers of revues were doing well, and *Castles in Spain*, the musical piece mentioned in the last chapter, was his answer. He worked on it all through the winter of 1915–16, and within a week of the opening of *Follow the Crowd* in February 1916, he had it finished: 'The whole ms.,' he told Hortense, 'most of the lyrics, 40 costumes, and 10 designs for the scenery.' He left it with Butt, with whom correspondence about it stretched from February to September, when still nothing was settled, and the following year he was showing it to Stoll. The difficulty seems to have been a lack of 'strong parts'. Like Beerbohm Tree and Oscar Asche, the revue artists had to be wooed and flattered, and three equally weighted couples put no one in the limelight.

At the same time, Weigall began to think about management himself. While writing *Castles in Spain*, he was also in discussion with Carl Leyel, his agent, about joining forces to create a species of variety theatre to be conducted, as Weigall's prospectus[1] says, 'on a new method'. Taking account of the wartime fact that the public, 'in its present restless mood', went less to the theatre than to music hall, variety and revue, this 'new method' took its cue from yet another form of entertainment that was proving increasingly popular – namely, the cinema. Just as in live forms of entertainment, the 'picture palaces' presented a series of short pieces; but the cinema was different in that these pieces were little plays: comedies and farces alternating with dramas and tragedies. There were no one man acts, trick cyclists, jugglers and the like. This was the model that Weigall and Leyel proposed to reproduce in their live variety theatre.

Film acting and scenery were also an inspiration:

> One of the chief attractions of film plays is the fact that though they might be remote from reality in conception they are presented in a setting that is very real, and are played by actors whose gestures are not conventionally melodramatic. The dramas presented at the proposed theatre, therefore, would be intensely dramatic and real. … Of course on the stage one cannot present the same lifelike scenic effects: but on the other hand the theatre has this advantage over the cinema – that it can present colour effects that will always remain outside the possibilities of moving pictures.

To take advantage of that – (Technicolor was not introduced until the early 1930s) – Weigall proposed a ballet as a feature of every show, and by way of variation 'a short opera or operette of a serious nature might be presented.'

The cinemas kept going through the early evening into the night, rotating their programme of short and medium-length plays. Tickets were cheap, smoking was allowed, and audiences dropped in and out. In the same way, Weigall proposed cheap seats and smoking for his theatre, with no fixed matinee and evening programmes, but a continuous performance, rotating twice in an evening. The show would be permanent, with one or two new items being introduced each month, thus providing opportunities for playwrights and composers besides giving employment to a permanent company of actors and actresses, a corps de ballet, a ballet master, an orchestra and a chorus. Standards would be high, special artists would be drafted in for individual items, and the company 'might soon obtain a reputation that would give it a name like the Irish Players used to hold, or like Miss Horniman's company [in Manchester] holds.'

One can hear the familiar voice of Weigall flowing along the tide of its own enthusiasm just as it always did in every scheme he ever proposed. Of course, neither Leyel nor Weigall had the capital to carry it through, so it was a question of trying to interest a third party with money – some £10,000 they thought. Various people were approached, a Mrs Chetwynd, for example, who obviously regarded the venture as a launching pad for her own career, but who gave it up in the end as 'her health would not stand the strain of continual work. It means all day and night and then the smoke!'[2] She had a point. Coolly examined, the whole idea of transferring to live theatre the format and general ambience of the cinema was unrealistic. Apart from the exhausting and mechanical concept of rotation, a drop-in show with inevitably noisy comings and goings was hardly likely to recommend itself to the first-rate playwrights, actors, dancers and musicians that Weigall hoped to attract. And if it did succeed in reaching the high standard he aimed for, there is a question whether an evening full of miniature masterpieces would be digestible.

Nevertheless, Leyel and Weigall did manage to interest two other possible backers, and got as far as looking at theatres to let. But they were always a few thousand short of what they needed. The prospectus that survives seems to have been Weigall's last attempt: the covering note is addressed to Mr Stoll, on the strength of Weigall's association with him in the *Bing Boys* and *Look Who's Here*. Stoll at least would have had the money, but the tale ends there. Another stillborn scheme.

Yet Weigall was never at a loss. At about the same period, he was meditating another scheme, more interesting than his variety idea in that it faces up squarely to the possibilities of cinema itself. During the months of work on the *Bing Boys*, he had come to know and admire Stoll's manager, Edward Foster, who reciprocated the feeling. One evening, seeing Weigall's book on modern Egypt in Charlot's room, Foster took it and devoured it at a sitting, writing immediately to say how much he had enjoyed it, especially the defence of Gorst: 'I used to hear a lot about him in India and very little of it was complimentary, and it is gratifying (strangely, in a way, because I have no personal interest in him) to read that in the opinion of men like you, he was not only a brilliant public servant ... but that he possessed high administrative ability and ideals.'[3]

The letter ends with a suggestion that after '*The Bing Boys* have binged or bunged themselves into a working proposition', they should meet and Weigall should '*tell me things*' about Egypt. The following month, Weigall wrote to Foster about a plan for 'cinema work in Egypt after the War'. The letter[4] is a formal elaboration of the whole idea, which is nothing short of establishing an alternative Hollywood in Egypt:

> The constant sunshine and the amazingly clear atmosphere make photography in Egypt always exceptionally brilliant, and in this respect the country is even better than California. Cairo and Alexandria are great commercial cities with every convenience at hand; native labour is cheap and all such matters as carpentry, temporary building, and the other necessary arts and crafts, could be carried out with cheapness and despatch such as one could never obtain in England or America. ...
>
> My idea would be to film during two winter seasons a big historical drama, a big modern Anglo-Egyptian drama, two or three short tales of modern or mediaeval or ancient life, and one educational film dealing with the monuments and sights of Egypt. ...

Compared with modern time-scales this seems astonishingly optimistic, indeed the whole plan is breathtakingly audacious. On the other hand, although Hollywood was fast establishing itself as the centre of film making, the field must still have seemed wide open.

Weigall then goes on to give examples under each heading. For the big historical drama he suggests, perhaps inevitably, the life of Cleopatra: 'The story is one which is thrilling to the highest degree. It is totally unlike Shakespeare's story, and totally unlike any dramatic version that has ever been advanced.' He has in mind something on as large a scale as D.W. Griffith's *Birth of a Nation,* a film about the American Civil War, which had made a huge success in 1914. Then, for the modern Anglo-Egyptian drama, a novel such as Robert Hichens' *Bella Donna* could be adapted, with settings on a Nile steamer and among the monuments at Luxor. The educational film is interesting. He says he has heard that 'lecture-films' do well in the States, and he proposes to write a lecture to be delivered by someone standing beside the screen.

As for the organization of the whole venture, Weigall is minutely specific, as with all his schemes: he estimates the cost of return fares to Egypt for the stars, their hotel bills, the daily rate for local extras, the cost of unbaked bricks and builder's wages. He points out that excellent 'ornamental plaster and cement work' can be carried out by Greek and Italian workmen, that Nile boats can be converted into Roman galleys, and that the desert is ideal for big crowd scenes. He himself knows the ropes, and could liaise with the Egyptian government, getting permissions and so on. The whole thing is imagined down to the last detail – down to the disused roller-skating rink he knows of in Cairo which could be converted into a studio. He believes that they should employ an experienced film producer, that Foster should be the business manager, and that he himself would advise on artistic and historical matters, design scenery and costumes and help with the preparation of the scenarios. There only remained for Foster to lay the whole thing before Oswald Stoll, 'or somebody', for the necessary finance. He wants to start right away writing and designing, so as to be ready to go out to Egypt the moment the war is over.

What Stoll thought of the plan, whether the war meant that no one felt able to think ahead or take risks, there is no knowing. But that is the last that is ever heard on the project. By the end of the war, Hollywood had gained an unstoppable momentum, and in any case an increasingly Nationalist Egypt was not as hospitable to European enterprise as before. But, stillborn or not, the idea is remarkable for recognizing the enormous potential of cinema at a time when many people of his class were inclined to turn their noses up at it.

All this time Weigall was working on his design commissions, and being swallowed up in the generally hectic atmosphere of the theatre – deadlines, last minute panics, all night rehearsals, first night nerves and next morning euphorias. It was hardly a regime for someone already dangerously swinging between peaks and troughs. Family life consisted of long distance arrangements, children to be met from trains and taken to Mimi, or sent back to Boar's Hill, or left with Geanie. Clothes would get forgotten, things had to be sent on, urgent messages passed. Colds and fevers went round and round the family, meetings would have to be postponed, and always there were financial emergencies.

This whole fragile structure required great powers of organization, and Hortense on Boar's Hill with three babies (the three girls, Geraldine, Zippa and Veronica were born within a year of one another in 1913, '14, and '15) seems gradually to have been losing her grip. On one occasion she posted a chicken to the vicarage at Shepherd's Bush where Alured was staying – a kind thought, but the chicken had gone off by the time it arrived, though 'the legs were all right,' wrote Alured. Weigall was not always so philosophical. Hortense's vagueness could sting him into furiously precise detail. In May 1917, when he was working on a Charlot revue called *Bubbly* at the Comedy Theatre, he wrote:

Darling, please *do* try to realize things, and don't live in a dream. For example your letter, written and posted on Saturday reached me of course today [Monday], and yet you ask me in it to phone 'before ten on *Sunday* morning'. Please try to realize that for the last fortnight, and all this week I have not one moment to do anything. I am up to my eyes in the new production. Please, *please* get that into your head. I mean, as regards Alured, for example, I can't arrange anything, and it is simply ludicrous your calmly asking me to bring him to Oxford. Do you really think that one can go off even for half a day when a new show is in preparation? ... Why telegraph to *me* about Alured? I only saw him for half an hour yesterday, by rushing madly out to the Vicarage between rehearsals. Yes, you know, we rehearse all day on Sundays as well. Why post his overcoat to *me*? Here it is, lying here, and I see no chance of returning it for the present ... I don't think you have the vaguest idea what work on a new show means.

He was right, she probably hadn't the vaguest idea. And, disapproving as she was, she was probably disinclined to try.

By the time Weigall was designing *Bubbly*, Charlot had begun to entrust all the scenery of a show to him. Weigall's scene for Stoll's revue *Look Who's Here*, in July 1916, was the last single-set commission he worked on. It was, according to the *Pall Mall Gazette* (18 July 1916), 'a highly imaginative and ingenious Watteau-transforming-to-Hampstead fête'; a 'picture of Toy and Fairyland', Grein called it, 'painted in eeriness' and 'the centre of gravity of the production'.[5] A friend adds another detail. 'I am haunted by its loveliness,' she says, ' How did you think of it? ... I loved the illuminated Pan.'[6] The scene formed the background to Ethel Levey, famous for her husky voice, singing in a black Pierrot costume, itself designed by Weigall, as were all the costumes in that scene: 'bizarre' creations, according to *The Stage* (20 July 1916), 'modern and partially futuristic'. A month later, the *Sporting Times* (12 August 1916) reported that his row of Corinthian columns was missing from the show, adding by way of explanation that a certain Lady Constance Stewart-Richardson was rumoured to want to buy 'the whole classic colonnade designed by Mr Weigall, and set it up in her big Chelsea studio.'

In the previous February, after Butt's show, Weigall had collapsed, as we have seen, in a state of nerves. This time he comes close again, telling Hortense that he has been 'in the depths of depression'. He doesn't actually say so, but one feels that the war itself must have played a part. Letters from friends were now filled with news about husbands and sons on active service, about promotions, deaths, and hospitals. The boy Gordon Jelf, his assistant in the Valley of the Nobles, whose sexual priggishness had so annoyed him, was killed in October 1915. Weigall urged Hortense to write kindly to Jelf's mother. There were Zeppelin raids over London in April 1915, and Weigall mentions others across England early in 1916 – 'I hear they did a lot of damage at Birmingham, Derby and elsewhere, which shows how far they can travel.' A letter from Mimi written from a soldier's home in Kent where her sister Florrie was working, speaks of the 'boys' there – playing chess, writing to their mothers, 'most of them are musical and play and sing beautifully': 'Oh the soldiers!' she exclaims. 'Guns, horses continually passing – we waved farewell to a lot of the men just crossing over.' And all day long they could hear the booming of the guns in France: 'It makes one feel so sad to hear them ... we are only 50 miles from the firing line.'

There is something grotesque about the dates mentioned so often here. The war and the theatre make two horribly yoked calendars: while Weigall was building models for his wordless play, the ill-fated Gallipoli offensive had begun and it wasn't until the run of Charlot's revue *Samples,* in December of that year, that the beaches were evacuated. In January 1916, while Weigall was preparing Butt's scene, the first Military Service Act was passed, compelling all unmarried men between the ages of 18 and 41 to enlist. In June, while he was arranging his contract for Stoll's *Look Who's Here*, the ship carrying his old chief, Kitchener, struck a mine and almost everyone on board, including Kitchener, was drowned. The most grisly conjunction is the Battle of the Somme in July 1916 with the run of that same revue.

It goes without saying that 'escape' in the theatre can only have been a very relative concept – to the people singing and dancing so blithely as much as to the audience. One black-edged letter to Weigall comes from Arthur Playfair, a comedian in many of the revues he designed for, thanking him for his condolences. The show went on, of course, but afterwards there was always 'the long grey line of motor ambulances waiting for the wounded at Charing Cross – what a sight it was to pass, almost every night, coming home from the theatre.'[7] So wrote the actress, Stella Patrick Campbell, and Weigall would have seen the same sight. There is a sentence in a letter to Weigall from J.M. Barrie, the creator of *Peter Pan*, which would probably have struck a sympathetic chord with most theatre people then: 'For myself, I don't find it easy to turn my mind to plays at present; all seems trivial besides the great thing.'[8] To some, the very idea of escape seemed obscene. As Siegfried Sassoon put it in a poem called 'Blighters':

> I'd like to see a Tank come down the stalls
> Lurching to ragtime tunes, or 'Home sweet Home',
> And there'd be no more jokes in Music-halls,
> To mock the riddled corpses round Bapaume.[9]

Weigall was reticent about his 'nerves'. He had once called his complaint 'agoramania', and his eldest son remembered that he suffered from claustrophobia too. His other children, whose memories go back to a later stage, confirmed that telephone boxes and the underground railway were places of horror to him. The two conditions do sometimes combine, and there had been a hint of it soon after his first attack in

1911. In December of that year, when he was preparing for his return to England on sick-leave, he wrote anxiously to Hortense to make sure that she booked his passage on the *Moldavia* – 'for it is 'one of the biggest boats (and my timidity hugs the thought of a *big* boat) ...' Did he fear a panic attack if he were cooped up on a small boat? One has only to think of his life in Egypt, tombs alternating with desert, to understand how such a cruel conjunction of fears might arise.

In April 1916, the Military Service Act of January was extended to everyone, unmarried and married, between the ages of 18 and 41. Weigall, aged 35, was now faced with a situation which filled him with dread and forced him out of his self-imposed silence on the subject. Application for exemption from military service, especially on the grounds of mental ill-health, was a lengthy affair involving hearings, medical examinations, and doctors' certificates. The correspondence relating to Weigall's case lasts from the middle of June to late August. At one stage he had to go for an examination at Reading Barracks, and was informed at the end of it that he would be re-examined in two months' time. It appears that he was not given the chance to explain himself on the first occasion, for there survives the draft of a letter which attempts to do so. After briefly explaining the Egyptian background to his illness, which he puts down to 'too much desert work under rather trying conditions', he outlines his symptoms:

I am unable to walk far along an open road, or to cross an open space such as Hyde Park, for example. If I do so I am seized with a kind of panic ... I cannot visit an unfamiliar part of the country, or walk down unfamiliar streets without the same result; and I may mention that I had a very distressing time in coming to the Reading Barracks, although I brought a certain cousin of mine to be with me.

I cannot travel in a railway carriage unless there is a corridor, and unless the train makes constant stops ... I cannot face an underground railway or a tunnel at all. I cannot enter a cellar or underground lavatory, or a lift, or any form of enclosed space for which the exit is not large; and in a theatre I can only sit in a seat near an exit. The hysteria when it comes takes the form of intense terror, which leaves me in a state of collapse.

He therefore asks to be excused coming to Reading again, offers to 'obtain the certificate of any nerve specialist you like to name', and mentions a certificate he has from a Dr Acland who was the chief officer of the Egyptian Government Medical Commission.

Dr Acland – now a consulting physician at St Thomas' Hospital – states that he has 'been acquainted with Arthur Weigall for some years' in Egypt 'where the trying climate and the conditions of his work led to serious functional disturbances of his nervous system'. He believes that active service would lead to a repetition of these disturbances and almost certainly to a complete breakdown, 'rendering him not only ineffective, but a source of anxiety to those with whom he was associated.'[10] Weigall was therefore exempted for the time being, though he had to go through the whole process again the following May, when previously exempted men were re-examined.

Shell-shocked soldiers sent back to the trenches may well have smiled grimly at Weigall's good fortune. Obviously there was a difference between accepting new cases of nervous disorder, and recycling old ones.

He was now free to return to his precarious existence, passing along the familiar streets of the West End, and attending rehearsals and performances in familiar theatres, always, one must suppose, from a seat near an exit. In fact he became entirely local, for in February 1917 he moved from the Fulham Road to a flat – 3 Cecil House, 41 Charing Cross – within a few hundred yards of all the theatres he worked in. From here his eldest son Alured remembered being taken to see Charlot's *See-Saw*, at the Comedy, the little theatre in Panton street, just round the corner from the Haymarket. For this revue, Weigall set his scene in Egypt for the first time since *Now's the Time*. It was for a ballet again, this time set in Cleopatra's palace at Alexandria. Two features of *See-Saw* stand out from the press reviews; the first was a touching little song sung by a muddy soldier fresh from the trenches. It was called 'I can't find a place for that', and it turns on the meanness of the service postcards distributed to the troops, in which they can indicate letters and parcels received, but little else. All ''Arry' wants to do is to tell his girl 'as 'ow I loves 'er', but he can't find a place for that. *The Observer* (17 December 1916) said that the song 'precious nearly makes some people cry.'

The other scene was Weigall's Egyptian ballet, glowing in the light of 'a sun unknown in England', wrote the *Star* (15 December 1916) 'the sun of Egypt, toned by blue Levantine skies.' The programme for *See-Saw* also lists him as one of the three writers, as well as one of the three set-designers, while his name appears alongside some of the songs – one of them called 'The Bye, Bye Rag' – as the lyricist. Writers and librettists could earn royalties, so that at long last, as well as a fee for the designs, Weigall received his percentage: 1½ per cent of all gross takings.[11]

His fees and royalties were never enough, however. He was running to keep still, and the edge was always near. Worse, Hortense always seemed to be pushing him over it. Beyond question she was a hopeless manager. Money slipped through her fingers with nothing to show for it. Local tradesmen learned to refuse her credit, her cheques bounced, and Weigall was sometimes seriously embarrassed. She herself seemed unaware of consequences, vague and distant. In a letter to Mimi, Weigall once wondered whether she was taking some kind of drug, and he went on to describe the scene that met him when he returned home one evening: Hortense, deep in a book, wrapped up in an eiderdown with a cold sardine supper on her knee, greeting him with a long, dreamy account of what she had just read – the fires unlit, the children ill and unwashed, the larder empty.

In fact Weigall, Geanie and Mimi were all frankly alarmed for the children's health. Alured, for example, was a particularly delicate child. At one point he became seriously ill, and Mimi took him off to the Vicarage. The boy had screaming fits, and Weigall wrote furiously to Hortense to say that he was taking him to a specialist: he thought he might be consumptive, and there had also been a 'discharge from his ears which has gone unnoticed for months' and which is 'very serious'. The curious thing is that, like everyone of her class at that period, Hortense was not without domestic help: there was always a live-in servant, and there was Nonie, the family's beloved

Guyanan nurse, who had been with them since Egypt. But, as one gathers from all the letters between the women of the family, servants were themselves a mixed blessing, and needed as much organizing and attention as anything else.

From Weigall's point of view, Hortense simply cut the ground from under his feet. At his most savage, he thought of her as a heartless bloodsucker, draining him of every penny while giving nothing in return. He missed the children, and he missed a home. What he longed for, he says again and again, was a smoothly running household that was a pleasure to come home to. A house in London would have brought the family within range, allowed Mimi and Geanie to keep an eye on the children, and saved him the rent of a separate flat. It might have been expensive, but then so was Melfort. In fact, by the summer of 1917 Hortense was obliged to give Melfort up. But she didn't move to London. She took a cottage in Fyfield, at a very low rent, about eight miles west of Oxford, where she and the children were practically inaccessible. The railway line did not run there, and there was no other public transport. Before cars were general, a village like Fyfield was the back of beyond.

It is difficult to get to grips with Hortense at this period. Her voice is so faint, and Weigall's so loud that there is a danger of interpreting everything from his point of view. But it does seem as though she were almost deliberately distancing herself from him – either that, or trying to force him out of London. She once told Geanie, her sister-in-law, that she wanted him to give up his career in the theatre. Perhaps she thought that by steering clear of London herself, she could tempt him away from it. As has been mentioned, she also probably wanted to avoid her in-laws. She was fond of them, but – like Weigall himself – they were exhaustingly active, interested and critical. Weigall was an extremely dutiful son and had on several occasions lectured Hortense on her duties towards his mother, particularly where the children were concerned. Once, when Hortense failed to mark Alured's birthday in a letter to Mimi, he went so far as to say that he regarded Alured as pre-eminently a Weigall, Mimi as the primary grandmother, and the Schleiter side as virtually incidental. In fact, it sometimes seems that Weigall almost thought of Mimi as his children's mother, rather than their grandmother. At any rate, Hortense must often have felt very much the outsider, and if she had wanted to escape this mystic Weigallism, she certainly wouldn't have been able to in London.

Apart from that, she was ill at ease in the fashionable world of Mayfair which now sought Weigall out, and which she would have had to entertain and be entertained by. Theatre people were one thing, alien to her of course, with their glamour, and late hours and familiar manners; but there were also a lot of smart people that Weigall knew from Egypt days. They went to his shows and wrote him flattering letters. He had lifted the curtain for them in Egypt, and now, as one of them wrote:

to think that [the scene] Toyland and our splendid Egyptian expeditions were arranged by the same – you. Toyland in *Bric-a-Brac* is as perfect a bit of staging and conception as one can ever see, but don't you remember how thrilled to the bone I was riding down into the Valley of the Kings on a wonderful night ... Not even you, I suppose, could stage such dramatic moments and scenes ... I never have and never shall see anything on the stage that sticks in my mind as the sights and sounds ... of places in Egypt you showed us. I always look back on those days as the happiest in my life ...[12]

No wonder Weigall was sought after. He was a magician, conjuring up beautiful sights and happy times. Even the miniature models in his studio exerted their spell. At the end of 1916, the *Daily Mirror* reported that Weigall had started 'a new fashion': 'One of our best-dressed women, who saw the models, was so charmed that she had a miniature of her boudoir made with the exact lighting.'[13] And so he was asked to country house parties, and invited, on coroneted stationery, to lunches and dinners at expensive hotels. These, incidentally, might have helped on the hungry days, though they might have increased his tailoring and laundry bills. Hortense knew from experience that Weigall was attractive to women, and she could scarcely have helped suspecting him now. By keeping right out of the way, she may have hoped to spare herself the details.

The irony was, that however much Weigall wanted Hortense to provide him with a smooth-running London household, he also knew that she was incapable of doing so. The house and children were only half the story. The blunt truth was that she herself was no longer presentable in any of Weigall's London circles. She was *insortable*, as the French say. Just when his costume designing had introduced him to a whole world of feminine chic, she had become an embarrassment. It wasn't a question of fashion; she was actually bedraggled. She had begun to offend Weigall, physically. Geanie saw this, and she took the opportunity to write to Hortense in an effort to save the marriage. This letter was written after the period described in this chapter, but it sheds light on a situation that had been developing for several years beforehand.

The occasion was the removal of Hortense from Fyfield into Oxford, where Weigall had been persuaded by Mimi and Geanie, anxious about the children, to join them. It was to be a new beginning, but the experiment could only work, Geanie saw, if Hortense herself could meet Weigall halfway. Geanie was obviously anxious not to seem interfering. In her letter, she reminds Hortense that they have often discussed delicate matters before, and that Hortense has always assured her that she did not resent such conversations. Once more, she says, 'I beg you to believe that my motive is purely for the happiness and success of this new plan.' The subject of clothes and appearance seems to have been an old one between them too, for Geanie refers to their difference of opinion as to how much these things matter. We have seen that Geanie was a sophisticated and worldly woman, and a modern reader, brought up with feminism, might well feel inclined towards Hortense's view of such things. But it needs to be said that Hortense herself wasn't making a feminist stand. She wasn't an Ibsen heroine, a Nora beating at the walls of her doll's house.

It is more likely that she took a high-minded view, and dismissed it all as vanity. On the other hand she knew that she was or had been beautiful, and she might therefore have felt it quite safe to be unworldly. Geanie must have hoped for some lingering self-regard and some memory of how much her beauty had always meant to Weigall, particularly to the artist in him, for she wrote:

Elegance – to use an early Victorian word – is what you most possess. I know of no one who can look more elegant than you can – and altho' I know that you disagree with the stress I put on this acquirement, you can never shake my belief in its worth. Arthur so often says 'How charming you look' and it seems to give him such pleasure, and *inspiration*, that if writing is to be his future career [he had by then started his first novel], surely it is worth considering ...

She reminds Hortense that Weigall happens to be peculiarly susceptible to these things, and to shudder more fastidiously than anyone she knows at dirt and untidiness. Furthermore she points to the fact that he has over the last few years associated with women 'who make it a lifelong study to enhance their charm by every form of attention to their dress, and complexion, hair and hands and feet and know to a nicety the value of scents and powders, tooth washes and the thousand and one things that go to make up that utterly feminine attraction that Eve began with the aid of a handful of fig leaves!'

All this reads very old-fashionedly now. But Geanie was of her time, as Weigall was in these matters. She probably made a tactical error with her 'thousand and one little things', for Hortense might well have felt that, if that's what it took, she'd rather not compete. But in fact Geanie was not trying to turn Hortense into a society lady; only to persuade her to do enough to keep Weigall faithful. She mentions a love affair that they both knew he had been conducting in London. This, she says, is over. The woman in question is now married. Hortense holds all the cards, she says, if only she will play them. Weigall wants to be a good husband and she could so easily win him: 'It is the extra five minutes ... that you grudge, but it's just that, together with the refinement and delicacy of a touch, that makes or ruins a woman's subtlety.'

The letter is a masterpiece of affectionate diplomacy. But Hortense, it appears, was unable to profit by it. One thing might have helped her – America and her own loving and uncritical American family. Her children remember her as a different woman on the occasions when she came back from the States, sparkling, happy, full of laughter. In one of her surviving letters, written years later from Chicago, Hortense makes the comment that 'after being so long absent from America, I have spent this year in soaking in America – like a dry sponge back in its element.' The letter is addressed (though possibly never copied out and sent) to an American poet she had been reading, Edgar Lee Masters. What she particularly admires in him, she says, is his 'love of Chicago', and continues with a rather surprising paean to urban beauty: 'Is there any city in the world with half its inspiration – with its beauty and its highness – its charm of sky and water and greenery – its clouds of steam and smoke (it's heresy to say it, but they are beautiful!) its noise and endeavour and its light-heartedness and enthusiasm. I have wanted to sit and click a typewriter in one of its offices – anything – to be a living part of it!'[14]

Weigall would have raised an eyebrow if he had seen this. It was after all he, the Englishman, who had this kind of gusto, and she, the American, who so signally lacked it. But he could have reflected that a woman in America was more a part of things, more liberated than in England, and that for an American woman, therefore,

England might have been doubly deadening. Hortense was out of her element there: domesticity of any kind was beyond her, but domesticity in England seems to have paralysed her. Later in her life she discovered the ideas of Gurdjieff and his disciple Ouspensky, both teachers of esoteric religious systems who became known in England during the 'twenties and 'thirties. According to her sons and daughters, Gurdjieff's teachings did eventually give their mother some sort of direction. But until then, gentle and sweet-natured as she was, she does seem to have been, for all practical purposes, a disaster.

This then was what Weigall felt himself up against, and by the middle of 1917 his letters become head-bangingly exasperated. At a distance, it was her financial sloppiness more than anything else that irritated him. It appears that she was now so deeply in debt that there was nothing for it but to take out a loan. In May 1917 Mimi and a certain Mrs Lambert, a wealthy friend of Weigall's, stood surety, a painful business for Weigall: 'You know,' he told Hortense, 'how bitterly I hate and detest having to ask her [Mrs Lambert] at all.' Hortense negotiated the terms with a Mr Griffith, terms which appear to have included staged payments by Griffith in return for a regime of retrenchment and repayment. She had a small income of her own, and Weigall continued to send her whatever he could spare from his earnings.

Weigall meanwhile had to earn as much as he could. His way of life obliged him to be constantly inventive, on the alert for anything that might turn up. The old spark of wild spontaneous enthusiasm was perhaps a little weaker now, but he kept it alive somehow. Fortunately he was by nature easily ignited, and now the political situation in England began to preoccupy him. 1917 was the grimmest year of the war at home, with serious shortages of food and fuel and rising industrial discontent. The Russian Revolution in March opened up the possibility of political agitation. In particular the idealistic peace terms that the Russians were proposing, with 'no annexations and no indemnities', contained, by implication, a suspicion as to the motives of the Allies in not negotiating a peace. As the historian A.J.P. Taylor put it: 'It was easy to allege that the war was dragging on for the sake of Alsace and Lorraine or the spoils of Turkey-in-Asia.'[15]

In May, the leader of the Labour party, Arthur Henderson, went to Russia and returned with the recommendation that his party should adopt the Russian peace programme too. A conference of socialist parties from all sides in the war was being promoted in Stockholm; Henderson proposed sending delegates; Lloyd George refused; the cabinet condemned Henderson; Henderson resigned, and thus the series of events was set in motion that led to the break-up of the Lib-Lab coalition and the establishment of a Labour party fighting in every constituency for an independent majority. Much of this lay in the future, but Weigall became intensely interested in the whole subject, not only in Labour's terms for peace, but in the Labour movement itself.

From an aside in one of his letters for May 1917, it appears that Weigall's continuing exemption from military service involved him in writing articles 'for the publicity

Dept. so as to show I am working for them.' It is not clear what this department was. The Ministry of Information, the government's propaganda machine, was not created until February 1918; before that there was the Press Bureau whose function was purely negative, censoring anything that might threaten national security. Nevertheless, Weigall does seem to be referring to a government body. He was busy 'doing writing work,' he says, 'especially on war subjects,' and he has a meeting fixed up with the editor of the *Evening Standard*. 'I am off on quite a new tack, being obsessed with the question of the views of the working classes as to the terms of peace, and I have so much to say that I am in quite a state of nerves about it.'

His excitement was fuelled by meeting Alan Gardiner again, who felt equally strongly on the subject, though there was room for argument between them. 'Alan Gardiner and his pacifist views', he told Hortense, 'have revealed so much that has to be contradicted and so much also that is sound sense. We've settled to lunch together every Wednesday for ever!! He hurls Labour literature at my head, and pamphlets and books, which if not convincing as to the need of peace, is certainly very enlightening as to the trend of public opinion amongst the people. I think some sort of upheaval is very near, and we must prepare for it: I am deeply impressed with [the] views of Labour and I think you will be too.'

It is an odd mixture of sentiments, at once sympathetic, patronizing and fearful. The article he wrote for the *Evening Standard* (5 June 1917) shortly afterwards shows the same caution. In it, he warns the government against falling into a 'Prussian' habit of autocracy, the very thing that the war was being fought against. The state in Britain is not an imposed authority, he says, but a condensation of the national will. Then, with awful bathos, he illustrates his argument by pointing, not to the withholding of workers' rights, but of beer. The whole subject is aired more seriously in his first novel, *Madeline of the Desert*, started a year later, a socio-religio-political romance set in Egypt and London, in which one of the set-piece scenes is a huge and frightening Labour demonstration in Trafalgar Square. As the Labour movement gathered pace, and the strikes became more widespread, there was plenty to talk about every Wednesday.

At the same time as politics, he was pursuing his enthusiasm for the cinema. As it happened, Charlot was setting up a film company and in the autumn of 1917 he made a trial picture scripted by Weigall who was also asked to be present during the shooting of it and to report back to Charlot at the end. Part of the script survives. He called it *Hidden Treasure* and it is a tale about a dastardly Professor bent on seizing an ancient treaure buried beneath a manor-house which he can only acquire by selling his beautiful ward (Phyllis Monkman) into the clutches of a loathsome money-lender. There is a haunted room with two or three rats in it (the rats, to Weigall's chagrin, were cut), a scene in which Miss Monkman dances in the moonlight under the trees, and another, improbable as it sounds, in which she reads the Bible to a woman on her sick-bed. In other words, there was plenty of scope for picturesque English interiors and exteriors, special effects, and dramatic incident.

The report makes fascinating, if painful, reading. As he had done in Egypt, Weigall found himself making the most elementary points: for example, that work must not begin on the first day the studio is booked, but at least a fortnight beforehand. The script must be studied; scenery, costumes and props, chosen and made; the sequence of shooting planned and so on. Actors should be contracted to wear what the producer decided and not what they liked; the lighting men should arrange their angles of shadow during rehearsals and not separately while the actors 'paid by the day, were kicking their heels'; the timetable and all relevant information for the next day should be pinned up the day before. All that was the easy bit.

The report is also about the aesthetics of film-making. This, he said, had been entirely overlooked. The producer – a man called Bannister Merwin – regarded as a complete waste of time, for example, Weigall's attempts to get the 'rags of moonlight', or the glow of embers to play upon Miss Monkman as she crept down the great stairs at dead of night. The dramatic possibilities of lighting, of close-ups, silhouettes, the length and range of camera shots, all these things required careful attention, Weigall wrote, and film budgets should allow for them. He cited Mr [D.W.] Griffith who, he has heard, 'makes six or eight photographs of every scene either by retakes or by using more than one camera, and he then selects the best for exhibition':

> He often expends 10,000 feet [of film] to obtain 1,000 of final result. That of course is unnecessarily fussy; ... [but] it is surely wiser to waste a few feet in trying various lightings of a scene, and taking short tests, than it is to rely on getting it right at the first attempt as we have done in the present production.

Altogether, it was a very inferior product that Mr Merwin finally presented to Charlot; but the whole exercise had been valuable.

It had set him thinking about the industry as a whole. American films were flooding the market. By the end of the war, Hollywood dominated the international film markets, about 70 to 80 percent of films shown in Europe being American imports. Weigall's report points out that England had potential advantages that were not being exploited: for example, old world architecture, from manor houses to cottages, the English landscape, English gardens, soft exterior lighting ('so infinitely preferable to the hard sunlight of California' – and to the light of Egypt, one wonders?), and 'a certain ease and grace and restraint in our actors and actresses':

> but instead of making use of them the English film companies try to compete with America along *American* lines ... We have not got the appliances or inventions or studios that the Americans have, and generally speaking our pictures taken by artificial light are not so good as those taken in the same way in America. But we have no chance to improve in this respect for a long time, and therefore I feel that our main energies ought to be turned to exploiting those things that we *have* got and in which we can assuredly beat the Americans.

Charlot must have been impressed by Weigall's report, for at the end of the year, just before the film was finished, Weigall told Hortense that 'Charlot has asked me if I will become director of his film department at a salary and work regularly on it.' He was in great need still. Whether he was ever paid for *Hidden Treasure* or his report, and whether the film was ever sold is not clear,[16] but during the filming he was desperate enough to try selling some Greek terracottas he had collected in Cairo: 'Spink came to see them yesterday, and though he would not buy them he said I ought to get £100 for them, and put me onto one or two people whom I am now sounding.' By October he had discovered he could only sell at public auction 'where I hear they would probably just now not fetch what they are worth – probably £50 or so, and so I hardly like to do that. I am still trying to find a private purchaser of course, but there seems little prospect. ... I am half starving here, and very wretched!' Whereupon, Hortense immediately sent him what she could – a pound – for which he thanked her, promising to 'return [it] when I come.'

There were air raids that autumn over London and some of these letters were written from the underground writing room of the Regent Palace Hotel, Piccadilly. A full moon was always an anxious time, but no one expected anything on the dark night of Friday, October 19th. That however was when a Zeppelin fell on Piccadilly Circus – 'We had forgotten all about Zepps – thought they had been abandoned as useless nowadays,' Weigall wrote. He happened to be in a nearby street, and had to 'run like a hare'. Swan and Edgars, the department store, was hit. 'In another two minutes or so I should have been at the actual spot, for I was on my way there. As it was, I walked afterwards over a sea of crunching broken glass, and saw pools of blood about.' What added to the wretchedness of this period was the fact that Hortense was now at Fyfield: 'I do wish you were more get-at-able, and that I could see the children more often,' he wrote mournfully. Their health seems to have been especially bad that winter, with sore throats being passed from one to the next, including Hortense herself.

In the circumstances, Charlot's offer was one he couldn't refuse. He hadn't had such a thing as a salary since Egypt, and here was Charlot offering him '£1500 a year and also ten per cent of the profits, which might mean another thousand or two with luck!' The studio was at a place called Garbrand Hall, in Ewell, Surrey, but for the moment he was operating out of Charlot's office at 6 and 7 Arundell Street, Coventry Street, West London. He couldn't tell when he was going to see any money: 'I don't like to press for it, and there are so many legal things to settle about the whole scheme that it takes time.' However, he was confident enough to tell her to pay the income tax bill that had just come in, and he sends her a pound with an apology for having 'kept it so long, but of course I'm very hard up still' – it wasn't, surely, last October's pound?

Meanwhile, he was reading short stories and novels for adaptation, sounding out authors, and approaching actors and actresses. With Englishness still in mind, he wrote to Rudyard Kipling, who referred him to his agent, but suggested that 'some of the stories from *Puck of Pook's Hill* and *Rewards and Fairies* might be of interest.'[17] Murder mysteries and sensational novels were also of interest. He was deep in books with titles such as *Who killed Mr. Bravo?* and *The End of her Honeymoon* by Marie Belloc Lowndes. This author also offered to send him her *Studies in Love and Terror*, a volume of short stories some of which, she thought hopefully, 'might expand to almost an unlimited extent.'[18] Another author, Philip Oppenheim, sent him a novel he had asked for, and hoped he would look at others: 'I am hoping very much that you will see a film in the "Bliss" adventures,' he wrote.[19]

It was obviously exciting for an author to be approached about film adaptations. Actors were not always so easy. Fred Terry, the much younger brother of Ellen Terry, wrote back with his immovable objection to the cinema as an actor's medium: 'No, when I am dead, I hope some people will remember the sound of my voice. You can't reproduce that, not even with machines. They kill the voice, as in my opinion, the cinema kills the personality of the actor. The very thing that probably endears him to his public on the screen may be against him.'[20] Synchronized sound was not achieved before 1927, but there had been earlier, unsatisfactory attempts to match sound to pictures by way of phonograph records. Actresses seem to have been less fussy than Fred Terry. One writes to say that she is 'most anxious to get any sort of work, and if you think I could be any good at film work it would be very nice of you to give me a chance to try.'[21] Even the great Mrs Patrick Campbell, for whom Weigall had recently designed a scene, wrote to ask whether his plans involving her were definite for the following month. She had been asked, she said, 'to take up a job (war-work) as inspector of [illegible] for aeroplanes', but she wouldn't take it if he definitely wanted her.[22]

Women, particularly attractive women, regarded films as one of their natural opportunities. Live theatre was seen in the same way, as a showcase or money-earner regardless of talent – Lily Langtry and the mime-dancer Ida Rubinstein are cases in point, or even (to bring it closer to Weigall) the Lady Constance Stewart-Richardson who had wanted to buy up Weigall's colonnade. She was a sportswoman with advanced ideas about education, and in order to finance her model school, had agreed with Alfred Butt to dance at the Palace Theatre in diaphanous draperies for £350 a week.[23] With the same amateurish assurance, glamorous women with no real qualification would assume they could be film actresses. Lady Cynthia Asquith, daughter-in-law of the previous Prime Minister, was one such, Lady Diana Manners another, both well-known beauties, and for different reasons hard pressed for cash. Much later in his life, after one of his own novels had been filmed, Weigall had at least one approach of this kind – from a Countess Schlippenbach, whom he had met in Egypt: 'I had to leave my husband about two years ago and he behaves pretty badly to me, leaving me nearly without a penny ... Fortunately my looks are quite what they used to be ... Personally I am not particularly keen on filming, but it is the only thing I can think of in order to find some work.'[24]

Once the preliminaries were over, Weigall moved down to Garbrand Hall permanently. His load was enormous. Either from inexperience or lack of money – or perhaps, after his disastrous time with Mr Merwin, from a desire for complete control – he seems to have been script-writer, set and costume designer, director, and casting director all in one. Distractedly he wrote to Hortense: 'A scenario takes at least 250 foolscap pages of close writing and most careful thought and arrangement and re-arrangement. Each scenario has to be written by me during the production of the previous one.' Then there is the scenery. 'I am designing and erecting all the scenes here – whole streets of Brittany houses, hotels, cathedrals etc; and all these have to have constant attention':

Then when the photographing begins [there was at least a cameraman] I have to produce all the acting myself, which means acting each scene myself in front of a looking glass 50 times before I can act it in front of the actors to show exactly what I want. Then there is all the business of fixing up contracts with authors, seeing the 'star' actors, and casting the whole thing.

In addition to that, Garbrand Hall itself became a sort of hotel for everyone connected with the filming, and anyone else Charlot, who was also living there, wanted to invite. 'Every weekend we have at least 15 people to lunch and dinner, and eight or nine staying in the house; and I have to play the part of host and housekeeper rolled into one.' In whatever time was left over, he was also designing most of the scenery and costumes for Charlot's next revue, *Tails Up*, which was to replace *Bubbly* at the Comedy. 'Thus I never have one moment to myself, and even to write a letter is difficult.'

Hortense was pressing him to come to Fyfield, just as she had done when he was in the middle of Charlot's *Bubbly* the year before. He was at his wits' end. His whole letter is really an attempt to din it into her, minutely, why exactly he is in this situation, and why, once in, he has absolutely no room for manoeuvre. In his novel, *The Not Impossible She*, he caricatures Hortense very cruelly, but one of the things he says about her comes from the heart of situations like this. He says that arguing with her was like arguing with something soft, a pillow for example. It was impossible to make any impression. So here, at the top of his voice, he reminds her that the whole point of giving up London and the theatre for this 'much more strenuous and more tedious work' is:

*solely* to make money, and my *SOLE OBJECT* IN MAKING MONEY IS TO ESTABLISH OUR HOME AGAIN, TO PAY MY DEBT AND YOUR DEBT ... AND TO PAY FOR THE CHILDREN'S EDUCATION.

Returning to lower case, he continues:

So long as you remain at Oxford or anywhere else that is not within an hour of Ewell, I *can't* come at all. It is not a question of finding time. There is *no* time. It is utterly impossible for me to come ... The wife of a soldier in India might just as well keep asking why he doesn't come to see her. The answer is that *she* must come out to see *him*.

He wanted her to find somewhere to live nearby, for 'it makes me very unhappy always to think of all the fun of the children that I am missing, and I feel the want of you very much.' Denny was now seven and Alured approaching eleven. The girls were five, four and three. The sight of someone else's daughter, aged six, sent him into a fit of acute loneliness. The trouble was that Garbrand Hall only rubbed it in. He had often been separated from his family, but in Ewell he was separated from everyone else he knew as well. It didn't help when Hortense gave as her reason for not moving that she would lose her friends. 'What about *my* friends? There is not one of them that I can see in this present work.' For once, he had to admit that he was feeling very sorry for himself.

But all this was nothing compared with what was about to break. Weigall's salary was to be paid quarterly, and the first payment had duly appeared. By the middle of April, when the next payment was due, he says he's living on the remains of the last quarter. By May the awful truth dawned. The financier for the whole scheme was a Mr Heistein,[25] who 'goes on putting off the proper financing of the scheme, and is more and more treating this place as a sort of summer resort ... I have not yet been paid and am getting rather short.' By the next letter, Heistein has explained that he had '£100,000 lying in London which he hasn't been able to touch owing to legal difficulties, and he thinks these will be overcome this week. But if they are not ...!'

Meanwhile it was becoming clear that not being paid was only a part of Weigall's troubles. The house itself, Garbrand Hall, had been taken in his name, bills had been run up, and tradesmen were becoming impatient. Weigall was in the front line of attack, and although 'I have a letter indemnifying me, from Charlot, in which he accepts all responsibility ... that merely means that creditors attack him through *me*.' Charlot also 'undertakes to see that I get paid for the full two years of the contract. But then '*he* is pretty rocky too, and any action I brought would simply lead to his bankruptcy; so all I can do is hang on and hope it will be all right. I can't sleep at nights and can hardly support the strain. I still expect and hope all will be well, but it is agonizing to face each day of writs and summonses and threats.'

Towards the end of July the whole disastrous enterprise was wound up. To Weigall's relief 'the landlord has taken back the house, and released me from the tenancy, so that's off my hands.' Charlot was close to bankruptcy, but agreed to pay Weigall a thousand pounds' compensation. Weigall of course couldn't force his hand, for fear of making him bankrupt, but he 'is giving me a written promise to pay so much a week according to what he can afford. We are good friends, of course, and I have treated him generously and he has been quite honourable about it all. It is only Heistein who has let him in so badly all round':

> It has been a time of really awful anxieties ... Every stick of furniture at Garbrand Hall has been sold of course. I had great trouble in getting my own things away, and of course expected to lose everything; but now they are safely stored. ... The trouble is that since I have not been paid a penny since January I owe all sorts of bills in London ... I feel as though I were slowly recovering from a terrible illness, but I'm not out of the wood, and if Charlot fails I shall be badly involved.

At least Charlot would pay him immediately some of the £100 owing him for *Tails Up* – 'enough to be getting on with.'

But there was no time to recover from the 'illness'. If he sought peace and quiet, it was only so as to have six or eight hours a day writing his novel. Fyfield was tiny and noisy. Before any visit there, there was always an anxious negotiation about a writing room for him – the boy's bedroom? the sitting-room between five and eight in the evening? the hall? Geanie was at that time living with a friend who had a farmhouse, called Vigo Farm, at Holmwood in Surrey. This was Olive Chaplin, a granddaughter of the actress Ellen Terry. Vigo Farm was now the obvious place for Weigall. So there he went and wrote steadily until the middle of October. It was a haven for him, for Geanie was prepared to study his needs in a way Hortense never could. In fact it was from here that Geanie wrote her delicate letter to Hortense. And in it she also stressed, along with the scents and powders, the importance to a writer of that elusive thing – a smoothly-running household.

# Chapter 18

## Novelist and film critic
## 1918–1922

1914 had, by coincidence, marked a turning point in Weigall's career. 1918 marked another, not as surprising perhaps, but significant. Just as the horrors in France and Flanders were coming to an end, Weigall too was delivered out of his nightmare into a life of quiet domesticity. At least domesticity was the idea.

Charlot avoided bankruptcy, it seems, and was able to pay Weigall his weekly sum. By the late autumn he had another revue in preparation, for which Weigall received a useful £150. It opened just before Christmas, and starred, among others, Gertrude Lawrence, with 'costumes and scenery under the supervision of Arthur Weigall'.[1] For the moment at least, the crisis seems to have passed and for the first time since Melfort on Boar's Hill, the family now settled itself somewhere large enough to take them all: Langdale House, Park Town, Oxford, a handsome Victorian building with a garden. The plan was that Weigall should now take charge of his neglected and disordered family, abandon his hustling theatrical life, and write novels. After Charlot's Christmas show, there was no more scenic work until August the following year.

The book which he had started at Holmwood, and had hoped to finish in October, was still not finished by Christmas, and since his publisher, Fisher Unwin, didn't publish until May 1920, he must have spent a portion of the following year on it. The lull must have been welcome. The war years had been an anxious, hand-to-mouth period for them all, full of private irritations and disappointment, scarcely mitigated – exacerbated, rather – by the huge public success that Weigall had enjoyed. And even though Weigall had not seen active service, there was the trauma of the war itself. Their eldest daughter, Geraldine, remembered her father, when she was five, announcing solemnly to Hortense that the war was over, and being bewildered by the sight of her mother sinking into a chair and weeping. There is a letter from Mimi to Hortense describing the first anniversary of Armistice Day at the Cenotaph in Whitehall which conveys something of the tide of sorrow that still engulfed the land:

As the clock struck 11, every bus stopped, also every taxi. Every man took off his hat and every woman seemed to be praying, and there were many many tears. It was the longest two minutes I have ever passed, some women knelt in the mud on the pavement and thousands had lovely flowers on their way to the Cenotaph – wreaths costing pounds and pounds and even little children carried high up on the men's shoulders had flowers in their hands. We were in the front row at the procession but it was the silence that was most awe inspiring. I would not have missed it for worlds.

News had come some months before from Weigall's old friend, Edward Madge, about the Peace Conference in Paris where he advised on Rumanian affairs. There was little to be hoped for there. 'I dined with Madge,' Weigall wrote to Hortense. 'He was most interesting after his experiences on the intelligence staff … He says it's all hopeless, and the quarrelling has been awful – that Wilson is a charming idealist, but has no knowledge of the intricacies of the European situation, and is floored at each argument and has to give in right and left. The French, he says, are fiends; and the peace, in his opinion is utterly rotten and unfair.'

Weigall must have felt a twinge of envy for his friend, now in the thick of things. His own life was so transformed, so domestic that, as he wrote to Mimi, 'The sort of work I do – writing and painting – keeps me so much at home, that I begin to feel as though I were the poor henpecked husband, minding the children.' And he did mind the children. Typically, he threw himself into it. Alured remembered that:

Punctuality was taken very seriously. Before every meal the maid would ring the bell twice. The first, to wash and get ready. Ten minutes later, the other, and if you were late for that, God help you. He even gave you what at school we called impots. Impositions. 'I must not be late', 'I must not forget', or something else to write out a hundred times.

Sometimes he went too far, and there is a rare glimpse of Hortense hitting back. 'He was at the sideboard, carving for lunch when she came in with all three girls dressed in frocks he hadn't seen before. He looked round and the only thing he said was, "Why are you late?" She said they had been trying on their new dresses for him to see. "How hateful of you," she said.' [2]

But he could also be fun, playing French cricket and Off ground safety with them, taking them all punting on the river, bicycling with the boys out into the countryside around Oxford. When they were away, with Mimi or Geanie, he wrote them letters full of the kind of gruesome detail that would delight them:

Today St Giles's Fair started and I'm sorry you missed it … [there was] a giant rat in a cage. It is said to be the largest rat in the world, and I can quite believe it, for it is as big as a large Persian cat. It has shaggy hair and a great, beastly, fat tail like a bit of thick india rubber piping, and two long brown teeth in the lower jaw. It is one of five caught in the trenches in France. The other four were gassed and killed, but this one survived, and after biting a soldier's nose off (so the man said) was caught and caged. It is a fearsome beast and must have scared the Tommies worse than any German.

Alured particularly remembered his deadpan sense of humour. At the end of a visit from Alan Gardiner, he watched the two men as they said goodbye at the door. 'A lump of dirty-looking Plasticine stuck on the end of an equally dirty-looking shaft of wood had been left on the hall chest by the children. Arthur handing it to him, saying in a matter-of-fact voice, 'Here's your stick'. Alan G. giggling all the way to the gate.'

Other friends came, and once Ronald Storrs, now Military Governor of Jerusalem, brought T.E. Lawrence. Weigall drew a caricature of them, with a comment about the extraordinary contrast they made: 'Storrs so full of good natured bombast' that the house seemed to clang with him even after he had left; and Lawrence so modest, walking behind Storrs, 'like a kitten behind a tom cat'.[3] This was in December 1920, and Lawrence was regarded as a hero for his exploits on the Hejaz railway against the Turks. Shortly after, in February 1921, he was appointed advisor on Arab affairs to the Middle East Department of the Foreign Office. Madge, Gardiner, Storrs, Lawrence – they were all making their way, becoming eminent in their different fields. Alured remembered his father telling him how 'one afternoon going back to his room and

Ronald Storrs (left) and T.E. Lawrence

opening the door, he was suddenly overcome by a gust of revolt, crying in his heart, "Here am I, *stuck in this back*water, at my age. Oh God help me." He was only 39.'

For all that he saw himself as home-loving, Weigall was in fact by nature restless. In one of his novels, *Bedouin Love,* he has a character who lives two lives, in each of which he calls himself by a different name – James Tundering-West in one and Jim Easton in the other. The first character, a country squire, is thoroughly domesticated, thoroughly English, steeped in the traditions of church and manor; by contrast, his *alter ego* is rootless, wandering, romantic, in love with a mysterious other woman called Monime. At bottom, this composite West-East person was himself, and his whole life was a demonstration of how much, when he was in the midst of one world, he longed for the other. Now that he was 'stuck', his only consolation lay in his imagination. Behind that door lay the first of four novels, published between 1920 and 1924, all playing upon the tensions between home and abroad, convention and freedom, society and the desert.

Weigall's children always maintained that he never took these novels seriously. They were potboilers with all the ingredients: beautiful heroines in Paris gowns, clean-living heroes in open-necked shirts, smouldering nights under the stars, life and death adventures, and so on. But the novels do also contain a lot of Weigall's thinking about contemporary life: the relations between men and women, the hypocrisy of current sexual morality, the gulf, as he saw it, between religion and morality, the overarching theme always being the battle between the material and the ideal. These are romances that were meant to make their readers feel intelligent. Their weakness lies in the fact they tried to make them feel profound as well. It may have been a shrewd calculation, to flatter an unsophisticated readership. The writer and traveller H.V. Morton, who was soon to become a close friend, thought so when he wrote once: 'I read two novels of yours during the holiday and admired your versatility to the point of adoration. Complete enjoyment of the novels was marred by the sight of your tongue firmly in your cheek!'[4]

Perhaps he was thinking of Madeline Rorke, the small but perfectly formed heroine of *Madeline of the Desert.* She is in love with a strong and decent Englishman who rescues her from her shallow self and introduces her to books. On the strength of a fortnight's reading, she then takes it upon herself to preach Christ's love and forbearance to a group of Labour and trade unionist activists visiting the ruins at Abydos. The Egyptian sunset falls on her face and she tosses back the unruly clusters of her hair as she discusses international affairs and labour relations in the light of Isaiah, the Epistles and the Gospels. Weigall makes her audience of rough northern men ('By gum, lass …') become rapt and spellbound. Madeline is perhaps the worst example of Weigall's line in facile profundity, but in general he does give his characters every opportunity to air his views.

Of course, when his hero is a traveller, an explorer, an ethnologist, a 'dweller in the desert' (one of his titles), Weigall's own personal perspective carries some conviction and can be made to sit comfortably and convincingly within the story. And the same goes for his feelings on returning to 'civilization'. But when his characters muse at length about, say, the nature of Woman, about Love and Marriage, about Englishness, race, patriotism and Empire and so on, the novels become propaganda – embarrassing propaganda at that. One longs for the moon to come out over the scented garden, for Lady Muriel to appear in her jewels, and for the hero to punch his rival's head in.

Which, of course, he does. Weigall is never dull. His creatures may be essentially unreal, vehicles for this or that opinion, but he twitches their strings with energy and he paints in the local colour, especially Egypt, with the same passionate exhilaration he showed in his *Travels in the Upper Egyptian Deserts*. It may be melodrama, but he carries it off with panache. Thus in *Madeline of the Desert*, the hero Robin finds himself unexpectedly stranded in an Arab village, at the mercy of a crowd baying for his Christian blood, and is rescued from certain death by the heroic Madeline who defies the mob – hatless, 'her hair ... tumbled about her flushed face ... with clenched teeth

By courtesy of Paramount Pictures

## THE
# DWELLER IN THE DESERT
## By ARTHUR WEIGALL

*POPULAR EDITION*

### 2s. 6d. net

A wonderful film of this thrilling story is now being shown.  SEE THE FILM & READ THE BOOK

*OBTAINABLE AT ALL BOOKSHOPS AND LIBRARIES*

PUBLISHED BY
T. FISHER UNWIN, LTD.  1 Adelphi Terrace, London, W.C.2

A publicity clip from the film based on Weigall's novel, *The Dweller in the Desert* and glittering eyes.' In *The Dweller in the Desert*, the heroine is carried to safety from feuding Bedouins, across the burning sands in the arms of the strong and silent man she has vowed never to speak to again (but whom, of course, she eventually marries). In *The Way of the East*, the cavalry officer hero climbs into his Egyptian beloved's apartment through a trap door in the ceiling, and then finds himself face to face with her Anglo-phobic ex-Etonian father at the head of a band of armed servants.

The scene is pure farce, but Weigall's comedy is not always as broad. He works in some nice stretches of dialogue, satirizing the kind of wit and snobbery he must have encountered across all those dinner tables. He also achieves some notable caricatures among his minor characters: parsons, for example, and bosomy Lady Bracknells; the falsely childlike Daisy in *Madeline of the Desert,* such a simple, skipping innocent, chattering on about fairies, but really interested only in seducing the hero; or the spooky mystic, Augustus Blake, based on Algernon Blackwood, invoking the ancient spirits of Egypt; or the politically incorrect but hilarious Egyptian women in *The Way of the East*, trying and failing to be western. Making allowances – huge allowances in the case of this last book which is all about race and 'stock', and whose ostensible liberal-mindedness cannot disguise its deep prejudices – these books are still entertaining.

So at any rate thought the public and many of the reviewers at the time. Of course an organ such as the *Times Literary Supplement*, reviewing along the strictest critical lines, could make nothing of them. But most papers commended him for his 'really convincing Egyptian background' (*The Observer*, 23 May 1920), the 'rare charm' of his scenery (*The Daily Mail,* 28 May 1920), and for his lively handling of incident. There was also a respectful interest in his ideas – *The Manchester Guardian* (4 June 1920) approved of his views on 'brotherhood in politics and religion' in *Madeline of the Desert*, for example. Clearly, in the case of *Madeline* these ideas were stronger stuff then than now. It had been turned down, he told Mimi, by one publisher who 'objected to the Christian and Labour teaching in it' and when Weigall's literary agent, John Farquharson, tried to interest the film company Famous Players-Lasky British Producers Ltd., they rejected it on the grounds that though 'powerfully written', the subject matter was 'delicate', and 'the religious questions raised ... would be rather dangerous for us to handle.'[5]

But he had gauged his public. Almost immediately after *Madeline* was published he started receiving fan mail: 'One of the finest books I have read,' wrote Nellie Cooper of Edgbaston, and Arthur Curtis of Barnes sent his 'sincere congratulations', adding that it was the first time he had ever written to an author. There was even a monk, from Chicago, who wrote to say that the book gave him 'exquisite pleasure and power to exorcise the demons of pain that delight to torture poor ailing humanity.'[6] The American edition came out later that year, and with the publication of his next novel, *The Dweller in the Desert* in January 1921, Weigall began to be hailed 'as a coming "bestseller" ' (*The Weekly Dispatch* 6 February 1921).

This second novel had 'all the elements for a big popular success', said the same paper, and *The Sunday Times* (20 February 1920) reluctantly agreed. While deploring all that was unreal and commonplace in the book, it conceded that it was sure 'to make an appeal, especially to the unsophisticated reader':

We can imagine sentimental ladies falling under the spell of his strong silent hero ... they will secretly envy his heroine her journey across the desert with the strong man as her sole companion, and find pleasure in those rides to the Pyramids under the stars of an eastern sky.

They did, and Paramount Pictures saw the possibilities. The American edition came out under the name *Burning Sands*, and that was the title of the film that was made of it the following year, starring Wanda Hawley and Milton Sills, and produced by George Melford. Weigall saw it, and groaned to Hortense that it was 'the worst picture I ever saw, and full of horrible mistakes, and *nothing* like my story. I wish I were rich enough to refuse to sell to America; but I have to think of the money.' In the circumstances he must have read with interest a letter from an American friend of Hortense:

'Over here' we are enjoying your success with quite truly American enthusiasm ... To have a novel a success in the 'movies' ... is certainly a huge advertisement ... You have certainly arrived with your novels at just the right time, as far as America is concerned, for the 'Sheik' [another film produced by George Melford, starring the matinée idol Rudolph Valentino] is in the zenith of his glory and even in the daily cartoons the flappers refer to their adolescent admirers as 'Sheiks' ... In return the 'Flapper' is called 'Sheba' ... so you had better turn us out a wondrous Sheba and let her dominate the book.[7]

It is ironic that at almost the same time, Weigall's old play 'Omar Khayam' had been rejected by the management of Drury Lane on the grounds that 'Eastern subjects have been touched upon too often in the last ten years.'[8] Just as the English theatre was running out of oriental steam the American cinema began to pick it up.

By now, his third novel, the James West/Jim Easton book, *Bedouin Love*, was out, and his press was better than ever, as he told Hortense, now in America visiting her family:

*Bedouin Love* is going extremely well ... not a single bad [review] since that rather sniffy one in the *Morning Post*. Even the *Times Literary Supplement* is enthusiastic. *The Daily Mail* gave me a great puff ... and the provincial papers have been wonderful – 'the finest novel we have read for many a day' – and so on. The publishers say it is just going into its 3rd edition, and that more than 6000 copies have already been sold, which is as much as *The Dweller* already. It is funny how differently Jim is taken. Some papers find him hard to understand; others talk of him as a 'real creation', and the *Observer*, to my surprise, calls him a real 'man's man'.

Still, even though the book is thus a success, I don't yet know if it is going to be a real "best-seller", though *John O'London's Weekly*, in its list of the current best-sellers compiled from information supplied by the leading booksellers, gives it among the four best-sellers at the moment.

His value to Fisher Unwin was increasing. In his next letter he reports sales for the cheap editions of his two earlier novels at '25,000 copies altogether, which is nearly

£300 to me; but I shan't see this for a year.' Unwin was now offering him a contract on his next two books 'for 20 per cent royalties and £350 advance on each', though a few months later, after *Bedouin Love* had gone into its fourth edition and had been sold to America, he received a better offer from Hutchinson: '£450 advance on each of my next three books, with 20 per cent and 25 per cent royalties … I may go over to them.'

Weigall's eye was on filming rights as much as on book sales. There is no record of what he received for *Burning Sands*, but in May 1922 *Madeline of the Desert* appears still to have been a runner, for there is correspondence about it from the film company, World's Master Productions Ltd, distributors for D.W. Griffith. The speed and style of these exchanges instantly conjure up a world of fast bucks and fat cigars. On May 1st 'E. Wertheimer' writes under a letter head consisting of five blue globes each bearing the title of a D.W. Griffith film, *Intolerance*, *Orphans of the Storm*, *Birth of a Nation*, and so on, asking Weigall to send him *Madeline*, and demanding to be dealt with direct, no agents. The next day a telegram arrives from 'Harry Reichenbach' offering 'fifteen hundred pounds Madeline of Desert answer Savoy Hotel'. Later the same day comes another telegram, this time from Wertheimer asking him to 'be at my office … eleven thirty tomorrow morning regarding madeline desert'. On May 3rd Reichenbach writes to say 'am glad you got a rise out of Wertheimer – whatever you do, ask him enough – he already has a sale. He never gambles. I hope you land him for a big lump.'[9] The rest of the story is lost, and there is no further reference to a film of *Madeline*. Perhaps Weigall overreached himself, or perhaps he groaned too loudly at the suggested treatment.

But £1500 would have lasted a long time, and one is not surprised to find him, all through the autumn and winter of 1922, writing anxiously about the possible sale of the film rights to *Bedouin Love*. Remembering his regret that film-makers didn't exploit the charm of the English countryside, its partial setting in rural Oxfordshire is perhaps a sign that he had been thinking about a film all along. But for all the soft grey walls of the manor house, the tilting mossy gravestones and the elms in the churchyard, there seems not to have been a bite, and he set to work almost immediately on the next novel, *The Way of the East*, and another scenic mix – London and Sussex alternating with Egypt.

The move to Langdale House had seemed at first glance to represent a lull, even a backwater, in Weigall's life. But in fact he made it into a whirlwind. Book followed book, one a year, and that was not all. In May 1921 he became the film critic for the *Daily Mail*. His recent filming experiences and the report he wrote for Charlot had not been entirely buried in the collapse of Garbrand Hall. In April 1921, *The Nineteenth Century* published an article of his on 'The Influence of the Kinematograph upon National Life' on the strength of which Lord Northcliffe, the proprietor of the *Daily Mail*, offered him a prominent column in which to promote the views contained in it.

In this article, Weigall admonished the 'intellectual public' for ignoring 'photoplays', and for speaking of them 'with contempt as being beneath the notice of persons of culture'. Whatever his educated readers may think of them, he says, films are a force to be reckoned with:

It is to be remembered that a popular photo-play is seen by scores of millions of persons throughout the globe: there has never before been such a means of publicity. The newspaper with the largest circulation on earth is a mere mouse in the presence of this mammoth, and the 'best-seller' in the book world is, by comparison, something still smaller. Even *Chu-chin-chow*, with the actors growing grey in their roles, cannot touch more than a small part of that vast public which views a successful film shown for the space of no more than three days at any one theatre.

This being so, he says, we must find out whether films are a force for good or bad. There then follows a version of the modern controversy about the influence of television on public morals. Much of it sounds quaint now, though his general objection to Americanization is still current. What is perhaps more interesting is his final appeal to his readers, cultured as they are, to wake up to the medium as an art form:

The photo-play can be a highly artistic performance and in it certain aspects of human character can be studied and presented with a clarity unsurpassed upon the theatrical stage. Through no other medium can the subtleties of facial expression be employed with such dramatic value ... The possibilities of the Kinema should arouse the enthusiasm of the artist to the highest pitch; for never before have the arts of literature, portraiture, scenic composition, drama, and music been capable of such interdependent combination.

Furthermore, as a record of the past, film is invaluable:

What adequate steps ... has the Government taken to secure the preservation of such records? Are proper archives being formed, so that our children's children may see with their own eyes the very scenes which we have witnessed? ... let us remember that there is no reason, if proper care be taken, why the people of the far future should not be able to be witnesses of the actual events of which they read in their histories. ... We of this age do not realize the power of the instrument which modern invention has placed in our hands ...

If only it had been invented by the ancients, he must privately have thought.

Weigall's film pieces in the *Daily Mail* became a crusade to promote the British film industry. He was prepared to praise the good and condemn the bad whatever the origin of the film, but all things being equal he wanted British films to take a larger share of the market, both at home and in America itself. He thought there was something good and distinctive about the British outlook, and he wanted films to be the ambassadors of the nation. He deplored the fact that American films tended to cast English actors in the roles of crooks and fools, and he feared that the casualness of American morals, as he saw it, would corrupt the British, especially the uneducated masses. In short, his standpoint was cultural imperialism abroad and social paternalism at home.

253

At the same time, he was convinced that artistically speaking Britain had something to offer that was as good as the best of Hollywood. He seized every opportunity to praise good British films: for example, something called the *Narrow Valley*, a simple tale of village life where 'the scenic effects are exquisite, the characterization is brilliant, the acting first rate, the photography well up to American standard ...'[10] By the same token – presumably with Mr Merwin in mind – he made a point of saying in the same article that the time was over when film makers could knock pictures together any old how. It was an art form with its own expertise, and it should be approached with serious professional understanding. At the risk of causing offence, he writes, it must be understood that 'British films will never gain a world market so long as illiterate, vulgar, inartistic, second-rate men have any principal part in the work.'

The trouble was that the market was skewed against the British film maker by the American system of block bookings, which required British 'exhibitors' (i.e. the picture palace owners), to book themselves up with American films for up to two years ahead. For every success included in these 'blocks', there were several that had failed in the States, the idea being to squeeze some return on them by dumping them on the British market. Because the public flocked to American films regardless, the exhibitors didn't dare hold out against the system for fear of losing business. The consequence was that British films were kept waiting, the makers (who weren't paid until their films were shown) went bankrupt, and unemployment followed. Weigall was outraged, and tried to rally the exhibitors to show a bit of mettle:

> I said to the representative of the British Cinematograph Exhibitors Association 'You have a huge membership. Why don't you all get together to fight the system?' He replied that there were still a great many exhibitors who did not belong to the association and that these blacklegs, as he called them, would have beaten the loyal theatres ...'[11]

This sort of campaign was meat and drink to Weigall. His articles attracted much public attention and, as he told his readers, shoals of letters every day. But reading his reviews of the films themselves – on the whole simple-minded moral and sentimental tales and melodramas – one wonders whether it was the work he would have chosen. It paid and he did it perhaps, as his son Alured observed, 'mostly, I suspect, as a prayer blessedly answered in a way which made it indisputably necessary for him to be somewhere else [i.e. not at Langdale House with Hortense].'[12]

The experiment of living as man and wife had clearly not worked. Hortense had not seized her opportunity, as Geanie had urged, and though Weigall had tried to introduce a domestic order of sorts, at the rate he had been working he had hardly had the time or energy for much more than peremptory discipline. By the middle of 1922, the two of them reached stalemate. Hortense's departure for America to visit her family looked natural enough. But it was a stand-off. At almost the same moment, Weigall gave up Langdale House, and moved the whole establishment to London, to 23 Cleveland Square, near Lancaster Gate – out of the backwater at last. London was where he had always wanted to be, and the idea first suggested to Hortense in 1913, of being able to offer a home to Geanie, was at last realized, almost ten years later.

So it was from here that the fate of *Bedouin Love* was anxiously followed, *The Way of the East* written, and his Omar Khayyam play adapted into a historical romance, *The Garden of Paradise*. Meanwhile, the British excavations being conducted by the Egypt Exploration Society at El Amarna, the city of Akhnaten, made a new edition of Weigall's *Life of Akhnaton* desirable. There were alterations to be made in the light of more recent scholarship, for example concerning Nefertiti, the existence of whose portrait head in Berlin was only just coming to light, though no photographs of it were yet available. He also added paragraphs here and there about the new material at El Amarna, in particular a wonderfully evocative section, several pages long, about the lakes and gardens, the painted palaces and mansions being uncovered by the excavators. It will be remembered that Alan Gardiner, H.R. Hall and others had urged Weigall to publicize their work in his new edition. Their hopes were handsomely realized; he took every opportunity to do so, and the very last sentence of his book is a plea on their behalf for more money.

Weigall was thus up to his ears as usual. Furthermore, Cleveland Square brought him back into theatrical circulation as well. Alured remembers the hours his father spent, not just in his study, but at the piano. For while Hortense was away, he developed a professional, and then a personal, relationship with a young Canadian pianist, Muriel Lillie. Muriel was the sister of Beatrice Lillie, their mother having brought both girls from Toronto to London just before the war with a view to launching them on musical careers. As we have seen, Beatrice had been taken on by Charlot, but Muriel had wanted to be a classical pianist, and had got as far as a recital at the Wigmore Hall. However, during the war, revue had sucked her in, as it had so many other artists, and in the wake of her sister's soaring popularity, she had turned to writing songs. With Bea to sing them her path was smoothed, and when she met Weigall she found her librettist.

Thus, during the early autumn of 1922, Weigall made a brief return to the theatre, a revue for which he was engaged to provide all the scenery, most of the costumes, and the lyrics for music composed by Muriel. This was the *Nine O'Clock Revue*, not produced by Charlot this time but by Dion Titheredge, 'a delightful man,' wrote Weigall to Hortense, 'and we worked together most happily.' 'Muriel now came regularly to the house,' Alured remembered, 'to try over with him whatever she'd composed ... He as regularly phoned for her to hum the tune again while he jotted down a ghost or dummy, any old words that fitted tune and rhythm, indispensable when hammering out the words he had in mind.' It was a relationship as different from his early years with Hortense as could be imagined: no goddess worship, no illusions, hard working, professional, collaborative. If Hortense was the last rose of a Victorian summer, Muriel was the first new potato of a modern spring. Temperamentally they were opposites too. Where Hortense was sweet and patient, Muriel was fiery and impetuous. Where one was all evasion and retreat, the other squared up like a fighting cock. Muriel's tantrums were legendary, but they were also an enormous relief.

That summer all was tranquil at Cleveland Square, and one of the songs that emerged was 'Susannah's squeaking shoes' which, sung by Bea Lillie, became a hit:

When I'm feeling lone and sad, and when I've got the blues,
I love to hear the squeaking of Susannah's Sunday shoes.
I hear them squeaking down the street, and squeaking up the stair,
There's not a sound of any kind to beat it anywhere.
I love the twang of the old banjo,
I love the haunting music of the piccolo,

Cover for the sheet music for 'Susannah's Squeaking Shoes'

I love the crying of the cockatoos,
But best I love the squeaking of Susannah's Sunday shoes.

In fact the whole revue was a hit, and Weigall's letter to Hortense – he was almost always able to *write* to her affectionately – reaches a pitch of excitement that recalls his first months in revue. 'We had a wonderful first night last Wednesday (the 25th) and everybody was enthusiastic. I've never read such a wonderful press ... They all say it is the success of recent years. Many of the papers talked of my scenery, and most of them talked about 'Susannah's Squeaking Shoes' and 'Banshee' and 'Little Flat' as being outstanding numbers.' Then comes a detailed description of the scenery, worth quoting because precise descriptions of his work are so rare:

That snow scene of mine looks really exquisite, and I have crowded every white light I could find onto it, so that it is dazzling. Then I have done a gold Chinese scene like my study wall – a gold back-cloth, the big tree (over my mantelpiece) cut out in front of it, and the rocks and a bridge etc, all in a sort of coppery glare of light against a black frame. It is beautiful. Then I have a Persian scene – just a girl seated in a doorway, with the sunlight on the plain white walls; and she holds a huge sort of carpet of vivid colours which is arranged in great folds across the stage. Then for Susannah I have a sort of silhouette effect, with the old mammy walking across the stage in shadow-graph, against a blue night-sky, and the chorus in moonlight in the front. Then another scene is the lights of London – a mass of little lamps and windows illuminated from behind, as though one were looking from a height across the city. ...

'Banshee' I have staged in a cottage interior, and it is intensely weird in the dim light and with the wind howling.

The whole thing had been got ready in the nick of time: 'I worked right through the last night, and then snatched an hour's sleep and was back at the theatre by 10 am and worked right through and only finished at 7.30 pm, just in time to dash home and get dressed for the performance.' At this point he drops Muriel's name in: 'Muriel and I sat together and agonized, she about the music and I about the scenery. Lots went wrong, of course, but nothing fatal. Poor Muriel, she has been like a lunatic; for the orchestra was bad to start with and she was often in tears.' To Alured he wrote more graphically that she 'stamped and cried and made the devil of a scene once or twice, but it did good and the orchestra is now much better.' The set-designer, Moira, in Weigall's novel *The Not Impossible She* is in fact based on Muriel. With Muriel's rages transferred from music to scenery, the character is a comic and affectionate tribute to the perfectionism that Weigall and she held in common.

Weigall's letters to Hortense about his successes, whether his books or his scenery, are always accompanied by a dose of accountancy. For example, a letter such as the one just quoted from, would contain calculations about the agreement he had struck – in this case a half of one per cent of the takings per week, which at full capacity – i.e. £1500 per week – would mean £7.10s a week, which across a year would be £350. It is as though it were understood between them that all the glory really boiled down to debt repayments and school fees. Lack of money is the endless refrain of the letters, a sleep-depriving, pounding anxiety, sharper at some times than at others, but never really overcome. Everything he touched turned to success, but not to gold. Or never to enough gold. If anything ground him down, it was that.

Things now took a surprising turn for the worse. Half way through August, Weigall was stunned by a letter from a moneylender called Passmore complaining that Hortense had sent him a dud cheque, part of her repayment on a loan of £60 taken out in May, shortly before she left for America. With interest, she now owed him £80. Weigall had known nothing of this, and wrote furiously to her to ask 'how on earth you came to borrow all this at a time when I was paying you huge sums each week also, and was paying every single bill as well, and when you had ... the monthly money from Griffith. I can't understand it ... I suppose your going away to America was just a sort of running away and leaving me to face the music.'

He insists that she start paying Passmore back immediately, and not to think of buying her return ticket to England until it is done. Three weeks later, she had still not replied and he wrote again very seriously lecturing her for 'taking so terrible a step as going to a money-lender, and not telling me and without knowing how you were going to pay him, and especially with being dishonourable about giving him a dud cheque.' He then gives her a minute picture of her household extravagance, as revealed in her account books, and describes down to the last penny how he has managed to cut costs to under half of hers. Incidentally, his description of the resulting upset among the servants shows just how crucial they could be:

> Of course there have been great rows. Nonie has been consistently loyal to you (for which I admire her) but consistently *dis*loyal to me (for which I do not trust her). She has abused Florence roundly, asking her how she can be so mean as to cut down expenses, and thus expose your extravagance. She said to Florence, 'You ought to have seen that the bills remained about the same, so that Mr Weigall would be satisfied' etc, etc.

The following month, another letter came from Passmore, and Hortense had to be begged again to 'settle up, and to *stop giving dud cheques*, which is *dishonest*. You must be honest at all costs, Hortense.'

This was really the beginning of the end of their marriage, though Weigall may not have realized it yet. It took more crises of the same sort, for example a large bill the following year for income tax arrears on Hortense's private income, and further evasiveness on her part. But the constant anxiety over money acted upon their relationship like a slow poison, far more debilitating than the problem that Geanie had tried to tackle. It struck at the very root of Weigall's existence, his ability to think and work and create. But that lay ahead. At this very juncture, true to the spirit of Weigall's old theme, the Present stepped in. Howard Carter's discovery of the tomb of Tutankhamun, at the end of November 1922, was a bolt from the Past, knocking out all thought of the Future. Nothing could have been more apt.

# Chapter 19

# Tut-ankh-Carter and TutCarnarvon
# 1923

On the 6 December 1922, Hortense received this letter from Weigall:

> I suppose you have read about Lord Carnarvon's great find at Thebes – the tomb of Tutankhamun, Akhnaten's son-in-law, with all the stuff intact, absolutely marvellous things, said to be worth in money alone five or six million pounds! The *Observer*, *Daily Mail*, and *Weekly Graphic* all 'phoned to me for articles, which I wrote and have made £30 out of it, so I hope he finds more! The inner chambers are all sealed up, and they can't even get at them for the piles of thrones, beds, chariots, etc. before the door. Wonderful jewels, the royal robes and crowns and everything! Our diggings missed it by about 50 yards in 1911!
>
> ... The *Nine O'Clock Revue* is still going well, but I am terribly off revues at present, and only want to be an Egyptologist again owing to this new find!

Hortense must have brightened. Here was something to put the theatre in the shade. The letter also has news of the current novel, and of *The Garden of Paradise*, but more to the point it has news of *Akhnaton* – 700 copies sold already ('This new find makes it almost out of date already! I tremble in case any of my theories are proved wrong!'); also about Butterworth publishing his collected essays and about Unwin republishing *Cleopatra*. All he wanted was to be an Egyptologist again, and the publishers were happy to cash in on the new public interest.

But it wasn't quite as an Egyptologist that Weigall became involved with the new find. As he explained to Hortense:

> You will be startled to hear that I am off to Egypt on Thursday. The *Daily Mail* has asked me to be present at the opening of the sealed inner chamber of the Tutankhamun tomb, which will be opened towards the end of this month. ... of course I jumped at their offer. I am to write three or four articles for them, and a particularly big one on the actual opening ...

Lord Carnarvon is in England now and we have exchanged very friendly letters. He is going out by the next boat after mine, I think. Meanwhile, at Luxor, Carter is removing and packing the stuff found in the first chambers, so as to clear the way to the sealed-up burial chamber. I expect it will be a formal opening with hundreds of people there, and the King of Egypt and all those sort of people. It will rest with Carnarvon whether I get actually asked to be part of the opening party, or whether (as I more expect) I shall have to wait a bit, and get Carter or somebody to let me look in a bit later. Anyhow I hope I shall see it before the newspaper men, who are sure to be there in dozens.

Weigall's frank excitement and his expectation that he would be accepted in Egypt as a colleague rather than as a 'newspaper man' were soon to be dashed. Carter was assembling a team which included Arthur Mace, lent for the purpose by the Metropolitan Museum. Both men had been involved one way or another with the story of Weigall and the statuette, and Weigall was reckoning without the acrimony of the archaeological world in general.

Carnarvon himself had never, as far as one can tell, been part of Carter's anti-Weigall campaign in Egypt before the war, but on this occasion his friendliness was a little disingenuous. As it later transpired he was even then negotiating with the *Times* newspaper – negotiations designed precisely to thwart men like Weigall. On returning to London after his first view of the tomb, Carnarvon had quickly begun to realize that here was a chance to make money. On Christmas Eve 1922, he wrote to Carter mentioning the possibility of a monopoly deal with *The Times*, as well as a contract with Pathé and others for the film rights: 'There is, I imagine,' he wrote, 'a good deal of money in this, what, I don't know, possibly 10-20 thousand ...'[1] In a piece he aptly named 'Tutankhamun and Co. Ltd', Weigall makes a point of Carnarvon's business acumen and illustrates it by saying that, in his innocence, he once 'wrote to him suggesting he should give the film rights to a certain educational firm which had the necessary organization for distributing the picture amongst the schools and institutes throughout the land, but I received a laconic reply from him that the price offered was the thing that mattered.'

Early in 1923, Carnarvon closed with the *Times*, and in return for £5,000 plus 75 per cent of the profits on sales of information and photographs to all other publications, gave that paper the sole publication rights to all material relating to the tomb. The *Times* gave itself permission to withhold up to 50 per cent of its news and photographs from sale altogether, and what was left was going to have to be bought by the world's press from the *Times* and printed a day late. The Egyptian press could have it free, but still late. Neither Carnarvon nor Carter were going to permit anyone, let alone ask Weigall or anyone else from a newspaper, to see anything before the *Times* correspondent had seen it first.

The precedent for this arrangement was the agreement reached with the *Times* by the Royal Geographical Society over the Everest Expedition the year before. But Carnarvon failed to take into account the crucial differences between Mount Everest and the Valley of the Kings. Where Everest was remote and unvisited, Luxor was a tourist centre, with comfortable hotels and bars and telephone lines. Besides which, Everest was not a piece of politically charged heritage, nor did it contain gold. Hordes of correspondents were, of course, an obvious inconvenience, just as all the aristocrats had been at the time of Yuya and Tuya. At the time, therefore, it must have seemed desirable to cut them out in favour of one outlet. In practice the plan was doomed.

It is worth quoting the relevant paragraph from the *Times* memorandum at some length, for when transferred to the public arena of the Valley of the Kings and the Winter Palace Hotel, it reads almost like a set of stage directions for the drama of looks and whispers, of sealed lips and locked doors that ran during the early months of 1923. It was signed on 9 January 1923, the day Weigall posted his letter to Hortense in which he speaks of Carnarvon's friendliness. It opens with the statement that the Earl appoints the *Times* as sole agents for the sale of all information about the tomb, and continues:

> The Earl hereby agrees that neither he nor his staff nor any persons authorized by him or them will knowingly communicate or permit to be communicated any such news articles interviews or photographs relating to any such exploration work ... to any person or persons company or companies other than the *Times* ... that neither the Earl nor his agents will authorize or permit personal friends acquaintances or other persons whatsoever to be present at any such exploration work or to inspect any of the results thereof unless such persons shall ... first pledge themselves to grant no interviews to and to make no communication and give no information whatsoever as to what such persons shall have seen or heard whether to representatives of the Press in any part of the world or to any persons whatsoever.[2]

Luxor was fuller that season than it had ever been before. An American steam ship company laid on three extra ships specifically for the journey to Egypt. The Reuters correspondent, Valentine Williams, recorded in his autobiography that the Winter Palace Hotel dining room 'glittered with the jewels and bare arms of beautiful women from all parts of Europe and America':

> The hotel split into two camps. Tourists who were friends of Carnarvon were unwilling to have any traffic with the other side, lest they might be accused of giving secrets away, and I did not blame them, although it diverted me to find people I knew quite well in London passing me by with face averted.[3]

Weigall's prominence in the hostilities between the press and Carnarvon's expedition is one of the few things that is remembered about him now. At the same time, very little is known with any exactness, and much colourful speculation has filled the gap. In his biography of Carter, T.G.H. James says that, in spite of some justification, the world's press behaved 'outrageously in bombarding the excavators with complaints and demands, in canvassing Lacau [Maspero's successor as Director General of the Antiquities Department] and the Antiquities Service to circumvent Carnarvon's arrangement with the *Times*, and in stimulating the Egyptian Press to feelings of outrage.' He also says that it was really Weigall who was responsible – 'The arrival of Arthur Weigall ... led to a serious deterioration in general relations with the Press'[4] – and in so doing he casts him as the villain of the piece.

In fact, whatever the excavators thought, the journalists never regarded Weigall as their ringleader. H.V. Morton of the *Daily Express*, thought that it was Valentine Williams who 'did most of the work; Weigall was always ready to share his archaeological knowledge; and I ... suggested that the three of us, instead of working in rivalry, should unite against the combine, which we did.'[5] These men, and others such as A.H. Bradstreet of the *Morning Post* and the *New York Times*, knew the implications of the monopoly agreement well enough without Weigall pointing them out. Huge circulations were threatened. According to H.V. Morton, he and his two colleagues from England 'probably represented more newspapers than any three men ever represented. My own allowance was ninety-six journals all over the Empire.'[6] Likewise, Weigall's articles were published not only in England, but throughout the United States by way of the North American Newspaper Alliance. Hortense was able to follow her husband in the Chicago papers and, as she explained to Alured, 'They are published all over America, so everyone is interested and it will make people interested in his books too.'

The discovery of the tomb promised to be one of the biggest news stories of the decade, so that when the *Times* agreement was announced, the newspaper editors simply decided to break it. H.V. Morton wrote that he, Valentine Williams and Weigall were 'sent out from England with instructions to break the monopoly by any means which seemed proper to them.'[7] As for the means, again the press could find their way to the Egyptian Government without Weigall. According to Williams, 'It was felt very strongly in some quarters that the Egyptian Government had no business to allow a single newspaper to monopolize a matter of acknowledged public interest and several of Reuters' correspondents enquired as to what steps Reuters proposed to take to fulfil its contractual obligations to its subscribers in the matter.'[8]

The issue of press freedom alone was therefore quite enough to account for ill-feelings between the two camps. Weigall's criticism of the monopoly agreement was wider. His experience of Egypt and of Anglo-Egyptian relations, together with his own ideals about the means and ends of Egyptology, gave him a different perspective. As Valentine Williams expressed it in a passage explaining his view: 'the granting of a monopoly of news in a scientific discovery to an individual newspaper for a financial consideration was a form of commercial exploitation unworthy of the traditions of science and hitherto unknown in the history of excavation.' He had, as we have seen, spent his years as Inspector trying to transform archaeology from a dream of hidden treasure into a disinterested science. Now Carnarvon had invented a new route back to the old pot of gold.

Weigall was dismayed, and in the end expressed his opinions vigorously in the *Daily Mail*. The consequence, according to Valentine Williams, was that:

The excavators were much incensed against Weigall, and his strictures led to his being virtually boycotted by the distinguished Egyptologists, some of them personal friends of his, who had come out to work on the tomb and were naturally partisan, a retribution which, I feel bound to say, Arthur bore with his customary smiling philosophy.[9]

In fact, if one looks at the evidence carefully, it is clear that the excavators had decided to boycott Weigall well before he had publicly declared his opposition to the monopoly agreement. The moment he arrived in Luxor, on January 23rd, Arthur Mace predicted that Weigall was 'going to have rather an uncomfortable time, as no-one is prepared to be cordial. Carter I know doesn't intend to let him to see anything.'[10] Lack of cordiality was the least of it. The atmosphere was poisonous. Carnarvon's half-brother, Mervyn Herbert, was perhaps more savage than most, but he came near the general sentiment of the team when he called Weigall 'the prince of swine ... [who] looks as complete a cad as he is.'[11]

T.G.H.James offers a plausibly personal motive for Weigall's supposed caddishness. Weigall, he says,

had returned to Luxor, unloved and unwanted. Any credit he might have expected for his work in the past on the Theban Necropolis was negated by what was seen as desertion to the ranks of the unprincipled Press. ... Sadly he felt rebuffed, and he exacted his revenge on former colleagues (even friends) by participating in, if not actually initiating, a campaign of hostile reporting in which scant credit was given to the excavators. ... here Weigall now was, in Thebes again, with Carnarvon and Carter in the ascendancy ... his sharp inquiring intelligence reacted poorly. He was obliged to ally himself with the hostile representatives of the newspapers with whom he could take some malicious pleasure in discomforting the excavators.[12]

The evidence points the other way. Weigall's letters – always frank – never betray the least sense that he felt unloved or maliciously inclined. On the contrary, Egypt exhilarated him, just as it always had done, and even in the thick of battle, he was able to report to Hortense:

It is really a glorious place, and I am awfully happy here, except that I find myself in a desperate political intrigue ... O, the delight of going up to the Tombs of the Kings again! Engelbach [the Inspector of Antiquities] and I came back up the 'chimney' and then over the cliffs and down the steep path onto the top of Der el Bahri ... I wish you were out here with me: you would enjoy seeing the old place again: it is really most beautiful, and the heat is glorious.

The letter also briefly describes the trouble over *The Times* agreement, but it does so without personal comment. In fact, when he wrote it, it wasn't even Carnarvon's commercial instincts that bothered him. At that moment, as the letter suggests, the principle of disinterested science was obliged to take second place to something far more urgent – the politics of the discovery.

On his arrival in Cairo, Weigall found a very different Egypt from the one he had known before the war. The Protectorate had been abolished and the promulgation of a new constitution was in the process of being negotiated. It was, however, too little too late. The British still dominated all levels of official life, and they were determined to retain control of important areas such as international relations, the Suez Canal, communications and the Sudan. A small standing army would remain. The Egyptians were impatient, the Nationalist party, the Wafd, was in the ascendant, and hostility to the British, which had always existed, was now outright and dangerous. 'O, the gloom of the Turf Club!' exclaimed Weigall to Hortense:

> All the English officials complaining that they couldn't get on with their work, owing to native opposition, and all either resigning or wanting to. A sort of dull lethargy of despair over them all. Somebody said to me, "The fact is – the soul has gone." Then there is this conspiracy to murder them, and nearly 20 have either been assassinated or wounded in the last year or so. Every man carries his revolver, and the Hall Porter at the Club hands the revolver to each man as he goes out, or puts it in the pigeon hole as he comes in. You can't go into the Mousky [the bazaar] without being insulted, and you mustn't go alone on any quiet road.

The discovery of the tomb of Tutankhamun by an Englishman couldn't have come at a worse time. The monopoly agreement only added fuel to the fire. The arrangement would oblige Carnarvon to exclude the Egyptian press from firsthand information about a tomb which at that moment they were very ready to invest with patriotic and ancestral feelings, and which anyway belonged to their own government. As the Egyptian Minister, Sirry Pasha, pointed out: 'It is an unheard of thing that the Egyptian papers should have to take all news of an archaeological discovery in Egypt from a London newspaper.'[13]

Added to that, there were rumours that Carnarvon and Carter were plundering the tomb. Of course they were not – though they were hoping to be granted good things by the Antiquities Department, and there would soon be acrimonious arguments over their 'rights' in the matter. But to the Egyptians, as was well known, there could only ever be one reason for not showing the world what you had found. As it happened, they had been given some grounds for suspicion. Shortly after the official opening of the ante-chamber the previous November, Carnarvon and his daughter Evelyn (Carter isn't mentioned in the accounts, but his presence was probably assumed) had indeed reopened an ancient robber's hole in the sealed up doorway to the inner burial chamber and had climbed through. They did so probably at night, thinks T.G.H.James, and without informing the Inspector of Antiquities for Upper Egypt, Reginald Engelbach. The question of how much they were to blame is debated still. But for the moment that is not the point. The point is that it had become known.

Carnarvon's daughter confided the fact of the clandestine entry to her uncle Mervyn Herbert, who recorded it in his journal, adding: 'The only others who know anything about it are the workmen, none of which would ever breathe a word to a soul about it.'[14] Anyone who had worked in the Valley, as both Carnarvon and Carter had, would have known that news of a discovery, accompanied by tales of untold wealth being spirited out, always found their way to the Theban villages. The result was, as Weigall told Carter in a letter he wrote soon after arriving in Luxor, 'the natives all say that you may therefore have had the opportunity of stealing some of the millions of pounds' worth of gold ... and already before I left London I was told of the intense feeling which you both aroused.'[15]

That Carnarvon should have risked causing these rumours indicated to Weigall how little he understood of the changed political situation. In fact one can see it plainly enough in just one sentence of Carnarvon's Christmas Eve letter to Carter. Commenting on the extraordinary public interest it has created, he puts it down to its being 'a private concern and that Englishmen are responsible for it'.[16] The fact that he was excavating not as a private man but as an agent of the Egyptian Government through its Antiquities Department does not cross his mind. Valentine Williams described Carnarvon as a typical example of a certain type of peer, very charming but having 'all the arrogance of his class in his approach to his fellow-man, particularly the Egyptians, whom he frankly despised and was at no pains to conceal it.'[17] The whole thing was thus a gift to the Nationalists and to anti-British feeling in general.

Weigall also realized that it would have been extremely easy for him, personally, to have hastened a showdown between Carnarvon and the Egyptian government. Reuters, as we have seen, was being asked to put pressure on the Egyptians. The *Daily Mail* was urging Weigall to do the same. After all, he knew his way around the Ministries. His views on the subject of Egyptian antiquities – that Egypt was the place for them – had now acquired a political resonance that would have made him very welcome. But as he wrote to Gardiner, whom he met in Cairo before continuing on to Luxor, he was not going to see 'the Prime Minister or anyone else for that matter, in deference to your argument', and that although he had just received 'another cable from London saying "impress on you importance of approaching matter through Egyptian ministry",' he would 'do nothing'.[18]

At first glance, such restraint seems unlike him. He had in the past used interdepartmental politics to gain his ends, and had played the British Agency against the French Department of Antiquities. But now two things stopped him. Firstly, British prestige was paramount with him, in spite of his sympathy with the Egyptians. And secondly, he had been shocked by the state of the Cairo Museum. The place had deteriorated sharply since he had last seen it, and there was a real danger that the things that Carter was bringing out of the tomb in pristine condition at Thebes were destined for damp and decay in Cairo. As he wrote in the *Daily Mail*, the objects that he and others had excavated in the Valley of the Kings 17 years before, and which had emerged 'in a blaze of gold ... absolutely new and untouched by time', were now 'tarnished, dingy and dropping to pieces':

> The building though modern is dilapidated and part of the roof fell in a short while ago, destroying many fine objects. If antiquities are removed from the tomb where they are perfectly safe and thrown pell-mell into an understaffed museum in the damp climate of Cairo and left to rot, excavation becomes utterly immoral ...[19]

Weigall therefore hesitated to make an alliance with anyone known to be rigidly against the export of antiquities. As it happened, the new Director General of Antiquities, Pierre Lacau, was just such a man. Times had indeed changed. Many Egyptologists, Weigall's friend Alan Gardiner among them, feared that Lacau would bring in a law prohibiting exports altogether, and that the funding for archaeological work from foreign museums would therefore dry up. Weigall's fear was more for the safety of the objects. Thus, in spite of pressure to do so, and the example of other correspondents, Weigall omitted to call on Lacau while he was in Cairo.

Weigall's plan was therefore to go to Luxor immediately, but to return to Cairo in time for Carnarvon's arrival from England, and to speak to him directly about the political dangers of the situation. By the same token, he wanted to be able to say something to Carter in Luxor while he was there, and knowing that an approach might be tricky, he asked Gardiner to think of a message 'to give me to deliver to Carter. That would be a friendly way of breaking the ice with him.'[20]

The ice was never broken. In 'Tutankhamun & Co. Ltd.', Weigall describes how Carter received him:

My old colleague ... informed me that the contract with the *Times* would oblige him to act towards me as my most bitter enemy during the ensuing weeks, that he would have to debar me from seeing the tomb or, as far as possible, any of the objects found, and that he would have to prevent my obtaining any information regarding the work, for fear that such knowledge as I possessed, if given to the public, might impair the value of the exclusive articles appearing in *The Times*.

Carter then advised Weigall against talking to Carnarvon, so he decided to stay in Luxor, write down what he would have said, and send it to Carter instead.[21] After all, they had known each other pretty well over the years, he probably did not realize Carter's role in trying to oust him from his job before the war, and there was enough common experience between them for Weigall to feel he could talk freely to him.

Winter Palace,
Luxor,

25th Jan., 1923.

Dear Carter,

When I met you the other day I explained to you that I found myself in rather an awkward position out here, but that anyway I wouldn't bother you at all, nor even ask for special consideration. I realized how harassed you must be and having myself been in charge of big finds of this kind I knew what you must be going through. You advised me not to go down to Cairo to see Lord Carnarvon and I am therefore going to write to you to give you some idea of what I should have said to him. ...

You, in the depths of old Tut's tomb, have probably not realized how bitter and dangerous the whole situation is, and this letter comes really as a sort of attempt to warn you and Lord Carnarvon of the danger. …

You are mistaken, he says, in thinking that 'British prestige in this country is still maintained':

and that you could do more or less what you liked just as we all used to do in the old days. You have found this tomb, however, at a moment when the least spark may send the whole magazine sky-high, when the utmost diplomacy is needed, when Egyptians may have to be considered in a way to which you and I are not accustomed, and when the slightest false step may do the utmost disservice to our country.

Things have come a long way, he might have said, since you and I sat under the palm trees at Saqqara and dispensed justice in colonial style.

He then raises the question of the monopoly agreement and the fact that it has opened both Carnarvon and Carter to the charge of being 'out for commerce at the expense of Egypt's "sacred dead"' – though he adds, with slightly cloying diplomacy, that he is prepared to give them the benefit of the doubt:

All sensible people must have seen of course that all you sold to the *Times* was the right to your private expert views on the find [he had not seen the contract]; but the newspaper world knew that in this case you could not sell this without shutting out of the tomb every single person connected in the most remote degree with a news-paper. They saw that if any Egyptologist came out here having promised, as all Egyptologists do from time to time, to enlighten the public through the medium of some one newspaper, he would be debarred from entering the tomb or getting one single word of information; and thus not only would science on the spot lose the aid of his advice or knowledge, but the public would lose the chance of obtaining from its particular newspaper firsthand information supplied without delay, unless it used the agency of the *Times*, which no self-respecting paper could do.

It wasn't, of course, Egyptologists that the newspaper world was worried about, but its own correspondents. Weigall is really talking about himself. He was, after all, the author of the life of Akhnaten, Tutankhamun's father-in-law, and was knowledgeable about the Tutankhamun period generally. And yet, he says, 'you had at once to slam the door in my face.' In *his* face especially, expertise from other sources being precisely the thing that would undercut the value of the *Times* articles.

But that apart, it is the political danger he stresses, a danger which he believes to be reaching some kind of bursting point. Contrasting the tomb with Everest, he recapitulates:

Here you had found a tomb belonging to the Egyptian Government, a tomb in a public place, under the immediate eye of native and foreign tourists, a tomb containing Egypt's "sacred dead", a discovery belonging in no way to you ... but to the whole world, especially to Egypt – Egypt seething with hatred of England ...

To retrieve the situation, he implores Carter to do three things:

Firstly, persuade Lord Carnarvon to declare publicly that he will not profit financially out of the contract with *The Times*, his expenses in the cause of science being so enormous. Next, show your workshop and its contents, as far as possible, to journalists so that they may tell the public what splendid work Lord Carnarvon is doing in preserving the objects found. And thirdly, persuade him to give to every journalist, and particularly to native journalists, the bare facts, at least on the day of the opening of the inner chamber, and *not* one day after *The Times*, which from a newspaper point of view, would be the same as not at all. Give *The Times* your own views and story of the opening, but give to every journalist at exactly the same hour the announcement of what you have found ...

In the light of later developments, this was sound and valuable advice. Whether he believed his own point about Carnarvon's 'enormous expenses' is doubtful; he offers it merely as worth a try. In fact, in 'Tutankhamun & Co. Ltd.', he was quite frank:

The oft-repeated statement – never I think made by himself – that his [Carnarvon's] expenditure in the cause of science has left him greatly out of pocket, is the merest verbiage. ... Excavation here [in the Valley of the Kings] is not expensive: I remember the entire work of excavation which led to the discovery of the neighbouring tomb of Yuaa and Tuau some years ago only cost about £80.

So far Weigall's letter to Carter is typewritten. But a hastily hand-written last page is added to it after the signature, announcing the imminence of the very explosion Weigall had feared: 'Since writing the above I have heard of this trouble about the Egyptian journalists tomorrow; and I should like to say that I personally have not applied for a permit to visit the tomb nor have had anything to do with the matter.'
What he is referring to is explained in 'Tutankhamun & Co., Ltd.':

The first incident of importance which happened after my arrival occurred on a certain day when Mr Carter was going down to Cairo by the night train to meet Lord Carnarvon. The Egyptian Government had been so annoyed by the excavator's attitude that, without consulting Mr Carter, they had invited a number of native journalists to proceed to Luxor and to enter the tomb, desiring thereby to show that they and not the excavators were the proprietors ... Mr Carter, however, acting loyally by the *Times* contract, was determined to thwart this move by locking the tomb and taking the keys down with him.

In the letter, Weigall warned Carter that (as he had just been saying) the consequences would be extremely serious for the British if he refused to compromise with the

Egyptians. The memory of Carter's obduracy after the Saqqara incident must have been in his mind :

> I implore you to forget all about questions of rights now and to regard the matter solely from a patriotic point of view. Simply ask yourself what is best for Anglo-Egyptian relations. The whole thing is too big and too serious for you even to bother about your unfortunate *Times* agreement ... This press view, I take it, has been engineered to test Egypt's rights in the tomb. You have been ignored and therefore insulted. But I beg you to keep your temper, and in view of the strained political situation, to pacify the native press as far as you can.

The story is continued in 'Tutankhamun & Co., Ltd.' Weigall followed up the letter by appealing in person. Carter, however 'was obdurate':

> Only an hour or two remained before his train was due to start; I and two Anglo-Egyptian officials ... wrote an urgent telegram to the Residency in Cairo explaining the situation; but just as it was being dispatched we received word that Lord Allenby [the High Commissioner] himself had earlier in the day telegraphed to Mr Carter advising him, apparently without avail, to leave the keys at the tomb.

In fact Weigall's own part in alerting the British authorities to the impending row and bringing their influence to bear may have been greater than he suggests there. For in the letter to Hortense quoted earlier, written at the end of this same day, he says:

> The Egyptian Ministry insisted that *native* journalists should be let in. Carter refused. There has been a devil of a row, in which I have been involved ... My one object has been to prevent a native row, and I have been in telegraphic communication with Allenby and the Ministers all day today, and have been arguing it out with Carter. It's too long a story to tell and I'm so tired.

In the end, Weigall actually pursued Carter to the station. The *Times* representative was there, and 'with peculiar misgiving' Weigall saw him, 'whispering to him to stick to his guns. Nevertheless I argued the matter with him once more, and at last to my great relief, just before the train started, he gave in and handed over the keys.' According to Weigall's son, Alured, the ending was even more of a cliff hanger, for the train had actually begun to move before Carter threw the keys onto the platform.

A crisis had been averted, at least in the short term. But in the long term neither Carter nor Carnarvon were prepared to take warning from Weigall's prescience, and the whole project continued on its way, dogged by suspicion and ill-feeling on all sides. The following season, there was indeed a lock-out, though on that occasion it was the Egyptian authorities who had the keys, and Carter who was locked out.

From all this it should be clear that Weigall concentrated his efforts, for as long as he was able, on the principals – Carter and Carnarvon. Far from lobbying and intriguing, his intention was to persuade them privately. On at least one occasion, his intervention had prevented a lock-out that might have had serious consequences. Needless to say, his advice gained him nothing but hostility. Thereafter, there was nothing for it, short of packing his bags, but to throw in his lot with the rest of the press and use his influence with the Egyptian ministries and the Antiquities Department. Even then, Weigall's dispatches to the *Daily Mail* do not amount, in T.G.H. James's words to 'a campaign of hostile reporting in which scant credit is given to the excavators'.

In fact it was not until three weeks into his five-week mission that he said anything about the situation at all. Until February 9th, his articles are all either background pieces about the history of the period, speculation about what the inner chamber will contain, descriptions of the things coming out of the tomb, or local colour pieces about the scenery, the tourists, the road being built in the valley, and the mounting excitement. The nearest he gets to a jibe at the monopolists is to say, on January 29th, that people have begun to refer to the Pharaoh as Tut-ank-Carter or TutCarnarvon. On the other hand, he puts in things like:

> A great debt is due to Mr Lythgoe, head of the Egyptological Department of the New York Metropolitan Museum of Art, who is directing neighbouring excavations, and who has lent an experienced staff. Mr Howard Carter ... also has much skill and ingenuity in such matters. Hence there is little likelihood that the treasures will perish.[22]

The following days saw the crisis of the near lock-out, but not a breath of it appears in his dispatches. And so it goes on, not a word throughout the days that Arthur Mace in his diary records as being 'rather lively':

> owing to Lord Carnarvon's agreement with the *Times*, which is much more drastic, now we have seen it, than we ever imagined ... The Winter Palace is a scream. No-one talks of anything but the tomb, newspaper men swarm, and you daren't say a word without looking around everywhere to see if anyone is listening ... Among them was Weigall if you please – very fat and oily, pretending to be a journalist only by accident so to speak.[23]

Fat and oily maybe, but he held his tongue. The provocation was considerable. Once, two years later, in the course of a letter to Gardiner, he speaks of his pleasure in recalling that 'you came up and spoke to me in the Valley at the time when I regarded myself as a lonely voice in the wilderness.'[24] It was clearly a brave act on Gardiner's part, and it speaks volumes about Weigall's personal situation.

As for his other friends and contacts, one wonders whether they too, like Valentine Williams's, would have had to pass him by with face averted. There is for example a letter from Mary Hunter innocently asking him, just as he used to be asked, to look after three friends of hers, Lady Juliet Trevor, Sir Louis Mallet and Sir Philip Sassoon: could he help them 'to see all they can see of the new discoveries – supposing Lord Carnarvon is not helpful.' [25] Would these three have had to choose between approaching Weigall and being cut by Carnarvon, or approaching Carnarvon and cutting Weigall?

On the 1st of February Weigall senses his readers might be getting restive for news about the opening of the inner chamber and has to admit that there has been a hitch. It had to do, he says, with the framing of the new constitution. There was tension in Cairo and neither Lord Allenby nor King Fouad, in whose presence Carnarvon wanted to make the opening, could leave the city. In fact, tension was mounting in the valley too. Carnarvon was guarding the secret of the day of opening. From a telegram sent to Weigall by the foreign editor, it appears that the *Mail* had instructed its lawyers to take out an injunction against the monopolists.[26] The journalists themselves were keeping watch on the tomb in case Carnarvon should steal a march on them. H.V. Morton describes an occasion when, convinced that the excavators were going to open it after dark, he stayed out all night on a hill overlooking the tomb – fruitlessly as it turned out, and dangerously too, for the rumours of gold had, he says, brought into the area a record collection of murderers, thieves and bandits from both deserts.[27]

Meanwhile a cat and mouse game was developing between the excavators and the Antiquities Department, and it was this that interested Weigall at least as much as the adventures of the press. Engelbach, the Chief Inspector for Upper Egypt, now found himself in very much the same position that Weigall had been in years before with Theodore Davis. Carter and Carnarvon resented Engelbach's efforts to supervize the excavation and kept him at arm's length. Perhaps Mervyn Herbert's diary reveals their attitude to him as it does to Weigall, for it refers to him as 'a filthy little fellow of German name'.[28] At any rate, there is evidence to suggest that they were trying to get him sacked.[29]

Maybe it was this that decided Weigall. Whatever it was, on 9 February 1923 the *Daily Mail* carried his denunciation of Carnarvon's monopoly agreement, his high-handedness towards the Antiquities Department, and his exploitation of the tomb for the purposes of private gain. The Department of Antiquities, wrote Weigall:

correctly assumes the right to inspect the tomb and have information regarding the progress of the work, and … [Carnarvon] suggests by a certain shortness of temper that the intrusion is resented.

The Government and the Department of Antiquities see things 'broadly and in principle' and are anxious to avoid creating a precedent which would 'loose into Egypt a hoard of loot-hunters … clamouring for the publicity which seems to bring such wealth in its train'. Lord Carnarvon, on the other hand, talks of 'news rights', 'film rights', 'photo rights', 'book rights' and how to keep them profitably exclusive, until the serious archaeologist, looking with anxiety into the future, is nauseated.' He only hopes that Lacau and Engelbach don't resign. He then winds up the article with a tribute – in case anyone should mistake his point – to the skill of the excavators:

Let it be understood that Lord Carnarvon's work on the technical side is above criticism, thanks particularly to the generous aid of the staff of the New York Metropolitan Museum of Art.

The battle was now open, and in its way Weigall seems to have enjoyed it. As he said to Hortense later: 'It was all great fun, but of course it was a real fight against Carnarvon and it all worked up in a crescendo to the opening of the sealed chamber – Carnarvon and *The Times* swearing we would not get one word of information, and we swearing we would get a story as good as or better than *The Times*.' After all he was still, as he had said of himself at Saqqara, 'prehistoric enough to love a good scrap'. He felt passionately about his argument, and he must have enjoyed the chance to give it a public hearing. In his next piece he acknowledged that he was now:

> regarded as [Carnarvon's] arch-enemy, for I have pointed out in these columns that the introduction of money-making into Egyptology is fatal to all the principles of scientific work, and I have said openly that I am eager to render abortive this monopoly of news in order to prevent such a transaction from ever being repeated.[30]

Now, as enemy number one, there was nothing he could not say, and he proceeds to tell his public about the campaign against Engelbach:

> The latest manoeuvre in Cairo has led to Captain Engelbach, the Chief Inspector of the Antiquities Department, being withdrawn to some extent from the Valley of the Kings because the interests of Egyptology were more important to him than those of private enterprise, and the native Inspector of Antiquities who happens to be a man appointed by me [was this Rushdy?] ... is to be joined at once by another native inspector who owes his rise to Mr Howard Carter ...[31]

The lobbying and intrigue were clearly not all on one side. In the same article he also informs his readers that Carnarvon has caused his coronet and monogram to be painted over the doorway to the tomb. At a little distance, he says, this looks remarkably like a skull and cross bones, earning the excavators the nickname, 'The Buccaneers'. He notes too the arrival in the valley of an American 'kinema operator' which caused consternation among the monopolists 'who intend to make a lot of money out of exclusive film rights' and had therefore to shut down work for the day.

From then on, Weigall kept his readers informed on both fronts – the tomb itself, and the battle of Carnarvon versus the journalists. On Thursday the 15th February he reported rumours that although Sunday was now named as the official day of opening, a secret entry before that day was expected. Then he goes on to describe the lion-headed beds as they came out, the heads:

> sculpted with great feeling and boldness, the gaunt cheeks, the hungry eyes, the pricked-up ears, and the conventionalized yet ragged mane conveying ... an instant and vivid impression of a sort of ferocious power.

On Saturday the 17th February his readers learned that Sunday was indeed a ruse, and that the opening had been made the day before, at an unexpected hour, and with very

272

few people present. At least the Antiquities Department had been represented by Lacau and Engelbach. For the rest of the gathering, Arthur Mace records Lythgoe (of the Metropolitan Museum), Herbert Winlock, Sir William Garstin and two or three native officials – '3 scrubby looking coons,' wrote Mervyn Herbert in his diary.[32] No one mentions the *Times* correspondent, and Weigall says he wasn't even in the valley. Apparently, as he explained to Hortense later, what had happened was that the Egyptian Minister for Public Works had 'refused to allow the *Times* man in at all till we could all go in.' Effectively, the monopoly agreement had been scuppered.

As for the other correspondents, Arthur Mace wrote that they were taken by surprise, having made no arrangements to file any messages back. He obviously didn't know about Valentine Williams's ingenious plan, devised precisely on the assumption that Friday would be the day. With a car hidden in the reeds by the Nile, and a chauffeur ready to rush him to the telegraph office, he had pre-written two cables, one to the effect that the chamber was empty, and the other saying that the king's sarcophagus had been discovered. As he hung over the retaining wall at the top of the entrance to the tomb, one of the official Egyptian representatives came out to relieve himself behind a rock. Williams seized his chance to play an old trick. By suggesting he knew more than he did, he managed to get the man to say what had been found – a magnificently decorated gold and blue sarcophagus. The news caught the 4:30pm London deadline that afternoon, and Lady Carnarvon first heard of her husband's great news from the *Evening Standard* before the opening party had left the tomb.[33] Weigall met his deadline for the next morning's edition, and his piece earned him a cable from the *Mail*: 'Thanks heartiest congratulations wonderful story difficultest conditions Marlowe [the editor]. Stop monopolists longer but unmore continuing yours which being commented everywhere Crawford.'[34]

He had written of the ancient belief that the dead were awakened after three thousand years, and that the tap of Carter's hammer on the wall of the inner burial chamber must have seemed to the Pharaoh within like the final summons to the Judgement Hall of Osiris. There is a note of melancholy in this piece, which he developed in his next article about Sunday's larger occasion, attended by the European and American V.I.Ps. In an essay published later that year for the collection *Tutankhamen and other Essays*, Weigall describes his feelings in very much the same words as he used in his *Daily Mail* articles:

> As for myself I sat for the greater part of the day upon a stone, like an old owl, brooding upon the strangeness of life, and as on Friday, my heart was heavy and my head full of dreams of other days ... The opening of this tomb still presented itself to my mind as the disturbing of a sleeping man ... It was as though he were somebody who had been left behind by mistake ... someone who was alone in an alien age, and who was being wakened to face thousands of staring eyes not filled with reverence but with curiosity.[35]

But the next day, Tuesday, February 20th, he was jubilant. He had at last entered the burial chamber, the first correspondent to do so since its opening, he says, and he had done it at the invitation of the Egyptian government, not of the excavators: 'At the time of writing the representatives of the *Times* have not yet been admitted.'

The season was coming to an end, and the tomb would soon be locked up until the following autumn. Tempers among the excavators were ragged. Carter had had a bad time of it and had sometimes wished the monopoly agreement had never been made. It was a pity that the advice that might have taken some steam out of the situation had come from the one man he was least disposed to listen to. As for Weigall, he had had the satisfaction of knowing that archaeological opportunists – as he would have called them – would probably think twice in future. But it had been at some personal cost. As he wrote to his son Alured from the boat, his time in Luxor had been 'a great strain and I'd like to have a holiday now'.

# Chapter 20

# American lecture tour; Carter again; and divorce
# 1923–1926

Perhaps it was on the boat home, in early March 1923, that Weigall wrote 'Tutankhamen & Co. Ltd.', the piece mentioned in the previous chapter. What it says about the situation as a whole is familiar; his only departure is in allowing himself a personal sketch of Carnarvon and Carter – a relief to the feelings, perhaps. Lord Carnarvon, he says, is:

> an odd mixture of Bohemian and plutocrat: a man who has seen a great deal of the underworld and is reputed to have pitted his brains against and outwitted the toughest bookies and 'crooks' on the turf. He is an adventurous soul, who goes his own gay way and seems to care not a jot for public opinion. His manners are notoriously bad; he is often thought to be insolent; and yet, in spite of many disadvantages, he manages generally to attain his objects, and he is regarded with affection by his friends.

Weigall had more sympathy for Carter:

> a man of good heart soured by ill-health ... he can be most charming, and yet is more generally thought to be intolerably rude [there follows a brief mention of the Saqqara incident and another, when he 'hit a native policeman and again caused a serious diplomatic incident by refusing to admit that he was in the wrong'] ... He is what is called "pig-headed", and yet, in spite of his blind obstinacy, he has a very charming side to his character.

Carnarvon died soon after Weigall wrote this, from an infected mosquito bite as we have seen, and no doubt that was why he never published the piece. It was not the moment. But it sounds as though he had been on the receiving end of much plain rudeness from both of them, so that he probably sailed away from his much-loved Egypt with a sense of good riddance.

When he reached England the atmosphere couldn't have been more different. He was pleased to find, as he told Hortense, that 'apparently the public has liked my articles, and the description of the actual opening caused quite a stir'. The *Daily Mail*

Lord Carnarvon

fêted him: 'Last night I was entertained to dinner by the Directors and Marlowe and a "distinguished gathering" and my health was drunk and I had to tell them the whole story of our fight, and altogether I seem to be the hero of the hour. I had no idea I had been so successful.' As Hortense had foreseen there was also a spin-off: 'Of course it has helped the sale of my books wonderfully – *Akhnaton* has sold over 3000 copies in the last few weeks, and the new book *The Glory of the Pharaohs* has sold out the first edition of 1500 copies and is well into the second edition, and it won't even be published till next Thursday!'

*The Glory of the Pharaohs* is a collection of essays, many of which had already appeared in the *Treasury of Ancient Egypt* and in periodicals, but with a few additions. After years of theatre work and novel-writing and cinema, it brought him again before his old public: those who had admired his *Travels in the Upper Egyptian Deserts* nearly 15 years before and whom he had since tried to educate on the subject of archaeological ethics. Here he strikes a balance: travel pieces, tales and legends retold from recently translated papyri, and comic tales of life in modern Egypt. The expeditions with his old friend from the police service, Norman MacNaghten, serve him well here. There is a piece on the alabaster quarries in the Wady Assiout, full of reveries about the Egyptian sunset, and another on the Wady Salamuni, where 'high upon a ledge of rock, a hundred feet from the valley, a small ruined building of unburnt bricks clung perilously to the cliff, and marked the site where a forgotten Coptic hermit had dwelt in the early centuries of the Christian era.'[1]

Once again, he describes the flowers, the birds, the rocks and the inscriptions of the desert, and that old sense of 'an atmosphere of expectancy ... a feeling that something lies waiting round the corner, a sense of elusiveness inviting a search.'[2] In among pieces of this kind Weigall includes a few critical essays discussing questions of the day – the dangers of Marinetti's futurist manifesto, the importance of history, the reasons for preserving the art and the monuments of the past, and so on. One in particular, mentioned earlier in these pages, is on the subject of his persistent concern, 'The Morality of Excavation'. Born out of his unpublished *Report on the Tombs of the Nobles*, it had originally appeared in 1912 in *The Nineteenth Century*, but now with the discovery of the tomb of Tutankhamun, certain points stood out again.

Discussing the phenomenon of European and American millionaires obtaining concessions to excavate in Egypt, Weigall makes the distinction between the romantic desire to find 'a king lying in state with his jewelled crown on his head', and the 'scientific' desire to extract historical information. To anyone reading that in 1923, the finger might seem to hover fairly close to Carnarvon. But perish the thought – Weigall adds a sentence to the original: 'What would have happened to the fragile objects found recently by Lord Carnarvon and Mr Carter in the tomb of Tutankhamun if those two gentlemen had not been trained archaeologists working for science and not for loot?'

One of his next points proved to be pertinent again, namely the danger of discovering more than the fieldworkers, scholars and museums could handle. There is so much already excavated, he says, that lies neglected:

Why excavate more remains until these are studied, unless the desired sites are in danger ...? Why fill up our museums with antiquities before public opinion has been sufficiently educated to authorize the employment of larger numbers of curators? ... It is to be remembered that in some cases the longer an excavation is postponed the better chance there will be of recording the discoveries adequately ...[3]

This book was in preparation before the discovery of Tutankhamun's tomb, and he did not take every last minute opportunity to highlight its relevance to the present situation. But at the end of the year, when his next collection, *Tutankhamen and other Essays* came out, he enlarged on the same issue of archaeological timeliness:

> The tomb ... was so safely buried beneath tons of rock that it was in no danger, and its treasures might well have been left to the better handling of a future generation ... Lord Carnarvon's excavations have suddenly sprung this mass of glorious relics of the past upon an unprepared present, and the grave question of how to hand them on intact to the future is one which, perhaps, has not been properly considered.[4]

The tomb of Tutankhamun was proving to be a test-bed for many of his ideas and principles, and as problems continued to arise from it during the next season – with Carter, the Egyptian authorities and the Antiquities Department at loggerheads – Weigall found himself in the thankless position of being able to say, 'I told you so.'

Yet, even though the discovery raised anxious questions, Weigall did not deny that it gave 'a great "lift" to Egyptology'.[5] The subject was now truly popular in the way he had always wanted it to be. His books and articles had been a long preparation for just this moment, and he threw himself back into his old role with relish. The book on Egyptian art that he had first talked about long ago, even before he left Egypt, was finally finished that spring: 'I have literally *slaved* this month,' he wrote to Hortense, 'and have finished my book on Egyptian art, with about 600 photographs and text. It is to be published both here and in the States in the early autumn' – in fact it didn't come out until the following year.

As with everything he did, this book was an attempt to wrest the subject from the specialists and give it to the general educated public. In his Introduction he made the point that the 'vast congestion of material' in the museums tended to be displayed with an eye to their archaeological rather than their artistic value, with the result that the public was 'baffled and depressed' by it. Masses of conventionally sculpted mortuary offerings and the like, which were never meant to have any 'more connection with art than a Victorian Christmas card', had given people the impression that Egyptian antiquities were mere curiosities. His book, he hopes, will show them some of that small fraction of ancient Egyptian sculpture and painting that deserves to be put alongside the work of the ancient Greek artists.

From statues to toilet utensils, here are photographs of anything which has the mark of an individual, expressive, and original hand. It is a personal choice, with personal captions: 'There is nothing except the style of workmanship by which to date [this limestone fragment],' he says in one place, 'but the general treatment of the king's face, especially the ears and eyelids, indicate pretty clearly that it belongs to the reign of Tutankhamen'; 'There is some very fine modelling under the chin and along the throat,' he says on another page, 'which can be felt with the hand but which is not easily seen by the eye.'[6] In black and white of course, and generally rather austere-looking by modern standards, it is still an impressive – and affectionate – tribute to the ancient Egyptian civilization. In a gesture of hope, he dedicated, 'in friendship and esteem', these 'works of art' to 'those who ought most to revere them, namely, their descendants, THE MODERN EGYPTIANS.'

*Tutankhamen and other Essays* was also put together that summer, some of the pieces recycled from earlier collections, but a good half of the book new. A revised edition of *Cleopatra* was brought out to stand alongside his revised *Akhnaton*. And now, there was the possibility of lecturing. The American circuit had always been fruitful ground for English speakers. Hortense in Chicago had recently attended a lecture given by Sir Frederick Kenyon of the British Museum and another by Ronald Storrs. Weigall wrote asking her to sound out some agencies there, and within a few weeks she came up trumps. In late March he received an invitation from James B. Pond of the Pond Bureau. Mrs Weigall had approached him, he writes, and 'I have made several investigations since then of the way in which you and your books have been received and I feel you could come to America and … be very well received.' He then adds:

> I am not going to overlook the fact that the one man who will have the biggest success right now is Howard Carter himself if he comes. If he comes, all other men must take second place and as no one knows whether Carter will come or not, this whole Egyptian field is a very dangerous thing to meddle with.[7]

Carter was being wooed by lecture agencies, but he couldn't in fact go to America until the end of the following season. The field was open, and Weigall was booked to give a minimum of 40 lectures at a minimum of $75 each (in the event, he gave 53 lectures), starting at the beginning of October 1923. Pond began advertising, and lining up newspaper interviews. As part of this pre-publicity, he wanted to exploit the story of the fight between the press and the monopolists. Weigall objected, and Pond replied:

> I now agree thoroughly with your reasoning with regard to making public the fight which was necessary for you to get the Tutankhamun story … We will therefore let this matter be forgotten and when you arrive you can give interviews about the work and about yourself and keep the secret history deeply buried.[8]

One can only speculate as to Weigall's reasoning, but it has been evident so far that his anti-monopolist argument involved a point of principle. An interview would have exposed the disagreement to whatever slant the interviewer cared to give it, and the chances were that it would emerge debased and personalized.

So he embarked for America with a clean slate, determined to forget the unpleasantness of the past season. It was his first visit, an adventure, and he soon found himself taken aback by how foreign the place was. To Hortense he was reticent and polite. It was, after all her country. But to his sister Geanie he confided that, although in a general way things 'don't seem so very different', nevertheless 'the *details* of life are *all* different.' What struck him immediately was the classlessness, or rather the middle-classness of America. It brought out the snob in him, to his own sheepish surprise. From Atlantic City he wrote:

At dinner last night at this magnificent hotel, I walked into the vast dining room early, ... hundreds and hundreds of empty tables and at each table sat a woman dressed in a white blouse and white skirt ... for a moment I was filled with horror in case these were sort of 'hostesses' and I would be introduced and expected to talk to the girl at the table I was led to. But she at once got up and handed me the menu, and proved to be a waitress ... I haven't any idea what it means, but I suppose it is that these women don't like to behave as waitresses, and pretend to be sitting at their ease. Most of them, I noticed, laughed and talked with the guests as they waited on them.

I haven't yet seen *anywhere* any *trace* of what might be called our walk in life and its ways. I've seen no really smart society women, but millions of neat typists or women of that class. I've seen no luxurious cars with people in evening dress, but millions of handy cars with people in business-like clothes.

This is all fine, of course and splendidly democratic; but to people accustomed to our sort of life (which is a life as detached as possible from the masses) it is all very awful, and at the same time one is almost ashamed of saying so.

Gradually, he began to feel more accustomed; the people who took care of him, put him up and drove him to his lectures were kind and enthusiastic. His letters to Hortense loosen up: 'I'm delighted with America, but *hate* your food, and all this mass of cream makes me sick. What with rich food, no ventilation, extreme heat, and no proper exercise, no wonder Americans are fat and yellow! But I like them, and they like me; and now that I know my way about I'm really enjoying it.'

He had hit his stride in his lectures too. The sinking stomach and dry mouth that afflicted him at first soon passed. As he told Geanie:

Last night I had a great lecture at Brooklyn, and talked to 1500 people. I have *no* nerves at all now, ... except that I am frightfully conscious when I am being dull ... and frenziedly rush the dull parts. I wish I could cut it down to less than an hour and a half ... I make them laugh several times, and it is great fun hearing that ripple each time. In fact it is great fun talking ...

By the second week of November, an audience of 1500 people was no longer exceptional. 2000 women undergraduates turned out to listen to him at Smith College, Massachussetts, and at Lowell, near Boston, he lectured to an audience of 4800. Another gathering in Boston where he talked soon after, 'applauded so much,' he told Hortense, 'that I had to go on and make a bow again afterwards.'

James Pond had nervously advised him beforehand 'always to keep [your lecture] as popular as possible for you will be speaking as a rule to general audiences which will want the popular side of this period rather than the scientific side.'[9] Pond needn't have worried. Weigall was accustomed to thinking of his public like that, and the manner of his delivery was in keeping. He had prepared a set of slides, his own photographs and drawings, round which he composed a lecture which took his audience by easy stages across the river from Luxor, past the Colossi of Memnon, past Der-el -Bahri and into the necropolis itself, casually slipping in bits of history by the way: the Colossi, he says, were 'set up by Amenophis III ... I want you to remember his name and date – he died in 1375 BC – because the excavations I am going to tell you about are all concerned with members of his family.'[10] To reach the Valley of the Kings you can go this way or that, he says, there I am (change slide) ' right at the summit looking down into the valley behind ... or [change slide] you can get there by the long road ... Here you see myself and some friends ... on donkeys.'

Once in the valley, he passes from tomb to tomb, telling the history directly now, taking the kings in order, why they were buried so richly, explaining their secret reburial away from the plunderers, and all the time keeping the slides moving every two or three sentences. The excavations he had charge of come in naturally – Yuya and Tuya, Queen Tiy and Akhnaten, Horemheb – and he describes the drama of their discovery just as he does, though more briefly, in his essays. He fits Tutankhamun in between Akhnaten and Horemheb, as part of the history, but not really as the centre or the climax of the lecture.

His style is relaxed, even chatty, though the lectures were written out, with numbered diagrams for the slides, every colloquialism included, and every 15 minutes ticked off. Presumably he came to know them well enough to manage without his text, but he wasn't taking any chances. It was a polished performance with all the appearance of improvisation. Occasionally he heightens the tone – for example, in the tomb of Horemheb 'our footsteps seemed to awake such thunders in these subterranean halls – it was an uncanny place, with the moving dark shadows cast by our lamps, and the hot breathless air ... and that extraordinary feeling of – how shall I put it? – of having stepped through a sort of hole in the curtain of Time.' The dramatic mixture of direct address ('how shall I put it?') with raised speech ( 'a hole in the curtain of Time') is nicely calculated.

And he always had an eye for intimate detail: 'In another box [slide change] there were some pairs of gloves – very modern looking gloves – one pair lined with fleece. You know the early mornings in Egypt in winter are very cold; and I expect when Tutankhamun went for his early morning spin in his chariot he needed warm gloves. One most curious find was a finger stall with two tape strings to tie it on with. It looks as though the king must have had a sore finger at the time of his death.' He would throw in a touch of sentiment: 'There were also a baby's cap and a child's glove, which may have belonged to the king when he was young. So pathetic they were.' As for comedy, perhaps the ripples of laughter were for when Maspero, 'a very fat man', got stuck in the opening they made just below the ceiling in the door to Yuya and Tuya's tomb. Or for Theodore Davis, who tapped Weigall on the arm just as he was about to climb the ladder from the well below Horemheb's tomb, saying '"Oh, please let me go in first: I have paid $1,000 for this sensation, and I do want to have it!"'

281

By the middle of December, Weigall had given thirty-eight lectures from Massachusetts to Washington DC, and in the midwest from Ohio and Michigan to Tennessee. It had been an extraordinary experience. In Tennessee, he tells Mimi, the hall had been so full that they had had to get him in by the cellars and up the baggage lift:

I was told afterwards that nearly three thousand people were squeezed into the hall and the next night was just the same only worse, and over a thousand were turned away, so they say. All the aisles in the hall were filled with people sitting on the floor, and at the back of the hall and all round the walls they were six or seven deep, standing … Of course, they don't know *me*, or come to hear *me*; but it's "old King Tut" that interests them.

America itself amazed him: the astounding wealth, the scale of its public institutions, the real implications of democracy, not just its clothes and cars and restaurants. All this made a deep impression. After giving three lectures at Urbana University he wrote to his mother:

What a country it is! Here is this great University, with 6000 men students and 3000 women students with every kind of subject taught – not only Greek and Latin, but every science – great greenhouses and nurseries for horticultural studies, vast farms with sheep and cattle for scientific farming, museums for geology and mineralogy, great hospitals for medical sciences, a huge musical academy, an art school, and so on, and all absolutely *free*. The students pay nothing at all: all the money comes from the state, and each state has its university …

They also have military training as part of all state universities, and I went to a parade, where I saw a march past, and O lor! – one felt that here was a vast democracy which soon will dictate to the world. All this education, all these facilities for learning every kind of science, all this *eagerness* to learn, all this wealth devoted to these democratic institutions, and all this military training and efficiency! – I feel we are being so outclassed.

He had been entertained at Urbana each evening by different departments – 'first it would be the classical professors, then the Orientalists, then the Political Economists and so on':

It is apparently their custom to advertise themselves always by systematically entertaining their foreign guests, and also their regular custom to settle down to make the guest talk and to squeeze him dry of information. It is as though they felt themselves rather detached from the world and pounced on every man from outside and picked his brains. All this entertaining of me, I mean, was *systematic*, and they admitted as much and said it was to broaden *their* outlook.

'I am so dog tired,' he wrote to Hortense, 'that all I want to do is to sleep.' When he wrote that, he thought he had only two more lectures to go, but Pond persuaded him to continue through Christmas and on up to January 25. Christmas was spent in New York where, as it happened, Charlot had just brought his new show to be opened in the new year, *André Charlot's Revue of 1924*, starring Bea Lillie and Gertrude Lawrence. On Christmas day, he told Hortense, he went over to the hotel where they were staying, 'and sat and talked to Beatrice Lillie and Gertie Lawrence ... They were both in bed in one room, but received me nevertheless! They were very depressed and nearly crying because they thought they wouldn't be a success here.'

But all turned out well. They were a smash hit, and their six weeks' booking was extended to nine months.[11] In his own way, Weigall had also been a hit. Pond wrote: 'My first prediction that you would make good and be liked has been more than borne out. Wherever you have gone people have been delighted with your lectures and have thanked me for sending you to them. You have made a genuine success. ... I am enclosing a copy of a quite marvellous letter which came to me from Cedar Rapids. There are very few lecturers who receive letters of this kind.'[12]

One shadow crossed his path. In December Howard Carter, enraged at the idea of Weigall lecturing on 'his' subject, issued a statement to the American press with the intention of discrediting him.[13] Carter had suffered much in the intervening months. The death of Carnarvon in April of that year had been a shockingly sudden end to a close partnership. The two men had often fallen out, but there had been a real friendship between them, and Carter was not a man to make friends easily. The fact that Weigall had attacked Carnarvon so soon before he died would have elevated Carter's hostility to him to an act of loyalty. Of course Carnarvon's death, though sad, was neither here nor there in relation to lecturing or publishing. The story of the tomb and its contents was no more his property after his death than it had been before. But however irrational, it was inevitable that the whole Tutankhamun project should become sacred, as it were, to Carnarvon's memory. When James Breasted heard that Weigall was to lecture in America, he was indignant and, in T.G.H. James's words, felt that it was 'a gratuitous insult to Carnarvon's memory'.[14]

James Pond wrote to Weigall to let him know that the *New York Tribune* had 'considered [Carter's statement] so injurious' that they would delete 'the maligning paragraph'. They wanted, however, 'to get in touch with you and have you attack Carter in return, but I told them of your attitude in the whole matter and they decided you were the bigger man of the two and thought it was better not to start an unpleasant controversy.'[15] But Weigall did write privately to Carter – his second big letter that year arising out of the Tutankhamun troubles.

In Weigall's earlier letter to him, written in Luxor, the suggestion had been that Carter's hostility was not real, but simply a necessary condition of *The Times* monopoly agreement. The letter he now wrote was plainer:

Last winter I was deeply opposed to the sale of your news rights to *The Times*, and to the general attitude of 'ownership' of the tomb which you adopted. It was quite a side issue that I happened to have agreed to write some articles for the *Daily Mail*, and found myself prevented by you from doing so with proper accuracy. It was also quite beside the point that you treated me without the courtesy due to a previous

Inspector who had been officially in charge of earlier work in the valley, and to whom you were under some old obligations.

The real point was that I opposed your publicity methods, and fought the *Times* contract as being in my opinion detrimental to the interests of Egyptology. That was a perfectly straight fight, which you yourself opened on my first day by telling me that you would have to be my bitterest enemy.

He then mentions the methods used by the monopolists to discredit him – methods 'which were by no means nice'. 'For example I heard that you had raked up an old story about me and a smuggled statuette ... And there were a great many other things of which I like to think that you were, after all, innocent. As far as I was concerned this was a fight on a question of principle, and at no time did the personal element come into it at all.'

He supports this claim by pointing to his latest publication, *Tutankhamen and other Essays*, in which 'I give you full credit for your fine work at the tomb', and also to his lectures in which he does the same. A glance at his lectures supports this. They positively showered compliments: James Breasted was 'in my opinion ... the greatest living Egyptologist'; Arthur Mace 'has probably done more than any other man for the preservation and cataloguing of the objects found in the tomb'; the aid of the Metropolitan Museum of New York was invaluable, and so on. To Carter he also explains that his lecture is not really a Tutankhamun lecture as such: that much of it is about the history of the valley as a whole, about his own work there, and about Tutankhamun as a historical figure. It is, therefore, only in part about the tomb itself and its contents. He assures Carter that the lecture is clear about his unofficial status in Egypt the previous season, and that he does not say 'one word in regard to any of our troubles ... because I think no useful purpose can be served by attacking your *principles* in public lectures.'

> Well, that then is the whole position ... In the face of the utmost provocation I have treated you with the greatest consideration and courtesy, and I expect the same from you. To me you seem like somebody who has been egged on by people's gossip and low-mindedness to think of me as a sort of enemy or rival or something. Please get that idea out of your head, and remember that no matter what you are prompted to say against me I shall continue to praise the things in you which I think ought to be praised, and to be silent about those things which I think are unworthy of you.[16]

On that virtuous note – Carter's reaction to it is not recorded – Weigall refers him to the chapter called 'The Future of Excavation' in his new book, *Tutankhamen & other Essays*.

This chapter contains, among other things, the substance of 'Tutankhamun & Co. Ltd.', – that is, the anti-monopoly argument – but with everything personal excised. Carnarvon's character is recorded simply as 'curious, interesting and charming', and nothing is said of Carter beyond the fact that he and his team did 'the best that this generation can do' to conserve the objects found in the tomb.[17] The argument, set out point by point, covers much the same ground as Weigall's Luxor letter to Carter, at the heart of which, apart from his objection to commercialization, lies his objection to secrecy.

This was ground long staked out as his personal territory, but the whole thing, he felt, needed saying all over again – not only because of Carnarvon, but because the habit of secrecy and possessiveness was still ingrained among scholars in general. Take the head of Nefertiti, for example. The Germans had 'for some unaccountable reason' been 'allowed to take it to Berlin' in 1913, and had since 'kept the matter as dark as night.' But photographs of it were beginning to circulate:

Less than a year ago an English Egyptologist showed me these pictures in profound secrecy, telling me that on no account must they be made public, lest a breach of etiquette be committed. Breach of fiddlesticks! All information regarding 'finds' made in excavations in Egypt should, if only for the sake of politeness, be at the disposal of the Egyptian nation as quickly as possible, and thence should be passed on to the world at large.[18]

And he did pass it on, for he had already included in his book on ancient Egyptian art a double page spread of the Nefertiti head photographed from three different angles.[19] The rest of the essay is an extended plea to archaeologists on the subject of politeness – a more sober version of the one he had made to Carter.

Egypt, he says, is no longer what it was, and foreign excavators must try to imagine what their labours look like from the other side; imagine what we would feel if Egyptians wanted to dig up Westminster Abbey. It is not just a matter of manners; there is a real danger that 'unless foreign excavators adjust themselves speedily to the new conditions in that country, they will cease to be given digging-concessions.' Carnarvon's proprietorial attitude may unwittingly have brought closer Lacau's proposed law forbidding the export of all antiquities from Egypt, but if it has, foreign excavators really 'have no cause for complaint'. 'They have freely filled their museums during the past years with antiquities obtained from Egypt, and their attitude now must not be one of outraged dignity but of gratitude for past favours and hope for continued indulgence.'[20]

He himself offers no opinion on Lacau's proposal. He sets out the pros and cons as expressed by both sides: the Egyptians say they are the rightful custodians of their antiquities; the archaeologists say that the antiquities belong to mankind not just to the Egyptians. The Egyptians say that the Cairo Museum can easily be made safe; the archaeologists say there is no guarantee of this. The Egyptians say that it is easier for Egyptologists to study the antiquities when they are massed together in one place; the archaeologists say that 'Egypt is very far away from the world's chief seats of learning, and that widely-spread collections mean widely-spread interest.' And so on, this way and that.[21]

The point he is making is that the rights and wrongs of the argument are, for the moment, irrelevant. The framework in which such matters are decided has changed:

foreign excavators now 'must not arrogantly demand their rights. They have none.' The whole language and spirit in which they approach the Egyptians must change too: they must 'endeavour to be more simple, more obliging, more gracious ... In vulgar language, they must get off their high horse.'[22] If Carter read any of this, it made no difference. He was by now so wedded to the notion of intellectual ownership that even information in the official Cairo Museum *Guide* about Tutankhamun objects on display seemed to him an infringement of his rights, and he threatened the Antiquities Service with legal action.[23]

In fact, what lay behind Carter's irritation was more than intellectual ownership. The whole question of the division of the contents of the tomb, which had been left purposely vague, was now beginning to surface, and Carter felt that the cataloguing of the objects as though they were the property of the Museum pre-empted the issue. After Carnarvon's death, the concession to clear the tomb had been extended to his widow, and Carter was determined to secure the full half share that he believed was her (though 'her' somehow blurred into 'his') right. But according to Carnarvon's contract, this 'right' apparently depended on the definition of the tomb's condition when found: if it could be called intact, then everything belonged to the Egyptian Government; if not, then half of the contents, after the mummies and the capital pieces, belonged to the concessionaire.

The long and complicated story of Carter's wrangles with the Egyptian authorities, together with the interventions of his sometimes exasperated supporters, is told by T.G.H. James.[24] As one follows their arguments, all bristling with indignation at Lacau's infamous new law, at the way Carter's 'rights' were being infringed, at his intolerable treatment at the hands of a petty and bureaucratic Egyptian government, one begins to see Weigall's point. Certainly, the authorities were harassing Carter. But then Carter was insisting on his rights. The whole quarrel was being conducted according to the old formula. Neither side behaved well; but the reality was – and no amount of foreign blustering could get round it – the Egyptians didn't have to.

On 13 February 1924 matters came to a head. The last straw had been the refusal by the Egyptian authorities to allow the wives of Carter's colleagues to view the tomb. Carter locked it up, posted a notice in the Winter Palace Hotel and, in effect, went on strike. A week later, on February 20th, the Minister for Public Works, Morcos Hanna, cancelled Lady Carnarvon's concession, and instructed Lacau to take charge of the tomb. For the moment, it looked as though Carter's future involvement with it was in the balance. Weigall had been anxiously following events.

Now in February 1924 and back in England, he found that everything he had said to Carter in both his letters, and everything he had published in his essay on the 'Future of Excavation in Egypt' was being borne out with embarrassing accuracy. On the 23rd of that month, Weigall published a letter in the *Daily Mail*, who printed it not with the letters but on a news page, repeating his warning against high-handedness. On the question of the division, he said that to insist on describing the tomb as 'ransacked' in order to qualify for the half-share was regarded by Egyptians as a 'quibble'. It would hasten the ban on exports, and the fault would lie with those

Egyptologists 'who have lacked the vision to see that a friendly, tactful and even self-denying attitude to the Egyptian nation is the first essential of their work.' He expressed sympathy for Carter, even though he had 'bungled the diplomatic side of the affair', and hoped he would be able to resume his work in the tomb next season.

Weigall speaks in this 'letter' of having lost many friends by his warnings, and one wonders how his friendship with Gardiner was faring. That glimpse of Gardiner, alone among the excavating team being prepared to speak to him during the previous season, suggests that perhaps it had survived the monopoly row. But now that their views were so divergent on the question of foreign rights over Egyptian antiquities – Gardiner being concerned above all to preserve the system of museum funding for excavations – the two men may well have cooled. If the tomb had a curse, it was in these broken friendships. Perhaps there was some small consolation in expressions of support, such as a letter from the Maharanee of Sarawak congratulating him on his piece in the *Daily Mail*:

I knew Lord C. rather well. Well, I don't say more. That lot have all been rude, undiplomatic and grasping. So glad at length the worm has turned! Of course Tutankhamun's remains being located is a fine important thing. But no greater and more important that yours and scores of others, although unlike Carnarvon you did not fill the Press with your exploits.

The letter ends with a final harrumph – 'So that's that.'[25] But that wasn't that for Weigall. Carter continued to pursue him.

This time, the problem was to do with the part Weigall played in the preparations for the British Empire Exhibition at Wembley, the great event of the year, to be opened by George V and Queen Mary on April 23rd. A replica of the tomb of Tutankhamun and its contents had been constructed as one of the exhibits, and Weigall had been the advisor to Messrs Aumonier and Son, who had made the objects in facsimile. The designs had been arrived at on the basis of photographs and drawings, and Carter, believing that these pictures were the property of the Carnarvon expedition, issued a writ against the Exhibition organizers on the grounds of breach of copyright. In fact, Weigall had already raised the matter of the replica with Carter in his letter the previous December in response to Carter's American press statement. He had explained then that he had been approached by the Wembley authorities, but that 'if you will enquire you will find that I advised them to apply to you, but they replied that you were not available; and so I agreed to act as advisor to them in this work.' It sounds as though Weigall, knowing Carter as he did, had taken pains to cover himself.

When the time came, therefore, he was well prepared, and he was able to show that the drawings and photographs were his own or those of friends and colleagues. There survives a series of notes[26] made no doubt in preparation for his defence, which indicate that 'everything brought out from the tomb was photographed from every angle by dozens of photographers. I will produce specimens of all these. Couches: my own snapshots and drawings. Beds, dummy, food boxes, chests, chairs, vases, chariots ditto.' A note next to 'chariots' elaborates: 'scenes of captives published by *Times* left out.' In other words, wherever his own photograph didn't include a detail which a *Times* photograph did include, that detail was still omitted. He also says that where his drawings were wrong, 'I was here scrupulously careful, and never changed it though I knew it was wrong.' For example, the lid of the tabernacle 'part in darkness at end is wrong.' Weigall had thought of everything, and when he and Aumonier declared in the *Daily Express* on April 22, a day before the Exhibition was to open, that they had not used the *Times*'s photographs, the writ was withdrawn. After that Carter, now in America on his own lecture tour, left him alone.

Weigall was now free to return to what he loved doing most: writing about ancient Egypt. Just before the discovery of the tomb of Tutankhamun, in early November 1922, he had written to his son Alured that he 'would rather write history than do anything else; but there is no money in it, so I have to do other things.' Tutankhamun had changed all that. Egypt had entered the bloodstream: Egyptian motifs in architecture, fashion, jewellery, biscuit tins, lamp-stands and so on were everywhere. There was a new appetite and a new audience. He had himself glimpsed it from the lecture podium. Now he signed himself up with The Lecture Agency, Ltd., and continued to lecture in England, billed as the author of the famous *Daily Mail* articles, as much as the 'former Inspector of Antiquities'. In May 1924 he lectured in Paris, where his revised edition of *Cleopatra* had been published in translation.

He could certainly make money out of popular history, and it looked now as though his reputation was high enough for him to make money out of something a little tougher. It is difficult to see how he had been able to fit it in, but he had already in America begun work on a history of Egypt, no less, and had negotiated a contract there which would give him, he told Hortense, '$2000 advance on delivery of the MS and I hope to get nearly as much from the English publisher too so I shall certainly go hard at it this year.'

He badly needed the money. Financially speaking, the last year had been a near thing. His success in America was important, as usual, for the cash as much as anything else. Shortly after he had got back from Egypt, he had received a demand from the Inland Revenue threatening proceedings unless he paid Hortense's income tax arrears for the year 1921-22. Five weeks later there had come another warning concerning arrears for 1922-23: unless he could pay £413, they would take summary proceedings. Somehow his lectures and novels paid enough for him to clear these arrears, but now, in April 1924, Hortense herself was due back from America. The trouble was that writing history needed not just time and money, but freedom from fury and exasperation. After two years apart, the prospects for resuming a happy life together were not good. Muriel was very much in evidence, and Hortense smelled a rat. As Weigall explained to Alured a year later when he had given up all pretence, even with his children:

She came back, you see, and found us all fairly jolly, and she came down like a ton of bricks and said, "NO, I am his wife. He is now quite well off, and this house is mine."

We went to Brighton for the holidays. I invited Muriel. Your mother objected. I insisted. She was beastly to Muriel, and Muriel said she would never put her foot in No. 23 [Cleveland Square] again. ... I immediately decided to let it. I revolted ... Your mother was again in debt and I had to pay up again and again; and now I said it must stop ...

The letter is a furious self-justificatory tirade, all the louder for the fact that in everyone's eyes, particularly in his children's, he knew he appeared to be in the wrong. What exasperated him more than anything was that technically speaking he was. 'She desires to appear as my wife and if I go away she will assume the attitude of the poor deserted wife. It is utter bunk! I am the poor deserted husband: I always have been.' But the world would never see it like that. Hortense, with five children, the youngest three aged ten, eleven and twelve, had all the cards. Nevertheless, he knew her too well to turn back now. It had in fact been a long time coming and, once faced, the conclusion was inevitable. He told Alured that he felt such 'burning resentment' against Hortense that he now wished she would divorce him.[27] In any case, whether she did divorce him or not, he said, he was never going to live with her again, nor see her unless by accident. He would get his own flat.

And so he did, 24 Haymarket, on the corner of Panton Street, in the heart of the West End where he had lived during his time in the theatre. Cleveland Square was given up, and Hortense moved with the children out of London again, this time to Mitcham, at that time a country village. And so they battled it out in their peculiar one-sided way, his sword against her pillow, for another 18 months, Weigall begging her more and more urgently for a divorce, and Hortense, evasive as ever, not answering his letters. At last, in August 1926, he made a move that stirred her into action:

Two or three times I have written to you to know what your attitude is in regard to the subject of our divorce, but you have not replied ... I feel very strongly that you have to a great extent ruined my life, and I am not going to allow you to ruin the years that are left to me. I have taken legal advice, and I find that if I establish my residence in France I shall be able to secure a divorce from you in the French courts [on grounds other than adultery]. This I intend to do unless you prefer to obtain a divorce from me in England.

Her reply was both pitiful and inadequate:

I have your letter of Aug 12th which I think hardly calls for a reply. I cannot think it so easy as you suggest to get rid of an innocent wife whom you know has done you no wrong but loved you dearly always,

Your Hortense.

Weigall's reaction to it can be found in his novel, *The Not Impossible She*, when Sebastian receives just such a letter from the Hortense-figure, Clotilde. He 'flung the letter from him in a frenzy of terror and exasperation. He felt a hot creeping sensation all over his head ... Did she write in this strain deliberately to suggest the unbroken continuity of their appalling marriage? ... Or was she mentally impervious to the new conditions? ... The thought once again brought back to him that sensation he had felt as a child, when he used to think that his 'tummy' had fainted.'[28]

Hortense also wrote to members of her family asking for advice, sometimes posting the letters, sometimes not. One reply, from a cousin Walter, probably sums up the views of most conventionally correct people:

> A divorce, it seems to me, should be resisted by you to the very end. It is ... long past the point when anything at all can be changed for your own self but you must protect the children. The woman in the case can be given no consideration whatever. Keep that before you. Failure to get what she wants will I believe destroy the relationship sooner or later.

In fact, one of the reasons Weigall was so anxious for a divorce was for the sake of 'the woman in the case'. Having monopolized Muriel for so long, he told Alured, he had spoilt her chances of finding a husband, and he felt that the only honourable thing was to marry her. The fear of scandal was damaging them both, in a way which, as he explained to Hortense, would in turn damage her: 'In the ambiguous position in which I now find myself, I do not care to go about or to see anybody, and my isolation is probably doing a lot of harm to my financial prospects; and I may say in passing that I would probably be able to give you a larger allowance if I were able to go about socially.' In the end, and much against her will, Hortense agreed to a divorce.

It was a bitter end to their marriage, to what had been the most desperate love of his life. There had been a time when her absence could make him physically ill – 'I actually ... break into a cold perspiration,' he had once told her, 'and feel that unless I rush about, I shall go raving mad.' This was not a romantic pose. It was a manifestation of an extraordinarily intense nature, of a sort of ravenous energy which itself, ironically, held the seeds of their final break-up. It is poignant to remember that he had almost predicted it at the very beginning of their courtship. 'O darling,' he had written to her from Saqqara in 1904, 'don't you see that my fault is that I throw myself too deeply into everything I do – that I love you too wildly, that I work too intensely ... You have never seen me so bursting with enthusiasm ... that I have to pace about the room.' Without any definite occupation herself, Hortense never did fully enter into the consuming, the driving and driven enthusiasms of her husband.

If, like Muriel, she had had something of her own, or if, like Geanie, she had been content with a supporting role, all might have been well. But she was neither one thing nor the other, and in the end he simply forged ahead without her. He was forced to keep looking behind him by her financial incompetence; but that very incompetence only drove him on faster. The deeper she involved him, the harder he had to work, until in the end there was no time left for her. In the last months before

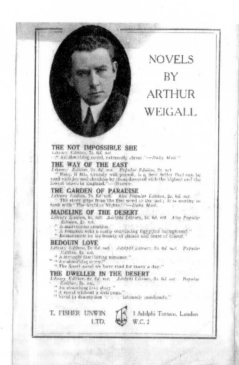

Publicity leaflet for Weigall's novel, *The Not Impossible She*

she agreed to the divorce, Hortense tried to draw him back by describing the charm – very real, as the children remembered it – of the house in Mitcham. But it was too late. 'My life is so occupied,' he replied, 'I am so everlastingly rushed for time, I have so much to think about, that I can find no place for this domestic picture as you see it. … I have to earn money to provide for you and the children as well as for myself, and I can't afford the time or the worry or the heartache to maintain a joint life with you.'

But although he wrung from her her consent to a divorce, relief from heartache eluded him. For once he could not shake off his deep sense of having been wronged, and his novel, *The Not Impossible She,* is in part a case for the defence. Self-justification is not a promising foundation for literature, and yet its bitter and savage conviction puts this novel into quite a different class from the others. It also offered a more plausible and integrated critique of society than some of his other novels. Weigall had, after all, lived much of Sebastian's life, and although the book is not great art, what he had to say about the complacency of the upper classes, the hypocrisy of the church, the emotionally crippling effect of the public school system, were said with feeling and inside knowledge. The book was widely praised in the press, by his friends, and in letters from readers. He himself took some pride in it as a piece of literature. But he had cruelly humiliated Hortense; and while she remained silent, and Mimi and Geanie tight-lipped, he knew his family would not forgive him for it.

# Chapter 21

# Egyptian chronology; English monuments
# 1925–1927

Weigall's mother and sister had long known that the marriage was not happy – that it had been precarious, in fact, even before Weigall left Egypt. Both had stepped in at times of crisis. In a hundred ways they had been a kind of anchor to Hortense, advising, lending money, sending clothes, looking after the children. When she was in America for so long, Mimi had been a second mother to them. However much she had been inclined to drift away, failing to write, to pay back debts, to involve herself with the children, somehow Mimi and Geanie had dragged her back into the family in spite of herself.

Now Weigall was cutting himself loose and in the most public and painful way possible. Mimi in particular felt it acutely. Though becoming more frequent, divorce was to most people unthinkable, a social and moral disgrace. Weigall's children say that their father lost many friends because of it. People were expected to take sides, even within the family. Geanie, who was determined to remain on terms with both Hortense and Muriel, felt she had to explain herself to Muriel. When Muriel and Weigall came to marry two years later in 1928, she assured her that she wished them well, and that she quite understood her brother's situation: 'He has had long years of misery with Hortense and no one who *really* knows could blame him for leaving her.' Hortense, she said, 'knows that I feel this – as I have not pretended to her that I take her side.' But all the same 'I have been sorry for her – as one is sorry for anyone so utterly hopeless – and I cannot break with her because of the children.' She then goes on to explain Mimi's position, and to beg Muriel to be understanding. 'She is old and conventional and she has made a God of Arthur – and in his effort to be loyal to you (quite rightly) he has had to be harsh with her and she feels that he no longer loves her. You can afford to be generous minded about her.'

In *The Not Impossible She*, Sebastian has painful religious discussions with his mother Amelia for whom divorce was not only bad in itself but somehow a symptom of the more general moral madness of the war: 'After all,' he makes her say, ' the nobler thing is sacrifice. It is a finer thing to renounce happiness than to obtain it.'[1] In vain Sebastian argues that it is hypocrisy to continue with an empty marriage and that there is no virtue in being miserable. He tries to persuade Amelia – just as Weigall persuaded himself in real life – that Clotilde doesn't really love him, and that apart from the inconvenience and expense of two households, she is perfectly happy without him. What makes the situation worse is that Sebastian wants to marry Moira. Although the re-marriage of divorcees was allowed in civil law, in the eyes of the church such a relationship was adulterous. Sebastian's stepfather, Jacob, the equivalent of Tony Craggs, takes a tolerant and, in his view, a truly Christian view of the matter. He welcomes them into his house, and declares his intention of marrying them. But there are mutterings among his parishioners, complaints reach the ears of his bishop, and he is summoned to explain himself. Even his servants become impudent.

In reality, things did not come to such a pass. There was no question of Weigall and Muriel being married by the Rev. Craggs. As for Weigall's view that Hortense would not really suffer, her silence makes it difficult to say. There is, however, a revealing letter from her to her cousin Walter about the divorce, written from the house at Mitcham, which suggests that Weigall might not have been far wrong:

It is very disappointing when one thinks of the life that we might so easily have enjoyed, with the children growing up and certainly a very adequate income if it had not been divided in keeping up *two* households! … There is nothing for it but to make the best of things as they are and I think that it is very much Arthur's loss that he has cut himself off from the life of his family. The children have a happy life here, I think, with their garden and their many pets and they are getting on very well at their various schools.

The slightly complacent tone is an uncanny echo of Weigall's Clotilde, and one wonders whether the picture of family happiness at Mitcham, that she paints so smoothly here, was like the one that Weigall had spurned so furiously a couple of years before.

It is at this point in the story that the younger generation begins to make itself heard and felt. Weigall never saw Mitcham, but he would have recognized only too well the description of it that his niece Betty, Geanie's daughter, sent to Alured at about this time. 'The house and garden were perfectly charming but the place was in such a mess and so filthy dirty it really didn't look at its best … They badly need you or someone to keep them going.' Betty was 18 in 1926 when this was written, and she was not alone in thinking that Alured, now 19, should take up the reins his father had dropped.

When Weigall announced his intention of never seeing Hortense again, he turned to Alured as the eldest child, and asked him to take charge of the household accounts. Perhaps he was remembering himself at the same age, qualified as an accountant and earning a salary. But Alured was not at all in his father's mould. Talented in many directions, he had grown into a strangely elusive young man. He had for a long time been the subject of intense interest and speculation among his parents, his grandmother and his aunt. More than with any of the other children, they had analysed and discussed his character, his taste, his piano-playing, his painting. They thought him variously a genius and a fool.

Weigall, who thought him a genius, enrolled him at the Slade School of Art. He was prepared to allow him the time, the travel and the training he needed in order to write, or paint, or act, or make music. But the boy dropped out of the Slade, refused to be helped or influenced, and seemed generally uninclined to devote himself to any of his talents, at least not in a formal or professional sense. To Weigall he was a bitter disappointment, all the more so for being much loved. The divorce brought one more complication into an already fraught situation.

Now, in reply to his father's request that he should keep an eye on things at home, Alured suddenly adopted a slightly solemn self-pitying tone, reproaching his father for abandoning his family and his responsibilities. It seemed somehow unlike him, and Weigall, reading between the lines, thought he could hear the voices of Mimi and Hortense in the background. His own letter in reply covers a lot of ground, rehearsing his grievances against Hortense, but it also sheds light on his feelings for the rest of the family. The sense of them as a weight, of their sympathy as a suffocation, is very strong, and he urges Alured not to be overwhelmed by their solicitude. The only way to survive, he tells him, is to:

fight against taking things too seriously. In life you must ... do your duty without letting yourself get submerged and without getting the feeling of weight on you. Do your job joyfully, and *fight* for your own individuality, especially when you are surrounded by women – I might almost say by too much love ... Keep your head above water ... [I urge you] to keep a light heart, and not to listen to the wails of the women.

It is almost as though Weigall were talking to himself as well. They both needed all the buoyancy they could find. Alured was the more vulnerable of the two at this stage, as we shall see, but Weigall did follow his own advice. He managed a smile, even though his teeth were probably gritted behind it.

One can see it in *The Not Impossible She*, which is a humorous as well as a savage book. Sebastian emerges from his disappointments and crises with a saving sense that tragedy is too grand a word for them. Moira herself is a help. Her fiery temper is one aspect of a generally fearless, deflating, and ironic character, and the two of them set off on their new life alternately shouting at each other and collapsing in fits of laughter. The real life Muriel was, equally, a tonic, at least in the short term, and one can see her influence in the rebellious and argumentative young women who dominate the novels that he wrote during the next few years.

All through his life, at times of emotional crisis, hard work had come to the rescue. At this period he was firing on all cylinders. Apart from *The Not Impossible She*, which occupied most of 1925, there was his much cherished project, his history of Egypt, which he eventually called *The History of the Pharaohs*, a work, as we shall see, of immense labour. In the novel, it becomes Sebastian's *History of the Early Emperors of Rome*, and his hero does indeed use it to keep his mind concentrated 'in very terror of the thoughts that lurked outside that refuge to affright him'.[2] But there is another point. Like Weigall's, though for different reasons, Sebastian's archaeological career has collapsed, and he is described as being 'mortified'. His *History* is intended as a way of re-establishing himself and his reputation. Weigall would never have admitted to being mortified, but Sebastian's hopes were probably his own. As usual, Weigall explained that his *History* was for the general reader, but in fact one could be forgiven for thinking that he was really writing for the scholars.

Each of the two volumes (he never completed the third) opens with, and is regularly punctuated by, long and forbidding chapters on the subject of chronology, then, as now, one of the knottiest and most controversial aspects of the study of ancient history. Instead of tempting his readers with dramatic incident and poetic description, Weigall hands them large hard pills to swallow, consisting of tables of dates, lists of reigns, and astronomical and calendrical explanations and calculations. Once, he would have argued that no historian should reveal the technicalities of his art. Now, it seems, the general reader is only too happy to 'apply his brains to the little puzzles which confront the historian'. Besides, Egyptologists should come clean, he says. Their chronologies are all hypothetical anyway, and the more the subject is aired the better: 'so that there may be as many amateurs at work as there are in other fields of art and science.'[3]

The trouble is that the problems were far from being 'little puzzles'. Weigall had first trailed the subject in his *Tutankhamen and other Essays*, in a piece entitled 'The problem of Egyptian Chronology'. There he had said that he was prompted to take the matter up because readers of the increasing number of books on Egyptian history were being confronted by discrepancies among Egyptologists:

Professor James Henry Breasted, of Chicago, and Professor Flinders Petrie, of London, differ to the extent of over two thousand years in the date they assign to the beginning of the First Dynasty, the former believing it to have occurred about BC 3400, and the latter about BC 5550.[4]

The piece had not attempted to offer solutions so much as to indicate the nature of the evidence and to demonstrate how inconclusive the arguments were on both sides. But during the following two years, despite the lecturing, journalism and novel-writing that were going on at the same time, the subject had become an obsession with him.

In the early part of this century Egyptologists had a much narrower base of evidence than they do now upon which to construct a chronology, and consequently they were obliged to set much greater store by what are now known to be suspect sources: in particular, a lost history of Egypt written by a certain High Priest called Manetho, living in the third century BC. Manetho compiled lists of Egyptian kings, sometimes giving the lengths of their reigns, and arranged them in dynasties whose lengths he also sometimes recorded. Unfortunately Manetho is only known in the quotations of later historians: Julius Africanus of the third century AD, and Eusebius,

Bishop of Caesaria about a century later. However, Africanus and Eusebius do not always agree with each other, and in any case, their information is often at variance with information derived from contemporary monuments.

Another list of kings, with reign and dynasty lengths, is provided by a document known as the Turin papyrus – or the Turin Canon, as it is sometimes called. This, however, though fuller and more reliable than Manetho, was badly damaged in the nineteenth century, and its gaps and obliterations have necessarily given rise to speculative reconstructions. Other king lists are recorded on the walls of temples and tombs at Abydos, Sakkara, Thebes and elsewhere, but these lists are incomplete, sometimes passing over kings and complete dynasties that appear in Manetho and the Turin papyrus. In addition to these there are two stone fragments – the Palermo Stone and the Cairo Stone, so named after the museums in which they now lie. These stones are inscribed on both sides not simply with lists of kings, but with the separate years of their reigns, set out in horizontal rows (or registers as Egyptologists call them) of numbered compartments, each compartment recording some event or events that occurred in that year, with the highest point of the Nile marked in a separate section beneath it.

However, lists and annals are not of themselves any use to chronology unless they can be related to some fixed starting point, which in turn can be related to our own system BC and AD. Egyptologists in Weigall's day were not agreed as to the fixed point from which to start counting, the differences between them arising ultimately from the fact that the ancient Egyptian calendar was itself defective. The Egyptians divided their year into twelve months of 30 days each, plus five 'intercalary days', to arrive at 365 days. They did not until very late in their history take into account the fact that the astronomical year is approximately a quarter of a day longer than 365 days. In other words they did not hit on the idea of a leap year every four years. With each passing year, therefore, their New Year's day fell behind, so that in four years it was a day behind, in twenty eight years a week behind, and so on. This was not immediately noticeable, but after a few thousand years the months denoting spring, summer and winter drifted completely out of alignment with the actual seasons. In his *Egypt of the Pharaohs*, Alan Gardiner quotes an ancient source complaining that 'winter is come in summer, the months are reversed, the hours in confusion.'[5]

At some point, the ancient Egyptians realized that they needed to find a fixed astronomical event as a New Year, and for this they chose the rising of the dog star Sirius – or Sothis as they called it – at dawn, at the moment it first becomes visible after a period of invisibility. This is known as the heliacal rising. However the problem of alignment with the calendar persisted, for of course the heliacal rising of Sothis occurs once every 365 days plus a quarter, thus falling a day later than the calendrical New Year once every four years, a week later every twenty-eight years and so on. The New Years of the two yearly cycles would coincide only once in every 4 X 365, or 1,460 years. Such an astronomical event, therefore, helps us only if there is an observation of it that links it both to the Egyptian calendar, and to our system BC and AD. Luckily, the second-century Censorinus recorded that such an observation had been made in 139 AD when the heliacal rising of Sothis coincided with the calendrical New Year's Day – that is, with the first day of the first month of the season of the Inundation. It thus became immediately possible for Egyptologists to calculate the occurrence of the same coincidence in cycles of 1460 years – (though Egyptologists explain that the cycle sometimes varies, and certainly the figures they produce are not multiples of 1460).

Early twentieth-century Egyptologists assumed that the establishment of the first calendar was associated with the beginning of one of these Sothic cycles, as they are called. The only question was which one. German scholars were particularly active in the chronological field, and one of them, Eduard Meyer, chose 4241 BC. William Flinders Petrie, on the other hand, threw the whole thing back another cycle. However, for reasons which will appear, both these chronologies seemed to other Egyptologists to be too 'long'. Nowadays, with much more evidence at their disposal, modern Egyptologists favour a date for the start of the first Dynasty of about 3000 BC.

As it happened, Weigall also advocated a more recent date, namely 3400 BC. Modern scholars would not now agree with all the stages in his reasoning, but he was the first to take one crucial step towards arriving at this shorter chronology. This was to sever the link assumed to exist between the Sothic and the calendrical New Year – in other words to free the search for the origin of the calendar from the specifically Sothic cycle as calculated backwards from 139 AD. He granted that at some point before Censorinus the two became associated, but he did not believe that that association marked or explained the establishment of the calendar in the first place.

Weigall proposed that this calendar was originally a farmer's calendar based upon the observed intervals between the yearly highs and lows of the Nile. Gradually, of course, the misalignment with the seasons began to be noticed, and the ancient astronomers observed that the rising of Sirius was reliable and stayed in step with the seasons. However, he points out that though risings of Sothis are mentioned in ancient times no particular connection is made between them and the calendrical New Year. In other words, although we can calculate the coincidences between the Sothic New Year and the calendrical New Year, there is nothing to show us when the ancient Egyptians started to do so:

All that can be said is that at some unknown period ... the astronomers made the discovery that the rising of Sirius was a good fixed point by which to regulate the year ... hence they began to celebrate the rising of Sirius as a New Year's Day, no matter with what date in the official calendar it happened to coincide ... They were dealing with two systems of reckoning, the Sothic Year and the calendar year; and they certainly noted the date in the calendar year on which the Sothic year happened to begin, but at what date they began to do so is not known ... we do not know when the rising of Sirius came to be regarded as New Year's Day, or when its coincidence with the first day of the first season [of the official calendar] came to be regarded as the beginning of a cycle.[6]

This insight is now attributed by Egyptologists to the German scholar Otto Neuge-bauer, who in 1938 – 13 years after Weigall's *History* – published a paper opposing Meyer's chronology along lines broadly similar to Weigall's.[7]

One of the reasons for wanting to establish a shorter chronology was the ancient record of a Sothic rising in the middle of the Twelfth Dynasty, in the seventh year of the reign of Sesostris III. This, combined with other recorded dates, yields a fixed date for that reign upon which all Egyptologists were and are agreed, more or less. According to Alan Gardiner it is 1872 BC, though according to Kenneth A. Kitchen, a modern expert on chronology, that date marks the beginning of Sesostris's acces-sion, not the seventh year after it. Weigall was further off, with 1990 BC. But which-ever date is right, the problem is roughly the same: the chronologies of Petrie and Meyer simply required too long a period between the First Dynasty and the Twelfth for the number of reigns as recorded in Manetho and the Turin Canon and on the Palermo Stone. Besides which, there were very few archaeological remains going back so far.

The business of calculating the years between the First and Twelfth Dynasties was itself problematical. At the beginning of this century, the Palermo and the Cairo Stones had been studied by the German scholars Schafer, Borchardt and Sethe, and found to be parts of a much larger tablet giving a complete year-by-year record of all the reigns of the first five Dynasties. The temptation for Egyptologists was to use the material provided by Manetho and the Turin papyrus and elsewhere to deduce the rest of the original. This is what Weigall did, with a steady reign-by-reign minuteness which belies the essential recklessness of the idea. By closely observing the conven-tions governing the layout of the existing fragments, he thought he could find a method of counting and measuring which would give him at least a hypotheses upon which to start:

> The size of the year-spaces differs in each year register of the Annals, and it seemed to me that this could only mean that the scribe wished to fit a definite amount of material into each register, and therefore in one case had to squeeze it together, and in another case had to space it out. Thus it seemed obvious that he wished to begin each register exactly at the beginning of some new reign, and to end it exactly at the close of a new reign, and to fit a definite number of reigns into a definite number of registers.[8]

This, at least, was a plausible working hypothesis. It has an intuitively 'right' feel about it. But this sense of being 'right' which always goes with intuitional thinking, imparts an air of absoluteness to the whole of Weigall's reconstruction, not only about its years, but its months and days. The pursuit of an exact chronology, down to the very days of the week, was not uncommon at that period. Meyer's earliest date was not just 4241 BC, but July 19th, 4241 BC. Modern chronologists are more cautious and usually allow margins on each side of a suggested date. But the earlier method, certainly in Weigall's hands, gives the exercise an obsessional quality which is strangely compelling, like following a mathematical detective thriller. To the scholars, whom he overturned with the same certainty left and right, it must have been infuriating. The reviewer for the *New Statesman* (25 July 1925) remarked that Weigall's theory 'involves throwing the camp of Egyptology in disorder', and that although the results were 'fascinating', his whole style was characterized by what he ventures to call 'dogmatism, for cocksureness is an impolite word'.

Not that Weigall's dogmatic approach arises entirely from his intuitionism. He supports his reconstruction of the Palermo Stone with an awareness of the scholarship of his day together with a wide knowledge of the contemporary sources of information. The following extract gives a taste of his method. He has just been explaining that his experimental choice of position for the Palermo fragment on the diagram of his reconstruction was made on the assumption that its second register recorded parts of the reigns of the first two kings of the First Dynasty: Menes and Athothis. Counting on from there, he continues:

In the eighth year-space (counting from the right) of the fourth register on the Palermo Stone, the event of the year is recorded thus: [hieroglyph]. I suppose there is little doubt, as Breasted agrees in his *Records*, I, § 125, that this means: "The hacking up or conquest of the fortress or fortified camp of the Host of Re; the hacking up or conquest of the fortress or fortified camp of Ha." We thus have here the record of a civil war; for the first name pretty certainly refers to On or Heliopolis, the city of Re, the Sun, and the second to an unidentified place called Ha, which was nearby. According to my experimental lay-out of the Annals, the year-space in which this event is recorded was the 363rd from the accession of Menes.

Now on a wall of the Ptolomeic temple of Edfu there is a representation of a famous wise-man, Iemhotpe, reading from a scroll the history of a civil war waged between the adherents of Horus and those of Set, which culminates in the two great defeats of the latter at [hieroglyph], these two very places, Heliopolis and Ha or Hat (Naville, *Mythe d'Horus*, Pl. XVIII, I). This war is there stated to have occurred in the 363rd of an era, which, as Newberry has pointed out (*Ancient Egypt*, 1922, II, p.42), must be that dating from the accession of Menes.[9]

After several pages of this kind of happy coincidence, the lay reader begins to fall under the spell. It is with an effort that one reminds oneself that at any given moment in the argument there are always a number of assumptions being made: that Manetho's figure for such and such a reign is a scribal mistake – modern scholars, incidentally, also assume scribal errors – or that he has mixed it up with the figure for the reign before, or that the year-spaces that we can't see here 'must have' gradually got bigger, and so on. It is a *tour de force*, after which Alan Gardiner's sensible warning comes as a salutary cold bath: 'Students cannot be too often warned how precarious such calculations must necessarily be.'[10]

Whatever the standing of Weigall's reconstruction, he made one other important discovery in the course of it that has become generally accepted – though again, when the same argument using many of the same examples was put forward much later, it was done without acknowledgement.[11] It was generally assumed in Weigall's day that the ancient Egyptians recorded the lengths of reigns in 'regnal years', not calendrical years. That is to say, the years of a king's reign were counted from the day of his accession, regardless of where in the calendrical year that fell. This, over very many reigns, can cause arithmetical havoc, the years lengthening and shortening at the changeover points like something out of *Alice in Wonderland*. As Gardiner pointed out:

> If, for example an accession fell on iii. 25 [i.e. 25 day of the third month of the Inundation] then in the reign in question 'year six, third month of the Inundation, day 23' would fall 361 days later than 'year six, third month of the Inundation, day 27.'[12]

At some point during the Eighteenth and through to the Twentieth Dynasties the years were counted in this way, but for most of Egyptian history it was not so. As Weigall points out in his second volume, unless this fact is understood all sorts of mistakes can be made as to the timing and duration of historical events. Something which, according to one system, appears to have taken place a few days after such and such an event, according to the other system would have taken place a year and few days after it.

The evidence that Weigall marshals (and after him, Gardiner) seems to make so solid a case that it is surprising that the system had not been previously observed. Though he gives other examples from later periods, the Palermo Stone offers perhaps the simplest illustration of the principle. On that stone, wherever the changeover point between two reigns is extant, the relevant year compartment records two fractions, the sum of which always comes to 365 days. The second fraction, however, is numbered 'year 1', however small a proportion of the whole, while the whole of the compartment after it is marked 'year two'. If 'year 1' is not a full year, the only reasonable assumption is that it was cut short by the arrival of the next calendrical New Year. Thus, if the previous king died three quarters of the way through the year before, the quarter that remained before the next New Year was counted as a full year for the purposes of calculating the length of the next king's reign. By the same token (so as not to count the first year twice, both as the first of the new king and the last of the old king), the old king was said to have ceased his reign on the last day of the calendrical year before his actual last year. In this way, the regnal years and the calendrical years were made to keep step with one another.

What particularly excited Weigall was that in one case – the year-space shared by the first two kings, Menes and Athothis – the fractions do not add up to 365 days. On Menes's side of the divided space, 6 months and 7 days is recorded, and on Athothis's side, 4 months and 13 days. In other words, 45 days are not accounted for. Weigall's explanation seemed to him to prove conclusively that it was Menes who instituted the ancient Egyptian calendar.

This is how it goes. At the beginning of Menes's reign the calendar had not yet been established. His years were therefore counted regnally, from the first day of his accession, whatever day that might have been in the calendar which didn't yet exist. The Palermo scribe had no other way of recording his reign than by giving its length:

62 years, 6 months and 7 days. His death occurred therefore on the 187th day of the 63rd year of his reign, those 187 days being counted, of course, from the 62nd anniversary of his accession, whenever that was. By that time, however, the calendar had been established, and the next king's reign had to be calculated accordingly. The calendrical New Year was due in 133 days time (i.e. 4 months and 13 days), so that was the time allotted to Athothis as his first year. The fact that 133 and 187 don't add up to 365 is hardly surprising. It simply means that the anniversary of Menes's accession fell well inside what was afterwards known as the calendar year – by 45 days, to be precise.

It is a neat and persuasive solution to what otherwise seems an inexplicable anomaly, and it does seem to point strongly to a change in the method of calculating the years at some time during the reign of King Menes. Some Egyptologists, for example Breasted, had been prepared to give Menes a more recent date than Meyer or Petrie, that is at around 3400 BC, while still agreeing with Meyer's 4241BC for the establishment of the calendar. Weigall was not therefore so much at variance with established scholarship; it was simply that he provided more solid grounds for rejecting entirely those chronologists who were inclined to connect the calendar with the Sothic cycle and to put them both, together with Menes, at the fourth or even the fifth millennium BC.

Weigall's whole chronological discussion branches out more widely and intricately than can be properly followed here. Notably, he had a 'solution' to offer to a problem that lay further on, in the period between the Twelfth and the Eighteenth Dynasties when Egypt was invaded by the Asiatic people known as the Hyksos. Some Egyptologists were inclined to limit this period to approximately two centuries, partly because of cultural resemblances between the Twelfth and the Eighteenth Dynasties and partly because the Sothic date-limit given to the Twelfth-Dynasty king Sesostris III narrowed the gap between that Dynasty and other known dates in the Eighteenth. However, the Turin Canon lists over a hundred kings for the period, which seemed too many to fit comfortably into so short a time. It was to allow for this number of kings that Petrie threw his chronology back a whole Sothic cycle. Another scholar, H.R. Hall, Deputy-keeper of Egyptian and Assyrian Antiquities at the British Museum, suggested in the 1923 edition of *The Cambridge Ancient History* that perhaps there had been a mistake in the original observation of the Sothic rising, or that there had been a change in the calendar introduced between the time of Sesostris III and the Eighteenth Dynasty. Hall still adhered to this view in 1932.[13]

The possibility that the Turin papyrus recorded overlapping and contemporaneous dynasties had been raised before by Breasted. Weigall took up the suggestion and argued it forcefully, giving for the first time in any detail the story of the Hyksos kings. As far as chronology goes, he claimed that the Hyksos Fifteenth Dynasty, established in the eastern Delta, ruled largely in parallel with the Egyptian Thirteenth and Fourteenth Dynasties in the rest of the country. The last two Hyksos kings then became overlords, their administrative centre now being further south in Memphis, with the Sixteenth and Seventeenth Dynasty kings of the other states as their vassals. Weigall's dates for these Dynasties do not tally with modern estimates, just as his date for Sesostris III did not, but the principle of parallel reigns came to be generally accepted. In 1961, Gardiner was able to say that 'all recent Egyptologists accept ... that the Canon's enumeration comprised many kings existing simultaneously, but presumably in widely different parts of the country.'[14]

Whatever Egyptologists thought of Weigall's chronology, that was only a part of his enterprise. The rest, after all, was the history itself. But here again, the general reader might have felt a little surprised, for Weigall's object, it seems, was to keep his public close to the sources. Weigall takes him on a dynastic journey, assembling for each Pharaoh all the known pieces of information: a bowl in this museum, a tablet in that, an inscription in a tomb, a graffito in a desert quarry. The texts of whole papyruses are given in full, where other histories tend to select and paraphrase. One is reminded of the style and format of his *Guide to the Antiquities of Upper Egypt*. And like that book, he seems to have assembled an astonishing quantity of information. It is as much a reference book as anything else, though when he comes to the Eighteenth Dynasty he does not resist the drama inherent in his material.

Here was the warlike Tuthmosis I, and his campaigns into Nubia and Syria. Never before had the Egyptian army fought in Syria and Weigall allows himself to imagine what it must have been like for the soldiers so far from home. He has them marvelling, on their return to Egypt, at such a Pharaoh who:

had led them to strange lands ... where they had sacked towns and cities curiously built, and had chased odd-looking people across fantastic landscapes: through gardens of outlandish flowers, through orchards of unknown fruit trees, over fields of peculiar grain, and into woods of amazing trees.[15]

Here too, was his powerful daughter Hatshepsut, her half-brother Tuthmosis II, and his son, Tuthmosis III. The feuds and rivalries, the ambitions and magnificence of these people are given the kind of treatment Weigall's readers had come to expect, though he never strays far from the monumental and documentary evidence. In the process, he also clears up a difficulty over the order of their succession that had long puzzled Egyptologists. It is a further instance of the neglect observed above that Gardiner should have ascribed to another Egyptologist, W.F. Edgerton in 1933, the very solution that Weigall had put forward six years before.[16]

In fact it is clear from these examples that the arguments and solutions that Weigall put forward were not all out on the wilder fringes. It is curious therefore that they were ignored by the scholarly world of his day, and since. He was reviewed, as usual, by the serious non-specialist press, by the *Spectator*, the *Athenaeum*, the *Times Literary Supplement* and so on, but the Egyptological periodicals were silent. The scholarly histories that subsequently appeared make no reference to him; he features in none of their bibliographies; and as we have seen, when some of his ideas emerged later, they did so as if for the first time.

Whether this was because his real scholarship was so mixed with conjecture that it was too difficult to sort them out, or to distinguish fruitful intuition from tendentiousness; whether it was because he had become identified over the years as a 'mere' popularizer; whether it was that he had been too long out of circulation, laying himself open to academic snobbery by becoming a part of slightly raffish worlds – the theatre, journalism, the cinema; whether it was that the old cloud under which he had left Egypt in 1914 had grown in the meantime and had been made blacker by his attacks on Carnarvon at the time of Tutankhamun; or whether it was because of the arrogant tone he adopted in the book – any or all these things might have contributed. As for his arrogance: his isolation was a serious drawback. His whole tone might have been more accommodating had he had colleagues. Like the outcast he probably felt himself to be, he seems to have preferred slamming his arguments down on the table, take them or leave them, rather than discussing possibilities and probabilities among fellows.

Altogether, these volumes make an odd mixture of difficult and minutely interrelating fact and conjecture, alternating with relatively expansive story-telling. As regards the first, the critics expected the general reader to be put off, and the scholar to raise objections; as for the second, they expected the scholars to think him merely 'popular'. Their own estimates varied. *The Times Literary Supplement* (10 October 1927), reviewing the book after the second volume came out, said that it missed 'the lighter touch of Mr Weigall's brush ... Mr Weigall himself ... [having] led us in other volumes to expect a magician, no matter how dry the bones might be.' It then added, rather minimally, that 'to the student, however, who wishes to have a comprehensive record by him of the chief doings of each king ... this is no disadvantage.' This was an unaccustomed form of praise for Weigall. On the other hand, the *New Statesman* (23 April 1927), after declaring that his new chronology was much strengthened by these pages (of the second volume), and commending him for his 'very full record', said that his narrative was 'everywhere enlivened by such human touches as his material affords', and that he was at once 'scholarly and glamorous'.

Weigall may have been disappointed at not being welcomed back into the scholarly fold, but he never let on. Sebastian's solemn hope of presenting his *History* to 'a grateful world', suggests a wry smile instead. And by the time his *History of the Pharaohs* was being reviewed or not reviewed, he had other fish to fry. Versatility was his saving. Now, with *The Not Impossible She,* he was in the public eye as a relatively serious novelist and social critic, and even more prominently – for things were moving on fast – as an unashamedly popularizing historian-guide-travel writer in the *Daily Mail,* on the subject of Roman, Anglo-Saxon and Norman Britain.

Here was a new field for Weigall. Just as in Egypt, Weigall was incapable of looking at his native landscape without seeing history too. During a long bicycle tour with his sons one summer in the early twenties, he had written letters not so much about the views and the pretty villages but about the signs he saw everywhere of the past. At Malvern, he notes, 'all the hillsides' are marked still with the old trenches dug by the ancient Britons in their wars with the Welsh tribesmen; and there are the old sacred springs of the Druids and their circles; here is the abbey built by the monks who turned springs into Christian places without realizing that they were carrying on long-forgotten heathen worship. A description of a ten-mile ride along the top of the Cotswolds 'under dark skies and a gale of wind behind us' quickly turns into a note about the crossroads where you could still see 'the old posts where the highwaymen were hanged; and the signs saying 'Ye Waye to Oxford' or 'Ye Waye to Warwick' just as they were written up in 1700.'

During 1926 and 1927 he wrote three series of articles for the *Daily Mail*, each series devoted to one of the three periods. It soon became apparent that these pieces, together with their appearance in book form, were attracting a huge following. Readers wrote in by the hundred: clergymen, retired military men, engineers, solicitors, city clerks, a pharmacist, a 'working man', school children, museum curators, men and women of all kinds, and of course archaeologists. They wrote to say how interested they were, and could he visit their church, their stone cross, their old bridge. They wrote to tell him that they came from Yorkshire, and could he tell them which Roman legion had been quartered there. They wrote to say that Burgh is not in Norfolk but in Suffolk, and that Ikleton is not in Suffolk but in Norfolk. They admonished him for saying 'England' when he meant 'Britannia'; they doubted that the Romans intermarried with the Anglo-Saxons; they queried his defence of William the Conqueror. They told him about local farmers who had ploughed up buried walls. They asked him about their surnames, and wondered about their descent. But more than anything, they wrote to say how eagerly they looked out for his articles, how much they wanted to know, how needed his work was. Could he give some motoring routes, could he publicize the plight of their ruined manor, could he come and lecture to their local historical society? The B.B.C. asked if he could be persuaded to give a series of six talks, at seven guineas a time, since they were about to develop the educational side of their work.[17] From all over the country came an outpouring of interest and opinion, of erudition and eccentricity – one correspondent signed himself a 'SAXON'.

With his usual feel for the public pulse, Weigall seems to have hit the very spot. He was tapping into people's abiding interest in their local patch, their church, their village, their county. They had most probably been brought up on Kipling, on *Puck of Pook's Hill*, where Roman legionaries step out of the hedges and knights clip-clop round the corner. Now the war had given them a rush of pride in Englishness, the landscape, ancestors and race. Over and above that, Weigall was riding the wave of the motorcar. A review of his pieces was as likely to appear in a magazine called *The Auto* as in *The Times Literary Supplement*. Cars were still luxuries, but mass production of Morris Minors and Baby Austins was beginning to change that. It was becoming increasingly possible to travel freely, to penetrate beyond the rail network, to arrange tours. By 1930 there were more than a million cars in private ownership, and well before that newspapers and weeklies regularly ran items about motoring and motoring holidays. The *New Statesman* had a feature called 'About Motoring', and in the *Spectator* there were motoring pieces signed by one 'C.A.R.'. At the same time books about the countryside proliferated. In one issue, the *New Statesman* reviewed *Sussex Pilgrimages* by R. Thurston Hopkins,

*Unknown Dorset* by Donald Maxwell, *Bypaths in Downland* by Barclay Wills, *People and Places in Marshland* by Christopher Marlowe, and *The Homeland of English Authors* by Ernest H. Rann.[18]

In his Introduction to *Wanderings in Roman Britain,* the collected edition of the first series of articles, Weigall confesses that the volume does not amount to a history as such, nor to a guide book, still less to a scientific treatise. It serves, he says, simply 'to show how much our cities and villages contain of the relics of a most inspiring epoch in the story of Britain.'[19] He had always been fascinated by the physicality of the past, but now, it seems, he had an axe to grind, a patriotic agenda to follow. If we could only realize, he says, 'the glories from which we have come, we shall turn our eyes with the more confidence to the greater splendours of character and world-wide usefulness towards which we are moving.'[20]

Talk of race and racial characteristics embarrasses us now. At that period people minded less. In his own naive way, Weigall had blundered about on some of this ground in relation to the oriental and occidental 'character' in his novel, *The Way of the East* (1924). There, bravely for the period, he had married his English hero to his Egyptian heroine. A modern reader would point out that the Egyptian Miriam's aristocratically white skin makes Weigall just as racist as if he hadn't. All the same it was a bold move, and he had driven his point home in the book in various speeches about the virtues of miscegenation. He could not, it is true, contemplate mixtures of white and brown or white and black. It is also true that his excitement at an English-Egyptian conjunction sprang from a sense of imperial glory of some sort – two great Empires, ancient and modern, coming together. But Colonel Romance, his oddly-named hero, is not altogether what one might expect from this.

There is a scene in the gardens of the Cairo Sporting Club, a little piece of England set down beside the Nile, in which the brass band strikes up Elgar's 'Land of Hope and Glory'. Colonel Romance 'suddenly became conscious of a sense of dramatic pride in his country.' He looks about him and notices to his fury that the few Egyptian club-members are laughing and talking through the music. By contrast, all his countrymen 'are intent: all had stopped smoking, or talking, or eating':

> There were dreams in their eyes, dreams of England's splendour. Conquered kings and beaten armies were parading before their inward vision; men from all over the earth were laying their tribute at the foot of the throne of the King-Emperor ...

The band stops and Colonel Romance suddenly recoils from himself in shame: 'He had caught himself out in a mental act of pure melodrama.' He curses the band, glares at his companion and exclaims, 'That's the sort of stuff that is poison to the world':

> It eggs one on to race-hatreds, and wars, and everything else that causes misery on earth. The Germans feel that sort of thing when they sing 'Deutschland uber Alles'. I'm never going to listen to a brass band again.[21]

And he stomps off to be alone.

If Weigall was capable of this kind of self-deflation, it is surprising to find him writing hymns to our island story and the splendours of worldwide usefulness – though 'usefulness' is an improvement on, say, 'domination'. One is reminded of his friend H.V. Morton's comment on his novels – that the only thing that marred them for him was the sight of Weigall's tongue firmly in his cheek. One is reminded too of the ribbing he got from H.R. Hall about Akhnaten, old Crackpot. But Weigall may have been in earnest in all these places even as he calculated his effects. It is probably just that ability that accounts for his popular appeal. It comes out with particular vividness in a letter he wrote to Alured just as he was researching the first series of his *Daily Mail* articles.

It was May 1926, during the General Strike called in support of the coal miners. Alured was at that time travelling in Italy, and Weigall describes for him the political situation at home. He had taken a train, for example, which had been driven by Lord Montague of Beaulieu, and the stationmaster at Waterloo had been Lord Charnworth. Weigall himself had been sympathetic to the demands of the coal miners, who were being asked to accept less pay and longer hours by the pit-owners, but he had opposed the General Strike on the grounds that it sought to over-rule the sovereignty of parliament. As he writes, the strike has just collapsed and Weigall explains how the Prime Minister, Baldwin, had:

adopted rather a religious note, quite sincerely, and called for national prayer; and whether one believes in that sort of thing or not, its sentimental and dramatic value was enormous. The Govt. commandeered the wireless ... and when the strike collapsed this broadcasting business was used with great dramatic effect. First came the announcement that the strike was over, then a message from the king was read, and then came Baldwin's speech, thanking God, and full of England and Christ and the Lamb of God and love Triumphant and then as he was finishing the organ rolled out and a great choir of voices swelled into an anthem about England and the throne of God and that sort of thing; and where I was, the crowd took it up and sang "O God our help in ages past".

So far the whole thing is described essentially as a piece of theatre. But then comes Weigall's own reaction:

Of course it was sentimental, so sentimental that most people nearly wept and I had a pain in my throat that *hurt*; but it was sincere, and I felt the enormous value of this religious strain in the national character.

He was both in and out of the emotional tide: the very word 'sentimental' seems to change meaning half-way through the sentence, at first denoting something hackneyed and then suddenly turning into a genuine emotion. Similarly in his own writing, he presumably knew he was using clichés, but he was more than half seduced by them himself. It is of course no coincidence that his *Daily Mail* pieces had a distinctly Baldwinesque feel to them. He was writing for a mass audience, for the same kind of people he had heard singing "O God our help in ages past": 'that vast body of the Middle Classes,' as his letter to Alured puts it, 'the shop-keepers, clerks, etc., with which Labour had not reckoned.' He knew what they were like.

But Weigall could never do anything, not even spin out clichés, without some twist. Like the patriotism of Colonel Romance in *The Way of the East*, Weigall's patriotism does not take quite the expected form. According to him, it is the mixture, not the purity, of race that has given the British people its best qualities. In Egypt he had liked the idea that the modern *fellahin* were descended largely without admixture – or so he thought – from the ancient Egyptians. A modern Egyptian brought you face to face with an ancient Egyptian. Now we find him celebrating the virtues of heterogeneity. The original Celts and Britons mixed with the Romans, he said, the Romans them-selves being a miscellaneous collection of nationalities from all over the Roman Empire; the Anglo-Saxons mixed with that mixture; and in their turn, the Normans did too. All this, he maintained, was achieved by virtue of those qualities of compro-mise and toleration and goodwill that in his view have always constituted the British character.

Weigall does not deny that there were wars and oppressions and rebellions; but overall the picture he paints is of relatively harmonious absorption. There was, however, one grain of sand in this smooth historical paste, namely the Germanic origins of the Anglo-Saxons. Weigall may have been happy to combine English with Egyptian blood, but he jibbed at the Germans. To overcome the problem he quotes seventh-, eighth- and even tenth-century sources indicating that there were still at these late periods populations of Britons as well as Picts and Scots and Latins in the island. The Anglo-Saxons may have defeated and enslaved the Britons, but they didn't exterminate them, and they probably intermarried with them. Furthermore, he says, the Anglo-Saxon period is characterized by 'a remarkable and gradually increasing refinement of mind ... contrasting them very favourably with their contemporaries on the Continent.' 'Did their undoubted intermarriage with the British,' he asks, 'foster in their character those qualities which now differentiate them so markedly from their Teutonic kin across the sea?' to which, of course, he expects the reader to answer 'Yes.'[22]

Thus, not only does Weigall dilute the Teutonic strain, but in one stroke he extends the indigenous lineage of his readers, the descendants of those Anglo-Saxons, and carries them back into further stretches of history, through four centuries of the Romans and beyond, 'for at least another 1500 years of more or less civilized life in Britain, and links us at length to the people who built Stonehenge.'[23] And these people were worthy ancestors; not, as the school books maintained, painted tribesmen capering on the shore to greet the ships of Julius Caesar. On the contrary, he says, their relics are of exquisite workmanship, gold and amber mounted daggers, gold bracelets, bronze hairpins, shaving razors, finely decorated mirrors, linen and wool. An Etruscan vase, Egyptian beads from the time of Tutankhamun, coins from France, and one from Carthage, show that they were traders and travellers over the rest of the known civilized world.

In this way, Weigall uses the actual remains to drive home his claim about the glories of Britain's history. Taking his readers from town to town, going over the walls and forts, the villas and churches, he points out the beauties and refinements, the sophistication of small domestic objects, the massive solidity and workmanship of the great Norman churches, all the time flattering his audience with the sense that these qualities are theirs too – by tradition, by blood, by whatever force lies in the current of a continuous and ancient history. In the process he covered many miles, sometimes by train, sometimes by car, and came to know many provincial museums. He made the best of their buckets and jugs, and if he was lucky, their torques and silver brooches. Wherever they were dingy and depressing, he rode his old hobby horse about the need for museums to 'attract and teach, not repel and disgust'.[24]

He also championed the cause of British archaeology, deplored the continuing loss of ancient remains, campaigned for money for excavations, and urged a more active role for the Office of Public Works. One can hear the old Inspector of Antiquities in him as he goes about: in Dorset, for example, the crypt of Sherborne Castle was being used as 'a sort of stable, and the pillar is covered with initials cut by local visitors ... a very memorial stone of rustic inanity.' At Christchurch near Bournemouth, the Norman remains in the tea-garden of the Kings Arms Hotel are covered with ivy. Somebody should tear it off.[25] At Letchworth, he would like to commend the local farmer, one Mr W. Hart, for giving up his field of brussels sprouts in order to allow excavations on his land:

He sees where so many farmers are blind, that since the genius of Britain is rooted in her British and Roman past, the dead who lie beneath his fields have a claim upon him both as a man of understanding and as a patriot; and he is willing to sacrifice something of his vegetable crop for their sake ...[26]

What Mr Hart made of that sentence is not recorded.

No one would use these books now in the way they might still consult his *Guide to the Antiquities of Upper Egypt*. But setting aside their outdated ideology, they convey their information lightly and vividly. In fact the *Manchester Guardian* (28 December 1926), in its review of *Wanderings in Roman Britain*, said, not unkindly, that they were 'an attempt to "film" the whole subject.' They have the trick, as with all Weigall's historical books, of bringing you up short against the past. For example, the old Saxon timber of Greenstead Church in Essex, he says, 'has heard the same words of divine worship spoken by the East Saxons in the Anglo-Saxon tongue as now, some 40 generations later, it hears spoken in English by the men of Essex.'[27]

Certainly these articles played a significant part in alerting the country to its heritage. If Weigall had known where it would lead by the end of the century, he might perhaps have hesitated. But in his day theme parks were undreamt of; it was more a question of where to find a decent guide book. As a sign of the times, here is a letter from a certain David Williams, a clerk perhaps, someone who sounds a little like Leonard Bast from E.M. Forster's *Howard's End*. Its grammar and spelling are preserved:

Sir,

Having just returned from my Summer Vacation, which I spent pottering about in those historical towns of Rye, Winchelsea and Hastings, I couldn't help being very interested in Arther Weigall's article on Norman England in Tuesdays Daily Mail. It seems rather a pity why so many holiday makers on the South Coast, do not avail themselves of the opportunity of visiting those towns which have so many buildings and relics that date back to and beyond the Norman Era.

I am forced to make this assertion for upon making enquiries at business today, I found that although nearly all my confreres had been to Hastings, only two had also visited the other towns I have mentioned. They to my surprise confessed that all they did was to walk through the streets, the idea of visiting any of the Historical places, did not occur to them.

That these places of maedevial interest are not visited on a larger scale than of yore I put down to the very poor advertising on the part of Hastings & Brighton's Corporations (not to mention the towns of the same vicinity).

As I intend to spend my next holiday in a similar manner, I would be grateful if one of your correspondents could let me know where I could obtain the necessary guide book which embraces all these towns which still have buildings of olden times.[28]

# Chapter 22

# The Old Brigade versus the moderns
# 1928–1929

Weigall's wanderings around England at this time might stand as a symbol of his way of life from now on. It is true that he had never really shared a settled life with his family, or not for long; but he had always hoped that he might. The Langdale House experiment in Oxford had been the nearest he had got to it, and Cleveland Square had offered a version of it, but with an important blank in the middle of the picture – the mother and wife, Hortense. Now the divorce erased the entire scene. Muriel and Weigall never had children of their own, and although in 1931 they did settle in London, in St John's Wood, their life until then was nomadic. For two years, from June 1929 to May 1931, they abandoned England altogether for America: going first to Hollywood, where Beatrice Lillie, now a very big star, was filming ('opposite an ostrich, a gorilla and George Grossmith ...,' she said[1]); and after that to New York. In both places, they lived in hotels.

Part of Muriel's attraction for Weigall may have lain precisely in the fact that she uprooted him. He had once warned Alured to beware 'the wails of the women', and the suffocation of too much love. He might have added, 'and too much admiration and ambition'. Muriel had never known him, as they had, during the Egyptian years, the period of his greatest promise, full of hope and idealism and solid achievement. Archaeological career-structures meant nothing to her. Weigall was not someone who might have been a Petrie or a Maspero or the Head of the Cairo Museum. Her life was in music and the stage, and in that field, Weigall had been a brilliant success. She was in no position to judge his standing among scholars, but he had written a lot of successful books, and it must have seemed to her that he had arrived. Ten years younger, she was the one with potential and a future, not he.

Theatrical and social success was now, after all, in the family. In 1920 her sister Beatrice Lillie had made an 'actress-weds-aristocrat' marriage, to Robert Peel, fifth in line to the baronetcy (the second baronet was the Peel who founded the London Metropolitan Police Force, in 1829) and the family possessed a vast seat, Drayton Manor, near Tamworth in the West Midlands. Not that Bea, as she was known, had any taste for the English aristocratic way of life. Soon after succeeding to the title in 1925, her husband died of peritonitis, and she retained the title Lady Peel, largely for its comic possibilities (in one of her sketches she speaks into a large lily trumpet which is meant to be a telephone: "C'est Lady Parle qui peel"). A son, Bobbie, had been born in December 1920, to whom she was devoted, keeping him in tow as much as possible in her constant travels between London, the Riviera, New York and Hollywood. Muriel loved him too, and she and Weigall often had the little boy to stay with them.

Meanwhile, Muriel's songs for Bea had been a success and she was now writing more – a musical piece, an 'operette' they called it, on which Weigall was collaborating with her. With Muriel shouldering some of the burden, he was at last taking life lightly. After years of anxiety and grind, he was happy. His sister Geanie wrote to her favourite niece and namesake, Geraldine, to say not only that Muriel was 'most striking looking and has a beautiful skin ... [and ] manages to look nice always,' but that 'she makes Arthur very happy and that is the principle of the thing.'

At the same time, though, the slate could never be wiped entirely clean. His two worlds jostled each other in his mind. Writing once to his three now teen-age daughters in England from his Beverly Hills hotel, he described his new way of life, swimming in the hotel pool, playing with Bobbie, going to parties, meeting unbelievably rich Americans and writing. Then he adds:

> I want to see you all so much, and I want to see Mimi and Auntie Geanie and everybody ... It's a mixed feeling having no home – rather horrifying, and also rather amusing. But I hate being away from Mimi for so long at a time; because much as she disapproves of me nowadays, I kind of feel blue when I don't see her. (O boy! – I'm sure growing so American these days!)

If Weigall had a home anywhere, it was where Mimi was. Once when he was at loggerheads with Alured, he confessed to feeling nonplussed at his son's avowed lack of feeling for him. He and Mimi, he said, were 'poles apart' in thought, but he loved her nevertheless. All the same, it wasn't easy. Mimi belonged in thought and habit to the pre-1914 world. It was as though the divorce had been not only from Hortense, but from his mother – or at least from everything she represented. Mimi now stood on the other side of a gulf wider than any that had previously divided the generations, and although Weigall was not exactly of the jazz-age, he had at the age of 45, decided to snap his fingers and kick up his heels. It was only half a joke when he wrote to his daughter Geraldine on her fourteenth birthday: '... the funny thing is that as you get older and older I grow younger and younger. By the time you are 20 you'll have to feed me from a bottle.'

And being the man he was, he couldn't very well not write about it. It was a fresh subject: the pre-war Establishment versus the moderns. Both seriously and frivolously, the books Weigall now began to write – farcical novels and a solid book on comparative religion – are an attack on the conventions. In one novel, he has a character say: ' "Every convention of society which is maintained by the feeling that it would be quite too too dreadful to upset it, is maintained by Magic. Top hats, for instance." '[2] It was top hats, or wedding rings, or marriage ceremonies and divorce laws in the novels; and in the serious book it was Church dogma and the sacraments.

In one case Weigall tipped his hat at a jaunty angle, in the other he puffed on his professorial pipe. But his object was the same in both.

Weigall was worried – or perhaps he was secretly hopeful – that the first of his new novels, *Saturnalia in Room 23* (1927), might shock people. Like the first act of Noel Coward's earlier *Private Lives*, it is set in a hotel on the Riviera, where his young couple, Camilla Worth and Peregrine Penny, are spending their honeymoon. In fact, we first meet them in bed, she wearing a cerise silk night-gown and he a pair of orange silk pyjamas – a scene both modest and shocking. But are they really married? Or are they living 'in sin'? Camilla's rich and childless aunt, Sally Worth, is an erstwhile suffragette violently opposed to marriage. Not a penny of her fortune will come to Camilla if she ever finds out that the pair are wed. On the other hand, none of Peregrine's inheritance will come to him if his father, a self-made businessman and Church alderman, hears that they aren't. The aunt and the father turn up separately and by chance at the same hotel, and the couple have their work cut out. Looking on in horror are Archdeacon Ribble and his preposterous wife, who believe that Camilla and Peregrine are unmarried, and that the noises of innocent merriment issuing from room 23, next to theirs, are saturnalian orgies.

The whole farrago of misunderstandings and cross-purposes that follows is designed to leave the supposed custodians of morality looking distinctly besmirched, eager to find sex and sin wherever convention appears to have been broken. The bright young things on the other hand – both here and in Weigall's next novel, *The Young Lady from Hell* (1929) – are shown to be essentially moral creatures. They banter about serious subjects and wear fashionable clothes, but there was no real reason for Weigall to think they might shock. As the *Aberdeen Press and Journal* (15 November 1927) put it: 'The story is worked out with delicate nuances of impropriety, but indeed for these days it is refreshingly proper.'

Everyone was agreed that the novel was clever and funny. *Punch* (30 November 1927) composed a doggerel verse about the couple's dilemma, and even the *Times Literary Supplement* (15 December 1927) primly conceded that 'the author manages to give it freshness and interest, thanks to his manner, which is light-hearted, somewhat cynical, and not infrequently flavoured with wit.' Under the title *Infidelity* the book was published in America, where it received wide and rather more robust coverage:

Mr Weigall has written as rollicking a yarn as has appeared between covers in a long time. It is a farce of the sheerest sort, lively and filled with verve, zipping along with a cheery gusto that will provoke smiles, chuckles and finally, downright guffaws.[3]

*The Sphere* (7 January 1928) called the book 'a holiday extravaganza', and it is possible that Weigall did write it on holiday. Since at least 1925 he and Muriel had been taking end-of-season breaks at the Hotel Beau Rivage in St Raphael on the French Riviera – an unmarried couple, really living 'in sin'. It was here, at any rate, that he corrected the proofs.

The Riviera had for some time been a wintering place for the British but, just as in Egypt, they had always gone north again in April. After the war, the pattern changed.

Americans began arriving and staying through the summer months, swimming and sunbathing, quite at home in the heat. Scott Fitzgerald describes this transformation in *Tender is the Night*, the hotels kept open for the foreigners, all stripped and roasting on the beaches. Geanie described beach life with some amusement in 1930 when she spent a summer as a guest in a smart Fitzgeraldian villa on Corsica: 'We lie on the beach all the morning, in and out of the sea, and I am already burnt scarlet, although I tried to keep in the shade ... But the girls here all look superb – almost black and almost naked. Even at meals they only wear trousers and a postage stamp.'

In October 1927, after completing his latest clutch of books and delivering any number of lectures, Weigall was doing the same thing, and writing about it to Alured: 'On calm days I bring down a tin plate to dive for ... or I take a log of wood in and fool about with that; or we all play about with a large ball in the water ... I'd like to do nothing for months and months.' But even if Weigall hadn't had to keep making money, one cannot imagine him doing nothing for long. In the same letter, he lets slip that, apart from the proofs of *Saturnalia*, he is also working on 'a little History of Egypt I've been asked to do for a cheap series (I'm not really doing more than a page or two a day, and even that is a bore).' He might also have mentioned, though perhaps he hadn't started them yet, a series of 30 articles for the *Graphic* magazine – sketches of figures from ancient history, which were collected and published in book form the following year, under the title *Flights into Antiquity*, and in America *Personalities of Antiquity*.

Writing was second nature to Weigall. It is almost as though his thoughts and impressions hadn't happened until he wrote about them. His advice to any of his children who showed promise was to turn writing into a habit. 'Make a point of writing about a thousand words a day,' he once told Alured, 'and keep what you have written, however bad.' Poor Alured! 'Keep a notebook', he wrote to his second daughter Zippa, 'in which you jot down all the odd or interesting things you notice, and your own feelings ... It is only a matter of habit – the habit of putting down into words the thoughts that come into your head, and the habit of writing down consecutive sentences.' It could be said that Weigall wrote too much, that he was facile. His work often cries out for an editor. But the *Graphic* pieces are short, informative, sometimes racy items, admirably calculated for their purpose.

Weigall defends his gossipy manner on the grounds that the writer of history:

> is always better served by the authentic reports of private conversations and the narration of events that have taken place behind closed doors ... history is poor stuff when it is based only on the record of events considered fit for public knowledge by contemporary censors.[4]

Here are portraits in miniature – Julius Caesar, the Queen of Sheba, King Arthur, Moses and others – as well as some short discourses on topics such as the building of the Great Pyramid, the origins of relic-worship, the desert hermits of Egypt, or the disaster at Herculaneum. Weigall's angle is usually quirky (Moses in Egypt would have been clean-shaven, close-cropped and perfumed; Arthur was probably Artorius, a

Romanized British general) always personal, and sometimes facetious. Julius Caesar, for example, was a dandy in his youth, who curled his hair, used rouge, and 'I take it that he powdered his nose.' Boadicea, he says, leaves him cold: 'Big, golden-haired women in tight jumpers always appal me.' What is interesting though, is that he is always close to his sources. Even Boadicea's jumper is shown to have been drawn from the original, in this case the Roman historian Dio Cassius who described her as wearing '"over her bosom a striped vest ... tightly pulled."'[5]

Many of Weigall's pieces are, in fact, perfectly straight, with scarcely a joke or flippant remark from beginning to end: the chapter on Pliny's country houses for example, the one on Harun-al-Rashid, or the story of Thutmose III's victory over the city of Megiddo, 'The first Armageddon'. The most frivolous thing about the otherwise serious and even moving piece on Aspasia is its title: 'The Lady Athens did not receive.' But although most critics said that they read the book with profit and enjoyment, taking it in the spirit in which it was written, he was attacked by some of the heavy-weights. Their criticism is interesting, for it defines what was regarded as 'respectable' history at that time.

Style and presentation were the main problem: the catchy titles, the *Graphic*'s slightly risqué illustrations, the jokes of course, and some of the expressions – *Lloyds List* (11 May 1928), for example, looked askance at the phrase 'riding hell for leather', to describe Zenobia fleeing the Romans. The critic of the *Spectator* (31 March 1928) said that the mere sight of some of the titles had inclined him to shut up the book without reading it, and *The Outlook* (16 June 1928) was especially upset by the illustrations, urging Weigall to 'remember that he owes it to himself to maintain the dignity of [his] solemn profession.' Both critics, however, did nerve themselves to read and even compliment him on the pieces, many of which, said *The Outlook,* are 'invigorating statements of important historical events ... fresh presentations of matters which many more famous historians have seen with duller wits.'

*The New Statesman* (24 March 1928), on the other hand, couldn't stomach anything at all. It wasn't just the titles, but the subject matter itself. It was 'regrettable', said the critic:

> that the growing interest of the general reader in the great story of the ancient civilizations should be catered for [by] ... papers as trivial as those on the epicene vagaries of Heliogabalus, the amours of Caesar, and the upbringing and rise to fortune of [the Empress] Theodora.

What Weigall had said about Theodora (to take that example) was that she had originally been a bear-keeper's daughter and had taken to the stage where she had become 'involved in all the horrors of that life which, in those days, was one of the lowest of the low.'[6] Weigall's crime was not that he was wrong, but that by taking the 'great' out of 'the story of the ancient civilizations', he had lowered historiography itself:

> Had the object of the book been to belittle the importance of historical and archaeological research, its tone could hardly have been worse, and adopted as it is by one claiming authority, it can only be described as deplorable.

In his present mood, Weigall would no doubt have been cheered. Here was another branch of the Old Brigade and this time he had managed to shock them.

Next in line for debunking was the solemn dignity of the Church. He had argued in *Saturnalia in Room 23* that the Church's attitude to marriage was primitive. If it was so in that particular, he seems to have asked himself, how does the rest of it stand up? As it happens, during 1927–28 there was much public and Parliamentary debate about the Book of Common Prayer. Weigall, typically, seized the occasion, and sweeping past this limited and local controversy, urged nothing less than a total overhaul of the Church – its theology, its teaching, and its ritual.

The claim made in the title of his book – *The Paganism in our Christianity* – was not new. Weigall was on well-trodden ground, and he acknowledges the work of other scholars in the field of comparative religion: most obviously James Frazer in *The Golden Bough*, and *Adonis, Attis Osiris*, but others too, such as J.M. Robertson in *Christianity and Mythology* and *Pagan Christs: Studies in Comparative Hierology*. What Weigall did was to take this tradition, work into it his own knowledge of the ancient Egyptian religions, and then condense, colour and point the whole thing for popular consumption. His aim, he said, was not iconoclastic, but on the contrary, restorative.

Weigall was careful to distinguish himself from the school of criticism that claimed that Christ's historicism was undermined by the pagan elements in his story. They are certainly there, he said, but they have only to be stripped away for the real man to stand revealed. His emphasis is on Christ the 'man', whose importance lay in his teachings and example, not in the miraculous manner of his birth, death, and life after death. The non-rational, supernatural parts of Christianity, together with the whole theology and ritual of the Church are, he pointed out, later accretions which derive from the pagan context in which the early Church defined itself. In his view, they obscure the true simplicity of Christ, and have survived only because people love the colour and drama of magic and superstition, and because they offer a distraction from the difficult task of understanding and obeying his teaching. They have no place, he insisted, in modern Christianity.

It was a no-nonsense, anti-sacerdotal approach, which recalls his old impatience with the idea of Egyptian mysticism. But, as many of the reviews pointed out, one didn't need to share it to be fascinated by the main substance of the book. *The Derby Daily Telegraph* (16 July 1928) complimented him simply for assembling 'in popular form and in small compass a vast amount of information about the Pagan cults of the Roman Empire which is not easily accessible to the general reader.' Quoting widely from the ancient historians and the early Christian commentators, Weigall presents the whole dramatis personae of the Christian story distributed, as it were, through the religions of the Mediterranean, North Africa, and occasionally of northern Europe and Britain. There, he argues, may be found any number of virgin mothers, divine families, holy trinities, and sacrificial sons all enacting the different episodes of Christ's life. In particular, the cults of Adonis, Dionysus, Atthis, Osiris, and Mithras, all feature sons of gods who are variously baptized, tempted in the wilderness, put to death, sometimes even crucified or hung in a tree, buried, some of whom then descend into hell, rise again, and ascend into heaven, and all of whom become the focus for stories of miracles, and for doctrines and observances remarkably like those that developed in the early Christian church.

The book was widely reviewed (a matter of course with Weigall's publications now). Most critics were impressed by the range of his knowledge and the clarity with which he conveyed it. Some grumbled at what they felt was his cavalier way with the Gospels, and at his habit of positively asserting what others had put forward more tentatively.[7] Generally, however, while being perfectly prepared to accept Weigall's charge of 'paganism', the critics couldn't feel as desperately about it as he did, and were bemused by his call for revolution.

He was pushing at an open door, it seems. As the *Oxford Times* (15 June 1928) pointed out:

A generation ago – when the Church was still doggedly fighting the scientific revelations of Darwin – this book would have been received with horror and disgust by all sections of Christendom ... Today ... it will not disturb, but strengthen, those who have a similarly 'revised' attitude to Christianity, whilst it will roll like water off a duck's back off those tenacious and water-tight sections of the Church which have been left undampened by half a century of criticism.

Weigall, with his vivid sense of history, had managed to shock himself. But it was never going to be easy to bring home to the unhistorically-minded that their Communion wafer and wine, for example, still reeked with the cannibalistic gore of sacrificial altars.

And then there were those who felt that there was something in these so-called 'heathen' religions after all, some instinct that Christianity did well to incorporate and express. *The Occult Review* (October 1928) made the point:

... while fully recognizing the sincerity and impressive scholarship of Mr Weigall, one cannot forbear suggesting to him in deep seriousness that some of the myths and mysteries of the pagan world may have found a place in Christian theology on their own merits, because they are true (actually or potentially) for all men in all ages, because no religious system would be complete without them ...

In fact, at an entirely unacknowledged level, the book is an unwitting endorsement of this view. His de-paganized version of 'Our Lord' or 'the Master', as he sanctimoniously takes care to call Jesus, is decidedly anaemic, a model of English decency. Only when Jesus backslides, as it were, and merges with one of his unwanted pagan counterparts – Dionysos – say does he begin to come to life. The cult of Dionysos fascinated Weigall, and he returns to it later in his *Life and Times of Marc Antony* where, with another glance in the direction of Jesus, it is clearer still how far his sympathies, if not his argument, lay on the pagan side of the question.

Naturally enough, the reviews of *The Paganism in our Christianity* were written by people already aware, more or less, of the research into comparative religion. But the subject was closer to the everyday lives of his readers than anything else he had

316

written (except, in a different way, the local history articles). One H. Russell Cotes from Bournemouth, wrote to thank Weigall for 'relieving me of a number of mental burdens' and J.W. Hamilton from Minnesota thought the book should be read 'by millions in many countries'. M.V. Hughes from Hertfordshire was also 'so deeply impressed', in particular by the chapter on the Resurrection, that he (or she) had written a narrative based on it. There was even a reader who wanted Weigall to write another book along the same lines called "The Paganism in Spiritualism": 'Someone ought to for it is becoming a menace to sanity.'[8]

Weigall would have sympathized with this last letter. His years in Egypt had acquainted him with some bizarre expressions of mysticism, from both Egyptians and Europeans. He once said that no fewer than 14 women had told him in confidence that they were re-incarnations of Cleopatra. Now, after several reprints of his *Life of Akhnaton* he attracted the interest of an esoteric group, the Theosophists, for whom the sun was an important a symbol. A certain Mrs Brettle from Sydney, for example, told him that she was his 'kindred spirit, who possesses the spiritual interpretation of all your Egyptian histories', and continued mystifyingly: 'I couldn't tell it to you or pass it on as an impenetrable veil of the highest knowledge of Theosophy is the lore and logic of the "Highest Spiritual definition" allowed mortal capacity of understanding, if Destiny ordains.' Weigall's reply to Mrs Brettle, or a draft of it, is interesting:

I have some idea of the religious and ethical views which you are trying to inculcate in me, and, in fact, I have a sort of leaning towards them, which would have led me in that direction ere now had it not been for a growing tendency towards a hardboiled practicality and away from all mysticism.[9]

One is reminded of his ambiguously expressed views on the malignancy of ancient Egyptian curses and spirits and again of similar ambiguities in his views about patriotism and race and the political uses of religion.

His next novel, *The Young Lady from Hell*, was written in a thoroughly hard-boiled humour. Here he throws a group of practical jokers into a household gripped by the contemporary craze for Black Magic and fairies and witchcraft and poltergeists. Weigall sets up a crazy plot which feeds the eager credulity of otherwise conventional people with a lunatic succession of incidents: a self-propelling dressing-table, a disappearing chicken leg, a collapsing sofa, peculiar malfunctionings of the electricity system and so on. Perhaps he prolongs the thing a little far; the nonsense seems to intoxicate him, and he keeps it twisting up to the last page.

The critics confessed to laughing out loud in public places, and warned readers to find somewhere private to read it.[10] Like Camilla in *Saturnalia*, Weigall's new heroine was pronounced especially appealing and *The Times Literary Supplement* (12 September 1929) went so far as to commend her to 'everyone feeling the years weigh heavily on them'. These two women belong to a new breed in Weigall's gallery of fictional females. Their men regard them as mates, rather than soul-mates, and although always feminine, they are neither mysterious nor cunning. They no longer yearn for

317

motherhood, nor inspire misty dreams of destiny and racial continuity. Small, neat, slim-hipped, fashionable, they speak their minds and make jokes. Weigall, for various complicated reasons, even calls the heroine of *The Young Lady from Hell*, William, and makes her get into scrapes, always tripping up and banging into things. To a modern reader she is not a little winsome, like the harum-scarum Cleopatra, but she represents an attempt – the best Weigall could do – to banish the holy dream of Womanhood that had so enslaved him 20 years before.

The Lillie sisters were a strong influence. Deflation was the whole point of Bea Lillie's comedy. Weigall would often have seen her, for example, in one of her most popular skits, dressed as Britannia, with a helmet rakishly tilted over her eyes, roaming the stage and singing:

March with me to the roll of the drum,
March to that rousing tune,
March with me to the call of the fife.
March, March, April, May and June.
Canada! Australia! South Africa!
To merely name a few.
Thirty days hath September
April June and November.
England is proud of you!

For another of her pieces, the curtain would rise to reveal her dressed in a long seductive evening gown, in which she would sing a romantic number. Then, after the applause, she would pick up her skirts and roller-skate off the stage. When Bea bobbed her hair, the new style became her trademark. Muriel never went so far, but her looks were similarly gamine and she shared her sister's ferocious honesty.

It was in this state of mind therefore that he and Muriel decamped for America: tired of the old world, impatient with its values, semi-detached from the family. Judging by the amount of critical coverage given him by the American press, he might well have felt that his public was at least as much American as English, and possibly more so. His comings and goings between New York and Los Angeles were announced as though he were a celebrity – 'Mr Weigall, Egyptologist, farceur, brother-in-law of Beatrice Lillie ...' His sister Geanie felt the full impact of his American fame once when she spent a holiday in Brittany with a woman who entertained both the English and American sets there:

Half the villas are owned by Americans ... and of course I am loudly announced as Arthur Weigall's sister and pounced upon and nearly eaten in their desire for information about you ... they have all read all your books and breathlessly await the last masterpiece ... They all know much more about you than I do! and ask obscure questions about Egyptology ... the English don't know so much – and Cora [her hostess] introduces me as Sir Archibald Weigall's cousin – you know – he was Gov. of Australia ...

At the same time Weigall never felt quite at home in America. In 1923 he had been impressed by the serious and worthy spirit in which the country used its enormous wealth. Now in the summer of 1929 it was another story. Hollywood money was seriously frivolous. He tells his daughters that he has been:

> trying to write some short stories and articles about this fantastically beautiful place and all the god-darned crowd of drunken lunatics who live here ... They're just like a lot of naughty children who have been given money suddenly and don't know where they are or what to do next ... They all just do their funny acts, and try to make each other laugh and then they all get drunk together, and somebody has to tell them next day that they had a good time ...

Bea's life was among these kinds of people, and since it was largely on her account that they were there at all, Muriel and Weigall were drawn into it, if only on the margins. Muriel, as has been said, was writing songs and working on her operette, and she hoped that her sister would either use the music herself, or get it placed somewhere. Relations between the two sisters were, however, difficult. Muriel was frankly jealous of Bea and adopted a disapproving manner which Bea resented. There is a letter from Weigall to Bea in which he comes loyally to Muriel's defence. Whether he ever sent it is uncertain. It may have been composed, like the one to Petrie long before, 'just to let off steam'. But quite apart from the light it throws on relations between the two sisters, the letter paints an intriguing picture, or rather caricature, of showbiz life. Weigall was at that time, as the letter makes clear, writing a biography of the Roman Emperor, Nero – and one can see why that period of history attracted him.

> Bea, you little daughter of Satan, with your beautiful white body and your burning lips! Muriel and I deeply resent your suggestion that we are respectable people in front of whom you feel uncomfortable. It is a scurrilous lie. Both of us, ever since we can remember, have been utterly depraved, and have habitually lived in sin; and it is a matter of perpetual astonishment to us that we now confine our depravities to the home circle. Our friends are all harlots, adulterers, lesbians, sadists, sodomites, pimps and dope fiends and dipsomaniacs and as we both like getting cock-eyed we have felt very scurvily treated by you because you never give us the opportunity to join you in your satanic revels.
>
> Muriel in particular resents your feeling that she is a spoil-sport and telling your friends that she is. If ever she has appeared to cross-question you or ask you where you are going, it is honestly because she hated being left out of any orgies that were going on; and most of her bitterness about you is due to the fact that you have never contributed one atom to her chances of having a hell of a time – and that's the truth.
>
> But apart from the matter of whoopee, I can't understand how you could have been so heartless as never to have asked your own sister and fellow-sinner to a single meal or other sinful amusement with you, all these six months, nor even to have come in to see what sort of brothel she is staying at or if she is comfortably bedded

out, nor to have shown the slightest interest in this really magnificently erotic operette she and her paramour have written, nor yet to have made a single enquiry about my Sex History of the Beast of the Apocalypse (Nero) which I am writing.

The least you can do, as one demonic Lillie to another, is to ask to come and hear her music before you go. The strange thing is that Muriel loves you very deeply and your indifference cuts her like a knife. She is always wounded. If you can't be bothered to be nice to her, for God's sake send her some dope to deaden the pain you so continually inflict.

Boo, you great big Bacchante.

Here is the modern Weigall – wicked but moral, naughty but nice. But it can't have been fun living with someone who was 'always wounded', and Muriel's temper threw a growing shadow over their lives. In fact it was her quarrelsomeness that Weigall's children particularly remember about her. When he returned for three months to England in the summer of 1930, he found himself in a tangle of awkward relationships among all the women of his family, and there were probably many scenes between himself and Muriel on that account.

Mimi and her husband Tony had by this time moved from Shepherd's Bush to the village of Heston on the outskirts of west London, where in 1927 Tony Craggs became the vicar of St Laurence's church. Geanie was as far out of London on the Kent side, in a rented cottage at Holmwood, which she knew well from her days at Vigo Farm with Olive Chaplin. Weigall and Muriel took a flat in central London from where they could keep in touch with everyone. But as he explained to his second daughter Zippa, he soon realized that nothing was so simple:

I have great difficulty in managing the various people and their jealousies and peculiarities – Mimi jealous of Alured's being with us; Muriel's jealousy of Alured's being with Mimi; Mimi jealous of Muriel and me; Muriel jealous of my being with Mimi; Tony anxious to be nice to Muriel but fearing the parish may be surprised at my matrimonial affairs; Mimi feeling out of it and hurt if Auntie Geanie and Betty and others congregate at my flat; Auntie Geanie hurt if I don't go down to Holmwood often; Mimi hurt if I do go there often; and so on and so on!

Meanwhile I am working hard at my new book *The Life of Marc Antony* which is to follow my *Nero* – and for a large part of each day I am living my own strange life in ancient Rome, with the door shut behind me on the present. In fact whenever things become too utterly impossible here ... I disappear mentally into Antony's house, and have a chat with him about the strange ways of women..

The 'American' pair made a commotion in the family wherever they went. When they went to stay at Holmwood, Geanie told her niece Veronica that they 'arrived with 14 boxes and a writing table at 11:30 at night!':

Since then, the cottage has swelled with their music and laughter. Muriel has the loft, where she composes everything except herself – and your father surrounded by books and writing sits in the window of the spare room and evidently gets inspiration from the cabbage patch their room overlooks. My attempts to induce them to come to meals are part of the day's work. I hammer on the gong at intervals for half an hour before food appears … I am now quite used to my door being flung open and each member of the party [Jack Rutter her semi-estranged husband, and Betty were both staying too] appearing in turn with their special grievance – Why is the bath water cold? … Why can't we have lunch at three? Why is it raining when the climate of America is so perfect …

Clearly Weigall's old habits of punctuality had loosened since Langdale House. Zippa and Veronica were 16 and 15 respectively when they received these confidential gossipy letters. It seems that as the members of the older generation became more strained in their relations with one another, they turned to the younger generation for relief.

Weigall's biographies of Nero and Marc Antony in 1930 and '31 were followed quickly by biographies of Sappho and Alexander in 1932 and '33. He worked with prodigious concentration and efficiency ('things' must often have been 'impossible'), for these are not slight or hasty works. Money too was a problem. He doesn't mention it, but in 1929 came the Wall Street crash, and that Christmas he wrote to his daughters from New York to say that he was writing his life of Nero 'with a calendar in one hand and my bank-book in the other, trying to make both ends meet.' All the same, he was enjoying the work, he said, and found his subject 'a most delightful and loveable character'. 'He poisoned his brother, murdered his mother, kicked his wife to death, set fire to Rome, and so on – so they say; but I interpret him quite differently, and don't believe any of this.'

It was typical of him to take a contrary line. Whitewashing Nero was even more perverse than finding in Cleopatra a pattern of marital fidelity. But it had always been his habit to put the cat among the pigeons.

# Chapter 23

# History again: beating the Philistines
# 1928–1933

What fascinated Weigall about Nero was not so much the moral case, for or against, but something else that had not until then been treated with any seriousness by historians: namely the fact that he was a musician, 'the first ruler in all recorded history', as the modern historian Michael Grant points out, 'and indeed almost the only one of any real importance, to consider himself primarily as a singer and stage performer.'[1]

Weigall puts great stress on 'the artistic temperament' in this biography, and one way and another it is a theme shared by the other biographies he published during the following years. His debunking exercises against the Old Brigade in the years immediately following the divorce were a natural enough reaction. Now he turns his back on them and gives his attention to the more congenial company of people who lived their lives, so he thought, by the light of the imagination.

Looking back, it was what he himself had done for most of his life. One cannot help realizing, as one reads these biographies, how much they are informed by his own character. All his energy and enthusiasm and daring sprang from the same vivid sense of life which – without pressing the analogy too closely – he found in Nero, Antony, Alexander, and more shadowily and tentatively in Sappho. Inevitably, these things cut across the conventional world – how deeply, the divorce and his present life in theatrical circles only served to emphasize – so that there is also in these biographies a sharp sense of contrast: Nero against the stiff-necked senatorial classes of Rome; Marc Antony against much the same, with Octavian to give the contrast extra edge; Alexander not so much against anything as alone with his sense of mystic destiny; and Sappho. ... well, Sappho against the moralizing of history.

As for Weigall, it is difficult to know exactly what his own dreams were at this time; there was no one to whom he was writing letters about them. It is possible that, after the elation of escaping the struggle with Hortense, there was a sudden stillness, like shutting the door on a noisy room. The time for grand schemes and crusades was past. He was writing, true, and at a furious rate. Perhaps that was enough. Besides, being a recognized writer carried its own built-in drag upon the spirit. Correspondence flowed in from readers and students all over the world, much of it requiring careful attention – though one hopes he never answered the woman who asked him to tell her what he thought was the 'greatest thing in life', and which he thought most important, heredity or environment, and please to say why. Many people wanted to know when he was going to publish his third volume of the *History of the Pharaohs*. There were also requests for lectures, and a stream of people wanting to translate his books, or dramatize them, or anthologize passages from them. The letters asking for photographs, autographs and biographical paragraphs for inclusion in compilations of famous authors must have given him a peculiar feeling of dreariness.

The time for consuming love seems also to have passed. Muriel was a fellow worker and could be a good companion. But she was never the passionate inspiration that the young Hortense had been. He had at one time been deeply excited by Alured, whom he believed to have the makings of a real artist. He never gave up hope, but he was bitterly disappointed in the young man's ability to realize his promise. As he wrote to his daughter Zippa:

> You know I love that boy, and it's quite painful to see him trying to say something intelligible, and stumbling over his words, when all the time I know that what's in his mind is worth hearing. He reminds me of primaeval Chaos. I keep thinking of "the Spirit of God moved upon the face of the waters" etc, and I wish to goodness some divine command "Let there be Light" would sound across that Chaos and enable him to see what he means and *say* it.

The same was true of his painting. Weigall had been sorry when Alured had dropped out of the Slade, and the only other practical thing he could suggest was set-design. When he and Muriel moved to London from New York in 1931, he offered to find him work in that line, and suggested that he try his hand at some scenes for Muriel's operette. Alured refused. Instead, he designed some sets of his own, with no connection to any particular play, but even these were few and took him ages to finish. The results were very beautiful, but Weigall realized that whatever the nature of his son's creativity, without that 'rush of ideas' he remembered so well in his own case, he would never be able to make a living out of it.

The truth was that Alured had had a breakdown not long before, and no one had known how to deal with it, beyond giving him what was known as a 'rest cure' – that is, putting him to bed and keeping him virtually in isolation in the care of a nurse. It doesn't seem to have done him much good. Geanie described the situation for Hortense. Alured, she said, was:

> a pathetic figure. Arthur says he has great talent – but the poor thing *can't* work – he falls asleep … altho' he spends hours over his table, he gets no further and the fact is he *can't* work … He is unhappy and looks white and blinking – and the *loneliness* of his soul is to my mind a tragedy … At the same time, it *isn't his fault*, I am sure of this. He can't help himself, and no one can help him.

It was a wretched time for both father and son. Weigall's 'cure' for his own breakdown had always been work and more work. Beyond that, he was out of his depth. He had told his daughter Zippa that he shut himself up with the ancient world as a relief from the jealousies of his wife, mother and sister. Perhaps it was a relief too from watching the slow, private torture of his son's soul.

For here were extrovert, vivid men and women, like himself, who plunged at life regardless. Nero was perhaps the most outrageous of them, neglecting the highest office in the whole of the civilized world for the stage, for poetry, for painting, sculpting, collecting works of art, and, after the fire of Rome, for his new palace surrounded by an Arcadian landscape made to his own design: 'Nobody but a poet,' wrote Weigall, 'would have thought of turning the centre of imperial Rome into a Garden of Eden.'[2] The old-fashioned patrician classes were scandalized by their Emperor, and deeply unimpressed by his establishment of Greek-style festivals for the arts and athletics. They got their revenge in the later accounts of their partisan historians, who blackened Nero's name even before the early Christian writers punished him for his persecution of their sect by naming him the Beast of the Apocalypse and Antichrist.

Weigall was not the first to question the impartiality of the Roman historians – Tacitus Suetonius and Dio Cassius. Long before, in 1863, a certain G.H.L. (presumably George Henry Lewes, the consort of George Eliot) had published in the *Cornhill Magazine* an article called, 'Was Nero a Monster?'[3] Looking dispassionately at the classical accounts, he had concluded that there was little in them that would stand the test of scientific proof. As it happens, G.H.L. was not concerned with the case for Nero, his article being really about the nature of scientific evidence and only about Nero by way of illustration. But he does say that if he had wanted to prove that Nero was 'a kind, gentle and in many respects admirable ruler', he could without much difficulty 'cite testimonies from his accusers which would somewhat stagger the reader.'

Forty years later in 1903, the historian B.W. Henderson took up the challenge, at least in respect of Nero's rule.[4] He doesn't go so far as to exonerate Nero himself, though he does note that he was not as cruel and bloodthirsty as some of his forebears. His main object is to show that under Nero the Roman Empire was, on the whole, relatively well governed. Neither G.H.L. nor Henderson give much space to Nero's artistic endeavours, beyond citing them as the reason for the odium in which he was held by the conservative, senatorial element in Rome. In order to bring home the horror and disgrace in Roman eyes of an Emperor who sang professionally on the public stage, G.H.L. asks his readers to imagine an acrobatic, tightrope-walking archbishop. Henderson is less picturesque, but he has little time for Nero's art. Coarse and brutal though the Romans were, he says,

> in the final issue ... there was a reasonableness in the Roman opposition to Nero's degenerate Hellenism, and in the Roman instinctive hatred of that Greek influence which should first corrupt and then divide the Roman Empire.[5]

Here was grist to Weigall's mill, and he took up the cause of Nero's Hellenism with enthusiasm.

Tacitus and his fulminations against the softening influence of music, the dangers of amorous dalliance, and 'the degradation of ... stage scenery' were a gift to Weigall.

From his relish in ridiculing him, one might almost think Nero was a modern, up against the dinosaurs of philistinism. It was a quality often noticed by the critics: the *Sunday Times* (24 September 1933), for example, reviewing his *Alexander*, said that 'Mr Weigall's ... aim is ... to show history to be the kind of thing that is always happening and will always happen'; and the critic for *Current Literature* (December 1931) said of his *Marc Antony* that 'it seems as if it all occurred last week'.

It was the pervasive atmosphere of his histories, conveyed in the very language Weigall used. Here, for example, he is describing the attitude to the new Emperor Nero of the young dandies and satirists of the time – the circle round Petronius, author of the *Satyricon*:

> They believed that he was not at all one of themselves: he was apparently a pious young man, entirely under the thumb of his virtuous and puritanical mother. He was not at all fashionable; he had no idea how to spend his money; the palace menage ... was deplorably stodgy and inelegant: in a word, he was ... probably a shocking Philistine. Yet Terpnus [a teacher of music and singing] was now telling them, on the contrary, that he was by nature an artist ... a romantic young fellow longing to break away from his humdrum life. The world of fashion was greatly intrigued ...[6]

The writing has a voice in it, in this case a slightly camp voice to match the fashionable young men: 'No *idea* how to spend his money ... dep*lo*rably stodgy ... *shock*ing Philistine ... *long*ing to break away.' It was not to everyone's taste, least of all to those who worried about the dignity of history. But dignified history – especially in school textbooks – had got itself a name for being 'stodgy' and there were many critics, including the one for *Current Literature*, for whom Weigall's histories were a breath of fresh air.

It was Weigall's habit to drive an argument to its limits. There is never any hidden agenda. As one critic said of him, he is like 'a brilliant barrister defending a doubtful case.'[7] This was of his Nero, but he is transparently partisan in *Marc Antony* too, where he clearly loathes Octavian and finds Cicero vain and self-serving. It is both his weakness and his strength. In pursuit of his case, he masters his brief and ransacks the sources for every piece of evidence he can find; his reading is therefore wide and thorough, and his books crammed with information and argument.

At the same time he must have it all ways. In Nero's case, for example, it is not enough that he should be an 'artist', but he must be good too. Or if not exactly good, then better than some of his predecessors – not difficult. He is not content with the fact that Nero murdered his mother Agrippina, for example, but he must show that it was really an act of mercy, to protect her from the public disgrace of being tried by the Senate for the murders that she was almost certainly about to commit. Weigall always manages to sound plausible, and he makes a good sentimental drama out of that episode. But one is not surprised at the scepticism of some of the reviews.

All the same, the *Sunday Times* (14 September 1930) hailed it as:

325

a human and historical document of singular value, such as no student of either history or of character should allow to pass unread, and such as perhaps no other historian now living could have accomplished.

And the idea was echoed in many other places, on both sides of the Atlantic:

> Whether we accept it or not, there can be no doubt about the quality of Mr Weigall's book. It is a brilliant book from start to finish, crammed with historical figures that are made to live again, and more thrilling than most novels.[8]

If the critics sometimes disagreed with his conclusions, they applauded the panorama, the great spread of people and plot he passed through on the way. Although he was writing for a popular audience, these books are not altogether light reading. Weigall is painstaking, and he asks his reader to follow him through intricate family trees, complicated factional alignments and realignments – in *Marc Antony*, he goes back 50 years before the birth of his protagonist, to the time of the Gracchi – through military engagements, tactics and plans of battle and, especially in *Alexander*, great stretches of geography. For all the human interest and vivid quotation, it is solid fare.

And, in a sense, even the vividness is solid. There is very little purple padding in these biographies – no room for it, in the dense weave of sources. As the *Bookman* (October 1933) noted of his *Alexander*:

> It reads like gossip. Until – after a glance at his references – one realizes that he has assembled everything that is known: the high words of statesmen, the final words of inscriptions, the chosen words of literature, down to the chat of the market place, a rude story, a popular song. All this he has gathered up, woven into its relations; until the whole appears like some huge embroidery, a tapestry, a display, with every intricacy, each scene, each turn of character or fate.

Everything interests him: an old tragedy about Nero's wife Octavia, for example, written by or based on the papers of his adviser Seneca. This is dismissed by Henderson as 'dismal and prosaic',[9] but in Weigall it becomes a significant document. A detail such as the name that Alexander gave to his first-born son is made to throw a sudden light:

> Had Alexander regarded himself as primarily King of Macedonia he would probably have named this first-born son of his after one of the great Macedonian kings – Karanos, Perdikkas, Amyntas, Philip or Alexander, for instance. In calling the child Hercules, however, he gave him a name which, having an almost universal application, befitted a king of vastly wider realms. In Egypt Hercules was recognized as one of the great hero-gods; in Crete he was highly honoured; in Phoenicia and Carthage he was identified with Melqarth; and even in far-off India he was said to be worshipped; while throughout Greece and the Greek colonies overseas he was regarded as the divine son of Zeus.[10]

But the reviewer for the *Near East* ( 28 September 1933), shook his head: 'This is not the way in which a serious historian writes.' Like his biography of Cleopatra, it was too full of speculation.

And just as in that biography Weigall saw significance in what others regarded as aberrant (Caesar's delay in Egypt, for example), so again he had a way of highlighting 'side-shows'. Hence Nero's music, or Alexander's visit to the oracle at Siwa in Egypt; or Antony's failure to cultivate Rome and win the imperial prize. Why, asks Weigall, after the death of Julius Caesar, when Antony and Octavian became rivals for power, did Antony concentrate his energies in the East, leaving the future Augustus to consolidate his power in Rome?

> In my opinion the answer is to be found in the statement of Suetonius that Caesar had often thought of transferring the capital of the entire Roman world to Troy, in northwestern Asia Minor, or to Alexandria, and that Rome was not a city "suitable to the grandeur of the empire".[11]

Weigall goes on to explain that Antony, having been Caesar's protegé and confidant and having possessed himself of his papers, may well have shared this notion. The countries to the west and north of Italy had never interested him. But along the eastern borders of the Mediterranean were:

> the wealthy and ancient cities and lands of Greece, Macedonia, Thrace, Asia Minor and Syria – and south of Syria, Egypt – which together formed a teeming hive of human activity ... In this rich and busy eastern area he had made himself fully acquainted with mighty cities such as Athens, Ephesus, Tarsus, Tyre, and Alexandria; and Italy had become to him but a faraway limb of this pulsing body.[12]

As Weigall tells it, Rome begins to seem like an irrelevance even to the reader. And when Antony sets his sights on Parthia, like Caesar before him and Alexander before them both, one sees the whole shape of the Empire changing in his imagination. The possibility that the Roman world might have shifted its centre of gravity eastwards fascinated Weigall here just as it had done in the story of Cleopatra and Caesar.

But what drew him to Antony in particular is something that Caesar never had – a Dionysiac quality that, in his view, aligned him emotionally and imaginatively with the east. Plutarch, not altogether approvingly, describes Antony's grand tours through Greece and Asia Minor as Bacchic, with excesses of all kinds, and actors, musicians and dancers following in his train. Weigall notes Plutarch's doubts, but he cannot help a fellow feeling with the Ephesians who came out to greet him dressed as Bacchantes and hailing him as Bacchus or Dionysus.

Nero as artist, Antony as Dionysus – with Alexander, it was the mysticism of his mother, Olympias. Weigall was not in fact the first to notice Olympias, and the reviewer of the *Times Literary Supplement* (2 November 1933) takes him to task for not mentioning the French historian Georges Radet, who in 1931 had come to much the same conclusion as Weigall. It is very possible that Weigall had not consulted Radet, for although his reading in the ancient sources was exhaustive, the more learned reviewers sometimes rebuke him for ignoring modern scholarship. But Radet apart, it was a novel approach. Olympias was, according to Plutarch, a mystic, if not actually a priestess, a fervent devotee of Bacchus who took part in the orgiastic rites associated with that god. Not only that, but she was the daughter of a king of Epirus (now northwestern Greece) and Epirus was close to Dodona, one of the most sacred oracles of the ancient world. It was dedicated to Zeus, consulted as frequently as Delphi, and twinned, as it were, with yet a third important oracle, at Siwa in Egypt, where the god Ammon was worshipped. Dodona and Siwa were each dedicated to different aspects of the same god: Zeus-Ammon, as he was called by the Greeks.

Weigall goes into some detail about these two gods and their different aspects, about the influence of Egypt on Greek religious beliefs, how it was spread by Greek mercenaries and merchants who had lived in Egypt, and about the temples to Zeus-Ammon in different parts of Greece and Macedonia. Both Olympias and Philip, he concludes, would have been familiar with the conjunction of these two deities. According to Plutarch, on her wedding night the mystically-minded Olympias believed herself to have been visited by Zeus in his guise as a thunderbolt. She also appears to have kept snakes and to have taken them to bed with her, and since a certain species of snake was sacred to the Egyptian god Ammon, the story grew up that she had been impregnated by that god. When Alexander was born, therefore, Olympias, following the tradition that mortal mothers may beget demi-gods, believed him to be the son, not of Philip, but of Zeus-Ammon. If Plutarch's information was right, and she was as passionate a mystic as her participation in the Bacchic rites would imply, Weigall believed her influence on Alexander's development to have been crucial:

> It is usual [he wrote] to regard the stories of his supernatural birth as being inventions introduced into the tale towards the end of his life, or later; but I consider that he was *brought up* in the belief that he was the son of Zeus-Ammon, the Graeco-Egyptian father-god.[13]

Alexander's habit of claiming celestial descent, and of linking himself, on his mother's side, with the semi-divine Achilles, was assumed by some historians merely to be part of his political shrewdness in playing to the gallery. J.M. Bury, whose *History of Greece to the death of Alexander the Great*, was published in 1900 and went into seventeen editions in the first three decades of the century, conceded that:

> It may well be that in Alexander's mind there was a vague notion that there was something divine about his origin, something mystical in his mother's conception, and that, like Achilles, he was somewhat more than ordinary man.[14]

But he lays no particular stress on the idea, and none on Olympias, explaining Alexander's ceaseless quest for dominion as the reasonable consequence of an admittedly extraordinary ambition to Hellenize the known world. The views of W.W. Tarn, in the

1927 edition of the *Cambridge Ancient History*, are also essentially rationalist. When, towards the end of his career, Alexander actually had himself proclaimed a god, Tarn argues that this had:

> no real bearing on his character for his deification had no religious import. To educated Greeks the old state religions were spiritually dead ... it was merely a political measure adopted for a limited political purpose ...[15]

Weigall had lived in a country where belief in superstition and magic still survived. Perhaps his feeling about Alexander was coloured by this, but at any rate, he was inclined to take him at his word, and to see in him a man of mystical imagination, intensely susceptible to the idea of his own miraculousness:

> In an age when the gods were thought not infrequently to beget sons by mortal women the distinction between being inspired and being begotten by a god was slight indeed.[16]

The heroes of these biographies were all public men for whom the world – nothing less – was their stage. For Nero the stage was also his world, and Weigall finds the same sense of theatre in the other two as well. As a historian, he handles them with a confidence and dash to match theirs. But Sappho falls into a different category: a private woman, a poet rather than a performer, and a lesbian. Weigall was on unfamiliar ground.

Sappho's poetry, in spite of being burnt in an early Christian bonfire, had never been entirely lost, and poets – Swinburne in particular – had celebrated her in translations and imitations. But the first scholarly edition of the surviving fragments wasn't published until 1882, followed in 1885 by an English translation of them by H.T. Wharton. From the 1890s onwards a new stimulus to the study of Sappho had come with the discovery at Oxyrhynchus in Egypt of previously unknown poems written on papyri used in making mummy cases. Together with the works of other classical authors who had survived in the same way they were published in the many volumes of the *Oxyrhynchus Papyri*, edited by two English papyrologists, Grenfell and Hunt, and in turn gave rise to further translations and studies during the next two decades. By the time Weigall started his biography of her, her work and life were becoming fairly generally available.

But there was a problem. As one of the syndicated American reviews of Weigall's book put it: 'Today, any reference to Sappho starts a snicker among those who profess to know that she stands for irregular sex relations.'[17] Geanie writing to her brother from Brittany, where so many of Weigall's American fans were entertained, confirmed the point. She told him how breathlessly they awaited his 'latest masterpiece' and how they 'roll the flavour of lesbianism round their tongues in a fever of anticipation – I excited them by saying we thought it might be banned in England and these women wrote off that night for copies.'

This is a reference to the notorious banning in 1928 of the lesbian novel, *The Well of Loneliness* by Radclyffe Hall, on grounds of obscenity. The trials in England and a few months later in America had attracted huge publicity. There had been crowds outside the courthouses, letters of protest from the literary world, everything, in short, to ensure that the book became a best-seller – at least in America where the ban was lifted on appeal. The Weigall children can remember reading it at Mitcham when they were in their teens. Lesbianism, or Sapphism as it was also known, was a part of the literary and artistic scene. But it had not, like male homosexuality, been a criminal offence. The escapades of Vita Sackville West and her various lovers were scandalous perhaps, but that was a privilege of the aristocracy. With a little discretion, lesbian households were tolerated. Weigall would have encountered the phenomenon himself, if only through Geanie.

Over the years Geanie had found herself gravitating more and more towards her women friends. Perhaps she knew men only at their worst: predatory, deceiving, or at best, comic. There is an entry in her Luxor diary which augured ill for any man:

> I do adore waking up here ... It's so lovely not to have a man in bed with me ... Why I ever married I can't imagine. I feel it more than ever here where the very air is full of electricity and life and all things are beautiful and husbands so easily forgotten!

Geanie never did manage to shake her husband Jack Rutter off, even though they were officially separated. He would turn up periodically, a pathetic case, self-pitying and debt-ridden, and Geanie would always give him a roof, even nursing him when necessary. Much of her correspondence with Weigall is about Jack, and how to find him some 'billet' abroad. In fact one of Weigall's more anxious family duties through all the years in Egypt and later was contriving to get Jack jobs and protecting Geanie's finances from him.

During the war Geanie had come to know Olive Chaplin, as has been mentioned, a granddaughter of the actress Ellen Terry. This friendship with Olive is understood by the family to have been lesbian. Through her she met Olive's aunt, Edy Craig, Ellen Terry's daughter, also a lesbian, who lived with Christopher St John (Christabel Marshall) and Clare 'Tony' Atwood, a painter, in a ménage à trois at Smallhythe in Kent where Ellen Terry had a cottage. There was a barn across the way from it, in which Edy produced plays, and Alured remembered being taken there, dressing up as Shylock with his cousin Betty as Portia, and acting scenes from the *Merchant of Venice*. Weigall knew all these people, and may well have met Radclyffe Hall herself, who also knew Edy Craig and her circle at Smallhythe. Olive Chaplin certainly knew her, for she became attracted to her partner, Una Troubridge, who found her 'a darling and very attractive', but remained faithful.[18] It was a small, even cosy, world, and no one of the next generation of Weigalls remembers any sense of scandal about Geanie's part in it. They were allowed to stay regularly with Geanie and Olive during the 'twenties, knew about the shared bedroom, and thought no more about it.

But although Weigall may have been privately unflustered, he would of course have known the attitudes of some of his readers – prurient, as Geanie reported, or outraged. When *The Well of Loneliness* was published, the *Daily Mail* (19 August 1928) had said that it 'would rather give a healthy boy or healthy girl a phial of prussic acid than this novel. Poison kills the body, but moral poison kills the soul.' In such an atmosphere, it is perhaps not surprising that those who wrote about Sappho took refuge in a lofty tone, either refusing to accept that she had been a lesbian at all, or denying that her sexuality had anything to do with her poetry.

Mary Mills Patrick, for example, who wrote a book about Sappho in 1912, thought her to have been 'a woman of high moral ideals' – i.e. not a lesbian. She must have been respectable, moreover, because she was known to have run an academy for young ladies: 'The fact that a man or a woman has been able to hold the position as head of an educational institution has always been considered without question a sufficient proof of integrity.'[19] One notes with interest that Mary Mills Patrick was herself the President of Constantinople College. Edwin Marion Cox, on the other hand, in his introduction to an edition of her poems in translation published in 1924, thought that 'it serves no good purpose to concern ourselves with the morality of her sentiments and conduct. We should rather concentrate our attention on the poetic depth, intensity and value of what she wrote, and upon its philological interest.'[20]

It was therefore with some trepidation that Weigall attempted to walk through this minefield. But before coming to Weigall's handling of the subject, there was another huge problem, namely that there was very little to say about Sappho anyway. Hardly anything is known, and what there is, is often so mixed up with legend that one can only guess. Weigall's answer – apart from guessing – was to use Sappho as an excuse for a wide historical and cultural overview of Greece, Asia Minor and the islands during her period, that is to say the end of the seventh and the beginning of the sixth centuries BC.

This he does by way of free association. For example, during Sappho's childhood, Lesbos was at war with Athens. The person who acted as arbiter during the armistice was Periander of Corinth, giving Weigall an opportunity to talk about sixth century Corinth under Periander. The next chapter turns to Athens itself, at the same period, its trade, its system of government, religion, art, the rise of Solon, and among other things his laws relating to women which contrasted with those current in Lesbos. The mention of Sparta in various connections offers another opportunity: a social system and a law-giver, Lycurgus, whose regulations concerning the relations between men and women were different again.

And so on he goes, round the cities and islands, the caves and shrines and temples, calling upon a huge variety of sources for stories and legends about the poets and singers, the philosophers, the rulers, and the travellers who had anything to do with any of these places at the time of Sappho. He brings in his beloved Egypt, and the subject of Egypto-Greek relations that so occupies him in *Alexander the Great*, because a brother of Sappho, Charaxos, exported wine to Naukratis, a Greek colony in Egypt. Sometimes Sappho herself is the excuse, for she visited Sicily, and was said to have gone to Samos, part of the Ionian Confederacy, a league of thirteen Ionian-Greek colonies south of Lesbos off the coast of Asia Minor – which, of course, get a chapter to themselves. And all the time he paints the picture: the mountains and coastlines, the flowers and smells. Circling in closer to Sappho Weigall has chapters on the town and domestic life of the period, containing learned little essays on houses, furniture, clothes, cosmetics, perfumes, food, feast days and music, dances and games. The whole thing is masterly, dense with information and yet passed off with apparent ease.

In among it all is Sappho, her circle of pupils, called her *hetaerae*, and her poetry – every surviving piece of which he manages to quote. Here Weigall's touch falters – not so much about the poetry, whose qualities he points out with discernment, and whose fierce passion he does not deny. But, although Weigall rejects Mary Mills Patrick's 'moral purity', he does introduce a shibboleth of his own: namely, refinement. All the places in her poems which mention soft clothes, bright colours, sweet smells, rose buds, nectar and so on, are pressed into service, together with all the charming possibilities of wood-land music and grassy dancing. What emerges is a 'strange, dark, dainty little person with … purple-black hair and … bewitching smile … a woman of such delicate and faultless refinement and of such intellectual culture that throughout antiquity she was regarded by connoisseurs as the very model of good taste.'[21] That's one way of putting it. She was actually regarded as a good poet. At least Weigall doesn't make her harum-scarum, but he does bring her very close to the other dainty little ladies that he put into his novels – all of whom, incidentally, are a collective swipe at Hortense.

The reason for this, of course, is Sappho's lesbianism. He doesn't shirk it, but he wants to make it tasteful. It may be 'aberrant', 'anomalous' perhaps, even 'unhallowed' – these are all words he uses – but among the flowers and meadows of Lesbos, or under starry skies to the accompaniment of nightingales, what could be less indeli-cate? But he is in difficulties, and his lapse into the old prose-poetry gives him away. On the one hand he must pay lip service to the *Daily Mail*. Sappho's biographer, he says, must approach her love for Atthis (one of her *hetaerae*):

> with hesitation, fearful of some apprehended poison blended in it with its sweet-ness and sorrow, doubting the poison, doubting himself for doubting it, aware that here in truth was love in its most overwhelming radiance, yet conscious too that this love had nothing in nature to justify its frenzy, nothing by which to make a demand upon the sympathies of ordinarily-minded men and women.[22]

On the other hand, he is not entirely 'ordinarily-minded' himself. It is a cunning phrase. He could have said 'healthily-minded', which was common at the time. But 'ordinary' shades easily into 'average' and even into 'mediocre'. No doubt uncon-sciously, he seems to suggest a certain distance between himself and those who cannot sympathize, offering a special dispensation for the unordinarily-minded.

But it is impossible to pin Weigall down. When he comes to the legend of Sappho's love for Phaon, a beautiful young fisherman whose faithlessness caused her, it was said, to fling herself from the Leucadian cliffs, Weigall embraces it eagerly as possible fact rather than fiction:

> This all-conquering passion … had swept through her sultry heart like a fresh breeze from the sea, and had purged it of the last lingering traces of its earlier anomalies, so that nothing now remained therein but a normal feminine instinct far more devastating than its perversity.[23]

And yet, he cannot let the matter rest there. Summing up at the end of the book, he returns to the subject of Sappho's 'anomaly', massaging it this way and that before finally letting it go. First he appeals to the different morality of her age, and warns against anachronism. Then, he tries excluding sexual matters altogether from the realm of moral judgement. As a parting shot, he makes an appeal to aestheticism which brings him round full circle to Edwin Marion Cox's lofty dismissal of Sappho's 'sentiments and conduct': 'Beauty,' says Weigall, '… must be appraised without any regard to the conditions which produce it: that is axiomatic in art … it is by her poetry that she must be judged.'[24]

From the point of view of his public, this equivocation may have been nicely judged. A blurry plethora of argument probably felt safer than a stark challenge. At any rate, he was thought by most critics to have handled the whole subject, as the *New English Weekly* (14 July 1932) put it, 'quietly, tactfully, but with justice to the truth of it all.' *The Lady* (9 June 1932) promised not to say much on the matter, only to warn off anyone hoping to find 'sensational details, about abnormal emotional states'. Having done which, it declared that it could 'joyfully recommend the book'.

A great deal of critical space was given to all these biographies: whole- and half-page spreads with photographs and illustrations in the British and American weeklies, long articles in the dailies there and in South Africa and Australia, scores of smaller pieces in the provincial journals, and when the French and German translations came out, full coverage in those countries too. Much of it is uncritical, enthusiastic retellings of Weigall's story, especially in the case of *Sappho* where many critics also fall into lush imitations of his lyrical style. It is one of the curses of honeyed prose that it so easily inspires saccharine imitators.

Taking it all together, the critical with the uncritical, the reviewers of *Sappho* gave him an easy ride. Even the *Times Literary Supplement* (16 June 1932), which complained that Sappho 'is no more than a date, a peg', conceded that the book was interesting for:

the freshness with which the atmosphere of the sixth and seventh centuries BC is reconstructed, in which Nebuchadnezzar, Sappho, Neco and Solon appear almost side by side.

'A vivid and detailed account of the life in the various States and communities … which went to make the haunting beauty of the early Greek world,' said *Everyman* (19 May 1932), and the *New York Sun* (7 June 1932), echoing the thought less sentimentally, added that 'his chapters on the Ionian life, describing such cities as Miletus and its philosopher inhabitants, are the sorts of things only a man saturated in his field could toss off.' This air of carrying his learning lightly – as 'gaily,' wrote the *Everyman* critic, 'as the youngest hiker his pack' – had always been Weigall's aim, and by typing out that particular review at the head of his publicity list of extracts, it would seem that he valued it above everything else.

# Chapter 24

# Shutting the door
# 1931–1934

During all these years of writing, the difficulty is to see Weigall himself. It is not just that he was no longer writing revealing letters; it is also that one feels that his 'real' self was more present in his books than anywhere else. It was there, alone not only with his characters but with his loyal public that he was most at home, most light-hearted, most sociable. Shutting the door on the present and having a chat with Antony was more than a whimsical manner of speaking. The irony was that Muriel herself was now the whirlwind – or rather the thunderstorm. After years in a marriage where he had been the centre of energy, the boot was on the other foot. Not that Muriel's energy was of the same kind as Weigall's. She merely threw things. Alured remembers him during the St John's Wood period in the garden quite often, writing at a table under the trees and gardening:

> Muriel rested then. There was peace. ... I was on the lawn one day while he mowed it, having developed a quiet back and forth continuous movement which wouldn't disturb her in the room directly above us ... unthinkingly I called out loudly to him 'What's the time?' Seconds later the window was flung up and the big bedroom clock hurled out ...[1]

Just as Hortense had retreated from Weigall, so Weigall retreated from Muriel. One has the impression of him at this time holding himself slightly apart – patient, resigned and faintly amused.

It comes across in his letters to his daughters. They are affectionate in a slightly shy way, mixtures of advice, nonsense and family news, rather in the vein of a favourite uncle than a father. Weigall had never been at home enough to get to know them as they grew up, and one can't escape the suspicion that he didn't especially try because they were 'only' girls. A great deal of thought had gone into Alured, his education and his future. If less thought had been given to Denny, it was only because he was more straightforward. When the family were at Cleveland Square, Weigall had written to Hortense describing his feelings for the two boys – Alured, full of genius he thought, but irritating to distraction; Denny less interesting to him because so much simpler, and yet enormously attractive:

so frank and bold and fearless in looking you straight in the face and getting what he wants by sheer assault. Den is a *beautiful* boy, I think, and has *the most fascinating* smile and wonderful merry rogues eyes, if you know what I mean.

But the girls in this letter are simply that – 'the three girls'. They were seven, eight and nine, and Weigall says nothing more about them beyond the fact that they're well, and 'quite nice'.

Now, in the late 'twenties and early 'thirties, they were in their teens and, in the family tradition, were beginning to write him lively and interesting letters. They had received a patchwork education – governesses, a spell at Wimbledon High School – and were now being 'finished' variously at schools and in families in Switzerland, France, Germany, and for Geraldine, in America as well. It is perhaps surprising that someone in many ways so modern-minded should have cared so little about how they were educated. On the other hand, he had never set much store by a formal, conventional education anyway. Decisions about the three girls seem to have been left largely to Hortense.

By the time he came back from America with Muriel, the girls were slipping out of range, often apologizing for not writing. He too had to apologize. 'I opened your letter in fear and trembling,' he wrote once to his daughter Zippa, 'expecting you to ask me why the dickens I hadn't written to you … Of course, I'm quite impossible as

Weigall's three daughters. From left to right, Veronica, Geraldine and Zippa

335

a father, don't you think? Never mind, I mean well.' In another letter he told her how pretty he had thought her when he last saw her – 'when you do your hair decently, quite charming in fact' – adding with rueful playfulness, 'I took such a fancy to you, and hope that we shall often meet again, and possibly even get to know each other.'

The only real emotion Weigall had for any of his children now was for Alured, and that was a bitter one. Since his father's return from America, Alured had been spending his days with him and Muriel in St John's Wood, miserably trying to make model scenes, and his nights at Heston with Mimi who adored him and made him feel a little less miserable. After a visit to her son one day, Mimi described the situation there for her granddaughter Geraldine:

> Alured, poor dear, is not himself in your father's company – father scolds him so! ... father, being such a worker, has no patience with the hours Alured takes to do a small amount of work ...
>
> However, he has just finished a beautiful scene, and father was so excited and pleased. ... Alured has a holy fear of his father! ... I am very unhappy.

It was a gloomy time for the family as a whole, with everyone very short of money. If Weigall had hoped that divorce from Hortense would release him from financial difficulty, the depression in America and Britain soon put an end to that. A letter to Hortense in the spring of 1932 explains the stark reality:

> My financial position is pretty rocky owing to the general depression here and in America; and for my new book, *The Life of Alexander the Great*, upon which I am now at work, and which is to follow *Sappho* ... I have only managed to get half the advance I got on the previous books. Articles seem to have dried up altogether, and I don't think there is much chance of my earning enough to save me from disaster ... I can just see my way for the next four months ... However one can but peg away and hope for the best ...

Geanie's case was no better. Jack Rutter's tea plantation was failing to pay dividends and 'unless I can raise money on life policies,' wrote Geanie, '– starvation.'

Mimi's unhappiness was not financial, but seemed to her equally apocalyptic. In December 1931 she had a bad fall which left her unable to walk and a prey to bouts of unaccustomed despondency:

> I find my gift for writing has gone and I never write at all in these days [she told Hortense] – I am a great trial to everyone ... such terrible depression – it is in our family – and poor old Arthur suffers with it as you well know ... I am glad to have [Alured] coming in each evening in time for supper and he is so good in helping me ... besides poor dear he seems to know the horrors of nerves and helps me ... but oh dear, he does want some money to buy a shirt or two, some shoes and clothes ... he is one of my causes of *nerves*, my dear.

With the publication of *Alexander the Great* in 1933, Weigall was now at the end of four years of intensive work. One would have thought it was time to pause. But the need for money never let him rest. The long-deferred third volume of his *History of the Pharaohs* was always listed among his publications as being 'in preparation', and his children say that they remember him at work on it. But first he had another book to see through the press. It will be remembered that one of the reviews of his *Sappho* had said that he carried his learning 'as gaily as the youngest hiker his pack'. It seems that the gaiety of his books was almost in inverse proportion to the desperation of his life. Now, anxious and hard up as he was, he produced the most light-hearted book he had ever written and the one for which he was most remembered after his death – *Laura was my Camel.*

It is a collection of stories about the animals he lived and worked with in Egypt: his aggrieved camel, Laura; his demented horse, Filfil; his amorous donkey, Cicero (who, like the Roman orator, loved the sound of his own voice); his clownish dog Pedro, and his holy cat, Basta, named after the goddess who was believed in ancient times to be incarnated in cats. In the course of describing these animals Weigall conjures up his old Egyptian life again, not romantically this time, but at its most cock-eyed and farcical. Laura was the beast that carried him on all his desert expeditions, and her antics suddenly throw a new light on those heroic journeys. As he mounted and dismounted 20 times a day to inspect the inscriptions in the rocks, we must imagine Laura watching him 'out of the corner of her eye until she caught me at a disadvantage.' She would scramble off her knees at a touch:

and unless my jump was perfectly timed she would either carry me up with her, hanging perilously by my hands to the saddle with one leg higher than my head, or else, if I had not yet grasped the pommel, up would go my one raised leg and likely as not I would be thrown on my back. If you lift your leg as high as you can and then get someone to jerk your foot upwards you will see what I mean.[2]

The trouble with camels, he said, is that:

they hate being camels, but they would hate to be anything else because in their opinion all other living creatures are beneath contempt, especially human beings. The expression upon their faces as they pass you on the road indicates that they regard you as a bad smell.[3]

But at least she wasn't an embarrassment. Weigall's dragoman duties among the grander tourists were perilous affairs, we discover, for his horse could not endure the fluttering of voluminous garments. Female dignitaries were especially at risk:

One day I found myself trotting politely beside a middle-aged, stout and excessively dignified German princess who was riding side-saddle and was wearing a white linen habit which had evidently shrunk in the wash, so that the buttons were all straining, though the skirt was still pretty long and full. Behind us rode a couple of German officers so stiff with etiquette as to be barely human.

The tossing of her skirt unfortunately caught the eye of Weigall's horse who made a grab at it with his teeth and tugged. The buttons popped, an officer hit the horse on the nose, and the horse bolted. Weigall's written apology received no answer.[4]

Tea in Weigall's Luxor garden could also be fraught. Once Weigall's cat laid a mouse on the plate of a visiting French antiquarian. 'The thing had almost gone into [the Frenchman's] mouth before he saw what it was and, with a yell, flung it into the air':

It fell into his upturned sun-helmet which was lying on the grass beside him; but he did not see where it had gone, and jumping angrily to his feet in the momentary belief that I had played a schoolboy joke on him, he snatched up his helmet and was in the act of putting it on his head when the mouse tumbled out on to the front of his shirt and slipped down inside his buttoned jacket.[5]

Surely some of these tales are embroidered. But they aren't all nonsense. He describes the ghostly duty of riding his horse round the temples and excavations at night, checking on the watchmen:

One night when we were returning home through the pitch darkness at a slow walking pace and both he and I were practically asleep, he stumbled and fell on his nose, and I woke up too late to prevent myself diving over his head ... it was then that Filfil revealed a real sense of comradeship, for he pushed his nose almost into my face, breathed heavily down my neck, nuzzled around my shoulders, and finally gave me a butt in the back with his head which clearly said, "For heaven's sake, get up ..."[6]

It is curious how, in the light of his imminent death, the book reads like a farewell to the places he loved most. The very last tale, in which he returns to Laura, ends on a note of frank nostalgia. He describes motoring with friends along an English country road one summer, half dropping off to sleep. Suddenly something lying on the road catches his attention. Before realizing what it is, the sights and sounds of Egypt break in upon his drowsy mind. A little further on the same thing happens again, and then again, the dazzle of Egypt getting stronger each time, until they round a corner and suddenly, there ahead, he sees:

a travelling circus, and at the tail of the procession, sure enough, there walked three gloomy camels who bleated their inconsolable vexation as, with grinding brakes, we swerved to avoid them.[7]

When the book came out in October 1933, Weigall was already very ill. Just when the *Sheffield Telegraph* (12 October 1933) was telling its readers how 'screamingly funny' it was, and the *Manchester Evening News* (28 October 1933) was chuckling at its 'delightful nonsense', Weigall was in acute pain. Exactly what had happened is explained in an unfinished letter, never sent, to his American agent, George Bye:

It started last June with back-aches and pains like lumbago, which kept me awake at nights; and then in July these pains developed into real spasms in the spine, and I found myself getting weak in the legs. Then the bladder began to get weak, and almost without my knowing it began to get fuller and fuller until suddenly I was in unspeakable agony, and the doctor arrived only just in time to draw off the water before the whole thing might have burst. I am now the world's champion bladderist, for believe it or not they drew off nearly nine pints ...

Well, after that the bladder stopped working altogether; and gradually my legs became paralysed and I took to my bed – tortured by agonies in my spine, unable to sleep and so shattered that I wept most of the time![8]

Muriel at that time had been 'dabbling', as Alured put it, in Christian Science and had refused to involve a doctor. Eventually she did but the trouble was already far advanced. It was October when Weigall wrote this letter, a few days after *Laura* had come out, and at that time he believed himself to be on the mend. He is anxious about not being able to deliver his next book, to be called *The Court of the Seven Cleopatras*, and could Bye break the news to the publishers and tell them it will be ready in the spring. Also could he tell Macmillan's that they can only have his *History of Egypt* if they can guarantee $500 in advance. This must have been volume three of his *History of the Pharaohs*. Soon after this letter, however, he had a relapse, and by the end of November there was talk of surgery.

Finally, in December he was moved to the London Hospital for an operation. It was a tumour and the family believes it to have been cancerous. For the next few days there was a constant coming and going of family. Weigall's daughters remember him calling for Hortense, and asking Geraldine to telephone her to come. He must have realized he was dying, and have wanted to make his peace with her. But the presence of Muriel paralysed them, for they feared a scene. Mimi, who was ill, came one day with Geanie, and Alured remembers being with them when they arrived:

Immediately inside the door, I stopped a nurse, asked how he was and she said, 'He's dead.' Pneumonia; 'but he never would have walked again'. It was a wretched party that came to Geanie's flat before separating to our different homes. Mimi and Muriel in tears, Muriel saying, 'I would have pushed him in a wheeled chair round the world' ... Back [home] Hortense had gone to bed. 'How is he?' she asked. I told her. She whispered, 'Oh my God,' and nothing more.[9]

Weigall was just 53 when he died. His last illness was extraordinarily intense, and his end rapid. It was like him.

Two months before, he had been planning and negotiating for his next books. And so it might have gone on – book after book with glamorous or notorious protagonists to catch the popular market, and perhaps soon the third volume of his *History of the Pharaohs*. But Zippa remembers him saying to her once in the St John's Wood garden that something had gone from his life. He had always taken intense pleasure in everything about him, trees, sunsets, the light, but now he had no feeling for these things.

He had nothing to live for, he said. Without intensity of feeling Weigall's life would have been a kind of death. It is fitting that he should have gone off abruptly then, and equally fitting that Egypt should have had the last word.

But Egypt, or at least Tutmania, played a posthumous trick on him. As we have seen, the newspapers seized the opportunity to run the story of the curse of Tutankhamun, and to suggest that Weigall was the latest victim. And there was more to come. For, on the 4th January 1934, the *Daily Express* ran a piece quoting the view of a 'famous Egyptologist' on the real cause of Weigall's death. The 'famous Egyptologist' turned out to be Ernest Wallis Budge, now Sir Ernest, of the British Museum, whose misla-belling of objects in the Egyptian galleries had so shocked Weigall more than 30 years before.

The article, by a certain Winifred Loraine, quoted Budge as saying: 'It is my firm belief that Arthur Weigall died the unfortunate victim of a curse. It was not, perhaps any royal curse, but one self-induced.' And Loraine adds this statement:

Mr Weigall, Inspector of Antiquities to the Egyptian Government when Lord Carnarvon discovered the tomb of Tutankhamun, died in penury in a London hospital as a result of hashish-eating and addiction to other drugs.

In the course of the rest of the piece, Budge is quoted again:

'Arthur Weigall ... was a disappointed man at the time of the Lord Carnarvon and Howard Carter excavations of the Tutankhamun tomb. He had tried to obtain employment under Lord Carnarvon which would permit him to conduct the exca-vations. His negotiations failed. Carter was chosen to conduct the work ... difficul-ties and failures obstructed the path of Arthur Weigall ever since the Tutankhamun discovery. He seemed to be the victim of some queer fate that never left him alone ... He died, I believe, the unfortunate victim of the curse of the failure and hard-ship which he himself had wished for others.'

The charge of drug-taking may have been a shot in the dark on Budge's part, on the assumption that since the theatre and film world were known for it – see Weigall's comic letter to Bea Lillie – the mud might be made to stick. The *Express* however seems to have got cold feet, for another edition of the paper omitted it and also the remark about Weigall wishing failure and hardship on others. However, it repeated the statement that Weigall was a disappointed man, that he had sought employment under Lord Carnarvon, and the slur – for it was intended as such – that he had died in penury. Two days later, it followed up with a long inside piece about superstition, developing Budge's idea that Weigall was haunted by a private curse, and incoher-ently rambling into a comparison between Weigall and Hamlet and Shakespeare. All of these men, says the journalist, were souls tortured by doubt, by the conflict between the material and the spiritual world, and all suffered from 'paralysis of the will'.

For once Muriel had cause to explode. She took herself with Alured directly to Budge and, as Budge wrote to the news editor of the *Express*:

> raved and stormed and threatened until I was tired ... At length thank God, they went. I never want to hear Weigall's name again and was his best friend as well as helper. ... Thornton Butterworth publisher might be able to tell you things ...[10]

The family was mystified as well as wounded. Alured wrote to the *Express* to point out the facts: that his father had retired from the post of Inspector in 1914 at a time when Howard Carter was already in charge of Carnarvon's excavations, and that he had never negotiated for employment under Carnarvon. Furthermore, he wrote, 'in view of his great output and vitality such phrases as "paralysis of the mind" are beyond comprehension.'[11] Muriel demanded an apology from the *Express* and a contradiction to the effect that there was no evidence of Weigall's death being the result of drug-taking, and that the period after the discovery of the tomb of Tutankhamun, far from being one of difficulty and failure, was marked by 'his most successful and highly paid work'.

*The Express* however declined to print it, and Muriel started proceedings for libel against the paper, claiming damages. Her solicitors duly applied to Thornton Butterworth in order to obtain whatever it was that Budge had hinted at, and received this baffled reply:

> Your remarks hereon and the copy of a letter from Sir Ernest E.A. Wallis Budge to the *Daily Express* of the 12th January 1934 come to me as a great surprise. I haven't seen Sir E.A.W. Budge for ages, I may say years. Furthermore I have never even heard it hinted that Weigall took drugs and I certainly have not heard 'any of the other nasty things that people have said'. I am entirely in the dark, and you may convey to Mrs Weigall this statement which I have made and made emphatically.[12]

Budge's animus against Weigall recalls Carter's. It is difficult to avoid the thought that it arose from professional resentment. In his outspokenness against the expropriation of Egyptian antiquities Weigall stood against everything that Budge stood for. Like Carter, Budge was also, personally, a difficult and cantankerous man and there were others who had crossed swords with him at one time or another. Petrie's name for him was 'Bugbear'.[13] One of Weigall's old detractors, the American scholar Herbert Winlock, who had written so gleefully in 1913 about Weigall's posting to a place where there were only a lunatic asylum and a water purification plant, had experienced the unpleasant side of Budge once when he was working in the British Museum. He wrote about it to Newberry, Weigall's old mentor:

> I think I happened to say to you last Sunday that I had never seen the disagreeable side of Budge. It may amuse you to know that yesterday I was treated by Sir Ernest

to 15 minutes worth of … the most ill bred bit of manners I have ever found in anyone who held a scientific position. It may amuse you because you know of other cases I believe, but for me it was thoroughly unpleasant …

Winlock had come across him in one of the galleries and had made a request to take some photographs for he needed 'uniform photographs of a series of coffins in London, Paris and Cairo'. Budge told him that he was always getting 'damn fool requests', and that Winlock was 'like all Americans trying to paint the lily and he for one wouldn't countenance such idiotic work.' He then began to talk sneeringly about foreigners and their 'unreasonable demands' – '"especially Germans and Americans, who it would seem were all thoroughly Germanized now"':

> It was a question then of hitting his puffy pink face or leaving and I took the cowardly course and said I preferred to drop the conversation and walked out of the Museum leaving him the centre of an admiring little group of sightseers who had beheld the British Lion blast the Germanized foreigner … I must say, so long as you have such a person at the head of your biggest institution I think you should look on Lacau [grumbled at for his strict anti-export laws] as a god sent angel of light. Lacau is difficult but he is a gentleman and Budge turns out to be a vulgar, ill-bred boor.[14]

During the summer of 1934 Muriel's solicitors assembled her case against the *Express* and by September the newspaper climbed down. They offered Muriel an out of court settlement of £500 and a public apology. Her solicitors gave their opinion that if she decided to continue proceedings she had a good chance of winning and of being awarded damages in the region of £1000.[15] But Muriel by then had had enough and settled. The apology duly appeared, somewhat grudgingly, in the *Express* for 22 October 1934. At last the family could lay Weigall's ghost to rest.

It had been an extraordinarily intense and crowded life, enough for several lives taken at a more ordinary pace. Once, in a letter to his son, Weigall had advised him always to think of himself 'as a potential force in the world'. The phrase seems to come straight out of the Victorian world into which he was born, but he used it like a born radical. He lived in a state of almost continuous battle. Whether the adversary was archaeological maladministration, the scholarly closed shop, the dealers and exporters of antiquities, the Establishment, the Church, whatever it was, he took them all on with a passionate belief that right was on his side.

At the same time, what appears to have struck people most about him, both personally and in his books, was his charm and good humour. During his life he would often receive letters from people he had never met who told him that, through his books, he had become their friend. Alan Gardiner had written about Weigall to his wife from Egypt, and in his obituary for the *Journal of Egyptian Archaeology* he wound up a generous account of his work on the same personal note: 'He had a highly original personality and was a delightful companion. No one could be dull in his company or fail to be amused by his witty and unusual outlook on things.'[16]

Though Weigall was born into the high imperialism of the 1880s, he died just as the Empire was beginning to unravel. Tutankhamun was in effect his turning point, the moment when western archaeology was obliged to get down off its high horse. Perhaps it took precisely Weigall's combination of radicalism and good humour to see it as such. He had always been an outsider, belonging and not belonging – in Mimi's slums, at school, among the Egyptologists and later in the theatre. As he said in his novel, *The Not Impossible She*, part of him wanted to be indistinguishable from the world, but in fact his feelings were all the other way. It makes him both of his time and ours. He could pass, as it were, in the fixed and formal circles of his day, the universities, the professions, the clubs and the 'best people'. But ultimately, in the face of any closed shop that mattered to him, his instinct was to break cover and, regardless of consequences, blow it open.

# Appendix

# The concession allowing Theodore Davis to dig in the Valley of the Kings

Direction Générale du Service des Antiquités

Autorisation de Fouilles Service des Antiquités

Je soussigné, Directeur Général du Service des Antiquités, agissant en vertu des pouvoirs qui me sont délégués, autorise par la présente M. Théodore M Davis, sujet Américain, résidant à ............... à exécuter des fouilles scientifiques dans la vallée des Rois, dans les terrains appartenants à l'État, libres, non bâtis, non cultivés, non compris dans la zône militaire, cimitières, carrières, etc, et en général, non affectés à un service publique, et aux conditions suivantes:

1 Les travaux de fouilles seront exécutés aux frais, risques et périls de M. Davis par les soins de M. Eduard R. Ayrton; celui-ci ne devra avoir aucune autre occupation, et devra se tenir constamment sur le champs de fouilles;

2 Les travaux seront exécutés sous le contrôle du Service des Antiquités qui aura le droit non seulement de surveiller les travaux, mais encore d'en rectifier la marche s'il le juge utile au succés de l'entreprise.

3 Si un tombeau, ou tout autre monument quelconque, vient à être découvert, M. Ayrton est tenu d'en aviser immédiatement l'Inspecteur en Chef du Service des Antiquités de la Haute Egypte à Luxor;

4 M. Davis aura le privilège d'ouvrir lui même le tombeau ou le monument découvert, et d'y pénétrer le premier.

5 Dès l'instant de l'ouverture, l'Inspecteur en Chef du Service des Antiquités placera sur les lieux le nombre de gardiens qu'il jugera nécessaire.

6 M. Davis, après avoir examiné le dit tombeau ou monument et pris les notes qu'il jugera nécessaire, le consignera à l'Inspecteur du Service des Antiquités ou à tout autre agent que le Service lui aura désigné.

7 M. Davis est tenu de rediger aussitôt un procès verbal indiquant les particularités observées au moment de l'ouverture et la place occupée par chaque objet, en y joignant des photographies et des dessins autant que possible.

8    M. Davis n'aura droit à aucun des objets renfermés dans le tombeau ou le monument découvert; ces objets, ainsi que le monument ou le tombeau restant la propriété du Service des Antiquités. M. Davis se réserve seulement de publier la trouvaille et il sera indiqué dans les catalogues du Musée comme ayant été l'auteur de la découverte.

9    M. Davis, une fois les fouilles terminées, est tenu de remettre à son frais dans un état satisfaisant de nivellement, tous les terrains sur lesquels il aura opéré.

10    M. Davis s'engage en outre:

A  à ne pas prendre d'estampage au papier humide sur les monuments coloriés;

B  à déposer au Musée, et, si possible, à la Bibliothèque Khediviale, un exemplaire des ouvrages, mémoires, tirages à part, receuils de gravures publiés par ses soins sur les objets découverts au cours des ses fouilles;

C  à livrer au Service des Antiquités, dans le délai d'un an à partir de la date ou les travaux auront pris fin: 1$^{er}$ un croquis, ou s'il y a lieu, au jugement du Service, un plan du champs des fouilles qui puisse être publié dans les annales du Musée; 2$^{me}$ une liste sommaire en référant à ce plan et indiquant la position des objets formant un ensemble, tels que sacrophages, barques, statues funéraires, verres, amulettes appartenants à un même sarcophage.

11    Toute infraction de part de M. Davis ou des ses agents, aux conditions ci-dessus énoncées, entrainera de plein droit sans mise en demeure ou formalité quelconque l'annulation de la présente autorisation. Le Service des Antiquités procédant par voie administrative fera cesser immédiatement tout travail et prendra les mesures qu'il jugera nécessaire pour ses interêts et pour la sauvegarde des monuments ou objets qui auraient été déjà découverts au moment de la cessation des fouilles, et ce, sans que M. Davis, ou quelconque de ses agents, ait droit à une indemnité ou à une compensation quelconque de quelque nature que ce soit.

La présente autorisation est valable pour un an à partir du 1$^{er}$ Novembre 1905.

Fait double au Caire le ...............................

Le Directeur Général du Service des Antiquités

Vu et accepté

la présente autorisation                      signé: G. Maspero

signé: Theo M Davis

Directorate General of the Department of Antiquities

Authorisation to dig

I the undersigned, being the Director General of the Antiquities Department, acting by virtue of the powers that have been delegated to me, hereby authorize Mr Theodore M Davis, an American subject resident at ............. to carry out scientific excavations in the Valley of the Kings, in areas that belong to the state, that are unoccupied, not built on, not cultivated, not included in the military zone, and that are not in use as cemeteries, quarries etc, and in general that are not assigned to any public service, subject to the following conditions:

1   The work is to be carried out at the expense and risk of Mr Davis under the care of Mr Edward Ayrton. The latter is not to take on any other commitment and is to be constantly in attendance on the site of the excavation.

2   The work is to be carried out under the control of the Department of Antiquitites, which shall have the right not only to oversee the works but also to correct their progress if it judges that this would be useful for the success of the enterprise.

3   If a tomb, or any other monument of any kind, is discovered, Mr Ayrton is required immediately to notify the Chief Inspector of the Department of Antiquities in Upper Egypt at Luxor.

4   Mr Davis shall have the privilege of himself opening the tomb or monument that is discovered, and of himself being the first to enter.

5   From the moment of opening the Chief Inspector of the Department of Antiquities shall place on the premises the number of guards that he considers necessary.

6   When Mr Davis has examined the said tomb or monument and has taken such notes as he considers necessary, he shall hand it over to the Inspector of the Department of Antiquities or to such other agent as the Department may designate.

7   Mr Davis is required to provide as soon as possible an account of the work, indicating the details that were observed at the time of the opening, and setting out the position of each object, together with as many photographs and drawings as possible.

8   Mr Davis shall not have any right to any of the objects enclosed in the tomb or monument that is discovered; such objects, together with the monument or tomb itself remaining the property of the Department of Antiquities; Mr Davis reserves to himself only the right to publish the finds, and he shall be shown in the catalogue of the Museum as having made the discovery.

9   Mr Davis is required, once the excavation has been completed, to restore at his own expense and to a satisfactory standard, all areas on which he has operated.

10  Mr Davis undertakes further:
A   Not to apply any wet squeeze to coloured monuments;

B To deliver to the Museum, and if possible also to the Khedivial Library, a sample of the works, memoirs, offprints, and editions of prints published under his auspices in relation to the objects found in the course of the excavations.

C To deliver to the Department of Antiquities, within one year of the date at which the works came to an end, 1$^{st}$ a sketch map, or if there are grounds, in the opinion of the Department, a plan of the site of the excavations, that can be published in the Annals of the Museum; 2$^{nd}$ a summary list referring to this plan and showing the position of the objects that form a group, such as sarcophagi, boats, funerary statues, vases, amulets that belong to an individual sarcophagus.

11 Any infraction on the part of Mr Davis or his agents of the conditions that are set out above shall without delay or formality of any kind constitute full grounds for and result in the immediate cancellation of this present authorization. The Department of Antiquities shall take administrative steps to cause all work to cease immediately, and shall adopt all means that it shall consider necessary to its interests and to the preservation of the monuments or objects that will have been discovered at the time that the excavations were stopped, and this without Mr Davis or any of his agents having any right to any indemnity or to any compensation of any kind whatsoever.

This authorization is valid for one year from 1$^{st}$ November 1905.

Made in duplicate at Cairo on ...........................

Director General of the Department of
Antiquities

Seen and accepted

the present authorization                                         signed: G. Maspero

signed: Theo M Davis

# Sources

## ABBREVIATIONS

ASAE: *Annales du Service des Antiquites de L'Egypte*
AW archive: *Arthur Weigall archive*
E.E.F.: Egypt Exploration Fund
G.I. : Griffith Institute, Oxford.
*JEA: Journal of Egyptian Archaeology*
JARCE: *Journal of the American Research Centre in Egypt*
MMA: Metropolitan Museum of Art, New York.
PRO: the Public Record Office, Kew, London.
PSBA: *Proceedings of the Society for Biblical Archaeology*
PSAL: *Proceedings of the Society of Antiquaries of London.*

## MANUSCRIPT SOURCES

The Arthur Weigall archive is held by the author.
The Griffith Institute in the Ashmolean Museum, in Oxford: the correspondence of Percy Newberry, Alan Gardiner and F. Llewelyn Griffith.
The Oriental Institute, The University of Chicago, Chicago: the correspondence of James Breasted.
The Metropolitan Museum of Art in New York: the correspondence of Arthur Mace, Albert Lythgoe, and some correspondence of Howard Carter.
The American Philosophical Society, Philadelphia: a transcription of Emma Andrews's diary, 'Journal of the Bedawin, 1889–1912'.
The Archive of American Art, the Smithsonian Institution, Washington D.C.: the correspondence of Joseph Lindon Smith.
Pembroke College, Cambridge: the papers of Ronald Storrs.
The Middle East Centre, St. Antony's College, Oxford: the diary of the Hon. Mervyn Herbert.
The Public Record Office, Kew, London: correspondence of Lord Cromer.

## BIBLIOGRAPHY

Aldred, Cyril, *Akhenaten, King of Egypt* (1988, revised edition; first published in 1968 as *Akhnaten, Pharaoh of Egypt*)
E.A.Ayrton, 'The Tomb of Queen Thyi', *PSBA* 29 (1907), 85f and 277f
Ayrton, E.R., Currelly, C.T. and Weigall, A.E.P., *Abydos. Part III* (London, 1904)
Baines, John, and Málek, Jaroslav, *Atlas of Ancient Egypt* (Oxford, 1984)
Bell, Martha R., 'An Armchair Excavation of KV55', in *JARCE* XXVII, 1990, pp. 97–137

Bentley, Juliette, 'Akhnaten in the Eye of the Beholder: do changing interpretations of the heretic King reflect contemporary values of his assessors?', in *Amarna Letters; Essays on Ancient Egypt ca. 1390–1310 BC* 3 vols, (San Francisco, 1991–1994), vol II, pp. 7–8.

Booth, Charles, *Life and Labour of the People of London* (London, 1902)

Breasted, James Henry, *A History of Egypt from the Earliest Times to the Persian Conquest* (London, 1906)

Brendon, Piers, *Thomas Cook. 150 years of Popular Tourism* (London, 1991)

Budge, Ernest A.W., *By Nile and Tigris*, 2 vols (London, 1920)

Bury, J.M., *The History of Ancient Greece* (London, 1959 edition)

Campbell, Stella Patrick, *My Life and Some Letters* (London, n.d.)

Clarke, Somers, 'Report as Local Secretary for Egypt', *PSAL*, 23 November 1907 to 24 June 1909. Second Series, vol XXII. 14 May 1908

Clayton, Peter, *The Rediscovery of Ancient Egypt: Artists and Travellers in the 19th Century* (London, 1982).

Cline, Sally, *Radclyffe Hall, a woman called John* (London, 1997)

Cochrane, Charles B., *Showman Looks On* (London, 1945)

Cox, Edwin Marion, *The Poems of Sappho with historical and critical notes, translations and a bibliography* (London, 1924)

Davies, Norman de Garis, *The Rock Tombs of El Armana*, 6 vols (London, 1903–1908)

Davis, Theodore *The Tomb of Siphtah* (London, 1908)

Davis, Theodore, *The Tomb of Queen Tiyi* (London, 1910)

Dawson, Warren R., and Uphill, Eric P., *Who was who in Egyptology* (London, 1972)

Dodson, A.M., 'Kings' Valley Tomb 55 and the Fates of the Amarna Kings' in *Amarna Letters : Essays on Ancient Egypt, ca. 1390–1310 BC* 3 vols, (San Francisco, 1991–1994) vol III, pp. 92–103

Dodson, A.M., 'The Burial of the Members of the Royal Family during the Eighteenth Dynasty', forthcoming in *Proceedings of the Eighth International Congress of Egyptologists* (Cairo, c.2001)

Drower, Margaret S., *Flinders Petrie: a Life in Archaeology* (London, 1985)

Edwards, Amelia, *A Thousand Miles up the Nile* (London, 1877)

Fagan, Brian M., *The Rape of the Nile; Tomb Robbers, Tourists and Archaeologists in Egypt* (New York, 1975)

Ferrero, Guglielmo, *The Greatness and Decline of Rome* 5 vols, translated by Alfred E. Zimmern and H.J. Chaytor (London, 1907–1909)

Gardiner, Alan, 'Regnal Years and the Civil Calendar in Pharaonic Egypt', in *JEA*, (31, 1945), pp. 11–28

Gardiner Alan, *Egypt of the Pharaohs* (Oxford, 1961)

Grant, Michael, *Nero* (London, 1970)

Griffith, F.Ll. (editor), *Egypt Exploration Fund. Archaeological Reports* (London, 1906–10)

Hall, H.R., *Ancient History of the Near East* (London, 1913; eighth revised edition 1932)

Henderson, B.W., *The Life and Principate of the Emperor Nero* (London, 1903)

Hoving, Thomas, *Tutankhamun, the Untold Story* (London, 1979)

Hughes-Hallett, Lucy, *Cleopatra: Histories, Dreams and Distortions* (London, 1990)

James, T.G.H., *Howard Carter: the Path to Tutankhamun* (London and New York, 1992)

Lauer, Jean-Philippe, *Saqqara, the Royal Cemetery of Memphis; Excavations and Discoveries since 1850* (London, 1976)

Lees-Milne, James, *Harold Nicolson, a biography, 1886–1929* (London, 1981)

Lewes, George (G.H.L.), 'Was Nero a Monster?' in *The Cornhill Magazine*, July-December 1863

Lillie, Beatrice, *Every Other Inch a Lady* (New York, 1972)

Loti, Pierre, *Egypt*, trans. W.P. Baines ( London, 1909)

MacCallum, M.W., *In Memory of Albert Bythesea Weigall* (Sydney, 1913)

Macgill, J.W. and Weigall, Mrs Arthur, *Seeking and Saving, being the Rescue work of the Manchester City Mission* (Manchester, 1889)

McIlney, David B., *A Gentleman in Every Slum; Church of England Missions in East London, 1837–1914* (Pennsylvania, 1988)

Mansfield, Peter, *The British in Egypt* (London, 1971)

Maspero, Gaston, *Les Temples Immergés de la Nubie* (Cairo, 1911)

Montserrat, Dominic, *Akhnaten: History, Fantasy and Ancient Egypt*, (London and New York, 2000)

Morris, James, *Heaven's Command; an Imperial Progress* (London, 1979)

Morton, H.V., *Through Lands of the Bible* (London, 1938)

Munro, H.H. [Saki], *The Chronicles of Clovis* (London,1911)

Newberry, Percy, *Life of Rekhmira, Vezir of Upper Egypt under Thothmes III and Amenhotep II circa 1471–1448 BC* (Westminster, 1900)

Nicolson, Harold, *Some People* (London, 1927)

Oman, Charles, *Seven Roman Statesmen of the Later Republic* (London, 1902)

Parker, Richard A., *The Calendars of Ancient Egypt* (Chicago, 1950)

Patrick, Mary Mills, *Sappho and the Island of Lesbos* (London, 1912)

Petrie, W.M.Flinders, *A History of Egypt*, 3 vols ( London, 1894–1896)

Petrie, W.M.Flinders, *Abydos. Part I* (London, 1902)

Petrie, W.M. Flinders, *Methods and Aims in Archaeolgy* (London, 1904)

Petrie, W.M. Flinders, *Seventy Years in Archaeology* (London, 1931)

*Rapports sur la Marche du Service des Antiquites de 1899 a 1910* (Cairo, 1912)

Rattigan, Frank, *Diversions of a Diplomat* (London, 1924)

Reeves, Nicholas, *The Valley of the Kings: the decline of a Royal Necropolis* (London and New York, 1990)

Reeves, Nicholas, *The Complete Valley of the Kings* (London, 1996)

Rohl, David, *A Test of Time* 2 vols (London, 1995–1998)

Romer, John, *The Valley of the Kings* (London, 1981)

Rose, John, *Tomb KV39 in the Valley of the Kings: a Double Archaeological Enigma* (Bristol, 2000)

Ross, E. Denison, *Both Ends of the Candle* (London, 1943)

Sassoon, Siegfried, *The Old Huntsman* (London, 1917)

Saterlee, Herbert, *J. Pierpont Morgan; an Intimate Portrait* (New York, 1939)

Sayce, Archibald Henry, *Reminiscences* (Oxford, 1923)

Short, Ernest and Compton-Rickett, Arthur, *Ring up the Curtain; being a Pageant of English Entertainment covering half a century* (London, 1938)

Sitwell, Osbert, *Great Morning* (London, 1948)

Sladen, Douglas, *My Long Life* (London, 1939)

Smith, Joseph Lindon, *Tombs, Temples and Ancient Art* (Oklahoma, 1956)

Steevens, George, *Egypt in 1898* (Edinburgh and London, 1898)

Storrs, Ronald, *Orientations* (London, 1937)

Tarn, W.W., in vol VI, of J.B.Bury, S.A.Cook, F.E.Adcock, (editors) *The Cambridge Ancient History* (1927 edition)

Tatham, John, *Borough of Salford: Annual Report of the Medical Officer of Health for the Year 1886*

Taylor, A.J.P., *English History, 1914–1945* (London, 1965)

Thompson, Kristin and Bordwell, David, *Film History, an Introduction* (New York, 1994)

Tyndale, Walter, *Below the Cataracts* (London, 1907)

Tyndale, Walter *An Artist in Egypt* (London 1912)

Weigall, Arthur, *Die Mastaba des Gem-ni-kai* (Berlin, 1905)

Weigall, Arthur, *Report on the Antiquities of Lower Nubia (from the First Cataract to the Sudan Frontier) and Their Condition in 1906–7* (Oxford, 1907)

Weigall, Arthur, *Travels in the Upper Egyptian Deserts* (Edinburgh and London, 1909)

Weigall, Arthur, *The Life and Times of Akhnaton, Pharaoh of Egypt* (London, 1910, revised ed., 1922)

Weigall, Arthur, *A Guide to the Antiquities of Upper Egypt* (London, 1910)

Weigall, Arthur, *The Treasury of Ancient Egypt* (Edinburgh and London, 1911)

Weigall, Arthur and Gardiner, Alan, *A Topographical Catalogue of the Tombs of Thebes* (1913)

Weigall, Arthur, *The Life and Times of Cleopatra* (London, 1914)

Weigall, Arthur, *A History of Events in Egypt from 1798 to 1914* (London, 1915)

Weigall, Arthur, *Madeline of the Desert* (London, 1920)

Weigall, Arthur, *Bedouin Love* (London, 1922)

Weigall, Arthur, *The Glory of the Pharaohs* (London, 1923)

Weigall, Arthur, *Tutankhamen and Other Essays* (London, 1923)

Weigall, Arthur, *Ancient Egyptian Works of Art* (London, 1924)

Weigall, Arthur, *The Way of the East* (London, 1924)

Weigall, Arthur, *The History of the Pharaohs 2 vols* (London, 1925–1926)

Weigall, Arthur, *The Not Impossible She* (London, 1926)

Weigall, Arthur, *Wanderings in Roman Britain* (London, 1926)

Weigall, Arthur, *Wanderings in Anglo-Saxon Britain* (London, 1927)

Weigall, Arthur, *The Grand Tour of Norman England* (London, 1927)

Weigall, Arthur, *Saturnalia in Room 23* (London, 1927)

Weigall, Arthur, *The Paganism in our Christianity* (London, 1928)

Weigall, Arthur, *Flights into Antiquity* (London, 1928)

Weigall, Arthur, *The Young Lady from Hell* (London, 1929)

Weigall Arthur, *Nero, Emperor of Rome* (London, 1930)

Weigall, Arthur, *The Life and Times of Marc Antony* (London, 1931)

Weigall, Arthur, *Sappho of Lesbos: her Life and Times* (London, 1932)

Weigall, Arthur, *Alexander the Great* (London, 1933)

Weigall, Arthur, *Laura was my Camel* (London, 1933)

Weigall, Rachel, *Lady Rose Weigall, a Memoir based on her Correspondence and the Recollections of her friends* (London, 1923)

Whymper, Charles, *Egyptian Birds* (London,1909)

Wilkinson, John Gardner, *The Manners and Customs of the Ancient Egyptians* (London, 1837)

Winlock, H.E., 'Materials used at the Embalming of King Tut-ankh-amun', in *Metropolitan Museum of Art Papers*, (New York, 1941)

Williams, Valentine, *The World of Action* (London, 1938)

Woolley, Charles Leonard, *As I Seem to Remember* (London, 1962)

# Notes and References

The letters of the Weigall family make up so much of the narrative of this book that to give a date for each one quoted would clog the pages with references. I have therefore omitted to give them, merely indicating in general terms when they were written.

## CHAPTER 1

1 *The Daily Express* (3 January 1934) had an article on the front page headlined 'Arthur Weigall who denied Tutankhamun's Curse, is Dead'; the next day it had a piece entitled 'A Curse Killed Arthur Weigall'. *The Daily Mirror* (3 January 1934) had 'Death of Mr. A. Weigall; Egyptologist who told Story of King Tut; That "Curse" '. *The Referee* (7 January 1934) simply headed its announcement with 'The Curse of Tutankhamun'.

2 The word 'native', either as an adjective or as a noun, was used generally and without question by Europeans at that period. It will occur in this book only when it is quoted from an original source, or in quotation marks when the attitude of the time is being referred to.

3 Arthur Weigall, 'The Malevolence of Ancient Egyptian Spirits', in *Tutankhamen and Other Essays*, (1924; first published in 1923), p.138.

4 'The Tomb of Tutankhamen', in *Tutankhamen and Other Essays*. Both quotations come from p.89.

5 'The Malevolence of Ancient Egyptian Spirits', p.157.

6 R. Engelbach, *Air Force News*, 17 February 1945, p.12. I am grateful to Nicholas Reeves for drawing my attention to this article.

7 Rachel Weigall, *Lady Rose Weigall, a Memoir based on her Correspondence and the Recollections of her friends* (1923), p.143.

8 In Exeter Cathedral there is a wall monument in memory of those from the 2nd Battalion of the 11th regiment who died in the Afghan campaign (1880–1881), on which is recorded the name of Captain and Paymaster A.A.D. Weigall.

9 M.W. MacCallum, *In Memory of Albert Bythesea Weigall* (1913), p.23.

10 These comments on Geraldine and Thomas Goodeve and Cecilia Wilson, come from a manuscript memoir that Arthur Weigall wrote for the family. AW archive.

11 In the following pages I shall refer to Sri Lanka as Ceylon because that is how it was known at the period described in this book.

12 J.W. Macgill and Mrs Arthur Weigall, *Seeking and Saving, being the Rescue work of the Manchester City Mission*, (1889), p.27.

13 Singalese and Indian children's nurses were known as ayahs.

14 'Alice and Florrie', an unpublished childhood memoir written by Alice (Mimi) Weigall.

15 MS memoir, AW archive. Weigall's recollections in the following pages come from this document and will not be further footnoted.
16 *Seeking and Saving*, p.28
17 See, David B. McIlney, *A Gentleman in Every Slum; Church of England Missions in East London, 1837–1914* (Pennsylvania, 1988)
18 Charles Booth, *Life and Labour of the People of London*, (London, 1902) First Series: Poverty. East, Central and South London, pp.287–8
19 Booth, *Life and Labour*, Third Series: Religious Influences, p.46.
20 John Tatham, M.D., *Borough of Salford: Annual Report of the Medical Officer of Health for the Year 1886*, p.66.
21 *Seeking and Saving*, p.60.
22 ibid., p.57.
23 *The Not Impossible She* (1926), p.29.
24 ibid., pp.30–31.
25 James Morris, *Heaven's Command; an Imperial Progress*, (Penguin edition, 1979), p.517.

## CHAPTER 2

1 MS memoir. AW archive. The following quotations describing Weigall's early life come from this document.
2 A schoolboy custom which meant that the victim was ostracized and shut out from all communication.
3 All the foregoing quotes come from *The Not Impossible She* (1926), pp.123–24.
4 James Lees-Milne, *Harold Nicolson, a biography, 1886–1929* 2 Vols (1981) Vol.I, p.9.

## CHAPTER 3

1 MS memoirs. AW archive. The following recollections of Weigall's school and university life are taken from the same document.
2 E. Denison Ross, *Both Ends of the Candle* (1943), p.299.
3 Undated letter in G.I. Newberry correspondence, 45/24, A.83.
4 20 July 1900. AW archive. Weigall pasted this letter, together with his own comments on it, into an exercise book in which he kept a record of his first archaeological ventures.
5 *PSBA* xxii pt 6, June 1900.
6 *The Morning Post*, 17 September 1900.
7 Quoted from Weigall's MS memoir.
8 17 September 1900. AW archive.
9 Undated letter in G.I. Newberry correspondence 45/28.

## CHAPTER 4

1 Flinders Petrie, *Seventy Years in Archaeology* (1931), p.8
2 The reviewer of the *Manchester Guardian* (20 April 1920) was amused by Budge's adventures, and only as an afterthought added: 'Some of the stricter archaeologists, however, may be permitted to drop a tear of regret for the sacrifice of material that is made to the collector's spirit, even though the collector be inspired by the worthy ambition of filling the British Museum with priceless treasure.'
3 *Seventy Years*. Both quotations come from p.19.
4 MS memoir. AW archive. The following account of Weigall's association with Petrie, his relations with Garstang and Mace and his journey to Egypt, is taken from the same document.
5 'Some Egyptian Weights in Prof. Petrie's Collection', in *PSBA*, Vol.23, December (London, 1901), pp.378–95.

6 Petrie, *Seventy Years*, pp.172–73.
7 ibid., p.25 and p.91.
8 ibid., see pp.176–78
9 This letter, marked A, 202a, was given to me by Margaret Gardiner, daughter of the Egyptologist, Sir Alan Gardiner, who possessed a number of early letters from Weigall to Newberry.
10 See E.R. Ayrton, C.T. Currelly, and A.E.P. Weigall, 'Tomb and Cemetery of Senusert III', Chapter III in *Abydos. Part III. 1904* (1904).
11 W.M. Flinders Petrie, *Abydos. Part I. 1902* (London, 1902): 'Mr Arthur Weigall came out for the first time and proved a most successful worker … he entirely superintended the men at the great southern tombs, which I only visited to give general direction … He also looked after the close of the temenos work, and drew some of the inscriptions …'
12 See chapter V of *Abydos. Part I.*
13 'Recent Excavations in Egypt' in *The Treasury of Ancient Egypt. Miscellaneous Chapters on Ancient Egyptian History and Archaeology* (1911), pp.170–71.
14 Pencilled letter from Petrie to Weigall, AW archive.
15 See Chapter III, in *Abydos. Part III*: 'The work of clearing away the debris … of examining the granite sarcophagus … of measuring and planning the place, was thought to be too great an undertaking for that season … the work was therefore discontinued …'
16 MS memoir. AW archive.
17 Undated letter in G.I. Newberry correspondence, 45/30.
18 A typescript of this letter was given to me by Margaret Gardiner.
19 Undated letter from Bissing to Weigall, AW archive.
20 See footnote 17.
21 See footnote 19.
22 Letter dated 3 June 1902. AW archive.
23 See footnote 11.
24 The result can be seen in A.E.P. Weigall, *Die Mastaba des Gem-ni-kai* (1905).
25 Autobiographical jottings. AW archive.
26 This and the following quotations come from letters to Hortense, to whom he was by then engaged, and who will be introduced in the next chapter. AW archive.
27 Letter from Petrie to Weigall dated 10 March 1904, referring to Weigall's help during the previous season 1903–4 season. AW archive.
28 Letters from Petrie to Weigall dated 23 January 1903, 26 December 1903 and 20 February 1904. AW archive.
29 Letter from Minnie A Stacey to Weigall dated 17 February 1903. AW archive.

## CHAPTER 5

1 Letter from Weigall to Breasted dated 17 October [1904]. Oriental Institute archives, Chicago University.
2 Letter from Breasted to Weigall dated 3 February 1905. Oriental Institute archives, Chicago University.
3 George Steevens, author of *Egypt in 1898*, (1898) quoted in Piers Brendon, *Thomas Cook. 150 years of Popular Tourism* (1992; first published 1991), p.231.
4 Pierre Loti, *Egypt*, (1909). For this picture of Cook's tourists and their Egypt, see pp.136, 141, 181, and 280ff.
5 *Rapports sur la Marche du Service des Antiquites de 1899 a 1910*, (1912), pp.119–20.
6 Letter from Somers Clarke to Francis Llewellyn Griffith dated 27 May 1899. G.I. Griffith correspondence, 22.
7 *Howard Carter: the Path to Tutankhamun* (1992).
8 Ed. F.Ll. Griffith, *Egypt Exploration Fund. Archaeological Report, 1909–1910* (London, 1910), p.18.

## CHAPTER 6

1 Letter from Mace to Weigall dated 21 January 1905. AW archive.
2 'Excavating in Egypt, where Rich Treasures sometimes reward the Digger', *Putnam's Magazine*, July 1909. This was reprinted in Weigall's collection of essays, *The Treasury of Ancient Egypt* (1911), as 'Recent Excavations in Egypt'.
3 Much of this material has been published in Julie Hankey, 'The Tomb of Yuya and Tuya: A Letter from Luxor, 1905', in *KMT*, summer 1998, Vol.9, No.2.
4 Entry for 13 February 1905 in Emma B. Andrews, "Journal of the Bedawin, 1889–1912". The American Philosophical Society. Emma Andrews was a cousin of Davis's wife.
5 Weigall seems to have added on a few centuries in his excitement.
6 Entry for 13 February 1905.
7 Smith, *Tombs, Temples*, pp.34–35.
8 Letter from Maspero to Weigall dated 29 May 1905, AW archive.
9 Letter from Maspero to Weigall dated 3 June 1905, AW archive.
10 Howard Carter had worked at Thebes for some years before becoming Inspector.
11 W.M. Flinders Petrie, *Methods and Aims in Archaeolgy*, (1904), p.179.
12 'The Morality of Excavation' in *The Nineteenth Century and After*, Vol.72 (August 1912), pp.382–96. Reprinted in a collection of his essays, *The Glory of the Pharaohs*, (1923).
13 Draft typescript memo to Dupuis, the Advisor at the Ministry of Public Works. AW archive. This document, undated but written probably in 1911, challenges the basis upon which concessions to excavate were granted by the Department of Antiquities (part of the Ministry of Public Works). AW archive.
14 Letter from Davis to Weigall dated 20 June 1905. AW archive.
15 See Appendix I.
16 For Whitaker see Chapter 13. Weigall mentions refusing concessions to Whitaker and Covington in his PWD memo (see footnote 13).
17 *Rapports sur la Marche du Service des Antiquities de 1899 a 1910*, (Cairo, 1912), pp.165–66.
18 Manuscript notes taken from office files 'with a view to writing my official experiences', 1914. AW archive.

## CHAPTER 7

1 'The Flooding of Lower Nubia' in *The Treasury of Ancient Egypt* (1911), pp.262–63.
2 *PSAL*, 28 November 1907 to 24 June 1909. Second Series, Vol. XXII. 14 May 1908, p.307.
3 Carter's report, Maspero's failure to press for money, and his own visit to Nubia are recorded in Gaston Maspero, *Les Temples Immergés de la Nubie: Rapports relatifs a la Consolidation des Temples* (1911). See respectively, pp.ix–xii; pp.xii–xiii; and p.xiii.
4 Arthur Weigall, *A Report on the Antiquities of Lower Nubia (the First Cataract to the Sudan Frontier) and Their Condition in 1906–7*, (1907), [p.i].
5 *PSAL*, (see note 2), p.304.
6 Weigall, *A Report on ... Lower Nubia*, pp.58–9.
7 ibid., pp.109–10.
8 ibid., pp.103–04.
9 This is the title Weigall gave to some manuscript pages on Maspero which he describes in a covering note as 'Notes for a book of reminiscences; these are about Maspero written in 1913; but I discontinued them because I felt they were rather unkind. A.W.' AW archive.
10 Archibald Henry Sayce, *Reminiscences* (1923), p.285.
11 G.W.Steevens, *Egypt in 1898*, (1898), p.99.
12 Maspero, *Les Temples Immergés*, pp.xii–xiii.
13 The relevant extract from the Public Works Department's Report is given in *Rapports sur la Marche du Service des Antiquites de 1899 a 1900*, Annexe A, pp.48–51.

14  PWD memo. AW archive.

15  ibid., (see note 2), p.303.

16  Ed. F. Ll. Griffith, *Egypt Exploration Fund. Archaeological Report. 1905–1906*, (1906) p.19.

17  This was a ceremony in which young women of the upper and upper middle classes were formally received at Court by the reigning monarch.

18  *E.E.F. Archaeological Report, 1905–1906*, p.19.

19  A draft manuscript entitled 'A Report on the Tombs and Mortuary Chapels of the Theban Nobles, and their Condition in 1911–1912'. This document gives a history of the work carried out at Gurneh by Weigall's predecessors and by himself. AW archive.

20  Arthur Weigall, 'A Report on the Tombs of Shekh Abd'el Gurneh and el Assasif', *ASAE*, Tome IX, (Cairo, 1908), p.120.

21  'When I first came to Upper Egypt ... [a] native actually had the audacity to warn me that any severity on my part would be met by destructions of monuments,' ibid., p.121.

22  ibid., p.121.

23  ibid., p.122.

24  'A Report on the Tombs and Mortuary Chapels ...' AW archive.

25  'Archaeology in the Open', in *The Treasury* (1911), p.296.

26  *Rapports sur la Marche du Service des Antiquites de 1899 a 1910*, (1912), pp.201–202.

27  See 'The Flooding of Lower Nubia', p.275 in *The Treasury*, pp.262–80.

28  Pierre Loti, *Egypt,*, trans. W.P. Baines, ( London, 1909), pp.286–87.

29  Arthur Weigall, *A Guide to the Antiquities of Upper Egypt* (London, 1910), p.359.

30  Quoted from the second edition, published 1888, pp.398–99.

31  Weigall's MS office file notes. AW archive.

32  The story is supplemented by another account of it in Weigall's PWD memo. AW archive.

33  Weigall's MS office file notes.

## CHAPTER 8

1  He expressed these views in 'The Flooding of Lower Nubia' in *The Treasury of Ancient Egypt*, (1911). See especially 266–276.

2  ibid., p.271.

3  Sayce, *Reminiscences* (1923), p.306.

4  'Akhnaton, Pharaoh of Egypt', in *Blackwood's Edinburgh Magazine*, October 1907, pp.470–482. It was reprinted in *The Treasury of Ancient Egypt* (1911) under the title 'The Tomb of Tiy and Akhnaton'.

5  Emma Andrews, "Journal", entry for 9 January 1907. The American Philosophical Society.

6  Theodore Davis, 'The Finding of the Tomb of Queen Tiyi' in *The Tomb of Queen Tiyi* (1910), pp.1–2.

7  'The Tomb of Tiy and Akhnaton' (see note 4), p.187. The following description of what they found in the tomb is taken from this essay.

8  Davis, 'The Finding of the tomb of Queen Tiyi', p.2.

9  'Akhnaton, Pharaoh of Egypt', *Blackwoods Edinburgh Magazine*, October 1907.

10  'A New Discovery in Egypt: the Recent Uncovering of the Tomb of Queen Tiy', *The Century Magazine*, September 1907.

11  Journal entries for 17 and 21 January.

12  Walter Tyndale, *Below the Cataracts* (1907), p.185.

13  Emma Andrews's journal entry for 17 February 1907: 'Theo was in Luxor this a.m. and Carter told him of various small and precious things which had been shown him by a native which had been stolen from Tiy's tomb. The man had told Carter that Davis could have them all for £400 – provided no attempt at arrest was made ... It is so humiliating to find that thieves have been among your trusted workmen.' The American Philosophical Society.

14 Journal entries for 27 January and 11 February.
15 'Akhnaton, Pharaoh of Egypt.' See note 9. The following account is also taken from this article.
16 Tyndale, *Below the Cataracts*, pp.193 and 195.
17 Or perhaps he was censored. See Weigall, 'The Mummy of Akhnaton', *JEA*, Vol. VIII, 1922, in which Weigall says that Davis edited Ayrton's piece.
18 'A New Discovery in Egypt …' See note 10.
19 For a brief survey of the changing ways in which Akhnaten's character has been interpreted during the last hundred years see Juliette Bentley, 'Akhnaten in the Eye of the Beholder: do changing interpretations of the heretic King reflect contemporary values of his assessors?', in *Amarna Letters; Essays on Ancient Egypt ca. 1390–1310 B.C.* 3 vols. (1991–94), II, pp.7–8.
20 *A History of Egypt from the Earliest Times to the Persian Conquest* (1906), p.356.
21 Petrie describes Akhnaten's religion as a 'refined and really philosophical worship'; of his ethics he writes: 'The customary glorying in war has almost disappeared … the motto 'Living in Truth' is constantly put forward as the keynote of the king's character … and domestic affection is held up as his ideal of life.' *A History of Egypt*, 3 Vols, (1894–1896), III, pp.214, 218–19.
22 These were placed in the tombs of Pharaohs, one for each of the cardinal points of the compass. In Tomb 55, two of these were found with Akhnaten's name unerased. Weigall doesn't mention them before 1922 when the revised edition of his biography of Akhnaten was published. He calls them 'foundation bricks'. See *The Life and Times of Akhnaton, Pharaoh of Egypt* (revised edition, 1922), p.xxv.
23 These bands went missing very early on. They are not mentioned in the catalogue of objects found in the tomb in Davis's publication (see note 6). In an article Weigall wrote for *JEA*, Vol.VIII (1922), he says he sent them to Cairo with everything else, and saw them subsequently in Elliot Smith's workroom there. He also remembers talking to Elliot Smith about them, and wonders whether they are somewhere in the museum, or whether they have simply 'disappeared'. In *Akhenaten, King of Egypt* (1988, revised edition; first published in 1968 as *Akhnaten, Pharaoh of Egypt*), Cyril Aldred says they were 'purloined by one of [Elliot Smith's] laboratory assistants', p.203.
24 See Martha R. Bell, 'An Armchair Excavation of KV55', in *JARCE* XXVII, 1990, pp.97–137. Cyril Aldred (see previous note) summarizes the development of scholarly opinion after Weigall in Chapter 18 of the revised edition of his biography (see previous note). This is not the place to unravel the arguments in favour of Akhnaten or Smenkhare: but as examples of the Smenkhare theory see both Aldred (ibid.) and Aidan Dodson, 'Kings' Valley Tomb 55 and the Fates of the Amarna Kings' in *Amarna Letters : Essays on Ancient Egypt, ca 1390–1310 B.C.* 3 Vols. (1991–1994) III, pp.92–103; and for the Akhnaten theory see Nicholas Reeves in *The Valley of the Kings: the decline of a Royal Necropolis* (1990), pp.44 and 49, and again in *The Complete Valley of the Kings* (1996), pp.120–121.
25 Letter from Sayce to Weigall dated 20 October 1907. AW archive.
26 Aldred, *Akhnaten* (1988), p.195.
27 See Appendix: The contract with Theodore M. Davis.
28 Both letters are in the AW archive.
29 E.R.Ayrton, 'The Tomb of Queen Thyi', *PSBA* 29 (1907), 85f and 277f.
30 *The Quarterly Review,* Vol.210, January to April 1909, pp.44–66, p.62.
31 G.I. Griffith correspondence, 362.

## CHAPTER 9

1 'A Nubian Highway', in *Travels in the Upper Egyptian Deserts,* (1909), pp.169–193. It originally appeared in *Blackwood's Magazine*, December 1907.

2 'The Eastern Desert and its Interests', in *Travels*, pp.1–27. Published originally in *Blackwood's Magazine*, November 1908.
3 ibid., p.12.
4 Whymper was a bird painter, and his book *Egyptian Birds* was published in 1909.
5 Walter Tyndale, *An Artist in Egypt* (1912), p.210.
6 'To the Quarries of Wady Hammamat', in *Travels*. See pp.50–51. Weigall was much struck by these abandoned blocks, for he mentions others – of breccia, granite and porphyry – in two other essays in *Travels*: 'The Eastern Desert and its Interests' and 'The Quarries of Mons Claudianus'.
7 'The Quarries of Mons Claudianus', in *Travels*, p.129.
8 'To the Quarries of Wady Hammamat', in *Travels*, p.54.
9 'The Eastern Desert and its Interests', p.1.
10 Undated letter from Norma Lorimer to Arthur Weigall. Weigall was obviously pleased with this letter, for he pasted it into his cuttings book. AW archive.
11 ibid., pp.6–9.
12 'The Imperial Porphyry Quarries', pp.100–02.
13 'The Red Sea Highroad', p.61.
14 'To the Quarries of Hammamat', pp.47–8.
15 'The Quarries of Mons Claudianus', pp.134–37.
16 'The Temple of Wady Abad', pp.159–60.
17 'To the Quarries of Wady Hammamat', p.35.
18 *An Artist in Egypt*, (1912) p.222.
19 See 'The Imperial Porphyry Quarries', pp.106–7.
20 *The Nation* (4 December 1909).
21 'To the Quarries of Hammamat', p.54.
22 'The Temple of Wady Abad', pp.157–58.
23 The mid-twentieth century debate about the origins of Egyptian civilization was called 'the Dynastic race' theory and drew upon differences in the nature of the remains between two pre-Dynastic cemeteries excavated by Petrie at Nakada north of Thebes. More recently, the Egyptologist David Rohl has used Weigall's copies as evidence for a theory about the prehistoric arrival in Egypt of a foreign people originating in the Euphrates valley. See David Rohl, *A Test of Time* 2 Vols. (1995–1998), Vol.2, Chapter 9. See also *The Followers of Horus Eastern Desert Survey*, Vol.I (2000), edited by David Rohl, which re-publishes Weigall's drawings.
24 'The Finding of the Tomb of Siphtah; the unnamed gold tomb; and the Animal Pit tombs', in Theodore Davis, *The Tomb of Siphtah* (1908), p.4.
25 AW archive.
26 AW archive.
27 See Appendix: The contract with Theodore M. Davis.
28 The following account comes in an article Winlock wrote, 'Materials used at the Embalming of King Tut-ankh-amun', *Metropolitan Museum of Art Papers*, (New York, 1941).
29 31 January 1908, AW archive.
30 AW archive.
31 'The Tomb of Horemheb', in *The Treasury of Ancient Egypt* (1911), pp.229–230. This article was first published in *The Century*, June 1909.
32 ibid., pp.231, 233, 234.
33 In a letter dated 8 December 1910, AW archive.
34 Letter dated 19 March 1908. Smithsonian Institution.

## CHAPTER 10

1 See the Foreword to his *Flights into Antiquity* (1928).
2 *Liverpool Daily Courier*, 20 April 1911.
3 In *The Treasury of Ancient Egypt* (1911).

4  'Archaeology in the Open', in *Treasury*, p.300.
5  'The Necessity of Archaeology to the Gaiety of the World', in *Treasury*, pp.67–8.
6  Letter dated 10 November 1902. AW archives.
7  See 'The Alabaster Quarries in the Wady Assiout', in *The Glory of the Pharaohs*, (1923), p.239. Although this piece was published much later, the expedition it describes took place in the summer of 1910.
8  *Report on the Antiquities of Lower Nubia* (1907), p.24.
9  'The Egyptian Empire', in *Treasury*, pp.31, 35.
10  ibid., p.37.
11  'Archaeology in the Open', in *Treasury*, pp.303, 306.
12  'The Temperament of the Ancient Egyptians', *Treasury*, p.90.
13  'Archaeology in the Open', in ibid., p.296.
14  For this and the preceding quotations illustrating Weigall's argument against museums see pp. 289–298 of 'Archaeology in the Open' in *Treasury*.
15  'Archaeology in the Open', p.287.
16  Letter from Cromer to Weigall dated 15 May 1911. AW archive.
17  The Introduction to *The Life and Times of Akhnaton* (1910), p.5.
18  ibid., p.275.
19  Letter dated 21 March 1908. Smithsonian Institution.
20  Letter dated 15 October 1909. AW archive.
21  The letter, dated 6 September 1909, is in the Griffith Institute archive, and is quoted in T.G.H. James, *Howard Carter, the Path to Tutankhamun* (1992), p.157.
22  The letter, dated 2 October 1909, is in the Griffith Institute archive, and is quoted by James, *Howard Carter*, p.157.
23  Letter dated 14 October 1909. AW archive.
24  Letter dated 15 December 1909. AW archive.
25  Letter dated 1 October [1908], G.I. Griffith correspondence, 362.
26  Joseph Lindon Smith, *Tombs, Temples and Ancient Art* (1956), p.81.
27  James, *Howard Carter*, p.138.
28  Undated letter, but from internal evidence March-April 1907. AW archive.
29  Letter dated I October [1908] G.I. Griffith correspondence, 362.
30  Letter dated 2 October 1908. AW archive.
31  AW archive.
32  James, *Howard Carter*, p.142.
33  *E.E.F. Archaeological Report, 1907–1908*, p.8.
34  *E.E.F. Archaeological Report, 1906–1907*, p.23.

## CHAPTER 11

1  Smith, *Tombs, Temples and Ancient Art*, p.22.
2  Letter dated 17 September 1907. AW archive.
3  Letter dated 17 November 1907. AW archive.
4  Letter dated 17 January 1908. AW archive.
5  Letter dated 28 December 1908. AW archive.
6  ibid.
7  Smith, *Tombs, Temples*, p.85.
8  James, *Howard Carter*, p.142.
9  Letter dated 28 April 1908. AW archive.
10  *E.E.F. Archaeological Report, 1909–1910*, p.18.
11  Memo dated 24 January 1909. AW archive.
12  'A Report on the Suffocation of five Persons in a Tomb at Gurneh on November 10th–11th 1905' in *ASAE* (1906), pp.11–12. Weigall tells this story again in 'Recent Excavations in Egypt', in *The Treasury of Ancient Egypt*, pp.182–3.

13 MS Report on the Tombs and Mortuary Chapels … 1911–12. AW archive.
14 MS Report on the Tombs and Mortuary Chapels … 1911–12. AW archive.
15 Letter dated 1 January 1908. GI, Gardiner MSS, AHG/42.355.25.
16 Letter dated 10 January 1909, GI, Gardiner MSS AHG/42.355.23.
17 *A Guide to the Antiquities of Upper Egypt* (1910), p.162.
18 Letter dated 25 April 1909. GI, Gardiner MSS AHG/355.24.
19 Alan Gardiner, *My Working Years*, (1962), p.17.
20 ibid., p.18.
21 Letter to 'Grandma and Grandpa' dated 28 December 1908. Smithsonian Institution.
22 Letter to 'Grandma and Grandpa and two little kidlings' dated 18 March 1909. Smithsonian Institution.
23 ibid.
24 This story was told me by Alan Gardiner's daughter, Margaret Gardiner.
25 Smith, *Tombs, Temples*, p.105.
26 See 'The Malevolence of Ancient Egyptian Spirits', in *Tutankhamen and other Essays* (1924), p.154.
27 Smith in *Tombs, Temples and Ancient Art* (1956), pp.109–113 and Weigall in 'The Ghosts in the Valley of the Tombs of the Queens', *The Pall Mall Magazine*, June 1912, pp.753–765. The *Pall Mall* piece contains long extracts from the verse play Weigall wrote.
28 Now their 'theatre' has been dug down to reveal a series of ancient walls to dam the water that used to flow there over great rocks and boulders. But at the beginning of the 20th century it had a flat floor of sand and gravel.
29 Three copies of this invitation survive, one in Hortense's hand (unfinished) one in Smith's, and the last in an unknown hand but signed with the four Weigall and Smith signatures. The invitation written by Smith is directed at the top to Howard Carter Esq, and Erskine Nicol Esq. AW archive.
30 Smith, *Tombs, Temples*, p.109.
31 Letter dated 25 January 1911. AW archive.
32 Letter dated 26 January 1909 addressed to 'Dear little Grandma and Grandpa'. Smithsonian Institution.
33 'The Malevolence of Ancient Egyptian Spirits', in *Tutankhamen and other Essays* (1924), p.151.
34 'People tell me that you are becoming more and more a kind of theatrical showman, with the temple for his theatre, and that everyone – natives and foreigners – ridicules both you who indulge yourself daily in these eccentricities and the Department that allows you to do so.' Letter from Maspero to Legrain dated 23 March 1911. AW archive. Maspero's second letter (not quoted here), in reply to Legrain's answer, is dated 27 March 1911.
35 *Tombs and Temples*, p.83.

### CHAPTER 12

1 See *JEA* 3 (1916), pp.147ff. However, Nicholas Reeves thinks that Carter may have been right, see *The Valley of the Kings* (1990) pp.3–5 and again in *The Complete Valley of the Kings* (1996), p.89.
2 'The tomb of Amenhotep 1st', in *Annales du Service des Antiquites* 11, 1911, pp.174–175.
3 John Rose, *Tomb KV39 in the Valley of the Kings: a Double Archaeological Enigma* (Bristol, 2000), p.151.
4 A.M. Dodson, 'The Burial of the Members of the Royal Family during the Eighteenth Dynasty', forthcoming in *Proceedings of the Eighth International Congress of Egyptologists* (Cairo, c.2001). I am grateful to Dr Dodson for allowing me to see an advance copy of this article.
5 Dominic Montserrat, *Akhnaten: History, Fantasy and Ancient Egypt* (London and New York, 2000). See particularly Chapter 4, 'Protestants, Psychoanalysts and Fascists'. I am grateful to Dr Montserrat for showing me the manuscript in advance of publication.

6  *Guide*, pp.380– 81.
7  Letter dated 31 July 1910. AW archive.
8  Letter dated 28 September 1910. AW archive.
9  Letter dated 19 March 1910. G.I. Gardiner MSS AHG/42 355.22.
10  Article by Dr Yunan Labib Rizk in *Al Ahram Weekly* (Cairo edition), 27 May– 2 June 1999.
11  Letter dated 30 May 1910. AW archive.
12  *The Outlook* (29 July 1911); see also *The Outlook,* (30 September 1911).
13  This lecture forms the first chapter in a collection of essays and speeches entitled *History as Literature,* (New York, 1913).
14  The following excerpts come from Geanie's Egyptian diary which was kept from 7 December 1910 ('my first day in Luxor') to 14 June 1911, three weeks after she left Egypt.
15  Telegram dated 28 February 1911. AW archive.
16  I have drawn the basic outline of the Atherton story from *The Times* of 17 July 1906, 20 January 1909 and 22 January 1909.

## CHAPTER 13

1  Letter to Gardiner, 10 January 1911. G.I.Gardiner MSS, AHG/42.355.22
2  p.118.
3  *Guide*, p.555.
4  Letter dated 10 January [1911], G.I.Gardiner MSS, AHG/42.355.21.
5  MS notes from office files. AW archive.
6  Letter dated 6 June 1911. PRO, FO 633,20.
7  MS notes from office files. AW archive.
8  Weigall enlisted the help of Norman McNaghten of the Ministry of the Interior, who wrote to his Ministry asking them to intervene with the Local Land Commission. MacNaghten sent a copy of this letter (dated 5 December 1910) to Weigall. AW archive. See also Weigall's E.E.F Reports for 1909–10, and 1910–11.
9  Letter dated 27 August 1910. AW archive.
10  Undated letter, but from the context probably January or February 1913. AW archive.
11  MS notes from office files. AW archive.
12  He puts this detail into an essay entitled 'Lower Nubia and the great Reservoir', in *The Glory of the Pharaohs*, p.207.
13  Ronald Storrs, *Orientations* (1943; first published 1937), p.53.
14  See *E.E.F. Archaeological Report, 1909–10*, p.18.
15  See note 4.
16  p.17.
17  Letter dated 8 December 1909. AW archive.
18  Letter dated 17 December 1909. AW archive.
19  Letter dated 4 October 1911. Extracts from this letter were given to me by Alan Gardiner's daughter, Margaret Gardiner.
20  G.I. Gardiner correspondence. See note 4.
21  Letter dated 'midsummer's day', [1911]. AW archive.
22  Letter dated 9 July [1911], G.I. Gardiner MSS AHG/42.355.15
23  Letter dated 3 August 1911. AW archive.
24  See note 21.
25  This is probably the MS document, so frequently referred to in these notes, entitled 'A Report on the Tombs and Mortuary Chapels of the Theban Nobles, and their Condition in 1911–1912.' Weigall gives Gardiner's name on the title page as well as his own, hoping perhaps that Gardiner's name would lend weight to his views.
26  PWD memo. AW archive.
27  Ronald Storrs mentions the loss of this statue: 'I can remember ... [Lord Kitchener's] expletives when he learnt that the superb and unique portrait group of the builder of the Third

Pyramid, Men Kau Ra ... and his Queen, a national monument of Egypt recently discovered by Dr Reisner, had been allowed to go to the Boston Museum.' *Orientations,* p.110.

28  See note 22.
29  Letter dated 18 October 1911, PRO, FO 633,20.
30  *By Nile and Tigris* (1920), Vol.I, p.74.

## CHAPTER 14

1  Undated letter, but from context September 1911. G.I., Gardiner MSS AHG/42.355.20.
2  In 1919 Edward Madge was on the intelligence staff of the Paris Peace Conference, advising on Rumanian affairs.
3  This extract from a letter dated 2 February 1913, was given to me by Margaret Gardiner.
4  *Orientations,* pp.110–111.
5  Frank Rattigan, *Diversions of a Diplomat* (1924), p.98.
6  Letter to his mother dated 12 May 1912. Pembroke College, Cambridge.
7  Edward Tuck wrote to Weigall on 18 February 1913 to thank him for three photographs 'of the ushabti statuette made in the likeness of Akhnaton, which I bought thro' you when in Cairo with your descriptive inscription on the wrapper.' AW archive. In Weigall's *Ancient Egyptian Works of Art* (1924), he publishes three photographs (on p.208) of an 'ushabti-figure of an unknown person.' The caption says that it was in the hands of 'M.Kitikas, a well-known Cairo dealer', that it was 'photographed for me in 1913' and that it was sold to a 'private collector'. He also says that he thinks that it represents Akhnaten himself. These photographs are almost certainly therefore of the figure sold to Edward Tuck.
8  Unless there is missing evidence to the effect that he did tell Maspero and the object was refused.
9  In 'Theban Thieves' in *The Glory of the Pharaohs* (1923), pp.316–320.
10  Undated letter, but from the context, written shortly before 14 November 1912 (see next note). Metropolitan Museum of Art.
11  Letter dated 14 November 1912. Metropolitan Museum of Art.
12  Letter dated 28 January [1913]. Metropolitan Museum of Art.
13  Though at some point, Weigall appears to have thought that it might have been Romano-Egyptian. The statuette makes a sly appearance in the biography of Cleopatra that Weigall was then writing, as a statue of Alexander Helios, Antony's son by Cleopatra, dressed in the royal costume of Media to mark the fact that Antony intended him to be that country's ruler: 'A figure has recently been discovered,' writes Weigall, 'which appears to represent the boy in this manner.' *The Life and Times of Cleopatra* (1914), p.293.
14  *J. Pierpont Morgan; an Intimate Portrait,* (1939), pp.507–8.
15  Two drafts of this document are in the AW archive.
16  Letter dated 30 January [1913]. G.I. Gardiner MSS, AHG/42.355.14.
17  'The future of excavation in Egypt', *Tutankhamun and other Essays,* (1924), p.33.
18  ibid., see note 16.
19  ibid., see note 16.
20  Letter dated 28 March 1913. AW archive.
21  ibid., see note 16.
22  This extract, from a letter dated 12 January 1913, was given to me by Margaret Gardiner.
23  Letter dated 26 [February 1913], G.I. Gardiner MSS, AHG/42.355.19.

## CHAPTER 15

1  Letter dated 23 April 1911. G.I. Newberry correspondence, 7/90.
2  Letter dated 30 January [1913]. G.I. Gardiner MSS, AHG/42.355.14.
3  Letter dated 10 January 1913. AW archive.

4  Letter dated 17 February 913. AW archive.
5  Letter dated 9 May 1913. MMA.
6  Letter dated 5 December 1913. G.I. Newberry correspondence, 46/7.
7  See below, [p.202–3].
8  Undated letter, probably January 1913. AW archive.
9  Charles Leonard Woolley, *As I seem to Remember* (1962), p.31.
10  Letter dated 21 November 1913. G.I. Gardiner MSS, AHG/42.69.42.
11  Letter dated 2 December 1913. G.I. Gardiner MSS, AHG/42.69.41.
12  ibid., see previous note.
13  Letter dated 1 January 1913. Oriental Institute archives, Chicago.
14  Copy of letter dated 10 October 1913. G.I. Gardiner MSS, AHG/42.355.12.
15  Letter dated 31 July [1909]. AW archive.
16  Letter dated 22 October 1913. G.I.Gardiner MSS, AHG/42.355.11.
17  Letter dated 22 November 1913. AW archive.
18  Letter dated 17 November 1913. G.I. Gardiner MSS, AHG/42.355.8.
19  There are several letters in the AW archive which show how closely Gardiner, Weigall and Mond were involved over the winter of 1912–13 in the creation of this post.
20  Charles Oman, *Seven Roman Statesmen of the Later Republic* (1902), p.331.
21  *Cleopatra*, p.96.
22  ibid., p.117.
23  *The Nation*, 29 October 1914.
24  p.10.
25  p.96.
26  *The Times Literary Supplement*, 18 June 1914.
27  Lucy Hughes-Hallett, *Cleopatra: Histories, Dreams and Distortions* (1990; Vintage edition 1991), chapter 10, 'The Child'.
28  *Cleopatra*, p.125.
29  Ferrero was the author of *The Greatness and Decline of Rome* (1907–1909), 5vols. Weigall quotes Ferrero's opinion in a footnote on p.157.
30  Letter dated 6 July 1914. AW archive.
31  These extracts come from undated letters signed by Renie Pes di Villamarina, which from the context were probably written some time in early 1913. AW archive.
32  Letter dated 11 January 1913. AW archive.
33  Extracts from two letters sent to Ronald Storrs on 14 and 27 February 1913. AW archive.
34  Letter dated 2 December 1911. PRO, F.O. 633.20.
35  Copy of letter dated 13 December 1911. PRO, F.O.633.20.
36  See Margaret S. Drower, *Flinders Petrie: a Life in Archaeology* (London, 1985), pp.280–285 and pp.293–295.
37  This and the following extracts are drawn from two versions in draft form of his proposal for an Institute of Archaeology in Cairo. AW archive.
38  I am grateful to Dr Mark Smith of the Griffith Institute Oxford, for drawing my attention to an article by Donald M.Reid entitled 'Indigenous Egyptology: the Decolonization of a Profession?' in the *Journal of the American Oriental Society 105.2* (1985). In it, the author gives a history of attempts by Egyptians to educate themselves in the language, history and archaeology of ancient Egypt, and of the frustrations they suffered at the hands of the Europeans running the Antiquities Service during the nineteenth and the early part of the twentieth centuries. Their suppression does indeed appear to have been extremely thorough, for I have not been able to find any reference in Weigall's letters or other documents to any of the scholars Reid mentions – Ahmad Kamal, for example, or Ahmad Najib – though, given Weigall's genuine desire to promote specifically Egyptian archaeology, one would have expected him to build on what was there if he had known of its existence.

39 *Orientations*, p.66. Storrs's discussion of the British in Egypt, of Gorst's policies, and of relations between the British and the Egyptians, is very interesting. See for example, pp.65–71 and pp.79–80.
40 Letter dated 12 December 1911. PRO, F.O.633.20.
41 Letter dated 5 May 1914. AW archive.
42 Letter dated 29 November 1913. G.I. Gardiner MSS, AHG/42.355.9.
43 Letter dated 9 September 1914. AW archive.
44 See for example an article in the *Times* for 9 August 1971, written after the signing of the agreement allowing the Tutankhamun treasures to be shown at the British Museum in London. The piece tells the story of the *Times*'s original involvement in the discovery, and mentions Weigall as the leader of the anti-*Times* faction, going on to state that as Inspector of Antiquities some time before, Weigall had 'lost his job when it was alleged that he was buying antiques for private collectors'.
45 Douglas Sladen, *My Long Life* (1939), p.153.
46 Letter dated 1 April 1914. AW archive.

## CHAPTER 16

1 Herbert L. Saterlee, *J.Pierpont Morgan; an Intimate Portrait*, (1939), p.571.
2 Letter dated 22 June 1920. AW archive.
3 Letter dated 3 May 1922. AW archive.
4 In *The Chronicles of Clovis* (1911).
5 *The Times*, 21 July 1911.
6 *The Times*, 17 October 1911.
7 Alured's memories. AW archive.
8 This spectacle is better known for its 1924 revival in New York with Lady Diana Manners doubling the part of the nun and the statue.
9 Osbert Sitwell, *Great Morning* (1948), pp.253–54.
10 Letter dated 30 July 1914. AW archive.
11 Ronald Storrs's uncle, one-time star of the Cambridge 'Apostles', editor of *The Pall Mall Gazette* and Conservative MP, on and off, until the Liberal victory in 1906.
12 Letter dated 11 September 1914. AW archive.
13 *The Not Impossible She* (1926), pp.315–316.
14 Letter dated 21 December 1914. AW archive.
15 Deneshwai (there are variant spellings) is the name of a village in Lower Egypt where in 1906 some British soldiers, out pigeon-shooting at the invitation of a local head man, overstepped the mark and shot some of the villagers' own birds. The locals were incensed, opened fire, and a uniformed officer was shot dead. Lord Cromer convened a special court which sentenced some of the villagers to execution and others to public flogging in the village itself: 'Excessive and medieval sentences,' thought Storrs (*Orientations*, p.64). There was a storm of protest not only from Egyptian Nationalists but in England and elsewhere. Bernard Shaw in particular wrote a damning account of the affair in his Preface to *John Bull's Other Island*.
16 *A History of Events in Egypt from 1798 to 1914* (1915), p.175.
17 *Truth*, 19 May 1915.
18 Letter dated 25 November 1915. AW archive.
19 Letter dated 3 June 1915. AW archive.
20 *The Sunday Times*, 19 September 1915.
21 *The Evening Standard and St. James's Gazette*, 20 September 1915.
22 *The Not Impossible She*, p.311.
23 *Reynold's Newspaper*, 5 December 1915.
24 Letter dated 20 November 1915. AW archive.
25 Letter dated 17 November 1915. AW archive.
26 Letter dated 27 September 1915. AW archive.

27  *Every Other Inch*, p.86.
28  Charles B. Cochrane, *Showman Looks On* (1945), p.201.
29  *The Observer*, 17 October 1915.
30  Letter dated 13 January 1916. AW archive.
31  *Sporting Times*, 21 April 1916.
32  'It is known of Mr Stoll that … he insists upon the entertainment that is funny without being vulgar,' *London Opinion*, 29 July 1916. The other managers would also have had to toe the line.
33  *The Stage*, 24 February 1916.
34  Note in the programme for *The Bing Boys*. AW archive.
35  T.G.H. James, *Howard Carter*, p.180.

## CHAPTER 17

1  The following quotations illustrating Weigall's scheme come from a copy of this document in the AW archive.
2  Letter dated 12 November 1915. AW archive.
3  Letter dated 2 April 1916. AW archive.
4  A copy dated 21 May [1915] is in the AW archive.
5  *The Sunday Times*, 23 July 1916.
6  Letter from Lady Eleanor Brougham whom he had kown in Egypt, dated 3 August 1916.
7  Stella Patrick Campbell, *My Life and Some Letters*, (n.d.), p.298.
8  Letter dated 20 August [?1915]. AW archive.
9  From 'Blighter' in his collection *The Old Huntsman* (1917).
10  Letter dated 23 August 1916. AW archive.
11  Letter from Charlot dated 18 December 1916.
12  Letter dated 30 December 1915. AW archive.
13  *The Daily Mirror*, 8 December 1916.
14  Undated, but written possibly some time in 1924.
15  A.J.P. Taylor, *English History, 1914–1945* (1970; first published 1965), p.128.
16  However Merwin did produce another film scripted by Weigall, called *Her Heritage*, also starring Phyllis Monkman (with Jack Buchanan) which was released in 1919. I am grateful to James Moore, who has been researching the life of André Charlot, for this information.
17  Letter dated 17 January 1918. AW archive.
18  Letter dated 19 January 1918. AW archive.
19  Letter dated 28 January 1918. AW archive.
20  Letter dated 31 January 1918. AW archive.
21  Letter dated 31 January 1918. AW archive.
22  Mrs Patrick Campbell thanked him for his scene in a letter dated 4 September 1917. The letter about her war-work is dated 15 March [1918]. AW archive.
23  Ernest Short and Arthur Compton-Rickett, *Ring up the Curtain; being a pageant of English Entertainment covering half a century* (London, 1938), pp.123–124.
24  Letter dated 30 May 1930. AW archive.
25  The names of Kristen Heistein, Bannister Merwin and Arthur Weigall all appear on contracts drawn up in April (Heistein) and August (Merwin and Weigall) 1917 by the André Charlot Film Company. Copies of these are kept among the Charlot Company Records, in the UCLA Archives, California. I am very grateful to James Moore and André Charlot's daughter, Joan Midwinter, for researching these records for me.

## CHAPTER 18

1  Programme note. AW archive.
2  Alured's memories. AW archive. The following glimpses of Weigall are taken from the same document.

3 Weigall's comment is written alongside his drawing.
4 Letter dated 19 September 1924.
5 Letter dated 26 July 1920. AW archive.
6 These letters are dated 16 April 1920, 7 June 1920, and 21 November 1920, respectively. AW archive.
7 Letter dated 27 October 1922. AW archive.
8 Letter dated 11 September 1922. AW archive.
9 Two letters and two telegrams dated 1,2,3, May 1922. AW archive.
10 *The Daily Mail*, 9 June 1921.
11 *The Daily Mail*, 18 June 1921.
12 Alured's memories. AW archive.

## CHAPTER 19

1 Letter dated 24 December 1922. MMA.
2 The whole agreement forms Appendix IV of T.G.H.James's *Howard Carter: the Path to Tutankhamun.*
3 Valentine Williams, *The World of Action* (1938), p.365.
4 James, *Howard Carter*, p.243.
5 H.V.Morton, *Through Lands of the Bible* (1938), p.267.
6 ibid., p.267.
7 ibid., p.267.
8 Williams, *The World of Action*, p.360.
9 This and the previous quotation come from Williams, *The World of Action*, p.363.
10 Quoted in James, *Howard Carter*, p.244.
11 Quoted from Mervyn Herbert's diary by James, ibid., p.251.
12 ibid., p.252.
13 Weigall quotes this in a letter to Carter dated 25 January 1923. MMA.
14 Quoted in James, *Howard Carter*, p.226.
15 See note 13.
16 See note 1.
17 Williams, *The World of Action*, p.361.
18 Undated letter, but from internal evidence written on 21 January 1923. G.I.Gardiner MSS. AHG/42.355.1.
19 *The Daily Mail*, 22 January 1923.
20 ibid., see note 18.
21 Letter dated 25 January 1923. MMA.
22 *Daily Mail*, 22 January 1923.
23 Quoted in James, *Howard Carter*, p.244.
24 March [?1925]. G.I.Gardiner MSS, AHG/42.358.14.
25 Letter dated 26 January 1923. AW archive.
26 Telegram to Weigall: 'Instructed Taylor take proceedings Cairo injunct monopolist from excluding press keep touch Taylor. Crawford.' AW archive.
27 H.V.Morton, *Through Lands of the Bible*, p.267.
28 Mervyn Herbert's diary. Middle East Centre, St Antony's College, Oxford.
29 See James, *Howard Carter*, p.242.
30 *Daily Mail*, 12 February 1923.
31 ibid., see previous note.
32 See note 28.
33 Williams, *The World of Action*, p.369. *The Evening Standard* for that day does indeed carry the news.
34 Telegram dated 17 February 1923. AW archive.
35 'The Tomb of Tutankhamen' in *Tutankhamen and other Essays*, p.97.

## CHAPTER 20

1  'A Ride to Wady Salamuni', in *The Glory of the Pharaohs*, p.253.
2  ibid., p.254.
3  These quotes come respectively on p. 101 and pp.105–06 of 'The Morality of Excavation' in *The Glory of the Pharaohs* (1923).
4  'The Future of Excavation', in *Tutankhamun and other Essays*, pp.32–33, 34.
5  ibid., p.34.
6  *Ancient Egyptian Works of Art* (1924), pp.222, 214.
7  Letter dated 16 March 1923. AW archive.
8  Letter dated 10 September 1923. AW archive.
9  Letter dated 21 September 1923. AW archive.
10  This extract and the following account of his lectures is taken from Weigall's own working copies. There were two versions of the lecture: a single lecture and a pair, for the same audience on two separate evenings. AW archive.
11  Beatrice Lillie, *Every Other Inch a Lady*, p.151.
12  Letter dated 7 December 1923. AW archive. Unfortunately, Pond's enclosure has not survived.
13  This incident is mentioned above, Chapter 10.
14  James, *Howard Carter*, p.270.
15  See note 12.
16  Ms draft copy in American notebook. AW archive.
17  'The Future of Excavation', in *Tutankhamen and other Essays* (1923), p.34.
18  ibid., p.31.
19  *Ancient Egyptian Works of Art*, pp.200–201.
20  These three quotations come from pp.23, 30 and 37.
21  ibid., pp.35–37.
22  ibid., p.35.
23  See James, *Howard Carter*, p.281.
24  Most notably in Chapter 12.
25  Letter dated 23 February 1924, AW archive. 'Maharanee' was the title bestowed upon the wives of the British governors or Rajahs who at that time governed Sarawak in the East Indies.
26  These notes appear in the same notebook in which he drew up the draft of his letter to Carter. See note 16.
27  Divorce at that time was only granted on the grounds of adultery, so he couldn't divorce her.
28  *The Not Impossible She* (1926), p.341.

## CHAPTER 21

1  *The Not Impossible She*, p.345.
2  ibid., p.380.
3  *The History of the Pharaohs* (1925–1926) 2 Vols., I, pp.xi–xii.
4  'The Problem of Egyptian Chronology' in *Tutankhamen and other Essays*, p.158.
5  Alan Gardiner, *Egypt of the Pharaohs* (1961), p.64.
6  Weigall, *The History of the Pharaohs*, I, pp.28–29.
7  See Richard A. Parker, *The Calendars of Ancient Egypt* (The Oriental Institute of the Univ. of Chicago, 1950), pp.51–52.
8  Weigall, *The History of the Pharaohs*, vol. I, pp.4–5.
9  ibid., vol. I, p.6.
10  Gardiner, *Egypt of the Pharaohs*, p.67. It doesn't appear, incidentally, that he has Weigall particularly in mind.

11  See Alan Gardiner, 'Regnal Years and the Civil Calendar in Pharaonic Egypt', *JEA*, (31), pp.11–28. (1945).
12  Gardiner, *Egypt of the Pharaohs*, p.71.
13  See his *Ancient History of the Near East* (1913; eighth revised edition 1932).
14  Gardiner, *Egypt of the Pharaohs*, p.150.
15  *A History of the Pharaohs*, Vol.II, pp.272–273. (Weigall called Vol.II 'A History …' and Vol.I 'The History …')
16  Compare Gardiner, *Egypt of the Pharaohs*, p.182–3, and Weigall, *The History of the Pharaohs*, II, pp.390–391.
17  Letter dated 18 November 1926. AW archive.
18  *The New Statesman*, 14 May 1927.
19  *Wanderings in Roman Britain* (1926), p.14.
20  ibid., p.332.
21  *The Way of the East* (1924), pp.294–96.
22  *Wanderings in Anglo-Saxon Britain* (1927), pp.41, 42.
23  ibid., p.18.
24  *Wanderings in Roman Britain*, p.109.
25  *The Grand Tour of Norman England* (1927) pp.76 and 85 respectively.
26  *Wanderings in Roman Britain*, p.97.
27  *Wanderings in Anglo-Saxon Britain*, p.156.
28  AW archive.

## CHAPTER 22

1  Lillie, *Every Other Inch a Lady*, p.215.
2  *The Young Lady from Hell* (1929), p.252.
3  *Columbus, Ohio State Journal*, 2 October 1928.
4  *Personalities of Antiquity*, 'The Reminiscences of Doctor Olympus', p.159.
5  ibid., the description of Julius Caesar comes on p.17; of Boadicea, on p.52; and the source in Dio Cassius, on p.46.
6  ibid., p.31.
7  See, for example, *The Spectator*, 7 July 1928.
8  Letters dated June 1929; 9 June 1930; 10 May1929; 3 July 1931; Mrs W. Wilson Leisenring, Hampstead, 21 June 1928. AW archive.
9  23 May 1930. AW archive.
10  *The Lady*, 12 September 1929; *Nottingham Weekly Guardian*, 5 October 1929.

## CHAPTER 23

1  Michael Grant, *Nero*, (1970), p.101.
2  *Nero, Emperor of Rome* (1930), p.233.
3  *The Cornhill Magazine*, July–December 1863, pp.113–128.
4  B.W. Henderson, *The Life and Principate of the Emperor Nero* (1903).
5  ibid., p.133.
6  ibid., pp.108–109.
7  *The British Weekly*, 9 October 1930.
8  *The Daily Herald*, 23 October 1930.
9  Henderson, *The Life and Principate*, p.149.
10  Weigall, *Alexander the Great* (1933), p.196.
11  *The Life and Times of Marc Antony* (1931), pp.370–71.
12  ibid., p.371.
13  *Alexander the Great* (1933), p.16.
14  J.M.Bury, *The History of Ancient Greece* (1959 edition), p.773.

15  W.W.Tarn, *The Cambridge Ancient History* (1927 edition), vol. VI, p.419.
16  *Alexander the Great*, p.215.
17  See, for example, the *San Francisco News*, 13 September 1932.
18  See Sally Cline, *Radclyffe Hall, a woman called John* (1997), p.334.
19  Mary Mills Patrick, *Sappho and the Island of Lesbos* (1912), p.100.
20  *The Poems of Sappho with historical and critical notes, translations and a bibliography* (1924), p.18.
21  ibid., p.179.
22  ibid., p.118.
23  ibid., p.297.
24  ibid., pp.313–314.

## CHAPTER 24

1  Alured's memories. AW archive.
2  *Laura was my Camel* (1933), pp.21–22.
3  ibid., p.15.
4  ibid., pp.86–87.
5  ibid., pp.106–107.
6  ibid., p.84.
7  ibid., p.128.
8  Letter dated 21 October [1933]. AW archive.
9  Alured's memories. AW archive.
10  Letter dated 12 January 1934. Included in the correspondence relating to the Statement of Claim. Weigall v. London Express Newspapers Ltd. AW archive.
11  Letter dated 7 January 1934. Included in the same correspondence (see note above). AW archive.
12  Letter dated 18 July 1934. Copy sent to Muriel from J. Chapman Walker, her solicitors.
13  See Margaret S. Drower, *Flinders Petrie*, p.125.
14  Letter dated 3 July 1920. G.I., Newberry correspondence 46/26.
15  Letter from Chapman Walker to Muriel, dated 13 September 1934. AW archive.
16  *JEA*, Vol.20, 1934, p.107.

# Index

Also available from Tauris Parke Paperbacks

# *Egypt's Belle Epoque*
## *Cairo and the Age of the Hedonists*
### Trevor Mostyn

Egypt's belle époque was a period of incredible extravagance during which the Khedive Ismail's Cairo became the mirror image, both architecturally and socially, of decadent Paris. The glamour and hedonism of the era reached its peak during the magnificent celebrations for the opening of the Suez Canal in 1869. But the splendour was short-lived. Only a year after the Suez Canal opened, the Second Empire in France collapsed and the Khedive's excesses plunged Egypt into crippling debt. Ismail was eventually forced to abdicate, leaving Cairo to the British who occupied Egypt in all but name.

Paperback, 216pp
ISBN 978 1 84511 240 0

*'This is an enthralling account of a period in Egypt's history now too often forgotten. Trevor Mostyn brings to life a glittering near century which opened with the Suez Canal and launched Cairo as one of the world's great cities.'*
Lisa Appignanesi

*'Egypt's Belle Epoque has the immediacy of oral history. This narrative depicts with wit and elegance the grandeur and decadence of a not so distant past. Trevor Mostyn writes as if he was himself a witness to the extraordinary events.'*
Moris Farhi

**www.taurisparkepaperbacks.com**

# *The Great Belzoni*
## *The Circus Strongman who Discovered Egypt's Ancient Treasures*
## Stanley Mayes

The truly extraordinary life story of Giovanni Belzoni – engineer, barber, monk, actor and circus strongman (where he earned his title, 'The Great Belzoni'), who became one of the giants of 19th century Egyptian archaeology. Sometimes maligned as a tomb robber, Giovanni Battista Belzoni is perhaps the most important and yet least remembered explorer and archaeologist of the last two hundred years. He was the first person to penetrate the heart of the second pyramid at Giza and the first European to visit the oasis of Siwah and discover the ruined city of Berenice on the Red Sea. In 1823, at the age of forty-five, Belzoni died of fever trying to reach the mysterious city of Timbuktu. There has never been a character quite like him in the history of exploration.

Paperback, 360pp
ISBN 978 1 84511 333 9

*'One of the most striking and interesting figures in the history of eastern travel.'*
DNB – The Dictionary of National Biography

**www.taurisparkepaperbacks.com**